Mark Wilson

Some say the real secrets of magic should never be revealed...

But I believe, if you are sincerely interested, you should have the finest, clearest instruction possible.

Over the years we have presented hundreds of television and stage shows. Now it's time to pass on what we have learned to you. That's why we created the **Mark Wilson Video Course in Magic.** I'll teach you hundreds of tricks and illusions, everything from simple close-up to the latest creations in the world of magic. Learning is easy and fast, just watch the video tapes.

Want to perform illusions?
If you like illusions, you should have the **Mark Wilson on Illusions** videos. Mark Wilson and the beautiful Nani Darnell teach you how to perform powerful illusions just as they did on television.

Want to see some great magic shows?

The Magic Land of Allakazam was the first network television magic series. Each half hour show features fast-paced openings, audience participation comedy magic, sleight of hand and at least one major illusion.

The Magic Circus television specials were the first prime-time full-color modern day magic shows. Mark, Nani and a glamorous cast perform 33 lavishly-produced illusions and many other powerful magic effects. Guest stars are the world's greatest magicians, Carl Ballantine, Shimada, Jay Marshall and Lefty and the Professor Dai Vernon.

We have more: **The Magic of Mark Wilson, The Magic of China,** and many others.

Need some magic props?
We also have a fine selection of **professional magic props**, as well as **classic memorabilia.**

To learn more and enter the wonderful World of Magic go to:
www.markwilsonmagic.com

To order call: (800) 367-8749
e-mail: mark@markwilsonmagic.com
P.O. Box 801839 Santa Clarita, CA 91380

Web site design by Presto Productions
www.prestoproductions.com

MARK WILSON'S COMPLETE COURSE IN MAGIC

RUNNING PRESS

PHILADELPHIA

ACKNOWLEDGMENTS

The contents of this course do not represent the efforts of only two, three, or a dozen individuals, but instead, of all those magicians of the past and the present who have labored so diligently to create, perfect, and present the art of magic.

Just as a stalagmite, buried unseen in a dark cave, builds from tiny drops into a towering structure, so has our art increased through the centuries, shrouded in a like darkness of secrecy, which remains a prerequisite to its growth.

With this course, you will join the ranks of those who have learned these inner secrets—and you must acknowledge and respect those whose contributions we enjoy. *Acknowledge* by being aware of the countless hours of study, work, and practice that have been expended by the magicians of the past to create our art. *Respect* the magicians of today, by never revealing any of these hard-earned secrets.

This, then, is the grateful acknowledgment of this course, *to the Magicians of all times and places*, for their countless contributions to the art of magic.

—M.W.

Copyright © 1975, 1981, 1988, 2002 by Mark Wilson

Hachette Book Group supports the right to free expression and the value of copyright.
The purpose of copyright is to encourage writers and artists to produce the creative works that enrich our culture.

The scanning, uploading, and distribution of this book without permission is a theft of the author's intellectual property.
If you would like permission to use material from the book (other than for review purposes),
please contact permissions@hbgusa.com. Thank you for your support of the author's rights.

Running Press
Hachette Book Group
1290 Avenue of the Americas, New York, NY 10104
www.runningpress.com
@Running_Press

Printed in China

Originally published in 1975 by Ottenheimer Publishers, Inc. for Courage Books,
an imprint of Running Press Book Publishers
Revised Edition: May 2003

Published by Running Press Kids, an imprint of Perseus Books, LLC,
a subsidiary of Hachette Book Group, Inc.

The Hachette Speakers Bureau provides a wide range of authors for speaking events.
To find out more, go to www.hachettespeakersbureau.com or call (866) 376-6591.

The publisher is not responsible for websites (or their content) that are not owned by the publisher.

Credits:

Course Coordinator: Larry Anderson; Assistant Course Coordinator: Don Wayne; Art Director: Julia Laughlin; Assistant Art Director: Manny Katz; Photographers: Terry S. Urie and Michael Wilson; Graphic Production: Susan Kennedy and Kathryn Capp; Digital Photography: Lincoln Bond; Contributing Writers (in alphabetical order): Larry Anderson, Fr. Jim Blantz, Earl Nelson, Tom O'Lenick, Peter Pit, David Roth, Brick Tilley, and Alan Wakeling; Special Contributing Author: U.F. Grant; front jacket photograph by Weaver Lilly

Library of Congress Control Number: 2002093018

ISBNs: 978-0-7624-1455-0 (paperback)

RRD-S

25 24 23 22 21

CONTENTS

Introduction 7
A Brief Biography 8
How to Add Magic to Your Life 14
The Benefits of Learning Magic 15
The Universal, International Appeal of Magic 16

Card Magic 17
Card Definitions 19
Card Handling Techniques 23
The Riffle Shuffle 24
The Table Shuffle 24
Dealing the Cards 25
The Card Count—Retain Order 26
The Card Count—Reverse Order 27
Spreading or Running the Pack in Your Hands 28

Self-Working Card Tricks 30
Automatic Card Discovery 31
Super Automatic Card Discovery 32
The Fantastic Five 32
Turnover Card 34
Double Turnover 36
The Double X Mystery 38
The Super Double X Mystery 39
The Super Anytime Double X Mystery 39
The Signed Card in Wallet 40
The Torn and Restored Card 42
You Do As I Do 44

The Hindu Shuffle 46
The Hindu Shuffle 47
The Hindu Glimpse 48
The Hindu Key Card Location 49
Spell-A-Name 50
Spell-A-Card 51
Spell-A-Card Outdone 51
The Hindu Flash Force 52
The Hindu Color Change 53
The Color Changing Decks (Two-Deck Version) 55
Hindu Shuffle—Bottom Stock Control 56
A False Cut 57
Hindu Shuffle Pick-Up Control 58
The Hindu Aces 59
Reverse Order Count Trick 60

Overhand Shuffle 61
The Overhand Shuffle 62
The Overhand Reverse Shuffle 63
The Card Case Escape 64
Overhand Shuffle Glimpse 66
Shuffle Control with Key Card 66
Overhand Shuffle Control—Top Card to Bottom 67
The Transferred Thought 67
The Overhand Slip Shuffle 69
The Card Through the Handkerchief 70
The Card Through the Handkerchief—Face-Up Method .. 72
Overhand Shuffle Card Control—Bottom Card to Top ... 72
Overhand Shuffle Control—Bottom Card to Top—Second Method
.... 72
The Overhand In-Jog Top Card Control 73
The Magnetized Card 73
Overhand In-Jog Control—Placing a Card at a Specific Location in the Deck 74
A Surprise Appearance 75

Forcing a Card 76
The Slip Force 76
The Slip Force—Second Method 77
10-20 Count Force 78
The Rollover Force 79
The Count Force 80
Roll Any Number 82

The Double Lift 83
Little Finger Break 83
The Double Lift 84
The Elevator Card 85
Riffle Revelation 86
Snap-It! 88
Color Changing Aces No. 1 89
Reversed Card in Deck 91
Sandwiched Aces 92
Thought Projection 95
A Clever Combination 96

The Glide 97
The Glide 97
The Glide—Alternate Method 99
Color Changing Aces No. 2 (Double Lift and Glide) 99
Oil and Water 101
Do As I Do Oil and Water 102
Birds of a Feather 102

Double-Backed Card 105
The Stubborn Card 105
Satan Behind You 106
The Perfect Card Force 108
The Two-Card Force 109
Insto-Transpo 110
The Perfect Card Location 112
You Can't Do As I Do (Five Cards) 114

Double-Faced Card 115
Two-Card Monte 116
New Card Monte 117
Forced Cards Reverse 119
Impossible Prediction 121
Four-Card Assembly 123

The Short Card 125
How to Make a Short Card 125
How to "Riffle" the Short Card to the Top 126
Short Card to Bottom—First Method 126
Short Card to Bottom—Second Method 126
Short Card to Bottom—Third Method 126
The Short Card As a "Locator" 127
The Surprise Discovery (Using the Short Card As a Locator) .. 128
A Weighty Problem (Using the Short Card As a Locator) 129
Quick Riffle Location 129
The Short Card Force 129
The Mystic Count Down 131
Cutting the Aces 132

Giant Cards 133
The Bigger Card Trick 134
Sympathetic Cards 135
The Applause Card 138
Double Applause Card 139
A Giant Mistake—First Version 140
A Giant Mistake—Second Version 141
A Giant Mystery 141

Special Card Tricks 143
Self-Reversing Pack 144
Self-Reversing Pack—Outdone 145
Grant's Superior Card Trick 146

Flourishes 148
One-Hand Cut—Basic Method 149
One-Hand Cut—First Variation 150
One-Hand Cut—Second Variation 151
One-Hand Cut—Second Method 152
Spreading the Cards—The Ribbon Spread 153
Ribbon Spread Turnover 154
Reverse Turnover 155
Turnover Pick-Up 156
Pressure Fan 156
Closing the Fan—Two-Hand Method 157
Closing the Fan—One-Hand Method 158
The One-Hand Fan 158
Springing the Cards 159
Arm Spread Catch 160
The Waterfall 161
Throwing a Card 162
The Boomerang Card 163

Genii Cards 164
The Genii of the Lamp 165
The Genii's Number 166
The Genii Predicts 167
The Sandwiched Genii 168
The Genii Saves the Day 170
Genii's Library 171

Money Magic 175
The Coin Fold 177
Coin Through Handkerchief 178
Coin Through Handkerchief—Second Version ... 180
Magically Multiply Your Money 181
Four-Coin Assembly 183
The French Drop (Using a Coin) 186
The Finger Palm Vanish 187
The Pinch or Drop Vanish 189
The Classic Palm (Using a Coin) 190
The Coin-Vanishing Handkerchief 191
The Coin-Vanishing Handkerchief—Second Variation 193
Grant's Super Coin-Vanishing Handkerchief 193
Super Dooper Versatile Vanisher 194
Coin Through Leg 195
Challenge Coin Vanish 196
Coin-A-Go-Go 197
Continuous Coins 200
Copper-Silver Penetration 202
The Shrinking Coin 204
Coins Across 206
Lapping—Pull-Off Method 209
The Coin in the Ball of Wool 209
The Expanded Shell Half-Dollar 212
Two Halves and Two Quarters 213
Two Halves and a "Half" Dollar 214
Coins Through the Table 216
Coins Through the Table—Alternate Method 218
The Coin Roll 219
The Roll Down 221

Money Magic—Bills 222
Roll the Bill 222
Bills From Nowhere 223
Bills From Nowhere—Version No. 2 224
The Torn and Restored Dollar Bill 225

Inflation 227
The Six-Bill Repeat 228
The Bill in Lemon 230

Rope Magic 235
Rope Preparation (Coring) 237
Cut and Restored Rope—First Method 237
Cut and Restored Rope—Second Method 239
Comedy Cut and Restored Rope 241
The Triple Rope Trick 242
Triple Rope—Multiple "Do As I Do" Knot 244
Triple Rope—"Times Two" 245
Double Restoration 245
Cut and Restored String 247
Threading the Needle 249
One-Hand Knot 251
The Melting Knot 251
Shoelace Rope Tie 252
The Rigid Rope 254
Equal-Unequal Ropes 256
The Great Coat Escape 258
Rope and Coat Release 260
Ring Off Rope 262
Impossible Rope Escape 263

Silk & Handkerchief Magic 267
Hypnotized Handkerchief 269
Fatima, the Dancer 270
The Dissolving Knot 272
The Knot Through the Arm 273
Handkerchief Through Handkerchief 274
The Penetrating Handkerchief 275
The Magical Production of a Handkerchief 277
The Vanish of the Handkerchief 279
The Universal Vanisher 281
The Serpentine Silk 282
The Serpentine Silk—Second Version 283
The Phantom 284
The Broken and Restored Match 285
Eggs From Nowhere 286
The Vanishing Glass 289
The Vanishing Glass—Impromptu Version 290

Impromptu Magic 293
The Jumping Rubber Band 295
Reverse Jumping Rubber Band 295
The Double Jumping Rubber Band—Version 1 ... 296
The Double Jumping Rubber Band—Version 2 ... 297
The Challenger Jumping Rubber Band 298
Linking Paper Clips 298
Linking Paper Clips With Rubber Band 300
Bag Tag Escape 301
Lifesavers on the Loose! 302
Cords of Fantasia 303
The Sucker Torn and Restored Napkin 305
Ring on Wand 307
The Jumping Match 309
The Flying Match 309
Dots Magic (Paddle Move) 311
Dots Magic—Impromptu Version 314
Glass Through the Table 314

Mental Magic 317
Three-Way Test 318
The Magazine Test 322
The Curious Coincidence 323
Million to One 325
The Gypsy Mindreader 326

The Center Tear 327
The Center Tear—"Standing" Variation .329
Spectrum Prediction .329
Spectrum Prediction—"Number" Variation 331
Ping Pong Prestidigitation .332
The Envelope Stand .334
The Envelope Stand—"Bank Night" Variation 335

Betchas .337
The Impossible Penetration .339
The Impossible Knot .339
The "Do-It-Yourself" Knot .341
Turned Up Glasses .341
Rubber Band Release .343
Knot in Handkerchief .344

Make At Home Magic .345
Vase of Allah .347
The Afghan Bands .348
The Utility Cone .350
The Sorcerer's Stamp Album (Svengali Book) .352
The Comedy Cut and Restored Paper (Clippo) .353
The Magic Card Frame .355
The Double-Walled Bag .357
The Double-Walled Bag—Vanish .358
The Double-Walled Bag—Transformation .359
The Sun and Moon .360
The Cut and Restored Necktie .362
Wine Glass Production .363
The Take-Apart Vanish .365
Confetti to Candy—First Version .367
Confetti to Candy—Second Version .369
Confetti to Candy—Third Version .370
Thank You Banner—First Method .371
Thank You Banner—Second Method .372
Thank You Banner—Third Method .373
Vanishing Bowl of Water .374
The Bunny Box .375
Production Box .376
The Square Circle .378
The Allakazam Hat—Introduction .379
The Allakazam Hat .380
The Allakazam Hat—A Variation .381
Magic Table .382
The Black Art Well .384
Mechanical Magic .385
The Dove Pan .385
The Foo Can .386
The Lota Bowl .388

Sponge Ball Magic .391
Sponge Sorcery .393
A Sponge Appears .393
The Flight to the Pocket .394
Guess Which Hand .394
Spectator's Doubles .394
Transposition in Your Hands .395
Impossible Penetration .397
The Spectator's Hand Revisited .397
Two in the Hand, One in the Pocket—Phase One 398
Two in the Hand, One in the Pocket—Phase Two 399
The Total Vanish .400

Billiard Ball Magic .403
The Classic Palm (Using a Ball) .405
The Classic Palm Vanish .405
The French Drop (Using a Ball) .407
Fist Vanish .408

Change-Over Palm .409
The Finger Roll Flourish .411
The Mark Wilson Billiard Ball Routine .412

Cups & Balls .423
Cups and Balls (Routine) .425
Penetration .425
Invisible Flight .428
Any Cup Called For .428
The Repeat Production .430
The Lemon Surprise .431

Magical Illusions .435
The Arabian Tent Illusion .437
The Haunted House .441
The Victory Cartons Illusion .446
The Mystery of the Magical Mummy .449
The Mystery of the Magical Mummy—Second Version 452
The Curious Cabinet Caper .453
Mummy's Casket .457
Who's There .460
Tip-Over Trunk .462
The Farmer and the Witch .464
The Suspension Illusion .469

Reputation Makers .472
The Challenge Coin Vanish .473
Cowboy Rope Trick .478
Magic For Campers .481
Tic Tac Toe Prediction .481
After Dinner Magic .483
The Ring on the Rope .484
Party Magic .486
Random Number Selector Mystery .490
Sales Magic Secrets .492
Your Magic Will Open Many Doors .493
Speeches and Presentations .493
If Your Customers Come To Your Business 493
Trade Shows and Networking .494
Magic Business Card Printing .494
The Magical Bottom Line .498
The Last Trick in the Book .498
The Chapstick Caper .498

Your Future in Magic .503

Dedication

Gratefully dedicated to two lovely and loving individuals without whom this would never have been written.My beautiful mother, Teta, for initially obvious reasons, but also for her continuing inspiration, and . . . My beautiful wife, Nani, who has given up so much . . . so that another prop could be purchased . . . another illusion built . . . another show successfully presented . . . another step taken in a journey toward some luminous, unknown goal . . . . . . and in the process has managed to raise our two fine sons, Mike and Greg, and make it all worthwhile.

If my magic were but real . . .

INTRODUCTION

Welcome to the wonderful world of magic! In the following pages I sincerely believe you will find the best illustrated, most easily understood, most completely developed method ever produced for learning the Art of Magic. All of the material was carefully selected, then written, rewritten, checked, and rewritten again. Over 50,000 photographs were shot—from these over 2,000 of the best were selected and then rendered as the line drawings which illustrate every move in the course. We have added a new section, "Reputation Makers," and sections on how best to use the magic you will learn in the course.

As you will see, most of the tricks have been divided into the following sections:

EFFECT—This is what the spectator sees—the mystery—the miracle—as performed by you, the magician.

SECRET AND PREPARATION—Describes the props that you will need, and the secret of how they work. Most of the items needed can be found around the house.

METHOD—This is the actual performance, explaining how you present the trick to the audience.

COMMENTS AND SUGGESTIONS—These are extra tips, suggestions, and ideas that will help you make each trick even more baffling and entertaining.

As you read and learn these great secrets, please remember and follow these four important rules:

(1) Never explain how a trick is done. If the audience knows the secret, then the mystery, the glamour, and the entertainment of the magic are lost.

(2) Never explain what you are going to do ahead of time. If the audience doesn't know what's going to happen, they won't know what to look for in advance and are much more likely to be baffled.

(3) Never repeat a trick for the same spectators. Once an audience has seen a trick performed, they have a much greater chance of "catching on."

(4) The most important rule of all: Always practice each trick before you present it.

Read the instructions. Practice with the props. When you can perform the effect smoothly and without hesitation, you are ready!

With the closely guarded secrets you will learn in this course, you can entertain your friends or a theater full of people, so there's an important point I must make. As a professional magician, I have promised never to reveal the inner secrets of magic except to those who are sincerely interested in learning our art. Before I open the door to these great mysteries for you, you must give me your word that, to the best of your ability, you will never reveal the secrets you learn to anyone.

You are not signing a legal document. It's a matter of honor and respect for the magicians who have gone before us. Maintaining these secrets is how we preserve the wonder and mystery of the art of magic, of which you will become a part.

Magic has taken my wife Nani and me around the world and helped us make friends everywhere. Now, with the complete course, you have taken the first steps on the road to the wonderful world of magic. With your pledge not to reveal these powerful secrets, I'm delighted to show you the way.

Happy Magic!

Mark Wilson

—Mark Wilson

A BRIEF BIOGRAPHY

Mark Wilson is not only a world-famous magician; he's also a producer, world traveler, teacher, author, businessman, creator of new approaches to sales and marketing, and the creative force behind an impressive display of television and stage attractions. Perhaps he's best known for his television appearances. *TV Guide* called him "the world's most televised magician," and it's easy to see why.

When James Mark Wilson was eight years old, he watched a magician perform and resolved then and there that the mystic art would be his own life calling. That ambition was furthered much sooner than he anticipated. Five years later, when he was a high school student in Dallas, Texas, where his family had settled, he took a part-time job at a magic shop called Douglas Magic Land and became the magic demonstrator.

Billing himself as Mark Wilson, he gave his first professional show at the age of thirteen before a Rotary Club for a modest fee of five dollars, confident that such engagements would increase in number and financial return. Gone were the golden days of vaudeville and the full evening magic shows that heralded such names as Blackstone, Thurston, Houdini, and Kellar, playing theaters from coast to coast and even embarking on world tours.

With a definite goal in mind, Mark enrolled in Southern Methodist University's School of Business Administration to major in advertising and marketing. He was positive that he could use magic as a means of selling products and services as well as entertainment, combining his knowledge of the art with his business training. That was proven when Mark linked the old art of magic with the newest form of communication, television.

After graduating from S.M.U, Wilson met beautiful Nani

A. Mark Wilson, fifteen years old and already an accomplished sleight-of-hand performer.

B. A twenty-year-old Mark, busy working his way through Southern Methodist University in Dallas, Texas.

C. In 1953, Mark won his first award—Most Outstanding Magician—at the Texas Association of Magicians Convention.

Darnell Arends, then a stewardess for American Airlines, who soon became his wife. With Nani's help, he was able to create, sell and present his first TV magic series, *Time For Magic,* sponsored by Dr. Pepper. The show debuted in February 1954 on WFAA-TV. It soon became the highest rated daytime show in Dallas.

Realizing, in 1958, that greater success could only be found with the major networks, Wilson began his efforts to sell the show as a network series. Success didn't come easily and he spent two years traveling around the country talking to every major advertising agency, kid-show sponsor and network executive he could corner.

After many months of meetings, phone calls, letters and presentations, sleepless nights and disheartening rejections, he received a call from the Kellogg Cereal Company who wanted to fully sponsor the show as part of the CBS Saturday morning lineup. Mark and Nani and their then six-year old son Mike left Dallas for Los Angeles to begin

production of *The Magic Land of Allakazam,* America's first network magic television series. The series began October 1, 1960 and aired for two years on the CBS network before being sold to the ABC network, where it ran for another three years. *Allakazam* was the first series ever aired on U.S. network television devoted exclusively to magic.

The Magic Land of Allakazam also set the standard for all future magic shows on television. Wilson always did his magic in front of a live audience, never used trick photography, and never allowed the camera to cut away during a trick, all to assure the home audience that magic was not accomplished through camera trickery … principles still used today on all major television magic shows.

In the 1970s, Mark Wilson produced and starred in six one-hour "Magic Circus" television specials, which were syndicated nationally by the Pillsbury Company. Later, in the 80s, he was host of *The Magic of Mark Wilson,* a half-hour, syndicated series co-starring wife Nani and the Wilsons' second son, 12-year-old Greg.

And when television and movie producers want magic, they know that Mark Wilson is the man to ask for. Once Mark and his creative staff have developed an appropriate concept, he turns to his vast warehouse, which houses the largest single collection of illusions (large magic props) under one roof in the entire world. In addition to his many "on camera" appearances, Mark has also often acted as magical creative consultant for many TV series and specials for all

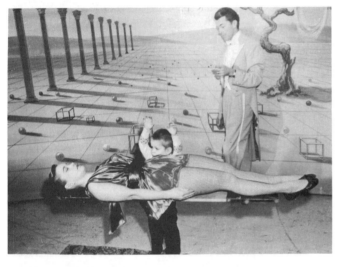

B

A

A. *Time for Magic,* Mark and Nani's first television series, made its debut in February, 1954.

B. A three-year-old Mike Wilson performs his first illusion.

C. Nani Darnell Wilson.

D. Mike, at four, picks up a few pointers from Dad.

C

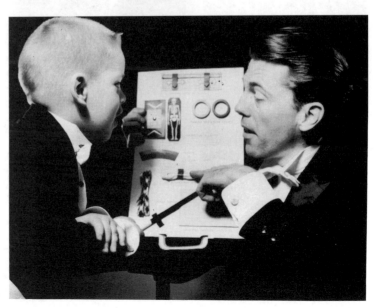

D

three television networks as well as most of the major motion picture studios.

Of particular note is *The Magician* television series for which Wilson provided all of the elaborate magic props, supplied story lines and script ideas and taught star Bill Bixby all of the magic for his role.

Mark has also instructed Hollywood's top stars in the performance of magic, working with such luminaries as Cary Grant, Tony Curtis, Peter Falk, Dick Van Dyke, John Denver, Jackie Gleason, Cher, Johnny Carson, and Burt Reynolds.

In addition to his television appearances, Mark has toured extensively, producing and presenting magic shows throughout the world. In 1980, Mark Wilson received one of the greatest honors ever given to any performer when he was invited by the government of the People's Republic of China to be the first Western entertainer to perform in that awakening country. It was a landmark event when Mark and Nani Wilson, along with a company of 20 people, a television production crew, and over two and a half tons of props, performed throughout China.

For the Chinese people this was their first opportunity ever to see an American performance, since no Western performers had appeared in mainland China in the 32-year history of the People's Republic of China. They called him the "Magical Marco Polo," and in the packed theaters where they appeared, Mark and Nani introduced the Chinese people not only to Western magic, but also to Western dance,

A

A. Greg Wilson enjoys performing with Mom and Dad.

B. Cary Grant presents the Magician of the Year award.

C. The *Magic Circus* television specials were syndicated throughout the world.

D. *The Magic Land of Allakazam* was the first national magic show television series.

E. *Allakazam!* Rebo (Bev Bergeron), Mark, and Nani.

B

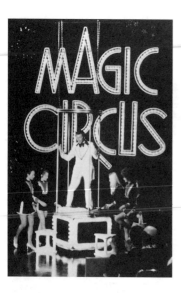

C

D

E

scenery, costuming, pacing, and showmanship.

So unique was this event that *Time* magazine carried both an article and photo coverage of Mark's advance visit to Beijing. China Central Television videotaped the show and aired it nationwide, another first for a Western performer. The government estimated that 200 million Chinese viewed *The Magic of Mark Wilson* television special, and the show has been rerun throughout China many times.

In addition, Mark reached out to the Chinese people by performing on location, another historic first. Mark entertained at agricultural communes and elementary schools, on trains, among workers tilling the fields, at the Children's Palace in Shanghai, in the Forbidden City and Tien An Mien Square in Beijing, in the courtyard of the Mausoleum of Sun Yat Sen in Nanking, and even on the ancient Great Wall. The tour produced three television specials, *The Magic of China* and *The Children of China,* and *The Adventures of a Young Magician* which aired on the CBS network and featured Greg Wilson co-starring with Bill Bixby.

Mark Wilson's work in China made him a celebrity there and, through the airing of his television series and specials in many countries, his fame has spread throughout the world. In 1983, he toured Southeast Asia, including Malaysia, Bangkok, Singapore, and Hong Kong, appearing in large theaters and giant arenas with an even larger cast and ten thousand pounds of equipment.

Mark Wilson authored *The Complete Course in Magic,* the highly-acclaimed volume which has been translated into Italian, French, Chinese and Russian. With more than three quarters of a million copies in print, it is the most popular book of magic instruction ever written.

Wilson has created and produced custom-designed magic productions for some of world's finest theme parks, world's fairs, and expositions, including: The Hall of Magic Pavilion at the New York World's Fair; ATT's Magic of the Telephone Pavilion at the Hemisfair; Disneyland; Disney World; Legoland; and all of the Busch Gardens Six Flags, and Kings Entertainment Parks.

Wilson's Magical Attractions are unique devices designed to attract, entertain and deliver commercial impact at trade shows. They include The Amazing Hand Machine, Man From Mars, Half Humanoid, Miniature Girl, Robot Girl, Miraculous Materializer, and Wilson's copyrighted Cinillusion©, which is the combination of a projected image of film or video, live action performers on stage and magic. Wilson has been issued five U.S. patents for these and other magical devices.

Mark Wilson and Nani Darnell's first son, Michael, born in 1954, graduated from the University of California, Berkeley with a Bachelor of Arts degree in 1977. In 1980, Michael was Road Show Manager for Mark Wilson's history-making tour of China, and became so fascinated by the Orient, he enrolled as a Chinese Language and International Business major in the graduate school of the University of Illinois, where he received the coveted Master of Business Administration degree. While studying for his degree, Michael attended the prestigious Peking University, living in Beijing for a year. Michael Wilson speaks fluent Mandarin, the official language of China, and now heads his own company, bringing international performers to the U.S. and

A

B

C

A. With Bill Bixby on "The Magician" set at Paramount Studios.

B. A giant billboard announces the appearence of the great American Magic Show in Bangkok.

C. Rehearsing with Dick Van Dyke.

booking U.S. entertainers overseas.

The Wilsons' younger son, Greg, was born in 1965, and he developed such an interest in magic that he became a skilled magician by the time he was eight years old, the very age at which his father, Mark, had first witnessed a magic show. In the early 1980s, Greg co-starred with his father and mother in *The Magic of Mark Wilson* series, which has delighted and baffled television viewers in many countries throughout the world. Greg is now an internationally recognized magician and illusionist carrying on the Wilson name.

In 1961, Mark Wilson brought a young college student, Johnny Gaughan, to Hollywood from Dallas where he had worked for Wilson. As John's great talent in design and woodworking became apparent, Mark made him supervisor of the Wilson workshop. John Gaughan now heads his own organization and is recognized as the leading expert in illusion design. John has built or supervised construction of almost all of the hundreds of illusions in Mark's warehouses, as well as for many other prominent magicians throughout the world.

Alan Wakeling, well known as a performing magician, joined Mark Wilson Productions in 1968 as Creative Director. Wilson credits Wakeling with the creation of many of his most effective and baffling magical presentations, including the Spiker, Excalibur, and Aquarian Illusions. After twenty-five years, Alan retired from Mark's company to pursue other endeavors including the building and restoring of exquisite automata.

Mark Wilson has become one of the world's most honored magicians. He is President Emeritus and former Chairman of the Board of the Academy of Magical Arts at the Magic Castle in Hollywood. Mark and Nani have received awards from major magic organizations throughout the world, including the Magician's Hall of Fame from the Society of American Magicians and Super Stars of Magic from the International Brotherhood of Magicians. Wilson was the first magician ever to receive two of the prestigious Magician of the Year awards from the Academy of Magical Arts, the magician's equivalent of winning two Oscars, and the Academy's top award, the Masters Fellowship. The readers of *Magic* magazine, America's leading independent publication for magicians, voted Mark Wilson one of the "Ten Most Influential Magicians of the 20th Century."

The eight-year-old boy who watched his first magic show with wide-eyed wonder has become the most well-known performer in the entire history of the ancient art of magic. But Wilson's world is not only one of magic, it encompasses the realm of producer, world traveler, teacher, author, businessman, creator of new approaches to sales and marketing, and the creative force behind a wide array of amusement park and stage attractions.

For a couple as diversified and talented as Mark Wilson and Nani Darnell Wilson, the greatest trick of all is finding the time to do everything.

A

B

A. Mark and his cast perform Robert Harbin's famous Zig Zag illusion on the Great Wall.

B. The "Magic Exchange." Magicians traveled from throughout China to exchange magic secerts with the magician from the west.

C. A Chinese boy is delighted by Mark's magic.

C

WALTER GIBSON (1897-1985): CO-AUTHOR

Walter Gibson was one of magic's most prolific journalists. As a young man, while working for the *Philadelphia Ledger*, he was commissioned to do a syndicated series of simple tricks, puzzles, and games. These caught the attention of Howard Thurston, who was then America's leading magician, and he engaged Gibson to prepare special booklets on magic to be sold at the Thurston show. Next, Gibson was working for Thurston on magical articles that were sold to popular magazines such as *The Saturday Evening Post* and *Boys' Life*.

Impressed with what he saw, Harry Houdini called on Gibson to prepare a series of three books to be published under Houdini's name. Only one had been completed at the time of Houdini's unfortunate death in 1926, but a few years later, the Houdini estate provided Gibson with all of Houdini's unpublished notes on magical methods. From those Gibson prepared two books under his own name—*Houdini's Escapes* and *Houdini's Magic*, which have become classics in the field.

Harry Blackstone, who had been one of Gibson's earliest magical friends and inspirations, contracted Gibson to write two books for him. Joseph Dunninger had Gibson pen books for him as well. Added to that, Gibson wrote innumerable magic books under his own name, and edited several different magic magazines throughout the course of his life.

Walter Gibson is probably best known as the creator of the character The Shadow, a hugely popular fictional crime fighter. Under the pen name Maxwell Grant, Gibson turned out 1,680,000 words of fiction during the year from March 1, 1932, to March 1, 1933, an all-time record for a year's wordage devoted to a single mystery character.

In 1966, a much younger mystifier was fast establishing himself as a master magician of the future. His name was Mark Wilson, and it was inevitable that he should later meet with Walter Gibson to discuss the shaping of magic in the years to come. When they did meet, their prime object of consideration was the comprehensive magic course that Mark Wilson was planning. They agreed that by combining the underlying principles of the past with the vast array of present methods currently available, future effects could be developed on a grand and lavish scale. Since then, they have cooperated to make the projected course the reality that it is today.

Walter Gibson's vast, highly respected literary output represents an immeasurable contribution to the art of magic.

U.F. "GEN." GRANT (1901-1978): CREATOR OF MAGIC

There is probably no other magician who has invented, devised, and improved more magic effects than U.F. "Gen." Grant. Practically every magician has performed at least a few (and often many) of Gen.'s creations. Certainly every modern magic catalog introduces some of Grant's remarkably marketable effects. Most assuredly this course owes a large debt to his fertile mind. As you progress in your knowledge of the principles of magic and their implementation, your respect and admiration will grow for this true master of magical invention—Mr. U.F. "Gen." Grant.

LARRY ANDERSON: COURSE COORDINATOR

By "magical" standards, Larry Anderson has attained a degree of pro in the art of magic, highly regarded by his peers. Larry first came to Wilson's attention at the age of nineteen, while still at the university in Minnesota. Mark required assistance with a large illusion show in the Twin Cities, and Larry's knowledge of magic, bearing, and hard work made him a stand out. Wilson was so pleased with his contribution, he flew Larry to California to be a full-time associate in his organization.

For this course, Larry, with the assistance of Don Wayne, coordinated the photography and artwork, and made valuable contributions in creative writing and rewriting, all essential to the result. Larry is now pursuing an acting and directing career, but still finds time to study, practice, and enjoy his first real love—magic.

HOW TO ADD MAGIC TO YOUR LIFE

I created the Complete Course in Magic because I believe that learning and performing really good magic can make your entire life better, just as it did mine. In the Course, you will find some of the most closely guarded secrets of the art of magic. In many ways, this book is similar to discovering a legendary volume of magical spells. Each trick is like an ancient incantation that will help you achieve some long wished for goal. (Watch out Harry Potter, here you come!)

Let me tell you a few of the things magic has done for me. As a youngster in school, I was shy … smaller than the other boys my age … not particularly good at any sport. Nobody hated me, but nobody seemed to like me very much either. I discovered I was not lucky enough to be inherently talented and certainly I was not an athlete. I was more of an introvert than a party animal, not particularly strong, and not as tall or well built as some of the other guys in my class. When they were picking a team for a ball game, I was not the first one chosen. I was all right scholastically, but my social life was lacking.

Then I saw a magic show. I was fascinated. I got books from the library. I studied everything I could find. Soon, I could do some simple tricks. I did some magic for a few kids at a class party … everybody gathered around … they liked my magic. More importantly, they liked me! The girls, as well as the guys, all seemed to like me more. I never expected this. The "magic" was working for me!

Then I figured out why it worked for me, and why it will work for you, too. When you show someone a really good magic trick, their first reaction is one of surprise and wonder …"How did you do that?"… followed by admiration and respect for you, the magician, "That was really good. Can you do something else?"

I began to be recognized as a magician. I began to stand out from the crowd. My confidence and feeling of self worth increased. I began to overcome my shyness. I was better able to deal with people. I became more successful in everything I did.

My life seemed to change, not immediately, but over time, as more people discovered what I could do. By the time I enrolled at Southern Methodist University, whenever I was invited to a party, I always had some magic in my pockets. I got invitations to a lot of parties. In fact, I was invited to so many parties, I couldn't attend them all.

Then I said to myself, "Wait a minute. They ask me to all those parties because I am a terrific guy. I don't need that "magic" anymore. They like me for who I am, not for my magic!" So, when I was beginning my sophomore year at the university, I took the tricks out of my pockets and stopped doing any magic at parties. I just went as myself. I didn't need that "magic!"

Sure enough, it worked! But not the way I thought it would. It worked in reverse. After a while, I was not invited to many parties. Then the invitations dwindled even more. That was not what I had expected. I had learned my lesson.

I put the magic back in my pockets. I did tricks for anyone who would watch. Sure enough, everything turned around. I was "popular" again. I was performing magic shows to help pay my way through college. I was asked to be the Master of Ceremonies for the annual homecoming show. My fraternity brothers elected me president of our chapter.

When I became a senior, in an attempt to gain more prestige for my fraternity, I ran for head cheerleader in the annual school election. I had never been any kind of cheerleader. I had no experience in leading thousands of people in "coordinated yelling." My opponent had a good track record as a cheerleader. I figured, "Okay, I won't win, but I will get some publicity for the fraternity." When the election was held, I won by the largest majority of votes of anyone running for any office that year.

The point of all this is, I'm sure none of these life shaping events would have ever happened if my fraternity brothers, the faculty members who produced that homecoming show, and my fellow students who voted for me in the election, had not known who I was. It wasn't, "Mark? Oh yeah, he's the short guy in my statistics class, I think." It was more like, "Mark Wilson. I remember him doing some magic at our sorority party last week. He might be a good head cheerleader. Maybe he could make the other football team disappear." … or whatever.

So, you see, it wasn't me, my athletic ability or my "wonderful" personality that gave me that recognition. It was because those people remembered who I was. And that was because of the magic.

I'm a lot older now. I have kept the magic in my pockets. I also have magic in my house, my office, and my warehouse. I have never left magic out of my life again. That's what magic did for me, and it will do the same for you.

Study this course, practice and rehearse the tricks, then try them on your friends. You will soon be recognized as a magician. Magicians make the impossible happen. There aren't many people who can make that claim. You will become a "special person" to your friends and to everyone you meet.

It really does happen. I've seen it hundreds of times. You will become more popular, your confidence will grow, your feelings of self-worth will increase. The magic will work for you. Here are a few of the many ways you can put the power of magic to work for you.

THE BENEFITS OF LEARNING MAGIC

You can meet people and make new friends. Your magic can help you "break the ice" and make new friends on a plane, in a restaurant, at the beach, just about anywhere. If there is someone you want to meet, perhaps he or she is across the room at any gathering, waiting near you in a line, or seated at another table in a restaurant, your magic will pave the way. Singles find it's an excellent way to meet members of the opposite sex.

You will be invited to many parties. As soon as your friends know you can perform magic, you'll be invited to every party. If you are not already known as a magician, do a trick or two for your host or hostess. They will ask you to do your magic for everyone at the party. You may just become the most popular person at the affair. The next time they see your name on a list of possible guests, someone will say, "Oh, yes, invite him. I still can't figure out how he did those amazing tricks at that last party."

You will be a sought-after dinner guest. With what you will learn in the course, you can do magic with objects found on any dinner table. Doing a few baffling tricks after dinner, along with the coffee, adds entertainment to the evening and assures your invitation to many more dinner affairs.

Sometimes, when dining in a restaurant, I do a few tricks for my friends at the table. Often the waiter will see what I am doing and ask if I will do a trick for him. When he is completely baffled, he will say, "Would you mind doing that for some of our other waiters?" When some waiters are gathered around, other dinner guests want to see what is going on and come over to our table to find out. So I warn you, if you are not careful, you can literally "take over" a small restaurant. I've had that happen many times.

You can be the family favorite. With just a few tricks, you can turn an ordinary family get-together into a special event. You'll find that magic has made you into a special person. A friend tells me his grandchildren are unanimous in saying, "I have two grandfathers. One does magic! And then there's that other guy."

Another example, is when mom says, with a great big smile, "Everybody climb into the car, we're going over to see grandma and grandpa." She doesn't want to hear, "Do I have to go, mom? We were just there last month." She's much happier when the response is, "Oh, goody, maybe grandpa will show me a new magic trick."

You can spread a bit of joy. Your magic can bring a few minutes of happiness to an orphanage, a children's hospital or a retirement home. You can be a great help at their next fund raiser. Church organization, civic clubs, underprivileged children's groups and many other charitable organizations are constantly looking for entertainment for their members. When you see that your magic brings smiles to those faces, it will be one of the greatest rewards you'll ever receive.

Your magic can help you set new sales records. Here's where your magic can really shine. If you call on clients at their offices or business establishments, a clever trick will brighten a receptionist's morning and give you an edge getting through to the boss. The right magic effect can emphasize your selling message and definitely add fun to a client's day. They'll be delighted to see you every time you call.

Or, if the customers come to your business, magic can help increase the selection of your establishment over your competition. "Let's go over to Joe's Place for our hamburgers. Maybe he will do one of those cool magic tricks for us." You'll find a whole section on applying magic to your sales later in this discourse.

You can make teaching interesting. Throughout the world, public interest in the art of magic has greatly increased, not only in watching magic, but also in learning how to perform it. With the knowledge you gain from this course, you may wish to become a magic instructor. There are many possibilities. The teaching of magic can be tailored to any group, selected and structured for their particular needs. As an example, check out what we suggest for summer campers in **Magic for Children.**

Many professional teachers have added magic to their course curriculums to entertainingly deliver educational material, emphasize particular learning points, maintain their students' attention in the classroom, or establish attendance-building, extra-curricular after-school activities.

You can make extra money in your spare time. There are many opportunities to make additional income with your magic. You don't have to be a full-time, professional magician to do it. You might want to become what we in the business call a "semi-pro." In your own neighborhood you can perform at birthday parties, bar mitzvahs, restaurants, retirement homes, anniversaries, sales meetings, office parties and all kinds of social affairs. There are many who have "worked their way through college" performing magic shows and many semi-pros who have magic as a secondary occupation, adding substantially to their income.

THE UNIVERSAL, INTERNATIONAL APPEAL OF MAGIC

Magic is a truly unique form of entertainment, appreciated by old and young alike. Magic knows no racial, geographic or language barriers. It is not even necessary to speak a country's language to perform magic and make friends in foreign lands. Presenting a few good magic tricks will make you welcome around the world.

Many times our personal experiences have illustrated to my wife Nani and me that the appeal of magic is truly universal and international. Universal because magic is equally appreciated by children in kindergarten, senior citizens in retirement homes, and every age in between. That appeal is also international, because magic works in any country in the world. Here's a perfect example of how the captivating power of magic is both universal and international.

In 1980, we were invited by the Chinese government to take our magic to mainland China. The invitation came from the Ministry of Culture, an agency of the People's Republic of China. At that time, they were in charge of all the performers in the country. China had been behind the "Bamboo Curtain" for 32 years, and the invitation came shortly after "joint recognition" between the U.S. and the P.R.C. Ancient China is the legendary home of magic.

We were the first "Western" entertainers allowed to perform for the people of China since the current government took control of the country in 1948. We had been preceded by a symphony orchestra and a ballet troupe, who performed one show in Beijing and another in Shanghai for government dignitaries and leading officials. We were to perform our illusion show in theaters in major cities and conduct the first ever "magic exchange" with Chinese magicians.

One part of the exchange was for us to teach the Chinese magicians the latest in western magic. That was easy for us. They hadn't seen any western magic for over three decades. (In a country of over a billion people, I was the only magician with a Zig Zag illusion!) The Chinese sorcerers would show us some of the classic Chinese wizardry handed down through the ages.

To us, the most important part of our visit was to see what "modern" China was like. We were going to a country that had been out of touch with the West for over thirty years. We spoke no Chinese. Their language, written in Chinese hieroglyphics, was totally unrecognizable to us as well. Our cultural backgrounds were entirely different. We were told different fairy tales as children and learned different nursery rhymes. Their music was cacophonous to us and ours equally strange to them. Almost all of the Chinese people we met and performed for had never seen anyone from the West. I'm sure our faces looked very strange to them. In the truest sense of the word, everything was as foreign to us as we were to the Chinese. And yet, our magic worked beautifully.

Because we wanted to meet as many of the people of China as possible, we performed not only in theaters, but also in communes, factories, schools, on trains, at national monuments, in parks, in Tiananmen Square, at the temple of Heaven, and on the Great Wall of China. The levitation of a young Chinese girl at the Great Wall was featured in *Time* magazine. Everywhere we went our magic got a warm welcome.

But it was in our appearances for smaller groups of Chinese that I could see their wonderful reactions. Several times I went alone to a public park and approached a group of old men, visiting in their retirement. I would say, "*Ne how*," which is Chinese for hello, the only word of their language I knew. Then I would then show them a magic trick.

The initial puzzlement on their faces turned to smiles. They understood immediately that what they were seeing was "magic." They commented in pleasure to each other. After several more effects, I could tell they were glad I came to see them. I had a feeling they would be telling stories about that Western man they met in the park for years to come.

The most important part of that experience was I could feel the warmth and friendliness created by the magic. I had that same feeling during our visits to children in grade schools, family groups in communes and workers in the factories. The wonderful response to our magic was certainly universal and truly international in this foreign land. Check it out, you'll see. Magic works everywhere.

That's what magic did for me, and it will do the same for you. Study this course, practice and rehearse the tricks, then try them on your friends. You will soon be recognized as a magician. Magicians make the impossible happen. There aren't many people who can make that claim. You will become a "special person" to your friends and to everyone you meet. It really does happen. I've seen it hundreds of times. You will become more popular, your confidence will grow, your feelings of self-worth will increase. The magic will work for you.

CARD MAGIC

★ ★ ★

Tricks with cards form a branch of magic entirely on their own. In fact, there are some magicians who specialize in card tricks and nothing else, due to the wide range of opportunities offered by that field. This applies to everyone to some degree, because from the moment you start doing card tricks, you naturally acquire a manipulative ability. The mere act of cutting and shuffling a pack of cards, then dealing it, demands skill of a sort. When you spread the pack, inviting someone to "take a card," or run rapidly through the face-up pack while looking for cards needed for some special trick, you acquire further facility. Next you may find fancy cuts and flourishes to your liking; and if you do, you will be on the road to becoming a card expert almost before you realize it.

There are many tricks involved in the discovery of cards selected by members of the audience. These depend upon a variety of methods, which enable you to keep a "jump ahead" of keen-eyed and keen-witted spectators. Basically, there are three ways of discovering a chosen card: One is to "force" it on the spectator, so that you know the card beforehand and thereby can predict it, name it, or produce a duplicate from some unexpected place. Another way is to "locate" the card by its position in the pack, so you can find it by simply looking through the pack or studying the cards as you deal them. The third way is to "control" the chosen card, by shuffles, cuts and other manipulations that enable you to reveal it at any time.

All three ways are covered in this section and each has its own variations depending on different degrees of skill. So, by switching from one method to another, you can leave your audiences utterly nonplussed. Here, you will be further aided by special devices described or supplied with this course. One is the "Short" card, which you can find or control by the sense of touch alone. Another is the "Double-Backed" card which is responsible for several special effects, including those where a card reverses itself in the pack. Also, there is the "Double-Faced" card which enables you to apparently transform one card into another.

None of these devices is suspected by your audiences, yet all can be added to a standard pack, enabling you to accomplish remarkable feats that would be impossible with an ordinary pack alone. All this will add to your growing reputation as a card master while simplifying your work to a marked degree. By adding some of the more elaborate effects described in this section, you can soon round out a program of card magic that will stand as a complete act in itself.

CARD DEFINITIONS

The following is a list of definitions of words or terms used in Card Magic. You will find many of these used in the Course. Each is listed with either a brief definition or a reference to the page in the Course where that particular sleight or term is described.

FULL DECK:
52 cards consisting of four suits, Diamonds, Clubs, Hearts, and Spades with 13 cards per suit from Ace through King. . .with the Joker as an optional 53rd card.

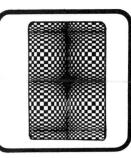

PATTERN BACK DECK:
Any deck with a *pattern* or *geometrical design* on its back.

TOP OF DECK:
When the deck is face down, the *uppermost* card or portion of the deck.

PICTURE BACK DECK:
Any deck with a "picture" on its back. The picture may be of anything such as a dog, a cat, or the Grand Canyon. Since these are mostly "novelty" cards, they are usually not well suited for magic effects except in special instances such as card fans.

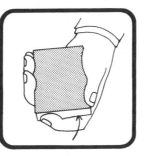

BOTTOM OF THE DECK:
The *lowermost* card or portion of the deck.

WHITE BORDERED BACK CARD:
Most "PATTERN BACKED" cards have a white border around the outer edge. (One notable exception is "Bee" brand decks.) A white border back is essential in the performance of many of the tricks described in this Course. This is because, when a card is reversed (turned *face up* in a *face-down* pack), it will not be noticeable because the white edges of the face are the *same* as the white border of the Pattern Back.

FACE:
The face of a card shows its value and suit.

SPOT CARDS:
Any card from Ace through Ten in any suit.

BACK:
The back of a card is the pattern or picture on the opposite side of the "face." The back design is repeated on all cards throughout the deck.

DEUCE:
Another name for a Two.

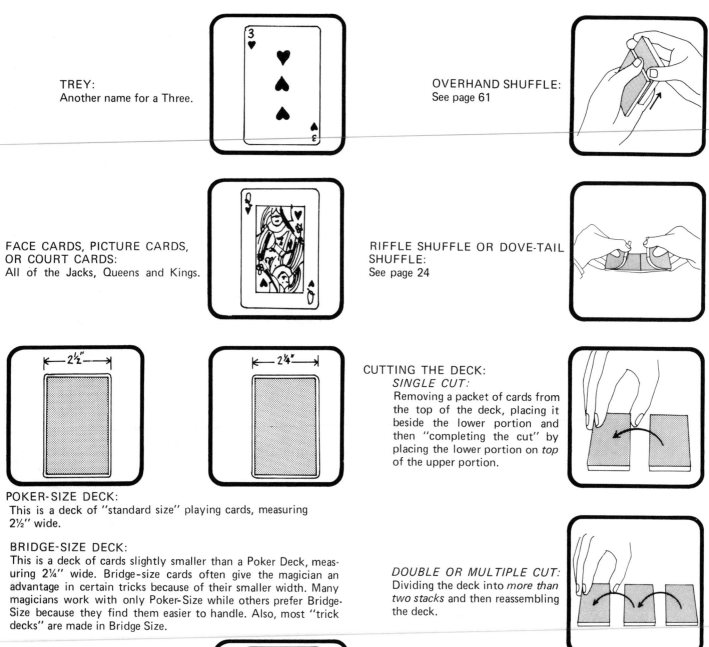

TREY:
Another name for a Three.

FACE CARDS, PICTURE CARDS, OR COURT CARDS:
All of the Jacks, Queens and Kings.

POKER-SIZE DECK:
This is a deck of "standard size" playing cards, measuring 2½" wide.

BRIDGE-SIZE DECK:
This is a deck of cards slightly smaller than a Poker Deck, measuring 2¼" wide. Bridge-size cards often give the magician an advantage in certain tricks because of their smaller width. Many magicians work with only Poker-Size while others prefer Bridge-Size because they find them easier to handle. Also, most "trick decks" are made in Bridge Size.

GIANT CARD:
An extra large card which is usually four times larger than a regular Poker-sized playing card.

MECHANICS' GRIP
A method used for holding the deck in the left hand for dealing. The left first finger extends around the *front* of the deck, the second, third, and little fingers around the right side, and the thumb on top (as shown). This is superior and more professional than the Standard Dealing Position in that the first finger keeps the cards "squared." The MECHANICS' GRIP should be used in almost all "dealing" tricks so that it becomes natural and easy. It is essential for more advanced sleights such as "Second" or "Bottom" dealing.

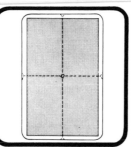

OVERHAND SHUFFLE:
See page 61

RIFFLE SHUFFLE OR DOVE-TAIL SHUFFLE:
See page 24

CUTTING THE DECK:
SINGLE CUT:
Removing a packet of cards from the top of the deck, placing it beside the lower portion and then "completing the cut" by placing the lower portion on *top* of the upper portion.

DOUBLE OR MULTIPLE CUT:
Dividing the deck into *more than two stacks* and then reassembling the deck.

FALSE CUT:
Any "cut" that leaves the deck *in the same order* as it was before the cut.

FALSE SHUFFLE:
Any shuffle which leaves the deck *in the same order* as it was before the shuffle.

DEAL THE CARDS:
Removing cards from the pack, singly or in groups. Although this is usually done with two hands, it can also be done with one hand.

One-hand dealing

STANDARD DEALING POSITION:
The pack is held in the left hand resting on the palm, with the fingers extending around the right edge of the pack and the thumb on top. From this position, the thumb is ready to push off cards across the tips of the fingers, so that the right hand can draw, or "deal," each card away.

STANDARD DEAL:
Cards are drawn off, one at a time, face downward, and placed on the table, each card going on the card before it. This *reverses* the order of the cards.

TURN-UP DEAL:
The cards are dealt singly from the top of the face-down deck but are *turned face up* as they are dealt. *This does not reverse the order of the deck.*

ONE-WAY DECK:
This is usually a "PICTURE BACKED" deck in which the back patterns may all be arranged so that they face *one way*. This type of deck may be quickly made into a "trick deck" by arranging the Picture Backs so they are *all* facing one way. Have a card selected...then merely *turn the deck around* so that when the card is returned, ITS "PICTURE" IS FACING IN THE OPPOSITE DIRECTION. Then, by running through the pack and looking at the backs, you can easily find the selected card.

FORCE:
Causing a spectator to select a particular card or cards *when he thinks he is making a FREE choice.*

See FORCES, Page 76

FORCING DECK:
A deck in which all of the cards are of the same value. (Usually the bottom or "face" card of the pack will be of a different value to mislead the spectators.)

TWO-WAY FORCING DECK:
A deck in which the *top half* is composed of cards all of the same suit and value while the *bottom half* is composed of cards all the same but of a *different* suit and value. Used for "forcing" two different cards by spreading the cards so that the *first* spectator selects from the *top* half and the *second* spectator from the *bottom* half.

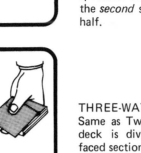

THREE-WAY FORCE:
Same as Two-Way Force Deck except deck is divided into *three* similarly faced sections.

50/50 FORCING DECK:
A deck in which the top half is all the same (forcing) cards and the bottom half is differing (regular) cards. With this deck, the magician may turn the pack face up to show that the cards are all different, as long as *he does not spread past the lower half*...and then turn the deck back, face down, and "force" a card *by having it selected from the top half.*

LOCATOR CARD:
Any card which can be used as a "key" to find some other card in the pack. Some examples of Locator Cards are:

Short Card, See page 125
Long Card, a card that is slightly longer than the rest of the pack. This card may be easily located because of its extra length.

KEY CARD:
Any card that can be used as a "locator" card.

CARD LOCATION:
Any method that allows the magician to "find" or "locate" a selected card after it has been returned to the pack.

DOUBLE-FACED CARD:
A specially printed "trick" card with a FACE on *both* sides.

REVERSE COUNT:
See page 27

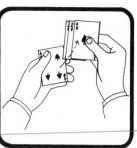

DOUBLE-BACKED CARD:
A specially printed "trick" card with a BACK on *both* sides.

SLEIGHT:
A *"secret"* move done with the cards which is not known to the spectators. . .such as Double Lift, Glide, etc.

MOVE:
A "move" may be either *secret* in which case it is a Sleight, or some movement of the cards which the spectators can "see," such as Cutting the Pack.

SET-UP
Any preparation done before a show (or in many cases *during* a performance) which arranges the cards in a special order or location.

BREAK:
See page 83

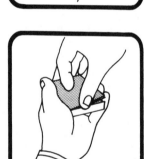

PREARRANGED DECK:
A deck which has been "set up" or arranged in some special order before the performance.

DOUBLE LIFT:
See page 84

STOCK:
Any portion of the pack containing cards which have been "set up" in a special order.

GLIDE:
See page 97

COUNTING THE CARDS:
See page 26

GLIMPSE:
Secretly noting a card while holding or shuffling the pack. See page 4 8

FLASH:
Allowing the spectator to "briefly see" the face of any card.

REVERSED CARD:
Any card which is *face up* in a *face-down* pack (or *face down* in a *face-up* pack).

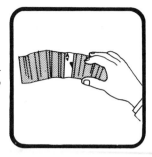

CONTROL:
Any method (usually unknown to the audience) that allows the performer to know the location of a particular card or cards in the pack. This term is used extensively in the Course and in most every instance refers to the return to the pack of the selected card by the spectator and the magician's ability to "Control" the card to the top, bottom or some other location in the pack where the magician wants it.

FLOURISH:
A display of skill with the cards. "Flourishes" are usually not tricks, although they can become important parts of some effects. Examples of flourishes are Fanning the Pack, Springing the Cards, the Ribbon Spread, One-Hand Cuts, etc.

GIMMICK:
Any *"secret"* device used to perform a trick. The audience is usually never aware of a "gimmick."

FAN OF CARDS:
A number of cards held in the hand in the shape of a fan.

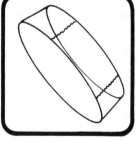

CARD DISCOVERY:
The climax or end of many card tricks wherein the spectator's card is revealed or produced in a "magical" manner.

THE "MAGIC LOOP":
A very useful article in many magic effects is cellophane tape. Cellophane tape is manufactured in two ways. One is the conventional tape with the "sticky surface" on one side; the other has the "sticky surface" on both sides and is called Double Stick tape. As you will see, Double Stick tape is quite helpful for magical purposes, particularly if the audience is unaware of its presence. However, if you wish to do any of the tricks that call for Double Stick tape and do not have any on hand, you can easily make your own by forming a "Magic Loop." This is done by taking a piece of the regular single-sided tape and forming it into a loop, as shown, WITH THE STICKY SIDE OUT. Now, by placing this on whatever surface you wish to apply the tape to, and by pressing the loop flat, you will have, to all intents and purposes, formed a piece of *Double Stick tape*. At various places throughout this Course, you will find the Magic Loop referred to. Now, with this knowledge, you can form a piece of Double Stick tape and perform the many magical effects possible with it from standard cellophane tape.

CARD HANDLING TECHNIQUES

Throughout all Card Magic, you will find that there are certain basic card handling techniques which are essential to your ability to perform card tricks. These include shuffling, counting, dealing, and spreading the pack. All of these techniques will not necessarily appear in each card trick, but there are very few tricks, for example, that do not require *at least* a shuffle. You probably already know one, but in Card Magic you will find that there are several kinds of shuffle. Most of them serve some special purpose, such as controlling the position of a card, and together they give you the opportunity to introduce *variety* into your card handling. Similarly, there are different techniques for dealing and counting which control card locations. The success of a trick frequently *depends* upon your skillful accomplishment of one of these manipulations. Therefore, you are urged to *practice ALL* of the following manipulations until you can do each one *smoothly, confidently,* and *without hesitation.*

Remember also, the mere appearance of skill and confidence in your handling of cards will add much to your audience's respect for your ability as a magician.

THE RIFFLE SHUFFLE

The RIFFLE SHUFFLE is probably the most widely used method of shuffling cards; and for that reason alone, you should be familiar with it. It is not difficult, but it will require some practice to perform it smoothly.

METHOD

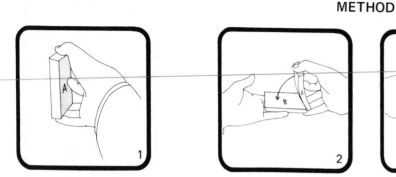

(1) Hold the pack in your right hand with your thumb at one end and your second, third, and fourth fingers at the other. The tip of your first finger should rest against the back of the top card of the pack. The pack should be held so that your right thumb is toward the ceiling with the face of the pack pointing to your left.
(2) Place the palm of your left hand on the bottom of the pack as shown. With your right hand, bend the pack outward and riffle about half of the pack with your right thumb, allowing the cards to fall forward onto the left fingers.

(5) Turn both packets face down and move the "thumb end" of each packet together. The backs of the second, third, and little fingers of both hands should rest on the top of the table.
(6) Slowly begin releasing (riffling) cards from *both* thumbs causing the cards to fall to the table and become <u>interlaced</u> at the inner ends. The ends of the cards should overlap about a half inch as they are "shuffled" together.

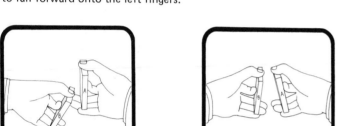

(3) Place the tip of your left thumb on the back of this new packet (B) and raise the lower end of Packet B *upward* until it clears Packet A in the right hand. As the end of Packet B comes clear, shift your left thumb to the right-hand end of Packet B.
(4) *The two packets should now be facing each other held with the same grip in each hand.* Your thumbs should be at one end of the packets, your first fingers resting against the backs of the packs and the remaining fingers at the opposite ends.

(7) When all the cards have been shuffled from both packets, push the two packets completely together and square the deck. This completes the RIFFLE SHUFFLE.

(8) Repeat Steps 1 through 7 in quick succession, executing the shuffle as many times as you wish, to thoroughly mix the cards.

THE TABLE SHUFFLE

This basic exercise is intended to show you how to shuffle a deck of cards in the proper manner. This is similar to, but considerably more "professional" than, the standard RIFFLE SHUFFLE. When working with cards, it is to your advantage to be able to mix the cards in a quick, graceful fashion and, since some of the best card tricks are performed while seated at a table, every magician should be familiar with the TABLE SHUFFLE. It gives your work an expert look, convincing your audience that even your simplest tricks are the result of great skill.

EFFECT

The magician divides the pack into two packets which he rests face down on the table. Lifting the *rear edges* of both packets, he begins to release the cards in succession causing their corners to interweave as they fall. He then pushes the two packets together and squares the pack, thoroughly mixing the pack.

METHOD

(1) Place the pack face down on the table in front of you and grasp the sides of the pack from above as shown. Using your thumbs, lift about half the pack from the top of the deck, near the middle.

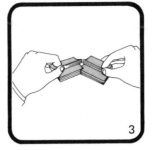

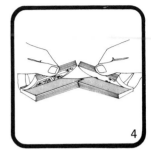

(3) Lift the inner edge of both packets with your thumbs and move the packets together so that the innermost corners will overlap slightly. Now, begin releasing the cards from your thumbs, allowing them to riffle downward onto the table so the inner corners of the cards weave together. (4) Here is a close-up view of the cards interweaving. The cards are released from your thumbs *interlacing at the corners only.*

(2) Now, separate the halves and place the packets on the table as shown. *The outer ends of both packets should be angled slightly toward you, to bring the innermost corners of the packets very close together.* Hold both packets with your *thumbs* along the *inner edge;* the *first finger* of each hand rests on the *top* of the packs, and your *remaining fingers* rest along the *outer edges.*

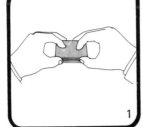

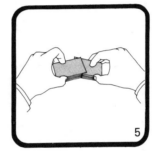

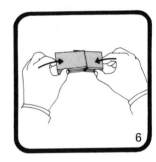

(5) Once all the cards have been released, . . . (6) . . . move your fingers to the extreme ends of both packets and push them together to form one complete "shuffled" pack.

(7) Repeat the shuffling process as many times as you like until all the cards in the pack have been completely mixed.

COMMENTS AND SUGGESTIONS

This type of shuffle, sometimes known as the "Dovetail Shuffle," is often used by gamblers or professional "dealers." Therefore, it is particularly effective when doing card tricks that have a gambling theme. Many gamblers, after completing the shuffle, will cut the pack by drawing out the *lower half* of the pack and placing it on *top* of the *upper packet.* As a magician, you can follow the same procedure, adding a natural and professional touch to your card work.

DEALING THE CARDS

Few actions are simpler than dealing cards from the top of a pack, but to do it smoothly, neatly and sometimes rapidly, the hands should work together, as described here.

METHOD

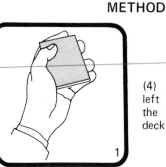

(1) Hold the deck in dealing position in your left hand, as shown in the illustration.

(4) . . . you relax the pressure of the left thumb on the top card allowing the right hand to carry it from the deck to the table.

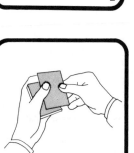

(2) With your left thumb, push the top card forward and to the right about an inch, and at the same time move the right hand toward the pack in readiness to receive the card.

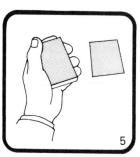

(5) The right hand then releases its grip on the card and leaves it on the table. The action can be repeated as often as necessary with each card desired.

(3) Now, grasp the top card between the thumb and fingers of the right hand, as shown, as . . .

COMMENTS AND SUGGESTIONS

With some tricks, you may deal the cards in a single pile, with others, you may deal them in a row or in some special formation. When dealing cards in a pile, one on top of the other, you will REVERSE THE ORDER of the cards as you deal them. This is known as the "Reverse Deal" which is very important with certain tricks that will be described throughout the Course.

THE CARD COUNT — RETAIN ORDER

EFFECT

This is a method of counting cards from one hand to the other, RETAINING THE CARDS IN THEIR ORIGINAL ORDER, which is important in certain tricks. Moves are shown with just four cards, all face up, so that each card can be clearly followed.

METHOD

(1) From the dealing position . . .

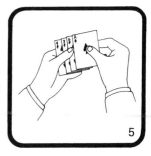

(2) . . . the left thumb pushes one card from the pack into the fingers of the right hand, as you count, "one."

(3) The thumb then pushes off a second card in the same manner, so that it comes BENEATH the first card in the right hand.

(4) The fingers of the right hand lift this card clear along with the first card, as you count, "two."

(5) Now, the left thumb pushes off card Number Three, again BENEATH the other two cards.

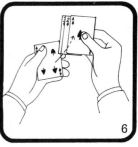

(6) The right fingers take this card along with the first two, lifting the three cards clear, counting out "three."

(7) Finally, the last card in the left hand is placed BENEATH the other three cards in the right hand . . .

(8) . . . as you finish the count with "four."

(9) NOTE: You have now counted the cards and are holding them as a separate group in your right hand — IN THEIR ORIGINAL 1-2-3-4 ORDER.

THE CARD COUNT — REVERSE ORDER

In all standard methods of counting, although you may not have thought of this before, the order of the cards is reversed. For instance, if you count cards one at a time from the top of the pack onto the table, the cards will be reversed. In other words, if you were to count through the whole deck, one at a time, the first card from the top, on the count of "one" would become the bottom card of the stack on the table. By the time you have counted all fifty-two cards onto the table, they would now be entirely *reversed in order* with the original BOTTOM card of the deck now the TOP card of the "counted" pack on the table. Also, when counting cards from one hand to the other, the cards will ordinarily be reversed in order. The following, using four face-up cards, explains the Standard Card Count Reverse Order.

METHOD

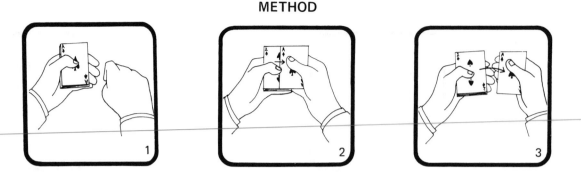

(1) With the pack in dealing position, (2) the left thumb pushes off one card, (3) which the right hand draws away as you count, "one."

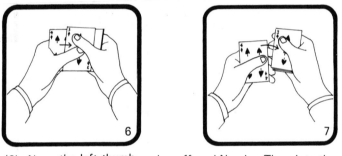

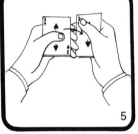

(4) Now, the left thumb pushes off card Number Two into the right hand ABOVE THE FIRST CARD, (5) as you draw them off together, counting out, "Two."

(8) The last card in the left hand is placed ON TOP of three cards in the right hand (9) as you finish the count with "Four."

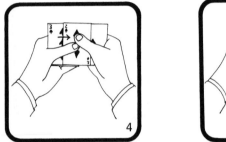

(6) Now, the left thumb pushes off card Number Three into the right hand ABOVE THE FIRST TWO cards. (7) You count out, "three."

(10) NOTE: *The right hand now holds the group of four cards in REVERSED ORDER 4-3-2-1 — instead of the original 1-2-3-4.*

SPREADING OR RUNNING THE PACK IN YOUR HANDS

This is a method of handling a pack of cards which will give your work a smooth professional touch. It is also a natural and effective way of having a spectator select a random card.

METHOD

(1) Hold the pack face down in your left hand with the fingers below and the thumb on top. The right hand waits alongside.

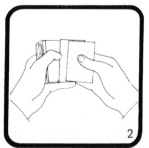

(2) With the left thumb, begin to push the cards from the top of the deck into the right hand.

(3) Continue this action as the right thumb and fingers grasp the cards that are pushed over by the left thumb. *YOU ARE NOW "RUNNING" THE CARDS FROM YOUR LEFT HAND TO YOUR RIGHT HAND.* Proceed until the cards are about evenly distributed between both hands.

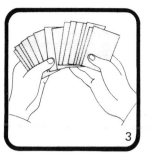

(5) From here, you can have the card returned to the pack, using any of the methods taught later in the course to "control or locate" the card. This spread should also be used when having someone draw cards for other purposes, as it thus becomes a natural procedure and helps you gain proficiency in your work.

(4) Offer the "spread" of cards to the spectator. Ask him to select a card and to remove it from the pack.

(6) Also, when looking for a particular card in the pack, you can see the spread with the cards face up, pushing the desired card (or cards) forward when you come to it.

SELF-WORKING CARD TRICKS

★ ★ ★

There are many excellent card tricks that practically work themselves and are nearly fool-proof from the magician's viewpoint yet are real bafflers where the spectators are concerned.

In this section we have assembled some of the best of these self-working mysteries which are both deceptive and easy to perform. Therefore you can concentrate almost entirely upon presentation, without worrying about any special "moves" or "sleights." Often, when a smart spectator is watching for special moves, you can really flabbergast him with a self-working effect.

So, make it your policy to include a few self-workers when the occasion demands. You may discover that such effects will be regarded as highlights of your program.

Most importantly, never neglect practice with a self-working trick, even though it seems unnecessary. If you fumble or hesitate, the effect will lose its impact. Always remember that a trick is only as good as you make it look!

AUTOMATIC CARD DISCOVERY

EFFECT

Perhaps one of the most puzzling of all card effects is when a magician causes a selected card to reverse itself and appear face up among the face-down cards in the deck. Here is one of the most basic and yet most effective means of accomplishing this feat.

SECRET AND PREPARATION

Simplicity is the answer here. The trick depends upon having the bottom card of the deck reversed from the start. (A) This can be set up before hand with the deck in its box or it can be executed easily and quickly at a moment when the spectator's eyes leave your hands as follows: (B) With the deck resting face up across the fingers of your left hand, your right thumb and fingers grip the ends of the pack from below as shown. Now, slide the pack toward the tips of the left fingers, at the same time tilting or rotating the deck up on its left edge. This leaves the lone card — in this case the Eight of Spades — still resting on the left fingers. (C) Continue the rotary motion until the right hand has turned the pack face down upon the Eight of Spades, which thus becomes a face-up card at the bottom of the pack, totally unsuspected by anyone. You are now ready to present the trick.

METHOD

(1) Spread the cards in your hands face down so that the spectator has an opportunity to freely select any card from the deck. Care must be taken here not to spread the cards too near the bottom of the deck, to avoid accidentally "flashing" the face up bottom card.

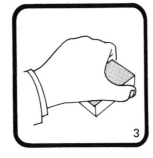

(2) As soon as the card is selected by the spectator, square up the deck in the left hand and ask the spectator to look at his card.

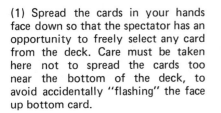

(3) *At the moment when the spectator's eyes are focusing on his card, the left hand TURNS COMPLETELY OVER and sets the deck of cards on the table. This action turns all of the cards in the deck face up, except for the "bottom" card which is now face down. Because of this single reversed card, it appears that the deck is still face down.*

(4) Leave the deck sitting on the table as you tell the spectator to show the card to the other members of the audience.

(5) When the spectator has shown his card, pick up the deck with the left hand, in its secretly reversed position. *Particular care must be taken here to keep the deck squared up so as not to "flash" the face up pack below the top single reversed card.*

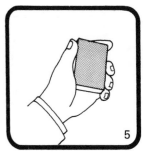

(6) Holding the deck firmly, ask the spectator to push his card face down anywhere into the deck. *Unknown to the spectator, he is really sliding his card face down into a face-up deck. (Except for the top card.)*

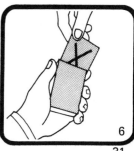

(7) When the spectator has inserted his card into the deck, place the deck behind your back and explain that since he touched only one card in the deck, that card will be a bit "warmer" than the other cards. State that, due to your highly trained sense of touch, you will be able to find his card and reveal it to him in a startling way.

(8) When you place the deck behind your back simply turn over the single reversed card and replace it FACE UP on the deck. *This places every card in the deck facing the same direction EXCEPT THE SPECTATOR'S CARD. It is the ONLY reversed card in the deck.*

SUPER AUTOMATIC CARD DISCOVERY

In performing the AUTOMATIC CARD DISCOVERY, here is another very easy and clever method for reversing the bottom card and secretly turning over the pack.

(1) It is not necessary to have the bottom card reversed before the start of the trick.

(2) After the spectator has selected his card from the deck, tell him to remember the card and that, after he replaces it in the deck, you are going to place the deck behind your back and locate his card in a very startling fashion....*at which time you DEMONSTRATE what you are going to do.*

(3) PLACE THE DECK BEHIND YOUR BACK. TURN THE BOTTOM CARD FACE UP. THEN TURN THE WHOLE PACK OVER SO THAT IT IS ALL FACE UP EXCEPT FOR THE ONE FACE-DOWN CARD ON TOP.

(4) Bring the deck out from behind your back. *You are now ready for the spectator to replace his card in the pack.*

COMMENTS AND SUGGESTIONS

With this method, you can perform the trick at any time with no previous "set-up." The spectator may even shuffle the deck himself before he freely selects a card. It only takes a moment to set up the pack behind your back as you "demonstrate" the first part of the startling way in which you are going to find the spectator's card. HOWEVER, WHEN YOU DO THIS "DEMONSTRATION," DO NOT TELL HIM THAT HIS CARD WILL LATER BE DISCOVERED FACE UP IN A FACE-DOWN PACK . . . YOU MAY ALERT HIM TO YOUR SECRET SET-UP. This method not only allows you to reverse the bottom card, but also to turn the pack over for the replacement of the selected card without any tricky moves whatsoever. When you first place the deck behind your back, just do it naturally, as if you were illustrating what is going to happen next. You can now present a very puzzling, self-working card trick that appears to require great skill yet is practically automatic in every respect.

THE FANTASTIC FIVE

EFFECT

This is a clever self-working card discovery utilizing a set up deck in its simplest form. The trick finishes with a double twist that will leave the onlookers completely baffled. Adding one surprise onto another is always a good policy, especially with card tricks.

A card is freely selected by a spectator and returned to the pack, by placing the card on top and giving the pack a cut. The magician then spreads the pack on the table, revealing that one card is face up. It is a FIVE. He explains that the face-up card, the Five, is his "Magical Indicator Card." Then he counts down *five* cards in the deck below where the face-up card was located. Turning up the fifth card, it proves to be *the card chosen by the spectator!* If that were not enough, he now turns the four cards that were *between the face-up card and the spectator's card....ALL FOUR ARE ACES!*

SECRET AND PREPARATION

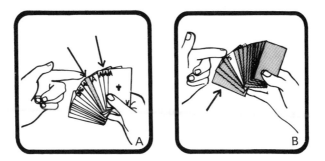

To prepare, run through the pack and remove the Four Aces and any Five-spot. This done, square up the pack and place the Five-spot *face up* on the bottom of the face-down pack and then place the four Aces *face down* below the Five. The first illustration shows the proper set-up with the pack held face up (A). The illustration (B) shows the pack held in its normal face-down position. Now, square up the pack and you're ready to begin.

METHOD

(1) Spread the pack and invite a spectator to select a card. Be sure not to spread the pack too near the bottom, accidentally exposing the face-up Five-spot.

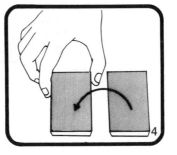

(2) Tell the spectator to be sure and remember his card. Square up the deck and place it on the table.

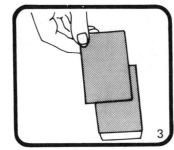

(3) Ask the spectator to place his card on top of the deck, (4) then to cut the deck, and (5) to complete the cut.

(6) *NOTE: Unknown to the spectator, when he cuts the deck, he places the four Aces and the face-up Five DIRECTLY ABOVE HIS SELECTED CARD.*

(8) Separate all the cards to the *right* of the face-up Five-spot.

(7) Explain to the spectator that something magical is going to happen. At the same time, spread the deck, face down, on the table. Call attention to the *one face-up* card in the deck.

(9) Explain that the face-up card is your "Magical Indicator Card" and that it will help to locate the card the spectator selected. Since the card is a FIVE, that must be a "clue." Count down five cards in the deck.

(10) Push the Five-spot, the four face down Aces below it, and the next card (the spectator's card) all forward from the pack.

(11) Turn over the fifth card and show it to be the card that the spectator selected.

(12) The spectator will assume that the trick is over. Not content with this, you turn over the four remaining cards TO REVEAL THE FOUR ACES. This second added surprise, the appearance of the Aces, adds greatly to the effect. This is also a good lead-in to any four-Ace trick.

COMMENTS AND SUGGESTIONS

Here is another presentation idea. After the spectator has returned his selected card to the pack and completed the cut, pick up the deck and give it a snap *before* you spread it along the table. Say that this will cause a card to turn over somewhere in the deck. When the spread reveals the face-up Five, count down to the chosen card. Turn it over, revealing it to be the spectator's selected card. NOW FOR THE ADDED TOUCH....you then gather up the upper and lower portions of the pack, *placing the "Aces" half of the deck on TOP.* Say, "Whenever I snap the pack a second time, something good always turns up"...SNAP!...."like the four Aces!" Then deal the four Aces from the top of the deck, TURNING EACH ACE FACE UP AS YOU PLACE IT ON THE TABLE.

TURN OVER CARD

This surprising effect is performed with a pack of ordinary playing cards. It can be done with a borrowed deck and requires *no skill or practice.* The trick depends on the use of a "key card" which is one of the most basic and simple methods used in card magic to locate a selected card in a pack of cards.

THE EFFECT

You have a spectator shuffle a pack of cards and cut the cards anywhere he wishes. Next, you tell him to look at the card he cut to— then complete the cut, thus burying his card in the deck. Now you take the cards in your hands *for the first time* and proceed to find the selected card.

SECRET AND PREPARATION

The secret of the trick depends entirely upon the performer secretly learning the bottom card of the pack before it is placed on the table to begin the trick. This card is called a "key card" because it is to be your key to the location of the selected card. In the following description we will assume that your key card (the card on the bottom of the deck) is the Two of Clubs.

THE METHOD

(1) If you use a pack of cards that is already in its case at the start, you can glimpse the bottom card as you remove them from the case. Just lay the pack face down and go right into the trick without a shuffle.

(2) Even better, if people want to shuffle the pack . . . let them. Often when a spectator is squaring up the pack after shuffling, he will "flash" the bottom card in your direction, not realizing it has anything to do with the trick.

(3) If you don't get a glimpse of the card during the shuffle, pick up the pack in your hands, turn it face-up, and begin running the cards from hand to hand, as shown.

Comment that the deck appears to be well shuffled and it would be impossible for you to know their order. Of course, here you see and remember your "key card". Now lay the pack face down on the table and you're ready to begin.

NOTE: In placing the lower half on top of the upper half, the spectator is also placing your "key card" directly above his chosen card. Ask the spectator to give the pack another complete cut and then to let someone else cut it also.

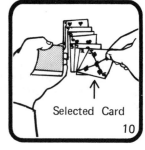

(8) When this is done, take the pack and begin dealing cards one by one on the table, turning each card face up. Tell the spectator that you are trying to get an impression of his card, *but he is not to say anything if he sees it,* or you will have to begin all over.

(4) With the pack lying face down on the table and the spectators satisfied that the cards are well mixed, ask someone to divide the pack into two parts.

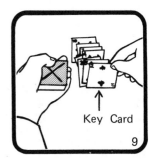

(9) As you deal cards one at a time from the pack, turning each face up, *watch for your key card,* the Two of Clubs. When it shows up, deal it on the table along with the others. You now know that the *next card* will be the spectator's card (the Five of Diamonds).

Key Card

(5) Tell him he can cut anywhere in the deck he wishes and to place the upper portion on the table. *Note that the card which the spectator has cut to, which will be his selected card, we have marked with an "X" in the illustrations to make it easier for you to follow. Of course, when you perform the trick, there will be no "X" on the card.*

(10) Deal the next card, the Five of Diamonds, but instead of stopping, just continue dealing as if you haven't reached the chosen card.

Selected Card

Spectator Looks At Card

(6) After he has cut the cards tell him to remove the top card of the lower half, *look at it, and remember it* and then to place it on top of the other half of the pack. Let's assume that the card is the Five of Diamonds.

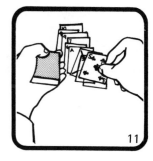

(11) After you have dealt a half-dozen or more cards, tell him you have received an impression and say: "The *next card I turn* over will be *your card.*" He will probably say you are wrong.

(7) Point to the lower half and ask him to put those cards on top of his card so it will be buried somewhere in the pack.

(12) But instead of dealing the next card off of the pack, reach among the face-up cards on the table and draw out the Five of Diamonds.

(13) Turn over the Five and lay it *face down* on the table and say: "I said the next card I *turned over* would be yours – and it is!"

Note: This trick is very effective because of its surprise ending! When the spectator sees you deal past his card he is sure that the trick has gone wrong. But when you actually do turn his card face down you really prove your "Magical" powers.

DOUBLE TURNOVER

In this card effect, the spectator plays such an active part that trickery seems impossible, yet the magical result is attained while the pack is practically in the spectator's hands. The secret is so simple – once you know it – you can fool an audience the first time you try.

EFFECT

The magician places a deck of cards on the table and invites a friend to remove the upper half of the pack for himself, while the magician takes the remaining lower half. Each puts his half behind his back and each removes a card at random. Each lays his half-pack on the table and looks at the card he selected. Then the magician and the spectator exchange their "selected cards" *without looking at each other's cards* and insert them face down into the respective half-packs – the MAGICIAN'S card in the SPECTATOR'S half-pack, and the SPECTATOR'S card in the MAGICIAN'S half. The full pack is immediately reassembled and both call out the names of the cards each has selected. The pack is spread face down on the table, and *both cards have magically turned FACE UP in the deck!*

METHOD

(1) Before the trick, give the pack a few cuts or a shuffle. In the process, casually spot the BOTTOM CARD of the deck, in this case the Five of Hearts, and *remember it*.

Glimpse bottom card

(4) Also remove any other card from your half. Turn it face down and bring it out from behind your back. To the spectators, this is *your* "selected" card.

Magician

Cards held behind back

(2) Lay the pack on the table and tell your friend to cut off about half the pack and hold it behind his back. You do the same with the remaining lower half.

Spectator takes top half

(5) *NOTE: The spectator does not suspect that your actions differ from his. In the illustration, your card, the Five of Hearts, is marked with an "M" ... the spectator's card, in this case the Two of Diamonds, is marked with an "X." The random card that YOU place on the table is marked with a "D" as it is a "decoy" that plays a special part, as you will see.*

(3) Instruct him to remove any card from his half, while you *supposedly* do the same. Actually you TURN YOUR HALF FACE UP. Then turn the card you glimpsed – the Five of Hearts – FACE DOWN *on top of the face-up packet.*

Cards behind magician's back

(6) Here you tell the spectator, "Look at the card you drew and remember it, while I do the same with my card." He looks at his card and notes that it is the Two of Diamonds. *You look at your card but it is not necessary to remember it ... just don't forget your "special" card, the Five of Hearts.*

(7) You continue, "Hold your card so I cannot see what it is, and lay your half of the pack face down on the table, just as I am doing. Do not tell me what card you selected. I also will keep my selected card a secret — FOR JUST A MOMENT."

(8) Here you bring out your half of the pack from behind your back and set it on the table. Your half appears to be the same as the spectator's half. ACTUALLY, ALL OF THE CARDS IN YOUR HALF ARE FACE UP EXCEPT FOR THE FIVE OF HEARTS WHICH IS FACE DOWN AT THE TOP.

(9) *NOTE: Care must be taken to place the cards on the table squarely so as not to "flash" any of the face-up cards beneath the Five spot.*

(10) Then you add: "Give me your card and you take mine, but I won't look at the face of your card and you don't look at mine. That way, only we will know which cards we took."

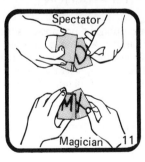

(11) Now with your half of the pack resting on the table, insert the SPECTATOR'S card into YOUR half near the center, *keeping your half well squared with your left hand.* Tell the spectator to push YOUR card face down into HIS half of the pack.

(12) *NOTE: At this point, your half of the pack has ALL its cards face up except for your face-down Five of Hearts ON TOP and his face-down Two of Diamonds NEAR THE MIDDLE.*

(13) Place your left hand over the top of your half in readiness to pick it up from the table, and at the same time, with your right hand, reach for the spectator's half-pack stating that you will add it to your own.

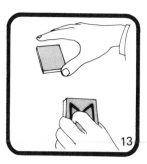

(14) At the exact moment your right hand picks up the spectator's packet, lift your packet from the table with your left hand and in the same motion, TURN YOUR HALF OVER. *Your half-pack now really is FACE DOWN except for the face-up Five of Hearts on the bottom.* This is the only "tricky" part of this effect. It does not require skill, merely the correct timing and should be well practiced before you present the trick.

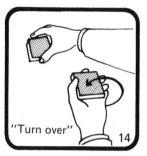

(15) Move your hands together and place the spectator's half on top of your half, squaring the halves together.

(16) *Now, the entire pack is face down, except for your Five of Hearts (on the bottom) and the spectator's Two of Diamonds, about a dozen cards above.*

(17) Cut the pack about one third of the way down in the deck and place this packet on the table.

(18) Complete the cut by placing the remaining two thirds packet on top.

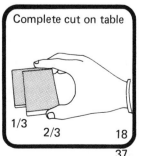

(19) As you do, say to your friend, "My card was the Five of Hearts, what was yours?" He replies, "The Two of Diamonds." Square the pack and riffle the ends twice with your finger. Say, "Good!. . .Now I'll make both cards magically reveal themselves."

(20) Ribbon Spread the pack along the table, face down, separating the cards rather widely. As you do, the two cards – the Five of Hearts and the Two of Diamonds – are seen to be FACE UP in the spread, for a startling climax.

COMMENTS AND SUGGESTIONS

When only a few spectators are present, it is not necessary to put the packs behind your back. Instead, you each can simply turn away, so that neither sees what card the other takes. This gives you an easy opportunity to note a card and place it face up on the bottom, while drawing out another card to serve as a decoy.

In either case, always use a pack with backs that have a WHITE MARGIN around the edges and be sure to keep the cards WELL SQUARED when handling your half-pack. Otherwise, a sharp-eyed spectator may notice the face-up cards in your supposedly face-down packet.

In turning your left hand over to bring your inverted half-pack to normal – as shown in Figs. 13 and 14 – you can cover the turnover by moving your left hand, with its packet, to the right. In this way you must reach *across* your left hand with your right hand in order to pick up the spectator's packet. That brings your right arm directly over your left hand, which does the dirty work under this cover.

THE DOUBLE X MYSTERY

EFFECT

Two spectators are invited to assist the magician. The magician gives the spectator on his left a pack of cards and a pen and asks him to place the pack behind his back and mark an X across the *face* of any card with the pen. The magician now gives the same deck and pen to the spectator on his right and asks him to mark the *back* of any card, also with the pack behind his back. The magician returns the deck to the person on his left and asks him to run through the deck and find the card with the X on the FACE, remove it, and hold it between both hands so that it is out of sight. This done, the spectator on the right is again given the deck and asked to find his card, the one with the X on the BACK. Upon searching through the deck, he finds that his card is missing. When the spectator on the left turns his card over, it is found to have an X on the back. It appears as if both spectators have chosen and marked the same card!

SECRET AND PREPARATION

The secret to this "coincidence" is so simple it's surprising. It all depends upon the unknown fact that the pen that the magician gives to the spectators just *doesn't work*. The best pen to use is of the felt tip variety. All that is required is to let it sit without the cap on until the tip is dried out. If a pencil is used, it is necessary to dip the tip of the pencil in clear varnish and allow it to dry overnight. This will prevent the pencil from making a mark on the cards although it appears to have a perfectly good "point." A drawback in using a pencil is that it does not make an easily visible mark on the card as does the felt tip pen. A ballpoint pen, which is out of ink, also works well but has the same "lack of visibility" as the pencil.

To prepare, remove any card from the pack and mark an X on both sides with a pen or pencil that really works and matches the special one you will use in the trick. The lines which form the X should appear irregular, as if the mark were made behind the back. Now replace the card back in the deck, and you're ready.

METHOD

(1) With two spectators to assist you, give the deck face up to the spectator on your left. Ask him to place the deck behind his back, to run through the cards, and without looking at it, to bring any card to the top of the deck.

(2) When he has done this, give him the prepared pen and instruct him to mark an X across the FACE of the card and then return the pen to you. Ask him to mix the cards behind his back so his card is lost somewhere in the deck. After he has done this, have him hand you the deck.

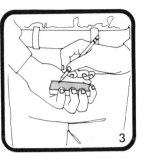

(3) Now turn the deck FACE DOWN and hand it to the spectator on your right. Instruct him just as you did the other spectator. But tell him to mark an X on the BACK of any card and mix the cards.

(5) *NOTE: Because of the prepared pen, neither spectator has made a mark on any card and both are unaware of the prepared X card in the deck.*

(4) When this has been done, take back the deck and put the pen away. Give the deck again to the spectator on your left, and ask him to look through the cards FACE UP and re- move the card he marked from the deck. Have him hold this card between the palms of his hands so no one else can see the card. *Actually, the reason for doing this is so that no one sees the X on the back of this card.*

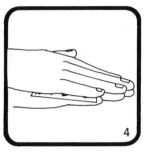

(6) This done, give the deck to the spectator on the right and ask him to do the same...."Please run through the deck and remove your card, the one with the X on the back." Of course, he will be unable to find his card.

(7) After several attempts, call attention to the fact that the only card missing from the deck is the one that the other spectator is holding between his hands. Tell the spectator on your left to look at the back of the card. It appears that the two spectators were some how able to freely select and mark the *very same card in the deck!*

COMMENTS AND SUGGESTIONS

It is a good idea at the start of the trick to run through the cards face up and show them to be an ordinary deck. In order to do this, it is necessary to have the secret X card close to the bottom of the deck. Then, run through the cards face up, supposedly to show that they are all different. Just be careful not to spread the cards near the position in the deck where the X card is located. The spectators will believe everything is on the up-and-up. You will be amazed at the effect that this trick has on an audience, as there appears to be no reason- able explanation for the astonishing results. Properly performed, no one will ever suspect the special pen as being the secret to the mystery.

THE SUPER DOUBLE X MYSTERY

One very subtle convincer, which can make this trick a COMPLETE baffler, is to introduce a duplicate pen (the one that REALLY made the X on the card), after the prepared pen has done the dirty work. Simply have the duplicate in your pocket and, after the second spectator has made his "mark," casually place the pen in the pocket with the duplicate. As the second spectator is looking for the card with the X, remove the unprepared pen and "help" him search by pointing to various parts of the deck with the "real" pen. Then just lay the pen somewhere in plain sight. Now *everything* can be examined.

SUPER ANYTIME DOUBLE X MYSTERY

With this method, you can perform the Double X Mystery at any time during your card routine....even though the deck has been used for a number of other tricks and even examined by the audience!

SECRET AND PREPARATION

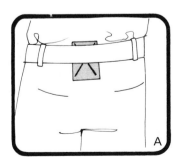
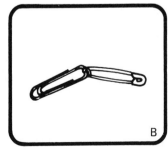
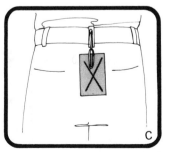

Before the show, place the X marked card either (A) under your belt behind your back or (B) in a "gimmick" card holder made from a safety pin and a paper clip. The special card is placed in the paper clip and the "holder" pinned inside the back of your coat (C) so that the card is just hidden by the bottom edge of your coat.

METHOD

(1) Have one of the spectators shuffle the deck. When he hands it back to you, place the deck behind your back to illustrate to your two assistants what they are to do....*it is now that you secretly remove the X card from beneath your coat and add it to the deck!*

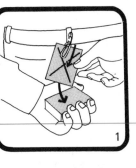

(2) Now you are ready to proceed with the Super Double X Mystery just as described.

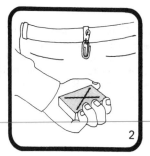

THE SIGNED CARD IN WALLET

Here is an effect which will cause spectators to give you credit for remarkable skill, yet no special moves or long practice is required. *Misdirection* is the main factor and even that becomes almost automatic, if you follow this timely, well-paced routine that has been carefully designed to baffle the sharpest spectators.

EFFECT

A card is selected by a spectator who signs his name on the back. The magician brings out his wallet which contains a "prediction" card which he has signed. When the "prediction" card is revealed, it is found to match the spectator's selection.

SECRET AND PREPARATION

For this trick you need a few simple props. First, an ordinary book-style wallet or checkbook. You will also need a pen, a small piece of either "double-faced" cellophane tape or regular cellophane tape made into a "Magic Loop" and a deck of cards. Also, you will need one duplicate card from another deck. It can be any card you choose, but for our explanation we will use an extra Four of Hearts. This card, known as the "prediction card," can be taken from a pack of a totally different design.

(1) Open the wallet or checkbook flat and place it on the table as shown. Next, sign your name across the back of the duplicate Four of Hearts and place it FACE DOWN on the LEFT SIDE of the wallet. *Now fold over the right side,* enclosing the card inside the wallet.

(3) With the taped side toward your body, insert the wallet in your left inside coat pocket.

(2) Turn the entire wallet over and place a small (1½-inch) piece of double-faced cellophane tape or a "Magic Loop" of regular cellophane tape in the center of this side of the wallet. Then turn the wallet back over to its original position. Be careful not to stick the tape to the table. See MAGIC LOOP, page 23.

Double Face Tape

(4) Place the pen in the same pocket. Look through the deck until you locate the Four of Hearts. (This has been marked with an "X" in the illustrations.) Remove the Four and place it on top of the deck. You are ready to perform a truly fantastic trick.

Four of Hearts

METHOD

(5) Spread the deck face down from hand to hand and ask a spectator to just TOUCH a card. *Emphasize that he has a completely free choice of ANY card.*

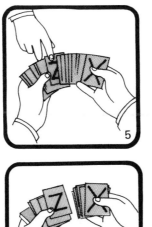

(6) When he does, separate the pack ABOVE the card (here marked with a "Z") that the spectator touched. Keep his "selected" card (Z) at the top of the left half of the pack.

(7) Deal this selected card (Z), *without looking* at it on top of the cards held in the right hand, explaining that you will move the chosen card to the top of the deck.

(8) Now, place the right-hand packet of cards on top of those in the left hand and square the cards up. *You should now have the selected card (Z) on top of the deck, with the Four of Hearts (X) directly below it.*

(9) Hold the deck in your left hand. With your right hand, bring the wallet from your inside coat pocket. Handle it in a casual manner, keeping the taped side toward you.

(10) Then, tilt the top (upper end) of the wallet toward your body, so the taped side is underneath....WITH YOUR RIGHT HAND, PLACE THE WALLET SQUARELY ON TOP OF THE PACK IN THE LEFT HAND.

(11) Hold the wallet against the deck with your left thumb while your right hand moves back toward the pocket for the pen. WITH YOUR THUMB, PRESS FIRMLY ON THE WALLET CAUSING THE TOP CARD (Z) TO STICK TO THE TAPE ON THE UNDERSIDE OF THE WALLET.

(12) With your right hand, remove the pen from your pocket and hand it to the spectator.

(13) *NOTE: Reaching back into your pocket supplies a perfect reason for momentarily leaving the wallet on the deck as a resting place as you bring the pen out to give to the spectator.*

(14) With your right hand, remove the wallet from the top of the deck to the table, SECRETLY CARRYING AWAY THE SPECTATOR'S CARD (Z) WITH IT. *The spectator thinks his selected card is still on top of the deck, but really the Four of Hearts is in its place.*

(15) Deal the top card – NOW THE FOUR OF HEARTS, onto the table, face down, to the left of the wallet. State, "I'd like you to sign your name across the back of your card to clearly identify your selection."

(16) Have the spectator sign the back of the tabled card....(which only you know is the Four of Hearts). When he is finished, replace the pen in your coat pocket.

(17)   Open the wallet to reveal your signed, face-down "prediction card." Remove the card from the wallet and place it, still face down, on the table next to the spectator's card.

Card with your name
17

(19)   Before turning the two cards over, pause a moment to tell your audience about the "Mysteries of ESP," thus building up the suspense a little before you turn both signed cards face up. Of course, your "prediction" proves to be correct making the mystery complete!

19

(18) *Pick up the wallet and place it back in your coat pocket thus getting rid of any evidence beforehand. Be sure to handle the wallet so as not to reveal (or unstick) the card held on the underneath side.*

COMMENTS AND SUGGESTIONS

This is a VERY STRONG mental effect in which no manipulative skill is involved. It should be presented in your own personal style.

NOTE: Some coats have the inside pocket on the right side, not the left. In that case, after placing the "touched" card on the top of the pack, transfer the pack from your left hand to your right. Then remove the wallet with your left hand and place it on top of the pack in your right hand. The procedure is then exactly the same.

THE TORN AND RESTORED CARD

EFFECT

A card is selected and signed by the spectator. The card is torn into four quarters, which are wrapped in a handkerchief and given to the spectator to hold. When the handkerchief is opened, all the torn pieces have VANISHED except for one corner. The magician picks up the deck and riffles it. The selected card JUMPS OUT of the deck COMPLETELY RESTORED, except for the missing corner. The spectator matches the corner to the card and finds that it is a perfect fit!

SECRET AND PREPARATION

(A)   Before the performance, tear off one index corner of an indifferent card. (You may discard this corner as you have no further need of it.) Place the torn card face down on top of the deck with the missing quarter at the lower left corner of the deck as shown. Place another card on top of the torn card to hide it. *(The torn corner card is now the second card from the top of the pack.)* Place a small rubber band in your right coat pocket.

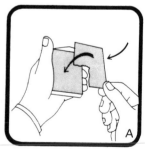

METHOD

(1)   Remove the pack from its case and hold the deck face down in your left hand. Riffle the end of the deck with your right fingers to allow the spectator to select a card. After he has removed a card, immediately place the deck FACE UP on the table.

(2)   As you do this, casually remove the card that is on the BOTTOM of the face up deck. (This is the card that was "hiding" the torn corner card.) Gesture with the card as you explain that the spectator could have selected *any* card. Return this card to the FACE of the deck.

(3) Take the spectator's card (X) and tear off one index corner. This should be approximately the same size as the quarter section already torn from the indifferent card.

(4) Return the large portion of the chosen card to the spectator and have him sign the face of the card. When he has done this, take the card from him. Pick up the deck and hold it in your left hand with its face toward the spectators so that they cannot see the other torn corner card on top. Place the selected card (X) face down on the top of the deck on top of "your" torn card.

(5) *NOTE: The torn corner of the spectator's card is at the upper right-hand corner of the deck (the opposite corner from your previously torn card). The deck may not be lowered so the spectators can see the top.*

(6) Now, ask the spectator to sign the torn corner of the card also, merely using his initials if he wishes. In fact, any identifying mark will do.

(7) While he is doing this, you apparently deal his card face down on the table. *Actually you press your right thumb upon the outer right corner of the pack and draw out the indifferent card from beneath the selected card.*

(8) THIS SWITCHES THE INDIFFERENT TORN CARD FOR THE SELECTED CARD, WHICH REMAINS ON TOP OF THE PACK, THE MOVE IS TERMED A "SECOND DEAL" AND THE MISSING CORNER OF THE SELECTED CARD MAKES THIS VERY EASY AND DECEPTIVE.

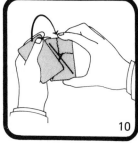

(9) As you deal the card onto the table, tilt the deck upward, toward your body, so the spectators cannot see the top.

(10) With the deck in this position, give the deck one cut to place the selected card (X) in the center of the deck. Lay the deck face down on the table, as you did before.

(11) Pick up the face-down indifferent card, *which the spectators think is their signed card,* and tear it into three pieces. Keep the pieces turned toward you so that no one can see the face of the card. The audience will suppose that you have torn the selected card into quarters.

(12) Pick up the corner of the selected card (X) and place it on the face of the torn pieces. Hold all the pieces in your right hand. In this way you can exhibit the pieces, both front and back.

(13) Cover the torn pieces held in your right hand with an ordinary handkerchief. With your right thumb, push the corner of the selected card a little higher than the pieces of the indifferent card.

(14) With your left hand, grasp the corner (X) of the selected card through the fabric. Carry the rest of the torn pieces downward in your right hand, concealing them in the bend of your right fingers. Thrust your right hand into your coat pocket.

(15) Leave the pieces in your pocket, bring out the band, and place it around the center of the handkerchief below the marked corner that the audience thinks is all four quarters of the selected card. Give the handkerchief to a spectator to hold and restate what has happened up to this point....*Now, for the Magic!*

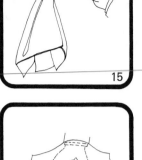

15

(18) Riffle the upper right corner of the deck with your right fingertips, keeping the pack tilted upward and forward, while the left hand retains its firm grip.

18

(16) Have the spectator remove the rubber band and spread the cloth. He will find *only* the torn corner, which he will recognize as the one he marked.

16

(19) The riffle action will cause the selected card (X) to jump half-way out of the deck. This is a very surprising effect, but only a prelude to the surprise that follows.

19

(17) Pick up the deck and hold it face down in such a way that the missing portion of the selected card is at the lower left. (The selected card, of course, is buried somewhere in the deck.)

Selected card in center of deck with torn corner here. 17

(20) Offer this card (X) to the spectator, letting him draw it from the deck himself. He will be amazed to find that the torn pieces of his own card have been magically restored!

20

(21) Have him match his torn corner to the card. It will be a perfect fit. THIS IS THE FINAL CONVINCER IN A TRULY GREAT CARD MYSTERY.

21

COMMENTS AND SUGGESTIONS

This feat of card magic was originated by the late Paul Le Paul and used for many years. It creates a startling effect, that is one of the best in magic. Give this the practice it deserves and you will have a card effect that will entertain and mystify all who witness it.

YOU DO AS I DO

As a "two person" trick, this is a real baffler. All you need are two ordinary decks of playing cards. It is a good idea to use packs with different colored backs, so that the audience can keep track of them as the trick proceeds.

EFFECT

Two packs of cards are thoroughly shuffled...one is shuffled by a spectator and the magician shuffles the other pack. The magician and the spectator then exchange packs and each selects a card, being sure that the other person does not see it. The cards are both replaced in their decks. The magician and the spectator exchange decks again and each finds the "duplicate" of the card he selected in the other pack. The spectator and the magician then place the cards that they have selected face down on the table. When the two cards are turned up, they prove to be identical!

SECRET AND PREPARATION

This is one of the finest self-working tricks in card magic. You need only two ordinary decks of cards, and the trick can be performed any time, anywhere, with no previous set-up. Let's assume that one deck has red backs and the other blue.

METHOD

(1) Place both decks on the table and ask the spectator to select either pack. *This is a free choice.* Let's assume that he takes the deck with the *red* backs. This leaves you with the *blue* backed deck.

(2) Tell the spectator that he is to please "Do As I Do"...and the first thing you will do is to shuffle your blue backed deck...so he should do the same with the red deck.

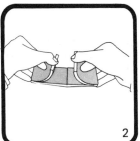

(3) As you complete the last shuffle, square up your deck as shown in the picture. As you do, turn the deck on its edge and "glimpse" the bottom card and remember it. Do not call attention to this, just remember the bottom card as it will serve as your "key card" for the rest of the trick. *NOTE: In the illustration, the Eight of Diamonds will be your "Key Card."*

Key Card

(4) Stress to the spectator that, to make sure that all is fair, you will trade decks with him so *you will be using a deck that he personally has shuffled.* Exchange decks with the spectator ... *UNKNOWN TO HIM, YOU KNOW THE BOTTOM CARD OF THE BLUE DECK HE NOW HOLDS.*

Magician 5

Spectator 5

(5) Instruct the spectator to spread the blue deck in his hands in front of him so that you cannot see the faces — just as you are doing with the red deck. He is to freely select any card from the deck and you will do likewise. Tell him it's best if he selects his "favorite card" and that you will do the same and select your "favorite card." *(To make the illustrations easy to follow, we have marked the spectator's card with an "X.")*

Magician 6

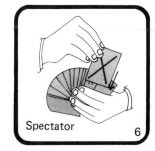

Spectator 6

(6) Explain to the spectator that he is to place the card he selected on the top of the deck (as shown in the picture) as you do the same with your card. It is not necessary for you to remember the card which you have selected at this point. *Just remember your "key card," the one that is on the bottom of the deck now held by the spectator — the Eight of Diamonds.*

Magician 7

Spectator 7

(7) Have the spectator square up his cards as you do the same. Then you each place your decks on the table.

(8) Tell the spectator to cut his deck, as you cut your deck, thus burying the selected cards somewhere in the middle of each pack. UNKNOWN TO HIM, THIS CUT PLACES THE BOTTOM CARD, WHICH IS YOUR "KEY CARD," THE EIGHT OF DIAMONDS, DIRECTLY ABOVE HIS SELECTED CARD.

(9) Have him complete the cut and then ask him to cut two more times, as you do the same. *Be sure that each cut is a "single cut" and that the cut is completed each time. No matter how many times you cut the deck, as long as each cut is completed before the next cut is started, the "key card" will stay next to the selected card.*

(10) Stress the fact that there's no possible way that you could know where his "favorite card" is now located in the deck and likewise he could not know where your card is either.

(11) Now trade decks with the spectator once more. You now hold the one you originally shuffled, the blue deck with your "key card."

(14) Tell the spectator to remove his selected card without showing its face and you will do the same. *Actually, you remove the card which you now know to be the one the spectator selected, the TWO OF CLUBS.*

(12) Tell the spectator to look through that deck he now holds (the red deck) and to remove the card which matches his "favorite card" — and you will do the same with the blue deck.

(15) Have the spectator place his card on the table and you place yours beside it.

(13) While he does this, you spread your deck until you locate your "key card," the Eight of Diamonds. THE CARD IMMEDIATELY TO THE RIGHT OF THE "KEY CARD" WILL BE THE CARD THE SPECTATOR SELECTED.

Key Card   Spectator's Card

(16) Say, "It would be quite a coincidence if we *both* had the same favorite card, wouldn't it?" Stress the fact again that you each have been doing the same "You Do As I Do." Now you and the spectator turn your cards face up at the same time. HE WILL BE AMAZED TO SEE THAT THE CARDS MATCH!

THE HINDU SHUFFLE

The "Hindu Shuffle" is ideally suited to the needs of present-day magicians, and therefore, is a manipulation that all card workers should acquire. Various factors stand out strongly in its favor. It is easy to learn, it is a legitimate shuffle in its own right, and it is especially suited to card tricks.

As you become familiar with the Hindu Shuffle, you will also find that it can be readily adapted to important magical purposes, such as Forcing, Locating, or Controlling desired cards — and all without suspicion on the part of the spectators.

Because of its speed and precision, the Hindu Shuffle will give your audience the impression that you are an accomplished performer. That is an important aim when presenting Card Magic. SOME OF THE SIMPLEST TRICKS CAN BECOME UTTERLY BAFFLING WHEN THE SPECTATORS SUPPOSE THAT SKILLED MANIPULATION IS INVOLVED.

THE HINDU SHUFFLE

This type of shuffle supposedly gained its name from the fact that it was occasionally used by Hindu magicians who were unfamiliar with the usual shuffling methods. Whatever its origin, other magicians found that it gave them a great advantage when performing close-up card tricks, as the pack can be handled under the very eyes of the spectators in a deceptive manner without fear of detection. Hence it is recommended as the first and most important step toward acquiring skill as a card manipulator.

EFFECT

The magician holds a pack of cards in one hand and with the other hand proceeds to shuffle it by repeatedly drawing cards off the top -- *from the end of the pack* -- instead of drawing them *sideways* as with the Overhand Shuffle.

METHOD

(1) Hold the pack face down near one end with your right thumb and fingers at opposite sides of the pack.

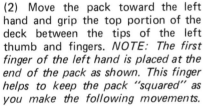

(2) Move the pack toward the left hand and grip the top portion of the deck between the tips of the left thumb and fingers. *NOTE: The first finger of the left hand is placed at the end of the pack as shown. This finger helps to keep the pack "squared" as you make the following movements.*

(3) With your right thumb and fingers, draw the bulk of the pack (B) out from beneath as you retain a small block of cards (A) with the fingers of your left hand.

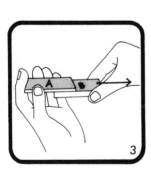

(4) As your right hand draws the bulk of the pack (B) clear, release the stack (A) in your left fingers, *so that it drops onto the palm of the left hand.*

(5) Again, move the hands together and grip another small portion of cards from the top of the pack (B) between your left thumb and fingers.

(6) Draw the bulk of the pack (C) from beneath the top stack (B). As soon as the pack is clear . . .

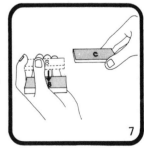

(7) . . . let the second stack (B) fall on the first stack (A) already lying in the left hand.

(8) Continue drawing off packets into the left hand until the right hand has only a small stack of its own (C), which you simply drop on the pack in the left hand.

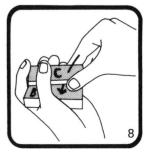

COMMENTS AND SUGGESTIONS

The shuffle should be executed at a moderately rapid pace, keeping the hands in continuous motion as you draw off the packets. This gives a polished and professional look. Because it is adaptable to various uses, the Hindu Shuffle is the basis for a whole series of clever but easy manipulations that will be described as we proceed. You will run into frequent mentions of the basic Hindu Shuffle and its more advanced forms throughout this series of lessons.

HOW TO USE THE HINDU SHUFFLE

Although the Hindu Shuffle *ACTUALLY MIXES* the pack, *it has many magical uses as well.* Once you have practiced and learned the regular Hindu Shuffle just described, you can use it to accomplish any of the three following purposes, which are indispensable in the presentation of good Card Magic.

(1)   LOCATING A SELECTED CARD . . . a card, freely selected from the pack is replaced wherever the chooser wishes . . . yet you can find the card in the "shuffled" deck. This uses a combination of a "key" card and the Hindu Shuffle. (Hindu Key Card Location and Short Card Location.)

(2)   "FORCING" A SPECIFIC CARD . . . a spectator has an apparently free choice of any card in the pack, but you "force" him to pick the one you want. (The Hindu Shuffle Flash Force.)

(3)   CONTROLLING THE LOCATION OF A CHOSEN CARD (OR CARDS) . . . after a card has been replaced in the pack, you can "control" it to the top or bottom of the deck while giving the deck an "honest" Hindu Shuffle. (The Hindu Shuffle Control.)

THE HINDU GLIMPSE

The Hindu Glimpse is a very useful and valuable move with the "Hindu Shuffle," enabling you to "sight" the bottom card of the deck secretly, in a natural manner that even the keenest observer will overlook.

EFFECT

The magician mixes the pack thoroughly, using the regular Hindu Shuffle. To keep the pack well-squared during this procedure, he taps the inner end of the left-hand packet with the right-hand pack pushing any protruding cards into place. This very action would seem to the spectators to eliminate the possibility of his seeing any cards in the pack, but actually it works to his advantage, enabling him to secretly note the bottom card of the right-hand packet.

METHOD

(1) Begin with the regular Hindu Shuffle, drawing off small blocks of cards from the top of the deck into the left hand.

(3) Then continue the shuffle pulling off small packets from the top of the right hand cards.

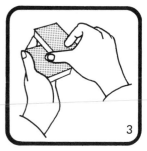

(2) As some point during the shuffle, when you hold about the same number of cards in each hand, turn the right hand packet at a slant, toward you, and tap the inner end of the left-hand packet in the pretense of "squaring up" the cards in that hand. This gives you the opportunity to sight the bottom card of the right hand packet ....the Two of Diamonds.

COMMENTS AND SUGGESTIONS

You only need a brief moment to glimpse the bottom card. Just make the move as a natural part of the shuffle. The Hindu Glimpse has many magical uses, as you will see.

THE HINDU KEY CARD LOCATION

Here is an example of a clever use of the Hindu Glimpse.

EFFECT

A spectator freely shuffles the deck as many times as he wishes and then has a free selection of any card. While the magician gives the deck a Hindu Shuffle, the spectator returns the card to the pack at any time that he wishes. The magician then shuffles the cards and gives them several cuts . . . yet he is still able to find and announce the spectator's selected card.

METHOD

(1) Let the spectator freely shuffle the deck as many times as he wishes so that you cannot know the location of any card.

(2) Ribbon Spread the cards on the table, or just spread them face down in your hands, so that the spectator may have a completely free selection . . . have him remove any card he wishes.

(3) Gather up the cards and begin the Hindu Shuffle. As you do the shuffle, glimpse and remember the bottom card of the packet in your right hand (THE HINDU GLIMPSE) . . . in this case the Two of Diamonds. This will be your "key" card in locating the spectator's card.

(4) Tell the spectator to look at his card (X) and remember it. Continue the shuffle and tell him to stop you when he would like to replace his card.

(5) When he says "Stop," have him return his card (X) to the top of the packet of cards in your left hand.

(6) You immediately drop the cards in your right hand on top of the left hand packet burying his chosen card in the pack. THIS PLACES THE TWO OF DIAMONDS (YOUR "KEY" CARD) DIRECTLY ABOVE THE SPECTATOR'S CHOSEN CARD (X).

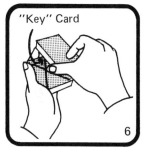

(7) Then give the deck a few single cuts or let the spectator make the cuts. Turn the deck face up and spread it between your hands. Act as if you are concentrating on the spectator's face. When you sight your "key" card, the Two of Diamonds, *the selected card (X) will be immediately to its right.* After a suitable period of time, announce the name of the card.

IMPORTANT NOTE

In using the "Hindu Shuffle Key Card Location" system just described, you may sometimes encounter a hesitant spectator who does not wish to replace his chosen card until you are about to drop your last few cards on top. That means that you may have to complete the shuffle and begin all over, which is perfectly natural. However, if that happens, your "key" card becomes lost. Just start the shuffle again and glimpse and REMEMBER a NEW bottom "key" card.

COMMENTS AND SUGGESTIONS

This is an example of using the Hindu Glimpse to get your "key" card next to the spectator's selected card in a very clever way, even though he has first shuffled the deck himself.

SPELL-A-NAME

When you have practiced the Hindu Shuffle and the Hindu Glimpse enough to where you can execute them smoothly and at a moderately rapid pace, you are then ready to learn the following mystery. Spell-A-Name applies the *first* use of the Hindu Shuffle as defined under LOCATING A SELECTED CARD in the "How To Use The Hindu Shuffle" section described earlier. Like many tricks involving a selected card, it depends upon the use of a "key" card, with its climax producing a distinctly different touch.

EFFECT

A spectator is given a free selection of a card from an ordinary pack. After his card is replaced in the pack, you give the pack several cuts and then turn the deck face up and run through the cards to show that they are thoroughly mixed. Next, you hand the pack to the spectator face down and tell him to SPELL HIS OWN NAME, letter by letter, dealing a card from the top of the deck for each letter. After he comes to the final letter of his name, you tell him to turn the *next* card face up. IT PROVES TO BE HIS CHOSEN CARD!

SECRET AND PREPARATION

As mentioned above, this is a trick in which the bottom card of the pack is remembered and used as a "key" card. Also, you must know beforehand the name of the person whom you intend to have select the card. Assume that you are performing the trick for a friend named "Larry Jones."

METHOD

(1) Spread the pack so your friend can remove one card. Then begin a regular Hindu Shuffle asking him to call "Stop" at any time during the shuffle. As you shuffle, glimpse the bottom card of the pack (see Hindu Glimpse). This card (the Five of Diamonds in the illustration) will be your "key" in locating the spectator's card in the pack.

(2) When he says "Stop," have Larry put his card face down on the lower half of the pack (the card marked "X" represents the chosen card).

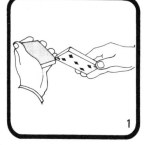

(3) When the card is replaced, drop the upper half of the pack on the lower so that your "key card" — the Five of Diamonds — comes directly over the chosen card (X).

(4) Now cut the pack several times to "lose" the card in the deck. Actually, as long as you give the deck only SINGLE CUTS, the selected card will not be separated from the key card. In fact, after you cut the deck — offer the pack to the spectator to cut as much as he likes. Make sure you specify he should make only SINGLE cuts.

(5) This done, turn the pack face up, remarking, "Your card is lost somewhere in the pack, so as I run through the deck, look for your card, but don't tell me when you see it!" With that, start "running" through the pack, thumbing cards from left to right, one at a time.

(6) When you come to your "key card" — the Five of Diamonds — start spelling your friend's name to yourself: "L-A-R-R-Y J-O-N-E-S" beginning with the letter "L" for the "key" card (the Five of Diamonds). *Continue spelling one letter of his name for each card you "run" from your left hand to your right.*

Key Card   Selected Card

(7) When you complete secretly spelling the name, separate the pack after the last letter ("S") in his name ("Jones") and ask the spectator if he has seen his card so far. *It is perfectly natural to gesture with your hands when asking this question, therefore, it should not arouse suspicion when you separate the pack at that point.*

"S" Card

(8) When the spectator replies "Yes" to your question, reassemble the pack; *but instead of placing the halves together the way they were, place the left-hand packet ON TOP of the right-hand packet.*

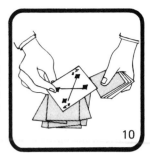

(9) Square the pack, turn it face down and hand it to your friend. Tell him to "Deal the cards one by one, *spelling your own name,* card by card."

(10) This he does, finishing his "spell" on your key card. The next card (X) will be his chosen card, which you tell him to turn over. He will be amazed to find that HIS name has found HIS card!

COMMENTS AND SUGGESTIONS

In this and in other similar "key" card tricks, when running through the pack, if you come to your "key" card before you are half way through the pack, "spell" the name and cut the rear portion of the front as usual. But instead of stopping there, run through the cards again before asking your friend if he has seen his card. When he says, "Yes," simply close the pack and hand it to him telling him to spell his name. The idea is to *let him see most of the cards in the pack BEFORE you put the question.* If he sees too few, the effect is weakened. Sometimes, in contrast, you may run through nearly all the cards before you come to your "key." This means you will not have enough remaining cards to spell your friend's name. In that case, simply close the pack and cut about a dozen cards from the face, to the back of the deck. Then start all over, running through the pack, in the usual fashion spelling your friend's name.

SPELL-A-CARD

EFFECT

This is an alternate version of "Spell-A-Name" which comes in very handy when you don't know the name of the person who selected the card. Rather than asking him his name and weakening the effect, you can switch to "Spell-A-Card."

METHOD

(1) Have a spectator select a card and return it to the pack; be sure to glimpse your "key card" in the usual fashion.

(2) Now, as you run face up through the pack, note the card JUST BEFORE THE "KEY" CARD. . .*this will be the spectator's card.* Let's suppose the spectator has selected the Five of Diamonds.

(3) As you run the cards from your left hand to your right hand, *secretly* spell the name of the spectator's card, letter by letter. . .F-I-V-E O-F D-I-A-M-O-N-D-S. . .passing one card for each letter BEGINNING WITH THE "KEY" CARD.

(4) This done, separate the pack at the proper location, just as you did in Spell a Name, as you ask, "Have you seen your card?"

(5) When he answers, "Yes," reassemble the pack, putting the left-hand packet on the top of the deck as before. *Thus you have secretly placed the selected card at the correct location to "spell out" its name.*

(6) Have the spectator spell the name of his card, letter by letter. When he turns up the next card, it will be his card. . .the FIVE OF DIAMONDS!

SPELL-A-CARD — OUTDONE

This version of SPELL-A-CARD offers an added feature which makes this a Double Mystery.

METHOD

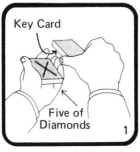

Key Card

Five of Diamonds

1

(1) Follow the usual procedure for Spell-A-Card by having a spectator select a card (the Five of Diamonds in the illustrations) and return it to the pack below your secretly noted "key" card (the Eight of Clubs).

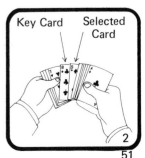

Key Card   Selected Card

2

(2) After the pack has been cut several times, run through the cards from the left hand to the right hand *face up* telling the spectator to make sure that the deck is thoroughly mixed. As in Spell-A-Card, when you come to the card *just before the "key" card,* you know that it is the selected card. Begin spelling its name, F-I-V-E O-F D-I-A-M-O-N-D-S, as you run the cards from your left hand to your right hand.

(3) Then, after spelling the Five of Diamonds, DO NOT CUT THE PACK AT THAT POINT as in the regular version. INSTEAD, note the NEXT card AFTER you have spelled the "selected" card, (the Five of Diamonds) and *secretly spell its name*, S-I-X O-F S-P-A-D-E-S, beginning with the next card above it (the Four of Hearts in the illustration).

(4) When you have finished secretly spelling this "new" card, cut the rear portion of the pack to the front and turn the pack face down as you state, "Here's something really magical. If I snap the end of the pack and spell out *any* card I have in mind, I find it. Take the Six of Spades for example." Here you deal cards, letter by letter -- spell S-I-X O-F S-P-A-D-E-S and turn up the next card, showing it to be the Six of Spades.

(5) Gather up the dealt cards, turn them face down and *put them on the bottom of the pack.* Now hand the spectator the deck and say "Here, try for yourself, spelling the name of the card you selected, whatever it happens to be. But don't forget to snap the end of the pack first, that's what works the magic".

(6) The spectator spells his card, F-I-V-E O-F D-I-A-M-O-N-D-S, and it's right there, just as you said, to complete the double surprise! Nobody will suspect that you set up your "spell" by merely looking through the pack, and when the spectator finds his own card in the same way, the audience will be completely amazed.

COMMENTS AND SUGGESTIONS

One advantage of this "Double Speller" is that, when *you* spell a card first, it makes the process easy for the other person to follow. ALSO, SINCE THE PACK IS IN THE SPECTATOR'S OWN HANDS, IT APPARENTLY PUTS THE CARDS BEYOND YOUR CONTROL.

THE HINDU FLASH FORCE

There are many ways of "Forcing" a spectator to select a certain card without having him realize it – but to do this naturally and repeatedly was formerly somewhat difficult. It took the "Hindu Shuffle" to produce a sure-fire way of "Forcing" a card at a moment's notice. Try the method that follows and you will see why.

EFFECT

During the course of a Hindu Shuffle, at any time the spectator requests, the magician pauses long enough to give the spectator a "flash" of a card in the pack. Though the magician keeps his own head turned so that he cannot possibly see the card . . . the magician has actually "Forced" the spectator to select the very card that the magician wanted.

METHOD

(1) Suppose you want to "Force" the Five of Diamonds. Place the Five on the bottom of the pack. Start the usual Hindu Shuffle, telling the spectator to call "stop" at any time he wants.

Five of Diamonds "force card" on bottom

(2) Continue the shuffle at the usual speed, pulling packets from the TOP of the cards in the right hand. *This leaves the Five of Diamonds at the BOTTOM of the right-hand cards.*

Force card stays on bottom

Five of Diamonds

(3) When the spectator says "stop," slant the right-hand packet toward him, showing him the face of the card on the bottom. THIS IS THE ORIGINAL BOTTOM CARD OF THE PACK, THE FIVE OF DIAMONDS!

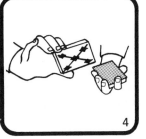

(5) Drop the right-hand cards on the cards lying in your left hand to bury the card the spectator *thinks* he has freely chosen from the deck. Actually you already know the card. YOU HAVE "FORCED" HIM TO SELECT THE FIVE OF DIAMONDS JUST AS YOU HAD PLANNED!

(4) *NOTE: Here is a view as the spectator sees it. Notice that the right hand is well forward toward the spectator to insure that the magician cannot see the card on the bottom. Tell the spectator to remember the card he has "selected."*

COMMENTS AND SUGGESTIONS

This is called a "Flash Force" because you simply "flash" the card before the spectator's eyes. But it is MORE THAN THAT. You can hold up the packet as long as you want. Just assure the spectator that you cannot see the card that he thinks is the result of HIS OWN FREE CHOICE, when he called "stop." When he is looking at the card, you should turn your head away to emphasize that you are the ONE PERSON who cannot possibly see that card. This is important, because it diverts the spectators' minds from the fact that you don't need to see it, BECAUSE YOU ALREADY KNOW IT. That is one use of "misdirection" – which you will learn to use more and more as you continue with the Course.

THE HINDU COLOR CHANGE

Here is a quick, baffling trick that makes a good opening number for a card routine. It depends upon the "Hindu Shuffle," so the skill that you have acquired in learning that important "move" can also be put to good use with this trick.

EFFECT

You take a red-backed pack of cards from its case and spread them FACE UP so that everyone can see that they are all different. Then, running through the face-up pack with a series of short cuts, you show the backs of the cards at frequent intervals. The spectators can see that all the cards have RED BACKS. Giving the face-up pack a "magic tap," you turn it face down and spread the cards along the table, and to everyone's astonishment, all the backs have turned from red to BLUE!

SECRET AND PREPARATION

All you need is a regular blue-backed pack and a *single red-backed card,* which you place on top of the pack before putting the deck in its box. You should use a RED CASE, as the pack is supposed to have RED BACKS at the start.

METHOD

(1) Open the box and bring out the pack face down, with the one red-backed card showing. Keep the cards well squared so you don't accidentally "flash" any of the blue cards beneath the top red card, as you remark, "Here is a pack of red-backed cards."

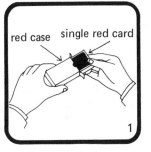

red case   single red card

(2) With that, you lay the box aside and turn the pack face up in your hands.

(3) Spread the pack *face up* in your hands showing the faces of the cards remarking: "As you can see, the cards are all different, as they should be . . ."

(6) *NOTE: Here you are simply combining the Hindu Shuffle with a REPEATED Flash Force while the pack is upside down. The audience thinks that you are cutting the pack at various places, showing a different red-backed card each time. Actually, you are always showing the SAME RED-BACKED CARD. Because of the "face-up" Hindu Shuffle, the red card remains on the bottom of the face-up right-hand packet. Do this deliberately and cleanly, keeping the pack well squared with each "flash" to prevent anyone from glimpsing a portion of a blue back during the process.*

(4) Now square the pack *face up* in the left hand and begin a regular Hindu Shuffle, but with the deck *face up.*

(7) As you complete the series of "flashes," drop the last few cards face up on the pack. Or, the shuffle can even be carried *to the very last card,* thus placing the single red card at the top of the face-up deck.

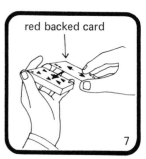

red backed card

(5) At various intervals throughout the shuffle, swing the right-hand packet away from you and tilt the back of the packet toward the spectators showing them the single red-backed cards as you say, ". . . and the backs are the same, red, as they should be."

(8) Square the face up pack and give it a sharp snap or riffle, saying you will change the backs from red to blue. With that, turn the pack face down (the single red-backed card is now face down at the bottom, or close to it) and spread or fan the pack *except for the last few bottom cards.* Apparently all the backs have magically changed from red to blue!

Single red back   All blue backs

COMMENTS AND SUGGESTIONS

(A) As already stated, the success of the effect depends upon keeping the upper packet well squared throughout the entire shuffle, so that the red-backed card can be shown repeatedly without exposing any blue card.

(B) To keep the packet square while shuffling you can tap it against the inner end of the pack, as described in the "Hindu Glimpse."

(C) When showing the blue backs at the finish, fan the cards from hand to hand, or spread them face down along the table....do just be careful NOT to spread the cards too close to the "secret" red-backed card. The simplest follow-up is to gather the pack and replace it in the case, which then goes in your pocket.

(D) As described later under A CLEVER COMBINATION, this makes a very good lead-in for DOUBLE THOUGHT....which also eliminates having to secretly get rid of the one red-backed card.

FINAL NOTE: By using a "short" red backed card (see "Short Card" section), after the color change, you can gather the out-spread pack, turn it face up and give it a Hindu Shuffle, this time flashing a blue backed card with each pause. Then turn the *back* of the pack *toward* the spectators and slowly riffle the cards, showing "all blue," as the short card will ride along unseen. Finally turn the pack face up in your left hand. With your right hand, riffle to the short card, and cut it to the face of the pack. Pick up the card case and dispose of the short red-backed card as described.

THE COLOR CHANGING DECKS
(Two-Deck Version)

In this modified version of the Hindu Color Change, you take the mystery one step further by adding a second pack of cards – of a different color – and convert the effect from a *color change* into a magical *transposition* of the two packs.

EFFECT

The magician removes a RED-BACKED pack of cards from its case and spreads them face up so that everyone can see that they are all different. Then, running through the face-up pack with a series of short cuts, he shows the *red* backs of the cards at frequent intervals, finally placing the pack face up on the table next to its *red box*. The performer then follows the exact same procedure with a BLUE-BACKED pack of cards, and places it face up on the table next to its *blue box*. The mystery begins when the magician removes one card from each pack. He places the one *red* card on the face of the *blue-backed* pack and the one *blue* card on the *red-backed* pack. Explaining that this causes the rest of the cards in both packs to "Follow the Leader," the magician turns over each pack and spreads it face down next to its correct colored box. The audience is amazed to discover that ALL THE BLUE-BACKED CARDS HAVE "MAGICALLY" CHANGED PLACES WITH ALL OF THE RED-BACKED CARDS!

SECRET AND PREPARATION

The only items required for this mystery are a *red*-backed pack of cards and its *red box* and a *blue*-backed deck and its *blue box* with a matching design. To prepare, remove a single *blue* card from the blue pack and place it face down on top of the *red deck*. Also, place a single *blue* card on top of the *red deck*. Now, place the red deck *(with the one blue card on top)* into the blue box; and place the blue deck *(with the one red card on top)* into the red box. You are ready to perform the COLOR CHANGING DECKS.

METHOD

(1) To begin, place both packs – in their boxes – on the table. Say, "I have two packs of cards, one red – and one blue."

Red Box   Blue Box

1

(2) Pick up the BLUE BOX and remove the pack of cards face down.... SO THE SINGLE BLUE CARD, WHICH MATCHES THE COLOR OF THE BOX, IS SEEN BY THE SPECTATORS. They will assume it to be an all blue pack. *NOTE: As you remove the pack from the box, keep the cards well "squared" so you do not accidentally shift the top blue card exposing the red cards below.*

2

(3) Place the empty blue box on the table and turn the pack over (face up). Run through the pack showing the faces of the cards.... say, "As you can see, all the cards in the pack are different, as they should be."

(4) Now square the pack face up in your left hand and begin a regular Hindu Shuffle, WITH THE DECK FACE UP. At various intervals throughout the shuffle, execute the repeated "Flash Force" as described in the HINDU COLOR CHANGE. The audience believes you are cutting the pack at *various* places showing a *different* card each time. Remark, "And the backs are all blue, as they should be."

4

(5) IMPORTANT NOTE: In this trick, (unlike the HINDU COLOR CHANGE, the Hindu Shuffle, MUST BE CARRIED TO THE VERY LAST CARD. As you complete the Hindu Shuffle, the left fingers draw off all the remaining red cards leaving the single blue card in your right hand. Finish the shuffle by dropping the blue card *on top of the face-up deck.*

(6) This done, square up the pack and place it face up on the table *next to the empty blue box* from which you removed it.

(7) Now, pick up the *red box* and remove the *"red"* pack *(actually the blue pack with the single red card on top).*

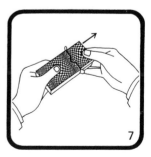

7

(8) Follow the same face-up Hindu Shuffle procedure using the repeated "Flash Force" showing the *red* card. Finish by shuffling the SINGLE RED CARD TO THE TOP OF THE FACE UP PACK. Square up this pack and place it face up on the table *next to the empty red box.*

8

(9) With the packs resting face up next to their "own" colored boxes, (10) lift the two "odd" cards (the single red card and the single blue card) from the face of each pack and transpose them – (11) PLACING THE RED-BACKED CARD ON THE REAL RED PACK AND THE BLUE-BACKED CARD ON THE REAL BLUE PACK. As you do this say, "If I move just *one* card from each pack and place it on the pack of the opposite color, the rest of the cards in each pack will "Follow the Leader."

(12) Pick up both packs – one in each hand – and spread them face down on the table *next to the box you first removed it from.* The audience will be amazed to see that THE BLUE CARDS HAVE MAGICALLY CHANGED PLACES WITH THE RED CARDS – RIGHT BEFORE THEIR EYES!

HINDU SHUFFLE -- BOTTOM STOCK CONTROL

In certain card tricks, it is important that during a shuffle, the bottom card, or a group of cards already on the bottom, are retained there for some future purpose. Here is a way of accomplishing that with the aid of the Hindu Shuffle, making this an important utility sleight that every card worker should learn.

EFFECT

To all appearances, the magician gives the pack a regular Hindu Shuffle. Yet, in this modified version, the bottom stock of cards remains undisturbed or "unshuffled." Despite that important difference, the magician can switch from this form of the Hindu Shuffle to another without any chance of detection.

METHOD

(1) Hold the pack in the tips of the fingers of the left hand, ready for the Hindu Shuffle.

(3) Once the right hand has drawn the center packet of cards clear of the bottom and top packets, *the left hand allows the top packet to fall onto the bottom packet.*

(2) Unlike a regular Hindu Shuffle, where the right hand begins by drawing off a group of cards from the BOTTOM of the pack, this time the right hand pulls out a section of cards from the CENTER, leaving the bottom group intact. The left hand retains the bottom stock *and* a small batch of cards from the top as in the usual Shuffle.

(4) Now, continue the regular Hindu Shuffle -- repeatedly pulling off small batches of cards from the right-hand pack until the shuffle is complete.

(5) The pack has now been fairly shuffled EXCEPT FOR THE SMALL BATCH OF CARDS WHICH REMAINS UNDISTURBED. You are also now set to repeat the Hindu Shuffle — Bottom Stock Control as often as you like.

A FALSE CUT

EFFECT

Many very good card tricks depend upon your knowing the bottom card of the pack or bringing a chosen card to the top. At that point, a suspicious spectator may want to cut the pack. So to prove that all is fair, your best policy is to beat them to it by cutting the pack yourself. You can do that with the following "False Cut" that looks like the real thing, but actually leaves the pack just as it was.

METHOD

(1) Hold the deck in the left hand between the tips of the left fingers and thumb.

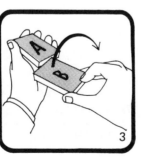

(2) With the thumb and fingers of your right hand, start to draw out about half the pack (B) from the lower part of the deck.

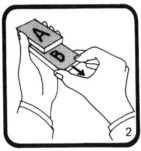

(3) As this lower stack (B) comes clear, sweep your right hand toward your body.

(4) Continue this sweep carrying the cards (B) in your right hand *up and over the top stack* (A) in your left hand.

(5) Place the packet in your right hand (B) onto the table and leave it.

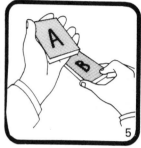

(6) Now with your right hand, take all of the cards (A) from the left hand and . . .

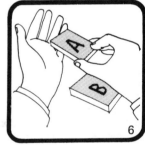

(7) . . . place them directly on top of the stack (B) on the table.

(8) It will appear as if the cards are fairly cut. Actually the order of the cards has not changed at all.

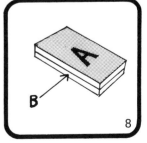

COMMENTS AND SUGGESTIONS

This False Cut should be performed at a moderate speed — not too slow and not too fast. Do not call special attention to it — *just do it as if you were cutting the cards in a normal manner.* Done correctly, no one will question it.

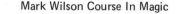

HINDU SHUFFLE PICK-UP CONTROL

This is one of the most deceptive and useful controls in all of Card Magic. If this sleight were the only one you used with the Hindu Shuffle, it would be well worth your time in learning it. The Pick-Up Control is not difficult to learn and, I am sure, you will be using it in many of your best card effects after you have mastered it.

EFFECT

A spectator returns a selected card to the pack while the magician is giving the deck a Hindu Shuffle. This apparently "loses" the card somewhere deep in the pack, yet the magician has secretly "controlled" the card to the top of the pack.

METHOD

Selected card on top of small packet

(1) Ask a spectator to select a card freely from the pack, either as you spread the pack between your hands — or you can let him take a card by telling you to "stop" during the course of a Hindu Shuffle.

(5) THE SELECTED CARD (X) IS THE TOP CARD OF THIS SMALL PACKET.

(2) While he is looking at his card, you square the pack and begin a new Hindu Shuffle, inviting him to replace his card any time he wants. You do the shuffle quite slowly, apparently to aid the replacement, *but actually to prepare for a simple but special move.*

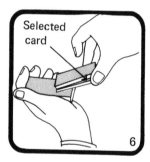

Selected card

(6) Continue the shuffle, drawing off cards from the top of the right-hand packet, *still holding the small packet on the bottom of the right-hand bulk of cards, always maintaining the "gap" between the two portions.*

(3) After the spectator has replaced his card (X) on the left-hand section of the pack, move the bulk of the pack held in your right hand above the cards in your left hand as if to merely continue the shuffle.

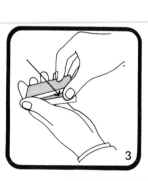

(7) As you finish the shuffle, *the left hand takes all the remaining cards ABOVE THE GAP . . .*

(4) NOW THIS IS THE IMPORTANT MOVE. As the left fingers slide off another packet from the top of the bulk of the pack, the tips of your right thumb and second finger squeeze inward, grip the sides *and pick up a small packet of cards from the lower left-hand heap.* Now carry this small packet away on the bottom of the right-hand bulk of cards. Keep a "break" or "gap" between that small batch and the upper bulk of the pack in the right hand.

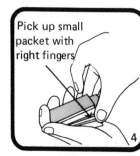

Pick up small packet with right fingers

(8) . . .while the right hand draws the little batch out from beneath . . .

(9) ...and drops it on the left-hand pack to complete the shuffle.

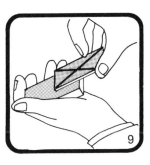

(10) Since the chosen card is the TOP CARD of that batch, it now becomes THE TOP CARD OF THE PACK. This means that YOU HAVE CONTROLLED THE CHOSEN CARD TO THE TOP OF THE PACK.

COMMENTS AND SUGGESTIONS

The Hindu Shuffle Control is one of the easiest and best ways to bring a selected card to the top of the pack. It also has many other uses ... and is one of the most valuable sleights that you will learn from this Course. Please study the pictures carefully. The most important move and the "key" to this entire sleight is in Step 4. This is when you pick up the small batch of cards, with the selected card on top, with your right thumb and fingers from the top of the left-hand packet. At the same time that you do this, you pull off a small batch of cards from the TOP of the right-hand packet, *just as if you were continuing the regular Hindu Shuffle.* This completely covers your "secret" pick-up. You then continue the Hindu Shuffle in the normal fashion until you get to the last small batch of cards with the selected card on top. Just place that packet as the last "shuffle" on the top of the deck in the left hand. Thus, you have secretly brought the selected card to the top. I have repeated the description of this sleight in "COMMENTS AND SUGGESTIONS" BECAUSE OF ITS IMPORTANCE. Once you have mastered the Hindu Shuffle and the Hindu Shuffle Control, you have opened the door to hundreds of wonderful, baffling mysteries with cards. If you are interested in performing card tricks, please practice and learn this important sleight.

THE HINDU ACES

As its name implies, this routine utilizes the Hindu Shuffle, with the Hindu Card Pick-Up Control as its "secret weapon." The more you practice it, the more you will like it ... and so will your audience!

EFFECT

The four Aces are removed from a pack of cards and given to a spectator to hold. As you shuffle the cards, Hindu style, he inserts the Aces at various intervals in the pack. When you finish the shuffle, you turn up the four top cards of the pack. All will be Aces!

METHOD

(1) From an ordinary pack of cards, run through the pack face up and remove the four Aces, placing them on the table. As you go through the deck, call attention to the fact that there are ONLY four Aces in the pack. Ask the spectator to pick up all four Aces and hold them face down in his hand.

(3) After the spectator has placed one Ace on top of the left-hand packet, continue the shuffle using the Hindu Pick-Up Control — secretly picking up a small batch from the top of the left-hand packet and maintaining a break between it and the bulk of the pack throughout the shuffle.

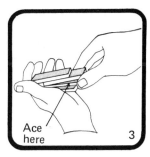

(2) Begin a regular Hindu Shuffle, drawing small batches of cards from the bulk of the pack into the left hand until nearly half the pack has been shuffled, and then stop. Now, move the left hand packet toward the spectator telling him to place any one of the four Aces on top of the packet. (The Aces have been marked with number "One" through "Four" in the illustrations.)

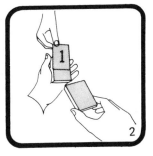

(4) When you have shuffled off all the cards above the break, the first Ace will have been secretly brought to the top of the deck with the cards in position to repeat the Hindu Shuffle.

(5) As you start the next Hindu Shuffle, draw about one-third of the deck (about 15 to 20 cards) from the top of the pack into the fingers of the left hand and STOP.

(7) This done, complete the Hindu Shuffle, using the Hindu Pick-Up Control, thus bringing both Aces to the top of the deck.

(6) Then, move your left hand toward the spectator and instruct him to place a second Ace on top of the packet in your left hand. *Unknown to the spectator, he will be placing this second Ace directly on top of the first Ace.*

(8) Repeat the entire process with the third and fourth Aces until all four Aces have been secretly controlled to the top of the deck. You can then reveal them in any manner you wish, or simply deal them face down on to the table, and turn each card face up, one at a time, to bring the mystery to a startling finish.

COMMENTS AND SUGGESTIONS

Practice this effect until you can do it smoothly, but not too rapidly, as you may have to pause occasionally to square the pack. When performing for a group of people, you can vary the routine by first handing each Ace to a different person. You then move from one to another, giving you a chance to square the pack before each replacement of an Ace, which is helpful with the "pickup."

REVERSE ORDER COUNT TRICK

In this quick, surprising way of discovering a chosen card, the person who selected the card plays an important part, which adds greatly to its impact on your audience. Once you have convinced people that a chosen card is hopelessly lost in the pack, merely naming it is not enough to impress them with your magic powers. You must make the card show itself in some unexpected way, and this is one of those ways.

EFFECT

After a card has been selected and shuffled back into the pack, you ask someone to name a number, preferably below twenty, though he can go higher if he insists. You count that many cards – say fourteen – face down on the table; then give the packet to the spectator and ask him to verify the count. When he comes to the final number – fourteen – you tell him to look at that card. When he turns it face up, he finds that it is the very card that he selected!

METHOD

(1) Begin by having the spectator select a card from a thoroughly shuffled pack. Ask him to remember it and return it to the pack during the course of a Hindu Shuffle. Using the HINDU PICK-UP CONTROL, bring the spectator's selected card to the *top* of the pack. (The selected card is indicated by an "X.")

(2) With the pack held in dealing position in the left hand, ask the spectator to call out *any* number from one to twenty, explaining that you will count down that many cards in the pack. When the spectator names the number, begin dealing the cards, <u>one at a time</u> in a pile, from the top of the deck onto the table—beginning with the spectator's card.

(3) *NOTE: Dealing the cards in this fashion – one at a time on top of each other – reverses the order of the cards as you count them. As explained in the Course, this is known as a Reverse Order Count, which, as you will see, is used to your advantage.*

(6) Instruct him to recount the cards in the same manner you did, one at a time in a pile and to count aloud as he does so. As the spectator recounts the cards, he is again <u>reversing their order</u>, placing them in the same sequence as when you began your count – WITH THE SELECTED CARD AT THE TOP!

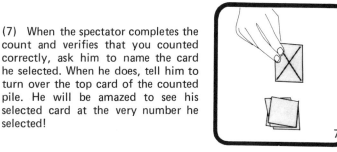

(4) Continue dealing and counting – one card for each number – until you have reached the number selected by the spectator.

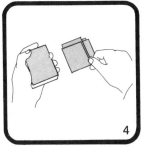

(7) When the spectator completes the count and verifies that you counted correctly, ask him to name the card he selected. When he does, tell him to turn over the top card of the counted pile. He will be amazed to see his selected card at the very number he selected!

(5) This done, give the pile of "counted" cards, face down, to the spectator as you say, "I have counted out the exact number of cards which you selected. Please count them yourself to verify that I have counted correctly."

COMMENTS AND SUGGESTIONS

Since no one knows that the chosen card is on top of the pack to start, the fact that the spectator reverses your count *back* to where it was originally will not seem to have any apparent bearing on the result. In a sense, this is a *"double reverse,"* the only difference being that you did yours knowingly, while he did his unknowingly. Clever and bold secrets of this type give Card Magic much of its appeal and the more you vary your program with surprise discoveries of chosen cards, the better your audiences will like it.

OVERHAND SHUFFLE

The "Overhand Shuffle" is the most common of all shuffles. The very simplicity of the shuffle makes it easy to locate and control certain cards, bringing them to top or bottom of the pack and retaining them there. For that very reason, it should be practiced until it becomes second nature, so that the various subterfuges can be introduced without arousing suspicion. By using the Overhand Shuffle constantly in card tricks as well as in card games, merely handling the pack gives you the opportunity to practice.

Hundreds of excellent tricks can be developed directly from the Overhand Shuffle, many of which have been included in the Card Section of this Course.

THE OVERHAND SHUFFLE

This is a simple, standard way of shuffling a pack of cards that you should use constantly when performing card tricks. It is both natural and convincing and is an honest shuffle. However, more importantly, it can be adapted to many special uses, such as "controlling" certain cards without the audience knowing it. These "controls," which will be taught later, are some of the most useful sleights in card magic.

METHOD

(1) Hold the deck with the thumb and fingers of your right hand.

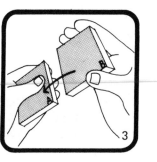

(2) Bring both your hands together. With your left thumb, from the top of the deck, pull off a block of several cards (indicated by the letter A), into your left hand, leaving the remainder of the deck (letter B) in the right hand.

(3) Separate your hands completely. Hold the block of cards now in your left hand (A) firmly between the left thumb and fingers.

(4) Lift your left thumb enough to allow the packet in the right hand to be reinserted into the "pull-off position." With the left thumb, pull another block of several cards (B) into the left hand on top of the cards (A) already in the hand, leaving the remainder of the deck (C) in your right hand.

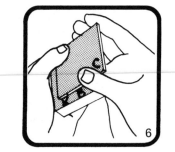

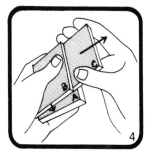

(5) Separate your hands, allowing the cards just removed (Block B) to fall on the cards already in the left hand (Block A).

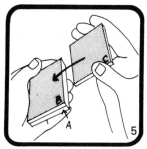

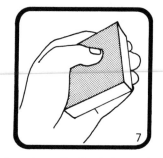

(6) Continue pulling off blocks of cards until all of the cards in the right hand (7) have been "shuffled off" into the left hand.

COMMENTS AND SUGGESTIONS

This is a natural way of shuffling a pack of cards and mixing it quite thoroughly . . . but it can also be easily diverted to magical uses . . . particularly in "controlling" cards on either the top or bottom of the pack or to a particular position in the deck. Therefore, easy as this shuffle is, you should practice it repeatedly until it can be executed without hesitation. This will enable you to perform the special variations as required.

THE OVERHAND REVERSE SHUFFLE

The Overhand Shuffle can also be done as a Reverse Shuffle. The movements are exactly the same as described in the Overhand Shuffle, except that the right hand holds the deck so that the faces of the cards are *outward* (with the back of the cards toward the right palm) instead of *inward* (with the faces of the cards toward the right palm). The operation of the Shuffle is the same. However, this Reverse has an important bearing on the "control" shuffles that follow.

THE OVERHAND IN-JOG CONTROL

EFFECT

This shuffle is very useful in controlling a selected card when the spectator returns the card to the pack. In addition, it can be used to bring a card to the top of the pack and also to keep it there. Yet all during the operation, the performer appears to be simply shuffling the pack in the normal Overhand fashion.

METHOD

(1) After a spectator has drawn a card from the pack and is looking at it, you start an Overhand Shuffle, drawing cards from the top of the pack with your left thumb. Tell the spectator to replace his card in the pack as you near the center.

(2) His card goes on the left-hand packet ... and, as you resume the shuffle, *bring your right hand slightly inward toward your body, a matter of a half an inch or so.* This is a simple action that might occur during any shuffle.

(3) With your left thumb, draw off a single card from the right-hand packet. Let this indifferent card fall upon the selected card, which is on the top of the left-hand packet. *The inward movement that you made in Step 2 will make this one card protrude slightly inward, toward your body, from the rest of the left-hand cards.*

(4) This single, "off center" card is called an "IN-JOG." You can prevent anyone from noticing it by now simply moving your right hand forward to its normal position and continuing your Overhand Shuffle. The remainder of the cards go into their regular position, "evened up" with the first cards shuffled.

(5) As more cards cover the "Jogged" card, they help to hide it from view, *particularly if they are shuffled in a somewhat irregular manner.*

(6) As you continue "shuffling off" blocks of cards, be sure that the In-Jogged card is not pushed back into the deck.

(7) Continue shuffling until all the cards in the right hand are held in the left hand.

(8) After you have completed the shuffle, the deck should look like this with the Jogged card protruding toward you. *Of course, since this is a secret maneuver, you do not call the spectator's attention to it.*

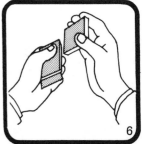

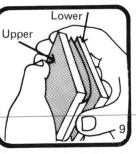

(9) You can now easily find the "Jogged" card *by pressing upward with your right thumb at the inner end of the pack.*

(12) Now, drop the packet in the right hand (with the selected card (X) on top) down in front of the cards held in the left hand. This is called a "throw" and to all appearances it adds a final and convincing touch to the shuffle.

(10) This upward pressure causes the deck to divide at the Jogged card ... by gripping the ends of the lower packet between your right thumb and fingers, you can lift the lower portion entirely clear of the rest of the deck.

(13) Actually, the "throw" brings the selected card to the top of the pack.

(11) With the right hand, carry the lower section completely over the upper section in the left hand.

COMMENTS AND SUGGESTIONS

Treat the Jogged card much as you would any other "key" card. Never appear to pay any attention to its position, which should be easy, since you are depending on your sense of touch alone. Make the shuffle look natural, even sloppy if you wish, for if you do it too neatly, you may lose track of the Jogged card. Don't worry if you pull down an extra card or two when making the "Jog." A little group of Jogged cards will function just as effectively as a single card, for when you press the lowest card of the group upward, the others will go along with it, and you will still be able to cut to the selected card and "throw" the packet to the top of the deck.

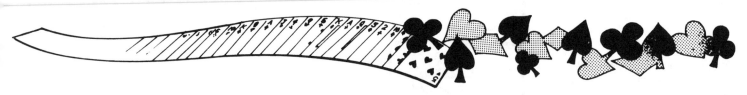

THE CARD CASE ESCAPE

Variety is an important factor in card tricks that end with the "discovery" of a card selected by a spectator. Many card discoveries, though clever, are too much alike to be presented on the same program, so it is a good procedure to inject something distinctly different. This effect falls into that category.

EFFECT

After a card has been selected by a spectator and shuffled back into the pack, the magician puts the entire pack into its box and closes the flap. Showing the box from all angles, he openly places it in his shirt pocket. Then, showing both hands empty, he reaches into his pocket. *He instantly removes the chosen card.* Immediately, he brings the card box from his pocket and gives it to the spectators, allowing them to open it for themselves and examine both box and pack. APPARENTLY, THE SELECTED CARD MANAGED TO PENETRATE THE CARD BOX UNDER ITS OWN POWER!

(1) Remove a regular pack of cards from its box, shuffle it, and have a spectator select a card. Tell the spectator to remember the card and return it to the pack. As the card is returned to the pack, use your favorite method to control it to the top.

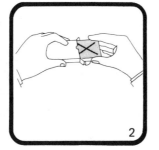

(2) Holding the pack in one hand, pick up the card box in the other. Replace the entire pack in the card box, making sure that the *top* of the pack (with the selected card on it) goes against the side of the box with the little "thumb slot" cut out. As you do this, say, "I will place the pack of cards into its card box, thus SEALING YOUR CARD INSIDE, SOMEWHERE IN THE DECK."

(3) Begin to close the lid of the box. As you do, *squeeze* the sides of the box containing the cards, as shown. This "squeezing" action will cause the top few cards of the pack to "bow" outwards against the top of the box, *making a small gap between each of the top few cards.*

(4) As you tuck the flap in, SLIDE IT BENEATH THE TOP CARD OF THE PACK (The spectator's card "X") as shown.

(5) Close the flap completely and transfer the box to your right hand.

(6) As you hold the case, *make sure the fingers of your right hand COVER THE THUMB SLOT,* thus concealing the visible portion of the spectator's card from view. With the pack held in this manner, you can display it casually on both sides before you proceed to the next step.

(7) After briefly showing the box, place it into your shirt or coat breast pocket as you remark, "With the pack sealed in its box and hidden in my pocket, it would be very difficult for me to find your card."

(8) Show your hand empty and reach into your pocket. Use your fingers to work the end of the spectator's card out of the box by pulling it from the "thumb slot." As soon as you have a good grip on the card, *immediately withdraw it from your pocket.*

(9) The back of the card will be toward the spectator, therefore, he will not know what card you have in your hand. Ask the spectator to name the card he selected. When he replies, turn the card in your hand face up and show it to be his card. IMMEDIATELY REMOVE THE PACK FROM YOUR POCKET AND TOSS IT ON THE TABLE FOR ALL TO EXAMINE.

COMMENTS AND SUGGESTIONS

The proper type of card case for this trick is one with a flap that slides in easily and rather deeply. Some short flaps will not stay in place while you are extracting the chosen card, so be careful, as you draw the card from its box, that the flap remains closed. As soon as *one hand* removes the chosen card from the pocket, the *other hand* can bring out the case and offer it for examination.

OVERHAND SHUFFLE GLIMPSE

The Overhand Shuffle Glimpse is a very useful and valuable move enabling you to "sight" the bottom card of the deck secretly during the course of an Overhand Shuffle. It becomes especially valuable in tricks where it is necessary to use a "key" card as it supplies a direct, natural manner in which to note the bottom card without suspicion.

METHOD

(1) With the pack held firmly in the right hand, begin a regular Overhand Shuffle, drawing off small batches of cards from the bulk of the pack into the left hand.

(2) Then, at some point during the shuffle when the left hand has just drawn off a batch of cards and both hands are separated, *tilt the upper edge of the right hand packet away from you* just enough so you can see the bottom card of that packet.

(3) You only need a brief instant to glimpse the card, so make the move seem natural without pausing or breaking the flow of the shuffle.

SHUFFLE CONTROL WITH KEY CARD

Whenever you are using a "key" card to locate a chosen card, you must be careful NOT to let anyone shuffle the pack, as that may separate the two cards. However, you can do an actual shuffle of your own, as follows:

METHOD

(1) In Step 6 of the Hindu Key Card Location, after you have dropped the upper half of the pack on the lower, placing the "key" card next to the selected card, begin an Overhand Shuffle, drawing off little packets of cards from the top of the deck with your left thumb.

"Selected" Card

"Key" Card

1

(3) Complete the shuffle by drawing off the lower cards in small packets again . . . then cut the pack as often as you want.

3

(2) WHEN YOU NEAR THE CENTER, DRAW OFF A LARGE BLOCK OF CARDS TOGETHER. *This section contains your two cards, the "key" card and the selected card. You draw off the large packet of cards so that they will not be separated.*

Draw off a large packet

2

OVERHAND SHUFFLE CONTROL — TOP CARD TO BOTTOM

EFFECT

With the Overhand Shuffle, you can "control" the top card of the pack and bring it to the bottom of the pack while apparently giving the deck an honest shuffle.

METHOD

(1) Your control card is on the TOP of the deck. Hold the pack in your right hand.

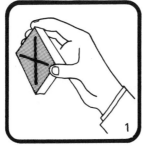

(3) Let it fall *alone* into the left hand.

(2) Start by drawing off ONLY THE TOP CARD with the left thumb.

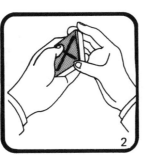

(4) Then continue the shuffle, pulling blocks of cards from the right hand with the left thumb on top of the "control" card, until all of the cards have been shuffled into the left hand. The "control" card will now be on the BOTTOM of the pack.

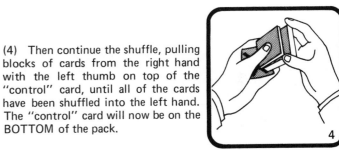

THE TRANSFERRED THOUGHT

Here is a card trick that will leave your audience believing in ESP, with the exception of one person, who will find himself "in the know," thanks to your choosing him as a helper. Actually, two spectators participate in the test, one as a "sender," the other as a "receiver," but the *sender* remains as baffled as the rest of the audience.

EFFECT

After a few remarks on Extra Sensory Perception (ESP), the magician invites two spectators to assist him in a test of thought transference. The magician tells *Spectator One* that he is the "Sender." He is to select any card from the pack and remember it, which he does. The Card is then returned to the pack, which is shuffled and put into its card case. The magician tells *Spectator Two* that he is to act as a "Receiver" by thinking of the pack and naming the *first* card that comes to his mind. After a brief period of concentration, *Spectator Two* announces the name of a card. To the surprise of everyone, especially *Spectator One*, that is the very card that was selected. The test can be repeated with the same remarkable result; and anyone who becomes suspicious of Spectator One is invited to serve as "Sender" himself. But no matter who tries it or how often it is repeated, *Spectator Two* always comes through with the correct card!

SECRET AND PREPARATION

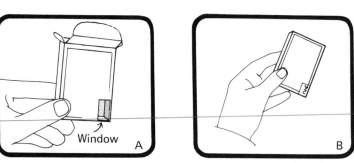

(A)   The secret of this trick depends upon the use of a specially prepared card box with a secret "window"! To make the *trick* box, with a sharp knife or razor blade, carefully cut a small rectangular opening or "window" in the lower right-hand corner of the <u>back</u> side of the card box. *This is the side which has the tuck flap attached to it.*

(B)   The "window" should be just large enough so, when the pack is inserted into the box, you are able to see the "index" with NUMBER AND SUIT VALUE of the <u>bottom</u> card of the pack. Place the box of cards in your coat pocket (or on your table with the "window" side down), and you are ready to begin.

METHOD

(1)   After a few brief remarks on ESP, invite two spectators to assist you in a test of Thought Transference. Have *Spectator One* stand at your extreme left and *Spectator Two* at your extreme right. Tell *Spectator One* that he will act as the "Sender" in this experiment and *Spectator Two* that he will be the "Receiver."

(2)   Take out the box of cards and remove the pack from the box. Then, place the box on the table with the WINDOW SIDE DOWN so it is concealed from view. *NOTE: In handling the box of cards, always be careful to keep the "window side" of the box facing down (toward the floor) so the audience cannot see that the box is specially prepared.*

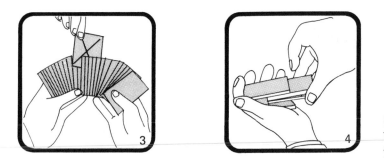

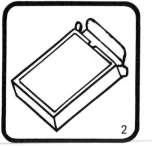

(3)   Run through the pack face down and invite Spectator One to select a card (X) from anywhere in the pack. Tell him to look at the card and remember it but not to show it to anyone else. (4)   Begin a regular Hindu Shuffle and have the spectator replace his card in the pack anywhere he wants. Then, using the HINDU PICK-UP CONTROL, bring the spectator's card to the top of the pack.

(5)   Now, begin a regular Overhand Shuffle, shuffling the spectator's card (X) from the <u>top</u> of the pack to the <u>bottom</u> as described in the OVERHAND SHUFFLE CONTROL – TOP CARD TO BOTTOM. As you shuffle off the remaining cards in the pack say, "Your card is now hopelessly lost in the pack."

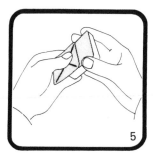

(6)   Holding the squared up pack face down in one hand, pick up the card box from the table ("window" side down) and insert the deck FACE DOWN into the box and tuck in the flap. *As you do this, the fingers of your left hand curl beneath the card box and cover the window from any possible view.*

(7)   By keeping the left thumb or fingers over the "window" in the corner, the box can now be shown casually on all sides. As you display the box, say to Spectator One, "I would like you to concentrate on the card you selected and try to 'send' a mental picture of that card to Spectator Two."

(8)   With that, turn your whole body to the right and face Spectator Two. As you do this, transfer the card box from your left hand to your right and hold it so the "window" faces him, enabling him to see the bottom card through the opening. Unknown to him, he is about to become your "confederate" in the trick. Now say, "I want you to concentrate as hard as you can and see if you can 'receive' a visual impression of the selected card. If so, what card do you see?" The illustration shows the spectator's view of the card box as you hold it in your right hand.

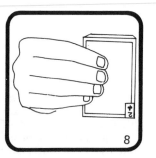

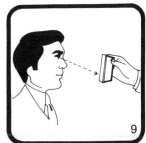

(9)   As you say this, look Spectator Two directly in the eyes and gesture with the card box <u>until you are sure he has seen the card in the "window."</u> If you play your part correctly, Spectator Two will "get the message" and will realize that <u>he</u> is now part of the deception. When he does, he will announce the name of the selected card! Once the test has succeeded, you will find Spectator Two more than happy to "receive" another image should you try the experiment again.

COMMENTS AND SUGGESTIONS

Repeating the trick will give Spectator Two another chance at "acting." Encourage him to play his part well. Once he realizes that he is "part of the act," he should cooperate in making the trick as mysterious as possible. If however, he becomes troublesome at any time during the trick, either choose another "receiver" or go on to the next trick. You can cover this easily by explaining to your audience that ESP experiments are never 100% sure and then move on to something else.

This trick is a good exercise in "controlling" the behavior of the spectator. Before beginning the trick, try to pick out someone who looks good-natured and cooperative. Treat this person with respect and kindness and he should help to make the trick a success.

If repeating the trick often, you can save time by simply handing the pack to a spectator — tell him to cut it anywhere and look at the bottom card. Have him turn the pack face down so you can place it into the card case without letting anyone see the bottom card other than Spectator One who chose it. You can even let the spectator push the pack in for himself, but your helper — Spectator Two — WILL NAME IT JUST THE SAME!

THE OVERHAND SLIP SHUFFLE

EFFECT

Once you are familiar with the standard "Overhand Shuffle," you can easily learn the "Slip Shuffle." The "Slip Shuffle" will enable you to retain the BOTTOM CARD ON THE BOTTOM OF THE PACK as the rest of the cards in the deck are being well mixed. To "control" the bottom card, proceed as follows:

METHOD

(1)   Hold the cards in your right hand in preparation for the standard Overhand Shuffle.

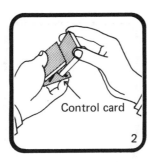

(2)   As you begin the shuffle in the regular way by drawing off the top stack of cards, the fingers of your left hand naturally rest against the bottom card of the pack . . . *this is the card (X) which you are going to control.* Press lightly against the face of the bottom card (X) with the left fingers. When you draw off the first stack from the top of the pack with the left thumb YOU ALSO DRAW OFF THE BOTTOM CARD (X) WITH THE LEFT FINGERS. Thus the "control" card (X) is added to the bottom of the packet being drawn off by the left thumb.

(3)   Here is a view from below of the left fingers "holding" the bottom card (X). *Note how the bottom card (X) is secretly being "slipped off" the bulk of the pack to retain its position at the bottom of the shuffled deck.*

(4)   From this point on you simply continue the regular Overhand Shuffle . . . Shuffling off small packets of cards from the bulk of the pack in the right hand onto the shuffled cards in the left hand. This "bottom control" can be repeated as often as necessary.

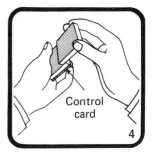

COMMENTS AND SUGGESTIONS

It is best to perform the Overhand Slip Shuffle with the left side of your body toward the audience. This keeps the faces of the cards away from the audience and prevents them from seeing that the bottom card *remains* on the bottom of the pack. Because this move is so natural and can be performed quite openly, there should be no suspicions aroused as the cards are being shuffled.

THE CARD THROUGH THE HANDKERCHIEF

Here is a classic of Card Magic that originally required considerable skill to perform. By eliminating the more difficult "moves," it has been reduced to a simple, direct presentation, without losing any of its masterful effect. Learn it now and you will still be using it, no matter how great a reputation you may gain as a card expert!

EFFECT

A card is selected and returned to the pack which is then thoroughly shuffled. The magician places it openly beneath the center of a fairly large handkerchief, proving that it would take x-ray vision to see through the cloth and find the selected card. Bringing the pack into view, the magician wraps it inside the handkerchief. Now, instead of trying to find the selected card, the wizard decides to let the card *reveal itself*. He starts to shake the handkerchief....amazingly, the chosen card *penetrates right through the cloth* and drops to the floor....while the balance of the deck remains wrapped in the handkerchief! The card and pack are then passed for examination along with the handkerchief, which is found to be intact.

METHOD

(1) Remove a regular pack of cards from its box, shuffle it, and have a spectator select any card. Tell him to remember the card and have him return it to the pack as you give it an Overhand Shuffle. When the card is returned to the pack, execute the OVERHAND SHUFFLE-IN JOG CONTROL, secretly bringing the selected card to the top of the pack.

(2) Hold the pack in dealing position in your left hand, with your thumb resting on top of the pack. (The selected card, the Two of Clubs, is on the top of the deck and has been marked with an "X" in the illustrations.)

(6) Bring the pack from under the cloth into view, leaving the selected card hidden beneath the handkerchief, resting loosely in your partially open left hand.

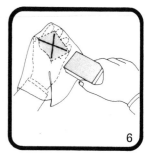

(3) With your right hand, drape the handkerchief over your left hand, so the pack is beneath the center of the handkerchief as you say, "It would be quite difficult for me to see through the handkerchief and find your card."

(7) Place the pack of cards in the center of the handkerchief, directly on top of the selected card. Then, square up the pack with your left thumb and fingers through the cloth even with the selected card hidden under the handkerchief.

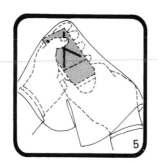

(4) Reach under the handkerchief with your right hand and grasp the inner end of the pack. (5) Now, pull all of the pack out from beneath the selected card. YOUR LEFT THUMB HOLDS THE SELECTED CARD IN PLACE, SECRETLY RETAINING IT IN YOUR LEFT HAND, UNDER THE HANDKERCHIEF.

(8) With your right hand, lift the edge of the handkerchief nearest you and fold this edge up and over the pack as shown. (9) NOW, GRASP THE DECK AND THE HIDDEN CARD BETWEEN THE THUMB AND FINGERS OF YOUR RIGHT HAND — THUMB BELOW, FINGERS ABOVE.

(10) Raise your right hand upward and forward, bringing the selected card into view on your side of the handkerchief. KEEP THE SELECTED CARD COMPLETELY HIDDEN FROM THE AUDIENCE'S VIEW. This leaves two loose flaps of cloth hanging down at both sides of the handkerchief.

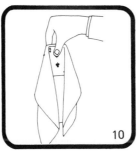

(11) With your left hand, grasp the left side of the handkerchief and fold it to the right, *across the pack, and the selected card, on your side of the handkerchief.* (12) Hold the fold in place with your left thumb. Then grip the entire pack with your left hand so your right hand can move away.

(13) Now, with your right hand, fold both flaps of the handkerchief to the left, across the pack, THUS WRAPPING THE PACK INSIDE THE HANDKERCHIEF AND THE SELECTED CARD OUTSIDE THE HANDKERCHIEF, BENEATH THE FOLDS AS SHOWN.

(14) With your right hand grasp all the cloth below the pack and hold it firmly together keeping the folds — and the selected card — securely in place.

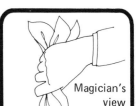

(15) Now, turn the whole affair completely over so the pack is "hanging" upside-down inside the handkerchief. Because of the firm grip your right hand has on the handkerchief, *the folds of the cloth retain the selected card in position (out of view) until you are ready for it to be revealed.*

(16) Gently begin shaking the handkerchief up and down causing the hidden card to slowly start to slide from its hiding place.

(17) To the spectators it will appear as if the card is actually penetrating through the cloth. Continue to shake the handkerchief until the selected card falls to the floor, or you can draw it clear with your left hand, just as it is about to fall and give it to the person who selected it.

(18) To finish the trick, grip the pack through the outside of the cloth with your left hand. You may then give the still-wrapped pack to a spectator—or—release the ends of the handkerchief from your right hand, which then spreads open the handkerchief and removes the pack. In any event, the pack and the handkerchief are now given to the spectators for examination.

COMMENTS AND SUGGESTIONS

Practice this effect until you can do it without fumbling or hesitation. Since everything is done "under cover," you can work deliberately without fear of detection, so it is wise to maintain a slow pace until you are fully sure of yourself. Don't rush when making the folds. Since everyone thinks that the chosen card is still deep in the deck, the more careful you are, the more impressed they will be.

THE CARD THROUGH HANDKERCHIEF — FACE-UP METHOD

In the Card Through the Handkerchief as just described, the spectator's card makes its appearance with the back of the card to the audience. Should you prefer that the face of the card be visible as the penetration takes place, the following adjustments must be made in handling the pack:

METHOD

(1) After the spectator's card has been controlled to the top of the pack, use the OVERHAND SHUFFLE — TOP TO BOTTOM CONTROL to bring the selected card to the bottom of the pack.

(2) Holding the pack face down in your left hand, start to drape the handkerchief over your left hand and in the same motion rotate the entire pack in your hand, turning it face up so the spectator's card is now on top of the face up pack. *Be sure that the pack is completely hidden by the handkerchief before turning it over.* From here, you proceed with the rest of the trick as described.

OVERHAND SHUFFLE CARD CONTROL — BOTTOM CARD TO TOP

EFFECT

In addition to controlling the top card to the bottom of the pack, the Overhand Shuffle Control can be worked in reverse to bring the bottom card to the top of the pack.

METHOD

(1) Hold the deck face outward as described in Overhand Reverse Shuffle. Your "control" card will be the Three of Diamonds, the BOTTOM card.

(3) *Draw off the front card by itself,* (the Three of Diamonds) with your left thumb.

(2) *NOTE: When working this method of the "top to bottom control," turn your body to the left so that the back of your right hand is toward the spectators. This keeps the bottom card from their sight.*

(4) Continue as already described, shuffling the rest of the deck on top of the Three. This will bring the bottom card to the TOP of the pack.

OVERHAND SHUFFLE

CONTROLLING BOTTOM CARD TO TOP — SECOND METHOD

With your LEFT side toward the spectators holding the deck in your right hand, begin the standard Overhand Shuffle. When you reach the last few cards in your right hand, pull off each card ONE AT A TIME with the left thumb. Thus, the BOTTOM card will be the last card remaining in your right hand and you just "shuffle" it on to the TOP of the pack.

COMMENTS AND SUGGESTIONS

This is superior in most cases to the first BOTTOM TO TOP CONTROL method described because you do not have to turn your other side (right side) of your body to the audience.

THE OVERHAND IN-JOG TOP CARD CONTROL

EFFECT

With this control, you perform what appears to be an ordinary Overhand Shuffle. Yet, when you finish, the top card of the deck is the same card as when you started.

METHOD

(1) The card you will "control" is on the top of the deck. Start the shuffle by removing a block of cards from the top of the pack with the left hand. The "control" card is now the top card of this packet.

(3) Then shuffle off the remainder of the deck in the regular manner, being sure not to disturb the "Jogged card." After all of the cards have been shuffled into the left hand, cut to the In-Jogged card as you did in Number 9 in the Overhand Shuffle In-Jog Control and throw the lower packet on top of the other cards in the left hand. The "control" card will now be back on the top of the pack.

(2) Immediately In-Jog the first card you shuffle off from the right-hand packet on top of the "control" card in the left-hand packet.

THE MAGNETIZED CARD

There are many ways in which a magician can discover a card selected by a spectator, but those in which the card actually *reveals itself* are perhaps the most spectacular. One of the most impressive is the "Rising Card Trick," which has been shown in various forms over a period of many years. Usually, special preparation is needed, but here is a quick and simple impromptu version that can be performed as a close-up mystery with surprising effect!

EFFECT

A card is selected and returned to the pack which is shuffled by the magician in the usual fashion. Holding the pack upright in his left hand, with its face toward the audience, the magician rests the tip of his right first finger on the upper end of the pack. He states that he will "magnetize" the chosen card and cause it to "rise" from the pack of its own accord. As the magician lifts his finger, the card obeys, rising slowly and mysteriously until it is almost clear of the pack.

METHOD

(1) From an ordinary pack of cards, invite a spectator to select any card, look at it and remember it. Using the HINDU PICK-UP CONTROL or the OVERHAND IN-JOG TOP CARD CONTROL, have the spectator return his card which you then control to the top of the pack.

(2) Hold the pack upright in your left hand with the thumb at one side and the fingers of the other side. THE BOTTOM CARD OF THE PACK SHOULD FACE TOWARD THE PALM OF YOUR LEFT HAND, AND THE BACK OF YOUR LEFT HAND SHOULD FACE THE AUDIENCE.

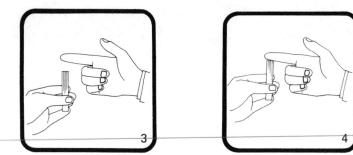

(3) With the pack held firmly in this position, extend the first finger of the right hand pointing it toward the audience. The remaining fingers should be curled into the palm of the hand. Hold your right hand about six inches above the top edge of the pack. (4) Then, slowly lower your right hand until the tip of the first finger rests on top of the pack as shown. Continue this up and down motion a few times as you say, "I will now attempt to magnetize the chosen card with my finger and cause it to rise from the pack on its own. Watch closely!"

(6) Without hesitation, slowly move the right hand upward *as you apply a slight pressure on the* back *of the spectator's card with the* tip *of the little finger.* This will cause the top card to slide "upward" and *appear* to be clinging to the tip of your right forefinger. (7) As the card slides upward, the tips of your <u>left</u> thumb and fingers serve as a "guide" or a "track" for the card during its rise.

(5) With that, lower the right hand until the first finger touches the top of the pack. When it does, straighten out your little finger so it touches the back of the spectator's card as shown. Because the spectator sees the pack from the front, the extended little finger will not be seen as it is hidden by the pack.

(8) When the card has risen almost to the top of the pack, move your right hand away. Let the left thumb and fingers hold the card secure momentarily before removing it with your right hand and tossing it out for inspection.

COMMENTS AND SUGGESTIONS

The important factor in this trick is to guard against "bad angles." If your audience is spread out, stand well back so that everyone will have a <u>front view</u> of the deck and be unable to see your little finger extended behind the pack. For "close-up" work, when performing for just one person, you can hold the pack *right before the spectator's eyes* giving him no chance at all to see past the edges.

OVERHAND IN-JOG CONTROL — PLACING A CARD AT A SPECIFIC LOCATION IN THE DECK

EFFECT

This "control" is very useful in placing a selected card at any number of cards down in the pack that you wish. Let's assume that for the particular trick you need the card fourth from the top.

METHOD

(1) With the selected card on top of the pack, begin a regular Overhand Shuffle drawing about half of the top of the pack into your left hand.

(2) Now, shuffle off *one at a time*, three cards on top of the selected card. DO NOT JOG THESE CARDS.

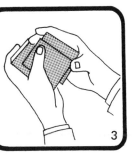

(3) Then, In-Jog the FOURTH card and shuffle the rest of the cards on top of it into the left hand.

(4) Cut the lower portion of the pack at the Jogged card and "throw" the lower block of cards to the top of the deck. The selected card will now be *fourth* from the top.

A SURPRISE APPEARANCE

This is a quick and clever card discovery using the Control just described.

EFFECT

The magician has the spectator select a card from the deck and then return it while he is doing an Overhand Shuffle. The magician states that he will bring the selected card to the top of the deck. After he fails three times, the selected card makes a surprise appearance.

METHOD

(1) Have a card selected and then use the Overhand In-Jog Control to bring the selected card to the top. Then using the Overhand Shuffle Control To Any Location just described, control the spectator's card so that it is FOURTH from the top of the deck.

(2) Give the deck a False Cut as previously described.

(3) Hold the deck in your left hand and state, "I will now bring your card to the top of the deck." Slap the deck with your right hand and then show the spectator the top card.

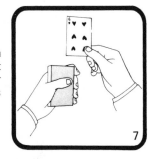

(7) NOTE: Each time you show a "wrong" card hold it with your right thumb and first finger and have your hand close to the top of the deck as shown.

(4) When you remove the top card to show it, just slide the card over to the right with your left thumb and then grasp the outer right corner of the card with your right thumb underneath and right first finger on top. Turn the card over as shown, TOWARD THE SPECTATOR, so that it is face up.

(8) As you show the third "wrong" card, push the top card of the pack, which is now the selected card (X), over slightly to the right.

(5) Ask him if this is the card he selected. Of course, his reply will be "No." Replace this card on the BOTTOM of the deck.

(6) Slap the deck again and show him the next card. Again, you have failed to bring the selected card to the top. Replace this card on the BOTTOM of the deck as well.

(9) As you display your third "mistake," grip the corner of the top card (X) between the tips of the third and little finger of your right hand.

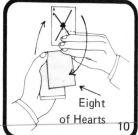

Eight
of Hearts
10

(10) Now, replace the third card on the TOP of the deck ... at the same time retaining your hold on the selected card (X) with your right third and little fingers. The selected card (X) will "pop up" unexpectedly facing the spectators ... held between your two fingers for a "Surprise Appearance."

FORCING A CARD

Forcing a card on an unsuspecting spectator is a sure way of bringing a trick to a successful conclusion. Since you already know what card will be chosen before you start, you can finish the trick almost any way you want — and the more surprising, the better. Try out the methods given in this section, and you will realize how effective they can be.

It is good policy to vary your forcing methods so that spectators will not become too familiar with your procedure. You will find additional forcing methods in the sections devoted to special types of cards, and these can be injected into your program whenever the opportunity arises, thus adding still more variety.

With most tricks, it is best to use a regular card location to reveal a chosen card, reserving the force for times when it is definitely needed. One such time is when a skeptical spectator wants to snatch the pack from your hands and shuffle it until you can't possibly find his card. If you force a card on such a customer, you won't have to worry about this shuffle.

There are many lesser forms of forcing applied to tricks involving the four Aces, the choice of different suits, or groups of cards. These are described in connection with the tricks to which they apply.

THE SLIP FORCE — FIRST METHOD

For a sure, deceptive FORCE, using any pack of cards, *this is one of the very best.* It depends upon a simple sleight known as the "SLIP," which can be learned quickly and performed almost automatically ... but it should be *practiced* until it becomes a smooth and natural move.

EFFECT

After shuffling a pack of cards, the magician holds it face down in his left hand. With his left thumb, he riffles the outer corner of the pack downwards. To a spectator, the magician says, "As I riffle the cards, please say 'Stop!'."

When the call comes, the magician grips the top portion of the pack in his right hand. Then, lifting that part of the pack upward, he extends the *bottom portion* in his left hand, so that the spectator can look at the top card of that packet ... the place where he called Stop! Apparently, this is a completely free selection, YET THE CARD HAS ACTUALLY BEEN "FORCED," thanks to the "SLIP"!

SECRET AND PREPARATION

The *top* card of the deck is the one which is "Forced" — therefore, it is necessary for you to know the top card beforehand. To do this, "glimpse" the *bottom* card using the OVERHAND SHUFFLE GLIMPSE or the HINDU SHUFFLE GLIMPSE. Then, shuffle the *bottom* card to the *top,* using either method of the OVERHAND SHUFFLE CONTROL — TOP TO BOTTOM. Once the top card is learned you are ready to begin. Also, in many tricks it is necessary to "Force" a particular card. In this case, position the card on top of the pack *before* you have the spectator make his "free" selection. (In the illustrations, the Force Card has been marked with an "X.")

METHOD

(1) Hold the deck in the MECHANIC'S GRIP dealing position in your *left hand.* Your left thumb is at one side of the pack, your first finger is at the front edge and the other three fingers are curled over the top of the pack at the right side.

(2) With your left thumb, bend the outer left corner of the pack downwards. Slowly begin releasing cards from the tip of the thumb, allowing them to spring "upwards" as shown. This is called RIFFLING THE CARDS. As you do this, explain to the spectator that he should call "Stop" at any time during the "riffle" and that he will take the card at the point where he stops you.

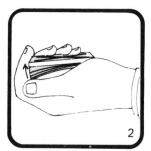

(3) Slowly begin riffling the cards and, when the call comes, you STOP. Without hesitation, move your right hand over the pack and grasp the *upper* packet of cards (above the point where you stopped) between your right thumb and fingers as shown. NOTE THAT YOUR *LEFT* FINGERS ARE CURLED *OVER THE TOP CARD OF THE PACK (X)*.

(6) The right hand *CONTINUES TO SLIDE OUT THE TOP PACKET* until it clears the edge of the "slipped" Force card (X), *WHICH FALLS ON TOP OF THE LEFT-HAND PACKET.*

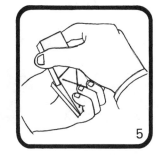

(7) Offer the left-hand packet to the spectator. Have him remove the top card, which is now the Force card (X), and look at it. You have now successfully "Forced" the card on the spectator using the SLIP FORCE. You can now reveal the name of the card in any manner you choose.

(4) Now, begin drawing the top packet upward. *The left fingers maintain a downward pressure on the top card (X).* (5) HOLD THE TOP CARD (THE "FORCE" CARD) *IN PLACE WITH YOUR LEFT FINGERS AS YOUR RIGHT HAND SLIDES THE TOP PACKET *FROM BENEATH IT.*

COMMENTS AND SUGGESTIONS

The great feature of the "Slip Force" is that it is absolutely undetectable when properly handled. As long as the back of your right hand is toward the spectators, the slip will be completely hidden. The same applies when the left hand tilts the pack well upward, with the bottom turned toward the audience. (See Slip Force — Second Method.) That is the very reason why you should get it exactly right. In your regular cuts, handle the pack as though you were about to do the "Slip" . . . then there will be no suspicion when the time comes to actually execute the SLIP FORCE move.

THE SLIP FORCE — SECOND METHOD

The Slip Force is one of the most useful and deceptive methods of having a spectator select a "Forced" card. After you have learned the Basic Method just described, here is a variation which can make the trick even more effective.

METHOD

(1) As in the initial description of THE SLIP FORCE, the top card (indicated by an "X") is the card that will be forced. Follow Steps 1 through 5 just as described in THE SLIP FORCE.

(3) *NOTE: Turning the hands over as you make the "Slip" hides the move completely from the spectator's view, EVEN IF YOU ARE COMPLETELY SURROUNDED.*

(2) When you get to Step 6, the right hand is sliding out the top packet as the fingers of the left hand hold the top card of that packet which will fall on top of the left-hand packet. At the same time this action is being executed, both hands turn their packets face up. The hands rotate in opposite directions, as indicated by the arrows.

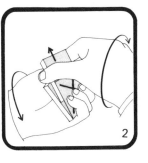

(4) At this point, the right-hand packet is face up and the left-hand packet is also face up WITH THE X CARD ON THE BOTTOM. Extend your <u>left</u> forefinger and point to the card on the <u>face</u> of the right-hand packet. Say, "I don't want you to take this card because <u>I know</u> what it is. . . ."

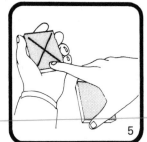

(5) With that, TURN BOTH HANDS OVER — BACK TO THEIR ORIGINAL POSITION. Extend your right forefinger pointing to the top card of the left-hand packet. Say, "Instead, take this one where you said 'Stop,' which no one knows."

COMMENTS AND SUGGESTIONS

As stated above, this variation should be learned <u>after</u> you master the "regular" Slip Force. When you can perform the regular "Slip" with ease, you can then add this "extra" touch which makes the SLIP FORCE *totally undetectable* under all conditions.

10—20 COUNT FORCE

EFFECT

The performer asks a spectator to call out *any* number between ten and twenty....stating that he will count that many cards from the pack onto the table. This done, the magician then *adds the two digits of the selected number* together to arrive at a total. He then counts *that many* cards from the top of the already dealt pile to arrive at a single card. The spectator is asked to look at that card and remember it. The performer automatically knows the name of this card which was really "Forced." The magician may now reveal the card in any manner he wishes.

SECRET AND PREPARATION

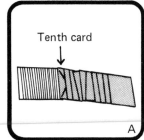

Tenth card

(A) Because of a simple but clever mathematical principle, this "Force" actually works itself. The only preparation necessary is that you know the TENTH *card from the top* of the deck beforehand. In the illustrations, this card is marked with an (X).

METHOD

(1) Hold the deck face down in dealing position in your left hand. Ask the spectator to name any number *between* 10 and 20. Suppose he says, "Thirteen." Count off thirteen cards, one at a time, face down in a pile on the table as shown. This dealing action *reverses* the order of the cards on the table. This places the "Force" Card FOURTH *from the top* in your new pile.

(2) Lay the pack aside and pick up the new pile of 13 cards in dealing position. State that you will add the figures of the chosen number...."13" ....(1 + 3 = 4) and count down *that many* in the pile.

(3) You do this with the following result: When you counted the original thirteen cards in a pile, you *reversed* their order as already stated. *Now, by counting four cards, one at a time, from that pile, you REVERSE THEM AGAIN. This system — which works with ANY NUMBER BETWEEN 10 AND 20 — causes the count to always end on the ORIGINAL TENTH CARD — your Force Card!*

(4) Place the remaining cards with the rest of the deck and ask the spectator to look at the top card of the pile of four and remember it. You have now successfully "Forced" a card using the 10-20 Count Force. You may reveal the selected card in whatever manner you choose.

COMMENTS AND SUGGESTIONS

The subtle mathematical principle which causes this effect to work can be easily understood by sitting down with the pack and trying out the various number combinations a few times. No matter what number the spectator selects *(between 10 and 20),* the result is always the same. The original *tenth card* from the top of the deck, always ends up as the "selected" card.

THE ROLLOVER FORCE

Here is a sure-fire method of "Forcing" a card where the actual handling of the pack seems so haphazard and disorderly that it appears impossible for the magician to have control over the position of *any* card in the pack. This makes for a very convincing "Force" which is ideal for any card worker's program.

SECRET AND PREPARATION

For the ROLLOVER FORCE all you need is an ordinary pack of cards with the Force Card on top. (In the illustrations, the Force Card is marked with an "X.")

METHOD

(1) Hold the pack face down, in dealing position, in your left hand. State that you wish to have one card selected from the pack at random; to make sure that this choice is not influenced by you, the magician, you will let *the pack itself* determine which card will be selected.

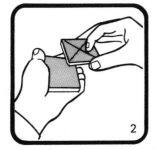 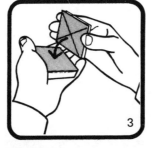 

(2) With that, you lift off the upper fourth of the pack (about 10 to 15 cards), (3) turn them over (face up), and (4) replace them on top of the face-down pack as shown. As you turn the packet over say, "To completely *confuse* the order of the pack, I will not only mix the cards — I'll turn some face up and some face down."

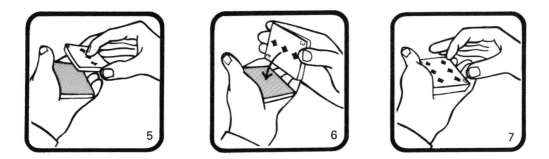

(5) Then, to make things *more confusing,* lift off nearly half the deck (20 to 25 cards), (6) turn these over as before, and (7) replace them on top of the rest of the pack.

(8) To add to all this....lift off another stack of cards, this time cutting closer to the bottom (about ¾ of the deck) and (9) turn them over, (10) replacing them on top of the remaining cards.

(11, 12, 13) You then state, "To confuse matters even further, I'll turn the whole pack over." — which you do.

(14) After turning the pack over say, "Now, we'll run through the pack and take the *first face-down card* that comes along." With that, you start to spread the pack, "running" the cards from your left hand to your right.

(15) The first face-down card you reach *will be the "Force" Card,* the Three of Clubs. The audience thinks it is just a random card. Have a spectator remove that card from the pack and look at it. When he does, you have successfully "Forced" the card....using the ROLLOVER FORCE.

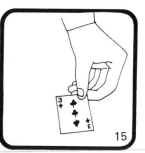

THE COUNT FORCE

The more card tricks you perform, the more you must depend on subtle, unsuspected devices like the "Force," which enables you to know beforehand what card a spectator will select. As with all routines, people may become familiar with a "Force" if it is repeated too often, which means switching to another forcing system is in order. Here is a very natural "Force" that will serve that purpose perfectly.

EFFECT

After shuffling a pack of cards, the magician asks a spectator to think of a number between 1 and 52 (corresponding to the number of cards in the pack). Whatever the number, the magician demonstrates how the cards are to be counted one by one into a pile and then gives the entire pack to the spectator to count for himself. He does, and without realizing it, he picks the very card that the magician "Forced" him to choose!

SECRET AND PREPARATION

(A) In this "Forcing" method the card to be "Forced" is the top card of the pack. This can be learned by first glimpsing the bottom card and then shuffling it to the top using either the Overhand Shuffle or Hindu Shuffle. Once the top card is learned by the magician, you are ready to begin the Count Force.

METHOD

(1) Holding the pack in dealing position in your left hand, ask a spectator to call out any number from 1 to 52, thus limiting it to the number of cards in the pack. Assume that the number the spectator names is 7. Begin dealing the cards one at a time from the top of the deck into a pile on the table, starting with the "Force" card.

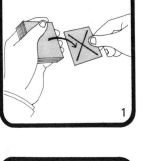

(4) Replace the seventh card back on top of the "counted" cards and then pick up the entire pile and place it on top of the bulk of the pack in the left hand. The Force card that was on top is now seventh down from the top of the pack because of the reverse order count. Now square up the pack and give it to the spectator to count for himself.

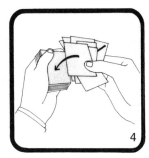

(2) As you deal, count each card aloud until you reach the spectator's number. By counting the cards one at a time in a pile, you reverse the order of the cards. You now have 7 cards in a pile on the table with the Force card at the bottom of the pile (seventh from the top).

(5) After the spectator does the count and looks at your "Force" card, tell him to gather up all the cards and shuffle the pack. You have now successfully forced the original top card of the pack.

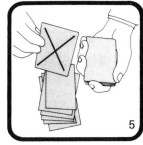

(3) State, as you deal, that you are merely demonstrating what you want the spectator to do. Explain that he should count down 7 cards as you have done and then pick up the sevventh card — the last one dealt — look at it, and remember it. Demonstrate this by picking up the seventh indifferent card and looking at it. It is not necessary that you remember this indifferent card.

COMMENTS AND SUGGESTIONS

In the preceding explanation, we used the number 7 as the spectator's selected number. The Force will work with any number; however, it is best to keep his choice under 20. Remember, it is necessary for you to first count cards one at a time to the selected number. This can be time consuming if the spectator has called number 46, for example. Also, it may tend to arouse suspicion for you to give such a lengthy demonstration for a simple counting process. Therefore, when asking a spectator to pick a number from 1 to 52, you can modify it by saying, "Let's make it from 1 to 16, as a time-saver." If the spectator should insist on a higher number, do this: Instead of counting the cards as a demonstration of what the spectator is to do, count down to the spectator's number and then give the spectator the counted pile and ask him to recount the cards to verify that you have counted correctly. When he finishes recounting the cards, tell him to look at the *last* card he counted and remember it. This, of course, will be the Force card.

ROLL ANY NUMBER

By now, you can see that a vital part of many tricks is "Forcing." In other words, the spectator is allowed to make certain "free choices," believing that the end result is a product of his own decision – out of the magician's control. Yet, no matter what choice the spectator may make, he will always make the selection which the magician plans. The following "Force" illustrates how you can cleverly maneuver the spectator, completely without his knowledge.

METHOD

(1) This Force uses a single die from any pair of dice. It will work with any *four* objects. To aid in the explanation, we will assume that the object to be "Forced" is one of four piles in a single row. The pile to be "Forced" should be in the third position from your left. The four piles are numbered A through D in the illustrations. THE PILE TO BE "FORCED" IS THE "C" PILE.

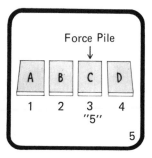

(2) Explain that the spectator should roll the die and that you will count its number along the row in order to choose a pile. This is done as follows:

(3) If the roll is "2," begin counting from the *right to the left*. Your count will end on the desired pile.

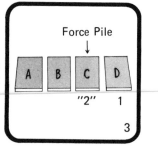

(4) If the roll is "3," begin counting from *left to right* to reach the correct pile.

(5) If the spectator rolls a "5," count from *left to right*. When you reach the end of the row on "4," continue the count BACK, from *right to left*, to land on the proper pile (C). NOTE: DO NOT COUNT PILE (D) AS "5".... JUST IMMEDIATELY START YOUR COUNT BACK FROM "4" ON PILE (D) TO "5" ON PILE (C), YOUR FORCE PILE.

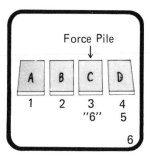

(6) If the roll is "6," count from *right to left* and then RETURN to the *right* to finish the count. NOTE: IN THIS CASE, YOU DO COUNT PILE (D) AS "4." THEN JUST CONTINUE AS IF STARTING FROM THE RIGHT, COUNTING PILE (D) AS "5" AND PILE (C) AS "6."

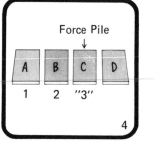

(7) The "Force" will not work with rolls of "1" or "4," *but such rolls make it all the better,* as they allow you to inject a clever twist that adds to the effect. If a "1" or a "4" turns up on the die, immediately say, "Good! We will use the 'hidden number,' the one that nobody knows!"

(8) With that, pick up the die, *turn it over,* and POINT TO THE BOTTOM NUMBER referring to this as the "Hidden Number." If "1" is rolled, the Hidden Number will be "6." If "4" is rolled, the Hidden Number will be "3." IN EITHER CASE, YOU END UP WITH A NUMBER THAT ENABLES YOU TO COUNT TO THE REQUIRED PILE.

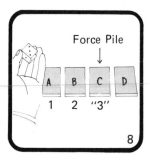

The following is a list of additional forces found elsewhere in the Course:

THE HINDU FLASH FORCE, see page 52

MAGICIAN'S CHOICE, see page 321

PERFECT CARD FORCE, see page 108

THE SHORT CARD FORCE, see page 129

THE TWO-CARD FORCE, see page 109

THE DOUBLE LIFT

Holding two cards together and exhibiting them as one is perhaps the oldest artifice in Card Magic. But it has attained new values in the comparatively modern sleight known as the "Double Lift." This maneuver is utterly deceptive in the hands of experts (many of whom have their own pet twists), but the basic principle is the same in all versions.

The Double Lift is one of the most effective and useful sleights in the realm of Card Magic, *providing it is not used too often or too boldly.* Originally intended simply to cause one card to "change" into another, newer and more subtle uses for the "Double Lift" were soon devised of which you will find a nice variety in this section. When worked in conjunction with other moves, the Double Lift is most effective, as results can be achieved that seem impossible — and all with an ordinary pack of cards.

THE LITTLE FINGER BREAK

This secret "move" is very important. The Little Finger Break has many uses....one of the most useful of which is to *prepare* for the DOUBLE LIFT....a simple sleight that is invaluable in the performance of MANY spectacular card tricks.

METHOD

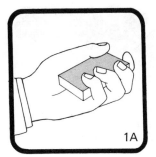

(2) Now, bring your *right hand* over the deck, right thumb at the inner end, your right first finger resting on top of the deck and your remaining fingers at the far end of the pack as shown.

(1) Hold the deck in dealing position in your left hand. However, unlike the regular dealing position (A) where the second and third and little fingers curl over the top of the deck (B), hold the deck so that just the *tips* of these three fingers extend above the right edge of the deck.

(3) With the ball of your right thumb, raise the inner end of the top card slightly off the top of the deck, then...

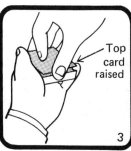

Top card raised

(4) . . .in the same motion, bend your right thumb inward *just enough to catch the edge of the second card* (the one just below the top card) and raise it also just slightly off the top of the deck as well.

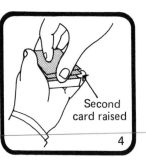

Second card raised

4

(5) *NOTE: The right first finger should apply a slight downward pressure on the top of the deck nearest the audience to assure that ONLY THE INNER ENDS OF THE CARDS ARE RAISED. From the audience view, it should appear that you are just holding the deck with both hands. ALL FINGER BREAKS ARE SECRET MOVES NOT KNOWN TO THE AUDIENCE.*

(6) When both cards are raised off the inner end of the deck, press lightly against the right side of the deck with your left little finger. This will cause the skin on the ball of the little finger to overlap the top edge of the deck just enough to hold a small "break" between the two "raised" cards and the rest of the cards in the deck.

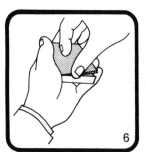

6

(7) Now relax your right thumb allowing the two lifted cards to come to rest together on the fleshy tip of your left little finger. You have now secured a "Little Finger Break" beneath the top two cards.

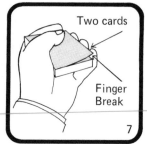

Two cards

Finger Break

7

(8) Move the right hand away and, at the same time, move the left thumb so that it rests on top of the pack with your left first finger curled around the front of the pack. Keep the "audience end" of the top two cards flush with the deck. The pack, from the audience point of view, should look completely natural.

8

COMMENTS AND SUGGESTIONS

The entire procedure of securing the Little Finger Break should be done deliberately in the pretense of squaring up the deck as it is held in the left hand. *NOTE: It is also important, after you learn the sleight, NOT TO LOOK AT THE PACK as you "make the break." This is another example of MISDIRECTION as the audience will look where you look. So make some comment and LOOK AT THE SPECTATORS when you make the secret move.*

THE DOUBLE LIFT

Once you have mastered the LITTLE FINGER BREAK to the point where you can execute the "move" quickly and without suspicion, you are then ready to learn one of the most fundamental and useful sleights in Card Magic — the DOUBLE LIFT. This multi-purpose sleight is one of the most deceptive and practical moves in Card Magic and its uses are many. Learn it well, as it will soon become the basis for many of your most baffling card mysteries.

METHOD

(1) As mentioned earlier, you must first learn the LITTLE FINGER BREAK....before you learn the DOUBLE LIFT. To execute the DOUBLE LIFT, first secure a LITTLE FINGER BREAK beneath the *top two cards* of the pack. (These two cards have been marked "A" and "B" in the illustrations.)

Two cards, A & B

1

(2) Now, bring your right hand over the pack....with your *thumb* at the *inner end,* your *first finger* resting lightly on *top,* and your *other fingers* at the *outer end* of the pack as shown. This is the same position your right hand was in after securing the LITTLE FINGER BREAK.

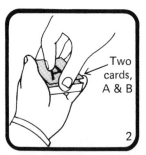

Two cards, A & B

2

(3) With the ball of your right thumb, raise the inner end of two cards ("A" and "B") you hold above the "break." Now, with your right hand, *lift BOTH CARDS together (as one) completely off the top of the pack.* Your right first finger should press lightly against the back of the card(s). This keeps them from "bowing" apart and holds their edges "squared" so *THE TWO CARDS appear to be ONE CARD.*

Two cards, A & B

(6) With the left thumb, deal the *real* top card ("A") off the pack where it is taken by your right fingers.

(4) Now, turn your right hand over, showing the face of the card(s). *NOTE: The audience believes you have simply picked up the top card of the pack and shown them the face of the card.* ACTUALLY, THE FACE OF THE CARD THEY SEE IS THAT OF THE SECOND CARD, THANKS TO THE DOUBLE LIFT.

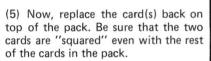

Two cards, A & B

(7) Set the pack on the table and turn this card face up, to show that the "top" card of the pack has magically changed to a different card....although we know better!

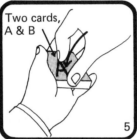

Two cards, A & B

(5) Now, replace the card(s) back on top of the pack. Be sure that the two cards are "squared" even with the rest of the cards in the pack.

COMMENTS AND SUGGESTIONS

To review, the effect to the audience is that you remove the top card with your right hand, show them the face of the card, and then replace it on top of the deck. You then take this card face down with your right fingers — *where it "magically" changes to another card.* This is only one of the countless uses of the DOUBLE LIFT. In fact, one of the *dangers* of the DOUBLE LIFT is that it is so effective, once you have learned to present it well, you may use it *too much.* But don't worry about that right now — just PRACTICE and learn this sleight well. As you will see, it will be of tremendous value to you as you progress through the Course.

THE ELEVATOR CARD

Here is an effect that depends on the DOUBLE LIFT in its classical and most direct form. It provides the right amount of misdirection to catch the average spectator off guard, making it a good addition to any card worker's program.

EFFECT

After shuffling a pack of cards, the magician casually turns the <u>top</u> card of the pack — say the Three of Hearts — face up and shows it to the audience. He turns the card face down and replaces it on <u>top</u> of the pack. Explaining that the Three of Hearts has a peculiar ability to "rise" to the top of the pack on its own accord, he deliberately takes the card from the <u>top</u> of the pack and inserts it into the <u>center</u> of the pack. Without hesitation, he snaps his fingers and causes the Three of Hearts to "elevate" itself back to the top of the pack. Somehow the card, buried deep in the pack, has found its way to the top, giving it the title of the *"ELEVATOR CARD."*

METHOD

(1) After thoroughly shuffling the deck, secure a LITTLE FINGER BREAK beneath the top two cards of the pack in readiness to execute the DOUBLE LIFT. This done, grasp the two cards (as one) between the thumb and fingers of the right hand. Perform the Double Lift by turning them over and showing the face of what the audience believes to be the top card (Three of Hearts in the illustrations). Now, replace the card(s) face down on top of the pack.

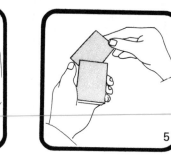

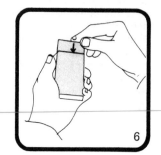

(5) Insert the *indifferent* card into the pack at the "break."
(6) Push the card all the way in until it is flush with the rest of the pack.

(2) Say, "An interesting characteristic of the Three of Hearts is that it has the peculiar ability to rise to the top of the pack by itself." Take the REAL TOP CARD from the top of the deck with your right hand as shown. *Be careful not to accidentally "flash" the face of this card exposing the fact that it is really an indifferent card.*

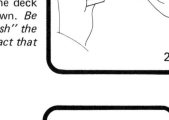

(7) Stating that the rest of the cards in the pack serve as an elevator for the Three of Hearts, snap your fingers and say, "The elevator card is now on top."

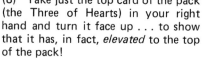

(8) Take just the top card of the pack (the Three of Hearts) in your right hand and turn it face up . . . to show that it has, in fact, *elevated* to the top of the pack!

(3) With the left thumb, riffle the outer corner of the pack downwards and stop somewhere near the center of the pack . . .
(4) . . .as you say, "Watch! I'll place the Three of Hearts here in the center and you'll see what I mean."

COMMENTS AND SUGGESTIONS

By adopting a casual manner when presenting this trick, you can be all "set" for the DOUBLE LIFT before anyone knows what to expect. While gathering cards or shuffling the pack after another trick, you are in an ideal situation to secure a LITTLE FINGER BREAK and move directly into the DOUBLE LIFT with any two cards that happen to be on top of the pack. As a neat bit of byplay, instead of snapping your fingers to bring the card to the top, you can *riffle* the outer corner of the pack slowly <u>downward</u> with your left thumb, saying, "This is the elevator going down. . . ." Then, after inserting the "top" card into the pack, you riffle the outer end <u>upward</u> with your right forefinger. Say, "And this is the elevator coming up!" Following that, you show the card back on top.

RIFFLE REVELATION

A very surprising "discovery" of a selected card, this is a basic application of the Double Lift already described, which can be presented at any time during your regular card routine.

EFFECT

A card is selected and shuffled back into the pack. The performer then shows that the selected card is not the bottom card or the top card, so it must be buried somewhere in the middle. He hands the chooser the top card, telling him to push it into the pack face down, while the pack is being riffled. Presumably, this card will "find" the chosen card...but it doesn't. The magician tries again and again fails. In desperation, the magician looks through the faces of the cards, wondering what could have possibly gone wrong. He asks the spectator what card he selected. When the spectator replies, the magician says, "Well that explains why we couldn't find your card in the deck.... it's the one you had in your hand all the time." To the spectator's surprise, the card he holds has magically changed into his selected card!

METHOD

(1) From an ordinary pack of cards have one card selected and returned to the deck. Using any of the methods you have learned, (the Hindu Shuffle Control, the Overhand Shuffle Control, etc.) bring the selected card (X) to the top of the pack.

(2) With the chosen card (X) on the top, grip the deck between the right fingers and thumb and turn the entire pack face up, calling the spectator's attention to the card at the bottom of the deck....as you say, "There's only a small chance that your card would be the bottom card of the pack, is this it?" Of course, the spectator will answer "No."

(3) Turn the pack over and hold it in your left hand in position to execute a Double Lift. However, before letting go of the cards with the right hand, secure a Little Finger Break beneath the top two cards of the deck.

Getting Little Finger Break

(4) *Now Double Lift the top two cards as one card* with the right hand. Turn the card(s) face up calling attention to what the spectator believes to be the top card of the deck....as you ask, "And is this your card at the top of the deck?" Again, the spectator will answer "No."

(5) REPLACE THE TWO CARDS ON TOP OF THE PACK. Then, with your right hand, take the top (selected) card (X) and hand it, *face down,* to the spectator....as you say, "With the aid of the top card, we will find the exact location of *your* card in the deck."

(6) Riffle the outer end of the pack with your right fingers as you explain that, as you riffle the deck, the spectator is to insert the end of his card into the pack anywhere he wants. Tell him that, when he does this, he will find the *exact spot* in the deck where his card lies.

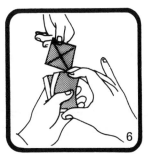

(7) Here is a side view as the spectator inserts the supposedly indifferent top card (really his selected card) into the deck as you riffle. Be careful not to let the spectator see the face of the card he holds and tell him NOT TO RELEASE IT — "Just hold it firmly."

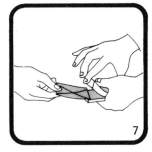

(8) After you have riffled the end of the pack and the spectator has inserted the card he holds into the deck, lift all the cards *above* his inserted card and turn this packet face up in your right hand to show the card at that point. Inform the spectator that the card on the face of the right hand packet should be his selected card.

(9) *NOTE: Be sure the spectator maintains his hold at all times on what he believes to be the indifferent card in his hand....when actually the card he holds is his own selected card.*

(10) Here you reassemble the deck and riffle the cards again, explaining that you will give *him* a second try at finding his card. When you are wrong again, act as if the trick has failed and you don't know why. Turn the cards face up and run through them as if trying to find his card.

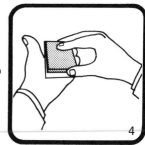

(11) Again, still puzzled at your failure, and without looking up from the cards, ask him, "What card did you take?"....when he replies, say, "Well that explains it, you were holding the card all the time." Of course, when the spectator looks, he will be surprised that the card has changed in his own hand, while he had control of it all along!

COMMENTS AND SUGGESTIONS

This is a good trick to use in which a chosen card is actually "found" by inserting another in the pack. When people want to "see it again," you can use the other instead.

SNAP-IT!

This quick way of "magically" changing one card into an entirely different card will create a real suprise when injected into a regular card routine and is guaranteed to keep people wondering what will happen next.

EFFECT

The magician removes the top card of the pack and shows it to be the Eight of Hearts. Turning the card face down, he gives it a "snap" with his finger. When the card is turned over, it is seen to have MAGICALLY CHANGED TO AN ENTIRELY DIFFERENT CARD!

METHOD

This is a classic utilization of the Double Lift.

(1) Hold the deck face down in dealing position in the left hand and with the help of the right hand, secure a Little Finger Break beneath the top two cards of the pack.

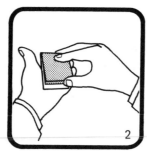

(2) With the right hand, execute the Double Lift *by picking up the top TWO cards as ONE CARD.*

(3) Turn the card(s) over showing the face of what the spectators believe to be the top card of the pack (the Eight of Hearts). As you display the card(s), say, "You will notice a peculiar characteristic of these playing cards."

(4) Replace the two cards on top of the packet and . . .

(5) . . . deal the REAL top card off the deck into the right fingers.

(6) Place the rest of the deck aside as you continue, "If I take the top card of the pack, in this case the Eight of Hearts, and give it a snap . . ."

(7) Holding the card firmly in the right hand, give the back of the face down card a sharp "snap" by hitting it with your left fingers.

(9) ... THE CARD HAS CHANGED FROM THE EIGHT OF HEARTS TO THE FOUR OF CLUBS!

(8) Say, "... it causes the card to change like this!" Turn the card face up to show that . . .

(10) Toss the card on to the table, just in case a suspicious spectator should want to examine it — and chances are he will!

COMMENTS AND SUGGESTIONS

Instead of the change as just described, you can add a clever twist by secretly placing two cards of the same suit on the pack with the lesser value card on top. For example: the Four of Diamonds on *top* of the pack, with the Five of Diamonds *just below*. Execute the Double Lift, replace the card(s) on the deck and remove the single top card and hold it in your right hand. PRETEND TO "KNOCK" ONE OF THE SPOTS OFF THE CARD BY SNAPPING IT. This can also be done with *any* two cards of the same suit, just remember to "knock-off" enough spots to correspond with the difference in the values of the two cards. If you're working standing up and have no place to lay the deck aside, simply strike the single card against the pack to "knock-off" the spots.

COLOR CHANGING ACES NO. 1

This is a novel and baffling version of the ever-popular "Four Aces" that can be presented in a quick, effective form, ending with a real surprise. In many Four Ace routines, extra cards are used....but here, *only* the Four Aces are involved making the entire trick clean, simple and most startling.

EFFECT

The magician displays the Four Aces. Then, holding them in his left hand, he deals the two red Aces, one at a time, face down on the table. To avoid any confusion, the magician openly shows the face of each red Ace *before* dealing it. This automatically leaves him holding the two black Aces. At the wizard's command, the Aces instantly change places. The spectators can even turn over the cards themselves, to find that the black Aces are now the two cards on the table, and that the magician holds the pair of red Aces!

METHOD

The only sleight necessary for this trick is the DOUBLE LIFT.

(1) From an ordinary pack of cards, remove the four Aces and place the rest of the pack aside. Display the four Aces to the spectators.

(2) Arrange the Aces in the following order: One black Ace on top of the packet (Ace of Clubs), the two red Aces in the middle (Ace of Hearts and Ace of Diamonds), and the other black Ace (Ace of Spades), at the bottom of the pile. *This should be done casually without calling attention to the fact that the cards are in any specific order.* (In the illustrations, the Aces have been numbered 1 through 4 to make them easier to follow.)

(3) Now, with the cards in their proper sequence, with your right hand place the fanned packet into your left hand...and, as you close the fan, *secure a Little Finger Break beneath the top two Aces* (the Ace of Clubs and the Ace of Hearts).

(4) You are now ready for the Double Lift.

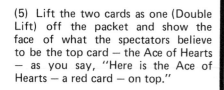

(5) Lift the two cards as one (Double Lift) off the packet and show the face of what the spectators believe to be the top card — the Ace of Hearts — as you say, "Here is the Ace of Hearts — a red card — on top."

(6) Replace the two cards on the packet and then deal the REAL top card — the Ace of Clubs — from the top of the packet to the table as you state, "I will place the first red Ace on the table."

(7) *This next step is very important.* REVERSE COUNT the remaining three Aces, one at a time, from the left hand into the right hand as you say, "That leaves one, two, three remaining Aces."

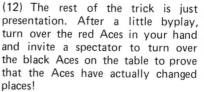

(8) The reverse count moves the two red Aces to the bottom of the packet and the remaining black Ace (the Ace of Spades) to the top.

(9) Now place the packet face down in the left hand as before and, as you square the cards, *secure a Little Finger Break beneath the top two cards* (the Ace of Spades and the Ace of Diamonds).

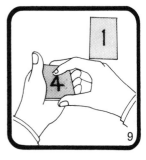

(10) Lift these two cards as one (Double Lift) off the packet and show the face of what the spectators believe to be the top card — the Ace of Diamonds as you say, "Here is the Ace of Diamonds....the other red card."

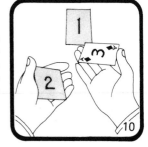

(11) Replace the two cards on the packet and deal the REAL top card — the Ace of Spades — from the top of the packet next to the Ace of Clubs already on the table as you say, "The second red Ace goes on the table with the first."

(12) The rest of the trick is just presentation. After a little byplay, turn over the red Aces in your hand and invite a spectator to turn over the black Aces on the table to prove that the Aces have actually changed places!

COMMENTS AND SUGGESTIONS

By handling the cards in an apparently casual manner, this trick can be built into an extremely deceptive mystery. Here is another clever procedure you can use when you do make the "set-up": After you have opened and removed the Aces from the pack and displayed them to the audience, hold them so that only you can see the faces as you arrange the Aces in their proper order. Say, "I'll put the black Aces in the middle and the reds on the top and bottom....although *actually the REDS go in the middle*. After showing the first red Ace and placing it (really the black Ace) on the table, when you reverse count the three Aces one at a time from the left hand to the right, you can call each card by its supposed color, i.e., "Black, Black, Red."

SPECIAL NOTE: In many cases, you can place the two "red" (really black) Aces DIRECTLY ONTO THE SPECTATOR'S OUTSTRETCHED PALM. After you deal each card to him, have him place his other hand flat on top of the cards. Apparently this is so that you can not do anything "tricky"....BUT IN REALITY THIS KEEPS HIM FROM LOOKING AT THE FACES OF THE CARDS. With this form of presentation, the Aces apparently change places while held tightly in the spectator's own hands!

REVERSED CARD IN DECK

Magically speaking, a "reversed card" effect is one in which a card mysteriously reverses itself by turning *face up* in a *face-down* pack. There are various ways of accomplishing this, all dependent on different methods. The one about to be described is particularly useful as it can be done with a borrowed pack.

EFFECT

A spectator is allowed to select a card at random from an ordinary pack. It is returned to the pack, which the magician shuffles. He then shows both the top card and the bottom card, asking if the spectator selected either. The reply is "no" in both cases, so the wizard exerts some magic power and causes the selected card to turn face up in the middle of the pack!

SECRET AND PREPARATION

Two basic sleights, already described, are combined to accomplish this result: The Hindu Shuffle Control and the Double Lift. The first is used to bring the selected card to the top of the pack; the second enables you to show two cards as one. If you have already mastered those sleights, you can easily perform this effect.

METHOD

(1) The spectator freely selects a card, which we will assume to be the Two of Spades. Have it returned and bring it to the top of the pack by the Hindu Shuffle Control.

(2) Under the selected card (indicated by an "X" in the illustration) is a second card (indicated by a "Z"). AS YET, YOU DO NOT KNOW THE IDENTITY OF EITHER CARD. *NOTE: The illustration with Step 1 shows the location of the "Z" card and is not part of the routine.*

Two cards ready for Double Lift

2

(3) *Get and hold a Little Finger Break under the two top cards in preparation for a Double Lift.* Tell the spectator to concentrate on his card, so that you can gain a mental impression. This distracts attention from the pack during your preparatory action.

Two cards ready for Double Lift

3

(4) Finally shake your head and say, "Your mental impressions are too weak. I want you to look at the top card and tell me if it is yours." With that, you remove the top cards, using the Double Lift to turn them face up and show them *as one.* The spectator sees the *second card* (Z) which in this case is the Four of Diamonds. He says, "No. That is not his card.

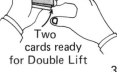

Two cards held as one

4

(5) *Place the two cards FACE UP on top of the pack, keeping them squared as a single card.* Hold the pack firmly in your left hand. Say, "So that isn't your card?" At the same time, point to the Four of Diamonds with your right first finger.

5

(6) Hold the two top cards — Z and X — firmly in position, as you say, "Well, let's look at the bottom card of the pack and see if that is yours."

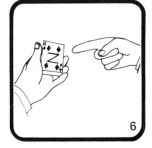

6

(7) Here, you turn the entire pack, face up, showing the bottom card — which we will assume is the Ten of Hearts. When you ask, "Is that yours?" the spectator again responds, "No." *At this point, you have all the cards face up except the two cards that you originally showed as the top card. They are FACE DOWN beneath the FACE-UP pack.*

Turn deck face up

7

(8) You next say, "Then neither the *top* nor the *bottom* card is the one you selected." As you are making this statement, with your right fingers, slide out the face down Four of Diamonds (Z) from beneath the pack.

8

(9) Turn the Four face up and display it beside the Ten. *This leaves the chosen card (X) FACE DOWN on the BOTTOM of the FACE-UP PACK.*

(12) Give the pack a complete cut, keeping both halves squared, as a slip here might allow a fleeting glimpse of the face up chosen card. Once the cut is made, THE SPECTATOR'S CARD WILL BE FACE UP IN THE MIDDLE OF THE PACK.

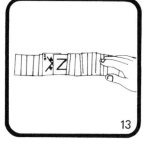

(10) Now, replace the Four of Diamonds (Z) *FACE UP on the bottom of the face-up pack. Thus, the Four goes back next to the still face-down chosen card.* As you do this, remark that, since the spectator's card is neither at the top or the bottom, it must be completely lost in the pack.

(13) So you promptly add, "It would be really magical if I could make your card *SHOW ITSELF* in the pack!" Spread the cards along the table and there is the chosen Two of Spades (X) face up among all the face down cards!

(11) Turn the pack over, face down, squaring the deck neatly, as you do. *The top card is now the Four (Z) while the chosen card (X) is FACE UP just below it.*

Turn deck face down

COMMENTS AND SUGGESTIONS

Actually, you do not know the chosen card before it reveals itself as described; but there is no reason why you have to know it, for if you follow the routine just as explained, the card will come up automatically. The only actual sleights — the Hindu Shuffle Control and the Double Lift — are executed at the very outset. From then on, it is only a matter of precision and close attention to detail. This gives you a chance to build up the effect as you proceed to the climax.

SANDWICHED ACES

Here is a baffling "Four-Ace" routine that people will talk about and want to see again. Once you have mastered it, you will probably keep it as a highlight in your program. Best of all, only a few special "moves" are required; and they fit into the routine so neatly that there is little chance that anyone will begin to suspect them.

EFFECT

The magician openly deals the TWO <u>BLACK</u> ACES face down on the table. The spectator then freely selects any card from the pack — say the Five of Diamonds. The Five is turned <u>face up</u> and "sandwiched" between the two <u>face-down</u> BLACK ACES. The three cards are then turned over as a group and placed on top of the pack.

Without hesitation, the magician spreads the top two cards showing that the Five of Diamonds has *vanished* from between the Black Aces. He deals the Black Aces onto the table and . . . immediately spreads the pack face down along the table — revealing the <u>TWO RED ACES</u> FACE UP IN THE CENTER, WITH A <u>SINGLE</u> FACE-DOWN CARD BETWEEN THEM. "I knew your card was sandwiched between two Aces," the magician declares. When a spectator turns over the face-down card, <u>it proves to be the missing Five of Diamonds</u>!

SECRET AND PREPARATION

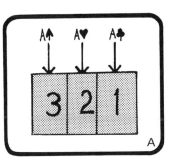

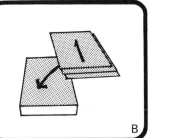

The success of this trick depends upon the proper set-up of the Four Aces in the deck before the trick begins. From a regular pack of cards, remove the Aces and arrange them in the following positions:

(A) Place the two <u>Black</u> Aces (Ace of Clubs and Ace of Spades) face down together and <u>one</u> of the Red Aces (the Ace of Hearts, in the illustrations) face down between them.

(B) Now, place this group of three cards on <u>top</u> of the face-down pack.

(C) Place the remaining <u>Red</u> Ace (Ace of Diamonds) <u>FACE UP</u> on the <u>BOTTOM</u> of the pack and you're ready. [In the illustrations, the Aces have been numbered 1 through 4 to make them easier to follow . . . (1) Ace of Clubs, (2) Ace of Hearts, (3) Ace of Spades and (4) Ace of Diamonds. The selected card is indicated by an "X."]

METHOD

(1) With the pack held in dealing position in the left hand, grasp the top card of the pack [the Ace of Clubs (1)] between the thumb and fingers of your right hand in the same grip as if executing the DOUBLE LIFT.

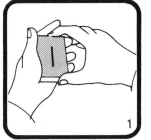

(5) Now, SECURE A <u>LITTLE FINGER BREAK</u> BETWEEN THE NEXT TWO CARDS ON TOP OF THE PACK [the Ace of Hearts (2) and the Ace of Spades (3)]. (6) <u>Execute a DOUBLE LIFT</u>, lifting both cards (as one) from the top of the pack. Turn them over showing the face of what the spectators believe to be the top card — the Ace of Spades (3). As you display the Ace, remark, "Here is the next card, the Ace of Spades. . . ."

(2) <u>DO NOT DO THE DOUBLE LIFT</u>, just pick up the Ace of Clubs and turn it face up . . . showing it to the audience. Say, "The top card of the pack is the Ace of Clubs. . . ."

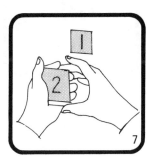

(7) Replace the two cards back on the top of the pack and. . .
(8) . . .immediately take the REAL <u>TOP</u> CARD [the Ace of Hearts (2)] from the top of the pack and place it face down next to the Ace of Clubs (1) on the table. Say, ". . .which I will place here next to the Ace of Clubs."

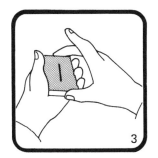

(3) Replace the Ace on top of the pack and, without hesitation,
(4) . . .take it with your right fingers and place it face down on the table. Say, "I will place it here on the table."

(9) *NOTE: As it stands now, you have <u>one RED</u> Ace and <u>one BLACK</u> Ace face down on the table, <u>which the spectators believe are the two Black Aces.</u> The other Black Ace is really on top of the pack and the last Red Ace is <u>face up</u> on the <u>bottom</u> of the pack.*

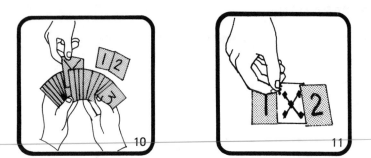

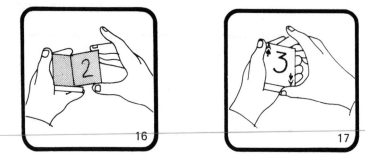

(10) Run through the pack face down and invite the spectator to select any card. When he does, square the pack and hold it in dealing position in the left hand. (11) Instruct the spectator to turn his card face up and slide it between the two "Black Aces" on the table, thus "sandwiching" his card between them.

(12) *NOTE: Be sure the spectator understands your instructions and does not pick up the Aces on the table. If you're not sure of the spectator, hold the two Aces face down in your hand and tell him to slip his card face up between them.*

(13) Now, secure a LITTLE FINGER BREAK under only the top card of the pack [the Ace of Spades (3)]. Because the attention of the audience is focused on what the spectator is doing, obtaining the Little Finger Break will go completely unnoticed.

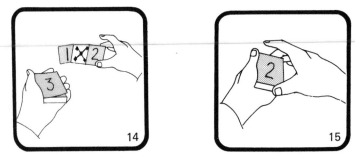

(14) Next, pick up the three cards on the table and (15) ... place them on top of the pack — ADDING THEM TO THE ACE OF SPADES — AND SQUARE ALL FOUR CARDS TOGETHER ABOVE THE BREAK.

(16) Without hesitation, turn over all four cards (as three) face up on the pack as shown. (17) *The two Black Aces will now be face up on top of the pack ... the spectator's card will be face down below the Aces ... and below that will be the face-up Ace of Hearts.*

(18) As soon as the four cards have been turned over, carefully take the two Black Aces [(1) and (3)] with your right hand and place them face up on the table. Remark, "Your card seems to have disappeared from between the two Black Aces." *Be sure when you deal the two Black Aces off the pack that you do not shift the face-down card below them accidentally exposing the face-up Ace of Hearts.*

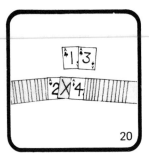

(19) HOLDING THE PACK IN YOUR HANDS, GIVE THE DECK A SINGLE CUT. THIS PLACES THE FACE-UP ACE OF DIAMONDS (THE BOTTOM CARD) DIRECTLY ON TOP OF THE SELECTED CARD AND THE FACE-UP ACE OF HEARTS BELOW IT. YOU HAVE AUTOMATICALLY "SANDWICHED" THE SELECTED CARD BETWEEN THE TWO FACE-UP RED ACES.

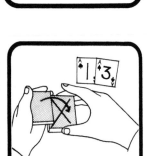

(20) All that remains is to spread the pack face down on the table revealing the two Red Aces and the face-down card between them. When the spectator turns over the "sandwiched" card, he will be amazed to see that his card has mysteriously appeared between the two RED ACES, the Ace of Hearts and the Ace of Diamonds!

COMMENTS AND SUGGESTIONS

Precision, more than skill, is the main factor in this mystery, so PRACTICE can make it perfect. In showing the *first* Black Ace, display it just as if you were doing a "Double Lift," replacing it on the pack and dealing it face down as a single card. Now, when you show and deal the Ace of Spades, your action is identical — so the "DOUBLE LIFT" will never be suspected.

DOUBLE THOUGHT PROJECTION

This is an exceptionally fine mental effect using only two ordinary packs of cards with contrasting backs....such as one red-backed deck and one with blue backs....and requires only one easily learned sleight which you have already been taught.

EFFECT

The magician runs through a deck of cards face up and asks a spectator to freely name any card in the pack. Assume that he selects the Seven of Diamonds. The wizard removes this card from the pack and turns it face down showing that it has a BLUE BACK. With that, he spreads the rest of the pack face down on the table revealing that every card in the deck EXCEPT the Seven of Diamonds has a RED BACK! Then, to take the mystery one step further, he spreads the BLUE-backed deck face down on the table to reveal a SINGLE RED-BACKED CARD right in the middle of the pack. When this card is turned face up, it is found to be the Seven of Diamonds FROM THE RED-BACKED DECK!

SECRET AND PREPARATION

The only sleight used in this amazing mystery is the DOUBLE LIFT.

You will need two "matching" decks of cards with different colored backs, say one red and one blue. Beforehand, remove a card from the blue-backed deck and place it on the bottom of the red-backed deck. In the illustrations this card is shown as the Four of Clubs, however, any card may be used. Then replace the red pack *with the one blue card,* in its case and have the blue-backed pack lying openly on the table. In fact, you can use the blue pack for a few preliminary tricks if you wish, as the absence of a single card (the blue-backed Four of Clubs) will not be noticed.

METHOD

(1) Bring out the case containing the red-backed pack and announce that you will *mentally* project the name of one card to the spectator. Fan or spread the cards FACE UP in your hands and ask the spectator to name any card of his choice. *Stress the fact that he has an absolutely free selection of any card.*

Blue backed card

(4) Reassemble the halves of the pack, placing the right-hand packet on top of the left-hand packet. *This leaves the spectator's card on the face of the deck with the blue-backed Four just below it.*

(2) When the spectator names a card, in this case the Seven of Diamonds, divide the pack into two sections at the place in the deck where his card is located. Keep the selected card at the top of the packet in your left hand. *NOTE: The Four of Clubs, THE SECRET BLUE-BACKED CARD is at the face of the right-hand packet.*

(5) At this point, get ready for the DOUBLE LIFT by securing a *Little Finger Break* beneath the Seven of Diamonds AND the blue-backed Four of Clubs under it.

(3) As you comment about the fact that his was a completely free selection, deal the Seven of Diamonds from the top of the left-hand packet *directly on top of the blue-backed Four of Clubs in the right-hand packet.*

(6) As you remark that the spectator could have selected any card in the pack, execute the DOUBLE LIFT and turn the two cards over *as one*, displaying the blue back of what the spectator believes to be his card, the Seven of Diamonds. ACTUALLY THE BLUE BACK HE SEES BELONGS TO THE FOUR OF CLUBS.

(7) Now to prove that you knew which card the spectator would choose all along, turn over the pack you are holding in your left hand and spread the deck face down on the table, showing them all to be red backed cards. *Be sure to keep the two cards in your right hand, WHICH THE AUDIENCE THINKS IS A SINGLE CARD, held firmly as shown.*

(8) Immediately pick up the blue backed pack (which has been sitting on the table all along) in your left hand and turn it face up.

(9) Place the DOUBLE CARD face up on the face of the blue-backed pack as you remark that the blue back Seven of Diamonds really belongs in the blue deck.

(11) Cut the deck burying the Seven of Diamonds somewhere near the center.

(12) The final proof of your Miraculous Powers comes when you now spread the blue backed deck face down to reveal one RED-BACKED card in the center of the deck.

(13) Remove the card and turn it face up to reveal it is the Seven of Diamonds... THE ONLY RED-BACKED CARD IN THE BLUE DECK.

(10) *NOTE: What the spectator does not know is that the Seven of Diamonds you have just placed on the blue-backed deck is really a red-backed card, thanks to your secret Four of Clubs! You are now set up perfectly to add a DOUBLE BARRELED impact to this mystery.*

A CLEVER COMBINATION

Here is a possibility for combining two very powerful card tricks into an excellent opening routine. The first is the HINDU COLOR CHANGE followed by DOUBLE THOUGHT PROJECTION. The routine goes like this.

EFFECT

FIRST EFFECT — The magician places two decks of cards on the table, both in their cases, one case is red and the other is blue. He opens the *blue*-backed case and takes out the pack of cards, showing that the faces are all different as they should be. But when he shows the backs to the audience, they are *red*. The magician explains that he obviously made a mistake after his last show and put the red-backed deck back into the blue box and the blue deck back in the red box. He further explains that there are two things he can do....ONE, he can remove the cards from both cases and replace them in their proper colored boxes OR,....and at this point he "taps" the red deck.... *he can change all of the red cards to blue and all of the blue cards to red.* He now spreads the "red" deck face down on the table. To the audience's surprise they see that ALL OF THE RED CARDS HAVE INDEED CHANGED TO BLUE. The magician then opens the red case and, sure enough, there is a red deck just as it should be.

SECOND EFFECT — The magician then proceeds to have a spectator touch any of the cards in the now blue-backed deck as he runs them from hand to hand face up. When he turns the selected card over, it is found to have a *red* back. THE SPECTATOR HAS SELECTED THE ONLY RED CARD IN THE BLUE-BACKED DECK. The red-backed deck is then spread and is found to contain *one blue-backed card,* and that card matches the very same card that the spectator touched in the blue-backed deck!

SECRET AND PREPARATION

As mentioned above, this is a combination of the HINDU COLOR CHANGE and DOUBLE THOUGHT PROJECTION. It makes an ideal combination because you already have the "extra" red card in the blue deck at the start of the routine. Just make sure that when you finish the last Hindu Shuffle before the deck "color change," that the *single* red card ends up on the *face* of the deck. This automatically gives you the "set-up" for Double Thought Projection. Complete the First Effect by removing the red deck from its case where it has been all along. You can then perform DOUBLE THOUGHT PROJECTION just as described. At the end of DOUBLE THOUGHT PROJECTION after the duplicate blue card is found in the red deck, the blue card can be returned ot its correct colored pack and *you have two perfectly ordinary decks ready for whatever additional tricks you wish to perform.*

COMMENTS AND SUGGESTIONS

Remember, at the start of the routine, the apparently red-backed deck, (really the blue deck with one red-backed card) is in the *blue* case. The remainder of the red cards (all except for the one red card in the blue case) are placed, as they should be, in the *red* case. This second "color change" of the *blue* deck in the *red* case is another good example of "misdirection," as the audience has never actually seen the color of the deck in the red box until you remove it to show that it has changed colors!

THE GLIDE

For directness, efficiency, and complete concealment, the "Glide" rates high among card sleights. Simple though it is, it does require practice to be done properly and convincingly. The Glide is an effective sleight, especially suited to beginners but equally valuable to all card workers, as it enables you to show a card and undetectably switch it for another. It is a most important move, and there are some excellent routines for it described in this section.

THE GLIDE

One of the simplest of card sleights, The Glide is also one of the most useful. With it, you can practically duplicate the work of some of the greatest card experts, without any chance of detection, as the vital move is entirely concealed from view. Some of the most deceptive card effects depend on the "Glide," so you can regard this sleight as a major step along the road to card magic.

EFFECT

You hold a pack of cards face up in your left hand, and call attention to the bottom card — say the Two of Clubs. Turning the pack face down, you draw out the bottom card with the tips of your right fingers and place it, still face down, on the table. When the card is turned over by a spectator, *the Two of Clubs has changed into a totally different card!*

METHOD

(1) Hold the pack *face up* in your left hand with the thumb at one side, and the fingers at the other. The tips of the second, third, and little fingers should curl over the top of the pack and rest gently, as shown, against the face of the bottom card (the Two of Clubs).

(2) *NOTE: YOUR FIRST FINGER REMAINS ON THE SIDE OF THE DECK AND DOES NOT TOUCH THE FACE OF THE BOTTOM CARD.*

(3) Turn the left hand over, toward yourself, rotating your hand at the wrist.

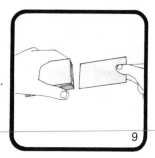

3

(9) Place the card on the table.

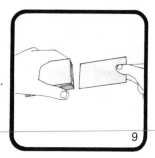

9

(4) As soon as the pack is face down, with the tips of your *left* second, third and little fingers, *slide the bottom card back,* so that it extends beyond the inner end of the pack about a half an inch. From underneath, the deck now looks like this.

4

(10) *NOTE: The audience believes you have just pulled the bottom card (the Two of Clubs) from the deck....really, you have removed the second card (the Eight of Spades).*

(5) From above, the pack should appear to be *completely natural,* with the back of your hand hiding the protruding bottom card.

5

(11) As the right hand places its card on the table, use the left fingers to return the "Glided" bottom card back to its original position flush with the rest of the pack. (See optional move described in Note 13.)

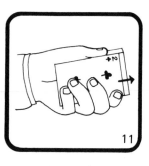

11

(6) Now, with your right hand, reach beneath the pack and press the tips of your *right* first and second fingers against the face of the now exposed SECOND CARD FROM THE BOTTOM (the Eight of Spades).

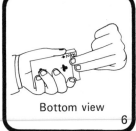

Bottom view

6

(12) The card on the table can now be turned over to show that it has magically changed to a different card.

(7) Begin to slide this card (the Eight) out from beneath the pack with the tips of your right fingers. When it is far enough out, place your right thumb on top of the card and draw it clear of the pack.

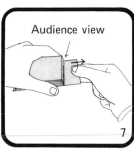

Audience view

7

13

(8) This is the view of the pack from the bottom.

8

(13) NOTE: As mentioned above in Step 11, if you find it difficult to return the Glided card to its original position using only the second, third, and little fingers of the left hand, you may wish to use this optional move: After the card has been removed by the right hand and is clear of the deck, extend your left first finger over the front of the deck. Then by a combination of pushing *back* with the left first finger and *forward* with the second, third, and little fingers, you will find that you can return the bottom card to its squared-up position on the bottom of the deck quite easily.

COMMENTS AND SUGGESTIONS

The "Glide" may be performed with only a few cards, rather than the entire pack, and still be equally deceptive. As you practice, you will find that only a very light pressure from your left fingers is required to "Glide" the bottom card back. Practice so that you can draw back *only* the bottom card, neatly and secretly, without having other cards tag along. Sometimes, you need a little more pressure, but always be careful never to apply too much. Also, many beginners, when learning the "Glide," hold the deck too tightly in the left hand. The pack should be held so that the back of the pack does not touch the palm of the left hand. Hold the deck so that just enough of your second, third and little fingers extend around the bottom of the pack to touch the face of the card to be "Glided." When working with a new or borrowed pack, test the "Glide" before using it, to get the "feel" of the cards. If necessary, the right fingers can actually take over the whole operation, by simply pushing back the bottom card and then pulling out the next, but this slows the action and should only be used in an emergency.

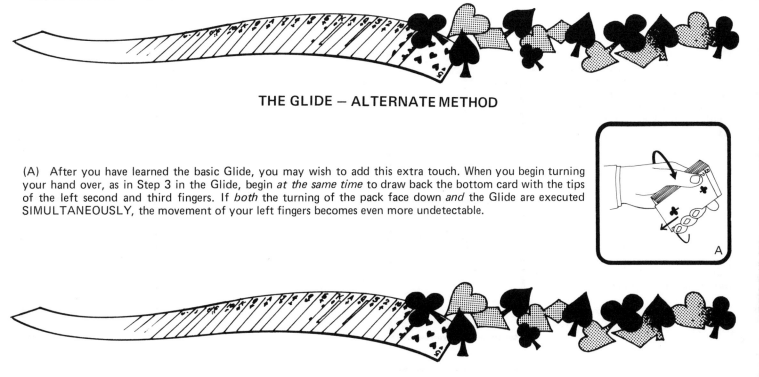

THE GLIDE — ALTERNATE METHOD

(A)   After you have learned the basic Glide, you may wish to add this extra touch. When you begin turning your hand over, as in Step 3 in the Glide, begin *at the same time* to draw back the bottom card with the tips of the left second and third fingers. If *both* the turning of the pack face down *and* the Glide are executed SIMULTANEOUSLY, the movement of your left fingers becomes even more undetectable.

COLOR CHANGING ACES NO. 2 — (Double Lift and Glide)

One good trick deserves another; and that rule applies to the second version of the "Color Changing Aces," which is very similar to the method already given. However, this version depends upon the "Glide" as its second move instead of another "Double Lift."

EFFECT

From the audience's view, the effect is identical with Color Changing Aces No. 1. The magician displays the four Aces. Holding them face down in a packet, he shows the face of both red Aces as he deals them on to the table. Holding the two black Aces in his hand, he commands the Aces to change places. When the cards are turned over, the black Aces are on the table and the magician is holding the red Aces!

METHOD

For this trick, you must do THE GLIDE and THE DOUBLE LIFT.

(1) From a regular pack of cards, remove the four Aces and place the rest of the deck aside. *(In the illustrations, the Aces have been numbered 1 through 4 to make them easier to follow.)* As you display the Aces, gather them into a packet and casually arrange them so that the Aces *alternate* in color — starting with a black Ace at the top of the face-down packet.

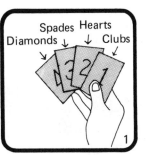

(2) As you place the packet face down in dealing position in the left hand, . . .

(3) ... obtain a Little Finger Break beneath the top two cards of the packet (Ace of Clubs and Ace of Hearts).

(4) Now lift these two cards as one (DOUBLE LIFT) off the top of the packet and show the face of what the spectators believe to be the top card — the Ace of Hearts — as you say, "Here is the Ace of Hearts — the top card of the pack."

(5) With that, replace the two cards on top of the packet and ...

(6) ... deal the REAL top card — the Ace of Clubs — from the top of the packet to the table as you say, "I'll place the first *red* Ace here on the table."

(7) NOTE: So far, this follows exactly the Color Changing Aces No. 1 routine (except for the color "set-up." Now comes the special added twist.

(8) Instead of doing a reverse count and another Double Lift, turn the packet face up in the left hand, in position to execute the Glide. As you do this, point to the bottom card of the packet (the Ace of Diamonds) saying, "And here is the Ace of Diamonds — the other red Ace."

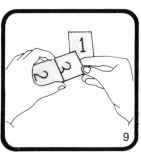

(9) With this, turn the packet face down and *execute the Glide* — DRAWING OUT THE CARD SECOND FROM THE BOTTOM (the Ace of Spades) instead of the "real" bottom card, the Ace of Diamonds.

(10) Place the card on the table as you say, "I'll put the Ace of Diamonds on the table along with the Ace of Hearts."

(11) At this point, the trick is really over; all that's left is presentation. After a little byplay, turn over the two red Aces in your hand to show that they have changed from black to red and invite a spectator to do the same with the black Aces on the table!

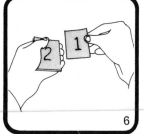

COMMENTS AND SUGGESTIONS

As you arrange the Aces in order: Clubs, Hearts, Spades, Diamonds, you can miscall their position by remarking: "Blacks in the middle; reds on top and bottom." Then, using the "Double Lift," you apparently deal one red Ace from the TOP. Then, *immediately* turn the packet face up and supposedly deal the other red Ace from the BOTTOM.

When "Changing the Aces," one good presentation is to hold one pair face down in each hand and slap their free ends together, with an up and down action. Then deliberately turn both pairs face up to show that they have "magically" changed places.

OIL AND WATER

"Dealing" tricks form a definite departure from other forms of card magic because they usually require only a small group of cards rather than a full pack. Also, they generally get away from the usual procedure of having a spectator select a card from the pack. As a result, "Dealing" tricks are very helpful toward making up a varied program. This applies particularly to this fine effect.

EFFECT

Six cards, three red and three black, numbering from Ace through Six, are arranged in alternating colors and number values. After displaying the cards in that manner, the magician turns them face down in his left hand and draws them out one at a time from the bottom and transfers them to the top, calling their colors, "Red — Black —" and so on. At intervals, individual cards are shown face up to prove that they are still in their alternating color order. The climax comes when the entire packet is turned face up and fanned. Amazingly, the cards have rearranged themselves in two separate groups; one composed of three black cards, the other of three red cards all in perfect number order from Ace to Six!

SECRET AND PREPARATION

THE ONLY SLEIGHT USED IN THIS TRICK IS THE GLIDE

(A) From a regular pack of cards, remove the Ace, Deuce, and Three of Diamonds, and the Four, Five, and Six of Spades. Now arrange the six cards so they appear in the exact order as shown. This done, you are ready to begin.

METHOD

(1) Fan the six cards face up and call attention to the fact that their number values are mixed and the cards alternate in color. Square up the packet of cards and hold them face up in your left hand in position for the Glide. Explain that, "Like Oil and Water, Red cards and Black cards just don't mix." *NOTE: Make sure that the spectator understands that the cards in your hand ALTERNATE in color.*

(2) As you display the Red Ace at the face of the pack, call out the word "RED." *Then, turn the left hand over so that the cards are face down.* Remove the card from the bottom, the Ace of Diamonds, with your right fingers.

(3) Place it on top of the packet. DO NOT DO THE GLIDE, simply remove the Ace from the bottom and move it to the top.

(4) With the left hand still face down remove the next card, the Five of Spades, from the bottom in your right fingers. To assure the spectator that this card is, in fact, a black card, with your right hand TURN THE FIVE OVER TO SHOW ITS FACE. As you do this, say, "BLACK." Turn the card back over and place it face down on top of the packet.

(5) Again turn the left hand over to show the face of the bottom card (Three of Diamonds) to the spectator, as you call out the word "RED." Immediately turn the packet face down and THIS TIME, EXECUTE THE GLIDE, actually drawing out the card SECOND from the bottom, the Four of Spades. Once the card has been removed from the "bottom," place it face down on top of the pack of cards.

(6) Still holding the cards face down in the left hand, draw out the bottom card of the pack, the Three of Diamonds, and hold it face down in your right hand. Pause for a moment as you call out the word "BLACK." DO NOT TURN THIS CARD FACE UP. Instead, place the card face down on top of the packet.

(7) With the packet still face down, remove the bottom card of the pack, the Two of Diamonds, and TURN IT FACE UP IN THE RIGHT HAND. Pause for a moment and call out the word, "RED." Then place this card face down on top of the packet.

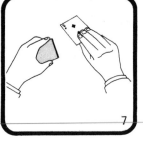

7

(9) *NOTE: Apparently you have just shown each card in the packet one at a time without disturbing their alternating color order or number order. Of course, you know different!*

(8) Finally, turn the packet face up, in position for the Glide, and display the face of the Six of Spades as you say, "BLACK." Then turn the pack face down and ONCE AGAIN EXECUTE THE GLIDE, actually removing the card SECOND from the bottom, the Ace of Diamonds. Place this card on top of the rest of the cards of the packet.

8

(10) All that remains is to fan the packet face up displaying that the cards have arranged themselves in numerical order and that, like Oil and Water, playing cards just don't mix.

10

COMMENTS AND SUGGESTIONS

Practice with the six cards until you memorize the routine as given and this trick becomes virtually self-working. Its only move, the "Glide," should be done smoothly and at exactly the same pace as when you are "really" removing the bottom card. The total routine has been carefully designed so that each time you display a RED or BLACK card, either on the bottom of the packet or in your right hand, you are psychologically convincing the spectators of the "honesty" of moving each card from the bottom to the top and away from the real secret.

DO AS I DO OIL AND WATER

This is a version of the "Oil and Water" effect involving audience participation. The working is the same, but you have a spectator follow your moves with a packet of cards arranged in the red, black alternating order exactly like your own. Although the spectator duplicates your moves exactly, your cards magically arrange themselves in separate groups, while the spectator's stay in alternate order, just as they started.

When done in that manner, this trick makes an excellent follow-up to the "You Can't Do As I Do," in which some face-down cards turn themselves face up during a similar type of deal. It can also be used instead of "You Can't Do As I Do," when you are performing for a group of people who have seen the five-card effect before. Actually, the two effects depend upon totally different principles, but to most observers, they appear to be practically the same. That serves as an excellent "throw off" to lead the audience away from the real secret.

You can enlarge the "Do As I Do" routine to include two or more spectators, giving each a group of six cards, half red and half black, so they can all go wrong together while trying to duplicate your magical procedure.

BIRDS OF A FEATHER

This is a modernized version of a card classic known as "Follow the Leader." Here, all difficult sleights have been eliminated, reducing the routine to a single, simple sleight — the "GLIDE" — with everything else working almost automatically.

EFFECT

From an ordinary pack, the magician removes five red cards, the Ace through Five of Diamonds, and five black cards, the Ace through Five of Clubs. Placing the Ace of Diamonds and the Ace of Clubs face up on the table to serve as "leaders," he deals the four remaining red cards face down on the red Ace and all the four remaining black cards face down on the black Ace. He then openly "transposes" the face-up Aces — and at his command, the two "Deuces" invisibly "jump" to the pile of the opposite color — each next to the Ace of its own suit. Next, the face-down piles are transposed and yet another pair of cards — this time, the "Threes" — follows suit in the same mysterious fashion, "magically" moving to their matching colored Aces. This is continued — transposing the piles in every possible combination. Yet each time two cards are turned up, *they prove to be a matching pair,* having "magically" changed places to appear next to the Aces of their own suits!

SECRET AND PREPARATION

From an ordinary pack, remove two groups of five cards — one group of red cards numbering Ace through Five, and one group of black cards of the same values. In the illustrations, all Clubs (black) and Diamonds (red) have been used. Place the two Aces face up on the table and casually arrange the remaining eight cards in a fan from left to right in the following sequence: Five of Clubs, Four of Clubs, Three of Clubs, Two of Clubs, Three of Diamonds, Four of Diamonds, Five of Diamonds, and Two of Diamonds. (See illustration for Step 1.) With the cards arranged in this order, you are ready to begin.

METHOD

(1) Display the eight cards in a face-up fan, pointing out that the cards are separated into two groups, RED and BLACK. Do not call attention to the numerical sequence of the cards. Shown casually, *they will not appear to be in any special order.*

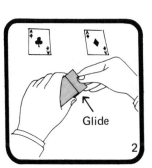

(2) Close the fan and turn all the cards face down. Hold the packet in your left hand in position for the GLIDE. Now, *execute the Glide,* apparently dealing the bottom red card (really the second from the bottom) onto the table next to the Ace of Diamonds. Say, "I will deal the RED cards here on the table next to their leader, the RED Ace of Diamonds.

(3) After dealing the second card from the bottom, *do not return the bottom "Glided" card back to its former position.* Instead, hold the card in its "Glided" position and *deal three more cards,* one at a time, apparently from the bottom of the pack onto the first card.

Deal from bottom

(4) Stop dealing after you have the four cards face down in a pile next to the red Ace. Because of the "Glide," *the last card dealt on the "red" packet is really a black card.*

(5) Square up the packet in your left hand (secretly bringing the "Glided" card even with the rest of the packet) and deal the remaining cards *from the TOP of the packet,* one at a time, onto the table next to the black Ace. As you deal these cards say, "All the BLACK cards go next to their leader, the BLACK Ace."

Deal from top

(6) *NOTE: As shown in the illustration for Step 6, unknown to the audience, you now have one RED card on top of the BLACK pile and one BLACK card on top of the RED pile, thanks to the Glide! If you have executed the Glide and the dealing correctly as described in Steps 1 through 5, the rest of the trick will work automatically.*

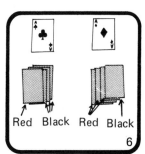

Red   Black   Red   Black

(7) Now exchange the positions of the two "leader" Aces. Say, "No matter how I change the Aces, the rest of the cards will 'Follow the Leader' and turn up in matching pairs."

(11) Now exchange either pile of face-up cards with the face-down pile of cards *diagonally across from it* as shown.

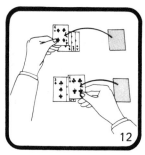

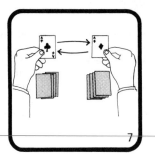

(8) With that, *turn over the top cards of both face-down packets.* These two cards will be the "Deuces" (twos) *which match in suit and color their new "leader" Aces.* Place the "Deuces" face up on top of their correct color "leader" Aces and continue.

(12) Turn over the top two cards from the face-down piles to show the matching "Fours" and place them on their respective "leader" packets.

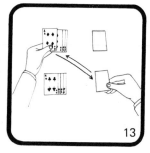

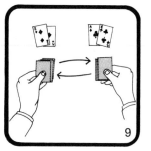

(9) Next, *exchange the positions of the two face-down piles.* Say, "Even if I switch the *piles,* it always works out the same."

(13) Now exchange the *other pile* of face-up cards with the single face-down card *diagonally across* from it as shown.

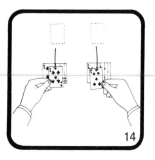

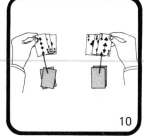

(10) Turn over the top card of each pile, revealing the "Threes," as they too follow *their* "leaders."

(14) Turn over the remaining two face-down cards. These will be the "Fives" which also match in suit and color to their "leader" packets!

COMMENTS AND SUGGESTIONS

After practicing this trick until you can present it smoothly and without hesitation, you can add the following touch: Instead of starting with the cards in a pre-arranged sequence, begin by openly shuffling the four red cards and place them face down on the table; then shuffle the four black cards and place them face down on the red cards. Since no one knows the bottom card, you can "Glide" it back and *show the faces of the first three red cards* as you deal them to the table. *The fourth card (really a black card) you deal on top of the red cards without showing it.* Now, deal the first three black cards in the same manner — showing their faces — dealing the last card (really a red card) *face down without showing it.* Those two final cards are the first to follow the leader. The rest of the cards travel automatically as already described. The one *disadvantage* to this method is when you turn over each set of cards to show that they have changed piles to match the color of their leaders, *the cards will not be matching pairs.* In the FIRST method, however, if you were to show the faces of the cards before you dealt them, someone might notice that the first red card you deal from the "bottom of the packet" is *not* the card they saw on the bottom when you showed the fan at the start.

DOUBLE-BACKED CARD

Many surprising effects are possible with the use of a Double-Backed Card which has been added to a regular pack without the knowledge of the spectators.

Most of the tricks you can perform with a Double-Backer would be impossible without it. Others would require difficult sleights to accomplish the same result. Those are two good reasons for including the Double-Backed Card effects in your program. None of the following mysteries requires any special skill, and each can be mastered with just a little practice.

After you have mastered these mysteries, add a little creative thinking of your own, and you may discover many new and amazing card effects which incorporate the Double-Backer as their "secret weapon."

THE STUBBORN CARD

This is an example of an easy "quick trick" involving a DOUBLE-BACKED card that can be used as a prelude to a more impressive effect, or even as a follow up to another trick. Such forms of byplay introduce a surprise element that will leave your audience wondering what can happen next.

EFFECT

A spectator is given a card and asked to place it *face down* into a deck held *face up* by the magician. Riffling the deck, the magician commands the card to turn face down of its own accord. Upon spreading the pack, the magician shows that all of the cards are face down. He can even count the cards separately onto the table to prove there is not a single face-up card among them.

SECRET AND PREPARATION

(A) Place a Double-Backed card on top of the pack and return the deck to its box. You are now ready to present the Stubborn Card as the opening number in your card routine. *NOTE: In this illustration and the others that follow, the Double-Backed card is indicated with the letter "D."*

METHOD

(1) Remove the pack from the box and spread the cards face down between your hands as you remark that all the cards in the deck are face down and that there are no "reversed" (face-up) cards anywhere in the pack.

(3) With that, turn the pack face up and spread it between your hands, asking him to insert his *face-down* card anywhere in the *face-up* pack. As he does, spread the cards still wider, proving that *every card is face up except his.*

(2) Square the deck in your left hand and deal off the top card of the pack. Hand this card *(really the Double Backer)* to the spectator, telling him to keep it face down, so you can show him how stubborn *any* card can be.

(4) After he has inserted the card, square the pack and turn it over, so that the pack is again face down. Here, you remark that no card likes to be face up in a face-down pack, and that his card is probably as stubborn as the rest. With that, riffle the end of the pack and then spread the cards between your hands telling him to watch for his *face-up* card.

(5) No matter how closely he watches, he won't see his card because THE "DOUBLE BACKER" APPEARS TO BE A REGULAR FACE DOWN CARD LIKE THE REST OF THE CARDS IN THE DECK.

(7)   Reassemble the two halves of the pack so the Double-Backed card will again be on top, just as it was at the start.

(6) To conclude the trick, turn the pack face up and start spreading through the cards saying, "There's no way of finding the Stubborn Card, since all the cards are face up and we don't even know what card it is!" As you spread the pack from left to right, tilt it toward yourself, so that you alone can see the Double-Backed card when you come to it.

COMMENTS AND SUGGESTIONS

You can now go into almost any other trick requiring a Double-Backed card, since it is handy on the top of the pack. The five-card "You Can't Do As I Do" is particularly effective as a follow-up to the Stubborn Card. You do not even have to cut the Double Backer to the top of the pack. Instead, you draw four random cards from the pack, casually showing their faces as you place them face down on the table. Finally, you add the Double-Backed card WITHOUT showing its "face" as you lay it down. You are then free to hand the pack to the spectator and tell him to remove any five cards he likes, just as you did.

SATAN BEHIND YOU

This begins as a "Do As I Do" effect and then develops into a "Do It Yourself" procedure on the spectator's part. Under your guidance, the spectator "magically" discovers a card that he previously selected, yet finds he cannot duplicate the trick on his own. As a mystery involving audience participation with a surprise payoff, this will add zest to any program of Card Magic.

EFFECT

Dividing a pack of cards, the magician gives one half to a spectator and keeps the other half for himself. He explains that the spectator is to "Do As I Do." The magician places his half behind his back, removes any card and looks at it. He then puts the card behind his back again and places it on *top* of his packet.

The spectator then does the same with his half. The magician then reassembles the pack, putting his half on top, burying the spectator's card in the middle. Now, the magician instructs the spectator to place the *entire* pack behind his back. The spectator is to remove the magician's card from the top, turn it face up, and insert it somewhere in the pack. The spectator then hands the deck back to the magician who *immediately* spreads it face down on the table. Near the center of the spread is the magician's face-up card which he removes *along with the face-down card just below it.* When the magician turns over the face-down card, *the spectator acknowledges it to be the very card he selected.*

SECRET AND PREPARATION

The only items required for this mystery are a regular pack of cards and one DOUBLE-BACKED CARD which matches the back of the pack being used. To prepare, place the DOUBLE-BACKED CARD on top of the pack and place the pack in its box. (The Double-Backed Card has been marked with a "D" and the spectator's card with an "X" in the illustrations.)

METHOD

(1) Remove the deck from its box and divide it into two fairly equal packets. Give the <u>lower half</u> of the pack to the spectator. Keep the <u>upper half</u> for yourself . . . it has the DOUBLE-BACKED CARD on <u>top</u>.

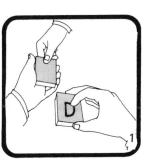

(2) Place your half behind your pack and withdraw any card from your packet. Tell the spectator to do the same. Instruct him to bring his card out from behind his back and look at it and remember it. . . . *He is to be sure you cannot see the face of his card.* As you say this, you also bring your card into view. Look at it and remember it (in this case your card is the Ace of Clubs). *Be sure the <u>face</u> of your card is toward you when you bring it out from behind your back.*

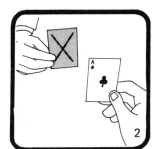

(3) When you have each looked at your cards, tell the spectator to return his card behind his back and place it on top of his packet. You *pretend* to do the same. Actually, when you replace your card, SECRETLY <u>TURN IT OVER</u> AND PLACE IT <u>FACE UP</u> ON THE <u>BOTTOM</u> OF YOUR PACKET.

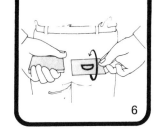

(4) Now, you both bring your packets back to the front. *Be careful not to "flash" the bottom of your packet, exposing the reversed card.* PLACE YOUR PACKET ON TOP OF THE SPECTATOR'S PACKET. Say, "If I place my packet on top of yours, your card will be buried in the middle of the pack." *Unknown to the spectator, this places <u>your face-up card</u> directly above his card.* The Double Backer still remains <u>on top</u> of the pack.

(5) Give the deck to the spectator. Instruct him to place the entire pack behind his back. He is to remove the top card *(which he <u>thinks</u> is your card . . . but is really the Double-Backer).*

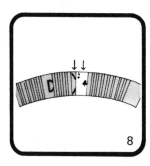

(6) He is to turn your card (really the Double Backer) "face up" and (7) . . . insert it anywhere in the pack.

(8) This done, tell him to bring the pack forward and give it to you. Without hesitation, spread the cards face down on the table as you say, "My card was the Ace of Clubs — here it is <u>face up</u> in the pack where <u>you</u> placed it. What was your card?"

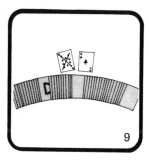

(9) Whatever the reply, remove the face-up card from the spread *along with the card directly beneath it* and turn that card face up! The spectator will be amazed to see that he has mysteriously managed to "locate" his card in the deck . . . ALL BEHIND HIS OWN BACK!

COMMENTS AND SUGGESTIONS

If you like, before you spread the pack on the table, you can <u>both</u> name your cards aloud. In fact, you can show your card to some other spectator before putting it behind your back; have the "participating" spectator do the same with his card. *Just be sure no one sees you place your card <u>face up</u> on the bottom of your packet.*

There is a slight chance that the spectator may happen to insert the Double Backer just below the face-up card, thus separating your card from his. So, as you remove the two cards from the spread, tilt them slightly so that you can "glimpse" the face of the lower card before removing it from the spread. If it happens to be the Double Backer, also remove the <u>next</u> card below it (which is the spectator's card). Then, remove the Double Backer from between the two cards and drop it on the pack, saying, "And here we have a 'mystery card,' with <u>my</u> card face up <u>above</u> it — and <u>your</u> card face down <u>below</u> it!"

THE PERFECT CARD FORCE

This can be termed as a "perfect" force, because if done deliberately and handled carefully, it defies detection. This is due to the presence of a "DOUBLE-BACKED" card which you secretly add to the pack beforehand, enabling you to accomplish what would otherwise be impossible. Hence it is a good method to have in reserve for some very special trick that *depends* on a successful force.

EFFECT

The magician asks a spectator to cut off a packet of cards — from a face-down pack. The magician takes the "cut" portion and turns it face up, placing it squarely on the rest of the face-down pack. He then gives the pack to the spectator and instructs him to run through the face-up cards until he comes to the *first* face-down card, where the spectator divided the pack. The spectator is asked to look at that card and remember it. ALTHOUGH THE SPECTATOR WAS FREE TO CUT WHEREVER HE WANTED, THE MAGICIAN ALREADY KNOWS THE CARD!

SECRET AND PREPARATION

The only items required for this force are a regular pack of playing cards and one DOUBLE BACKED card that matches the back design of the cards in the pack.

(A)   To prepare, place the card to be "Forced" FACE UP on top of the face-down pack. (In the illustrations the Eight of Spades is the "Force" card and is marked with an "F.") Directly above this, place the Double-Backed card. (The Double-Backed card is marked with a "D.") The face-up Eight of Spades is now *second* from the top *hidden by the Double Backer.* Square up the pack, and you are ready to begin.

METHOD

(1)   Place the pack face down on the table and ask the spectator to divide the pack into two parts. Tell him that he can cut *anywhere* in the deck he wishes — and to then place the upper portion on the table. *Stress the fact that the spectator is cutting the pack at a location of his own free choice.*

(2)   *NOTE: IT IS VERY IMPORTANT HERE THAT THE SPECTATOR CUT THE CARDS NEATLY SO AS NOT TO ACCIDENTALLY SHIFT THE DOUBLE BACKER EXPOSING THE FACE-UP FORCE CARD BENEATH IT. FOR THIS REASON, IT IS WISE FOR YOU TO DEMONSTRATE BE- FOREHAND HOW THE SPECTATOR SHOULD DIVIDE THE PACK INTO TWO "NEAT PILES."*

(3)   This done, pick up the packet the spectator cut off the deck. CARE- FULLY TURN THE PACKET OVER, AND REPLACE IT FACE UP ON TOP OF THE REST OF THE PACK. Say, "By placing these cards face up on top of the face-down cards, we will mark the location where you divided the pack."

(4)   *NOTE: This automatically reverses the Double-Backed card and the secret face-up Eight of Spades and makes them the first two cards of the face-down portion of the pack.*

(5)   Pick up the pack from the table and hand it to the spectator. Tell him to run through the pack until he reaches THE FIRST FACE-DOWN CARD — WHERE HE DIVIDED THE PACK.

(6)   He is to remove that card from the pack.

(7) The <u>first face-down card</u> he *arrived at was your "Force" card, the Eight of Spades.* After he removes the card, tell him to reassemble the pack and give it to you. YOU HAVE NOW SUCCESSFULLY EXECUTED THE <u>PERFECT CARD FORCE.</u>

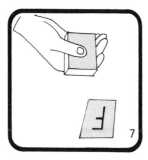

COMMENTS AND SUGGESTIONS

The "Force" can be ruined if the spectator handles the cards too carelessly and the top (Double-Backed) card slides from the pack, exposing the face-up "Force" card beneath. *Therefore, if you are not sure of the spectator, you will do better to handle the pack yourself.* Simply riffle the outer end slowly and let the spectator insert his forefinger; or have him lift up a portion of the pack at the outer end as *you* hold the cards. Either way, *you* then divide the pack at the point he selected and carefully turn the whole group face up on the pack. Then immediately square the deck with your hands. You are then ready to let the spectator run through the cards until he comes to the one that he thinks is his "free" selection.

THE TWO-CARD FORCE

While this can be classified as a "Force" involving a Double-Backed card, its effect is so strong that it can be presented as a prediction trick in its own right. No skill whatever is required, yet the performer will be given credit for a near miracle. This trick alone makes it worthwhile to include "Double-Backed" card effects in your program.

EFFECT

The magician gives a sealed envelope to a spectator and says that it contains a "Double Prediction." He then takes a pack of cards from its case, and handing the top card face down to another spectator, he explains that this card is to be used as an "indicator." *Turning the squared pack face up,* he tells the spectator to insert the indicator card *face down* ANYWHERE he wishes in the pack. This done, the magician turns the pack back over and runs through the now face-down deck. When he comes to the *face-up* "indicator" card. The spectator is asked to remove the two cards on both sides of the indicator and looks at them. When the envelope is opened, IT CONTAINS A SLIP OF PAPER WITH THE NAMES OF THOSE TWO CARDS!

SECRET AND PREPARATION

The only requirements for this mystery are a regular pack of cards and a single Double-Backed card which matches the back design of the cards in the pack. To prepare, write the names of any two cards on a slip of paper. These will be your "Force" cards. Seal the piece of paper in an envelope and place it in your pocket. This done, run through the pack of cards and find the two "Force Cards" and place them together, face down, somewhere near the center of the face-down pack. NOW REMOVE ANY INDIFFERENT CARD AND PLACE IT FACE UP BETWEEN THE TWO FACE-DOWN FORCE CARDS. Finally, place the Double-Backed card on *top* of the pack and you're ready. (In the illustrations, the Double Back card is indicated by a "D" and the two "Force" cards by "F.")

METHOD

(1) Begin the presentation by removing from your pocket the sealed envelope. Say, "In this envelope is a slip of paper with a double prediction." Place the envelope on the table or hand it to a spectator to hold and pick up the pack of cards.

(2) Holding the pack face down in dealing position in the left hand, deal the top card (the Double Backer) from the top of the pack into your right fingers. Give this card to the spectator, asking him to hold it face down — without looking at it — as it will be used simply as an "indicator" card.

(3) Now TURN THE PACK FACE UP and tell the spectator to insert the indicator card FACE DOWN anywhere he wishes in the pack.

(6) Run through the face down pack until you come to the face up Six of Clubs in the center as you say, ". . . and here is your face-up indicator card, the Six of Clubs."

(4) NOTE: The spectator will believe that when this card is replaced "face down" in the "face-up" pack, it will be the ONLY reversed card in the pack. What he doesn't know is that the card he holds is a Double Backed card....and that you have previously reversed one card (the Six of Clubs) in the pack beforehand.

(7) Ask the spectator to remove the two cards on either side of the face up indicator card. THESE ARE YOUR TWO "FORCE" CARDS WHICH MATCH THE PREDICTION ON THE SLIP OF PAPER IN THE ENVELOPE.

(5) After the spectator has inserted the indicator card (the Double Backer) into the pack, TURN THE PACK OVER (FACE DOWN). Say, "When I turn the pack over, your indicator card will become the only face-up card in the pack, right?"

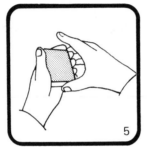

(8) Tell the spectator to turn the two cards face up. Then, to complete the mystery, ask another spectator to open the envelope and read the "Double Prediction"!

COMMENTS AND SUGGESTIONS

Another way of handling the insertion of the indicator card is to give the entire pack, face down to the spectator and tell him to put the pack behind his back. Then tell him to remove the top card with his right hand, *turn it face up,* and insert it anywhere into the pack. This done, you can even let *him* spread the pack along the table to find the face up indicator. In this modified version, *he* actually turns over the Double-Backed card, but since it is behind his back, no one can see that it is a Double Backer.

ADDED NOTE: You can also use this method to force a single card. Simply state that you will use whatever card happens to show up face to face with the indicator card. When you come to the face-up card you set up beforehand, remove it with the card above and let the spectator look at that card without showing it to you. YOU WON'T HAVE TO SEE IT, BECAUSE YOU ALREADY KNOW IT!

INSTO—TRANSPO

Three elements are combined to produce this super mystery: A Double-Backed card, a Double Lift and a simple but deceptive turnover that provides a final touch. Each element strengthens the others and the mystery itself is built around an element of "misdirection" designed to aid all three.

EFFECT

The magician gives a spectator a free choice of any card in the pack. The spectator signs his name on the face of the card and gives it to the magician, who places it *face down* on the table. Now, the *spectator* runs the pack from hand to hand and the *magician* selects one card from the pack. The magician signs the face of his selected card and *lays it face down beside the card signed by the spectator.* FROM THAT MOMENT ON, THE MAGICIAN NEVER TOUCHES THE CARDS. The magician, commands the two cards to change places. When the spectator turns both cards over, HE HAS THE MAGICIAN'S SIGNED CARD, WHILE THE SPECTATOR'S SIGNED CARD IS WHERE THE MAGICIAN'S CARD SHOULD BE!

SECRET AND PREPARATION

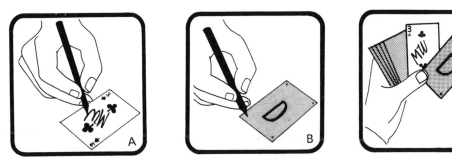

All that is required for this baffling mystery is a regular pack of cards and a matching Double-Backed card. *To prepare,* (A) Remove any spot card (for the illustrations we will use the Three of Clubs), from the pack and sign your name or initials across the face of the card with a marking pen. (B) Next, make a small pencil mark in each of the four corners *on both sides* of the Double-Backed card. The marks should be just dark enough so you can see which card is the Double Backer as the cards are run from hand to hand. (C) To set up, place the initialed card (the Three of Clubs) FACE UP on top of the face-down pack. On top of this, place the Double-Backed card (in the illustrations the Double-Backed card is marked with a "D"). Now square up the deck and you are ready to begin.

METHOD

(1) Run the cards from hand to hand and ask the spectator to select a card. Be careful not to separate the cards too near the top and expose the *face-up* card second from the top.

(2) After the spectator freely selects a card (the Four of Diamonds in the illustration), square up the pack and ask him to sign the face of his card with your marking pen.

IMPORTANT NOTE: The following Steps, 3, 4, and 5, are very important and are the real secret to the mystery. Follow them carefully.

(3) While the spectator is signing his card, with the help of your right hand, OBTAIN A LITTLE FINGER BREAK BELOW THE TOP TWO CARDS OF THE PACK (THE DOUBLE BACKER AND YOUR *FACE-UP* INITIALED CARD BELOW IT).

(4) When the spectator has signed his card, place it *face up* on top of the deck, *adding it to the two cards above the Break,* and square all three cards together.

(5) *Almost immediately turn over all three cards (as one) face down on top of the deck.* Turning the three cards as one is called a "Triple Lift." WHEN THE THREE CARDS ARE TURNED OVER, BECAUSE YOUR CARD (THE THREE OF CLUBS) WAS FACE UP, IT WILL APPEAR TO BE THE BACK OF THE SPECTATOR'S SIGNED CARD.

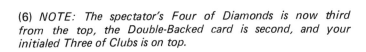

Three cards turned as one

(6) *NOTE: The spectator's Four of Diamonds is now third from the top, the Double-Backed card is second, and your initialed Three of Clubs is on top.*

(7) Now deal the top card (really your initialed card), face down on the table as you say, "I'll place *your* card on the table in front of you where you can keep close watch on it all the time."

(8) This done, give the pack one complete cut — cutting as close to the CENTER as possible. This buries the Double-Backed card and the spectator's initialed card near the middle of the pack.

(9) GIVE THE PACK TO THE SPECTATOR and ask *him* to run the cards from hand to hand, as you did, so that *you* may select a card FROM THE CENTER OF THE PACK.

(12) DO NOT LET THE SPECTATOR SEE THE FACE OF THIS CARD. Pick up the marking pen and *pretend* to sign your name or initials on the face of the card. *The spectator will believe this card was a random selection and that you are simply signing your own name on the card.* After you have supposedly signed the card, place it face down on the table in front of you.

(10) As the spectator does this, *watch closely for the small pencil dots on the Double-Backed card.* The Double Backer is your "Key" card in locating the spectator's signed card in the pack.

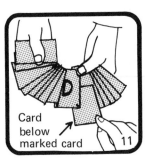

Pencil dots   10

(13) The trick is now over. The rest is just presentation. State that you will command the two cards to change places. Then, after a little byplay, turn over your card to show that it has changed places with the spectator's signed card. Of course, when the spectator follows suit, his card will bear your signature thus completing THE IMPOSSIBLE TRANSPOSITION!

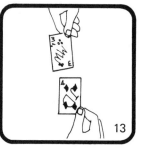

(11) When you spot the "Double Backer," REMOVE THE CARD DIRECTLY BELOW IT. *This is the spectator's original selected card with his initials on the face!*

Card below marked card   11

COMMENTS AND SUGGESTIONS

The real secret of this trick comes very early, before anyone suspects it; namely, while the spectator is signing his chosen card. Since the pack is not involved at that moment, you have ample time to "set" the two top cards with a Little Finger Break in readiness for the replacement of the spectator's card. Then you can easily do the "Triple Lift" when you turn over the top three cards AS ONE CARD.

In preparing the Double-Backed card, make the pencil marks rather light, so that they will not be noticed unless you are looking for them. As mentioned, it is a good idea to put the dots *on both sides* of the Double Backer; otherwise, you will have trouble if you put the Double Backer wrong side up. Afterward, you can erase the pencil marks. Some Double-Backed cards may not exactly match the color of the deck that you are using. With such a card, you may not need the pencil marks, as you can spot it by its off-color shade when the pack is spread.

THE PERFECT CARD LOCATION

EFFECT

The magician hands a spectator a deck of cards. While the magician's back is turned, the spectator cuts anywhere in the deck. He is told to look at the card to which he cut and remember it. The spectator then loses the card in the pack by cutting it again. When the magician turns around, he immediately spreads the deck face up on the table. One card is found turned over in the deck. The magician explains that this card is his special "Finder" card, which always manages to locate a selected card. Sure enough, the selected card is found to be the one card directly beneath the "Finder" card.

SECRET AND PREPARATION

This trick actually works itself. The only preparation needed is to have a matching "Double Backed" card on the top of the deck before the trick. The deck is then placed in the box and you are ready to perform. *NOTE: In the illustration, the Double-Backed card is marked with a "D."*

METHOD

(1) Remove the deck from its box and casually spread the cards face down on the table. This subtly shows that there are no face-up cards in the pack, *but do not call attention to this now.* Explain to the spectator that this is a very "special" card trick in which *he* will do all of the work but that *you* will still get all of the credit.

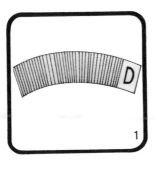

(2) Gather up the cards and hand the deck *face down* to the spectator. Explain that you will now turn your back and give him instructions which he is to follow.

(3) With your back to the spectator, tell him to cut off as many cards as he wishes from the top of the deck.

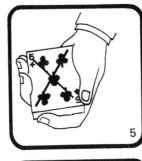

(4) He should *turn these cards over* (face up) and replace them on the deck, *on TOP of the remaining face-down cards.*

(5) Tell him to look at and remember the card he cut to . . . the card which is now *face up* on top of the deck. *(In the illustrations, this card is the Five of Clubs and is marked with an "X.")*

(6) Now, instruct the spectator to run through the deck UNTIL HE LOCATES THE POINT AT WHICH THE FACE-UP CARDS MEET THE FACE-DOWN CARDS. Have him separate the cards at this point.

(7) *NOTE: Unknown to the spectator, when he separates the cards, the Double-Backed card now becomes the top card of the face-down portion.*

(8) Tell him to turn over the face-up cards so that they are ALL FACE DOWN and to replace them ON TOP of the other face-down cards. This apparently returns the deck to its original "all face down" condition. *However, this actually places his selected card, the Five of Clubs, directly above the Double-Backed card.* All of this is done while your back is to the spectator.

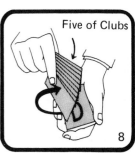

Five of Clubs

(9) Instruct the spectator to give the cards several complete cuts, thus mixing the cards thoroughly. *Be sure that these are "single" cuts and that they are each completed before he cuts the deck again.* When he has cut the deck as much as he wishes, turn and face the spectator. EMPHASIZE THAT, SINCE THE VERY START OF THE TRICK, THE SPECTATOR HAS HAD THE CARDS IN HIS OWN HANDS AND YOUR BACK HAS BEEN TURNED . . . YOU COULD NOT HAVE SEEN ANYTHING HE HAS DONE.

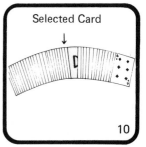

(10) Immediately spread the pack FACE UP on the table. One card will appear to be reversed in the deck (actually the Double-Backed card). Call attention to the reversed card, and explain that in every deck of cards you always have one special "Finder" card.

Selected Card

10

(11) As you talk, draw out the card directly *beneath* the "Finder" card. THIS IS THE SPECTATOR'S CARD and the mystery is complete.

11

COMMENTS AND SUGGESTIONS

The audience will be especially puzzled at this one because AT NO TIME DURING THE TRICK DO YOU HANDLE THE DECK after you hand it to the spectator... Until you spread the pack on the table and show the reversed "Finder" card RIGHT NEXT TO THE CARD THAT HE FREELY SELECTED.

YOU CAN'T DO AS I DO

(FIVE CARDS)

Audience participation is an important phase of today's magic and it reaches a peak where tricks of the "You Do As I Do" category are involved. For that reason, this five-card fooler should prove ideal.

EFFECT

The magician deals five cards to a spectator and five cards to himself, each group being dealt face down. The magician then moves cards from the top of his packet to the bottom, turning some face up and keeping others face down, while the spectator does each move exactly the same with the cards in his packet. The magician then spreads his cards, showing ALL FIVE FACE DOWN, saying that the spectator's packet should be the same. But when the spectator spreads his cards, he finds ONE FACE UP! This happens every time the routine is repeated, no matter how closely the spectator follows the magician's pattern.

SECRET AND PREPARATION

This trick practically works itself. It all depends on the use of ONE DOUBLED-BACKED CARD among the magician's five cards. To set up, place the Double-Backed card in the deck, ninth from the top. With the Double-Backed card in this position, all that is necessary is to deal the top five cards to the spectator and then five to yourself, one at a time, on the table. This will automatically reverse the order of the cards and place the Double-Backed card *just below the top of your five cards*. Therefore, with the card in the ninth position, place the deck in its box and you are ready to begin.

METHOD

(1) Deal the cards out as described above so the spectator holds five regular cards face down and you hold five cards with the Double-Backed card in the second position from the top. Fan the cards open and tell the spectator to be sure that his cards are all FACE DOWN like yours. (In the illustration, the Double-Backed card is marked with a "D.")

(2) Explain to the spectator that he is to move each of his cards EXACTLY AS YOU DO, one by one. Your first move is to turn the top card of your stack face up and place it on the bottom of your stack. *NOTE: Be sure that the spectator moves each of his cards just as you do on this and all the following steps.*

(3) Second, take the next card off the top and place it on the bottom, this time without turning it over. *Unknown to the spectator, this card in your stack is the Double-Backed card.*

(4) Third, remove the top card, turn it face up, and place it on the bottom.

(5) Fourth, move the next card from the top to the bottom without turning it face up.

(6) At this point, you stop to make sure that the spectator has followed your moves correctly. Fan your cards open and tell the spectator to do the same. Your cards should appear with the two face-up cards sandwiched between the face-down cards. *The spectator does not know that you have the Double-Backed card in the center.* When the spectator fans his cards, they will appear in the same sequence as yours.

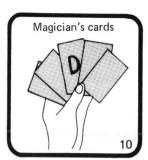

Magician's cards

(7) Now close your fan of cards and instruct the spectator to follow your next moves exactly. First you turn the top card over and leave it face up on top of the stack.

(10) This is the point in the trick where you reach the pay off. When you fan your cards, all five cards will be face down.

(8) Now turn the ENTIRE STACK OF FIVE CARDS over in your hand.

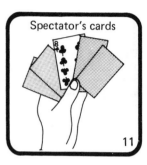

Spectator's cards

(11) However, when the spectator does the same, one card will appear face up in the center of the face-down cards....leaving no possible explanation for this mysterious occurance.

(9) For the final move, turn the top face-up card face down on the stack.

NOTE: When the trick is over, it can be immediately repeated merely by shifting the top card of your stack to the bottom, thus placing the Double-Backed card in the proper starting position for the effect.

COMMENTS AND SUGGESTIONS

Often, the routine can be ended exactly as described; in that case, you can compliment the spectator for having made such a good try; then gather the cards and go on with something else. Or, another trick involving a Double-Backed card can very well be introduced, since you already have one in the pack. Another possibility is to invite other spectators to try along with your original victim, dealing them five cards each and turning the trick into a form of "group participation." When they all find they can't do it, the laugh is on everybody instead of just your one original spectator. You conclude the operations by gathering their packets along with your own.

DOUBLE-FACED CARD

The legendary Burling Hull introduced some revolutionary principles which were unique to Card Magic when he developed the "Double" card. These principles are used to a great extent today because they enable magicians to perform "miracles" without the long hours of practice required to accomplish the same result through Sleight-of-Hand.

The Double-Faced Card is a great aid to the card worker because it can be added to almost any borrowed pack to produce effects that could not be duplicated without it. To change one card into another, or cause a card to turn face up in the pack become simple matters when a Double-Facer is secretly put to work.

TWO CARD MONTE

Tricks involving special cards are extremely baffling when injected into a series of effects performed with an ordinary pack. When a touch of skill is added, you can sometimes gain seemingly impossible results; and that rule applies to the following trick.

EFFECT

From a pack, the magician removes two contrasting cards; one red card and one black card which he places back to back. After turning them over several times, showing both sides, the performer takes the face-up red card in one hand and puts it behind his back, keeping the face-down black card in his other hand. When he asks which card he put behind his back and the spectator replies, "The red card," the magician brings it into view only to find it has changed to the black card. This is repeated, several times, always with the same result: Whichever face up card he puts behind his back invariably changes places with the face-down card in his other hand, unless the magician deliberately decides to keep them as they were. Always, both cards are under his magical control!

SECRET AND PREPARATION

The secret to this mystery is in the cards, themselves, as *both* cards used in the effect are special cards. *One is a Double-Faced card; the other is a Double-Backed card.* The Double Facer shows a black card on one side (Five of Clubs in the illustrations) and a red card on the other (Ace of Hearts). First you must learn the very important "secret" move which is the basis of the entire trick. This move will be referred to as the MASTER MOVE and it is executed as follows:

METHOD

(1) Hold the two cards together partially fanned in your right hand with your thumb on top and your first and second fingers beneath as shown in the illustration.

(2) With the cards held in this position, slide the top card (the Double Backer) to the *left* with your thumb and *in the same motion,* slide the bottom card (the Double Facer) to the *right* with the first and second fingers. THIS REVERSES THE POSITIONS OF THE TWO CARDS IN THE FAN.

(3) At the same time this sliding action is executed, the right hand turns completely over — so the back of the hand is up — as if to show the face of the other card. To the spectators it will appear to be the face of the other card, thanks to the secret sliding action which transposes the positions of the two cards. *NOTE: The sliding motion of the two cards will go undetected due to the more extreme motion of the right hand as it turns over.*

(4) Now, reverse the process exactly turning your hand back over, and the cards will again appear as they did when you started.

(5) Now that you have learned the MASTER MOVE, you are ready to actually perform the Two-Card Monte as a trick. Begin by placing the two cards together with the Double Backer on top of the Double Facer in position to execute the MASTER MOVE.

(6) Show the two cards on both sides, using the MASTER MOVE as you say, "For this trick, we use two cards, one black card and one red card, such as the Five of Clubs and the Ace of Hearts."

(7) Now, grasp the Double Facer in your left hand and place it behind your back. *Be careful not to accidentally "flash" the other side of the Double Facer as you handle the card.*

(8) Ask the spectator to name the card which remains in your *right* hand. Of course, he will answer "The Ace of Hearts." Before bringing the card from behind your back, *secretly turn it over so the Ace of Hearts side is face up.*

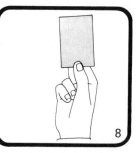

(9) Bring it into view as you say, "No, I'm sorry, I have the Ace of Hearts behind my back. You must not be watching closely enough."

(10) With that, place the Double Facer *beneath* the Double Backer in position for the MASTER MOVE. You are now ready to repeat the Two-Card Monte again, as often as you like.

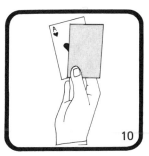

COMMENTS AND SUGGESTIONS

A neat way to begin the Monte trick is to have the Double Backer on top of a pack of cards and the Double Facer on the bottom. Remove the pack from its case and deal a row of three face-down cards from the top; THEN TURN OVER THE PACK and deal three cards face up from the bottom. Place two of the ORDINARY cards face to face and turn them over a few times; then do the same with the other ordinary pair. Finally, settle on the "third" pair – the Double Backer and Double Facer – and replace the others back in the pack. This will help avert any suspicion of the two trick cards, as they look just like the ordinary pairs.

NEW CARD MONTE

EFFECT

Two cards are removed from an ordinary pack and shown front and back. Both cards are then placed inside the card box. The performer openly removes one of the cards and places it in his shirt pocket. Now, to the amazement of the spectators, the two cards magically change places. From his pocket, the performer brings the card that was in the card box....a spectator opens the card case and finds the card that the performer put into his pocket! Everything can then be examined.

SECRET AND PREPARATION

(A) For this trick, you use one of the specially printed DOUBLE-FACED cards described earlier. In the illustrations, the Double-Faced card has the Seven of Hearts on one side and the Ten of Spades on the other side.

(B) Before beginning the trick, place the "Double Facer" in your shirt pocket *and remember which side of the card is toward the audience* (in this case the Seven of Hearts in the illustrations). You are now ready to begin.

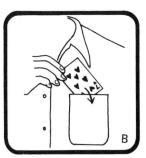

METHOD

PHASE I - THE SET-UP

(1) Remove an ordinary pack of cards from its box. Leave the box open and lay it on the table with the flap *facing up*. Now run through the cards face up and find the two cards which match those printed on your Double-Faced card (Seven of Hearts and Ten of Spades). Casually remark, "For this we need two cards. Any two will do – let's use the Seven of Hearts and the Ten of Spades."

(2) Remove the two cards from the pack and set the rest of the deck aside. Now place the Seven and the Ten *back to back* with the Seven of Hearts facing up as shown.

(3) Insert the two cards into the card box *with the lid facing up* as shown – close the lid, and place the box on the table. Now tell the audience: "If I openly remove one card from the box, and place it in my pocket, it would be easy for you to tell me which card remains in the box, right?"

(4) As you say this, open the lid and remove the Seven of Hearts from the box and place it in your shirt pocket with the face of the Seven toward the audience. Be sure to place this card BEHIND THE SECRET DOUBLE FACER which is already in your pocket.

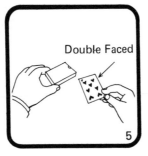

Regular Card

Double Faced

(5) Ask the audience to name the card which remains in the box. Of course, the answer will be the Ten of Spades. With this, REMOVE THE DOUBLE FACER WITH THE SEVEN SIDE SHOWING from your pocket and place it on the table next to the box as you remark, "That's right. I can see that you are watching me closely."

Double Faced

(6) *NOTE: Because the Seven of Hearts side of the Double-Faced card was toward the audience, they will believe this is the same card which you just placed in your pocket. Be careful not to "flash" the other side of the Double Facer as you remove it from your pocket.*

(7) As soon as the Double Facer is on the table, open the lid of the box and remove the Ten of Spades. Turn it face up as you remark: "That was easy. Now I'll make it just a little more difficult."

Regular Card

Double Faced

PHASE II - THE TRANSPOSITION

(8) Repeat the same actions as in Steps 2 and 3, apparently placing the two cards back to back – except this time TURN THE TEN OF SPADES FACE DOWN AND PLACE THE DOUBLE-FACED CARD WITH THE SEVEN SIDE "UP" ON TOP OF THE TEN. Place the two cards in the box and close the flap.

118

Double Faced

(9) *NOTE: You have apparently just repeated the same action of placing the two cards back to back and putting them in the box.*

(10) *This next step is an important part of the trick.* After you have placed the cards in the box, pick the box up off the table as you close the lid. Then, as you place the box back on the table, casually TURN IT OVER so that *the flap is now facing down.* This turns the regular Ten of Spades face up in the box with the "Ten" side of the Double-Faced card *face up beneath it.*

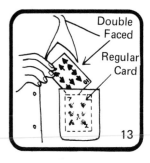

(11) Tell the audience that you will remove one of the cards from the box and place it in your pocket — and, as before, they are to remember the position of both cards. Open the lid of the box and remove the *bottom card* —THE DOUBLE FACER WITH THE TEN SIDE SHOWING. To the audience it will look as if you are removing the regular Ten of Spades, leaving the Seven of Hearts in the box.

(12) As soon as the Double-Faced card is out of the box, lay the card on the table and *immediately close the lid of the box so that the audience will not see the regular Ten of Spades inside.*

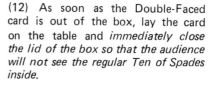

(13) Pick up the Double-Faced card and place it in your shirt pocket BEHIND THE REGULAR SEVEN OF HEARTS that was left in your pocket. Do this openly as you say, "Keep close watch on the position of both cards — and don't let me fool you."

Double Faced

Regular Card

(14) After the Double-Faced card is in your pocket, lift the box slightly off the table in the tips of your left fingers and shake it lightly back and forth, remarking "If I do this, do you think it could have any effect on the position of the two cards?" No matter what the answer, reach into your shirt pocket and REMOVE THE FRONT CARD — THE REAL SEVEN OF HEARTS. Place it on the table next to the box.

(15) Then, immediately open the lid of the box and remove the real Ten of Spades — or better yet, have the spectator do it himself, thus, completing the impossible transposition!

COMMENTS AND SUGGESTIONS

If you start by taking the pack from the card case, you can already have the two matching cards — the Seven of Hearts and Ten of Spades — together at the face of the pack. It would then be quite natural for you to take them as the first two cards in hand. In Step 8, after you place the real Ten of Spades back to back with the Double-Faced Seven of Hearts, if you keep the two cards squared together, you can turn them over to show the face of the Ten of Spades. Then, when you turn them over again with the Seven of Hearts face up, you can casually spread the cards to let the audience see the back of the Ten of Spades.

NOTE: If the card may be seen through the material of your shirt pocket because it is too "transparent," you may use your inside coat pocket or your pants pocket instead. If you use your pants pocket, be sure to remove the Double-Faced card before you sit down as you might crease it.

IMPORTANT POINT — *Another very strong feature of this effect is that the Double-Faced card is NOT in the deck at the START or at the CONCLUSION of the trick. Thus, everything can be handed for examination!*

FORCED CARDS REVERSE

For a double-barreled mystery, this must be given top rating. It fulfills our old saying that "One good trick deserves another," by repeating itself under conditions that would normally be impossible without the secret presence of a "special card." Read the effect closely, and you will appreciate its impact on the average audience. Then try it yourself and prove it!

EFFECT

A spectator selects two cards by cutting anywhere in the pack. As the magician shuffles the pack, he asks the spectator to replace *both* cards face down in the pack. This done, the magician *immediately* Ribbon Spreads the pack face down across the table. There, staring face up in the middle of the pack is THE FIRST CARD THE SPECTATOR LOOKED AT AND REPLACED FACE DOWN!

All this is done very openly, leaving the audience quite amazed. The performer removes this revealed card and replaces it in the pack face down. The magician then asks the spectator if he would like to see the miracle again. When the spectator says, "Yes," the magician again *immediately* spreads the pack of cards face down on the table displaying THE SECOND SELECTED CARD, FACE UP, IN THE MIDDLE OF THE SPREAD!

SECRET AND PREPARATION

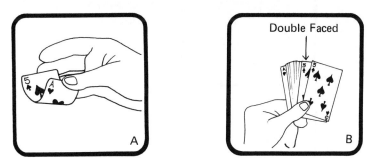

(A)   For this trick, you need an ordinary pack of cards and one DOUBLE-FACED card. In the illustrations, the Double Facer has the Ace of Hearts on one side and the Five of Spades on the other. To prepare, run through the pack and remove the two regular cards that match those shown on the Double-Faced card.

(B)   Place one of these regular cards (the Ace of Hearts in the illustration) on *top* of the deck and the other regular card (the Five of Spades) on the *bottom* of the pack. *The Double-Faced card goes second from the bottom* with the "Five" side facing the same direction as the rest of the cards in the pack. The illustration shows this clearly. Now, place the deck in its box and you are ready.

METHOD

(1) To begin the presentation, remove the pack of cards from its box and place it face down on the table in front of the spectator.

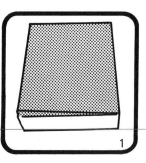

(2) Ask him to divide the deck into two parts. Tell him he can cut *anywhere* in the deck he wishes and to place the upper portion on the table. *Stress the fact that the spectator is cutting the pack AT A LOCATION OF HIS OWN FREE CHOICE.*

(3) Now, *you* pick up the LOWER packet of cards from the table and place it *cross-wise* on top of what was originally the UPPER packet.

(4) THIS PLACES THE ORIGINAL TOP AND BOTTOM CARDS (ACE OF HEARTS AND FIVE OF SPADES) TOGETHER IN THE CENTER OF THE PACK WHERE THE TWO HALVES CROSS. *The spectator believes they are two random cards which he cut to in the middle of the pack.*

(5) Stall for a few seconds with a statement such as, "Rarely are two randomly selected cards of the same suit. Let's check yours." Then lift the crosswise portion of the pack and remove the bottom card of that pile (Five of Spades) and . . .

(6) . . . place it face down on the table. *At the same time, place the cross-wise portion of the pack on the table next to the rest of the pack.*

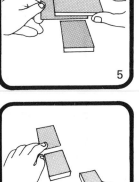

(7) Next, remove the *top* card (Ace of Hearts) from the other packet and place it next to the Five already on the table.

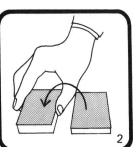

(8) YOU HAVE NOW "FORCED" THESE TWO CARDS. Ask the spectator to look at the two cards he "selected" and to remember them. Reassemble the pack, making sure to place the original *lower* portion of the pack BENEATH the original *upper* portion, THUS RETAINING THE DOUBLE FACER ON THE BOTTOM OF THE PACK.

(9) When the pack is reassembled, begin a regular Hindu Shuffle. Instruct the spectator to call "Stop" any time he wishes to replace one of the two "selected" cards back in the pack.

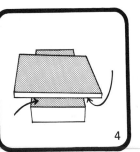

(10) When he says, "Stop," extend the left-hand packet toward the spectator and instruct him to place either one of the two selected cards on top of that packet.

(11) This done, continue the shuffle and instruct the spectator to call "Stop" when he would like to replace the second card. When the call comes, stop the shuffle and have the spectator replace the second "selected" card.

(12) *NOTE: Just do a regular Hindu Shuffle as it does not matter where the spectator replaces the cards.*

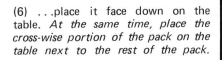

(13) After the second card is replaced, reassemble the pack *by placing the right-hand packet on TOP of the left-hand packet* and square up the pack.

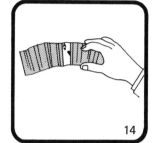

13

(16) With the pack *face up* in your left hand, insert the Double Facer – *Ace of Hearts side up* – into the center of the deck as shown. The spectator thinks you are merely replacing the card "correctly" back in the pack.

16

(14) Riffle the ends of the pack a couple of times as you say, "The easy part of the trick is to make the *first card* turn face up in the deck, LIKE THIS!" Spread the pack face down on the table to reveal the first card (REALLY THE DOUBLE-FACED ACE OF HEARTS) *face up* in the face-down spread.

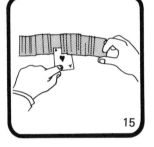

14

(17) Say, "But the difficult part is to find the SECOND CARD." Now turn the pack face down and once again spread the cards on the table – *revealing the face-up Five of Spades (REALLY THE FIVE OF SPADES SIDE OF THE DOUBLE-FACED CARD).*

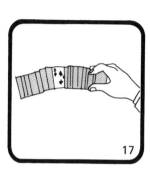

17

(15) Remove the Double Facer from the spread. Gather up the rest of the pack and *turn the deck face up. Be careful not to accidentally "flash" the other side of the Double-Faced Ace as you handle it.*

15

(18) Both cards have instantly and magically reversed themselves in the pack without any false or suspicious moves of any kind. The spectator will be left speechless.

COMMENTS AND SUGGESTIONS

Since no moves or sleights are required other than the regular HINDU SHUFFLE, your only concern is the handling of the DOUBLE-FACED card. Let the spectator cut the pack at the start, but be sure to *complete the cut yourself,* keeping the pack well squared to prevent the Double-Faced card from showing at the wrong time. If you intend to continue on with other tricks, you must dispose of the Double-Faced card. One easy way is, with the Double Facer on the face of the pack, start to put the pack in your coat pocket as if you were finished. With your thumb, push the Double-Faced card off the face of the pack into your pocket. . . . Then, "remembering" another trick, bring out the pack and continue with your routine.

IMPOSSIBLE PREDICTION

Any effect involving a *Prediction* should be treated strongly from the spectator's angle. Instead of trying to outwit the audience, the magician is dealing with a fixed result that "nothing can change." So, giving the spectator a chance to change it, only to find that he can't, becomes a real convincer, as you will see in the effect that follows.

EFFECT

The magician displays a small, sealed envelope, which he places upon the table. He brings out a pack of cards and allows a spectator to divide the pack into two piles so that *either of two cards* can be taken from the point at which the pack was cut. THE SPECTATOR IS ALLOWED FREE CHOICE OF EITHER CARD. After the spectator makes his decision, the magician opens the envelope and removes a *single* face-up card. When the spectator's card is turned over, IT PROVES TO BE THE SAME SUIT AND VALUE AS THE PREDICTION CARD. The envelope may be immediately examined to prove that it contains no other card and the pack may be inspected to show that it has no duplicate cards.

SECRET AND PREPARATION

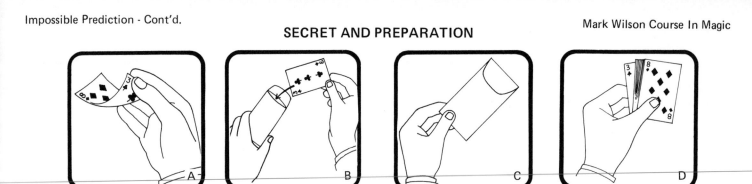

For this effect, in addition to a regular pack of cards, you will need (A) one Double-Faced card (the Three of Clubs on one side and the Eight of Diamonds on the other in the illustrations) and an envelope large enough to contain the Double Faced card. This can be any envelope as long as it is opaque. Small "coin envelopes", which are available in stationery stores, work well for this effect. (B) Place the Double Faced card in the envelope. BE SURE TO REMEMBER WHICH SIDE OF THE DOUBLE FACED CARD FACES THE FLAP SIDE OF THE ENVELOPE (THE THREE OF CLUBS). (C) Seal the envelope and place it in your pocket. (D) Next, remove from the deck the two regular cards that match your Double Face card, the Eight of Diamonds and the Three of Clubs. Place one of the cards on top of the deck (Three of Clubs) and the other on the bottom (Eight of Diamonds). Square up the pack, place it in its box, and you're ready.

METHOD

(1) Explain that, for this effect, you will enter into the realm of *mentalism,* rather than magic. Remove the envelope from your pocket as you say, "I have sealed a prediction in this envelope". Hand the envelope to a spectator to hold or place it on the table so everyone can see it.

(5) After a few seconds, pick up the crosswise portion of the pack and remove the *bottom* card of that pile (Eight of Diamonds) and . . .

(2) Remove the pack from its box and place it face down on the table. Ask someone to divide the pack into two parts; telling him he may cut anywhere in the pack he wishes. He is to place the "upper" packet that he cuts off, beside the "lower" packet which remains on the table. Stress the fact that the spectator is cutting the pack at a location of his OWN FREE CHOICE.

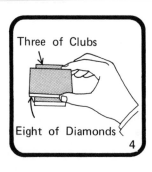

(6) . . . place it face down on the table.

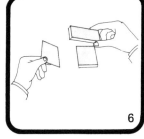

(3) Now you pick up the LOWER packet of cards from the table and place it crosswise *on top* of what was originally the UPPER packet.

(7) Next, remove the *top* card (Three of Clubs) from the other packet and . . .

(4) THIS PLACES THE ORIGINAL TOP AND BOTTOM CARDS (EIGHT OF DIAMONDS AND THREE OF CLUBS) TOGETHER IN THE CENTER OF THE PACK WHERE THE TWO HALVES CROSS. *The spectator believes they are two random cards which he cut to in the middle of the pack.*

Three of Clubs

Eight of Diamonds

(8) . . . place it next to the Eight already on the table.

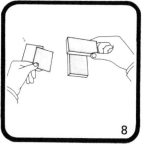

(9) Reassemble the pack and explain to the spectator he has a FREE CHOICE of *either* of the two cards he cut to. Ask him to choose one of the two cards and give him every opportunity to change his mind.

(12) Now ask the spectator to turn his card over so that everyone can see, FOR THE FIRST TIME, the card he freely selected from the pack. Pick up the prediction envelope and tear off the end.

(10) When the spectator is satisfied with his selection, (let's assume he takes the Eight of Diamonds), SHOW HIM THE FACE OF THE CARD HE DID NOT SELECT and replace it in the pack. Pick up the prediction envelope saying, "I hold in my hand the prediction envelope which has been on the table (or held by a spectator) all along."

(13) Then, holding it slightly above the table, tilt your hand enough so the Double Facer slides out of the envelope onto the table. Your prediction card will match the spectator's card exactly!

(11) Using the flap on the envelope as your "key," lay the envelope on the table next to the spectator's card so that the side of the Double Facer that corresponds with the spectator's selection is *face up* in the envelope.

(14) Immediately hand the envelope for examination proving that there are no other cards inside. While the spectator's attention is on the envelope, pick up the Double Facer and place it in your pocket and hand out the deck for examination.

COMMENTS AND SUGGESTIONS

From the very start, this effect offers a series of options that you can introduce as you see fit. It is a good plan to vary these, so you can stress a different factor when working for people who may have seen the effect before, thus giving it something of a "new" look. For instance, one idea is to have someone sign their name on the envelope before you bring out the pack. This keeps the envelope identified throughout the effect and eliminates the possibility of your "switching" it for another. As another neat touch, when the spectator cuts the pack into two separate piles side by side, *lay the envelope on top of the upper pile* and tell the spectator to "complete the cut." The spectator is then to choose either of the cards above and below the envelope. This is quite deceptive, giving the impression that you inserted the envelope somewhere near the middle of the pack, instead of between the top and bottom halves. At the finish of the routine, you can open the envelope and remove your prediction card BEFORE the spectator turns over his card and hand the envelope out for inspection right away. Or you can just leave the envelope on the table, bring out another pack of cards, and add the Double Facer to that pack as though it belonged there. Later, some suspicious spectator may snatch up the envelope, only to find it empty.

THE FOUR-CARD ASSEMBLY

This is a classic card effect and a favorite with many of the great card workers. The method given here is one of the best and has the added advantage of requiring absolutely no skill, so you can perform it immediately after reading the instructions.

EFFECT

From a pack of cards, you take four cards of the same value — for example, the four Aces — and lay them in a face up row. You now deal three cards face down on each of the four Aces, giving you four piles of four cards each. One pile — is chosen and placed in front of a spectator on the table. The other three piles are gathered together and returned to the pack, which is cut a few times and turned face up. Now, you give the deck three snaps or riffles and, when you run through the pack, the three Aces are gone! To the spectator's amazement, he finds that the three missing Aces have joined the one Ace in his pile giving him all four Aces.

SECRET AND PREPARATION

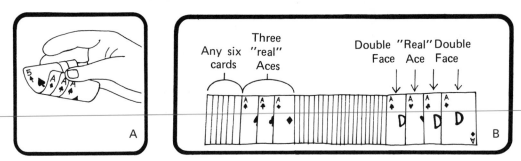

(A) The trick depends upon three Double-Faced cards, each showing an Ace of a different suit on one side and an indifferent card on the other. (For convenience, in the illustrations, we are supposing that one side of each of the Double-Faced cards are: Ace of Diamonds, Ace of Clubs, Ace of Spades.) (B) Beforehand, arrange the pack as shown. The three Double-Faced cards are at the bottom of the pack in the *first, second,* and *fourth* positions with the regular Ace of Hearts in the *third* position. On the top of the pack, place any six indifferent cards above the three remaining regular Aces. Thus, the other three "real" Aces are in the *seventh, eighth,* and *ninth* positions from the top of the pack. Now square up the deck and place it in its box and you are ready to begin. (C) *NOTE: In the illustrations, the Double-Faced cards are marked with a "D."*

METHOD

(1) Bring out the pack and remove it from its box saying, "For my next surprise, I need four cards all of the *same value.* Let's use the four Aces. I'll deal them face up in a row on the table." Turn the deck face up and deal the four Aces on the bottom of the deck (really three Double-Faced cards and one regular card) face up on the table from left to right. *This places the regular Ace (the Ace of Hearts) in the third position from your left.*

(4) Once you have "forced" the pile of regular Aces, gather the three remaining piles on top of one another and add them to the top of the face-down pack just as they are. The fact that the "Aces" are face up, while the other cards are face down, does not matter, as you will see.

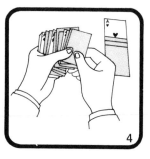

(2) Now turn the pack face down and deal three indifferent cards *from the top of the pack* onto the "Ace" at the left end of the row (the Double-Faced Ace of Diamonds). Then deal three more cards on the next "Ace" (the Double–Faced Ace of Clubs). Deal the next three cards on the real Ace (Ace of Hearts). THE THREE CARDS YOU JUST DEALT ONTO THE "REAL" ACE OF HEARTS (NUMBER 8, 9, 10) ARE THE OTHER THREE "REAL" ACES, THUS BRINGING ALL FOUR REGULAR ACES TOGETHER IN THIS PILE. Finally deal three more cards on the last "Ace" (the Double-Faced Ace of Spades) at the right end of the row.

(5) Square the three piles on top of the pack and give the pack several cuts. Then *turn the pack face up* and give it a few more cuts. Finish by giving the pack three fast riffles or snaps as you say, "One snap (or riffle) for each Ace in the pack."

(6) With that, spread the pack *face up* on the table, or run the cards from hand to hand to show that the Aces have vanished from the pack. By now the repeated cuts (face up and face down) will have your audience too confused to suspect that they are seeing the "backs" of the Double-Faced vanished Aces!

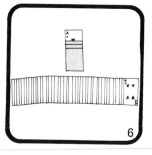

(3) This done, it becomes necessary to "force" the spectator to choose the pile of cards containing all the regular Aces. Use any of the appropriate "Forces" described in the Course. (The "Magician's Choice" or "Roll Any Number" are particularly good here.)

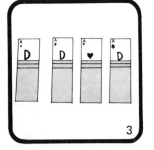

(7) Now turn over the remaining three face-down cards to reveal that all four Aces have amazingly assembled in one pile! This, of course, applies to whatever value cards you may be using instead of Aces.

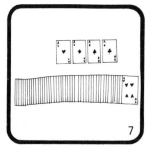

COMMENTS AND SUGGESTIONS

Beforehand, remove from the pack the three regular cards that appear on the "other sides" of the Double Facers. Then, when the pack is spread face up on the table to show the "Aces" have vanished, none of the spectators can spot any "duplicate" cards in the pack.

THE SHORT CARD
HOW TO MAKE A SHORT CARD

The "SHORT CARD" is one of the most useful devices ever designed for Card Magic. It can be used for "Locating," "Forcing," or even "Vanishing" a card, yet it will pass totally unsuspected by even the keenest observers. As its name implies, it is a card which is "shorter" than those in the rest of the pack and can be simply and easily prepared with any deck.

METHOD

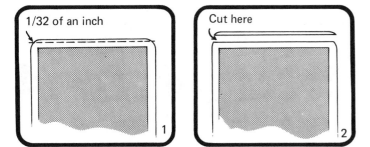
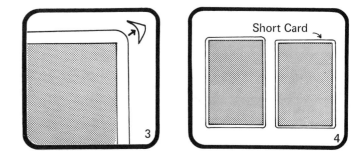

(1) To make a SHORT CARD, first draw a ruled line one-thirty-second of an inch from *both ends* of a standard playing card.
(2) Then, with a pair of good, sharp scissors, carefully trim off the ends using the ruled line as a guide.

(3) Next, "round" all four of the cut corners so they will match the corners of the "regular" cards in the pack. *NOTE: For "rounding" the corners, a pair of curved manicure scissors is helpful, but ordinary scissors will also work. Just cut the corners very carefully.* (4) This illustration compares a Short Card with a regular card from the same pack. As you can see, it would be difficult for anyone to detect the Short Card mixed among the regular cards in a pack.

(5) Some magicians carry a pair of small "fold-away" scissors with them, to use with a *borrowed deck.* All you have to do is to secretly pocket a card from the borrowed deck. Then work some trick — such as a "mental" effect — in which you *leave the room.* While outside, you cut the end from the card and round the corners. You can then return the card to the pack later. The pack can still be used by its owner in regular card games, without the players ever realizing that one of the cards has been "shortened."

COMMENTS AND SUGGESTIONS

For purposes of practice, you can make your first Short Card from the Joker (or the Extra Joker, if the pack has one). In this way, you can then either add the Joker when you wish to do a Short Card trick — or you can later "shorten" any other regular card after you have learned how to use your "practice" Short Card.

HOW TO "RIFFLE" THE SHORT CARD TO TOP

No matter where the Short Card may be in the pack, you can find it almost instantly *by sense of touch alone* in a number of ways. (In all of the following illustrations, the Short Card is indicated by an "S.")

METHOD

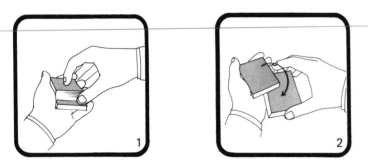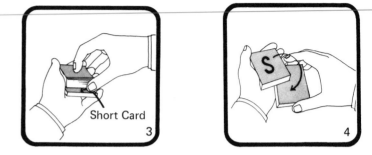

(1)   Square the shuffled pack and hold it in "dealing position" in your left hand. Cut the pack a few times by "riffling" the inner end of the deck with your right thumb.   (2)   Stop your "riffle" about half-way through the pack and transfer the remaining upper half to the bottom of the pack to complete the cut.

(3)   On your *last cut,* when you "riffle" the inner end of the pack upward with your thumb, if you *listen* and *feel* with your thumb, you will notice a slight "SNAP" when you reach the Short Card. When this happens, STOP YOUR RIFFLE. Then, make your cut, lifting off all of the cards *above* the Short Card. (4)   Complete the cut by placing this upper packet beneath the lower, as shown. *This puts the Short Card on top of the pack.*

SHORT CARD TO BOTTOM

In some tricks it may be necessary to control the Short Card to the *bottom* of the pack instead of to the top. This can be done in several ways:

FIRST METHOD

Bring the Short Card to the *top* of the pack as just described in SHORT CARD TO TOP. Then, using the OVERHAND SHUFFLE — TOP TO BOTTOM CONTROL, *shuffle* the *top* card (Short Card) to the *bottom* of the deck. Now you have not only placed the Short Card where you want it, on the bottom of the pack, at the same time you have convinced the spectators that all the cards in the pack are well mixed.

SECOND METHOD

A second method of bringing the Short Card to the bottom of the pack is simplicity itself. After your "riffle" which places the Short Card on top, simply turn the pack *face up* in your left hand. Then proceed with the instructions for SHORT CARD TO TOP as described. This brings the Short Card to the *top* of the *face-up* pack — and — *if you turn the pack over,* the Short Card will be at the *bottom!*

THIRD METHOD

Of the three methods described, this is the cleanest and quickest method of getting the Short Card to the bottom of the deck, although it will require a bit more practice. In Method No. 1, you have to riffle the card to the *top* and then *shuffle* it to the *bottom.* In the Second Method, the deck must be held face up, in which case the Short Card may be noticed — particularly if you are doing a number of tricks in which the same Short Card is used. This Third Method avoids both of the "shortcomings" (pardon the pun) of the previous two methods.

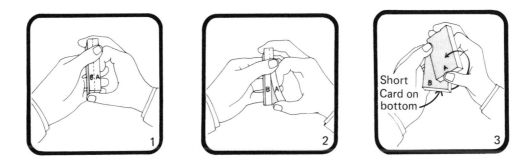

(1) Hold the deck in your left hand as if you were starting to perform an Overhand Shuffle. Your right hand grasps the deck with the first finger on the face of the pack, your other three fingers cover the outside end, and your thumb is at the end nearest you as shown. (2) Now, riffle the deck *downward* — starting with the top card — with your right thumb. When you get to the Short Card and hear and/or feel the "Snap," STOP YOUR RIFFLE. (3) Then, either cut the bottom portion to the top of the pack or Overhand Shuffle the bottom portion to the top of the pack, *leaving the Short Card on the bottom.*

THE SHORT CARD AS A "LOCATOR"

Once you have controlled the Short Card to the top of the pack, you can use it effectively as a "Locator" for finding other cards as well. This is highly baffling to those spectators who think they have followed a trick up to a certain point, only to find that it goes completely beyond their idea of "how it's done." This is a combination consisting of the Short Card and the Hindu Shuffle, which is always effective, as each helps the other to gain results which neither could gain alone.

EFFECT

A card is freely chosen from the pack. The spectator who took it is allowed to replace it wherever he wants. The magician gives the pack a thorough, genuine shuffle; then causes the card to appear on top of the pack; or finds it in some other unaccountable way. In brief, this method can be used as a very baffling "card control" in many standard tricks.

METHOD

(1) A Short Card is already in the pack and is brought to the bottom by the riffle method described under the "Short Card." From then on, the trick is handled in conjunction with the Hindu Shuffle and standard riffle shuffles.

(3) This gives you ample time to square the pack in readiness for the Hindu Shuffle. Don't actually begin the shuffle until the spectator is about ready to return his card to the pack; otherwise, you may have to go through the shuffle more than once, which is apt to slow the action.

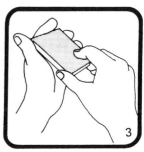

(2) With the Short Card on the bottom of the pack, spread the cards and let the spectator take any one he wants. Tell him that he can show the card to the audience before returning it to the pack.

(4) Proceed with the regular Hindu Shuffle, drawing back the lower portion of the pack with your right hand. *Keep the Short Card on the bottom of the packet in your right hand as you draw off small batches of cards with the fingers of your left hand.* Tell the spectator to say "stop" at any time during the shuffle.

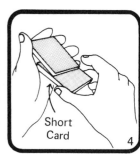

(5) Let the spectator return his card (X) on the portion of the pack resting in your left hand. Then drop the right-hand packet on the left-hand cards, as with the Hindu Shuffle Location. In this case, the Short Card becomes the "key" card, as it is placed directly upon the selected card (X).

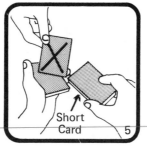

(8) After each shuffle, square and tap the pack. Finally riffle the inner end *upward* with your right thumb. You will note the *click* when you come to the Short Card. Cut the pack at that point. The Short Card (S) will stay on top of the lower packet.

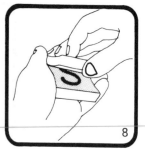

(6) Now square the pack, cut it, and give it a regular riffle shuffle, riffling the ends of the two halves of the pack together. This can be repeated and it *will not* separate the two cards, as the Short Card (S) will ride along with the longer selected card (X).

(9) In cutting, place the right-hand packet beneath the left-hand packet, which will automatically bring the Short Card (S) to the top, with the selected card (X) just beneath it. Thus, you have used your "key" card to bring a chosen card to the top *without* looking through the pack; and you have legitimately shuffled the pack as well!

(7) *NOTE: You should try this shuffle a few times to see how well it works. Be sure to tap the end of the pack on the table, to make sure that the Short Card is "down" in the pack.*

(10) Since you now know the position of the selected card in the pack you may proceed with any "discovery" that you wish.

COMMENTS AND SUGGESTIONS

The Short Card as a Locator can be used in any trick where you must first bring a chosen card to the top of the pack. In Step 10, the selected card (X) is actually *second* from the top, but you can handle that quite easily. One way is to turn up the top card, asking if it was the card the spectator took. He says, "No," so you push the Short Card face down into the middle of the pack, saying that you will find his card in a most mysterious way, *which you are now prepared to do!*

THE SURPRISE DISCOVERY
Using the Short Card as a Locator

(1) For an immediate and effective "discovery" of the chosen card, you can proceed as follows: Take the Short Card (S) from the pack, removing it face down with your right hand. Tap the Short Card on top of the pack, and tell the spectator that this will cause his card to "rise to the top of the pack."

(3) Now have the spectator turn up the tabled card (X). To his surprise, it will be the very card he took! Or, if you prefer, you can have him name his card and let someone else turn it up. This will dumbfound all the spectators, particularly those who did not see the spectator's card when he removed it from the pack.

(2) Since the selected card (X) is already there, the trick is really done; but for added effect, you should thumb the top card (X) onto the table; then casually replace the Short Card (S) on top of the pack, as though it had played no real part in the trick.

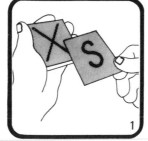

A WEIGHTY PROBLEM

Using the Short Card as a Locator

Here is another good effect using the Short Card as a Locator. When the selected card is second from the top, directly under the Short Card, cut a dozen or more cards from the bottom of the pack to the top. Then start dealing the cards *face up* from the top of the pack, one at a time, stating that, "Since the spectator is concentrating on the particular card that he selected, it will add an infinitesimal amount of weight to the card. Through long study and practice, I can tell which card he took just by this small bit of increased weight." Deal the cards one at a time pretending to "weigh" each card on the fingertips of your right hand before you turn it face up. You don't actually know the chosen card, but when you turn up the Short Card, you know that the spectator's card will be next — so you will have no trouble "weighing" it, and then announcing that, "This is the card you selected." *Only then* do you turn the card over to show the sensitivity of your magical fingers — as you comment that the spectator certainly is a "heavy thinker."

QUICK RIFFLE LOCATION

This form of the "Short Card Location" is very effective when done briskly and convincingly. It forms a nice variation from the usual "location."

METHOD

Have the Short Card either on the bottom or on the top to start. While the spectator is looking at his card, cut the Short Card to the center of the pack. Then, riffle the pack for the card's return — *but stop at the Short Card.* The spectator's card is replaced in the pack where you stopped — *on top of the Short Card.* You can then locate the Card by riffling the Short Card to the top of the pack. This automatically brings the spectator's card to the bottom where you can reveal it in any manner you wish.

THE SHORT CARD FORCE

As stated before, the "Forcing" of a card on an unsuspecting spectator is essential in many tricks. This means that not only must you have several methods at your disposal; you should also take advantage of any "special" device that can render forcing more effective. The "SHORT CARD" meets both of these qualifications, as it can be forced on a spectator almost automatically, leaving him totally unaware that the Force took place.

EFFECT

The magician gives a pack of cards a thorough shuffle and even hands it to a spectator so he can do the same. Then, gripping the pack firmly in his left hand, the magician riffles the outer end of the pack with his right fingers, telling the spectator to call "Stop!" while the riffle is in progress. Cutting the pack at that point, the magician extends the lower portion to the spectator, telling him to look at the card where he called "Stop." *When he does, the spectator will be looking at a card that was just "Forced" on him without him even realizing it!*

SECRET AND PREPARATION

The only requirements for this Force are an ordinary pack of cards and one SHORT CARD which matches the rest of the cards of the pack.

129

METHOD

(1) To prepare, place the Short Card somewhere near the center of the pack. (In the illustrations the Short Card is indicated by an "S.") Square up the deck and you are ready to begin.

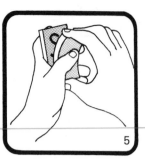

(5) When the spectator understands what he is to do, slowly start to riffle the end of the pack. TRY TO TIME THE RIFFLE SO YOU NEARLY REACH THE SHORT CARD JUST WHEN THE SPECTATOR IS ABOUT TO CALL "STOP."

(2) Hold the pack face down firmly in your left hand with the outer end of the pack extending half-way out of your hand.

(6) When the "Stop" call comes, *allow the Short Card AND ANY REMAINING CARDS BELOW IT to quickly riffle onto the lower packet of cards.* This should be done deliberately as if a few extra cards "just happened" to riffle after the spectator said "Stop."

(3) Move your right hand over the pack and grip it between your thumb— at the inner end — and your first and second fingers at the outer end towards the spectator.

(7) Divide the pack at this point and extend the *lower* packet toward the spectator. Instruct him to remove the top card and look at it. YOU HAVE NOW SUCCESSFULLY EXECUTED THE <u>SHORT CARD FORCE</u>. The "Forced" card can now be shuffled back into the pack and revealed in any manner that you wish.

(4) Explain that, as you riffle the end of the pack, the spectator is to call "Stop" at any time during the "riffle." Demonstrate this by riffling the end of the pack a few times.

COMMENTS AND SUGGESTIONS

Since you already know what card the spectator will take, you can use the "Force" for a prediction effect. Simply write the name of the Short Card on a slip of paper, fold it, and give it to someone beforehand, to be opened after the Force. You can also "reveal" the card by pretending to read the spectator's mind, or by producing a *duplicate* of the Forced card from some unexpected place.

Another way is to "discover" the card by bringing it to the top of the deck *after the cards have been thoroughly shuffled by the spectator.* Simply riffle the Short Card to the top of the deck and turn it over, showing it to be the spectator's card. Or, since you have the chosen card on top, you can reveal it in a variety of ways, described in other areas of the Course.

THE MYSTIC COUNTDOWN

Here is another baffling effect using the SHORT CARD. The result is gained so smoothly that you will have your audience puzzled from start to finish . . . and the routine can be repeated with equal impact. Try it a few times and you will probably make it a regular feature in your program.

EFFECT

After shuffling a pack of cards, the magician hands the deck to a spectator. The wizard tells him to start dealing cards, one at a time, from the top of the pack onto the table into a face-down pile. The spectator is to stop dealing wherever he wants, look at that card, replace it face down on the pile, and drop the rest of the pack on top. The magician then squares the pack and gives it a few cuts. He then uses the top card to flip over the card just below it — WHICH PROVES TO BE THE SPECTATOR'S CARD.

SECRET AND PREPARATION

The only items required for this mystery are an ordinary pack of cards with one SHORT CARD. To prepare, place the SHORT CARD on the bottom of the pack and place the deck in its box. (In the illustrations the SHORT CARD has been marked with an "S" and the selected card with an "X.") You are ready to begin.

A

METHOD

(1) Remove the pack from its box and shuffle the cards. Use the OVERHAND SLIP SHUFFLE to retain the SHORT CARD on the bottom of the pack.

(2) NOTE: As an alternate method *you can even have the spectator shuffle the cards himself.* After taking the pack back, riffle the SHORT CARD to the top of the pack. Then bring it to the bottom by executing the OVERHAND SHUFFLE — TOP CARD TO BOTTOM.

(3) With the SHORT CARD on the bottom of the pack, give the pack to a spectator. Instruct him to start dealing cards, one at a time, from the top of the deck in a pile on the table.

3

4

5

(4) Explain that he can stop dealing wherever he wants. (5) He is then to look at the top card of the "dealt" pile and remember it.

(6) After he looks at and remembers the card, tell him to return it to the top of the "dealt" pile and place the rest of the pack on top of the dealt cards, burying his card into the deck. UNKNOWN TO THE SPECTATOR, THIS PLACES THE BOTTOM CARD OF THE PACK (THE SHORT CARD) DIRECTLY ABOVE THE SELECTED CARD (X).

Short card

6

(7) After he has reassembled the pack, instruct him to give the pack as many <u>single</u> cuts as he wishes. *It is important that the spectator give the pack only <u>single</u> cuts so as not to separate the SHORT CARD and the selected card in the pack.*

(8) When the spectator is satisfied that the pack is thoroughly mixed, take the deck and give it a few more single cuts. Say, "Using my extra fine sense of touch, I can find your card merely by cutting the pack. Watch!" Suiting your action to your words, riffle the SHORT CARD to the top of the deck. THIS PLACES THE SELECTED CARD (X), WHICH IS DIRECTLY BENEATH THE SHORT CARD, <u>SECOND FROM THE TOP.</u>

8

(9)   Now, take the SHORT CARD from the top of the pack in your right hand. Then, using the SHORT CARD as a lever, turn over the <u>second</u> card which is the selected card (X), face up on top of the pack — as you say, "Here is your card."

COMMENTS AND SUGGESTIONS

Instead of placing the SHORT CARD on the bottom of the pack beforehand, you can easily get it there at any time during a series of card effects by cutting it to the top and shuffling it to the bottom using the OVERHAND SHUFFLE CONTROL — TOP CARD TO BOTTOM. You can keep it there with a "Table Shuffle" by simply releasing the bottom few cards first, as you riffle the ends of the two halves together. For a repeat, this trick is set up perfectly, truly a magician's dream! After flipping the chosen card face up on the pack, you are still holding the SHORT CARD. Simply slide it <u>underneath</u> the pack, where it becomes the bottom card . . . ready for a repeat of the "Mystic Countdown."

CUTTING THE ACES

People are always impressed by card tricks involving the four Aces, particularly when a performer shows his ability at finding an Ace in a pack that has been shuffled and cut. This ranks with the fabled feats of famous gamblers, yet you can accomplish the same effect with very little skill.

EFFECT

Without looking at the faces of the cards, you shuffle the pack and cut it repeatedly. In the course of the shuffling and cutting, you turn up an Ace and place it on the table. Continuing, as you shuffle and cut the cards, you find the three remaining Aces in the same baffling fashion.

SECRET AND PREPARATION

This is a perfect example of a trick demonstrating your ability to control the location of cards in a deck while it is being shuffled. *The success of this trick depends upon the use of a SHORT CARD.*

(A)   To prepare, place the Four Aces on top of the pack with the Short Card just above them, making the Short Card the top card of the pack. Now, place the pack back in the box and you're ready to begin. (In the illustrations, the Aces have been marked "1, 2, 3, and 4" and the Short Card is indicated by an "S.")

METHOD

(1)   Remove the pack from the box and start by giving it a regular Overhand Shuffle. *Be sure that the first batch of cards you shuffle from the deck consists of a dozen cards or more to retain your five card "set-up" in its original order.* Once this first batch of cards has been "shuffled off," continue shuffling the rest of the cards in the pack upon it.

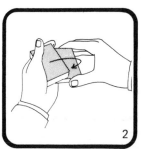

(2)   After the pack has been shuffled, cut about one third of the pack from the top of the deck to the bottom. You have now fairly shuffled and cut the pack leaving your set-up — the Four Aces and the Short Card — somewhere near the center of the pack in their original order.

(3) Square up the pack in your left hand. With your right thumb at the rear end of the pack, riffle the end of the pack from bottom to top until you "feel" the Short Card.

(7) Now with the left thumb, push the first Ace from the top of the pack face onto the table and replace the Short Card face down on top of the deck. *(This places the Short Card back on top of the three remaining Aces.)*

(4) Here you cut all the cards above the Short Card to the bottom of the pack, thus bringing your set up to the top.

(8) Square the pack and do the Overhand Shuffle, again making sure that the first batch you pull off contains the Short Card and the three Aces. Cut and riffle as you did before bringing the Short Card to the top and use it again to turn up the second Ace.

(5) Take the Short Card from the top of the deck with your right hand. Now with your left thumb, push the first Ace (1) a little to the right so that it protrudes about an inch off the right side of the pack.

(9) After dealing the second Ace face up on the table, replace the Short Card on the pack and repeat the same "shuffle, cut and riffle" routine, bringing up the third Ace.

(6) Using the Short Card as a lever, raise the right side of the first Ace, causing the Ace to hinge on its left edge. Continue rotating the Ace on edge with the Short Card until the first Ace is turned completely over (face up) on top of the deck.

(10) As the suspense increases, repeat the procedure with the fourth Ace and deal it on the table along side the other Aces and the effect is complete. You have cut all the Aces to the top of the pack!!!

GIANT CARDS

Giant Cards represent a comparatively new type of magic that has come into popularity. Since the cards are *four times* as large as ordinary playing cards, they have little in common where manipulation is concerned, and their added thickness makes the giants still more cumbersome to handle. However, they can be dealt face down or face up and shown fanwise like smaller cards, which makes them adaptable to certain tricks.

Giant Cards can also be identified by suit and value, so that the discovery of chosen cards in *giant* size can be worked in conjunction with cards from ordinary packs. Such tricks will be found in this section along with other effects of a more varied nature.

Most important is the use of Giant Cards when performing for larger audiences where smaller card effects would be less effective and those of the "card table" type would be lost entirely. The bigger the audience, the bigger the cards is the rule in this case, just as with any other magical appliances.

When working before smaller audiences, you can reserve a Giant Card trick for a "smash" ending to a regular card routine. Always, people are impressed by a climax that tells them that the show is over, and a Giant Card finish will fill that purpose perfectly.

THE BIGGER CARD TRICK

A bit of comedy usually adds spice to a mystery and this trick stands as a good example. By having it ready, you can inject it at a timely moment, dependent on the mood of your audience. It can also serve as a prelude to a more ambitious effect.

EFFECT

A card is selected and returned to the pack, which the magician shuffles and places in a paper bag. Showing his right hand empty, he thrusts it into the bag, announcing that he will find the chosen card by his "magic touch." He brings out a card, such as the Three of Clubs, and shows it triumphantly, only to have the chooser say it is the wrong card. The magician asks the spectator if his card was a "bigger" card, to which he replies, "Yes." The Wizard tries and fails again — the card is still not "big" enough. This third time the magician is successful and brings out the chosen card, the Nine of Hearts, which is not only "bigger" in value, but proves to be FOUR TIMES BIGGER in size, for it emerges in the form of a Giant Card!

SECRET AND PREPARATION

(A)   All that is required for this effect is a regular pack of cards, an ordinary paper bag, and one Giant Card. The Giant Card should be a Seven or higher in value.

(B)   Place the Giant Card (the Nine of Hearts in the illustrations) inside the paper bag.

(C) Then fold the bag flat and place it aside. Find the Nine of Hearts in the regular pack and place it in position in the pack ready for one of the card "forces" you have learned.

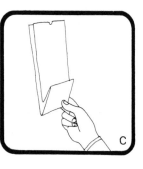

METHOD

(1) Begin by "forcing" the Nine of Hearts by any method you have learned. After the audience has seen the card, have it returned to the pack and have the pack thoroughly shuffled by a spectator. When he returns the deck to you, thumb through the deck and say something like "Well you have mixed them well....so thoroughly that I certainly couldn't find your card just by looking. *So I'll find it without looking at all!*" AS YOU RUN THROUGH THE DECK, PICK ANY TWO "SMALLER" VALUE CARDS AND PLACE THEM ON THE TOP OF THE PACK.

(4) Actually, grasp the top card of the deck (the Three of Clubs in the illustration). After a few seconds, remove the Three and show it to the audience triumphantly as you remark, "Here is your card." Of course, the answer will be that it is not. Act puzzled for a moment and then ask, "Was yours a bigger card?" The spectator will, of course, reply "Yes."

(2) Now pick up the folded bag and shake it open. Be careful to keep the Giant Card inside the bag as you do so. Place the deck into the bag. Do not disturb the cards as you put them in so that you will be able to find the two "small" cards on top of the deck.

(5) Place the Three aside and repeat the procedure, again removing the "smaller" second card from the top of the pack.

(6) Now even more puzzled, reach into the bag as you say "Even bigger?" Then remove the GIANT Nine of Hearts and ask, "Well, is this big enough?" The audience will not only be surprised that you have found the correct card, but also that it has grown to four times its normal size!

(3) Once the cards are in the bag, announce that you will attempt to find the selected card by your magic touch alone. With this, reach in the bag and pretend to grope around as if searching for the spectator's card.

COMMENTS AND SUGGESTIONS

Handle the paper bag casually as though it had nothing really important to do with the trick. Also, if you present the effect in a serious vein, as if you were honestly attempting to find the spectator's card through your sense of touch, it will turn the climax into a real comedy surprise when you produce the much "bigger" card.

SYMPATHETIC CARDS

Here is a really "magical" effect performed with any standard pack of cards and a "GIANT CARD." No special skill is required — *proper timing* is the important factor. Therefore, the trick should be carefully rehearsed until you are familiar with the entire procedure. After that, the presentation will become almost automatic. You, yourself, may be amazed by the way it will mystify your audiences — even at the closest range — for the trick depends upon a subtle principle that truly deceives the eye.

EFFECT

The magician displays an ordinary deck and asks a spectator to shuffle it until the cards are well mixed. Holding the pack face down in one hand and a Giant Card face down in the other hand, the wizard begins dealing cards, *one at a time,* onto the back of the Giant Card. He then, in turn, tosses the cards, *one at a time,* into a pile on the table.

This is continued, card by card, as the magician tells the spectator that he should give the order to "Stop!" *at any card he wishes.* When he does, the magician remarks what a "magical coincidence" it would be if *both* the Giant Card *and* the card from the pack at which the spectator stopped were *identical.* The magician then turns both cards face up — REVEALING THEM TO BE EXACTLY THE SAME!

SECRET AND PREPARATION

The only items needed for this effect are a GIANT CARD and an ordinary pack from which the "duplicate" of the GIANT CARD is removed in advance. To prepare, place the Giant Card face down *on top* of the regular-size "duplicate" card. Hold both cards in your right hand — with your fingers beneath holding the "duplicate" small card and your thumb on top of the Giant Card. (In the illustrations, the Giant Card and its "duplicate" are the *Ace of Hearts.* The "duplicate" regular-size Ace of Hearts is indicated with an "X.") You are now ready to begin.

METHOD

(1) Hand the pack to a spectator to shuffle. Pick up the Giant Card *and (secretly)* the "duplicate" regular card in your right hand. Hold the two cards face down above the table, as shown. Be careful not to show the face(s) of the card(s). *NOTE: For a clever method of pre-setting the Giant Card and its "duplicate" before the show — which makes the "pickup" of the two cards quite easy — please see COMMENTS AND SUGGESTIONS at the end of this trick.*

(2) After the spectator is satisfied that the cards are well mixed *and* you have the GIANT CARD and its "secret" smaller duplicate held firmly in your right hand, pick up the shuffled deck in your left hand. Hold the pack in "dealing position" as shown in Step 1. *NOTE: You may find it easier to position the shuffled pack in your left hand <u>first</u> — then pick up the Giant Card and its secret "duplicate." In that case, just reverse Steps 1 and 2. In any event, you should now be in "dealing position" ready for the next step.*

(3) Tell the audience that you are *not* going to show the face of the Giant Card. Explain that you are doing this for a special reason, since the object of the mystery is for the spectator to magically determine the *suit* and *value* of the Giant Card *without knowing it.*

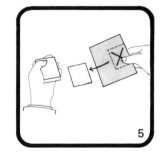

(4) Deal the top card from the pack in your left hand, face down, onto the back of the Giant Card as shown. (Just push the card from the top of the pack onto the back of the Giant Card with your left thumb.) (5) Pause a moment — and then *tilt* the Giant Card, allowing the smaller card to slide off the Giant Card and drop, *face down,* on the table.

(6) With your left hand, deal the next (top) card from the pack onto the back of the Giant Card *in exactly the same way.* After a brief pause, your right hand tilts the Giant Card, letting the smaller card slide off on top of the first card already on the table. Continue thumbing off cards, one by one, onto the back of the Giant Card, then let them slide onto the pile of cards on the table.

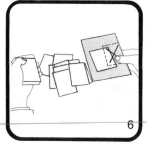

(7) Explain to the spectator that he is to say, "Stop!" *at any time as* you deal through the deck. *NOTE: Be careful that none of the regular cards turns face up as you slide them from the Giant Card onto the pile of cards on the table.*

(8) When the call comes — STOP! If you are in the middle of a "deal," or if you are sliding one of the regular cards onto the pile on the table, ask the spectator *which card* he is selecting — thereby indicating that you are giving him *every opportunity to make a "free choice."* Whatever his final decision, see that the "selected" card is positioned on the back of the Giant Card as shown in Step 6.

(9) *NOTE: Here is the situation at this point: The GIANT CARD is held in your right hand. It acts as a "tray" for the spectator's freely selected card which rests on the Giant Card's back. Unknown to the audience, with your right fingers, you are holding, UNDERNEATH the Giant Card, the secret "duplicate" regular card which matches the Giant Card.*

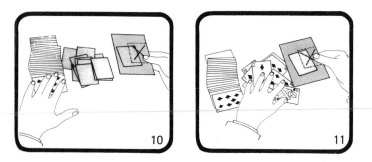

(10) Now spread the remainder of the cards which you are holding *in your left hand* FACE UP on the table with your left hand. As you spread the left-hand packet face up, remind the spectator that he could have selected *any of those cards.* (11) Now, pick up the pile of cards *already dealt,* and turn *them all* FACE UP. Casually spread them on the table as shown. State, "If the spectator had 'stopped' me sooner, he would have gotten *one of those.*"

(12) As you make the statement about the "already dealt" cards in Step 11, your left hand moves its fingers *beneath* the Giant Card. With your left fingers, hold the regular "duplicate" card against the bottom of the Giant Card. Your left thumb holds the spectator's "selected card" above. *This allows your right hand to release its grip on the Giant Card and the secret "duplicate" card.*

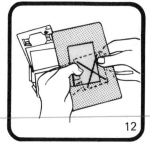

(13) Now, with the first finger of your right hand, point to the "selected" card lying *on top* of the Giant Card. Say, "Out of *all* the different cards in the pack, *this* is the card you chose." *NOTE: In transferring the Giant Card from your right hand to your left hand, you have subtly convinced the audience that all is "fair" — as both hands are obviously quite empty.*

(14) THE FOLLOWING THREE STEPS (14, 15, and 16) ARE THE MOST IMPORTANT AND DECEPTIVE PART OF THE ROUTINE — STUDY THEM CAREFULLY. Your right hand now returns to its former position so that the *fingers of your right hand* also hold the "duplicate" card under the Giant Card. Your left fingers now *release* their hold on the "duplicate" card — *but your left thumb continues to press against the spectator's "selected" card on top of the Giant Card as shown in Step 12.*

(15) You now begin THREE actions that take place *simultaneously:* FIRST, *both hands* begin tilting the *audience end* of the Giant Card upward; SECOND, at the same time, your *right fingers* begin to draw the secret "duplicate" card to the right, *off the face of the Giant Card;* THIRD, with your *left thumb,* retain the spectator's "selected" card *on top* of the Giant Card.

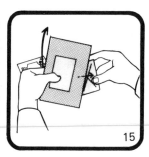

(16) Continue rotating the Giant Card so that the face of the Giant Card is toward the audience. *You secretly retain the spectator's "selected" card on top of the Giant Card with your left thumb. With your right fingers, draw the hidden "duplicate" card, face up, fully into view.* YOU HAVE NOW UNDETECTIBLY SWITCHED THE "SELECTED" CARD FOR THE SECRET "DUPLICATE" CARD. To the spectator, it will appear that you are merely turning his card *and* the Giant Card face up at the same time. *This is a very deceptive and totally convincing move.*

(17) *NOTE: At this point, the spectator's "freely selected" card is hidden UNDER the face-up Giant Card. The "duplicate" regular card, which matches the Giant Card, is face up in your right hand. TO YOUR AUDIENCE, IT WILL APPEAR AS THOUGH THE "DUPLICATE" CARD CAME OFF THE <u>BACK</u> OF THE GIANT CARD INSTEAD OF FROM <u>BELOW</u>.*

(19) Drop the "duplicate" regular card face up on the Giant Card — PROVING THAT THE SPECTATOR HAS MIRACULOUSLY PICKED THE EXACT DUPLICATE OF THE GIANT CARD FROM THE PACK!

(18) Now, casually place the Giant Card *face up on the face-up pile of cards on the table.* THE HIDDEN "SELECTED" CARD FALLS UNNOTICED BENEATH THE GIANT CARD AND BECOMES ANOTHER OF THE MISCELLANEOUS FACE-UP CARDS IN THE PILE OF CARDS ON THE TABLE.

(20) The trick is now over. However, at this point you can add a subtle touch by picking up the Giant Card and its "duplicate" from the table and handing them to the spectator. As you hand them to him, *turn both cards over,* showing the backs to be unprepared. The original "selected" card lies forgotten in the mass of cards on the table.

IMPORTANT NOTE: This entire, very clever effect hinges upon the "Secret Move" (Steps 14, 15, and 16). This is when you secretly "switch" the spectator's freely "selected" card for the "duplicate" card under the Giant Card. Here is the sequence *as seen by the spectators:*

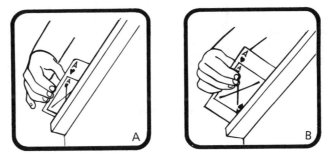

(21) As described in Step 14, your right hand moves to the Giant Card and your right fingers grasp the secret "duplicate" card and press it against the bottom of the Giant Card. Then, both hands start to rotate the Giant Card face up *toward the spectator.* (22) Your right fingers begin to slide the "duplicate" card off the face of the Giant Card. Your left thumb maintains its pressure on the selected card on top of the Giant Card. (23) The selected card is now hidden by the Giant Card as your right hand continues sliding the "duplicate" card to your right. (24) Your left hand drops the Giant Card and the selected card face up on the pile of face-up cards already on the table. Your right hand displays the "duplicate" small card *as if it were the freely "selected" card.*

COMMENTS AND SUGGESTIONS

If you wish to perform this effect *during* your card routine, rather than at the start, you can use the following clever set-up: (A) Place the GIANT CARD *and* its regular "duplicate" on the edge of the table so that they *both* overlap the edge. You may then present any card effects which do not involve the "duplicate" card. When you are ready to present the SYMPATHETIC CARDS . . . (B) . . . reach over with your right hand and pick up the Giant Card *and the secret "duplicate"* card as shown. You are now all set to present this extremely clever close-up mystery. If more convenient, you may also place the Giant Card and the secret "duplicate" card on a book, ashtray, or some other handy object that is already on the table, rather than placing the two cards on the edge of the table. Just be sure that *both* the Giant Card *and* the secret "duplicate" can be easily picked up at the same time.

IMPORTANT NOTE: In the "switch" of the "duplicate" for the spectator's card, *timing is the key factor.* For best results, you should *practice in front of a mirror.* The "draw-off" should begin as the edge of the Giant Card is level with the eyes of the spectators. That is the time when the *ends* of ALL THREE CARDS are toward the spectators. At that instant, the spectators lose sight of the BACKS *before* they see the FACES. When your right hand draws the card to the right, as it comes into view, LOOK AT IT. *All of the eyes of the audience will follow* — never suspecting that the card they are watching came from the FRONT and not the BACK of the Giant Card. This is another excellent example of *MISDIRECTION.*

THE APPLAUSE CARD

This is a surprise ending for a card routine in which a clever trick is followed by a comedy gag. Audiences appreciate such touches and, even if you have patterned your program along serious lines, it is often good to conclude your show with a "magical" comedy closing effect such as this one.

EFFECT

A spectator selects a card and returns it to the pack, which is thoroughly shuffled. The magician announces that he intends to produce the chosen card by using his "sense of touch" alone, as he places the pack in his inside coat pocket. After several "wrong" cards are removed, the magician reaches into his pocket and brings out the spectator's card, but it is now a giant size! When the audience applauds, a banner drops from beneath the big card saying, "THANK YOU."

SECRET AND PREPARATION

(A) The props needed for this effect are a deck of cards, a jumbo card and a piece of light colored paper approximately two feet long and three inches wide. With a heavy marking pen, print the words THANK YOU or some other appropriate phrase such as GOOD BYE, or APPLAUSE, down the length of the paper, allowing enough blank space (about half the length of the jumbo card) at the top of the piece of paper before beginning your lettering. Then, pleat the strip of paper, "accordian fashion" as shown.

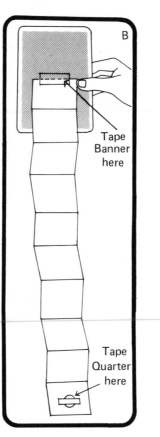

Tape Banner here

Tape Quarter here

(B) Attach the top of the banner to the center of the back of a giant card, in this case the Four of Diamonds, with a piece of tape as shown. Also, tape a quarter to the "unlettered" side of the banner near the very bottom. This will act as a weight and cause the banner to open quickly.

(C) This done, fold the banner and hold the pleated banner against the back of the giant card. Place the giant card in your inside coat pocket with the face side of the card toward the audience. You are now ready.

METHOD

(1) From a regular size pack of cards, force the Four of Diamonds on the spectator using any of the forcing methods previously explained. After the card is noted by the spectator and shown to the rest of the audience (but, of course, not to you), let him replace the card anywhere in the deck and have any member of the audience thoroughly shuffle the pack.

(2) Ask the spectator if he is satisfied that his card is lost in the shuffled deck and you could not possibly know where it is (as, indeed you do not!). If he wishes, he may even shuffle the deck again. When he is completely satisfied, state that your "super sensitive" fingers will now find his card while the deck is completely hidden from view in your pocket. Place the deck in the same inside coat pocket that contains the giant card.

(3) NOTE: When you take the shuffled deck back from the spectator, casually look at the first two cards on the face of deck to make sure that neither is the Four of Diamonds. If either of them is the Four, just remove the cards from the top of the deck instead of the face of the deck in Step 4.

(4) Reach into your pocket and remove one of the regular cards that you know is NOT the Four of Diamonds. Display the card triumphantly and ask him if you are correct. The spectator will reply, "No." Say that this is an extremely difficult trick and you will try again. Remove the second card, and, with a bit less confidence, ask the spectator if this is the one. Again the response is "No."

(5) You now become even more embarrassed....you might say something like, "I hope none of you have any place you were planning to be soon as we have fifty cards left to go." Then, ask the spectator to help by concentrating on his card. "Just make a BIG mental picture of it." Reach into your pocket and get ready to remove the GIANT CARD. Be sure to hold the pleated banner with your thumb so that it does not unfold.

(6) Ask him to name his card out loud and AT THE SAME TIME remove the giant card.

(7) As you show the huge Four of Diamonds and the spectator acknowledges that you have at last found his card, say something like, "Well, I see you really did make a BIG mental picture!"

(8) The unexpected appearance of the giant card will always get a laugh and applause. As the spectators react to this first surprise, draw back your right thumb and allow the banner to unfold to reveal your, "THANK YOU" message. This is sure to get an even greater response from your audience.

COMMENTS AND SUGGESTIONS

This particular card trick can be seen by a large group of a hundred or more people, particularly if you leave the stage and go into the audience to have the card selected. Then have the spectator show the card to the rest of the audience while your back is turned. Have him replace the card in the deck and return to the stage. If more convenient, you may also have a spectator join you on the stage for the selection of the card and the follow-up comedy "discovery." This is a very clever comedy effect as well as good magic and makes an excellent closing number for your show.

DOUBLE APPLAUSE CARD

It is possible to tape two or more pleated banners on the same Giant Card for a repeated comedy effect. For instance, the first banner can say "THANK YOU" and the second "BOTH OF YOU" — or for a birthday party, "THANK YOU" and then "HAPPY BIRTHDAY MARY," etc. After the first banner falls, simply tear it off and set it aside still keeping the second banner in place with your thumb. Then move your thumb allowing the second banner to fall for the double-barreled impact. When using more than one banner, tape them directly above one another so you are able to hold them both in position with your thumb and release them one at a time. You can also print the second message on the back of the banner. Then just turn the card around after the audience reads the "front side" of the banner. In this case make the banner "double" to hide the quarter you are using as a weight. Audiences always enjoy clever bits of comedy along with their magic and the Applause Card is excellent for this type of effect.

A GIANT MISTAKE — FIRST VERSION

Comedy effects add a light touch to a card routine, so it is always wise to have a few ready for the right occasion. Here is one that should bring a "big" laugh as it takes a "big" card to do it.

EFFECT

This is similar to the "Applause Card" trick except that it has a different comedy ending. A spectator selects a card, remembers it, and returns it to the pack. The magician states that he will find the selected card by his "sense of touch" alone and places the deck in his inside coat pocket. The wizard reaches into his pocket and draws out several "wrong" cards (just as in the "Applause Card" trick). In desperation, he asks the spectator to "form a BIG picture of the card in your mind"....the magician then reaches into his pocket and starts to draw out a "giant" Seven of Spades! Pausing with just the top half of the large card in view, the magician asks, "Was this your card?" The spectator replies "No," stating that he took the FIVE of Spades. The magician responds, "Then this IS your card" and draws the Seven completely from his pocket, showing it to be only a *part* of the jumbo Seven of Spades, bearing ONLY FIVE SPOTS!

SECRET AND PREPARATION

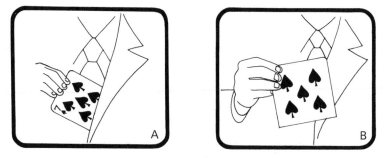

The only requirements for this effect are a regular pack of cards and one Giant Card.

To prepare, cut off a portion of the Giant Card, reducing its value from that shown on the card to the "spot" value of the card you will later "Force" on the spectator. In the illustrations, the Seven of Spades has been cut to show FIVE spots instead of SEVEN. Other combinations that make an effective change are: A SIX-spot changed to a FOUR-spot, a NINE changed to a SEVEN, a TEN changed to a FIVE, a THREE changed to a TWO, etc. No matter what combination you choose, remove from the regular pack of cards the card that matches the "lowered" value of your prepared Giant Card. Place this card in the position in the deck for your favorite "Force." Put the "cut" Giant Card in your inside coat pocket and you're ready.

METHOD

The working of the trick is exactly the same as the "Applause Card" trick....except that you use the comedy "cut" card instead of the Applause Card.

COMMENTS AND SUGGESTIONS

When you first start to show the "top" part of the Giant Card coming from your pocket, hold the card as shown in Illustration A. Then when you remove the card completely from your coat, cover the index number of the card with the tips of your fingers as in Illustration B so that only the spots on the face of the card are visible. Then, point to the spots on the card and count them out loud, proving that you have humorously "discovered" the spectator's card!

A GIANT MISTAKE — SECOND VERSION

Here is another clever method of presenting this effect.

METHOD

From the regular pack of cards, "Force" the card that matches the prepared jumbo card using your favorite method. Ask the spectator to show the card to all the members of the audience and then to return the card to the pack....then have him thoroughly shuffle the cards so that there is no chance for you to know the location of his card in the pack. Now, (instead of placing the deck in your pocket) explain that you will attempt to find the spectator's card by EXTRA-SENSORY PERCEPTION, as he concentrates upon it. As you say this, start running through the pack face up as if looking for the spectator's selection. Then, after several wrong guesses, confess that you seem to be having some trouble reading the spectator's mind. Explain that whenever this happens, you always have "THE MAGICIAN'S SPECIAL *WHAT-TO-DO-IF-A-TRICK-GOES-WRONG* TRICK." With that, reach into your inside coat pocket and triumphantly start to remove the jumbo Seven from your coat — but withdraw the card so that only *half* of the card is visible.

Ask, "Is THIS the card on which you are concentrating?" Of course, the answer will be "No." Ask the spectator what the card was that he selected and, when the answer comes, remove the jumbo card completely from your coat pocket as you say, "Then this IS your card."

COMMENTS AND SUGGESTIONS

You can also do a clever impromptu version of this comedy effect on a small scale by simply carrying the cut portion of a normal sized card taken from an old pack. In this version, the "half card" can be brought from your shirt pocket, the outside pocket of your coat or even your wallet.

A GIANT MYSTERY

Here is a mystery that goes well beyond the scope of many card effects; therefore, you may wish to use it as a *special feature,* possibly the finale of your routine. You could also use it as an encore, on the theory that when people are eager for you to shown them "one more trick," it should not only be something *different,* but also something *big.* This striking effect meets both those qualifications.

EFFECT

Starting in a conventional manner, the magician has a spectator select a card from the pack, remember it, and return it. After the pack is thoroughly shuffled, the magician decides to make the card reveal itself in a very unusual way. For this purpose, he uses two large pieces of stiff cardboard. He shows the boards on both sides, finally placing them together and resting them on the table. The magician explains that he will make the chosen card appear *between* the panels. After some byplay, he separates the two panels only to find that the card has failed to materialize. So, again he shows the two boards and places them together for another try. This time, he succeeds "in a big way" — for when the boards are separated, a GIANT CARD, a duplicate of the very card the spectator selected, is found between them!

SECRET AND PREPARATION

Required for this effect are a regular deck of cards; two pieces of stiff cardboard or artist's construction board, approximately eight inches by ten inches; and a Giant Card.

(A) On one of the cardboard squares, attach a Giant Card with glue, Double Stick tape, or a "Magic Loop." For clarity, *the prepared board is a DARKER color than the unprepared board in the illustrations.* We will call the side of the prepared board that has the Giant Card attached to it, the "face" of the prepared board.

(B) To set up, place the regular board on top of the "face-up" prepared board with the Giant Card side of the prepared board "face up." The regular board should be "angled" slightly to the right so that the four corners of the prepared board show beneath it. Now place the two boards on your table in this position.

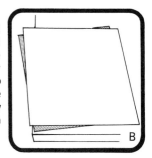

(C) From a regular pack of cards, remove the card that matches the Giant Card (in this case the Ten of Hearts) and place it at the position in the deck ready for your favorite "Force." Now place the deck in its box, and you are ready to begin.

METHOD

(1) Remove the pack of cards from its box and "force" the Ten of Hearts on a spectator using any of the methods you have learned. Tell the spectator to remember the card, and after he has returned it to the pack, he is to shuffle the deck until the cards are thoroughly mixed.

(7) Your left fingers grip the prepared board as both hands begin to pull the boards apart as shown.

(2) Place the pack aside and pick up the two cardboard panels in your left hand, thumb on top, fingers beneath, saying, "I have here two pieces of cardboard."

(8) When the two boards are completely apart . . .

(3) As you say this, grasp the two boards in your right hand – fingers on top, thumb beneath – and *turn both cards over,* toward the audience.

(9) . . . TURN THE REGULAR BOARD (IN YOUR RIGHT HAND) OVER – toward yourself – to show the other side of the board saying, "As you can see, they are the same on both sides."

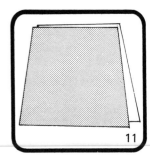

(4) THE PREPARED BOARD IS NOW ON TOP "FACE DOWN."

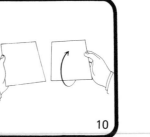

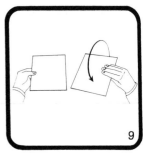

(10) With that, TURN THE RIGHT HAND "REGULAR" BOARD BACK TO ITS ORIGINAL POSITION. SLIDE THE TWO BOARDS TOGETHER PLACING THE PREPARED BOARD ON TOP OF THE REGULAR BOARD and (11) put the boards on the table.

(5) Without hesitation, pull the two boards apart, *keeping the top prepared board in your right hand and the regular board in your left hand.*

(12) *NOTE: As you execute this series of movements, the audience will believe they have seen all sides of both panels of cardboard and will be convinced that everything is on the level.*

(6) As soon as the two boards are apart, *place the regular board on top of the prepared board and SLIDE IT TO THE RIGHT COMPLETELY ACROSS THE TOP OF THE PREPARED BOARD into the tips of your right fingers.*

(13) Pick up the pack of cards and state that you will attempt to make the chosen card appear between the two boards. Toss the pack face down on top of the boards as if to cause the selected card to "penetrate" between them.

(14) Place the deck aside and pick up both boards. Separate them so that the *regular* board is in your left hand and the *prepared* board is in your right. Since no card is found between the boards, tell your audience that you must have made a "minor" error, so you will attempt the feat once more.

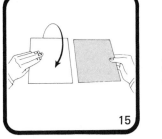

(18) This time, however, instead of immediately placing them on the table, grasp the boards in your right hand, fingers on top and thumb below, and TURN BOTH BOARDS OVER. THIS PLACES THE PREPARED BOARD ON THE BOTTOM WITH THE REGULAR BOARD ON TOP HIDING THE NOW "FACE-UP" TEN OF HEARTS.

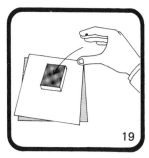

(15) As you make this remark, TURN THE LEFT-HAND PANEL OVER TOWARD YOURSELF showing the other side of the regular board as if hoping to find the selected card there.

(19) Place both boards on the table and pick up the deck. Explain that you expect the trick to "work" this time as you toss the cards onto the boards.

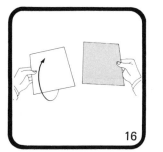

(20) Place the pack aside, and pick up the boards. Separate them to reveal the Giant Ten of Hearts as you say something like, "When this trick works – it works in a big way!"

(16) Turn the left-hand panel back over to its original position.
(17) NOW, SLIDE THE TWO BOARDS TOGETHER. PLACE THE PREPARED BOARD ON TOP OF THE REGULAR BOARD.

COMMENTS AND SUGGESTIONS

The beauty of this effect lies in its certainty. This is another reason why it is a good effect to use as a *finish* or an *encore*. IT CANNOT FAIL IF YOU REHEARSE IT TO THE POINT WHERE EVERY MOVE IS SECOND NATURE. The smoother the routine, the more deceptive it becomes. Simply follow the steps as described and the big climax will take care of itself automatically.

SPECIAL CARD TRICKS

Certain card tricks can be classified as "special" because they depend on methods or procedures that are somewhat unusual. Since they belong in no other category, they deserve one of their own and the term "Special" most adequately defines it.

In a sense, these are advanced card tricks — not necessarily because they are difficult to perform — but because they are the type that a performer is apt to add to his program *after* he has mastered tricks of a more general nature. So test these "specials" by incorporating them into your regular program, one by one, and see for yourself how effective they are in enhancing the overall variety of your card mysteries.

SELF-REVERSING PACK

EFFECT

The magician shows an ordinary pack and begins to demonstrate various ways used to shuffle cards. Finally, taking the pack in both hands, he gives it a peculiar shuffle by repeatedly mixing batches of *face-up* cards with *face-down* cards until the whole pack is a hopeless jumble. Then, giving the pack a single tap, he spreads the cards on the table and shows that the entire pack has regained its normal order with every card in the deck in its original face-down position.

METHOD

(1) Begin by demonstrating various different shuffles used with a pack of cards, such as Overhand Shuffle, Hindu Shuffle, Riffle Shuffle, etc.

(2) Square the pack and hold it face down in your right hand with your thumb on top. Slide a small batch of cards from the top of the deck into your left fingers, which grip them as shown.

(3) Now turn your left hand over, so that its cards are face up. Then your right thumb slides another batch of face-down cards from the TOP of the pack BENEATH the face-up cards in the left hand.

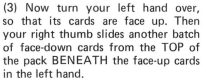

(4) The left hand turns over again *retaining its grip on both of the packets that have been slid off.* The right thumb then pushes more cards from the TOP of the deck to the left, so that the left hand (now thumb upward) can use its fingers to take these along BENEATH its group.

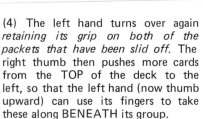

(5) This process of sliding batches of cards from the TOP of the pack to the left BENEATH the cards held in the left hand continues as the left hand alternately turns over to receive some face up and some face down. This is repeated until all the cards in the right hand have been transferred to the left.

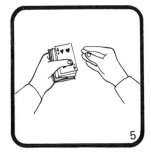

(6) *NOTE: Actually, instead of mixing the pack, YOU ARE DIVIDING IT INTO TWO SECTIONS, BACK TO BACK. The face-up cards are never really intermingled with the face-down cards, although to the spectators it appears that is the case.*

(7) Square the pack, remarking something like "The cards are now hopelessly mixed, with batches of face-down cards among the face-up cards." To further demonstrate the "mixed up" nature of the deck, cut DEEP in the pack and turn your right hand palm upward stating: "Here you see some cards back to face—" as you show the *face* of the card on the right-hand packet and the *back* of the card on the left-hand packet.

(8) Now reassemble the two halves and cut the pack again; but this time you cut NEAR THE TOP of the pack. Turn the right hand palm upward adding, "And here are cards that happen to be face to back." Show as in Step 7, but since you now are in the top half of the pack, the right-hand packet will show a *back* while the left packet will show a *face*.

(9) Again reassemble the pack and cut it once more. This time cutting at the spot WHERE THE TWO GROUPS MEET BACK TO BACK. You will find this easy to do. Because of the natural bend in a deck of cards, when a portion of the deck is reversed on itself, it leaves a definite "break" between the two sections....making it very simple to find. When you locate the spot where the halves meet, separate the two sections and TURN THE RIGHT HAND PALM UPWARD, saying, "And here are some others that are back to back."

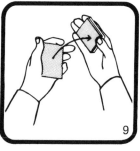

(10) *Now, instead of turning the right hand palm downward to replace the packet the way it was, REASSEMBLE THE PACK LEAVING THE RIGHT-HAND PACKET PALM UPWARD. Just slide the right-hand packet on top of the left-hand packet. By this maneuver you have turned the upper half (the face-up cards) face down on the rest of the face-down pack. ALL OF THE CARDS ARE NOW FACE DOWN.*

(11) Holding the pack in your left hand say, "Now for some real magic; One little tap" – tap the pack with your right forefinger – "and all those mixed up cards turn *face down,* as they were originally–" Spread the pack face down on the table to show ALL BACKS; your "magic tap" worked!

COMMENTS AND SUGGESTIONS

No real skill is required for this effect, as the "sloppier" the shuffle looks, the better. You should practice it, though, in order to do it rapidly, thus convincing the audience that you have really mixed face-up cards with face-down cards all through the pack. Also, your rapid action will be hard to follow, so if a spectator tries to duplicate your shuffle, he will get the cards really mixed.

SELF-REVERSING PACK — OUTDONE

EFFECT

A card is selected, noted and returned to the pack which is then shuffled by the magician in an apparently ordinary manner. Then, holding the deck in both hands, the magician gives the pack a very peculiar "slip-slop" shuffle, carelessly mixing *face-up* cards with *face-down* cards in a hopeless jumble. Then, with the aid of a single "magic" tap, the pack is spread on the table showing that all the cards in the deck have turned face down, with one exception....THE CHOSEN CARD IS FACE UP IN THE CENTER OF THE PACK!

METHOD

(1) Using methods you have learned, have the selected card (in the illustration, the Five of Hearts) returned to the deck and control it to the bottom of the pack. This can be done effectively by bringing the card to the top of the pack using the "Hindu Shuffle Pick-Up Control." From there it can be brought to the bottom by the "Overhand Shuffle, Top Card to Bottom."

(2) Another neat way is to have the card returned to the pack in the course of the "Hindu Shuffle." As the card is replaced, you "glimpse" the bottom card (Hindu Glimpse) which then becomes your "key." Give the pack a few single cuts, apparently "losing" the card completely. Now look through the pack and say you will try to find the chosen card . . . which you *actually do,* thanks to the *"key."*

(3) Run through the deck, holding the cards so that only you can see their faces. When you come to the chosen card, shake your hand and say that you just can't find it—so you will do another trick instead. Tell the spectator to remember his card anyway, as you may be able to locate it later on. With that, you cut the pack, bringing his Five of Hearts to the top of the face-up pack. Now turn the pack over so it is the bottom card of the face-down pack.

(4) *NOTE: Whichever method you use, be careful when you turn the pack face down, so that no one sees that the chosen card (the Five of Hearts) is on the bottom; you are ready to proceed with the "Self-Reversal."*

(5) With the chosen card at the bottom of the pack, begin the "slip-slop" shuffle, repeatedly sliding off batches of cards (some face up, some face down) from the left hand into the right hand, as already described in the Self-Reversing Pack.

(6) The slip-slop shuffle is continued until only a few cards remain in your right hand. Then, when the LEFT HAND is in its THUMB DOWNWARD position, the right thumb pushes THE CARDS REMAINING IN THE RIGHT HAND onto the bottom of the pack EXCEPT THE BOTTOM "SELECTED" CARD (indicated by the "X"), which is still held in the right hand.

(7) After the left hand turns over (thumb upward) *the right hand places its single card (the chosen "X" card) ON TOP OF THE PACK* — beneath the left thumb, as though to complete the hit-or-miss shuffle, which now looks "sloppy" indeed.

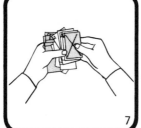
7

(9) Then, with the last cut, repeat the procedure where you divide the pack between the back-to-back sections and reassemble the deck. *All the cards in the pack will now be face down except for the chosen Five of Hearts (X), which is face up in the center of the pack.*

9

(8) Square the deck, remarking that the cards are hopelessly mixed, as you proceed to cut the pack (once near the top and once near the bottom) to show how some cards are "face to back" and some "back to face," as described in the Self Reversing Pack.

8

(10) Immediately spread the pack face down on the table, showing all backs except for the single face-up Five of Hearts in the middle!

10

GRANT'S SUPERIOR CARD TRICK

Here is a triple mystery created by "Gen" Grant, whose ingenious card effects are becoming classics in their own right. In this particular effect, the magician starts by pretending to show the spectators how a trick is done, which is an excellent way of misleading them from the *real* secret. From there, the trick builds to the *TRIPLE CLIMAX*. This trick should usually be reserved for a spectator who has some small knowledge of magic, and perhaps is aware of the "key" card principle. In this case, "a little knowledge" turns out to be a very "baffling" thing.

EFFECT

The magician has a spectator select a card and replace it in the pack. The magician then shows the audience how easily a "selected" card can be found by simply noting the card above it and watching for that card to appear when the pack is dealt. Proceeding along that line, the magician deals the *chosen* card face down to the spectator, then deals an *indifferent* card to another person, and keeps the *"key"* card for himself. But when the faces of the three cards are shown, ALL HAVE MAGICALLY CHANGED PLACES!

SECRET AND PREPARATION

(A) The only special item needed is an extra card with the same back design as the pack that you intend to use. This extra card is a DUPLICATE of a card already in the pack with the same color back and back design. Assuming that the *duplicate* card is a Four of Diamonds, remove the *regular* Four of Diamonds from the pack and place *both* cards on the bottom of the deck. In the illustrations, we will call the bottom Four "A" and the next Four "B."

A

(B) Also remove *any* indifferent card from the deck. (For the illustrations we will use the Ace of Hearts.) Place it *in your shirt pocket,* WITH ITS BACK TOWARD THE AUDIENCE. You do not even have to know the name of this odd card.

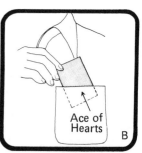
B

METHOD

(1) To begin, spread the pack face down and ask a spectator to take a card, telling him that you will "teach" him how to do a trick. (In the illustrations, the selected card is marked with an "X," and we will assume that it is the Six of Spades.)

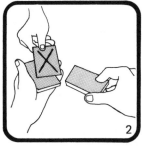

(2) While the spectator is looking at his card, square the pack and begin a regular HINDU SHUFFLE by drawing off half the pack in your left hand. Tell the spectator to replace his card (X) on that half of the pack.

(3) Now, deliberately turn the right hand packet *face up,* SHOWING THE FOUR OF DIAMONDS (A) on the bottom of that packet. Say, "All you have to do in order to find any selected card is secretly note the bottom card of the upper packet before you place it on top of the selected card (X). The Four of Diamonds will be my secret "locator" card in this trick."

(4) Place the right-hand packet face down upon the left-hand packet. Call to the audience's attention that this places the "locator" card (A) next to the "spectator's" card (X). Remind the viewers that your "locator" card is the Four of Diamonds and tell them to watch for it as you deal the cards.

(5) Holding the pack in your left hand, begin dealing cards one at a time, (6) face up on the table, placing each card on the one before. You can do this rapidly at first . . .

(7) . . . then, *slow down as you near the center of the pack,* and continue dealing until you reach the FIRST Four of Diamonds (B). The other DUPLICATE Four (A) is just below it, *the top card of the packet you hold in your left hand.*

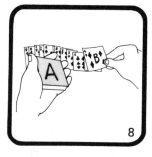

(8) When you turn over the FIRST Four of Diamonds (B), deal it on the row of face up cards, saying, "That's *my* locator card, the Four of Diamonds, which means *your* card is next."

(9) *NOTE: UNKNOWN TO THE SPECTATOR, THE "NEXT" CARD IS THE DUPLICATE FOUR OF DIAMONDS (A), WHICH HE NATURALLY ASSUMES TO BE HIS CHOSEN CARD (X), SINCE HE SAW YOU PLACE THE FOUR OF DIAMONDS JUST ABOVE IT.*

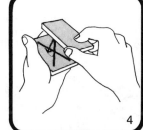

(10) Deal the top card (A) on the table in front of the spectator saying, "There is *your* card, just below the Four of Diamonds, so I want you to keep *your* hand on it." *HE DOES, NEVER SUSPECTING THAT INSTEAD OF HIS CARD (X) HE HAS THE DUPLICATE FOUR OF DIAMONDS (A).*

(11) Now, turn to *another* person and deal the *next card* (X) face down on the table in front of him. Tell him to put his hand on it. State that since NO ONE knows what this card is, you will call it the *"mystery card."* ACTUALLY, IT IS THE CARD CHOSEN BY THE FIRST SPECTATOR, THE SIX OF SPADES (X).

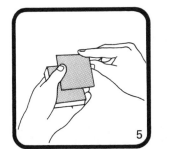

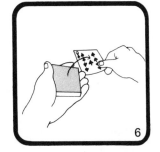

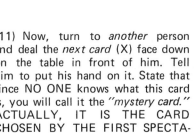

(12) Say to the first spectator, "You now have YOUR CARD, which YOU ALONE know." Turn to the second person and add, "And you have the MYSTERY CARD, which NOBODY KNOWS." Then, pick up the face-up Four of Diamonds (B) from the row saying, "Since EVERYBODY knows MY CARD, I'll put it in my pocket."

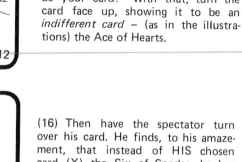

(15) "Wait! This isn't my card!" Turn to the first spectator and add, "It must be your card!" With that, turn the card face up, showing it to be an *indifferent card* – (as in the illustrations) the Ace of Hearts.

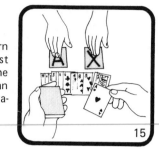

(13) With that, turn the back of *your* Four toward the spectators and slide it into your shirt pocket with your right hand.

(16) Then have the spectator turn over his card. He finds, to his amazement, that instead of HIS chosen card (X) the Six of Spades, he has YOUR "locator" card, the Four of Diamonds (A). Say, "Why, that's my card! What was your card?"

(14) IN THE SAME MOVE, grip the indifferent card that you placed there beforehand and bring it out IMMEDIATELY. Glance at it with a puzzled frown and say,

(17) The spectator will answer, "The Six of Spades." With that, turn to the *second* person and say, "Let's see your MYSTERY card that NOBODY knows!" He turns it over, revealing the *first* spectator's chosen card, the Six of Spades (X). THIS IS THE CARD WHOSE NAME THE FIRST SPECTATOR HAS JUST REVEALED FOR THE FIRST TIME ... WHICH, SO FAR AS HE KNEW, WAS KNOWN ONLY TO HIM ... and the climax is complete.

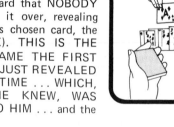

COMMENTS AND SUGGESTIONS

This is not *really* a three-way change, because only *two* cards, the one chosen by the first spectator and the card you showed as your "locator," *actually change places*. The fact that the second person's *"mystery card"* is missing and you come up with the *odd* card is sufficient to make it look like a magical "round robin."

Revealing the indifferent card IMMEDIATELY is very important because *before suspicion can be aroused,* you spring the twin surprises of the "locator" card *and* the selected card, both showing up where they don't belong. The cleverest part is that your duplicate "locator" (B), Four of Diamonds, is now safely hidden in your shirt pocket, leaving only a complete pack which can be examined by the spectators, enabling you to proceed with whatever other tricks you wish.

FLOURISHES

Fancy flourishes with cards date far back to the self-styled "Kard Kings" of the vaudeville era. Houdini himself had lithographs showing him performing a myriad of masterful card flourishes.

One thing is certain, card flourishes are sure to impress your audience. Whatever practice you give to such manipulations is time well spent. Your audience will recognize your skill and respect it.

THE MORE YOU PRACTICE THEM, THE MORE YOUR CARD WORK WILL IMPROVE IN GENERAL, MAKING YOUR ENTIRE PERFORMANCE MORE EFFECTIVE.

ONE-HAND CUT — BASIC METHOD

To many people, sign of a real card expert is the ability to "cut" a pack of cards using only one hand. It appears difficult, but it's really much easier than it looks. Try it and you'll see!

METHOD

(1) Hold the pack between the tips of your thumb and fingers as shown. Your first finger and little finger are at the opposite ends of the pack. Your other fingers and thumb are at the sides as shown. Be sure your thumb and fingers point *almost straight up.* Also, hold the deck at the *tips* of your fingers to form a deep "well" between the deck and the palm of your hand.

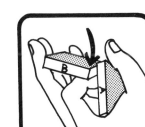

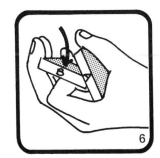

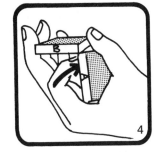

(2) To begin, bend your thumb just enough to let the *lower half* (which we will call Packet A) of the deck drop into the palm of your cupped hand. The upper half remains held between the tips of your thumb and your two middle fingers. (We will call this Packet B.) Your little finger will help to keep the cards from sliding out of your hand.

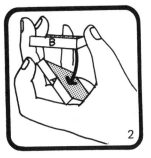

(5) Now, gently extend your fingers just enough to allow the edges of the two halves to clear so that your thumb releases Packet B which drops on top of your curled first finger. (6) By curling your first finger lower into your hand, Packet B will come down with it. *Packet B now becomes the lower half.*

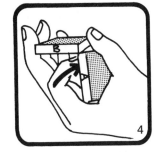

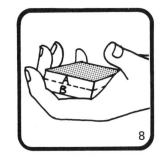

(3) Bring your first finger below the lower half, Packet A, and push the packet upward, sliding it along the bottom card of the upper half, Packet B. (4) Continue pushing the edge of the lower half, Packet A, *all the way up* to your thumb as shown.

(7) Slowly begin closing up your hand — bringing both halves together — with Packet A *on top* of Packet B. (8) Extend your first finger around the end of the pack, squaring the halves into place. YOU HAVE JUST DONE A ONE-HAND CUT!

ALL OF THE ILLUSTRATIONS ARE FROM THE AUDIENCE POINT OF VIEW WITH THE DECK HELD IN THE LEFT HAND.

COMMENTS AND SUGGESTIONS

Although this "Flourish" appears quite difficult, once you take the deck in your hand and follow the steps as shown in the pictures, you will find the ONE-HAND CUT quite easy to do. It is best, particularly when first learning, to use the narrow, Bridge-size cards rather than the wider Poker-size. After you have mastered the sleight, you may wish to try it with the larger cards. You can also then begin to practice the variations that follow.

ONE-HAND CUT — FIRST VARIATION

This is the first of two variations of the "ONE-HAND CUT — BASIC METHOD" enabling you to display your dexterity while also serving as a step toward other card manipulations involving the same basic sleight.

EFFECT

Holding a pack of cards in one hand, the magician starts a simple ONE-HAND CUT, but pauses during the early stage to turn it into a "three-way" cut. Steadily, he transposes the bottom, center, and top portions of the pack. This makes an impressive ornamental flourish when the three sections drop neatly into place.

METHOD

NOTE: In all ONE-HAND CUTS, you may hold the deck in either your right or your left hand, whichever is easier for you. ALL OF THE ILLUSTRATIONS ARE FROM THE SPECTATORS' VIEW WITH THE DECK HELD IN THE LEFT HAND.

(1) Begin by holding the pack in the same position as you did for the regular ONE-HAND CUT. Your first finger and little finger are at opposite ends of the pack; your two middle fingers and thumb are at the sides. Be sure that your fingers and thumb point "up" or slightly to the "right" if this is easier for you. Also be certain, as before, that you have formed a deep "well" between the deck and the palm of your hand.

(2) Unlike the regular ONE-HAND CUT — where the pack is cut into two *equal* sections — in this modified version, begin by bending your thumb just enough to let the *lower third* (Packet A) of the deck drop into your cupped hand. Your little finger will help to keep the cards from sliding out of your hand.

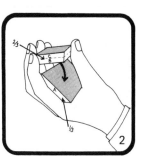

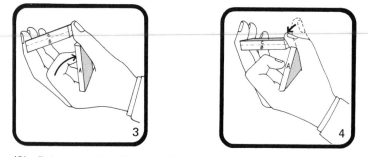

(3) Bring your first finger *below* Packet A and begin pushing its edge *upward* toward your thumb as shown. (4) Continue pushing Packet A all the way up to your left thumb. The top edge of Packet A will contact your thumb near the "bend" of the first joint of the thumb.

(5) *NOTE: Your hand now holds the bulk of the deck (the remaining two-thirds) between the tip of the thumb and your fingers — while the bottom third of the deck (Packet A) is held between the "bend" of your thumb and the palm of your hand as shown in Step 4.*

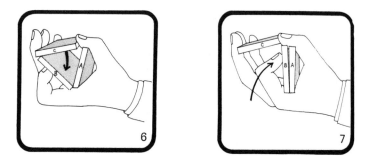

(6) With the cards held firmly in this position, relax the tip of your left thumb allowing *another third of the deck,* Packet B (the middle third), to *drop* from the bulk of the pack *into your cupped hand.* (7) Once again, bring your first finger below Packet B and push it upwards toward your thumb until it is all the way *up against the bottom of Packet A.* The remaining third of the deck, Packet C, is still being held by the tips of your thumb and fingers as shown.

(8) Now, release your thumb tip from Packet C and allow its top to clear the top edge of Packets A and B. *You can help the packets to clear by pushing the bottom of Packet B with your first finger.* Packet C will come down with it into your palm. *Packet C now becomes the LOWER THIRD of the pack.*

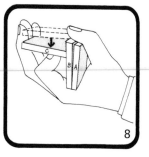

(9) Now, slowly begin closing up your hand, bringing all three sections together to complete the cut. (10) Finally, extend your first finger around the end of the pack and square the deck as the sections settle into place. You have just executed the ONE-HAND CUT — FIRST VARIATION.

COMMENTS AND SUGGESTIONS

Practice this flourish with a narrow, Bridge-sized pack, as it is much easier to handle than the wider "Poker" deck. Later, you can switch to the wider size if your fingers are long enough to handle it easily. *The dropping of the center section, Packet B, is the vital point,* because your thumb must hold both Packets A and C in place until your first finger releases Packet B. If Packet A should accidentally drop during that maneuver, that's OK — just let it fall on top of Packet B and complete what would then be a slightly different "cut" than you had originally planned.

THE ONE-HAND CUT — SECOND VARIATION

This is another variation of the ONE-HAND CUT that can be used interchangeably with the one already described. The two cuts can also be worked in combination, starting with one, and ending with the other, all in the same sequence.

EFFECT

In this triple cut, the magician divides the lower section into two packets and lets the upper third drop in between. This can be repeated several times, either in slow motion, or at a rapid speed once the knack is acquired. Either way, it increases the audience's admiration of the magician's skill.

METHOD

(1) In the usual One-Hand Cut style, hold the pack between the tips of the thumb and fingers of either hand. The first finger and little finger are at opposite ends of the pack, the other fingers and thumb are at the sides. Be sure the fingers point straight up (or nearly straight up if this is easier for you). Just be sure to form a deep well between the deck and the palm of your hand.

(2) To begin, bend the thumb just enough to let the lower *two-thirds* of the pack drop into the cupped hand. The little finger will help to keep the cards from sliding out of your hand.

(3) Bring your first finger *below* the bulk of the pack and push its edge upward, *sliding it along the bottom of the upper third of the pack.* Continue pushing the lower section all the way up to the ball of the thumb as shown.

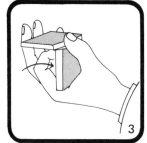

(4) *Here your left thumb retains hold of HALF of the bulk of the pack* as you begin to open your first finger, *allowing the other half to DROP BACK DOWN into your hand.*

(5) As the packet falls into your hand, relax the grip of the tip of your thumb on the top third of the pack, and *allow it to fall into the hand BETWEEN the two packets already formed.*

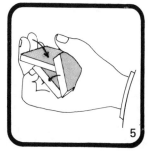

(6) Slowly begin closing up your hand *bringing all three packets* together to complete the cut. Finally, extend your first finger around the end of the pack and square the pack as the three packets settle into place. You have just done the ONE-HAND CUT, SECOND VARIATION.

COMMENTS AND SUGGESTIONS

Along with serving as an ornamental flourish, this variation of the ONE-HAND CUT fulfills a useful purpose. With it, you can "bury" the top card of the pack somewhere in the middle of the deck. Then, as you call attention to that fact, the audience doesn't realize that the bottom card remains the same and can, therefore, be used as a "key" in a trick that follows.

THE ONE-HAND CUT — SECOND METHOD

In this "ONE-HAND CUT," the technique is somewhat different from those already given, as the pack is held in an entirely new position to start. This forms an interesting contrast to the previous methods, which, in itself, is a good reason why you should include it among your "Flourishes."

EFFECT

Holding the pack upright in the crook of his thumb, the magician cuts the lower third into the tips of his fingers, bringing both sections upright with a wide space between. He then cuts another section of the pack from his left thumb and "folds" the lower third between it and the top packet. This completes a very neat *triple* cut in which all three sections of the pack go into action almost simultaneously, having a very strong effect upon the observers.

METHOD

(1) The pack is held upright in the left hand. One edge of the pack is held by the *ball and first joint of your left thumb* and the other edge is *wedged deeply into the palm* at the very base of the thumb. *NOTE: STEPS 1 AND 2 ARE SHOWN FROM THE SPECTATORS' VIEWPOINT.*

(2) With the pack held firmly in this position, curl the left fingers up against the face of the pack, *except for the second finger which is brought OVER the top edge of the deck next to the thumb.* With the second finger in this position, draw away the *lower third* of the pack as shown.

(3) HERE IS THE SAME ACTION AS SEEN FROM YOUR VIEWPOINT. Note that, as the second finger draws its packet away from the bulk of the pack, the other fingers are curled against the face of the pack. We will call this Packet A.

(4) Pull Packet A all the way down against the curled fingers and then . . .

(5) . . . GRIP PACKET A BETWEEN THE SECOND FINGER ON TOP AND THE FIRST AND THIRD FINGERS UNDERNEATH. Slowly begin to straighten out the left fingers, lifting Packet A upwards, swinging it out from beneath the bulk of the pack. This is a view of the completed action from your viewpoint. *Packet A is now held firmly between the second finger and the first and third fingers. Meanwhile, the bulk of the pack is still held tightly in position by the left thumb.*

(6) Now relax the left thumb enough to allow *half* of the pack it holds (Packet B) *to fall into your hand* as shown. THE ILLUSTRATION IS FROM YOUR POINT OF VIEW.

(7) Curl the left fingers inwards, placin Packet A on top of Packet B.

(8) Now begin to close up your hand. *Bring the cards held by the thumb (Packet C) down onto the rest of Packet A . . .*

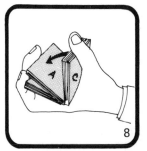

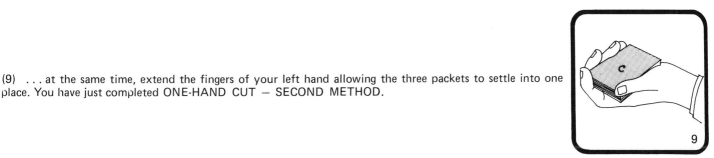

(9) ...at the same time, extend the fingers of your left hand allowing the three packets to settle into one place. You have just completed ONE-HAND CUT — SECOND METHOD.

COMMENTS AND SUGGESTIONS

A BRIDGE-SIZE PACK is highly helpful for this cut, as the thumb has a "long stretch" to hold the pack upright in the crook of the thumb. The narrow Bridge-size pack is also helpful in supplying the space needed *between* the first two packets (A and B) when they are levered apart. In this form of the One-Hand Cut the *bottom* card is buried into the pack, while the *top* card remains in place. In this way, it differs from the previous version where the *bottom* card remains in place.

SPREADING THE CARDS — THE RIBBON SPREAD

EFFECT

In the performance of card tricks, it is often necessary to spread the entire pack of cards across the table so all of their backs or faces are visible to the spectators. The following describes the method for executing a "Ribbon Spread" which looks very nice and demonstrates your ability to handle cards skillfully.

METHOD

NOTE: The Ribbon Spread is difficult to do on a slick or hard surface. However, it is quite easy on a soft, textured surface such as a felt top table, a rug, a heavy table cloth or the magician's "Close Up Mat."

(1) Place the deck on the table face down slightly bevelled at the side of the deck as shown.

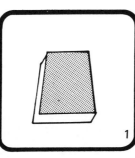

(3) Now with a slight downward pressure of the hand, move your arm and hand to the right. The cards will begin to spread apart evenly FROM THE BOTTOM OF THE PACK as you slide the bulk of the pack along the table.

(2) Lay all four fingers of your right hand across the top of the pack, with the tips of the fingers extending over the bevelled edge.

(4) Continue this sliding motion releasing cards from the bottom of the pack until all of the cards are evenly spread in a "ribbon pattern" along the table.

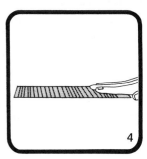

COMMENTS AND SUGGESTIONS

In practicing the Ribbon Spread, be sure you have a soft surface and remember that the sliding motion of the hand must be smooth and unbroken in order to achieve even spacing between the individual cards. The motion should not be done too slowly either. A moderately fast movement is most effective for the best results. As always, *PRACTICE* is the key to success.

RIBBON SPREAD TURNOVER

This is an ideal flourish to use when doing card tricks at a table. Though easily learned, it gives the impression that you are displaying great skill. Always take advantage of such opportunities . . . they create a lasting impression on the audience regarding your work. It's all part of the game called MAGIC.

EFFECT

The magician takes an ordinary pack of cards and spreads them in an even row *face down* along the table. Then, by *tilting up* one end of the spread, HE CAUSES THE ENTIRE ROW OF CARDS TO TURN *face up!*

METHOD

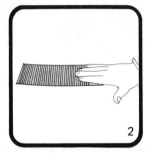

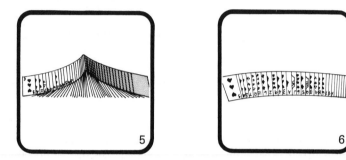

(1) Set the pack *face down* on the table in preparation for the RIBBON SPREAD. (2) RIBBON SPREAD the pack from left to right as described earlier. *The cards in the spread must be evenly spaced. . . . Any "gaps" or "breaks" in the spread will disrupt the TURNOVER.*

(5) Rotate the card on its edge until it turns over (face up) *causing all of the cards above it to "follow the leader" as they begin to TURN OVER in sequence.* (6) The TURNOVER will progress throughout the spread until *all of the cards* are FACE UP, as shown.

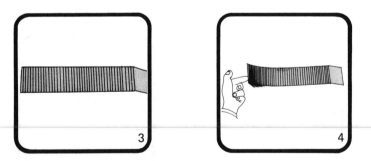

(3) The completed spread should look like this . . . *until the TURNOVER.* (4) Now, with your left fingers, raise the *outer edge* of the card on the *left end* of the spread . . . tilting it "up" on its edge as shown.

COMMENTS AND SUGGESTIONS

This is the "basic" TURNOVER. A rather easy and most impressive flourish. To add even more to your display of skill, you can incorporate the two following variations.

REVERSE TURNOVER

After completing the TABLE SPREAD TURNOVER, you may immediately reverse the procedure as follows:

(1) With your *right hand,* lift the card at the far *right end* of the now face-up spread. Using this card as the "pusher" card, pivot it on its edge... (2) ...causing the cards to repeat the TURNOVER... (3) ...this time back to their original *face-down* position.

COMMENTS AND SUGGESTIONS

By placing your left hand at the left end of the spread and your right hand at the right end of the spread, you can "flip-flop" the cards back and forth as they TURN OVER in rotation — first, *face up* — then, *face down* — making not only a remarkable display of skill, but also a very pretty picture.

TURNOVER CONTROL

This is another even more intriguing use of the TURNOVER, which is particularly good when used *between* effects in your card routine. This is also a most spectacular way of showing that the deck is "ordinary" . . . composed of "all different" cards.

METHOD

(1) First remove any card from the deck and place it on the table. Then perform Steps 1 through 5 in the RIBBON SPREAD TURNOVER. When the cards have "turned" to approximately the middle of the spread, pick up the card you removed and hold it, as shown, in your right hand. This card will be used to "control" the sequence of the TURNOVER in the following manner:

(2) You will find that, as you carefully touch the *edge* of the single card in your right hand to the "peak" of the TURNOVER, you can very easily "control" the sequence and direction of the TURNOVER. For instance, you can now *reverse* the TURNOVER by moving the single card *back to the left* as shown. *As you move the card to the left, keep the edge of the card touching the new, constantly changing "peak."* This can be done back and forth as often as you wish, as long as the cards remain evenly spread on the table.

(3) The single card is then used to "control" the TURNOVER all the way over to the *right end* of the spread . . . where the cards will fall *face up* . . . as they did at the conclusion of the regular RIBBON SPREAD TURNOVER.

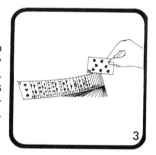

TURNOVER PICK-UP

A *spectacular conclusion* to the TURNOVER can be accomplished by using the single card that you have used to "control" the rotation of the cards as follows:

METHOD

(1) As you control the TURNOVER to the right end of the spread with the single card, just before the last card in the spread "flops" to the table, quickly insert the "control" card *between* the falling spread and the table as shown.

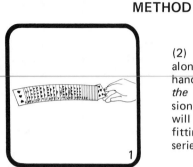

(2) Then, *use the card as a "scoop,"* along with the fingers of your right hand to *gather up all of the cards in the spread* as shown. At the conclusion of this "pick-up," the entire deck will be face up in your right hand. A fitting conclusion to a spectacular series of flourishes!

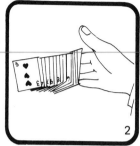

COMMENTS AND SUGGESTIONS

As mentioned, all of the four TURNOVER flourishes depend upon the initial table spread of the cards being *evenly spaced,* without any breaks or gaps. Thus, you must first learn to do the RIBBON SPREAD well before adding these very effective extra touches. The combination of the RIBBON SPREAD . . . the RIBBON SPREAD TURNOVER . . . the REVERSE TURNOVER . . . the TURNOVER CONTROL . . . and concluding with the TURNOVER PICK-UP, is easily learned with a relatively small amount of practice. It is quite spectacular and can be used to attract attention, as well as to display your skill as a card manipulator. One final word: As emphasized in the RIBBON SPREAD, the surface on which the SPREAD TURNOVER is best presented is one which is *soft* and has a "texture," such as a tablecloth, felt table top, a blanket, or, ideally, a Magician's Close-Up Mat. This type of surface enables you to spread the cards evenly. It also keeps the cards in place so they will not slip as they rotate "over" during the TURNOVER.

PRESSURE FAN

Giving your performance a professional look should be a primary aim when taking up card magic. Shuffles and cuts should all be done smoothly and neatly, as a prelude to fancier moves. This applies specifically to the PRESSURE FAN, which follows.

EFFECT

Holding the pack squared in one hand, the magician deftly spreads it in a circular fashion across the fingers of his other hand — finally displaying it in a broad "fan" — with the index corners of the cards showing evenly throughout its colorful span.

METHOD

(1) Hold the pack by the ends between the tips of the right thumb and fingers. Your thumb is at the center of the lower end and your first, second and third fingers are across the upper end as shown. Your little finger rests lightly on the side of the deck.

(3) To begin the fan, squeeze the fingers of your right hand downward, BENDING THE CARDS OVER THE LEFT FOREFINGER.

(2) With the cards HELD FIRMLY IN THE RIGHT HAND, place the pack *against the fingers of the left hand* in the position shown. The ball of the left thumb rests at the middle of the lower end of the pack. *NOTE: The right hand is not shown in the drawing in order to show more clearly the exact position in which the pack is HELD AGAINST THE LEFT HAND BY THE RIGHT HAND.*

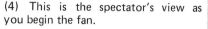

(4) This is the spectator's view as you begin the fan.

(5) Then IN ONE CONTINUOUS MOTION – allow the cards to start "springing" from the right fingertips as the right hand begins to rotate the pack to the right. The left thumb acts as a pivot point holding the lower left corner of the pack.

(7) . . . as you continue to "spring release" cards in succession until the fan is complete. This action is shown from the point of view of the audience.

(6) Continue the CIRCULAR MOTION of the right hand *around* the tips of the left fingers and *down* the side of the left hand. . .

(8) There is only one secret in making a good Pressure Fan, and that is – PRACTICE. First attempts at making the Fan may be very discouraging – the cards may "bunch up" and not spread far enough or evenly, or they may even "spring" completely out of your hands! But, little by little, you will eventually get the knack of making an evenly spaced, beautiful fan. Most importantly, remember that a good Pressure Fan is accomplished by a *rapid, unbroken, sweeping* motion of the right hand – and PRACTICE is the answer!

COMMENTS AND SUGGESTIONS

The amount of pressure necessary to make the fan depends considerably upon the pack you are using. A brand new, high-quality pack can be fanned with a light touch but will need more "bending" pressure by the right thumb and fingers. With a new, "clean" deck, the cards are smooth enough to spread evenly and stiff enough to resist pressure. The more a pack is shuffled and used, the more flexible it becomes, and the pressure must be *decreased* proportionately. Also, as the deck is "soiled," it becomes more and more difficult to get the cards evenly spaced.

CLOSING THE FAN – TWO-HAND METHOD

All of the illustrations are from the <u>spectators' viewpoint</u>.

(1)   To close the fan, curl the tips of your right fingers around the extreme left edge of the fan as shown.   (2)   Then, in one continuous motion, sweep your right hand in an arc around the left fingers causing the cards to start to collect against the fingers of your right hand. (3)   Continue to sweep the fan closed until all the cards have gathered together into a single packet, thus completing the procedure.

CLOSING THE FAN — ONE-HAND METHOD

The simple action of closing the PRESSURE FAN can be as impressive as the fan itself — particularly when executed *without the aid of the other hand,* as described below.

METHOD

(1) Begin by forming a Pressure Fan as described earlier. The four fingers should be flat against the face of the pack with the thumb pressing inwards at the pivot point on the back of the fan.

(2) To close the fan, shift your left first finger so that its fingertip rests on the face of the first card AS CLOSE TO THE OUTER EDGE OF THE FAN AS POSSIBLE.

(3) With a slight amount of pressure from your left first finger on the face card of the deck, begin to push your finger in a circular motion . . . upwards and to the right . . . as you slowly begin to close the fan.

(4) Continue pushing the fan closed and open the remaining fingers of the left hand when necessary, allowing the first finger to sweep the cards downward as they collect in succession against the heel of the hand until the fan is closed.

THE ONE-HAND FAN

Though basically a Card "Flourish," this is also a useful move in connection with various tricks. That makes two good reasons why you should practice it, as each will add a professional touch to your work.

EFFECT

Holding a pack of cards face front between the thumb and fingers of the right hand, the magician, with one deft move, instantly spreads the pack in a broad fan, showing the index corners of the cards in colorful fashion. Closing the fan and turning the pack over, he fans them again, showing the backs spread evenly, allowing a spectator to select a card — an excellent opening move for many card effects.

METHOD

(1) Hold the pack in your right hand with your thumb on the face of the pack and your fingers flat against the back. Position your thumb at the lower right-hand corner of the pack as shown.

(2) Here is a view of the pack from the other side. Notice that your fingers only cover half of the length of the pack.

(3) Now in one smooth, continuous motion, start to *slide your thumb upwards. AT THE SAME TIME, curl your fingers inwards and downwards,* as the pack begins to spread out in the form of a fan.

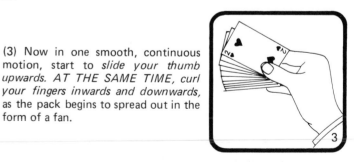

(4) Continue sliding your thumb upwards as the fingers continue pushing the cards in a sort of "smearing" motion down the heel of the hand until they curl into the palm....almost forming a fist with the cards held tightly between. When your thumb and fingers have reached this position, the fan should be fully formed as shown.

(5) NOTE: Your *fingers* are responsible for forming the *lower half* of the fan and the *thumb* is responsible for forming the *upper half*. DO NOT BE DISAPPOINTED IF YOU CANNOT MASTER THE ONE-HAND FAN IMMEDIATELY. Careful practice will teach you exactly how much pressure to exert with the thumb and fingers in order for the cards to distribute properly from the top and bottom of the pack, forming an evenly spaced fan.

(6) Here is a view of the completed fan from the other side. Notice the right fingers have curled into the palm of the hand to form a fist.

COMMENTS AND SUGGESTIONS

In tricks where you are using half a pack or less, fanning is just as effective as with a full pack, as all the cards in the half-packet can be spread out evenly and more of each card will show. Even when doing a trick with only a few cards — such as the Four Aces — using a ONE-HAND FAN to show their faces has a striking effect and adds to your style as a performer. You may also wish to learn the fan with both hands. Then, by splitting the deck and holding half in each hand, the *two* fans will form a truly spectacular display.

SPRINGING THE CARDS

This fancy flourish is the basis for many other flourishes with a pack of cards. It is one that should be practiced first on a limited scale (springing the cards only a short distance) with a pack that can be handled easily and comfortably. Then, you can gradually increase the scope of this manipulation.

EFFECT

The magician holds a pack of cards lengthwise between his thumb and fingers. By applying steady pressure on the pack, he causes all the cards in the pack to "spring" in succession from one hand to the other — in mid-air! This has a very impressive effect upon the audience, as the cards form a colorful cascade that can cover a surprising distance.

METHOD

(1) Hold the pack lengthwise in your right hand ... with your thumb at the lower end and your first, second, and third fingers at the upper end. The pack should be held close to the tips of the fingers as shown.

(3) With the pack held firmly in your right hand, squeeze your thumb and fingers together, bending the cards inwards toward the palm of your hand and move the right hand about three inches above the "cupped" left hand.

(2) Your left hand is held palm up with the fingers spread wide — pointing upward. This forms a sort of "trap" to catch the cards as they cascade from the right hand into the left.

(4) Continue to squeeze the pack inwards as you begin to RELEASE THE CARDS FROM THE TIPS OF YOUR RIGHT FINGERS sending them springing, one by one, from the right hand into the awaiting left hand.

(5) *NOTE: The left hand should be positioned so that, as the cards arrive in the hand, the outer ends of the cards hit the <u>left first fingers</u> ... which prevents them from shooting out of the hand onto the floor.*

(7) When the bulk of the pack has arrived in the left hand and only a few cards remain in the right, move your right hand toward your left hand, gathering all the cards in between to conclude the flourish.

(6) As the cards start to "spring" from one hand to the other, GRAD-UALLY BEGIN DRAWING YOUR RIGHT HAND FARTHER AWAY — a few inches at first — then more and more. No matter what distance you will eventually achieve, ALWAYS BE-GIN WITH THE TWO HANDS CLOSE TOGETHER. Then, draw the right hand away as the cards "spring" into your left hand.

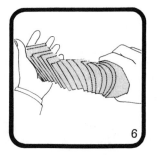

COMMENTS AND SUGGESTIONS

In first practicing the "spring," place your left hand just below your right hand and spring the pack for a distance of only a few inches. Your purpose is to gain the knack of springing the cards smoothly and evenly without losing any of them. Once you learn to release the cards in an even stream, <u>with practice</u> you can then spread your hands a foot or so apart. When you first practice, it is best to use <u>soft, flexible cards</u> ... an "old" used deck works well.

It is also a good idea to practice over a bed, as a certain amount of failure is inevitable at first. One final suggestion: If you swing your body from left to right during the "spring," the distance effect between your hands is further exaggerated, *creating the illusion* that the cards cover a distance of eighteen inches to two feet.

ARM SPREAD CATCH

One of the most spectacular of card flourishes, this also appears to be one of the most difficult. Proper technique, attention to detail, and a reasonable amount of practice combine toward impressive results in this special branch of magic that blends juggling with wizardry.

EFFECT

The magician spreads a pack of cards lengthwise along his left arm from the base of his fingers to his elbow. With the cards neatly set in place, he gives his arm an upward toss and *at the same time,* makes a long, inward sweep with his right hand, "SCOOPING UP" THE ENTIRE PACK OF CARDS IN MID-AIR WITHOUT DROPPING A SINGLE CARD.

METHOD

(1) Hold the pack in your right hand, with the thumb at one end and the fingers at the other. Extend your left arm, palm up, and hold the pack slightly above the fingers of the left hand. Bend the entire pack inwards toward the right palm (this is the same "bending" by the right hand as in "SPRINGING THE CARDS").

(2) Slowly begin to release the cards from the *tips* of the right fingers onto the left hand ... and, AT THE SAME TIME, move your right hand down the length of your left arm. The cards should begin forming an even spread along the left arm.

(3) Continue releasing the cards from the fingertips along the left arm until *all* the cards have been spread. With practice you can attain a spread which extends from the tips of the left fingers to the elbow.

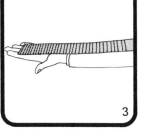

(6) With an upward lifting and tossing motion of the left arm, *gently throw the entire spread of cards into the air* as shown.

(4) *NOTE: After the cards are spread along the arm, it is necessary to keep the arm VERY STILL to keep the cards from falling.*

(7) WITHOUT HESITATION, and in ONE CONTINUOUS MOVEMENT, swing your entire body to the left and, with a long sweeping motion of the right hand, begin gathering or "scooping up" the cards *in mid-air* from one end of the spread to the other.

(5) With the cards neatly set in place, position your "cupped" <u>right</u> hand near the left fingertips, at the beginning of the spread, in readiness to catch the cards.

(8) With practice you should be able to catch the entire pack without any cards falling to the floor. At first, practice the Arm Spread Catch using a half-pack and a shorter arm spread. Then, gradually add more cards until you can perform the flourish with a full pack, spread from the tips of the fingers to the elbow.

COMMENTS AND SUGGESTIONS

In early trials, as you practice "springing" the cards along the arm, the spread may prove too irregular for an "effective catch." In that case, simply lower the left arm rapidly and let the pack slide down into the cupped left hand. This is a neat manipulation in itself, so you can use it as a preliminary "warm-up" before the catch.

THE WATERFALL

EFFECT

The magician grasps the entire pack in his right hand with his left hand cupped beneath it. Skillfully, he begins to release the cards in rapid succession, causing them to cascade downward, one at a time like a "Waterfall" into his waiting left hand. The flourish reaches its conclusion after the entire pack has made its impressive journey through the air into the magician's left hand.

METHOD

(1) Grasp and hold the deck lengthwise in your right hand with your thumb at one end of the pack and your four fingers at the other end. Your right fingers and thumb should be straight with only the edges of the top card touching your right hand.

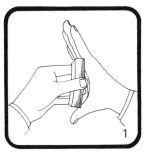

(2) *Keeping your fingers and thumb straight,* slowly squeeze them together so that the cards bend *inward* toward your right palm. This action is very similar to Springing the Cards except here, the object is to get a small amount of space between each and every card as you hold the pack.

(3) The special grip described here allows the ends of the cards to "spread" *along the length* of your thumb and fingers. Done correctly, the cards should "fill up" all the open space between your thumb and fingers. Careful practice will teach you just how to bend the pack to secure this small gap between the individual cards.

(6) At the same time, move your left hand *downward* as the cards continue to fall from your right hand. If you release the cards in an even flow, they will resemble a Waterfall as they cascade from one hand to the other.

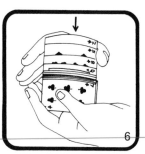

(4) With the cards held in this manner, you are ready to begin the Waterfall. Position your cupped left hand directly below your right hand in readiness to receive the cards as they fall. The illustration shows the proper position of both hands at the beginning of the flourish. *This and all the following steps are shown from the audience point of view.*

(7) *To achieve maximum distance between your hands, move your right hand up a few inches at the same time you move your left hand down. With practice you can attain a Waterfall of eight to twelve inches — or even longer.*

(5) Slowly begin to spread open your right thumb and fingers — releasing the cards in succession *from the face of the pack.* This action causes the cards to fall into the left hand in an even flow.

(8) When nearly all cards have been released from your right hand, quickly move your hands back together, squaring up the cards, to complete the flourish. You are now prepared to repeat the Waterfall as many times as you wish. Your audience will be more than convinced that you possess great skill as a card manipulator.

COMMENTS AND SUGGESTIONS

The real secret of the Waterfall is *your intial grip on the pack* shown in Step 1 and Step 2. The cards must be spread evenly along your thumb and fingers. At the start, practice the flourish with your hands very close together. Then, as you begin to acquire the "knack" necessary to release the cards in an even stream, move your hands farther apart. When selecting cards to use for this flourish, it is a good idea to experiment with different decks. Choose cards which bend easily enough for you to space them evenly in your hand. If you practice this flourish with a deck that suits you well, you will be pleased at the progress you will make in achieving a perfect "Waterfall" effect.

THROWING A CARD

Many famous magicians, most notably Herrmann, Thurston, and Raymond, have intrigued audiences throughout the world with their ability at "Scaling" cards to the highest balconies of the largest theaters. How far you can go toward achieving a similar result will depend upon how much practice you are willing to devote to this very impressive flourish.

EFFECT

Upon concluding his card routine, the magician offers several cards for examination by "Scaling" them across the room to different members of the audience. This is done in a smooth, graceful manner, sending the cards skimming into the air while the audience watches in amazement as they whiz by.

METHOD

(1) Holding the card in the proper "throwing position" is essential in attaining effective results. There are two "correct" positions and you should try them both to see which works best for you. (The other "optional" holding position will be described in the next effect.)

(2) To place the card in the first position, clip the very end of the card between the first and second fingers of your right hand as shown. Do not allow the card to "droop," but hold it firmly so that it is level with the fingers at all times.

(3) Here is the card held in proper "throwing position" as seen from the spectator's point of view.

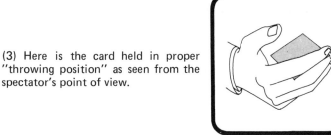

(4) Start by bending *all four fingers inward,* until the lower right edge of the card touches the heel of your hand. This is shown from above.

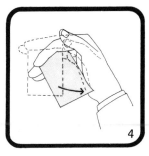

(5) In the same movement, *bend your wrist inward,* toward yourself, as far as it will go.

(6) Now, to make the actual throw, snap your wrist "open" AS HARD AS YOU CAN. AT THE SAME TIME, *straighten out your fingers* and release the card to send it spinning out of your hand.

COMMENTS AND SUGGESTIONS

Keeping the card level with the fingers and maintaining a consistent wrist action are essential factors in developing the "throw," which can cover a long range once the knack is acquired. When aiming for higher levels, the hand must be kept "on target" and the force of throw increased. Along with accuracy, the practiced performer can propel the cards an impressive distance by combining a *throwing motion of the arm* with the action of the wrist as a means of gaining still greater distance.

THE BOOMERANG CARD

After demonstrating his skill by throwing playing cards great distances into the audience, the magician begins throwing cards toward the ceiling only to have them sail out into the air and return to his hand, much the same as a Boomerang.

METHOD

(1) In order to achieve the "Boomerang" effect, the card should be held either in the position described in THROWING A CARD or in this new position as follows: Hold the card at one end between the tips of the right thumb and fingers as shown. Grip the card near the outer right corner between your right thumb and second finger. Your first finger rests against the left corner of the card to serve as a pivot point to start the "spinning" action of the card as it leaves the hand.

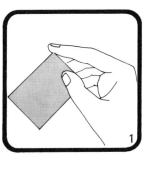

(2) With the card held in this position, it can be sent spinning out of the hand using the same arm and wrist action as described in THROWING A CARD.

(3) To achieve the BOOMERANG effect, hold the card in either "throwing" position. Then, instead of throwing the card out of the hand on a level plane, throw it at an upward angle of 45 degrees or more, *with just enough force to send it only a few yards away from you.* In throwing the card, concentrate on obtaining as much spin as possible. This is done by "snapping" your hand back *toward your body just before you release the card.* Your first finger on the outer right corner acts as the pivot point to aid in starting the card in its spin as it leaves your right hand.

(4) Once the card has reached its maximum distance in the air and begins its downward fall, it will return to you instead of falling straight down to the floor. This is due to the 45-degree angle of the card in the air. With practice you will be able to cause the card to return directly to your hand where you can catch it between your thumb and fingers.

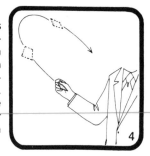

COMMENTS AND SUGGESTIONS

Practice the BOOMERANG CARD until it can be done with neatness and precision. Performed properly, it creates an impression of great skill and dexterity. A certain amount of failure is inevitable at first, but once you develop the knack of THROWING A CARD, the BOOMERANG should come quickly and easily.

GENII CARDS

In contrast to tricks with regulation playing cards, the "Genii" tricks require a special type of card. Since the Genii Cards are handled somewhat like playing cards, they have been included in this section.

While several tricks may be performed with the "Genii Cards," all depend upon the same simple, but deceptive, move. Although this move is excellent, you should not perform more than one Genii trick at any performance. It is better to keep a few Genii tricks in reserve, so that on your next show you can switch to another.

This keeps people wondering just what to expect, which is an important factor in all magic. If you wish, you can use the Genii Cards for an introductory trick, or inject them as an interlude during a program of effects with playing cards, and you will always be on the safe side.

The Genii Cards and their routines were specially devised for use with this magic course, which means that they will be entirely new to many people who see them. This gives you, as the performer, a real advantage over your audiences from the start — so make the most of it!

You may have the Genii Cards and the special half-cards printed on business card-sized stock at a local printer. Because spectators will be asked to write on the full-sized Genii cards in most of the following routines, we suggest a number of these be printed. Approximately 20 of the half-cards will last a long time.

THE GENII OF THE LAMP

In this very basic form of the Genii, the only "props" needed are the cards themselves. The effect is that a Genii mysteriously appears thanks to the magic of Aladdin's Lamp.

EFFECT

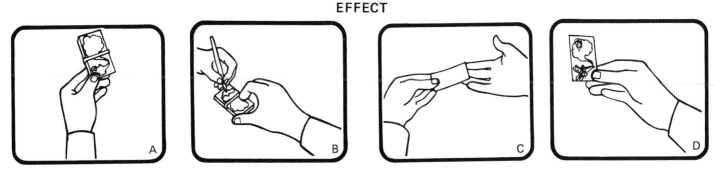

(A)   You show a stack of cards with a rubber band around it. The top card shows a magic lamp giving off a cloud of smoke, but no Genii.
(B)   Remarking that this represents Aladdin's wonderful lamp, you invite a spectator to write his initials in the lamp. You then remove the card and state that whenever Aladdin rubbed the lamp, his Genii appeared.   (C)   Holding the card face down in one hand, you rub the lamp with the fingers of your other hand.   (D)   After a few rubs, you turn the card over showing that the Genii himself has "magically" appeared in the cloud of smoke and the spectator's initials are still in the lamp!

SECRET AND PREPARATION

This basic trick, and all other tricks with the Genii cards, depend on a simple, natural movement which secretly switches one card for another. We call this the "Master Move". Here is the explanation of the trick and how the "Master Move" makes this a real mystery.

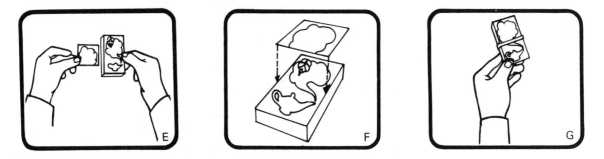

(E) A special half-card showing only an empty cloud is used, shown here next to the packet of regular full-sized cards. Approximately ten full-sized cards should be used to make up the packet. (F) Before the trick, one half-card is placed on the packet so that it covers the cloud portion of the top card with the Genii in it. (G) Now, put the rubber band around the cards so that the half-card is held firmly in place and its bottom edge is completely hidden by the rubber band. Once the half-card is in position and held there by the rubber band, the top card of the packet looks like a full-sized card showing a lamp, a cloud, and nothing else. Use only one half-card when you set up the packet for the trick. Save the others for spares.

METHOD AND MASTER MOVE

(1)   You show the packet to a spectator, and ask him to write his initials in the lamp of the top card.

(2)   Now for the Master Move: Holding the packet in your left hand as shown, you lift up the lamp end of the initialed card with your right finger.

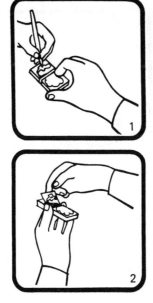

(3)   Now, your left hand starts to turn the packet over as you begin to pull out the Genii card with your right fingers.

(4)   Here is the action as seen from below. The spectators see the back of the packet instead of the face. Everyone is sure you are drawing out the initialed card.

The Genii of the Lamp - Cont'd.

(5) As the card comes clear, both the packet and the card have been turned all the way over so that no one can see their faces. Although you *have* actually drawn out the initialed card, the secret half-card remains on the packet. Place the packet face down somewhere out of reach, or drop in your pocket, so that no one will learn about the half-card.

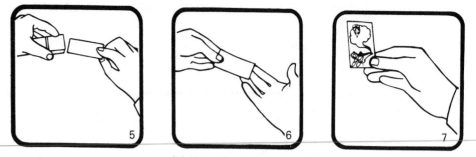

(6) Hold the initialed card face down in your left hand. Place your right fingers under the card and rub the lamp a few times. (7) When you turn the card over, the Genii is found to have "magically" appeared in the cloud of smoke!

COMMENTS AND SUGGESTIONS

Through this Master Move, you have secretly switched what the spectators thought was the original Genii card for another; yet the change seems impossible because the person who wrote his initials on the card will find that they are still there. This is something of a miracle in its own right, and when used in association with other effects, it becomes even more sensational. These added details will be covered in the Genii tricks that follow, all using the Master Move just described.

THE GENII'S NUMBER

In this trick, the Genii does magical mathematics and predicts a chosen number. And he does it very well, as you will see.

SECRET AND PREPARATION

(A) Before the trick, write the number "1089" in the cloud of the top Genii card; (B) then cover it with the empty half-card and place a rubber band around the packet.

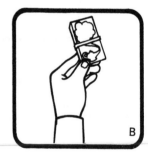

METHOD

(1) Have a spectator write his initials in the lamp as you did in the Genii of the Lamp trick.

(2) Remove the initialed card using the Master Move (actually removing the "1089" card) and place it face down on the table.

(3) Lay a pad and pencil beside it.

(4) Now tell the spectator: "I want you to write a number of *three different figures,* any number between one hundred and one thousand, without letting me see it." Let's say that he writes "318."

(5) You continue: "Now reverse that number and subtract the smaller number from the larger." *NOTE: Here you tell him if the answer is less than a hundred to leave a zero in front of it so he will still have a number with three figures.*

(6) As soon as he has done the subtraction, you state: "Now reverse your answer and write it just below." When he does this, tell him: "I want you to add those two numbers so you will get a *grand total.*"

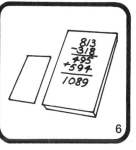

(8) Explain that you will call upon your invisible Genii to check the spectator's arithmetic. Pick up the Genii card and place it face down on top of the pad. Then, pretend to catch the Genii out of the air and slip him between the pad and Genii card.

(7) You then tell him to circle the grand total, and lay the pad down beside the Genii card.

(9) After a few moments, ask the spectator to turn over the card. He does, and to his amazement, the Genii has appeared *showing* the same number as his slip: 1089.

COMMENTS AND SUGGESTIONS

Whatever the original three-figure number, the grand total will always be 1089, unless the original figures are all alike, as 333 or 555. That is why you tell him that he is to write a number with *three different figures.* When subtracted, they will always produce numbers that, when reversed, and added, will total *1089.* In some cases, like 463 minus 364, the subtraction gives him 99. That is why you tell the spectator to put a zero in front of anything under 100, so if he makes it 099 and reverses it to form 990, the two will add up to the usual 1089. If he should get some other total, simply check his figures for him and he will find that the Genii was right all along!

THE GENII PREDICTS

In this Genii trick, along with the packet of Genii cards, you need an ordinary pack of playing cards, which may be borrowed for this effect.

EFFECT

The magician shows the Genii Packet with the rubber band around it. The top card shows a magic lamp giving off a cloud of smoke, but no Genii. A spectator writes his initials in the lamp of the top card of the Genii Packet, which is then removed from the packet and placed face down on the table. A card is chosen by the spectator from the pack, and placed on the table beside the Genii card. The magician then picks up the Genii card. Keeping the Genii card face down, the performer reaches beneath and, with his finger, "rubs" the lamp a few times. When the card is turned over, both the Genii and the words "Three of Clubs" have mysteriously appeared in the cloud. When the "chosen" card is turned over, it is the Three of Clubs....PROVING THE GENII'S PREDICTION TO BE CORRECT!

SECRET AND PREPARATION

Before the performance, write the name of any card, say the "Three of Clubs" in the cloud section of the top card of the Genii Packet. Cover this top card with the half-card and place the rubber band around the packet. Then, go through the pack of playing cards, find the Three of Clubs and move it to the position in the pack ready for your favorite force. The ROLLOVER FORCE or SLIP FORCE described in the Card Section of the Course both work well for this effect. (In the illustrations, the Three of Clubs has been marked with an "X" to make it easy to follow.) Place the pack in its card box or simply have it lying handy on the table and you're ready to begin.

METHOD

(1) Lay the Genii Packet face up on the table and place the pack of playing cards face down beside it.

(2) Pick up the Genii Packet and point out the empty cloud on the top card stating that "The Genii, who usually lives in the lamp, apparently isn't home today." Then, ask a spectator to write his initials in the lamp.

(3) That done, you remove the initialed card from the packet *(actually the prediction card)* using the MASTER MOVE, and place it face down on the table.

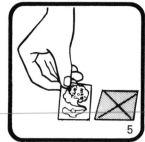

(5) Tell the spectator to turn over the Genii Card and see if the Genii has anything to say. When he does, he will see that the Genii has appeared and has written "Three of Clubs" in the cloud.

(4) Put away the rest of the Genii Packet and pick up the pack of playing cards. State that you wish to have one card selected at random from the pack. With that, force the Three of Clubs on the spectator, using whichever method you have decided upon. Have the spectator place his "chosen card" face down on the table next to the Genii Card.

(6) When the spectator turns over the playing card, the Genii's prediction proves correct!

COMMENTS AND SUGGESTIONS

In this Genii routine, *after* you have drawn out the Genii Card and placed it on the table, you can let the spectators see the packet of Genii Cards face up. Since the half-card is still in place and has no writing in the cloud, it will be mistaken for the second Genii Card. Just make sure that the rubber band is still in proper position *hiding the edge* of the half-card. If the half-card has slipped from place, put the packet away without turning it face up. A quick glance will tell you which to do. *Also, if you use a pencil to write the Genii Prediction, you can later erase it and use the Genii Card over again.*

THE SANDWICHED GENII

EFFECT

This is similar to the "Genii Predicts." In this trick after the spectator has initialed the lamp he places the Genii card in the center of a deck of playing cards. When the deck is spread the spectator finds that the Genii has not only mysteriously appeared, but he has also "magically" written the names of two playing cards in the cloud of smoke — and when the spectator looks, he finds that *these are the two playing cards that are next to the Genii card in the deck!*

SECRET AND PREPARATION

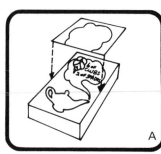

In addition to the Genii cards, you will need a regular deck of playing cards. (A) Before you perform the trick, with a pencil write the names of any two playing cards in the cloud of smoke on the top card of the Genii card packet. Let's suppose that you write the "Six of Clubs" and the "Two of Spades." This is now your *Genii prediction card.* (B) Then cover your "prediction" card with one of the "empty cloud" half-cards and put the rubber band around the packet. Now, from the deck of playing cards, remove the Two of Spades and the Six of Clubs. (C) Put the Six of Clubs on the top and (D) the Two of Spades on the bottom of the deck of playing cards and place the deck back in the box. Now you are ready to perform the trick. *NOTE: In the illustrations we have marked the Six of Clubs with the letter "A" and the Two of Spades with the letter "B" to make them easier to follow.*

METHOD

(1) To begin the presentation lay the Genii packet face up on the table with a pencil and the box of playing cards. Remark that the Genii who *usually* lives in the lamp must not be home, so ask a spectator to write his initials in the lamp of the top card.

(2) Remove the initialed card using the Master Move (actually removing the prediction card) and lay it face down on the table. Put the rest of the Genii cards in your pocket or just lay them aside.

(3) Tell the spectator to write his name on the back of the Genii card. While he is writing, pick up the deck of playing cards, remove it from the box and set it on the table next to the Genii card.

(4) Now, ask the spectator to divide the deck into two parts. Tell him he can cut anywhere in the deck he wishes, and place the upper portion on the table on the other side of the Genii card.

(5) *NOTE: Stress the fact that the spectator is cutting the pack at a location in the deck of his own free choice!*

(6) Then, tell him to place his Genii card face down on top of this new pile (which places it on top of the Six of Clubs).

(7) Now tell him to place the lower half of the deck on top of the Genii card, thus burying it in the deck. (This now places the Two of Spades which was on the bottom of the deck — directly above the Genii card.)

(8) *NOTE: At this point, the Genii card has been "sandwiched" between the Six of Clubs and Two of Spades, while the spectator thinks he has merely placed the Genii card in the deck at the spot to which he has freely cut.*

(9) Now say that you will have to call upon the Genii to help with this trick. Explaining that the Genii is always invisible when he's not at home, pretend to spot him in the air and reach out and catch him in your hand. Then pretend to slip the Genii into the pack of cards on the table.

(10) Pick up the pencil and lay it on the end of the pack and say: "This Genii is very intelligent. He can even write if he has a pencil." Move the pencil forward, sliding it completely across the top of the pack; then lay the pencil aside.

(11) "That gave the Genii time to write a message. Let's find him and see if he did." With that, you spread the pack along the table.

(12) Push the Genii card out of the deck along with the card just below it (A) and the card just above it (B) as shown.

(13) "I'll just turn over the Genii card, and we'll see what the Genii knows." When the signed Genii card is turned over, the names of the two playing cards are seen in the cloud with the spectator's initials still in the lamp.

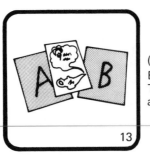

(14) You then turn over cards A and B showing the Six of Clubs and the Two of Spades, which makes the amazement complete.

COMMENTS AND SUGGESTIONS

As in the previous trick, once you have drawn out the previously prepared Genii prediction card, you may allow the spectators to see the face of the packet of Genii cards. As long as the half-card is still in place and securely bound by the rubber band, they will think they are seeing the second Genii card in the packet. Be sure to glance at the face of the packet, though, to be sure the rubber band is still hiding the edge of the half-card.

THE GENII SAVES THE DAY!

EFFECT

In this GENII CARD effect, the magician makes a prediction, writing it in the Genii's cloud. When the prediction goes wrong, the Genii magically "fixes" it, producing a *double surprise.* Again, the MASTER MOVE is used along with the "Force" of a card from a regular pack of playing cards.

SECRET AND PREPARATION

To prepare, before the show, write the name of a playing card — say "Three of Clubs" in the cloud section of the top Genii card. Cover this with one of the "blank" half-cards and place the rubber band around the packet. From an ordinary pack of cards, remove the Three of Clubs and place it at the correct position in the pack ready for any of the "Forces" you have learned.

METHOD

(1) State that you are going to make a "prediction" — you will predict the very same card that a spectator will later select from an ordinary deck of playing cards! So, you OPENLY write the name of some other card — say the Five of Hearts — in the Genii's cloud, stating that this is your prediction.

(2) *Actually, your prediction is written on the half-card which no one knows about.* You then have the spectator put his initials in the lamp to identify the "prediction" card.

(3) Now, go through the Master Move, laying the Genii card (actually the Three of Clubs prediction card) face down on the table and place a coin or other small object on top of it. The half-card with your "Five of Hearts" prediction remains on the Genii packet.

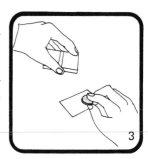

(4) *NOTE: Placing a coin or other small object on the Genii card is important as it discourages anyone from turning the card over until you're ready.*

(5) Drop the Genii packet in your pocket and bring out the pack of playing cards. Remove the pack from its box and "Force" the Three of Clubs on the spectator using the force you are set up for.

(6) Ask the spectator to look at the card he selected and see if your prediction is correct. When he does, he sees that you are wrong, since he saw you write "Five of Hearts" on the Genii card and the card he selected is the Three of Clubs.

(7) That's when you call on the invisible Genii for help — *and the Genii does help.* Remove the coin and ask the spectator to turn over the prediction card. He will find that the Genii has "magically appeared" AND has changed your prediction to the "Three of Clubs," THE SAME CARD HE SELECTED! *HOORAY FOR THE GENII!*

COMMENTS AND SUGGESTIONS

This effect is "super" for three reasons. *One,* it fulfills a prediction; *two,* it mysteriously changes one prediction into another; and *three,* it proves you are right when the spectator thinks that you are wrong. All these combined will have your audience trying to figure out three things at once, which is sure to leave them totally baffled.

One word of caution. You must keep the packet of Genii cards FACE DOWN after the Master Move so that no one will see the "false" prediction on the half-card. Just drop the packet in your pocket and you will find that by the end of the trick, the spectators will have forgotten the packet completely.

GENII'S LIBRARY

EFFECT

The magician has a spectator write his initials in the lamp on the face card of a packet of Genii cards. The picture on the card shows a magic lamp giving off a cloud of smoke — *but no Genii.* This done, he removes the initialed Genii card from the stack and places it face down on the table.

The magician then displays an ordinary paperback book and "riffles" through its pages inviting the spectator to call "Stop" at any time during the riffle. When the call comes, the magician inserts an envelope into the book to mark the exact page selected by the spectator. The spectator is then asked to note the word in the text located in the upper right corner of the selected page.

In an attempt to locate the Genii *and* learn the selected word, the Genii card is partially inserted into the book for only a brief moment. When the card is removed and turned face up, it shows that *both* the Genii and the exact word which was selected from the text have "magically" appeared — with the word written in the Genii's cloud of smoke!

SECRET AND PREPARATION

(A) Carefully cut one page from the center of the paperback book you plan to use and place it on your table, with the *front* of the page (that is, the odd-numbered side of the page that was originally facing the front of the book) facing up. This done, apply a very thin strip of rubber cement along the "binding" edge of the page *and* on the top edge of the envelope as shown.

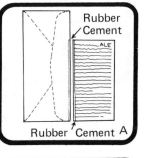

(B) Allow the cement to dry on both surfaces and then attach the glued edge of the page to the glued edge of the envelope. Be sure that the edges of the page are *exactly even* with the left side and lower edges of the envelope. Although this is difficult to describe in written form, it is really quite simple to make. Just study the pictures and you will see exactly how to make this "special" envelope prop which is the key to the entire trick.

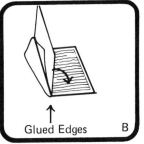

(C) NOTE: The envelope should be *longer* and *wider* than the book page, so that when it is turned over, the page will be completely hidden from view beneath the envelope.

(D) After the glue has set, insert the prepared envelope into the book so that the "secret" page is lined up with the rest of the pages in the book. If this is done correctly, everything should appear natural from all angles. It will look like a book with an envelope stuck in its pages.

(E) Next, write the prediction word from the "force" page (the page you have glued to the envelope) in the cloud of the top card of the Genii packet. Then, cover this with the half-card and place the rubber band around the entire stack.

(1) To begin, place the packet of Genii cards on the table and bring the book into view, casually showing it on both sides. Then, turn the book "face up" and remove the envelope with your right hand. *Make sure not to flash the attached page as you do this.*

(7) Immediately lay the book on the table and pick up the initialed Genii card.

(2) Pick up and display the packet of Genii cards. Have a spectator write his initials in the lamp of the top Genii card as usual. Remove the initialed card using the Master Move (actually removing the prediction card). Place the card face down on the table.

(8) *NOTE: Picking up the Genii card at this time is actually a clever ruse to let you set down the book with the "special" envelope inserted into it. If you did not use the Genii card here, then there would be no reason for you not to show the spectator the page he selected.*

(3) Pick up the book in your left hand and riffle through the pages with your left thumb. Explain to the spectator that he may say "Stop" at *any time* during the riffle.

(9) Slide the Genii card *face down* through the pages of the book. Say, "I will now attempt to locate the Magic Genii within the pages of this book — where he frequently visits on vacation. If we're lucky, perhaps he will also reveal to us the word that you select-ed." After this bit of byplay, replace the prediction card *face down* on the table.

(4) When the call comes, stop riffling and (5) insert the envel-ope into the book where the spectator called stop. Be sure to insert the envelope so that the "bottom" of the envelope is lined up evenly with the bottom edge of the book. Also, insert the envelope *all the way* into the book <u>so that the glued edge of the envelope</u> and the secret prediction page are wedged securely into the binding of the book.

(10) *NOW HERE IS THE MOST IMPORTANT MOVE IN THE TRICK.* Pick up the book and open it (11) so that the book hinges open <u>*between*</u> the envelope and the secretly attached page. The envelope should cover the left-hand portion of the book, exposing the front side of the attached "force" page. Point out to the spectator the *last word* in the *top line* of this page (actually the "force" word) and ask him to <u>remember that word</u>.

Force Page

(6) Without hesitation, gently tap the bottom edge of the book on the table. This squares up the envelope (and the hidden page) with the rest of the pages of the book.

(12) *NOTE: Do not look at the page or the word as you do this. Hold the book away from you so that it faces the spectator and you obviously cannot see the "freely selected" page. Unknown to the spectator, you have now "forced" him to choose a word which he thinks is the result of his random selection.*

(13) Close the book and *remove the envelope,* bringing along the secret page. Immediately place the envelope aside, or better yet, into your coat pocket, *making sure not to expose the secret page as you do.*

(14) To bring the mystery to its close, ask the spectator to call out the word he selected. When he does, turn over the Genii card revealing *both* the Genii *and* the word written in the cloud that *exactly matches* the word "selected" from the text of the book!

COMMENTS AND SUGGESTIONS

Be sure and use a book which *does not open out flat* for this trick. A "paperback" book is best. This is because, if the book opened wide, the spectators might notice that the page he "freely selected" is *actually glued to the envelope.*

Do not call any unnecessary attention to the envelope during the presentation. Handle it as if its *only purpose* is to mark the selected page in the book. Then, after it has done its work, place it in your pocket and continue. By the end of the trick, the audience will most likely forget that you ever used any additional "props" other than the book.

SPECIAL NOTE: Since all of the Genii tricks use the same magical principle, the half-card and the Master Move, you should present only one of the Genii tricks at any one performance. This is an example of Rule 3. . .NEVER repeat a trick for the same spectators.

Money Magic

★ ★ ★

Tricks with coins date back almost to the beginning of magic, and they are as popular as ever today. Coins are always handy if you want to borrow some for impromptu work. If you carry a supply of your own, you will be equipped for feats of really surprising wizardry. Tricks of both types are covered in abundance in this section.

Some good coin tricks are quite simple, others require a great deal of practice while of the best depend on basic moves that are quite easy to learn and a number of them will be described in detail in this section. Your knowledge of such sleights will enable you to build up highly effective coin routines without going into more difficult manipulations which have created the impression that coin work is for "experts" only. Even some coin flourishes come easily with reasonable practice and those, too, have been included in this section.

By putting coin effects into your general programs, you can learn as you go, expanding your coin routines until they become all-inclusive. Even before then, you should become sufficiently "money minded" to go in for tricks with folding currency. So some of those have been included in this same section, to be used as required. The same rule applies both to coins and bills: When performing either type of money magic, stress the fact that you use ordinary means-in some cases, borrowing them, thus proving that skill, not trickery, is the great factor in your work. The more you have them believing that, the more wonderful your money magic will appear.

THE COIN FOLD

The magician borrows a coin from a member of the audience and has it marked by its owner for later identification. A small sheet of paper is then folded around the coin so it is completely enclosed within the paper. This little package can even be tapped on the table so the audience can hear that the coin is actually inside. At all times the folded paper remains in view of the spectators — yet the magician causes the coin to vanish from within the paper — which he tears into pieces. He then reproduces the coin from his pocket, the spectator's lapel, or anywhere he wishes.

SECRET AND PREPARATION

No special items are required for this effect. The coin, however, which can be borrowed, should be large enough for an effective vanish. A half-dollar or dollar-sized coin works well and is easily visible even at some distance. The piece of paper used should measure approximately 4 x 6 inches.

METHOD

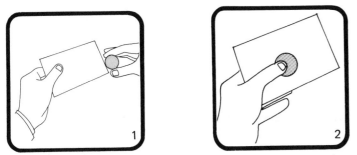

(1)   Borrow a coin from a member of the audience and have the spectator mark the coin with a permanent ink marking pen for later identification. This done, hold the paper in your left hand and display the coin openly at your right fingertips. You remark, "I will seal the borrowed coin within the folds of this piece of paper." (2)   Place the coin in the center of the paper and hold it there with your left thumb and fingers as shown.

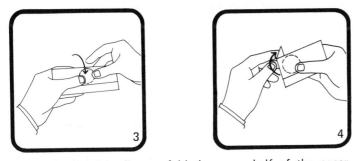

(3)   With the right fingers, fold the upper half of the paper *toward you* as shown — completely over the coin — so that no part of the coin is visible to you or the spectators. (4)   Next, fold the left side of the paper — *away from you* — against the back of the coin. This seals the coin in the paper at the *left side*. Do not fold the paper tightly against the edge of the coin. Instead, leave about a quarter inch of "play" between the fold and the left edge of the coin.

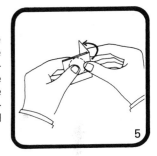

(5)   Now fold the right side of the paper — *away from you* — against the back of the coin so it overlaps the left-hand fold. This seals the coin in the paper from the *right side*. Again, leave another quarter inch of "play" between the crease of the right fold and the right edge of the coin.

(6)   *NOTE: At this point, the coin is sealed in from all sides except for the bottom edge of the paper, which remains open. In making the folds, be sure to maintain enough pressure on the coin through the paper to keep it inside, so it won't slide out the open bottom edge.*

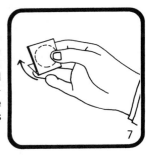

(7)   The last fold is the most important. If you folded the bottom edge upward — *toward you* — it would seal the coin inside. Instead, the last fold is made upward — *but toward the audience* — leaving the bottom edge of the package open. This provides a means of escape for the coin.

(8)   When the last fold has been made, press the paper firmly around the edge of the coin *leaving a distinct impression of the coin outlined on the surface of the paper*. This impression is important. It will later convince the audience that the coin is still wrapped securely within the folded package.

(9) Hold the small package with the tips of your right fingers. Tap the edge of the folded paper on the table allowing the spectators to "hear" the coin inside. Say, "The coin is now securely sealed within the folded paper. If you listen, you can even hear it."

(13) *NOTE: As the folded package is transferred from the right to the left hand, if you wish, instead of leaving the coin in the right hand, you can place your hand casually in your right pants or coat pocket where you leave the coin to be reproduced later. In this way, the right hand will be empty as you move on to the next step.*

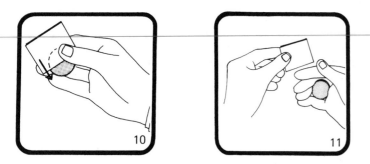

(10) To make the coin "vanish," you do the following moves: Hold the folded paper with the "opening" pointing downward toward the base of the fingers. Relax the pressure of your right thumb and fingers and the coin will slide out of the bottom of the paper into your right hand — where it remains hidden in your curled fingers. (11) After the coin drops into your hand, take the package with your left fingers. Your right hand falls casually to your side with the coin held secretly in the Finger Palm position as shown.

(14) Bring both hands together in front of you and tear the paper in half. (The illustration shows how to hold the coin in the Finger Palm position as you tear the paper.) Toss the pieces onto the table. You can even tear the paper into many pieces to prove, without a doubt, that the coin has truly "vanished." The coin can then be reproduced from your pocket — or, if you still hold the coin in the Finger Palm position, you can produce it from the spectator's coat lapel, tie, or anywhere you desire.

(12) With your left hand, casually display the folded package to the spectators, who believe that the coin is still wrapped inside. *This is where the outlined impression of the coin becomes so valuable.* As you display the paper, casually show both sides, *allowing the spectators to see the impression made by the coin,* thus proving the presence of the coin.

COMMENTS AND SUGGESTIONS

The Coin Fold is a standard method for vanishing a coin and can be used in conjunction with many coin routines where the vanish of a coin is necessary.

COIN THROUGH HANDKERCHIEF

Here is a clever effect using a pocket handkerchief and a coin (a half-dollar is a good size to use).

EFFECT

The magician displays the coin at the tips of his right thumb and fingers. He then drapes the handkerchief over the coin so that the coin seems to penetrate the fabric of the handkerchief, without leaving a trace of a tear or a hole. The magician can then hand both the coin and the handkerchief for examination.

METHOD

(1) For this effect you may use your own handkerchief, but the trick is stronger if you utilize a borrowed one. In either case, first display the coin by holding it at the tips of your right thumb and first two fingers. Your fingers and thumb are pointing *up* with one side of the coin facing the audience.

(2) With your left hand, drape the handkerchief over the coin *and over your right hand.* The coin should be under the center of the handkerchief.

(3) With your left hand adjust the handkerchief around the coin. At the same time, underneath the handkerchief, secretly lift a small bit of cloth behind the coin with your right thumb and fold it around your left thumb as shown.

(4) Remove your left hand, leaving the small bit of handkerchief "nipped" between your right thumb and the back of the coin. This places two layers of fabric between the right thumb and the coin.

(5) Now, grasp the front edge of the handkerchief with your left hand, lifting it up, back and completely over the coin. This action will expose the coin to the spectators, supposedly to assure them that the coin is still in its original position.

(6) THE FOLLOWING MOVE IS THE REAL SECRET OF THE TRICK: With your left hand, grasp BOTH EDGES of the handkerchief and lift them both up and over the coin as shown.

(7) The effect on the spectators will be that you simply exposed the coin for them to show that it was still there and then re-covered it with the handkerchief as before.

(8) *In actuality you are now holding the coin OUTSIDE the back of the handkerchief.*

(9) With the left hand, grasp the coin through the now doubled over fabric and remove your right hand as shown. It will appear to the audience as if the handkerchief is draped completely around the coin.

(10) With your now free right hand twist the lower part of the handkerchief around the coin.

(11) As you twist the handkerchief, the shape of the coin will become visible under the fabric.

(12) You may also adjust the cloth over the exposed "Back" of the coin and show the handkerchief on all sides, if you wish.

(13) Now, slowly push the coin upwards in the handkerchief as your left hand comes over to take the edge of the coin as it "penetrates" the handkerchief.

(14) You may now hand both the handkerchief and the coin for examination.

COIN THROUGH HANDKERCHIEF — SECOND VERSION

This effect will appear exactly the same to your audience as the first COIN THROUGH HANDKERCHIEF, yet *the METHOD is entirely different*. But because it is so direct and bold, it will fool anyone who might know the first method just described. This is another example of an ingenious mystery devised by "Gen" Grant.

EFFECT

The magician displays a Half-Dollar between the tips of the fingers of his right hand. The left hand holds a handkerchief which he drapes over both the coin *and* his right hand. Then, with his left hand, he grips the coin through the cloth from the outside, holding it there while his right hand is withdrawn from beneath. The right hand again grasps the coin — this time *through* the material. Now he moves his left hand down and grasps the "hanging" corners of the handkerchief while his right continues to hold the coin. The magician gives a sharp downward jerk to the handkerchief — and the coin "penetrates" completely through the cloth, leaving no trace of a hole.

METHOD
ALL OF THE FOLLOWING ILLUSTRATIONS ARE AS SEEN BY THE MAGICIAN.

(1) Hold the coin by the tips of your right finger and thumb as shown. Pick up the handkerchief with your left hand.

(4) Your left hand then grips the coin through the cloth, *from the outside,* between the thumb and fingers as shown.

(2) As you display the coin, begin to cover it with the handkerchief. Notice that your left hand holds the edge of the handkerchief by the *side,* not by the *corner*.

(5) Now, as you withdraw your right hand from beneath the handkerchief, you really *keep the coin in your right hand* and *secretly* bring it down below the rear edge of the handkerchief. Your left hand holds the handkerchief at the center, AS IF IT WERE STILL HOLDING THE COIN THROUGH THE CLOTH.

(3) When the coin is completely covered, the *front* edge of the cloth (the edge toward the spectators) drapes a little *lower* than the *back* edge. *This leaves the handkerchief a bit shorter in back than in front.*

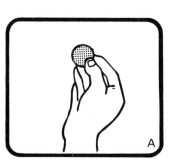

(6) With your right hand, bring the coin up *behind the handkerchief* and SLIDE IT UNDER YOUR LEFT THUMB — "clipping" the coin *behind* the cloth, out of the spectators' view.

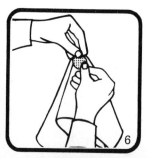

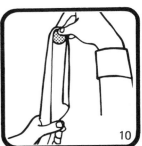

(7) With the right fingers, *pretend* to adjust the folds of the *right* side of the handkerchief by sliding your fingers down along the cloth.

(9) Then, with your left fingers, *pretend* to adjust the *left* side of the handkerchief, sliding the fingers down the cloth as before.

(10) Now gather all four corners of the handkerchief into your left hand. Your right hand still holds the coin *behind* the cloth.

(8) Bring your right hand back up to the center (top) of the handkerchief and *transfer BOTH the coin AND the handkerchief from your left fingers to your right fingers, still keeping the coin hidden behind the cloth.*

(11) Hold the corners tightly in your left hand. Then "jerk" the handkerchief **sharply** downward — *out of your right hand. Pull the handkerchief AWAY from the coin — WHICH REMAINS HELD BY YOUR RIGHT FINGERTIPS.* The coin has apparently penetrated the center of the handkerchief! The handkerchief and the coin can then be tossed to the spectators for examination.

COMMENTS AND SUGGESTIONS

As bold as this may seem, performed correctly, every movement is natural and, therefore, accepted by even the sharpest observers, who are looking for quick or suspicious movements. Rehearse it first by *actually leaving the coin under the handkerchief* and going through the rest of the "Steps" just as described. Then repeat *the very same action,* following the "magical penetration" routine given here. *When both look the same,* you will be ready to present this second version of the COIN THROUGH HANDKERCHIEF.

MAGICALLY MULTIPLY YOUR MONEY

For a neat, close-up effect, this is ideal, as it can be set up in a moment and performed almost anywhere — provided the spectators are close enough to appreciate it fully. As a result, it makes an excellent "close-up" trick — but it also can be worked quite as readily while standing.

EFFECT

The magician displays a "Nickel" between the tips of his right thumb and first finger. The other fingers of his right hand are *open wide.* Everyone can see his hand is quite empty except for the Nickel.

Showing his left hand to be equally empty, the magician slowly grasps the Nickel with his left thumb and first finger. For a brief moment, both hands hold the coin at the fingertips — then the hands draw apart in a slow, outward motion. The audience is amazed to see *two Half-Dollars* emerging instead of the Nickel. When both hands are separated, each unmistakably holds a real Half-Dollar, proving that his money has multiplied *twenty times over.* THAT'S MAGIC!

SECRET AND PREPARATION

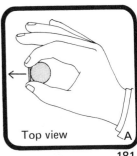

Top view

The entire effect depends upon an artful form of concealment, which is simplicity itself, yet so deceptive that no one will suspect it. Skill is reduced to a minimum. So just follow instructions and see for yourself — which you can do quite nicely by testing the routine before a mirror.

To prepare, hold the two Half-Dollars *edgewise* (horizontally) near the tips of your right thumb and forefinger, keeping the two coins together. Now, place the Nickel *upright* (vertically) between the tips of the same thumb and forefinger. Center the Nickel against the outer edge of the Halves. With the coins held firmly in this position, you are ready to begin.

METHOD

(1) As you face the spectator, position your right hand full front before him, showing him the Nickel *at his eye level.* The spectator will not see the Halves hiding edgewise behind the Nickel if, *and only if,* your hand is held so the Halves are parallel to his line of vision — hidden "edgewise" behind the much smaller Nickel. Illustration A shows the starting position as it would be seen *from slightly above.* Note how the Nickel masks the Half-Dollars since the edges of the Halves are at the *exact center* of the Nickel.

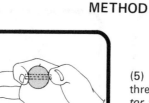

(5) All in the same action, "tip" the three coins upright *toward the spectator* with your left thumb and first finger. The coins are all held together in a stack, *with the Nickel "hidden" in back.*

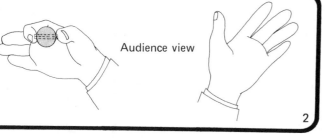

Audience view

(2) From the spectator's view, your right hand is so obviously empty (except for the Nickel) that any suspicion would be directed toward your left hand — which you now show just as empty — front and back.

(6) Without stopping, grip the stack between your thumbs and fingers and begin drawing the two Halves apart. Your *left* hand draws the *front* Half-Dollar to the left while your *right* hand draws the *rear* Half-Dollar *and the Nickel* to the right.

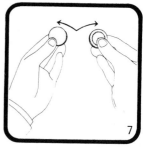

(3) Slowly and deliberately, bring your hands together, with the thumbs and forefingers of *both hands* pointing toward each other. The remaining fingers of both hands should be slightly opened to give the spectator a clear view of your "empty" hands. *NOTE: Keep your hand "level" with the spectator's eyes so that he does not see the concealed Halves as you turn your hand.*

(7) Your right thumb keeps the Nickel hidden behind the rear Half-Dollar — retaining it there as you separate the two Halves. To the audience, the Nickel will appear to have "magically" *enlarged* AND *doubled* before their eyes — in an instant!

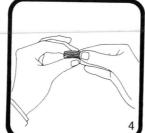

(4) As your hands move closer together, your left thumb comes *beneath* the coins, pushing the lower edge of the Nickel inwards, *rotating the Nickel up against the bottom Half-Dollar* — ALL THREE COINS ARE NOW HORIZONTAL. This is the *one moment* when the coin(s) are out of the spectator's direct view.

(8) The coins are then drawn completely apart and shown as two Half-Dollars at the fingertips of each hand. Be careful not to accidentally "flash" the hidden Nickel when displaying the two Halves to the audience.

COMMENTS AND SUGGESTIONS

This is a brief but baffling effect. The only question left concerns the disposal of the Nickel, which would spoil the mystery if seen. When seated at a table, after displaying the Half-Dollars, bring both hands near the edge of the table and dip your right hand a little behind your left hand. This hides your right hand momentarily. At that moment, your right thumb releases the Nickel, letting it fall into your lap. *NOTE: This is one method of LAPPING.* Both hands then come forward and toss their coins on the table. The hands can be shown completely empty, proving that the Nickel is no longer there. If you are standing, just place the "right-hand" Half in your pocket (along with its "secret" Nickel) and proceed with any effect using the other, "left-hand," Half.

FOUR-COIN ASSEMBLY

This highly effective table trick is performed with the simplest of objects: four coins, either half-dollars or quarters; two pieces of cardboard about 3 x 5 inches ("index" cards work nicely); and a napkin or fairly thick handkerchief.

EFFECT

A handkerchief is spread on the table and four coins are placed near the corners, with the two cards lying along with them. Picking up the cards, the magician shows various ways in which they can be used to cover any two of the coins. After deciding on diagonal corners, he takes the uncovered coins, one at a time, under the handkerchief and causes each coin to mysteriously penetrate the cloth under the card at the Corner A. At the end of the trick, *all four coins appear under the card* — including the coin at Corner D — WHICH THE MAGICIAN APPARENTLY NEVER TOUCHED DURING THE ENTIRE PERFORMANCE.

METHOD

The presentation depends upon a well-designed routine that directs the spectator's attention away from the few simple moves required. By following it with the actual items, all the details can be easily learned and mastered:

(1) Begin by laying out four coins, one on each corner of the cloth, as shown. The cards are tossed on the handkerchief as you say, "Here are *four* coins, *two* cards and *one* handkerchief."

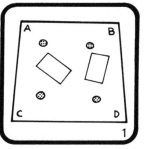

(2) Pick up a card in each hand, thumb on top, fingers below, and cover the two coins at Corners C and D. Say, "I can use these cards to cover the two coins in this row."

(3) Lift the cards and move them to cover the coins at Corners A and B. Say, "Or I can cover the coins in this row."

(4) Next, your right hand again moves to cover the coin at D, while your left hand moves its card from A across to B. State, "Also, I can cover two coins at the sides."

(5) Here, as you cover the coin at D, YOUR RIGHT THUMB PRESSES DOWN ON THE LEFT EDGE OF THE COIN SO THAT THE FINGERS OF YOUR RIGHT HAND CAN SLIDE UNDER THE COIN AND SECRETLY PICK IT UP AND HOLD IT AGAINST THE CARD.

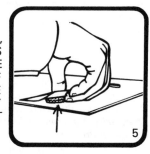

(6) *NOTE: When you "secretly" pick up the coin, it is important that your right fingers make as little motion as possible. Your right hand should look completely natural with no suspicious movements that might give you away. ALSO, YOU WILL FIND THE "PICK-UP" MUCH EASIER TO DO IF YOU ARE PERFORMING ON A SOFT SURFACE, SUCH AS A CLOSE-UP MAT.*

(7) Your left hand draws its card toward you, SLIDING IT OVER THE RIGHT-HAND CARD, as if to cover the coin at Corner D.

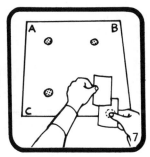

(8) Then, your right hand draws its card toward you, HOLDING THE COIN UNDER IT AS SHOWN IN THIS VIEW FROM BELOW. Your left hand leaves its card at D *over the exact spot where the "stolen" coin was located.*

(9) Your right hand then places its card over the coin at Corner A, LEAVING WITH IT THE COIN THAT IT SECRETLY BROUGHT FROM D. Leave the cards at A and D as you comment, "Or I can cover two coins, 'criss-cross,' like this."

(10) *Note the "build-up" and timing up to this point. By covering C-D, then A-B, then B-D, you "condition" the observers to expect another simple placement of cards. The fact that the left hand is moved first, showing the coin at B, will cause people to think they also saw the coin at D before the left-hand card covered it.*

(11) Remark that you have now covered coins at the diagonal corners (A and D). *Pick up the coin from C with your right hand and lift that corner of the cloth with your left hand as shown.* State that you will now magically "push" the coin up through the cloth, causing it to join the coin under the card at Corner A.

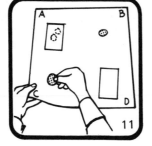

(12) Here you make another secret move — AS YOU MOVE YOUR RIGHT HAND UNDER THE CLOTH, SECRETLY CLIP THE COIN BETWEEN THE TIPS OF THE FINGERS OF YOUR LEFT HAND. Your right hand should continue its forward motion under the cloth to Corner A without pausing, as you secretly transfer the coin from your right to your left hand.

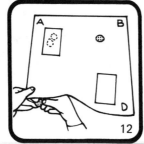

(13) Here, the "secret transfer" of the coin is shown from a different view.

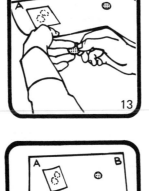

(14) When the now empty right hand is under the coin(s) at Corner A, make a slight upward "flicking" movement with the right fingers, causing the coins under the card to clink together. Explain that the coin has just "penetrated" the cloth and joined the coin under the card.

(15) The right hand is now removed from under the cloth and casually shown empty as it reaches to turn over the card at Corner A. THE LEFT FINGERS STILL HOLD THE CLIPPED COIN, BUT KEEP IT HIDDEN BENEATH THE HANDKERCHIEF.

(16) The right hand now turns over the card at Corner A, and, in the same motion, moves the card toward your left hand *bringing it directly over Corner C.*

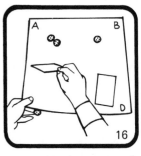

(17) In one continuous motion, YOUR RIGHT HAND SLIDES THE CARD UNDER YOUR LEFT THUMB ....AS THE LEFT HAND DRAWS THE CLIPPED COIN FROM UNDER THE CLOTH, PRESSING IT UP AGAINST THE CARD.

(18) Then, the left hand places the card over the two coins at Corner A, SECRETLY ADDING THE COIN IT HOLDS UNDER THE CARD.

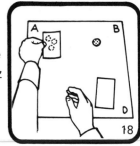

(19) Your left hand returns to Corner C and lifts the cloth while your right hand picks up the coin at Corner B. Announce that you will push another coin up through the cloth.

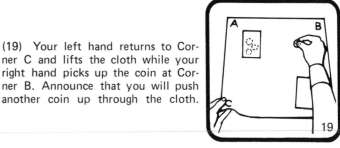

(20) Place your right hand under the cloth the same as before, WITH YOUR LEFT FINGERS CLIPPING THE COIN AND STEALING IT AWAY, AS YOUR RIGHT HAND GOES BENEATH THE CLOTH.

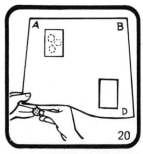

(21) The right hand then pretends to push the coin up through the cloth under the card at Corner A (also with a clink).

(24) As before, the right hand transfers the card to the left hand, which secretly carries the coin away beneath the card. Place the card over the three coins at Corner A, just as before, secretly adding the fourth coin. *(NOTE: Be careful not to let the "secret" coin clink against the other coins as you lay the card down.)*

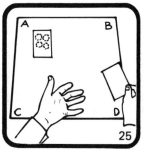

(22) Remove your right hand from beneath the cloth, then lift the card at Corner A.

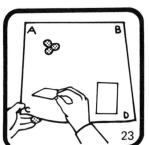

(25) With no more coins in view, you remind the audience that one coin is still under the other card at Corner D. So you command it to join the other three. When you lift the card at Corner D, the spectators see, to their amazement, that the coin has really gone!

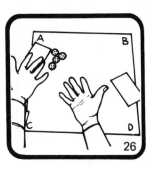

(23) As you reveal the *three* coins, turn the card over toward your left hand, which has the clipped coin ready. Remark, "And another coin has come up through!"

(26) Use your left hand to lift the card at Corner A, showing all four coins there, making the mystery complete!

COMMENTS AND SUGGESTIONS

The entire routine should be practiced until it can be done smoothly, and without hesitation where the "secret moves" are concerned. You may experiment with other patterns of covering the coins that work well in directing attention away from the right hand when it secretly picks up the coin at Corner D. For example: Cover the coins at A and B, then bring the right-hand card down to D, so that A and D are covered. Now the left hand moves its card from A to B, while your right fingers secretly pick up the coin at D — *all attention is naturally centered on the left-hand card.* From there simply proceed with the usual routine. Keep alert for audience reactions whenever you present this excellent close-up mystery, and other ideas will suggest themselves.

SLEIGHTS WITH COINS

The following four effects are "pure" *sleight-of-hand* and are all done with an ordinary object that you almost always have with you — a *coin*. After you have mastered them, you will not only have acquired several great effects that can be presented anywhere and anytime, but also you will have opened the door to a multitude of additional, truly sensational Magical Mysteries. Most important of all, you are beginning to learn two of the basic prerequisites to becoming an expert magician — *Dexterity and Misdirection.*

THE FRENCH DROP
Using a Coin
METHOD

MAGICIAN'S VIEW

SPECTATORS' VIEW

(1) Hold the coin level between the tips of your left thumb and fingers. All four fingers and the thumb of your left hand should point *upward.* Your fingers should be held *close together* so the audience cannot see between them.

1A

1B

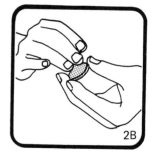

(2) Your right hand approaches from behind to apparently take the coin by sliding your right thumb beneath and your right fingers above the coin. Your left hand should be held as shown from the "Spectators' View" (right side of page), so the coin can still be seen.

2A

2B

(3) Now the fingers of your right hand close over the coin — covering the coin as shown.

3A

3B

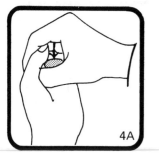

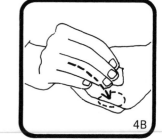

(4) As your right hand pauses momentarily, your left thumb *releases the coin* so that it "secretly" *drops* into the bend of your left fingers.

4A

4B

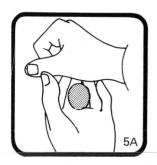

(5) Without hesitation, your right hand closes into a fist *as if taking the coin* from your left fingers.

5A

5B

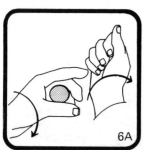

(6) Then, in one continuous motion, *turn both hands over* (see arrows) — as you turn your body to the right. (Just twist your left hand inward, toward your body, so the coin stays hidden from view, and *at the same time,* turn your right hand so that its *closed fingers* face the audience.) As you rotate your hands, your left first finger casually points toward your right hand. *Follow your RIGHT HAND with your eyes* — IT IS SUPPOSED TO CONTAIN THE COIN.

6A

6B

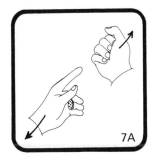

(7) As your right hand moves away, casually let your left hand fall to your side with the coin held secretly in its curled fingers. *Your eyes should remain fixed on your right hand at all times. This is MISDIRECTION.*

(8) Slowly begin to make a "rubbing" motion with your right fingers, as if to rub the coin away. Then, open your hand to show the coin has "vanished."

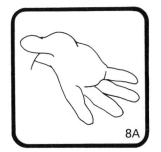

THE FINGER PALM VANISH

EFFECT

In this vanish, the coin is actually retained *in the same spot in your left hand* from start to finish. This allows you to perform the sleight either swiftly or slowly, as you prefer. The instruction is given with TWO sets of illustrations. . . . Those at the *left* show how it appears to you, the *performer;* those at the *right* represent the *spectators'* view.

METHOD

MAGICIAN'S VIEW   *SPECTATORS' VIEW*

(1) Display a coin lying on the finger of your right hand, as shown.

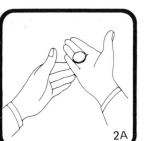

(2) Your left hand is held palm up, about waist high, with your left fingers pointing just to the right of the center of your audience. Your right little finger rests across the tips of your left fingers.

MAGICIAN'S VIEW

SPECTATORS' VIEW

3A

3B

(3) The right hand starts to turn over toward you. *At the same time, curl your right fingers inward just enough to hold the coin securely in the right fingers,* as shown. The coin is now in the FINGER PALM position.

4A

4B

(4) Tip your right hand over even more, as shown . . . right now is the moment when the coin "should" be falling into your left hand. *Actually, the right hand secretly retains the coin in the FINGER PALMED position.*

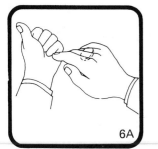

5A

5B

(5) Your left fingers close, *as if they contained the coin.* Your right hand begins to move away from your left hand with the coin secretly FINGER PALMED.

6A

6B

(6) As your left hand closes into a loose fist, your right hand pauses briefly, pointing the first finger toward the closed left hand, which carries attention by moving away to the left.

7A

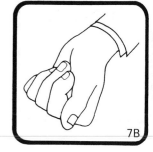

7B

(7) Lower your right hand casually to your side . . . *as your eyes follow your left hand.* . . . THIS IS MISDIRECTION.

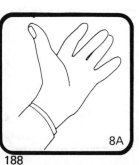

8A

8B

(8) The left hand is now "on its own." It apparently squeezes the coin into "nothing" and opens to show that the coin has "vanished."

THE PINCH OR DROP VANISH

MAGICIAN'S VIEW   **METHOD**   *SPECTATORS' VIEW*

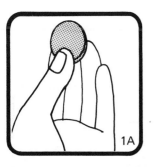

(1) Hold a coin at the tips of your left thumb and first three fingers so it projects straight upward. Keep your fingers *close together* so that the viewers cannot see between them. The palm of your hand faces you.

(2) Your right hand approaches your left hand as if to grasp the coin.

(3) The right hand continues to move until it *completely covers the coin* as if to remove it from between your left thumb and fingers.

(4) As soon as the coin is concealed by the right fingers, your left thumb releases its "pinching" grip, *allowing the coin to slide secretly down to the base of the left fingers.*

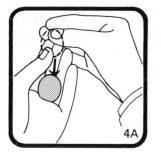

(5) The coin remains concealed in your left hand, held in the FINGER PALM position. Your right hand moves away, *apparently taking the coin with it.* As you move your right hand away, *keep your eyes "fixed" on your right hand,* as if it really contained the coin. *The audience's attention will follow your right hand* — while you casually drop your left hand to your side with the coin secretly held in its fingers.

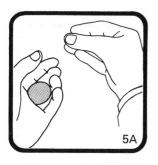

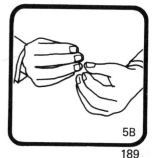

MAGICIAN'S VIEW

SPECTATORS' VIEW

6A

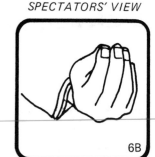

6B

(6)   With the back of the right hand still toward the audience, "rub" your thumb and fingers together as if to "dissolve" the coin in your fingertips.

7A

(7)   Finally, open your hand and show it empty to complete the "vanish."

7B

NOTE: In Steps 6 and 7 of this "vanish," your right hand *does not* close into a fist. It appears to "take" the coin from your left hand and then "pretends" to display it — before grinding it into "nothing."

COMMENTS AND SUGGESTIONS

In Steps 5, 6, and 7 and in all other Sleight-of-Hand vanishes where the coin is *apparently* transferred from one hand to the other, it is *ESSENTIAL that your eyes follow the hand which apparently contains the coin*. This is one of the most basic and important examples of *"MISDIRECTION."* In fact, in this case, where you *look* is as important as the *sleight* itself. THE AUDIENCE WILL LOOK WHERE YOU LOOK. Therefore, when you practice this or any other similar sleight, you should first practice *really* taking the coin away in your right hand. This will accomplish two things: FIRST, you want the audience to believe that you are taking the coin in your right hand when you are really concealing it in your left. Therefore, the more *natural* this move looks, the more your audience will "believe." Thus, *by really taking the coin,* you will discover for yourself exactly how the move should look *when you perform the sleight.* SECOND, and of equal importance, you will see that, if you *really* take the coin in your right hand, *that is where you will look.* You would *not* take the coin in your *right* hand and *look* at your *left.* All of the moves in the PINCH VANISH are fully illustrated. Stand in front of a mirror — hold the coin at the tips of your left fingers — *then, really take the coin in your right hand.* Do this a number of times. Make your actions correspond to the pictures on the right-hand side of the page. Just make the "pickup" motion in an easy and natural way. THEN, still standing in front of the mirror, try the *sleight.* As you "pretend" to take the coin, let it slide down into your left hand, as shown on the *left* side of the page. By using the mirror and the two sets of illustrations, you can see exactly how this sleight will appear to you *and* to your audience. And always remember your *MISDIRECTION* — ALWAYS LOOK AT THE HAND THAT *SUPPOSEDLY* CONTAINS THE COIN!

THE CLASSIC PALM
Using a Coin

This is probably the oldest and most basic of all coin sleights used to conceal a coin in the hand in a natural manner. It is also one of the most difficult to master....but, once learned it will be of great value to you — not only with coins, but with other objects as well.

METHOD

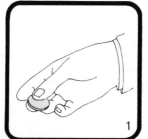

1

(1)   Place a coin on the tips of your two middle fingers and hold it there with the tip of your thumb.

(2)   Remove the thumb and bend your fingertips inward, sliding the coin along the underside of your thumb until it reaches your palm. As you slide the coin into the palm, *stretch your hand* open so the muscles at the base of your thumb and little finger are fully expanded.

2

(3) Press the coin *firmly into the palm* and *contract the muscles* of your hand inward — thus gaining a grip on the edges of the coin. Draw your thumb inward only as far as needed to retain the coin comfortably. Too much "grip" will make your hand appear cramped and tense.

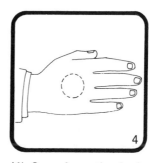

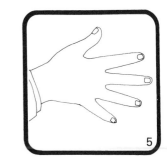

(4) Seen from the back, the hand should look relaxed and natural, with the fingers close together. (5) Avoid the common fault of holding the coin too tightly and spreading the thumb and fingers wide, as shown here. This will only give away the fact that you are "hiding" something. Only when the hand looks natural will you be above suspicion and thus have mastered the Classic Palm.

COMMENTS AND SUGGESTIONS

The basic magical term "Palm" comes from this method of concealment, as the coin is actually gripped in the *palm* of the hand. Keep practicing it until you can place the coin in just the right position. It will then become "second nature" and will prove extremely useful. Once the knack is acquired, coins of various sizes can be retained. It is a good idea to use the hand containing the palmed coin for various gestures such as snapping the fingers, pulling back the sleeve, or picking up articles from the table. These natural actions will direct attention *away* from the hand as people will automatically assume that it is empty. NOTE: The object being "Palmed" must be placed in the CLASSIC PALM position with the aid of only the finger and thumb of the hand doing the "Palming" — with no help from your "other" hand. You should also practice this important sleight so that you can "Palm" objects in *either hand* with equal ease.

MASTER COIN MYSTERIES

Now that you have learned four basic coin sleights — The French Drop; The Finger Palm Vanish; The Pinch Vanish, and The Classic Palm — you are ready to move ahead to the outstanding *Master Coin Mysteries* that follow.

THE COIN-VANISHING HANDKERCHIEF

EFFECT

The magician borrows a coin from a spectator and has it marked for future identification. The magician places the coin under a pocket handkerchief and gives it to a spectator to hold. Under these conditions, *even though the volunteer can feel the coin through the fabric of the handkerchief and the audience can plainly see its shape,* the performer causes the marked coin to *VANISH right from under the spectator's fingertips!*

SECRET AND PREPARATION

The following method for the vanish of a coin or any other small object has many uses, as you will find later in the Course.

(A) For this you need an inexpensive pocket handkerchief. Place the handkerchief flat on a table. Place a coin of the same size as the one which you will later borrow from the spectator on the lower right hand corner of the handkerchief.

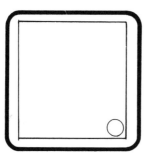

(B) Now cover the coin with a small square piece of matching fabric (a piece cut from a duplicate handkerchief is perfect). Sew the four edges of the small square of cloth to the handkerchief. THE COIN IS NOW HIDDEN INSIDE A SECRET POCKET YOU HAVE MADE IN THE CORNER OF THE HANDKERCHIEF.

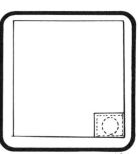

(1) Put the prepared handkerchief into your pocket or lay it on your table. If you can do so, it's a nice touch to wear it as a part of your wardrobe. If worn in your top coat pocket, as an example, it subtly influences your audience into assuming that the handkerchief is not a "magical prop."

(2) Borrow a coin from a spectator which duplicates the coin hidden in your handkerchief. Bring him up on the platform with you and have him mark the coin for identification. Stand your volunteer to your left and remove your pocket handkerchief.

(3) Hold the borrowed coin between your left thumb and first fingers, with your fingers and thumb pointing "up" and one side of the coin toward the audience. With your right hand cover the coin *and* your left hand with the prepared handkerchief. THE CORNER WITH THE SECRET POCKET SHOULD BE ON THE SIDE OF THE HANDKERCHIEF *THAT IS TO-WARD YOU,* AS SHOWN.

(4) Grasp the hidden coin with the right thumb and fingers and, *with your right hand, lift the corner with the concealed duplicate coin up under the handkerchief.* POSITION IT <u>NEXT</u> TO THE BORROWED COIN.

(5) At this point, you substitute the hidden coin for the marked coin BY FINGER PALMING THE MARKED COIN IN YOUR LEFT HAND. With-draw your left hand holding the bor-rowed coin as shown.

(6) *NOTE: Either your right or your left hand can be used for Finger Palming and removing the borrowed coin — just use whichever hand is easier for you and whichever works best for the "reproduction" of the coin that you have set up. In the illustrations, your left hand is shown palming the spectator's coin while your right hand holds the handkerchief and the "secret" duplicate coin.*

(7) Now grasp the "secret" coin through the fabric of the handkerchief with your left hand. Remove your right hand from beneath the hand-kerchief as you hold the coin with your left thumb and fingers. Then, with your right hand, twist the cloth around *below* the coin. *Make sure that the spectators don't get a "flash" of the marked coin that is Finger Palmed in your left hand.*

(8) Grasp the handkerchief beneath the coin with your right hand and offer the cloth-covered coin to a spectator to hold. Just act natural and remember that the audience's attention is on the duplicate coin which is now under the handkerchief. Ask the spectator to hold *his* coin through the fabric of the handkerchief as you (a) either casually drop the coin into your pocket or (b) place the coin in position for its mysterious reappearance — (as in THE COIN IN THE BALL OF WOOL).

(9) When you are ready for the "vanish," ask the spectator if he can still feel his coin under the handker-chief. He will reply, "Yes."

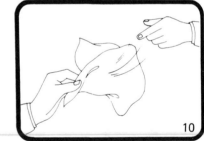

(10) GRASP ONE CORNER of the handkerchief and "jerk" the handkerchief and the coin away from the spectator's grasp. *It will appear as if the coin has "vanished" from the spectator's fingertips.*

(11) Casually show the handkerchief on both sides and replace it in your pocket. You may now reproduce the borrowed coin in any manner you wish. A number of very clever effects using this "vanish" are described later in the Course.

THE COIN-VANISHING HANDKERCHIEF — SECOND VARIATION

EFFECT

The effect is the same as the COIN-VANISHING HANDKERCHIEF, except that in this case, the borrowed coin is further "secured" in the handkerchief before the Vanish by a rubber band.

SECRET AND PREPARATION

In addition to the specially prepared COIN-VANISHING HANDKERCHIEF, you will need a small rubber band which you place in your left coat pocket.

METHOD

(1) Proceed as in the Coin-Vanishing Handkerchief through Step 9.

(2) As the left hand leaves with the Finger Palmed marked coin, reach into your coat pocket and remove the rubber band, *leaving the coin in your pocket.*

(3) Place the rubber band around the handkerchief *below* the coin as shown.

(4) *NOTE: The reason for the rubber band is twofold. First, it permits a natural way in which to dispose of the marked coin in your pocket temporarily. Second, it prevents the spectator from visually inspecting the contents of the handkerchief while he is holding the coin.*

(5) When you are ready for the Vanish, ask the spectator if he still has the coin in his grasp. After he answers "Yes," *remove the rubber band.* Then, quickly snap the handkerchief out of his hand as usual.

COMMENTS AND SUGGESTIONS

The addition of the rubber band can come in handy to cover what might otherwise be a "suspicious" move when you pocket the borrowed coin. The rubber band could also be placed in the location where the marked coin is going to be reproduced, say in the box holding the COIN IN THE BALL OF WOOL. This would give you a natural reason for going to the box and inserting the coin in the slide before the audience is aware of trickery of any kind.

GRANT'S SUPER COIN-VANISHING HANDKERCHIEF

"GEN" GRANT

Here is a clever variation for the specially prepared COIN-VANISHING HANDKERCHIEF. The construction of this handkerchief is different in that the "secret" coin, which is concealed in the corner of the handkerchief, is *removable.* The handkerchief can therefore be adapted to *many different tricks* requiring the vanish of various sized coins or other small objects.

METHOD

(1) Purchase two identical pocket handkerchiefs. Open one of them flat on your table as shown. (2) Cut a 2" square from the corner of the second handkerchief and place it over the matching corner of the first handkerchief.

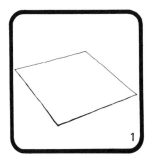

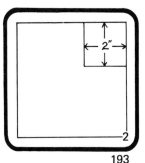

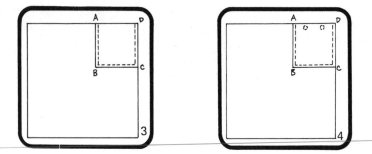

(5) IMPORTANT NOTE: The most important value of this specially prepared handkerchief is that you can now insert *any coin or small object* into the secret pocket. A ring, coin, or folded up dollar bill are just a few examples of the small items which can be vanished by this versatile and inexpensive piece of magical apparatus.

(3) Sew *three* of the edges of the small square of cloth (indicated by dotted lines in the illustration) to the first handkerchief. Leave the outside seam, A to D, *open. NOTE: The unhemmed edges of the corner patch, A to B and B to C, should be turned under before sewing to prevent the cut edges from fraying.*

(4) This done, sew two small dress snaps on the inside hem of the "open" seam (A to D), as indicated. You now have a secret pocket in the corner of the handkerchief which will safely conceal a coin or other small object inside.

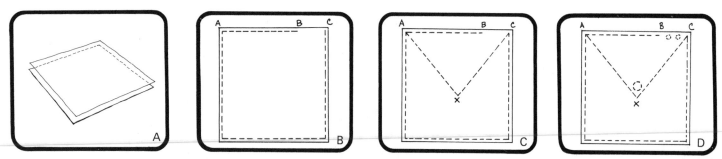

SUPER DOOPER VERSATILE VANISHER

Here is an even more versatile and deceptive "Vanishing" Handkerchief. It combines all of the best features of the previous special handkerchiefs and adds another improvement as well.

EFFECT

The effect is the same as the COIN-VANISHING HANDKERCHIEF.

SECRET AND PREPARATION

(A) Purchase two identical pocket handkerchiefs that are made with a colorful pattern or design. (A common "bandana" works well.) Place one on top of the other as shown. (B) Sew the two handkerchiefs together along the four sides and leave the top hem open at one corner. This opening is between Points B and C in the illustration. The opening should be about two inches wide or slightly larger than the object you intend to vanish. (C) Also, sew the handkerchiefs together as indicated by the dotted line in Illustration C. The stitching from A to X to C forms a "V-shaped" pocket *inside the handkerchief.* Point X should be slightly below the exact center of the handkerchief. (D) Sew two small dress snaps inside the open hem between B and C as shown. Any size coin (or any other small object) may then be inserted into the opening and sealed inside with the snaps. In the following description, you will be "vanishing" a coin, so place a coin that matches the one that you wish to vanish inside the secret pocket and you are ready to begin.

METHOD

(1) To vanish the coin, grasp the handkerchief in both hands at Corners A and C and snap it open. The "hidden" coin will automatically position itself *in the center of the double handkerchief.*

(2) Drape the handkerchief over your left hand so the hidden coin rests on your open left palm. Place the borrowed coin *directly on top* of the hidden coin as shown.

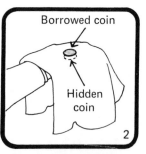

Borrowed coin

Hidden coin

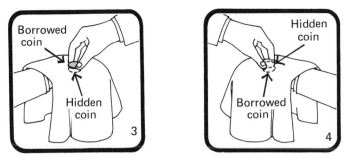

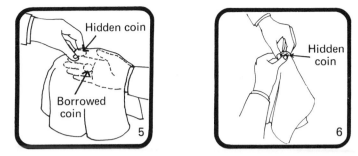

(3) With the fingers of the right hand, hold the borrowed coin and the secret duplicate in place. (4) Turn the entire affair upside down so that the handkerchief falls over your right hand and the coin(s).

(5) Now with your left hand, grasp the *duplicate coin* through the fabric. At the same time, your right hand allows the spectator's coin to fall into the Finger Palm position as shown. (6) Casually withdraw your right hand (and the spectator's coin) from beneath the handkerchief, as you ask the spectator to grasp "his" coin (really the duplicate) through the fabric of the handkerchief. At this point, your right hand, which secretly holds the borrowed coin concealed in the curled fingers, can be casually placed in your right pocket where it leaves the coin to be reproduced later.

(7) When you are ready to "vanish" the coin, grasp the bottom corner of the handkerchief and give it a sharp downward tug — pulling it from the spectator's grip. The duplicate coin is retained within the double handkerchief giving the impression that the borrowed coin vanished from between the fingertips of the volunteer.

COMMENTS AND SUGGESTIONS

There are three advantages to this type of "vanishing" handkerchief: First, you may insert any small object into the secret pocket to be "vanished." Second, because the duplicate is located in the center, the placement of the object under the handkerchief as described in Steps 3 and 4 is very natural. Third, the "V" type pocket is so constructed that a somewhat larger or bulkier object may be used and will still not show after the vanish because of the size of the "secret" pocket and the location of the object *in the center of the handkerchief* after the vanish.

COIN THROUGH LEG

EFFECT

The magician apparently causes a half-dollar to magically pass completely through his right leg.

METHOD

All that is required are an unprepared half-dollar and mastery of the FINGER PALM.

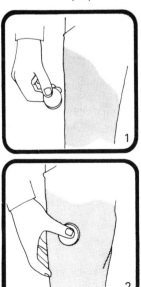

(1) Display a half-dollar to your audience. The coin is held between the thumb and fingers of the right hand. Now lower the coin to your right side, next to your right trouser leg and slightly above your right knee.

(2) Place the coin on your leg as shown. Your right thumb holds the coin *against* your trouser leg just above the knee.

(3) Bring your left hand over beside the coin. With the fingers of *both* the right and left hands, lift a portion of the trouser fabric *up and under* the coin.

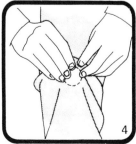

(4) Now, *fold the cloth that you have just pulled under the coin UP AND OVER THE COIN.* The left thumb holds the fold of cloth in place.

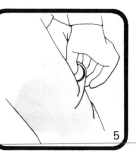

(5) This is how the coin and folded cloth should look to you.

(8) *NOTE: The right hand will appear to be empty, while the left hand is apparently still holding the coin behind the fold of cloth in your trouser leg.*

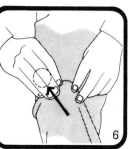

(6) As soon as the coin is covered by the fold in the trouser leg, THE THUMB OF YOUR RIGHT HAND SECRETLY PULLS THE COIN UP BEHIND YOUR RIGHT FINGERS.

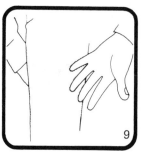

(9) NOW FOR THE "VANISH." The left hand releases the fold of cloth in the trouser leg. The fabric will drop revealing the "vanish" of the coin. Turn your left hand over to show the audience that it is empty.

(7) You now FINGER PALM the coin in your right hand. Move your right hand away and, slowly and deliberately, place it behind your right leg.

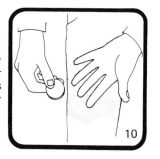

(10) With your right hand, slowly withdraw the coin from behind your right knee. Apparently, the coin has gone "magically" right through your leg!

COMMENTS AND SUGGESTIONS

This is a very clever and easily learned "sleight" which can be used as a trick in itself as just described . . . or for the *Vanish* of a coin, as explained in the next effect, which can be useful in other coin routines.

CHALLENGE COIN VANISH

EFFECT

The magician displays a coin and places it in a fold of cloth on the leg of his trousers. A member of the audience is allowed to feel the coin to see if it is still there. Yet, under these seemingly impossible circumstances, the coin vanishes completely.

SECRET AND PREPARATION

(A) Place a "duplicate" of the coin you intend to vanish in your right trouser pocket.

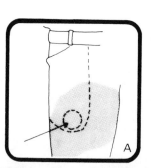

METHOD

Proceed exactly as in the COIN THROUGH LEG, through Step 5.

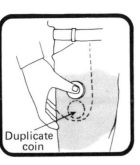

(1) However, when you place the coin which will vanish on your leg in Step 1 this time position it *directly above* the "secret" duplicate coin in your right pants pocket. *NOTE: Because of the location of the duplicate coin in your pocket, it will be necessary to place the "vanishing" coin slightly higher on your pants leg than in the COIN THROUGH LEG.*

Duplicate coin

(4) Now proceed to "steal" the coin away in the FINGER PALM position as explained in Step 6 in COIN THROUGH LEG.

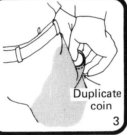

(2) Now, when you fold the cloth up around the coin, make sure that the duplicate coin is in the fold of cloth ON TOP OF THE COIN WHICH WILL VANISH.

Real coin

Duplicate coin

2

(5) Ask the spectator to feel and see if the coin is still there. *When he does, he will feel the duplicate coin which is in your pocket.* THIS GIVES YOU IDEAL "MISDIRECTION" TO SECRETLY DROP THE FINGER PALMED COIN INTO YOUR RIGHT COAT POCKET.

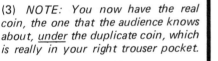

(3) *NOTE: You now have the real coin, the one that the audience knows about, under the duplicate coin, which is really in your right trouser pocket.*

Duplicate coin

3

(6) After the spectator is satisfied that the coin is still there, merely let the fold of cloth drop as before. You may then show both hands to be completely empty. The coin has vanished.

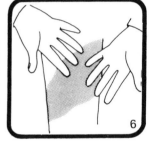

6

COIN-A-GO-GO

EFFECT

The magician borrows a half dollar from a member of the audience. The spectator is handed a black grease pencil with which to mark the coin. Working at very close range, the performer causes the coin to vanish right before the spectator's eyes, utilizing the pencil as an impromptu wand. The magician shows both hands to be unmistakably empty, and even hands the pencil to the spectator to examine. Then, to bring the mystery to a happy conclusion, the magician simply taps the back of his left hand with the pencil and magically reproduces the marked coin.

SECRET AND PREPARATION

This is a very good impromptu trick. Carry a grease pencil, marking pen, ballpoint pen, or just a regular lead pencil in your left inside coat pocket, and you are always ready to perform. To insure the proper working of the effect, do not use a coin smaller than a quarter. Only one sleight is used, the "Finger Palm" which you have already learned. After you have mastered this move, this routine will become an excellent addition to your impromptu program.

METHOD

(1) Borrow a half-dollar from a spectator and have him mark it with the pen or pencil. Let's suppose you are using a pencil. After the spectator is satisfied that he will be able to identify the coin later, replace the pencil into your left-hand inside coat pocket.

(5) ...finally ending up with the half-dollar enclosed in the left hand.

(2) Place the coin on the palm of your right hand.

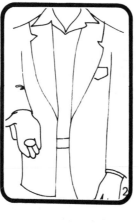

(6) Reach into your inside coat pocket with your right hand and retrieve the pencil.

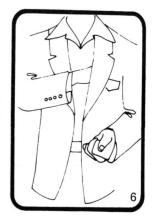

(3) Now toss the coin from hand ...

(7) Point the pencil at your left hand and ask the spectator to call "heads or tails."

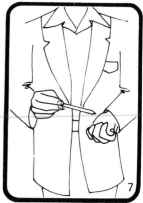

(4) ... to hand ...

(8) After the spectator makes his choice, open your left hand and allow him to verify whether or not he was correct. *NOTE: All of the preceeding has nothing to do with the actual working of the trick but adds greatly to the "misdirection," as you will see.*

(9) In any event, you tell the spectator that you would like to try it again. Replace the pencil in your pocket and once again toss the coin back and forth from hand to hand. However, on the last "toss," when you apparently throw the coin into the left hand, execute the Finger Palm with your right hand. *Secretly retain the coin in your right hand as your left hand apparently closes over the coin.*

(10) Now the effect should be exactly the same as before as far as the spectator is concerned. With the coin concealed in your right hand, reach into your coat for the pencil. THIS TIME, HOWEVER, DROP THE COIN DOWN THE TOP OF YOUR LEFT SLEEVE AT THE INSIDE ARMHOLE OF YOUR COAT. The coin will fall down your sleeve to your left elbow and will remain there as long as you keep your left arm bent as shown.

(11) The above move should be accomplished smoothly. As you remove your right hand from your jacket, bring the pencil into view and once again use it to point to the left hand. Ask the spectator to call heads or tails. Since every move you have just made duplicates the first run through, the spectator will have absolutely no reason for doubting the presence of the coin in your left hand.

(12) After the spectator has made his choice, slowly open the hand and reveal the startling vanish of the coin. HAND THE PENCIL TO THE SPECTATOR AND SHOW BOTH HANDS TO BE COMPLETELY EMPTY.

(13) Lower your left arm to your side as you ask the spectator to return the pencil.

(14) The spectator's eyes will be diverted by the pencil as the marked coin falls silently into your left palm. Take back the pencil from the spectator as you close your left hand around the coin.

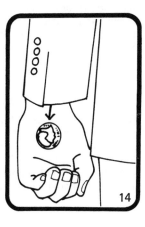

(15) Raise your left hand to waist level and tap it with the pencil.

(16) Slowly open your hand revealing the magical reappearance of the coin. Have the spectator identify the half dollar as being the original borrowed coin and thank him for his assistance.

CONTINUOUS COINS

Catching coins from the air and dropping them in a high hat was long a classic among old-time magicians. Coins are still with us, and to produce them magically in endless fashion is even more wonderful when done at close range. In this modern version, you either borrow a handkerchief or use one of your own and begin to extract countless coins from its folds to the amazement of your audience.

EFFECT

The magician's hands are unmistakably empty as he removes a handkerchief from his breast pocket. This handkerchief is draped over his right hand. The left hand is shown to be empty as the handkerchief is transferred from his right hand to his left. The audience is surprised to see a large silver coin has "magically" appeared in the folds of the handkerchief! Removing the coin, the magician places it into his right side trouser pocket. He now transfers the handkerchief back to his right hand. Another coin is seen to materialize from the center of the handkerchief. After pocketing this second coin, the magician increases his pace – producing coin after coin in an apparently unlimited supply. Finally, the performer sets his handkerchief aside and removes the coins from his pockets. The spectators see them shower from both of his hands into a container on the table.

SECRET AND PREPARATION

The only sleight needed for this clever bit of skullduggery is the "Finger Palm" and some practice so that you present the routine smoothly. It will be necessary for you to perform the Finger Palm with both your left hand and your right hand, which you should find quite easy to learn as you practice. The items needed to present this effective mystery are: An ordinary pocket handkerchief, twelve coins (half-dollars are recommended for visibility — even silver dollars if you have large hands), and a glass or metal bowl which you place on your table. Put the handkerchief in your coat pocket or simply have it already on the table. Place six of the coins in your left trouser pocket and the other six in your right trouser pocket. Now you are ready.

METHOD

(1) Remove the handkerchief and display it on both sides. SHOW CLEARLY THAT YOU ARE NOT CONCEALING ANYTHING IN EITHER OF YOUR HANDS OR IN THE HANDKERCHIEF.

(2) Now, position your right hand as shown — all of your fingers and thumb should touch at the tips and all are pointed "up."

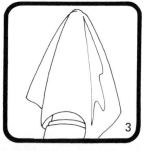

(3) *With your left hand, drape the handkerchief over your right hand. Make sure that your right fingertips are near the center of the handkerchief.*

(4) Show your left hand to be empty, then grasp the center of the handkerchief with your left fingertips as shown.

(5) The object of the next move is to reverse the positions of your hands. That is, to cover your left hand with the handkerchief and to free your right hand. With the left fingers grasping the center of the handkerchief as shown in Step 4, THE RIGHT HAND THROWS THE HANDKERCHIEF OVER THE LEFT HAND. The left hand turns over, assuming the same position previously held by the right. The left hand is now covered by the handkerchief.

(6) You then "pretend" to see something protruding from the center of the handkerchief. Your right fingers grasp the phantom object. *By keeping the back of your hand to the audience, they will assume that you are holding some item that they cannot see.*

(7) Without hesitation, place the imaginary object into your right hand trouser pocket. YOU NOW SECRETLY FINGER PALM ONE OF THE SIX COINS IN YOUR POCKET IN YOUR RIGHT HAND.

(8) *NOTE: The total action here must be timed so that you give the impression of putting something INTO your pocket not REMOVING something.*

(9) Now bring your hand out of your pocket. *Keep the back of your hand toward the audience which will effectively conceal the Finger Palmed coin.* Grasp the center of the handkerchief with the right fingertips as shown.

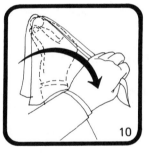

(10) Once again, you are going to "reverse" hand positions – this time covering your right hand, *which contains the hidden coin,* with the handkerchief. The left hand throws the handkerchief over the right hand as the right hand turns over assuming its original position.

(11) *NOTE: The audience is unaware of the coin now palmed in your right hand. At this point you have successfully "loaded" your first coin into the handkerchief.*

(12) Once again, you pretend to see something protruding from the center of the handkerchief. But this time, the *left* fingers grasp the phantom object.

(13) You promptly thrust this newly found item into your left trouser pocket as in Step 7. While your hand is in your left pocket, FINGER PALM ONE OF THE SIX COINS LOCATED THERE IN YOUR LEFT HAND AND REMOVE YOUR HAND. Then, with the coin secretly held in the Finger Palm, reach for the center of the handkerchief with your left fingertips.

(14) *This next move is important.* WITH YOUR LEFT FINGERS AND THUMB GRASP THE HANDKERCHIEF IN THE CENTER AND ALSO GRASP THE HIDDEN COIN THROUGH THE CLOTH, THE COIN THAT IS UNDER THE HANDKERCHIEF IN YOUR RIGHT HAND.

(15) *NOTE: Make sure not to "flash" the Finger Palmed coin in your left hand during this action. It must look as if you are only grasping the handkerchief, when in reality you are also lifting the hidden coin out of your right hand.*

(16) Now repeat the moves described in Step 5. However, this time the result will be the SUDDEN APPEARANCE OF A HALF-DOLLAR IN THE CENTER OF THE HANDKERCHIEF! *The "appearing" coin is held through the cloth by the left fingers.*

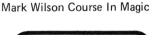

(17) Grasp the coin and display it between the right thumb and fingers as shown. Then place the coin into your right-hand pocket. ACTUALLY, AS SOON AS YOUR RIGHT HAND IS INSIDE YOUR POCKET, FINGER PALM THE COIN. Then withdraw your hand with the secretly Finger Palmed coin. *The effect is that you left the coin in your pocket since your hand will appear to be empty when you bring it out.*

(18) NOW, WITH YOUR RIGHT FINGERS AND THUMB GRASP THE CENTER OF THE HANDKERCHIEF AND THE COIN HIDDEN UNDERNEATH IN YOUR LEFT HAND. Repeat Step 14 for the *left-handed* production of the next coin.

(19) These moves are repeated between the right and left hands until you have apparently produced a dozen coins.

(20) Finally, discard the handkerchief, reach into both trouser pockets and grasp all of the coins. Remove your hands and allow the coins to shower from your palms into the receptacle on your table. At this point, your audience will be completely convinced that you actually produced *all* of the coins from your empty hands and the equally empty handkerchief, *when in reality you accomplished the effect using ONLY TWO COINS.*

COMMENTS AND SUGGESTIONS

The usual way to conclude this effect is simply to spread the handkerchief and give it back to its owner, telling him you hope that he can get the same results later on. If it is your own handkerchief, put it in your pocket and then go on with your next trick, letting the audience wonder where the coins could have come from.

A clever effect is to have coins of different values and sizes in each pocket. Then, after producing and pocketing several half-dollars, you can switch to a dollar sized coin in your right pocket and begin producing those. Your left hand could then switch to a large copper coin — such as an old English penny. You can finish by switching to a dime or a nickel giving you an excuse for ending the production, since the coins are dwindling in size, indicating that the magic must be running out.

COPPER-SILVER PENETRATION

EFFECT

The magician requests the assistance of a spectator and asks that he stand to his (the performer's) left. The magician removes two coins from his trouser pocket. One of the coins is an English Penny, the other an American Half-Dollar. Both of these coins are the same size, but the copper Penny contrasts attractively against the silver Half. The coins are handed to a spectator for examination. The performer then displays an empty pocket handkerchief and wraps the silver Half in it. The Half-Dollar, wrapped in the handkerchief, is given to the spectator to hold. The magician calls the audience's attention to the English Penny. The magician then "invisibly" throws the Penny toward the handkerchief. To everyone's surprise, THE VANISHED PENNY IS HEARD TO MAGICALLY PENETRATE THE HANDKERCHIEF AND FALL ALONGSIDE THE HALF! The spectator is asked to open out the handkerchief to verify the coin's arrival.

SECRET AND PREPARATION

In order to present this effect, it will be necessary for you to have mastered the FINGER PALM and the FRENCH DROP or any other "sleight-of-hand" vanish of a coin. You will also need two English Pennies, one Half-Dollar and a Pocket Handkerchief. *(If you do not have two English Pennies, see COMMENTS AND SUGGESTIONS at the end of this trick.)* Fold the pocket handkerchief and place it into your inside coat pocket. Place one of the English Pennies next to the handkerchief so that you will be able to grasp it easily. Then, put the Half-Dollar and the "duplicate" English Penny into your right trouser pocket.

METHOD

(1) Ask for the assistance of a volunteer from the audience and have him stand to your left. (This will give you the most protection from "accidental exposure" during the presentation.)

(2) Remove the Penny and the Half from your right trouser pocket and give them to the spectator for examination.

(3) While he is busy examining the coins, reach into your inside coat pocket with your left hand and secretly *Finger Palm the duplicate Penny.* As soon as the coin is securely palmed, grasp the handkerchief and bring it into view. *Make sure the spectators do not catch a glimpse of the hidden coin as you display the handkerchief.*

(4) After showing the handkerchief, hold it in your left hand . . . *this disguises the fact that you are also concealing a coin in that hand as well.*

(5) Ask the spectator for the Half-Dollar. Hold the coin by your *right* fingertips and display it to the audience. Now, transfer the Half so that it is held by your *left* fingertips. YOUR LEFT HAND IS NOW HOLDING THE HALF-DOLLAR IN PLAIN VIEW, THE DUPLICATE COPPER PENNY IN A FINGER PALM, <u>AND</u> A CORNER OF THE HANDKERCHIEF. The illustration shows the positions of the three objects.

(6) Your right hand now grasps the bottom corner of the handkerchief and "snaps" it free of your left hand. Then cover your left hand and the coin(s) with the handkerchief. *NOTE: Position the handkerchief so that the Half-Dollar is near the center of the handkerchief.*

(7) With your *right fingers,* grasp the Half-Dollar *through the fabric* and lift the coin out of your left fingers.

(8) *Now, under cover of the handkerchief, with your left hand, secretly place the Finger Palmed Penny into the palm of your right hand.* THE ENGLISH PENNY STAYS UNDER THE HANDKERCHIEF as your right fingers curl around the handkerchief AND the Penny and HOLD THE PENNY THROUGH THE FABRIC UNDER THE HANDKERCHIEF AS SHOWN.

(9) Have the spectator grasp the Half-Dollar *through* the fabric of the handkerchief. As he does this, *slide the Penny down, inside the handkerchief,* as you continue to hold the Penny with your right fingers.

(10) *Turn the handkerchief parallel to the floor....* Then slide your right hand to the right end (where the corners are) of the handkerchief. As you slide your hand, LEAVE THE PENNY IN THE MIDDLE AREA as shown.... The Penny is now in the handkerchief between *your* right hand and the *spectator's* hand holding the Half-Dollar.

(11) *Immediately reach up with your left hand and HOLD THE PENNY IN PLACE* by grasping the handkerchief *in the middle* as shown.

(12) Ask the spectator to hold the handkerchief with his free hand somewhere between your right and left hands as shown. *NOTE: Since the duplicate Penny is being held by your left hand, he cannot accidentally feel the Penny.*

(13) You can now remove your hands from the handkerchief. *As long as the spectator holds his hands apart and the handkerchief level with the floor, the hidden Penny will stay "in place."* Pick up the other "visible" Penny and display it in your left hand.

(14) Reach over with your right hand and execute the FRENCH DROP. As you know, this move will lead the audience to believe that the Penny is in your closed right hand ... *when actually it is "secretly" being held in your left hand.* (NOTE: If you prefer, any other "vanishing" sleight may be used here.)

(15) Move your right hand, supposedly containing the Penny, above the handkerchief being held by the spectator. You are about to "slap" the handkerchief free of his right hand. To accomplish this correctly, be sure to strike the handkerchief *as close to the Half-Dollar as possible.* Make a sharp downward motion with your right hand. *Open your hand just before it hits the handkerchief.*

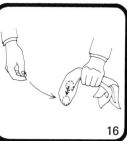

(16) The handkerchief will fall free of the spectator's *right hand,* CAUSING THE HIDDEN COPPER COIN TO FALL INTO THE CENTER OF THE HANDKERCHIEF AND STRIKE THE HALF-DOLLAR. To the spectator and to the audience, it appears that the Penny penetrated the handkerchief and joined the Half-Dollar.

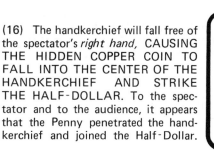

(17)   The spectator is told to unfold the handkerchief. He will discover *both* coins in its center. While he is examining the coins, secretly drop the duplicate Penny into your pocket.

COMMENTS AND SUGGESTIONS

This is an excellent Sleight-of-Hand trick. Although it requires a bit of practice to get all of the moves and the timing correct, it is well worth the effort. IF YOU DO NOT HAVE TWO ENGLISH PENNIES, YOU MAY SUBSTITUTE ANY TWO HEAVY COINS. Foreign coins are best since you can get more "contrast" between the coins. However, two American coins may be used as well . . . for instance, one Half-Dollar and two Quarters, or one Silver Dollar and two Half-Dollars. In this case, it is better to use the smaller as the "duplicate" coin, as these are the two that are involved in all of the "Palming." The different sizes will not matter since the spectator "feels" only *one* coin (the larger coin) when he holds the coin under the handkerchief. Thus, the difference in size will not be noticed. Just be sure that the "duplicate" coin is heavy enough to fall within the handkerchief when it makes its mysterious appearance with the other coin.

THE SHRINKING COIN

EFFECT

The magician borrows a finger ring from one spectator and a half-dollar from another. He also requests that these two members of the audience assist him on stage as he presents his next mystery. He has the spectators stand beside him . . . one spectator on his left side, the other on his right. The magician now removes a handkerchief from his pocket. The borrowed half-dollar is wrapped securely in the center of the handkerchief and one of the spectators threads the four corners of the handkerchief *through* the finger ring . . . *imprisoning the coin in the handkerchief.* Each of the spectators is asked to hold two of the corners of the handkerchief (one in each hand) and to stretch the handkerchief out between them so that it is parallel to the floor. The magician reaches underneath the handkerchief and grasps the ring and the imprisoned coin. He then asks the spectators to gently pull on the corners of the handkerchief. To the amazement of all, *the coin slowly penetrates UP THROUGH THE RING.* The ring is now free and is removed from under the handkerchief by the magician . . . and the coin lies on the handkerchief held between the two spectators. All of the items can be examined . . . the ring and coin are returned to the spectators, along with the magician's thanks for their assistance.

SECRET AND PREPARATION

All that is required for this effect is a pocket handkerchief, a half-dollar, and a finger ring, all of which are quite ordinary. You must also be able to perform the COIN THROUGH HANDKERCHIEF trick. No preparation is necessary as THIS IS A COMPLETELY IMPROMPTU MYSTERY.

METHOD

(1)   Borrow a half-dollar and a finger ring from members of the audience. You will also need the assistance of two spectators. If they are the same ones who lent you the borrowed articles, so much the better.

(2)   Remove your pocket handkerchief and display the borrowed half-dollar. Now, WRAP THE COIN IN THE CENTER OF THE HANDKERCHIEF AS DESCRIBED IN THE <u>COIN THROUGH</u> HANDKERCHIEF TRICK (Page 178). *As you know, the "special" way in which you wrap the coin leaves the coin on the OUTSIDE of the handkerchief. To the audience, it appears as though the coin is securely held INSIDE the handkerchief.* Follow the COIN THROUGH HANDKERCHIEF routine only through Step 10, then STOP. *Do not perform the "penetration" of the coin through the handkerchief.*

(3)   Now hold the handkerchief and coin with both hands as shown. *Be sure the side of the handkerchief that was <u>toward you</u> in the COIN THROUGH HANDKERCHIEF, Steps 8 and 9, where a portion of the coin might be visible, is resting next to your left fingers, so the spectators cannot see that the coin is not REALLY inside the handkerchief.*

(4) Now have the spectator thread the four corners of the handkerchief *through* his finger ring as shown. As he does this, retain your grip on the coin with your left hand. *Also, hold the handkerchief ABOVE the coin with your right hand, as shown, so the handkerchief does not "untwist" revealing the coin.*

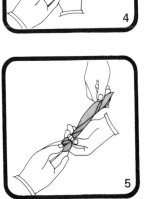

(5) After the spectator has threaded the ends through the ring, tell him to slide the ring down the handkerchief until it rests tightly against the wrapped coin. *This will lock the coin into position and KEEP THE HANDKERCHIEF FROM UNWRAPPING.*

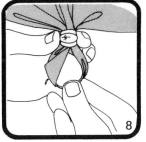

(6) Ask the spectators to hold the four corners of the handkerchief as shown. The handkerchief should be level with the floor. The coin and ring are hanging underneath the handkerchief.

(7) *NOTE: To the spectators, it appears that you have placed the borrowed coin underneath the handkerchief. Then a spectator has threaded his own ring over the corners of the handkerchief imprisoning the coin in the center of the handkerchief. Since the coin is much LARGER than the INSIDE of the ring, there is apparently no way for the coin to escape.*

(8) Now, using both hands, reach underneath the outstretched handkerchief. Grasp the ring with the thumb and first finger of your left hand. Work the ring slightly *upward* so that you gain a bit of slack in the handkerchief. With the right hand you can now slip the coin free of the handkerchief as shown.

(9) IMPORTANT NOTE: FROM NOW ON, UNTIL THE COIN "PENETRATES" THE RING (Step 17), HOLD THE CENTER OF THE HANDKERCHIEF WITH YOUR LEFT HAND SO THAT THE SPECTATORS ARE NOT AWARE THAT YOU HAVE REMOVED THE COIN.

(10) *Under the handkerchief, secretly FINGER PALM the coin in your right hand.* Then, as your right second and third fingers hold the coin FINGER PALMED, your right first finger and thumb pull the ring off the handkerchief and place it in your left hand . . . so that the ring may be held by your left third and fourth fingers as shown

(11) *NOTE: As pointed out in Step 9, BE SURE TO MAINTAIN YOUR GRIP ON THE FABRIC WITH YOUR LEFT THUMB AND FIRST FINGER so that the spectators are unaware that either the coin or the ring has been removed.*

(12) Bring your right hand *with the secretly FINGER PALMED coin,* out from beneath the handkerchief. MOVE YOUR RIGHT HAND DIRECTLY OVER THE CENTER OF THE HANDKERCHIEF AS SHOWN.

(13) *The following step is most important.* YOUR RIGHT HAND NOW <u>SECRETLY DROPS THE COIN</u> INTO THE "WELL" IN THE CENTER OF THE HANDKERCHIEF (which the audience *thinks* is made by the ring and coin). Under the handkerchief your left fingers open momentarily to let the coin into the "well."

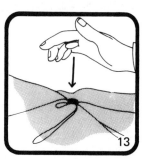

(14) The drawing in Step 13 shows the right hand held "high" above the handkerchief. This is only TO ILLUSTRATE THE "MOVE." When you are ACTUALLY PERFORMING THE TRICK, your hand should be resting DIRECTLY ON TOP of the fabric when the "drop" is made.

(15) When the coin is "dropped" into the well, the left fingers open to receive it and then close around the coin and the fabric. To the audience, the handkerchief appears just as it did before. Your right hand continues to move over the handkerchief, apparently smoothing out its folds. This "smoothing" move is used before and after the "drop" as MISDIRECTION for what you are really doing, which is secretly bringing the coin from beneath the handkerchief and dropping it into the "well."

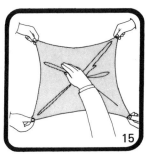

(16) *NOTE: At this point, the spectator's borrowed ring is held by your left third and fourth fingers UNDER the handkerchief. The coin is now ON TOP of the handkerchief in the "well." Your left thumb and first finger hold the handkerchief closed over the coin so that all appears as it did at the start.*

(17) As your left hand continues its hold on the ring and coin, have the spectators gently pull on the four corners of the handkerchief. With your left fingers, *let the coin slowly appear from the well* as it works its way up through your left fingers. *TO THE AUDIENCE, IT WILL APPEAR THAT THE COIN IS PASSING THROUGH THE RING,* WHICH IS MUCH SMALLER THAN THE COIN.

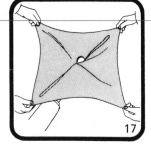

(18) When the coin is completely on top of the handkerchief, and the handkerchief is stretched "flat" between the two spectators, with your left hand slowly and dramatically bring the ring from under the handkerchief. Drop it next to the coin on the outstretched cloth. The effect is two-fold. The coin has passed *through* the much smaller ring, which also *releases* the ring from the handkerchief. You may now pass all of the articles, the ring, the coin, and the handkerchief, for examination ... as you thank the spectators for their assistance.

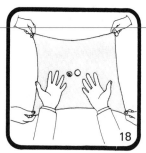

COMMENTS AND SUGGESTIONS

This is a very clever adaptation of the Coin Through Handkerchief move. It is particularly misleading for the spectators since the "effect" is that the coin does not *penetrate* the handkerchief but passes *through* the ring instead. The outstretched handkerchief forms a perfect "cover" when you secretly palm the coin and slip the ring off the handkerchief. This makes an ideal close-up effect since it may be performed at any time and uses small borrowed articles, all of which may be examined. The effect works particularly well if performed so that the handkerchief is held over a low table (such as a coffee table) at which you and the other participants are seated. If performing for a larger group, have the spectators who are holding the handkerchief "tilt" the side nearest the audience slightly downward so that the handkerchief is "angled" toward the spectators. This will allow you all of the cover necessary and also keep anyone from seeing under the handkerchief as you perform this Miniature Miraculous Mystery.

COINS ACROSS

EFFECT

The magician is seated at a table. From his pocket he removes six coins and places them on the table, arranging them in *two* rows of *three* coins each. The performer gathers three coins into each hand and – "magically" causes THE THREE COINS FROM HIS RIGHT HAND TO TRAVEL ONE AT A TIME INTO HIS LEFT HAND.

SECRET AND PREPARATION

In order to present this classic Sleight-Of-Hand effect, you must first have learned the CLASSIC PALM. Since this mystery is presented as a *close-up* trick, you should practice until you can perform the "Palm" easily. You also will need seven *identical* coins. Be sure to pick a coin of the size that is the easiest for you to palm. (Either quarters, half-dollars, or silver dollars, depending upon the size of your hands.) Place the seven coins in your right pocket.

METHOD

(1) Reach into your pocket and remove the coins. As you do, secretly CENTER PALM ONE OF THE COINS. Arrange the six remaining coins on the table into two rows of three as shown. In the illustrations, we have lettered the six coins on the table "A," "B," "C," "D," "E," and "F," and the seventh, palmed, coin "G."

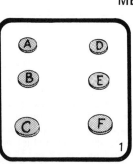

(2) With your right hand concealing the seventh coin, G, reach across the table and pick up the *first* coin from the *left* row (A).

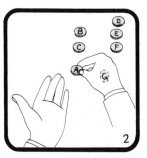

(3) If the "angles" permit (if the audience is located in front of you), you may now display Coin A at the tips of your thumb and fingers of the right hand while still concealing the palmed coin, G, as shown here. The fingers and thumb of the right hand *point up* and the palmed coin is concealed from the audience. If, on the other hand, you are surrounded by spectators, then just keep your right hand with your palm toward the table as you place the coins into your left hand.

(4) Throw this first coin, A, into your open left hand.

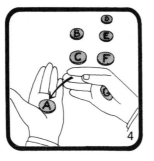

(5) With your right hand still concealing Coin G, reach across the table and pick up the *second* coin, B, from the left-hand row.

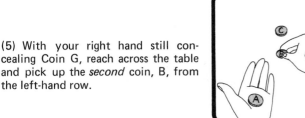

(6) Throw Coin B into your open left hand alongside Coin A.

(7) The right hand picks up the *third* and last coin, C, in the left-hand row. Coin G is still hidden in your right palm. *NOTE: Watch your "angles" to be sure that you do not FLASH the palmed coin, G, during any of Steps 1 through 7.*

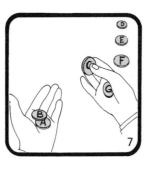

(8) This time, when you throw the third coin into your left hand, SIMULTANEOUSLY RELEASE THE PALMED COIN, G, SO THAT BOTH THE THIRD COIN, C, AND THE PALMED COIN, G, GO INTO YOUR OPEN LEFT HAND TOGETHER.

(9) Close your left hand IMMEDIATELY around the four coins and turn your hand over. AT THIS POINT, THE AUDIENCE BELIEVES THAT YOU HAVE SIMPLY COUNTED THREE COINS INTO YOUR LEFT HAND.

(10) *NOTE: Although the illustration in Step 8 shows Coin C on top of Coin G, this is not necessarily the way the coins will land. Just drop both coins as one and immediately close your hand.*

(11) With your left hand apparently holding the three coins from the left row (really four coins), the right hand starts picking up the three coins (D, E, and F) still on the table.

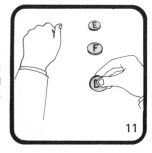

(12) Pick up the first coin, D, and display it in your right hand. AS YOU DO, POSITION THE COIN IN YOUR HAND IN READINESS FOR THE CLASSIC PALM.

(13) Now, close your right hand and turn it over. USE YOUR FINGERS TO PUSH COIN D INTO THE CLASSIC PALM. Pick up the two remaining coins (E and F) with your thumb and fingers. Then close your right fingers around all of the coins.

13

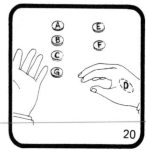

20

(20) Casually show your left hand empty — but be sure the spectators are not aware of Coin D hidden in your right hand.

(14) MAKE SURE TO KEEP THE PALMED COIN D SEPARATED FROM THE LAST TWO COINS (E and F).

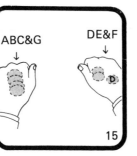

14

NOTE: At this point, the spectator will believe that each hand contains three coins.

(21) YOU HAVE JUST LEARNED THE BASIC SEQUENCES IN CREATING THIS EFFECT. From this point on the basic moves are repeated starting from Step 2 through Step 9.

(22) The right hand picks up the four coins from the left row one at a time and throws them into your open left hand. AS YOU THROW THE LAST COIN, G, THE CLASSIC-PALMED COIN D IS ADDED TO THE OTHER FOUR COINS IN THE LEFT HAND.

(15) Now make a slight "throwing" motion with your right hand in the direction of your left hand. Loosen your left fingers so that the coins in your left hand will "clank" together. Tell the spectators that one of the coins has "magically" traveled to your left hand.

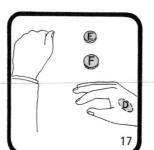

ABC&G   DE&F

15

(23) Then the right hand picks up the two remaining coins on the table. THE FIRST, COIN E, IS PLACED IN THE CLASSIC PALM. *Be sure to keep the second, Coin F, separated from the first, Coin E, as in Steps 13 and 14.*

(24) Make the "throwing" motion with your right hand. "Clink" the coins in your left hand to signal the mysterious arrival of the fifth coin.

16

17

(16) The right hand, WHILE RETAINING COIN D IN THE THE CLASSIC PALM (17) places the other two coins (E and F) on the table.

(25) The right hand places only one coin (E) on the table, keeping the other coin (F) in the Classic Palm. The left hand then spreads the five coins on the table.

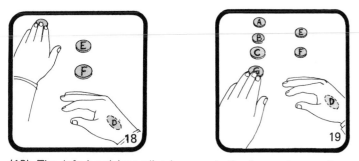

18

19

(18) The left hand immediately spreads the four coins on the table. (19) The effect is that one coin traveled "magically" from your right hand to your left hand.

(26) Now, repeat Steps 2 through 9 as you place the five coins into your left hand. SECRETLY ADD THE PALMED COIN E FROM YOUR RIGHT HAND ON THE FIFTH "THROW."

(27) At this point you will be left with *one* coin on the table. For this you use a special method of Lapping called the "Pull Off" Method. Steps 28, 29, and 30 describe this method of Lapping.

LAPPING — PULL-OFF METHOD

EFFECT

The magician picks a coin up from the table and it *vanishes completely* from his hand!

SECRET AND PREPARATION

The following "Vanish" describes how this useful sleight is used for the magical transposition of the last coin in COINS ACROSS.

METHOD

(1)   Cover the last coin with your right-hand fingers and slide it toward yourself as if you were going to "scoop" it up into your hand. (2)   *Instead of actually picking up the coin,* (3)   ALLOW THE COIN TO FALL UNSEEN OFF THE BACK EDGE OF THE TABLE ONTO YOUR LAP — as your right hand continues the "scooping" motion with the fingers apparently closing around the coin.

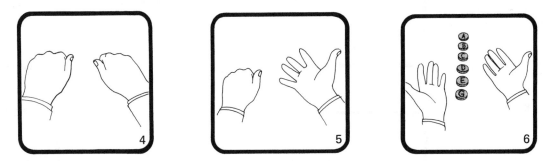

(4)   Now hold both hands closed on the table in front of you.   (5)   Lift your right hand above your left and apparently "rub" the coin *through* the back of your left hand. Then show your right hand empty.   (6)   Now dramatically spread the six coins onto the table.

(7)   While the spectators are examining the six coins, casually retrieve the extra coin from your lap. Add this coin to the six on the table as you gather them up to put them away, or secretly drop it in your coat pocket as you continue your "close-up" routine.

THE COIN IN THE BALL OF WOOL

The following effect is one of those classic tricks that deserves your very best effort.

EFFECT

The magician borrows a quarter from a spectator in the audience and asks him to mark the coin so that he can identify it at a later time. (A black grease pencil carried in the performer's pocket is good for this purpose.) The magician removes his pocket handkerchief and wraps the coin in its folds. The volunteer is given the folded package to hold. He can and does confirm the presence of the coin by feeling it through the fabric.

EFFECT Cont'd.

A ball of wool is freely shown to the audience and dropped into a clear glass. (In the illustrations and the written instructions, we will use a brandy snifter; however, any glass of the correct size will do.) A second spectator is asked to hold the glass containing the yarn ball high enough so that all can see. Returning to the first spectator, the magician causes the borrowed coin to vanish from the handkerchief. The performer explains that, since the first volunteer has apparently lost the borrowed coin, the magician must give him a chance to recover it. The performer grasps the loose end of the yarn ball and passes it to the first spectator. As the volunteer pulls on the yarn, the ball unwinds, spinning merrily in the brandy snifter held by the second spectator. A matchbox bound with rubber bands is found in the center of the wool ball. The second spectator is asked to remove the box from the snifter and open it. The spectator's marked quarter is found inside the box!

SECRET AND PREPARATION

(A) In order to present this effect, you will need the following items: 1) a ball of wool (heavy knitting or rug yarn is good for this), 2) a common "penny" matchbox or some other small box, 3) a brandy snifter or other transparent container large enough to contain the yarn ball, 4) a "Vanishing Handkerchief" of any of the types already described (in this case a quarter is placed in the "secret" corner), 5) four small rubber bands, and 6) a special coin "slide" which may be constructed as follows:

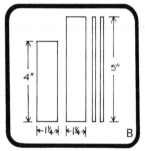

(B) Cut four pieces of heavy cardboard (1/16" thick is about right) as shown. The two narrow strips and one of the wide strips should measure approximately 5 inches in length. The shorter piece should be cut about 1 inch shorter.

(E) Open the drawer of the empty matchbox and . . .

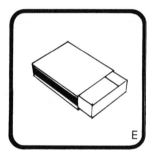

(C) Now glue the four pieces together to form a tube. When finished, the slide must be large enough to allow a quarter to pass completely through it without binding.

(F) . . . insert the blunt end of the slide into the open drawer.

(D) The short side of the tube makes it a simple matter to insert the coin into the tube.

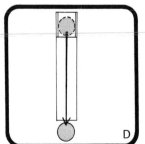

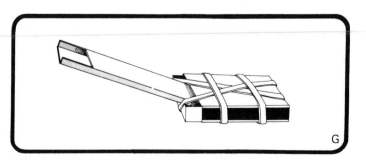

(G) Wrap the four rubber bands around the box as shown. *NOTE: The rubber bands serve two purposes. The first is to hold the slide in position in the matchbox, and the second is to close the box after the slide has been removed.*

(H) Wrap the matchbox with the yarn until you have formed a ball with the matchbox hidden in the center. This must be done loosely in order not to create a bind in the tube or prevent its easy removal.

(I) Attach the yarn ball and tube to the rear edge of your table or on the back of a chair. The important thing to look out for here is that the ball must not be visible to the spectators. If necessary, throw an attractive drape over the table top prior to attaching the prepared ball to its rear edge. In the event a chair is used, be sure the back is solid. In any event, no one should get a glimpse of the coin slide.

(J) Put the brandy snifter on top of your table or on the seat of the chair (depending on the method you have chosen) and pocket the "special" Vanishing Handkerchief. You are now ready to present a very startling mystery.

METHOD

(1) Borrow a quarter from a spectator and have him mark the coin for future identification. While this is being done, remove the special handkerchief from your pocket and spread it over your left hand. The coin previously concealed in the handkerchief should now be in the rear right-hand corner of the special handkerchief as previously explained.

(2) Take the now "marked" coin from the spectator and place it in the handkerchief. *Really retain the marked coin secretly in your right hand as you bring up the duplicate quarter to take its place.*

(3) Allow the spectator to hold the handkerchief containing the duplicate coin. The spectator's marked quarter is Finger Palmed in your right hand.

(4) *NOTE: See Vanishing Handkerchief, Pages 191 to 195.*

(5) Ask for the assistance of a second member of the audience. At this point the first volunteer holding the wrapped coin should be standing to your left. Have the second spectator stand to your right.

(6) With the left hand, reach for the brandy snifter. During this move the right hand grasps the rear edge of the table as if to steady it. *When the left hand lifts the snifter into the air, the right hand secretly drops the marked coin into the tube at the rear of the table.* Immediately hand the snifter to the spectator standing to your right.

(7) Go back to your table, reach behind it and grasp the ball of wool and *pull it down and off of the slide.*

(8) Display the ball to the audience and drop it into the empty brandy snifter, hand the glass to the second spectator.

(9) Return and ask the first spectator if he is still holding his coin through the handkerchief. After he agrees, jerk the handkerchief from his grasp and show that the coin has vanished. Display both sides of the handkerchief.

(10) As the second spectator holds the brandy glass, grasp the loose end of the ball of yarn and hand it to the first spectator. Instruct him to unravel the ball. As he pulls on the brandy snifter will spin in a very attractive manner.

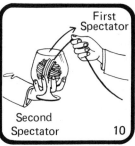

(11) When the wool has been exhausted, the matchbox will be left inside the brandy snifter. Take the brandy snifter from the second spectator and pour the box into his hand.

(12) Instruct the spectator to remove the rubber bands and open the box. He discovers the marked coin inside. Have him return the coin to the lender for positive identification.

COMMENTS AND SUGGESTIONS

Properly presented, this is one of the finest tricks in magic. Here are some additional important points:

(A) *The audience is never aware of the "slide."*

(B) *The slide can be made from cardboard as described or, if you are handy with tools, from a thin sheet of metal which can be cut with tin snips and bent into the correct shape. The slide, matchbox and ball of yarn, can also be purchased if you do not wish to make them yourself.*

(C) *The small box can either be a matchbox or a small box with a hinged top. Either will be automatically closed by the rubber bands when the slide is removed.*

(D) *In Steps 6 and 7, if you are working surrounded or if it is more convenient, you may have the ball of yarn with the slide in place inside a box or even in a paper bag which is sitting on your table. In this case, after the first spectator is apparently holding the coin under the handkerchief, just put both of your hands, one of which contains the palmed quarter, into the box or bag. Drop the coin down the slide and remove the slide from the ball of yarn. Then bring out the ball cupped in both hands.*

(E) *If you use a "grease pencil" to have the spectator mark the quarter, be sure that you do not rub off the mark while carrying the "palmed" coin in your hand or inserting it into the slide — because if you do, NO ONE will ever believe that the coin inside the ball of yarn, inside the sealed matchbox is the SAME quarter that you borrowed from the spectator. You may wish to have the coin marked by having the spectator "scratch" it with some sharp object like a knife.*

(F) *When the first spectator is pulling on the end of the yarn, as the second spectator holds the brandy snifter, have them move several feet apart as the yarn unravels. This presents a very interesting and dramatic picture to the audience.*

(G) *AFTER the ball of yarn is in the brandy snifter and BEFORE the coin has "vanished" from beneath the handkerchief, emphasize that THE SPECTATOR IS HOLDING HIS MARKED COIN AND THAT YOU WILL NOT TOUCH OR GO NEAR THE BRANDY SNIFTER OR THE BALL OF WOOL UNTIL THE CONCLUSION OF THE TRICK — AND BE SURE THAT YOU DO JUST THAT.*

(H) *Allow the spectator to remove the rubber bands from the matchbox, DO NOT TOUCH THE BOX AT ANY TIME UNTIL AFTER THE MARKED COIN HAS BEEN REMOVED AND IDENTIFIED.*

Follow the above rules and you will have, not just another magic trick, but one of the classic miracles of our art.

THE EXPANDED SHELL HALF-DOLLAR

This is a special "gimmicked" Half-Dollar which has been hollowed out until all that remains is the mere "shell" of the original coin. Then the edges of the Shell Half are "stretched open" just enough so that it will fit perfectly over any "regular" Half-Dollar. Thus, a "real" Half-Dollar can slip in or out of the shell easily, without binding. When the Expanded Shell Half is over a "real" Half, they appear to be only one coin. NOTE: The Expanded Shell Half-Dollar is an improvement over the gimmicked coin that was originally made and which is still available, called a "Shell Half-Dollar." In this instance, the hollowed out coin *has not been* *"expanded"* so that it is impossible to fit a "real" Half inside it. Although Regular Shell Halves are available, in most instances everything that can be done with a Regular Shell Half can be done with an Expanded Shell Half. In addition, there are many other tricks that can *only* be done with an Expanded Shell. Thus we recommend that, if you are going to purchase one of these special coins, you make the extra investment and obtain an Expanded Shell Half.

TWO HALVES AND TWO QUARTERS

This clever coin sequence uses the EXPANDED SHELL HALF-DOLLAR. As you will see, some very mystifying coin tricks can be done with a Shell Coin. Here is one of the best.

EFFECT

The magician shows *two* half-dollars, held at his fingertips. He begins to slide the coins over and under each other. During this action, one of the half-dollars *visibly* changes into TWO QUARTERS. The magician is left holding *one* half-dollar and *two* quarters, which he displays freely.

SECRET AND PREPARATION

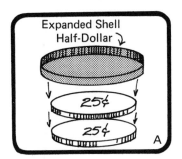

(A) Place two quarters inside the Expanded Shell Half.

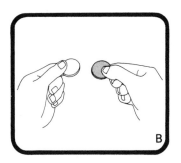

(B) Hold both halves as shown, with the Shell Half in your right hand. (In the illustrations, the Shell Half is a <u>darker</u> <u>color</u> so that you can follow it in the routine.) Your right first finger holds the Shell from beneath and prevents the quarters from falling out, and your right thumb holds the Shell from above. The left hand holds the "regular" coin in the same way. Both hands are held at waist level, with the coins parallel to the floor. Now you are ready.

METHOD

(1) Place the right-hand coin (Shell) on top of the left-hand coin.

(2) With the right thumb, push or slide the Shell coin to the left. Use the left fingers to push the lower coin into the right fingers. *You have now "reversed" the positions of the coins.*

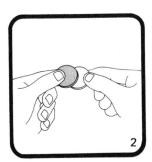

(3) Separate your hands. The coins are held as they were at the beginning, but now *the left hand holds the Shell with the quarters inside, and the right hand holds the regular half-dollar.*

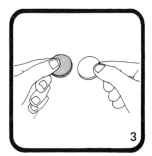

(4) Place the right-hand unprepared coin on top of the gimmicked coin.

(5) Repeat the "sliding" over and under motion described in Step 2. *This brings the Shell Half back into the right fingers, and the regular half back into the left hand.*

(9) SLIDE THE REGULAR HALF-DOLLAR INTO THE SHELL. THIS WILL AUTOMATICALLY DISPLACE THE TWO QUARTERS. Again, this is shown from underneath.

(6) Separate your hands. The coins should be in the same position they were in at the start of the trick. NOW FOR THE MAGIC!

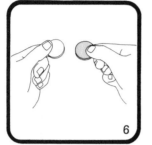

(10) Press the regular half-dollar UP INSIDE THE SHELL with your left thumb and first finger. Grasp the two quarters between your right thumb and first fingers.

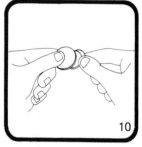

(7) Again, place the Shell coin on top of the regular half so that it overlaps slightly. HOWEVER, THIS TIME YOU SECRETLY INSERT THE REGULAR HALF DOLLAR BETWEEN THE SHELL AND THE TWO QUARTERS.

(11) Separate your hands. *You now hold the regular half-dollar, covered with the Shell in your left hand. The right fingers hold the two quarters.*

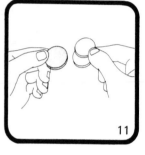

(8) Here is how this action looks from underneath. Note that the quarters are *under* the "regular" coin.

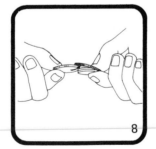

(12) Turn your hands over to show the opposite side of the coins. The Shell-covered half-dollar will appear as *one coin* in your left hand. To the audience it appears you have "magically" *changed* one of the half-dollars into two quarters.

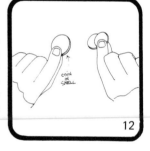

COMMENTS AND SUGGESTIONS

The entire sequence takes only a few seconds and the change of coins should appear *INSTANTANEOUS*. The change is quite visual and startling because you apparently do not use any extra coins and because the handling is so clean.

TWO HALVES AND A "HALF" DOLLAR

EFFECT

This is a clever variation of the TWO HALVES AND TWO QUARTERS routine. The only difference in this routine is that you substitute "half" OF A PAPER DOLLAR BILL for the two quarters. Instead of going from *two* halves to *one* half-dollar and *two* quarters ... you "magically" change one of the halves to one "half-dollar" ... meaning *half of a paper dollar bill*. This works well as a startling comedy effect.

SECRET AND PREPARATION

Expanded Shell Half-Dollar

Dollar bill torn in half and folded.

A

(A) Tear a dollar bill in half, fold it, and place it inside the Shell just as you did with the two quarters in the effect first described.

METHOD

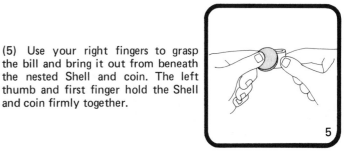

(1) Display the coins as in the previous routine. The gimmicked coin is held in your right hand.

(5) Use your right fingers to grasp the bill and bring it out from beneath the nested Shell and coin. The left thumb and first finger hold the Shell and coin firmly together.

(2) Execute Steps 2 through 7, as in the previous routine. *You will find it considerably easier to hold the bill inside the Shell than it was to hold the two quarters.*

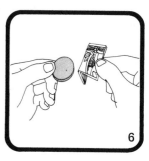

(6) Your right fingers open out the torn bill. You can use the left second and third fingers to help.

(3) NOW INSERT THE UNPREPARED COIN INTO THE SHELL **BETWEEN** THE SHELL AND THE FOLDED BILL. This shows the action from underneath.

(7) Once the half-bill is unfolded, turn both hands over as you did in Step 12 of the previous effect. The sequence is finished. The clever and impossible climax can make this into a fine "comedy" effect to add to your coin routine.

COIN IN SHELL

(4) The unprepared coin will slide into place inside the Shell and will force the folded bill out of the Shell.

COINS THROUGH THE TABLE

EFFECT

The magician, who is seated at a table, shows four Half-Dollars. He places them on the table with each coin slightly overlapping the next. He then scoops up all four coins in his right hand and taps the edge of the stack on the table. Immediately, the coins are spread to reveal only *three* coins left in what was a stack of four. Showing his other hand empty, the magician reaches beneath the table and brings the missing coin into view — it has apparently "magically" *penetrated through the top of the table!* This feat is repeated with the remaining coins, one at a time, until all four coins have passed through the table.

SECRET AND PREPARATION

This routine utilizes an Expanded Shell Half-Dollar. *NOTE: In the illustrations, the Shell is darker in color so you can follow its moves during the routine.*

METHOD

FIRST PENETRATION

(1) You will need four regular Half-Dollars and one Expanded Shell Half. Place the four regular coins in a row near the edge of the table in front of you. Unknown to the viewers, the coin on the left is the Shell-covered coin.

(5) Now, grip the last coin (the one with the Shell over it) in the same manner, by the edges between your right thumb and first finger, *just as you did the first three.* (6) However, this time, when you slide the coin(s) off the edge of the table, LET THE REGULAR COIN SECRETLY FALL OUT OF THE SHELL INTO YOUR LAP, where it remains held between your legs.

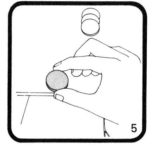

(2) With your right thumb and first finger, grasp the coin at the far right by the edges as shown. Then, slide the coin toward you *until it clears the edge of the table.*

(7) Without pausing, place the Shell with the other coins so that it overlaps the uppermost coin in the row. *The audience believes the Shell is an ordinary coin like the others.*

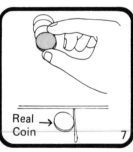

Real Coin →

(3) Now, move the coin forward and <u>place</u> it near the center of the table. Be sure to place the coin — do not <u>drop</u> it — on the table.

(8) Call attention to the four coins on the table as you casually show both hands empty. NOW FOR THE MAGIC!

(4) Repeat this action with the next two coins, sliding each coin off the edge of the table and then <u>placing</u> it on the first coin so that its outer edge *overlaps the coin beneath it.* Repeat the *placing* and *overlapping* with the third coin.

(9) Place your left arm beneath the table as if reaching to the spot *directly below the coins.* What you <u>really</u> do is to *secretly pick up the coin from your lap* as your hand travels under the table. Explain to the audience that the reason you are placing your hand underneath is to "catch" the first coin as it falls through the table.

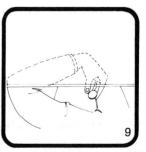

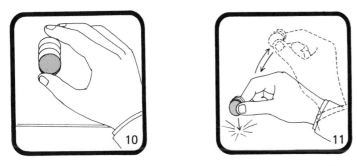

(10) With your right finger, square the row of coins on the table into a single stack. *This causes the Shell to drop down over the top coin in the row.* (11) Pick up the coins by tilting the stack on its edge and grasping the coins firmly with the fingers of your right hand. Without hesitation, raise your right hand. Then, with a downward motion, *gently* (so you do not bend the edge of the Shell) tap the edge of the stack on the table. Say, "Watch as I send one of the coins *right through the table!*"

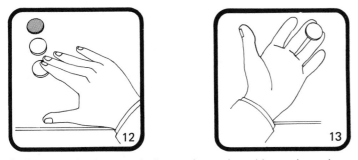

(12) Immediately spread the stack on the table to show that only three coins remain. *Be careful not to accidentally separate the Shell from the regular coin it now covers as you spread them on the table.* Practice will teach you how to handle the Shell correctly. (13) Now, bring your left hand from beneath the table *with the coin you picked up from your lap.* Display it and say, "That makes *one* coin that has passed through the solid table." PLACE THIS COIN ASIDE and go on to the next step.

SECOND PENETRATION

(14) Position the remaining three coins (and the Shell) in a row near the edge of the table just as you did in Step 1. The Shell-covered coin should be at the left end of the row as shown.

(15) Now, follow the same moves as you did in Steps 2 through 12. However, this time you are performing the sequence with *three* coins instead of four. Here is a recap of the moves:

The three coins are slid, one at a time, from the table and then placed in an overlapping row. On the last "pick-up," secretly drop the Shell-covered coin into your lap. Your left hand goes under the table again and picks up the "lapped" coin, as your right hand squares the three coins (two and the Shell) into a stack. You then "tap" the stack on its edge, to "magically" make the second coin penetrate the table — just like the first.

(16) Spread the stack on the table to reveal only *two* coins. Bring your left hand into view with the "lapped" coin. Having completed the penetration, PLACE THIS SECOND COIN ASIDE WITH THE FIRST.

THIRD PENETRATION

(17) You are now left with two coins (and the Shell) on the table. Position both coins near the edge of the table with the Shell-covered coin at the left end of the row as in Step 1.

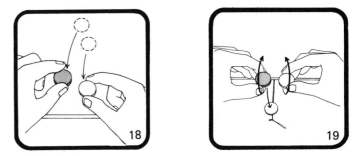

(18) Holding one coin in each hand, move *both* coins back to the table edge at the same time. (19) When the Shell coin reaches the edge, *let the regular coin drop into your lap.*

(20) Display the two coins (really one coin and the Shell) one in each hand. (21) Transfer the left-hand coin to your right hand so that the two coins overlap, *with the Shell in front* as shown.

(22) Place both coins on the table. *Do not let the Shell fall over the "real" coin.* (23) Now rest your right hand on its edge near the coin and Shell as shown in the illustration. Your right hand should be about an inch or so away from the *right edge* of the Shell coin.

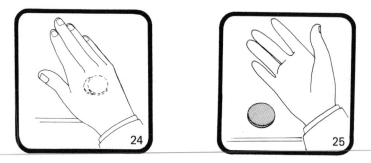

(24) Now, lower your right hand, palm downward, on top of the coins. Then, shift your hand slightly to the left, *causing the Shell half to fall over the regular coin.* At the same time, make a "rubbing" motion as if causing the coin to penetrate the table.

(25) As soon as you feel the two coins nest together, rotate your right hand upward — back to its former position — to reveal only *one* coin remaining on the table.

(26) Bring your left hand from beneath the table with the "lapped" coin as if it has penetrated the table. PLACE THIS THIRD COIN ASIDE and continue with the next step.

FOURTH PENETRATION

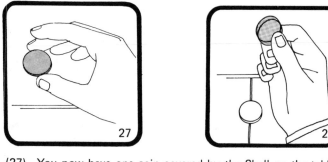

(27) You now have one coin covered by the Shell on the table. With your right thumb and first finger, grasp the coin by the edges and slide it toward you until it clears the edge of the table.

(28) As usual, *the regular coin will drop unnoticed into your lap.*

(29) Now, instead of placing the last coin on the table, hold the coin (really the Shell) in your right hand in position ready for the FINGER PALM VANISH. As you hold the coin in your hand say, "This is the only coin left." *Be careful not to expose the "inside" of the Shell coin as you display it to the audience.*

(30) Execute the FINGER PALM VANISH by apparently taking the Shell coin from your right hand into your left hand. Really the coin is retained in your curled right fingers. *Direct the attention of the audience toward your left hand,* which supposedly holds the coin. *This is MISDIRECTION.* Say, "Follow the last coin closely and see if you can spot the moment when it actually penetrates the table."

(31) As you say this, reach your RIGHT arm beneath the table as if to catch the coin when it falls through. ACTUALLY, YOUR RIGHT HAND SECRETLY PLACES THE SHELL COIN ON YOUR LAP AND PICKS UP THE REGULAR COIN THAT IS ALREADY THERE.

(32) In a sharp, deliberate motion, slam your left hand down onto the table as if to <u>force</u> the coin through the table top. Immediately raise your left hand to show that the coin is no longer there.

(33) Without hesitation, bring your right hand into view with the regular coin as if it were the coin that penetrated the table. Place this coin on the table with the three others, and the mystery is complete. All can now be examined *as the Shell Half remains in your lap for you to secretly dispose of later.*

COMMENTS AND SUGGESTIONS

This is a brilliant piece of coin manipulation and is well worth the practice it takes to perform it smoothly. Remember to always <u>place</u>, never <u>drop</u> the Shell on the other coins, since the Shell does not "sound" like a real coin if it is dropped.

COINS THROUGH THE TABLE
FOURTH PENETRATION — ALTERNATE METHOD

DAVID ROTH

Here is an alternate method for making the last coin (really the Shell) penetrate the table. This can also be used as a very clever trick by itself with a single coin and an Expanded Shell.

METHOD

(1) After you have completed Steps 27 and 28 of the Coins Through the Table — with the real coin secretly on your lap and the Shell coin held by your right hand — <u>place</u> the Shell coin on the table near the edge in front of you.

(2) Now, with your right hand, appear to push the Shell coin forward on the table. Actually, *you do not move the coin at all* — you leave it in its original position near the edge of the table. The fingers of your right hand are held close together as if they cover the coin.

(3) Your right hand moves forward as if pushing the coin along, really leaving the coin in its original position. The Shell is now under your hand near the wrist. *The audience thinks that the coin is under your fingertips.*

(4) Spread your right fingers to show that the last coin has vanished. *Without moving your right hand,* bring your left hand, which has retrieved the coin from your lap, from beneath the table. The fourth coin has apparently penetrated the table.

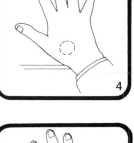

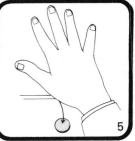

(5) Place the coin in your left hand on the table. *At the same time,* slide your right hand back over the rear edge of the table. As you do this, press gently down on the Shell with the heel of your hand. This will cause the Shell to slide over the edge of the table and fall, unnoticed, into your lap.

(6) Once the Shell is hidden in your lap, you may show both hands empty, and all may be examined.

THE COIN ROLL

Though this is strictly an ornamental flourish and not a magical effect, it belongs in every coin manipulator's program. When you are doing coin tricks, it is always wise to impress your audience with your skill causing them to believe that the simplest of your routines must depend upon your remarkable dexterity.

EFFECT

The performer demonstrates his dexterity as a magician by causing a half-dollar to roll from finger to finger across the back of his hand. When it has finished this surprising run, it drops from sight beneath his little finger and pops up again between his thumb and first finger, only to repeat its remarkable roll. He does this repeatedly, so that the coin really seems to come alive, rolling of its own accord. When the magician performs the COIN ROLL deftly, it will surely dress up his coin routine giving the appearance of great professional dexterity.

METHOD

NOTE: So that you can follow the coin as it "rolls" over the fingers, we have added the letters "A" and "B" to the opposite edges of the coin.

(1) Hold the coin by Edge A in your right hand between your thumb and first finger as shown.

(2) *Push the coin up and release the thumb,* allowing the coin to "roll over" the back of the first finger near the knuckles.

(3) *Lift the second finger* and allow it to clip the right-hand Edge B of the coin. The coin will assume a temporary position clipped between the first and second fingers.

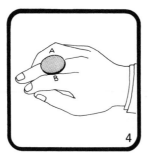

(4) Without stopping, *raise the first finger* which pushes the coin on to the back of the second finger.

(5) *Lift the third finger* and grip Edge A which allows the coin to roll over the second finger. The coin will again assume a temporary "clipped" position between the second and third fingers.

(6) Without stopping, and by tilting the hand, the coin is allowed to fall onto the back of the third finger.

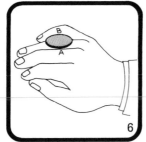

(7) *Lift the fourth finger* and clip Edge B of the coin. The coin will now be temporarily held between the third and fourth fingers.

(8) Move your little finger up and allow the coin to drop or be pulled down by the little finger through the opening between the third and little fingers. The majority of the coin is now protruding from the palm side of the hand—clipped between the third and little fingers.

(9) Move your right thumb to a position beneath the coin.

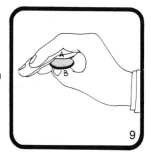

(10) Release the coin and balance it on the ball of your right thumb.

(11) Move your thumb under your fingers and transfer the coin back to the original starting point at the base of the first finger.

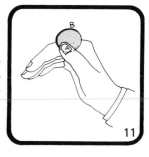

(12) Now you can push the coin up over the knuckle of the first finger and begin the entire sequence again. You may repeat the same set of moves as many times as you wish.

COMMENTS AND SUGGESTIONS

Along with its value as a flourish, the COIN ROLL is highly helpful toward developing skill in sleight-of-hand, as it limbers your fingers so they can execute difficult moves with speed and precision.

It will require considerable practice on your part in order to master the COIN ROLL. Depending upon the size of your hand, you may wish to use either a quarter or a silver dollar instead of the half-dollar. Also, although all of the "moves" are described in detail above, you may develop a slightly different technique that is better for your hand. Some performers, through a great deal of practice, are able to roll more than one coin on the same hand — or to roll one coin on the left hand and another on the right hand at the same time. But don't expect to master either of these variations quickly. One great advantage of this type of flourish, however, is that although it requires a great deal of practice, you may practice it while you are doing something else — watching television, listening to the radio, traveling — at any time when your hands are free and you will not disturb anyone if you drop the coin — *which you surely will as you learn this flourish*. Once learned, it is a great "attention getter" as you idly *sit rolling a coin back, up and around your fingers!*

THE ROLL DOWN

EFFECT

The performer, during a coin routine, displays a stack of four coins. Suddenly, the coins "roll down" his fingers until each coin is held *separately* between the fingers of the magician's hand.

The ROLL DOWN might be classified as a *MASTER FLOURISH*. Once learned, it can truly demonstrate your skill as a manipulator. We recommend the use of half-dollars (or silver dollars if you can manage them) for two reasons. The flourish with larger coins appears to be more difficult (in truth it is easier) and visually, a larger audience can see the effect.

METHOD

(1) Begin by placing four stacked coins in your right hand, holding them between your thumb and first finger. The palm of your right hand should be up, as shown.

(4) *NOTE: It is important that you master Steps 1, 2, and 3, before moving on to Step 4. The security with which Coins A & B are held between the third and fourth fingers will determine the success or failure of the next steps.*

(2) Now bend your second finger into your palm and tilt your hand slightly to the left.

(5) With Coins A & B held between your third and fourth fingers, lift your second finger and grip the edges of Coin B and Coin C. Your thumb applies pressure to Coin D.

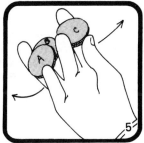

(3) The object at this point is to allow the top two coins (A & B) of the stack to slide (or be rotated by the little finger) to the left and wedge themselves between the third and little fingers.

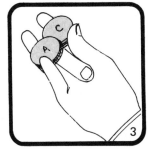

(6) Slowly straighten out your fingers. Your thumb pivots Coin D to the *right* as your little finger pivots Coin A to the *left*. The second finger rolls in between Coins B and C holding their edges.

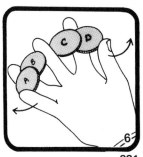

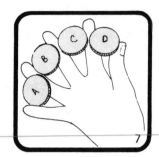

(7)   The coins are now in position ... DRAMATICALLY DISPLAYED BETWEEN YOUR FINGERS.

COMMENTS AND SUGGESTIONS

If you have followed each of the above steps with the four coins in your hand, you will have discovered that this is *not* an easy flourish to learn. But, <u>with practice, it can be mastered.</u> The obvious display of skill will be instantly recognized and appreciated by any audience.

MONEY MAGIC
BILLS

ROLL THE BILLS

For a close-up mystery, this is a real puzzler. It's a good one to perform when someone asks you to "Do A Trick" and you're not really prepared.

EFFECT

The magician lays two bills on the table — say a One-Dollar bill and a Five-Dollar bill — so they form a "V." With the One on top, he calls the audience's attention to the fact that the One-Dollar bill is on *top* of the Five. The magician then begins "rolling" the two bills together, starting at the point of the "V." While he is rolling the bills, the magician asks the spectator to place one of his fingers on the corner of the One-Dollar bill and another finger on the corner of the Five. The spectator now has both bills *pinned to the table*. So far, so good — with no chance for deception. But now, when the magician unrolls the bills, *the FIVE is on top of the ONE,* yet the spectator still has his fingers on both bills. AND THAT'S IMPOSSIBLE!

METHOD

(1)   Lay the two bills on the table with the One *on top* of the Five as shown. *Notice that the One is a bit further forward (toward the spectator) than the Five. This illustration is from the MAGICIAN'S VIEWPOINT.*

(2)   With the first fingers of both hands, start rolling the bills together beginning at the point of the "V." NOTE: In this step and all of the following steps, all of the illustrations are from the *SPECTATOR'S VIEWPOINT.*

(3)   Continue rolling the two bills until just a small part of the corner of the Five remains in view — then STOP. As shown, *more of the corner of the One shows* because it was placed further forward in the initial layout (Step 1).

(4)   STEPS 4 AND 5 ARE THE SE-CRET MOVE. As you continue to roll the bills forward, open the fingers of your left hand over the corner of the Five. Apparently you are merely holding the bills as you roll them, but actually you are *hiding the corner* of the Five from the spectator's view as shown. At the same time, point to the corner of the One with your right hand. Ask the spectator to place his left finger on that corner to hold it in place.

(5) As he does this, place your right finger on the *center* of the roll of bills and roll them slightly forward. The corner of the Five, which is hidden by your left fingers, *flops over*. In other words, this corner goes beneath the rolled bills and does a *forward flipover* back to its original position on the table. *This is unknown to the spectators,* as it is hidden by your left hand.

(8) Ask the spectator to place his *right finger* on the corner of the Five. *Emphasize that he is pinning the corners of both bills to the table.*

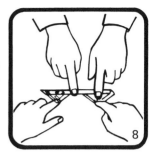

(6) This is a view of the action as shown *from the side.* Notice how your left fingers cover the "secret" *flipover* of the corner of the Five.

(9) All that is left now is for you to unroll the bills as shown. As a result of the "secret" flipover of the corner of the Five, the position of the bills will be reversed — with the Five-Dollar bill now *on top* of the One-Dollar bill!

(7) Now, still holding the roll of bills with your right finger, lift your left hand and point to the corner of the Five.

COMMENTS AND SUGGESTIONS

It is not necessary to use bills of different values in order to perform ROLL THE BILLS. If the two bills are the same, simply turn one of them over and you have bills of different colors (one black and one green). So that the trick will be easily followed by the spectator, be sure to point out which color is on top *before you start* rolling the bills. For that matter, it is not even necessary to use bills at all — different colored slips of paper will work just as well.

BILLS FROM NOWHERE — First Version

The following effect makes an excellent opening number for your act. The magician enters and walks briskly down stage center. He shows his hands to be unmistakably empty. Then, holding his hands together, a quantity of One-Dollar bills "magically" appears from out of the magician's empty palms!

SECRET AND PREPARATION

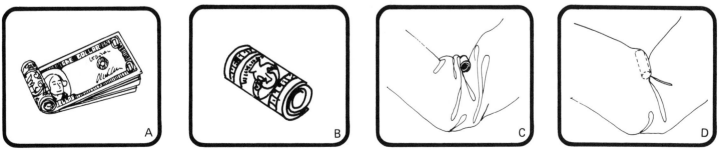

You must be wearing a suit or sport coat in order to present this effect properly. (A) Make a stack of 5 or 6 one-dollar bills. . . (B). . .and roll them into as "tight" a roll as you can. (C) Place the roll of bills into the crook of your LEFT elbow. (D) Then, pull the fabric of the coat sleeve up and over the bills. *Keep your arm slightly bent in order to hold the roll of bills in place.*

(1) With the bills "loaded" as described, make your entrance and face the audience. As you make your opening remarks, reach over with your *left* hand and grasp your *right* coat sleeve at the crook of your elbow. Pull the sleeve back, clear of your right wrist as you show your RIGHT HAND IS UNMISTAKABLY EMPTY.

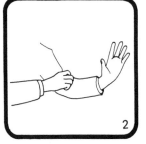

(5) Now hold both of your hands in front of you at shoulder height with your left hand in front of your right hand. *This position will give you maximum coverage for the next move.*

(2) Now reach across with the *right* hand and grasp your *left* coat sleeve at the crook of the elbow and pull that sleeve back and clear of the left wrist as you show your LEFT HAND EMPTY.

(6) Using the thumb and fingers of *both* hands, unroll the bills so that they begin to appear at the top of your fingers.

(3) DURING THIS MOVE, IT IS VERY NATURAL FOR YOUR RIGHT FINGERS TO SECRETLY "STEAL" THE CONCEALED BILLS FROM THE FOLD IN YOUR JACKET.

(7) After unrolling the bills halfway, suddenly pull the left hand down so that the thumb of the left hand unrolls the bills the rest of the way from the bottom ... leaving the open bills in the right hand. Fan the bills and display them to the audience.

(4) The roll is held in your right hand between your fingers and palm as shown.

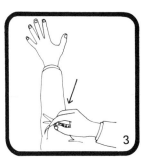

BILLS FROM NOWHERE — VERSION NO. 2

EFFECT

The magician reaches into his pocket and removes his wallet. Opening the wallet, the performer removes a single one-dollar bill. After replacing the wallet, the magician clearly demonstrates that, other than the *one* bill, his hands are absolutely empty. By suddenly slapping the bill against the palm of one hand, THE SINGLE BILL MAGICALLY MULTIPLIES INTO A QUANTITY OF NEW ONE-DOLLAR BILLS!

SECRET AND PREPARATION

Place a single bill into a "secretarial" wallet or check book and put the wallet into your inside coat pocket. Prepare a stack of bills as described in Steps A, B, C, and D in BILLS FROM NOWHERE, Version 1.

METHOD

(1) With the bills loaded into the crook of your left arm, reach into your coat pocket and remove your wallet. Take out the single bill and display it to the audience. Clearly show your hands to be empty except for the one bill.

(4) Without hesitation, grasp your right sleeve at the crook of the elbow and pull this sleeve back until you bare your right wrist.

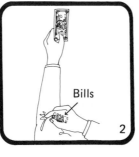

(2) Now, with the bill in your left hand, reach over with your right hand and grasp your left coat sleeve at the crook in the elbow. Pull the sleeve back until your left wrist is bare. AS YOU PULL BACK YOUR SLEEVE, <u>SECRETLY STEAL THE HIDDEN BILLS INTO YOUR RIGHT HAND</u> (as in Step 3 of the First Version).

(5) *NOTE: The spectator will have seen BOTH of your hands empty except for the single bill, which has constantly been in view.*

(6) Now, *behind the visible bill,* unroll the hidden bills.

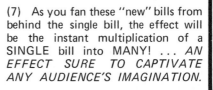

(3) With the roll of bills hidden in your right hand, transfer the single bill from your left hand to your right fingers. Place the single bill <u>in front</u> of the roll. The "secret" roll of bills will be effectively hidden behind the single bill as shown.

(7) As you fan these "new" bills from behind the single bill, the effect will be the instant multiplication of a SINGLE bill into MANY! ... *AN EFFECT SURE TO CAPTIVATE ANY AUDIENCE'S IMAGINATION.*

THE TORN AND RESTORED DOLLAR BILL

EFFECT

The magician displays a One-Dollar Bill front and back ... and then proceeds to tear the bill into two parts. Not satisfied with just the halves, the performer puts the two parts together and tears through them both. He now has four separate pieces of a once-whole bill. He folds the torn pieces neatly into a small square package. Then he makes a magical gesture over the small green bundle.... When he opens it, the audience is amazed to see that all of the pieces have mysteriously joined together to restore themselves into a completely undamaged bill.

SECRET AND PREPARATION

You will certainly want to practice this trick using "stage money" or "play money." Or, you may merely cut some pieces of paper to the correct "dollar bill" size for practice purposes. When performing for an audience, you may prefer to use real bills. This certainly strengthens the effect.

(A) Take one of the bills and place it flat on a table. Now, "accordian pleat" the bill into seven equal parts as shown. *NOTE: On a "real" dollar bill, the FACE of the bill is printed in black while the BACK is printed in green. To make the rest of the steps clear, they will be described using a "real" bill.*

(B) With your bundle now folded into seven pleats, *one* of the outside surfaces of the packet will show part of the bill's *face* (dark side) while the *other* surface will show part of the bill's *back* (green side). Place the folded bill with the *back* (green side) next to the table. The *face* (dark side) is on top. Now fold over one-third of the left side of the bill to the center as shown.

(C) Now fold the other end (right side) of the bill over as shown. This last fold should bring the corner of the back (green side) of the bill to the top of the folded package. The complete folded package should appear as shown.

(D) If the preceding three steps have been done correctly, you should have a small flat package approximately three-quarters of an inch square. Now glue this packet to the back of a duplicate bill. NOTE: If you use rubber cement, the bills can be easily separated after the show. Position the bills as shown here. *The glue is applied to the third of the bill that was NEXT TO THE TABLE when you folded the bill in Step C.*

METHOD

In the illustrations, to make the two bills easy to follow, the secret bundle has been colored darker than the open bill that you first display to the audience.

(1) Display the dollar bill to your audience, holding the bill opened out between the thumbs and fingers of both hands. Your left thumb serves two purposes: *First,* it keeps the duplicate folded bill from opening, and *second,* it conceals the folded bill from being seen by any spectators located on the sides.

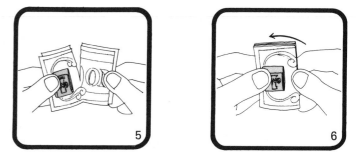

(5) Grip the two halves between the thumb and fingers of both hands and tear <u>both</u> halves as shown. (6) Again, place the torn pieces in the right hand, IN FRONT of the pieces in the left hand . . . and square the packet. To you, the torn pieces and the "secret" duplicate bills should appear as shown here.

(2) *NOTE: You may wish to start the routine by holding the bill in your right hand with your right fingers on the side of the duplicate bill . . . COMPLETELY HIDING IT FROM SIGHT. In this way, you may show the bill on BOTH sides. Then, turn the face of the bill to the audience and transfer your grip on the duplicate bill from the fingers of the right hand to the thumb of the left hand.*

(7) *NOTE: A neat touch here can be added by first placing the torn pieces in the right hand to the rear of the packet held in the left hand. The four pieces can then be spread in a small fan and shown on both sides. The pieces at the rear will conceal the folded duplicate bill. Then, in squaring up the packet, you replace the rear pieces to the front and continue as follows.*

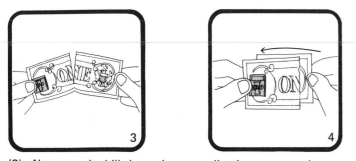

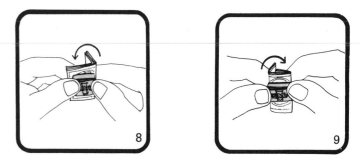

(3) Now tear the bill down the center line into two equal parts as shown. (4) Place the *right-hand half* of the bill IN FRONT of the *left-hand half*.

(8) Fold the *right*-hand edges of the torn pieces *forward* so that they are even with the right side of the secret folded bill as shown. (9) This done, fold the *left*-hand edges of the torn pieces *forward*, even with the left edge of the secret bill.

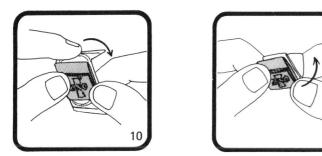

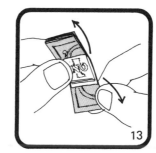

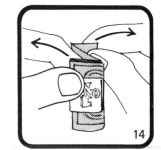

(10) Now fold *down* the *top edges* of the *torn pieces* even with the *top edge* of the *secret bill.* (11) Lastly, do the same with the *bottom edges,* folding them *upwards* even with the *bottom edge* of the secret bill. *NOTE: You have now created a folded package of the torn pieces that matches exactly in size and shape the duplicate "whole" bill behind it.*

(13) Make a *magical gesture* or say an appropriate *magic word* and begin unfolding the top and bottom thirds of the *whole bill* as shown. (14) When these portions have been unfolded, grasp the right-hand edge of the pleated bill with your right thumb and first finger. YOUR LEFT THUMB HOLDS THE FOLDED TORN PACKET AGAINST THE BACK OF THE BILL AS SHOWN.

(12) Folded in this way, the *total package* gives the impression of being *only* the folded pieces of the original bill. This makes it easy to casually *turn the package over* showing both sides of the torn bill. WHEN YOU FINISH SHOWING BOTH SIDES, BE SURE THAT YOU END WITH THE DUPLICATE "WHOLE" BILL IN FRONT AND THE FOLDED TORN PIECES TO THE REAR.

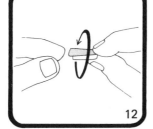

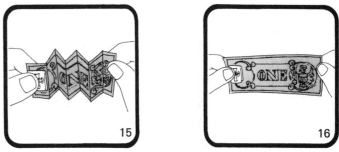

(15) Now, by pulling your hands apart, the duplicate bill unfolds so quickly it will seem to the spectators as if the torn pieces are instantly restored. (16) Briefly display the restored bill. Then fold it in half back over the torn pieces . . . thus eliminating the possibility of accidentally exposing the torn packet as you return the "restored" bill to your pocket.

INFLATION
PETER PIT

Here is a baffling "Cut and Restored" routine that is particularly effective when performed with "real" Dollar Bills. You can use play money, stage money, blank checks, or any form of printed paper about the size of regular currency.

EFFECT

The magician openly displays two Dollar Bills and places them back to back. He then cuts through the center of both bills with a pair of scissors — unmistakably cutting the two bills into four "halves." Without any suspicious moves, the *magician instantly restores both bills to their original condition right before the eyes of the astonished spectators!*

SECRET AND PREPARATION

(A) Place two new or nearly new Dollar Bills face down on a table with the "green" side up. (B) Apply a thin layer of *rubber cement,* about a half-inch wide, down the center of the back (the "green" side) of each bill. When this is dry, add a *second coat* of cement and allow it to dry also. (C) Next, sprinkle a little talcum powder on the "cement covered" area on each bill. Spread the powder over the entire surface of the cement with your finger, or better yet, a soft brush. You will notice that now the "treated" areas of both bills *will not stick to each other* because of the powdered surface. Put the bills in your wallet or on your table and you are ready to perform this very clever close-up mystery.

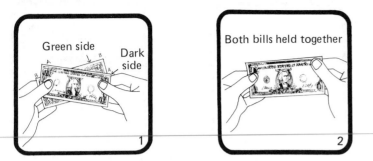

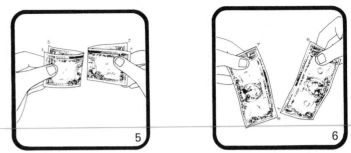

(1) Begin by removing the two prepared bills from your wallet and casually showing both sides of the bills. Place them *back to back* as shown. (We will call the bill nearest you "Bill A," and the one nearest the spectators "Bill B.") (2) Square up both bills. *Be sure that the cemented areas are touching each other.*

(5) With the thumb and fingers of both hands, separate the "halves" of the bills and ... (6) ... shake them open. Because of the rubber cement, *the halves in each hand will stick together at the cut edges* giving the illusion that the four "half" bills have "fused" together — TO FORM TWO COMPLETE BILLS!

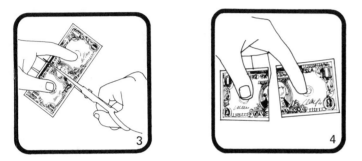

(3) Hold *both bills* with the thumb and fingers of your left hand as shown. With your right hand holding the scissors, carefully cut through the center of both bills. *Make sure that you cut within the areas covered by the cement strips.* Done openly and deliberately, there will be no question in the audience's mind that both bills have actually been cut in half — *which they have.*
(4) Place the scissors aside. Grasp the halves on the right sides of the cut in your right hand (one-half of Bill A and one-half of Bill B) and the left side's two halves (the other two halves of Bill A and Bill B) in your left hand.

COMMENTS AND SUGGESTIONS

Done well, this "quickie" is a real eyepopper. First practice with stage money or with newspaper cut to the size of Dollar Bills. In this way you will find out just how much rubber cement and talcum powder to apply. Then, if you wish, you can try it with "real" bills. These should be new and crisp and fit together neatly for Steps 2 and 3. Don't worry about losing money when using real bills, as the halves can be mended with transparent tape, just as with any torn bills.

THE SIX-BILL REPEAT

If you can throw away your money and still keep it, that would be *REAL MAGIC* ... like "having your cake and eating it too." That is exactly what you do with the "Six-Bill Repeat" — or it is at least what you appear to do. The best part of this effect is that the surprise increases with each repeat, which is quite unusual as most tricks lose their impact after they have been performed once. This makes the "Bill Trick" an outstanding number in any program, as you will find out for yourself when you perform it.

EFFECT

The magician removes his wallet from his inside coat pocket and takes out a number of one dollar bills. Counting them one-by-one for the audience, they see that he has *six* dollars. Dealing *three* of the bills on the table, the performer calls to the spectator's attention that simple mathematics would dictate that he has just *three* bills left in his hand. After all, three from six leaves three, doesn't it? Well, not in this case, for when the magician recounts the money, he finds he still has *six* one dollar bills. The performer keeps discarding three bills — only to find that each time he is "magically" left with six. This continues until a sizable amount of money is displayed on the table.

SECRET AND PREPARATION

We will assume that you will be using stage money for this effect, although real bills can be prepared in the same way.

(A) The secret lies in four special "envelope" type bills which you must construct. The first step is to cut the corner off of four bills as per Fig. A.

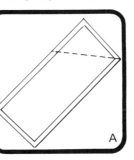

(E) Insert three unprepared bills into the "envelope" bill. Be sure that the unprepared bills all face in the proper direction and are correctly aligned so they match the printing of the "envelope" bill.

(B) Place the long edge of one of the cut bills next to an unprepared bill as in Fig. B. Be sure that the unprepared bill is *face down* and the the cut bill is *face up.*

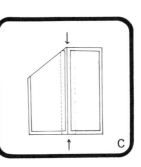

(F) Make up three more "envelope" bills and insert three regular bills inside.

(C) With a strip of cellophane tape, tape the edges of the bills together.

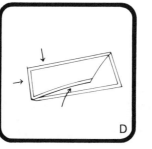

(G) Arrange the four *loaded* envelope bills and add two unprepared bills to the front of the final stack.

(D) Fold the cut bill down on top of the unprepared bill. Now, by taping the narrow edges at the left end of the bills, you have created an "envelope." *NOTE: To hide the tape on the narrow edges, first, fold the tape with the sticky side out and tape the narrow edges INSIDE the bills.*

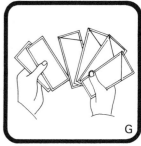

(H) Square up the stack so that the diagonal cuts of the prepared bills are at the top and facing in your direction. Place the bills in a "secretary" type wallet (or a business letter size envelope) and you are ready to perform.

METHOD

(1) Remove the bills from your wallet and hold the stack in your left hand. Slowly and deliberately count the bills into your right hand, *making sure not to disturb their original order.*

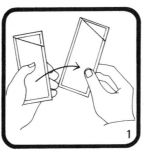

(2) At the completion of the count, all six bills should be in your right hand with the four prepared envelope bills still facing you.

(3) Square up the stack and transfer all to your left hand.

(4) Now count off three unprepared bills, *pulling them out of the top envelope bill one at a time.* Count them aloud, "One, Two, Three," as you place them on the table.

(5) You are now left with an empty envelope bill at the rear of the stack. MOVE THIS ENVELOPE TO THE FRONT OF THE STACK *(audience side)* and give the remaining three bills a deliberate snap with your fingers. As you do this, remark, "By placing the *back* bill in the *front* and giving the packet a *magic tap,* it magically doubles the amount of money left in my hand."

(6) Then slowly count the bills as before (Step 1), demonstrating the "magical" restoration to six bills.

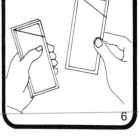

(7) It is important that during the "counts" you maintain the order of the two regular bills and the four envelope bills. In other words, from your point of view you should now have in your right hand, starting from the side nearest you, three "loaded" envelope bills, two regular bills and one empty envelope bill. In the illustration the bills have been purposely fanned open to show more clearly their position at this point in the routine.

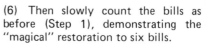

(8) This process continues until all of the loaded envelopes have been emptied. All in all, twelve "new" dollar bills make their magical appearance. The effectiveness of this illusion is enhanced by repetition, which does not normally hold true in presenting a trick. But in this case, the audience becomes more and more involved as the effect progresses.

COMMENTS AND SUGGESTIONS

This trick is quite effective and the props can be made quite inexpensively, and it can be seen by a large audience. The entertainment value of the trick lies in the "patter" story that you devise to accompany it. Here is an example:

"I saw an ad in a magazine for the Mark Wilson Course In Magic. The ad said that one of the tricks I would learn if I studied the course is how to count, one-two-three-four-five-six dollar bills — and then remove one-two-three - - and I would still have one-two-three-four-five-six dollar bills left. So I ordered the Course and while I was waiting for it to come, I wondered how you could possibly have one-two-three-four-five-six dollar bills, remove one-two-three and have one-two-three-four-five-six dollar bills left. When I received the Mark Wilson Course, sure enough, after I practiced the trick I learned how to count one-two-three-four-five-six dollar bills, remove one-two-three and still have one-two-three-four-five-six dollar bills left." You have now emptied three of the envelope bills, you have one "loaded" envelope left. Your patter continues: "And now I am going to tell you the secret. Instead of starting with one-two-three-four-five-six dollar bills, you really have one-two-three-four-five-six-SEVEN-EIGHT-NINE bills to start with. AND THAT'S HOW THE TRICK WORKS." The last count of nine — the comedy explanation — is performed by counting the first three bills from the last envelope bill and *then counting the envelope bills as well* onto the table.

NOTE: When you count the bills in the final "nine count," be sure to place the envelope bills on the table so that the "cut side" of the bills is face down so they will not be seen by the audience.

THE BILL IN LEMON

The BILL IN LEMON is one of the great "classics" of modern magic. That claim is supported by the fact that several famous magicians have featured it as the highlight of their individual programs. There are several different versions of this mystery. In the clever method described here, no special skill is required, which makes it ideal for new students of magic as well as advanced practitioners.

EFFECT

From a bowl containing three lemons, a spectator is given a free choice of whichever one he wants. The selected lemon is then placed in an ordinary paper or plastic bag and the spectator holds the lemon throughout the entire presentation. _After the lemon has been selected and is securely held by the first spectator,_ the magician borrows a dollar bill and writes its serial number on the back of a small envelope. He then inserts the bill into the envelope, seals it, and gives it to a second spectator to hold. He then recaps exactly what has happened up to this point. Then, the spectator holding the envelope is told to tear it open and remove the borrowed bill. When he does, _instead of the bill,_ he finds an I.O.U. for one dollar, _signed by the magician._ The first spectator is given a knife and asked to cut open the selected lemon, _which has remained in his custody at all times._ Inside the lemon, he finds a tightly rolled dollar bill. When the bill is opened, its serial number is found to be exactly the same as the number written on the envelope, proving that the _borrowed bill_ has magically travelled _from the envelope to the inside of the freely selected lemon._

SECRET AND PREPARATION

For this amazing effect, you will need the following items: a stack of a dozen or more envelopes (small "pay" envelopes are best, however, any small opaque envelope can be used), three lemons, a bowl, a dollar bill, your handwritten I.O.U. which is the same size as a dollar bill, a rubber band, some glue and a small paper or plastic bag. (A transparent plastic bag is best.)

HOW TO PREPARE THE ENVELOPES

(A) To begin, write the serial number of _your_ dollar bill on the back of one of the envelopes near the lower end as shown. For future reference, this envelope has been marked with an "O" in the illustrations.

(F) Then place Envelope X (the one with the flap cut off) directly on top of Envelope O, concealing the serial number from view.

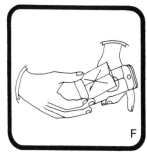

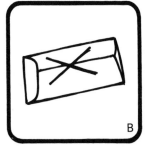

(B) Then, _carefully cut off the gummed flap from another envelope._ This envelope is identified with an "X" in the illustrations. (C) This is how Envelopes X and O should look at this point.

(G) Now, square up the envelopes and place the rubber band around the entire stack. _Done properly, the gummed flap of Envelope O will appear to be the flap belonging to Envelope X._

HOW TO PREPARE THE "SPECIAL" LEMON

(H) First, _carefully_ remove the "pip" from one of the lemons with the point of a knife. _Do not throw the pip away as you will need it later._

(D) Fold the I.O.U. and insert it into Envelope O. (E) Place Envelope O on top of the stack of regular envelopes so that the written serial number is facing up as shown.

(I) Then, using a smooth, round stick (like the kind used for candied apples), or any similarly shaped slim long object, carefully make a hole in the center of the lemon as shown. This will *expand the inner core area of the lemon* and make the necessary space to accommodate a rolled bill. *Be careful not to go too far and puncture the skin at the other end of the lemon with the stick.*

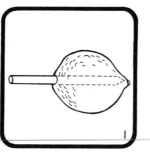

(L) Push the rolled bill *completely into the lemon.* Use a small dab of glue to fix the pip back on the lemon (model airplane glue works well). *Be sure that you have written down the serial number of the bill before you insert it into the lemon.* When you glue the pip back in place, adjust it so that it hides the small hole in the end of the lemon.

(J) *NOTE: If a wooden stick of this type is not available, certain kinds of ball point pens and some pencils are* <u>thin enough</u> *to make the correct sized hole in the lemon. The important point here is that whatever object you are using be thin enough so that it does not puncture the inside "juicy" portion of the lemon when it is inserted.*

(M) Finally, place the prepared lemon (marked "X" in the illustrations) in a bowl with two "ordinary" lemons. *Be certain that you are able to distinguish the "prepared" lemon ("X") from the other two at a glance.*

(K) Now roll the dollar bill into a tight, compact cylinder.

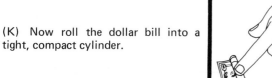

(N) NOTE: There may be some special "blemish" on the prepared lemon that you can remember — or you can make a small mark with a black pen or pencil on the lemon that will not be noticed by the audience.

(O) Place the bowl of lemons, the stack of envelopes, the pencil, the knife, and the small bag on your table. YOU ARE NOW READY TO PRESENT THIS CLASSIC MYSTERY.

METHOD

(1) *FIRST, THE "FREE" CHOICE OF THE "SPECIAL" LEMON:* This is accomplished by "forcing," using the MAGICIAN'S CHOICE, which is described in detail on **Page 321** of the Course. In this force, the spectator *believes* he is given a free choice of any of the three lemons, when *actually* you cleverly maneuver him to select the special Lemon X. After he has made his "selection," pick up the small bag from your table. Hold the bag open and have the spectator drop the lemon inside. Tell him to hold the bag tightly so that the lemon *he selected* cannot get away!

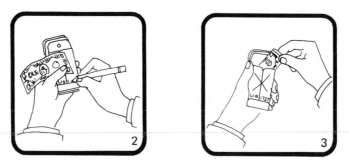

(2) *NOW FOR THE BILL AND THE ENVELOPE* — Borrow a dollar bill from some member of the audience. Explain that you will write its serial number on the top of the stack (Envelope X). As you "pretend" to copy the number from the borrowed bill, you <u>actually</u> write *any number you wish on the envelope,* as it will automatically be "switched" for the correct serial number which is now hidden on the second in the stack, Envelope O. (It is best if you remember the <u>first letter</u> of the serial number of *your* bill as this is the most obvious thing that the audience might see and remember.) Just casually copy the number (with *your* first letter) of the <u>borrowed bill.</u> Remember, the audience, at this time, does not know what trick you are going to perform — so they will not pay particular attention to the serial number now <u>if you do not call special attention to it.</u> (3) This done, fold the borrowed bill to about the same size as your I.O.U. Then openly insert it *into the flapless Envelope X.* Be sure that everyone sees that the bill is definitely going into the *top envelope of the stack.* Be careful not to expose that Envelope X <u>does not have a flap.</u>

(4) *NOTE: Inserting the bill into Envelope X requires some practice in the handling of the envelopes so that you can do it smoothly and not arouse suspicion. It may be helpful to remove the rubber band before attempting to insert the bill into the top envelope. This depends on how tight the rubber band holds the packet of envelopes.*

(10) Immediately place the rest of the envelopes in your pocket, eliminating the possibility of anyone discovering that a switch was made. Now, seal Envelope O and give it to a spectator to hold.

(5) Once the bill has been inserted into Envelope X on the top of the stack, grip the uppermost flap (actually the flap of Envelope O) between your right thumb and fingers — and draw this envelope from the rest of the stack.

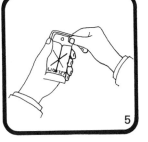

(11) This done, ask the person holding the sealed envelope to raise it toward the light *so he can see that the bill is really there.* Of course, what he actually sees is the outline of your I.O.U.

(6) What you are really doing is drawing out Envelope O instead of Envelope X, but you hide that move from the spectators BY TURNING THE STACK COMPLETELY OVER AS YOU DRAW THE ENVELOPE CLEAR.

(12) Now ask the first spectator if he is still holding the bag with the lemon inside. When he says he is, ask him if there is any way *anything* could have gotten inside the bag with the lemon. After he replies, recap what has happened up to this point. Explain that first you had *one* of three lemons selected and that *that lemon* has been securely held by a member of the audience *at all times.* Now take the two remaining lemons from the bowl and toss them to other members of the audience. This will strengthen the effect later after the borrowed bill is found inside the selected lemon. The spectators may even cut open these "ungimmicked" lemons which will only increase the mystery.

(7) This makes a *perfect switch* of Envelope X, the one containing the borrowed bill, for Envelope O, the one that contains your I.O.U.

(13) Now, emphasize that you *then* borrowed a dollar bill from someone in the audience — AFTER THE SELECTED LEMON WAS SAFELY IN THE BAG HELD BY THE SPECTATOR. The serial number of the bill was recorded on the outside of an envelope and the bill sealed inside. Emphasize again that THE ENVELOPE, WITH THE BILL STILL SEALED INSIDE, IS NOW HELD BY THE SECOND SPECTATOR.

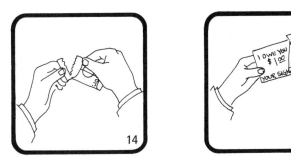

(8) Once Envelope O is entirely clear of the rest of the stack, . . .
(9) turn it "flap side up" so that the serial number that you previously wrote on Envelope O is clearly visible to the spectators. The audience will be convinced that *it is the same envelope* and that everything is aboveboard.

(14) NOW FOR THE MAGIC! *Really the trick is already done, but the audience doesn't know it!* Ask the second spectator to tear open the envelope and remove the bill. (15) When he does, *he finds your I.O.U. instead.*

(16) Next, give the knife to the person holding the bag with the lemon inside. Tell him to remove the lemon from the bag. <u>After</u> he removes the lemon, *take the bag from him and hold it in your hand.* With your other hand, give him the knife and ask him to cut the lemon open. (It's even better if he uses a pocket knife borrowed from someone in the audience!) As he cuts the lemon, instruct him to "rotate" the lemon around the knifeblade as if it had an inner "core" which he did not wish to cut.

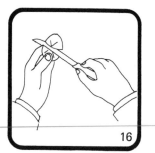

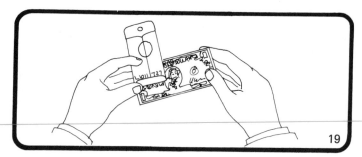

(19) <u>After</u> *the bill is removed from the lemon by the spectator,* take the lemon "halves" from him and *drop them into the bag.* Put the bag on your table or casually toss it off stage. (This subtly gets rid of the "gimmicked" half of the lemon so that it is not lying about where someone might pick it up and examine it later on.) Then, have the spectator compare the serial number on the bill he found in the lemon with that of the now "vanished" borrowed bill which was written on the envelope. HE WILL FIND THAT THE NUMBERS ARE IDENTICAL — proving that the borrowed bill has "magically" gone from the sealed envelope into the freely selected lemon — A MAGICAL MIRACLE! Take back your I.O.U. in exchange for the borrowed bill and thank the spectators for their assistance.

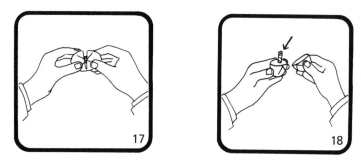

(17) When the spectator draws the halves of the lemon apart, . . .
(18) he finds the bill imbedded in the center! EMPHASIZE THAT <u>YOU HAVE NEVER TOUCHED THE LEMON</u> SINCE IT WAS SELECTED FROM THE BOWL.

COMMENTS AND SUGGESTIONS

Be sure to write down the serial number of *your* bill <u>before</u> you load it into the lemon. Also, have the first letter of the serial number written somewhere handy for quick reference in case you forget it. You can strengthen the effect even more by really writing the *complete serial number* of your "loaded" bill on Envelope X. To help you remember it, you may write the number *very lightly* so that no one can notice it on the back of Envelope X before the show. Another subterfuge for "remembering" the number is to have the number already written near the center of the envelope and then cover it with a wide rubber band. You can then shift or remove the rubber band as you "pretend" to copy the number from the borrowed bill. If you use this method, be sure to keep the stack of envelopes turned toward you as you write. Then, after the number is written, since it *matches identically* the previously written number on Envelope O underneath, *you may display the stack freely to the audience.* As for the rubber band, its main purpose is to keep the envelopes neatly in place during the early handling of the stack. It does not have to be removed from the stack during the performance as it may prove helpful for the "switch," *if it is not too tight.*

Another suggestion is to use an *orange* instead of a lemon. As an orange is somewhat larger, it is easier to load, and you can easily withdraw the "pip" from the orange before inserting the bill.

It is a good plan to get *several* people to offer you a bill for the trick so *you can pick the one that <u>most closely resembles</u> the age and "wear" of the bill already in the lemon.* Also, don't give the owner time to note the serial number, as you are going to give him back *your* bill instead of the one you borrowed from him.

As you can see, this is one of the truly great tricks in magic. You can build your reputation on this one trick alone — so <u>study</u> it and <u>practice</u> it before you <u>perform</u> it. Add your own touches — emphasize the "impossible" nature of what the audience is seeing — and always protect the truly marvelous secret of THE BILL IN LEMON.

ROPE MAGIC

★　★　★

Here is a highly popular branch of modern wizardry that has grown by leaps and bounds, for a very good reason. Simple tricks with rope can be done any time, anywhere, in an impromptu fashion, making them ideal for beginners who can later graduate into more elaborate "rope work" suitable for platform or stage. With ropes, once you have learned a good trick, it invariably paves the way to another, gradually enabling you to build a reputation as well as a program.

Originally, rope magic was confined chiefly to "Trick Knots" that puzzled spectators but did not actually mystify them. A new era arrived with the "Cut and Restored Rope," which soon became popular with stage magicians, although for a long time it was the only rope trick on their programs. However, various methods were soon devised, so that audiences were continually deceived by new versions with unexpected twists. This led to improvements that were baffling even to magicians who depended on the old-time routines; and that rule prevails today.

Now, instead of merely cutting a rope in half, a magician can cut it into several pieces before restoring it. Short ropes can be tied together with knots that disappear, leaving one long rope. Stretching short ropes to various lengths is another specialty, and knots can be made to come and go in amazing fashion. Though every rope has an end, there seems to be no end to rope tricks, and that is why you will find this section of very special value. It will teach you rope magic as it stands today, so that your program will represent a long step toward the rope magic of tomorrow!

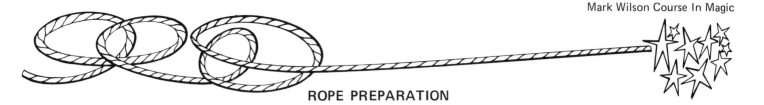

ROPE PREPARATION

In performing Rope Magic, there are several "tips" you should know about the preparation of the rope to achieve the most effective results in practice and presentation.

CORING: In certain tricks it is important that the rope be extremely flexible — even more so than it already is. In that case, you can do what is known as "Coring" with many types of rope — especially the soft cotton rope used by magicians. If you look at the end of some types of rope, you will notice that the rope is constructed of a woven outer "shell" which contains an inner "core." This core is made up of a number of individual cotton strands running the entire length of the rope. To remove the core, first, cut off a piece of rope and spread open the threads of the outer "shell" at one end. With your fingers, firmly grasp the strands of cord which make up the core. Now with your other hand, get a firm hold on the outer shell near the same end and start pulling the core from within the rope's outer shell. As you pull the "core" and slide the outer "shell," you will find that the shell tends to "bunch up" and then bind, making it difficult to pull out the inner core. When this happens, grasp the rope just below the "bunched up" shell and pull the shell *down along the length of the remaining core* until the shell is "straight" again — with the empty shell extending from the other end of the "core." Then pull another length of core out from within the outer shell until it "binds" again. Continue this process of pulling and "unbunching" until the core has been completely removed from within the shell of the rope. Discard the core. This leaves you with the soft, flexible outer shell of the Rope. To the audience, however, *the rope will appear just the same as before you removed the core.*

FIXING THE ENDS: Another suggestion which will aid in maintaining the appearance of your rope, particularly if it has been "Cored," is to permanently "fix" the ends of the rope so that they will not fray (come apart). This can be done in several ways.

(1)   A particularly good method is to dip the end of the rope into a small amount of *white glue* and allow it to dry over night. This will permanently bond all the loose fibers together and prevent them from unraveling.

(2)   Another substance which works well for this purpose is *wax* or *paraffin*. The wax is melted and the ends of the rope dipped into the liquid wax and allowed to dry. This method has the advantage that wax requires only a short period of time to dry and your ropes can be prepared only minutes before a performance.

(3)   Another method which works well is to "tie off" the ends of the rope with regular *white sewing thread* after the rope has been cut to the desired length. Simply wrap the thread around the ends of the rope and tie the ends tightly to keep the rope from unwinding.

(4)   One final method is to wrap a small piece of white *adhesive tape* or *transparent cellophane tape* around the ends of the rope. Because tape is more easily visible, however, it may draw undue attention to the ends of the rope and distract from the effect being presented. The "tape method" is a good, fast way to get your "rehearsal" ropes ready.

CUT AND RESTORED ROPE — FIRST METHOD

This effect has become a magical "classic" in its own right and is one with which every magician should be familiar. Most all versions of the CUT AND RESTORED ROPE are based upon the same simple method. Once you have learned it well, you can continue with other forms of the trick described later in the Course.

EFFECT

The magician displays a six-foot length of rope. He then forms the center of the rope into a loop in his hand and cuts it there — explaining that the rope must first be divided into *two equal* sections. However, it becomes immediately evident — first to the audience and then to the magician — that the two resulting lengths of rope are not the same length, much to the dismay of the performer. Somewhat frustrated, the magician ties the cut ends together with a simple knot — and then winds the rope around his hand. After a little "magic," the performer unwinds the rope to show that the knot has "dissolved" — leaving the rope COMPLETELY RESTORED!

SECRET AND PREPARATION

The only items required for this effect are a length of rope, a coin (or some other small object), and a pair of sharp scissors. To prepare, place the coin in your right trouser or jacket pocket. Have the scissors on a table nearby. This done, you are ready to begin.

(1) Display the rope to your audience, holding the ends between the thumb and fingers of your left hand, so that the center of the rope hangs down as shown. NOTE: There are *two key locations* on the rope that will help greatly in explaining the secret of the CUT AND RESTORED ROPE. The *first* is a point about four inches from the end of the rope. We will call this "Point A." The *second* is the *true center* of the rope — this we will call "Point B."

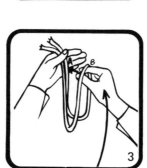

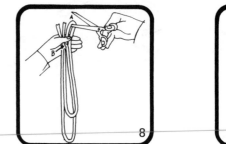

(8) With the scissors, cut the rope at Point A. Say, "I'll cut the rope at the *center,* which makes *two ropes exactly equal* in length." (9) After the cut the audience will see *four ends* projecting above your left hand. Point A has now been cut into *two parts* as shown.

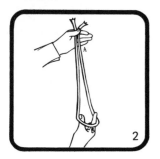

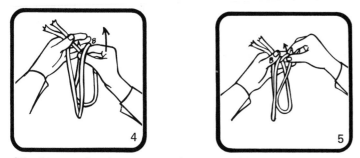

(2) Insert your right thumb and first finger through the center loop, Point B, from the *audience side* of the rope as shown. *NOTE: Your right thumb and first finger are pointing upward and slightly back toward you as you insert them into the loop.* (3) With your right hand, bring the rope up toward your left hand, keeping the loop, Point B, draped loosely over your right thumb and first finger.

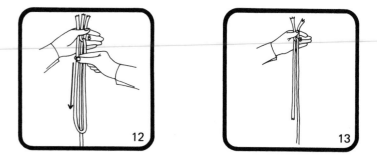

(10) With your right hand, draw the end at the *far right* away from your left hand and (11) drop it. As you do this say, "That is *one* rope . . ."

(4) As your hands come together, your right thumb and first finger grasp the rope *at Point A* as shown. (5) HERE COMES THE "SECRET MOVE" WHICH MAKES THE TRICK WORK. Now, pull Point A upward so that it forms a small loop of its own, which you hold between your right thumb and first finger. At the same time that you pick up Point A, tilt your right fingers downward so that Point B — *the real center of the rope* — slides off your right fingers into the cradle of rope formed when you lifted Point A into a loop. STUDY THE ILLUSTRATION FOR STEPS 4 AND 5. *NOTE: Steps 4 and 5 must be hidden from the spectators by your left hand.*

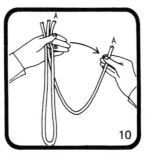

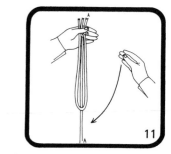

(12) Grasp the end of the rope at the *far left* and (13) let it fall next to the first as you say, ". . . and here is the *second* rope." At this point it will become obvious to the audience that the "two" ropes did not come out equal in length as you had intended. Pretend to be puzzled and somewhat frustrated at the results; as you say, "Something seems to have gone wrong; the rope must be cut into two equal pieces." *NOTE: The two ends of the short piece of rope that project above your left hand look like the ends of two separate long ropes. The real center of the rope (Point B) is looped over the short piece of rope.*

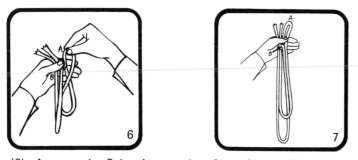

(6) As you raise Point A upward to form the new loop, your left thumb keeps the real center, Point B, down in your left hand, out of view of the spectators. (7) This new loop, Point A, takes the place of what the audience still believes is *the real center of the rope,* Point B — since your left hand concealed the "secret" switch.

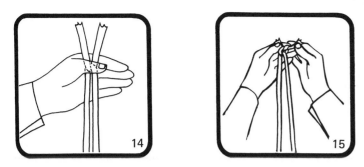

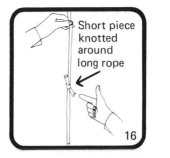

(14) As an optional "convincer," you can add the following move to prove that you actually have "two separate pieces" of rope. Cover the interlocking loops at Point B with your left thumb. Then swing your left arm out to your left side so that the palm of your left hand is facing the audience. This lets you casually show *both sides* of the cut ropes — while your left thumb hides the fact that the upper ends are really the ends of a short loop — not the ends of two long ropes. Then swing your arm back to its former position in front of your body and continue with the next step. (15). While your hands conceal the true condition of the ropes, *tie the ends of the short rope around the center of the long piece of rope at Point B.* Be careful not to reveal that you really have <u>one long rope</u> and <u>one short rope</u> while tying the knot.

(16) This done, you can now openly display the rope to the audience, as you call attention to the knot which is tied slightly "off center." (17) Then, starting at either end, begin to wind the rope around your left hand. What you really do, however, is *slide the knot along the rope* with your right hand as you continue the winding process. Keep the knot hidden in your right hand as you slide it along.

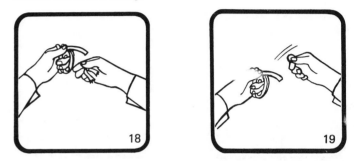

(18) As you complete the winding, *slide the knot off the end of the rope.* Hold the knot secretly in your curled right fingers. Without pausing, dip your right hand into your pocket, remarking, "I will now need my magic coin" (or whatever small object you are using). With that, *leave the knot in your pocket* and bring out the coin. Wave it over the rope as you make some remark about the "Magic Coin." (19) Now, release the coin in your pocket and uncoil the rope — showing that the knot has vanished and the rope is COMPLETELY RESTORED! The rope can then be tossed to the audience for examination.

COMMENTS AND SUGGESTIONS

The length of the rope used in this trick can vary from three to eight feet. It is a good plan to start with a *long* rope, as with each performance the rope loses several inches. When it finally becomes too short to be effective, discard it and use another long rope or save it for some other trick in which a "short" rope is used.

CUT AND RESTORED ROPE — SECOND METHOD

EFFECT

The performer draws a long piece of rope through his hand and asks a member of the audience to call "Stop" to select a point anywhere along the length of the rope. When the call comes, the magician cuts the rope at the spot indicated by the spectator. After displaying the two pieces of rope, the performer decides that the rope served a more useful purpose as one long piece. As if by magic, the performer *instantly restores the rope back to its original condition!* The presentation can end at this point, or be used as a lead-in to a series of other rope effects.

SECRET AND PREPARATION

As in the First Method, the rope is unprepared. Again, the only items required are a sharp pair of scissors and a piece of soft rope about five or six feet in length.

METHOD

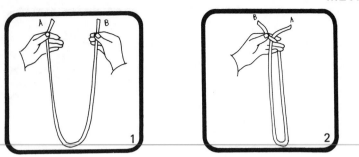

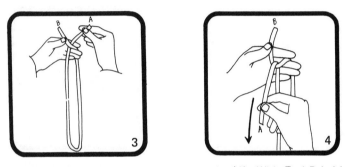

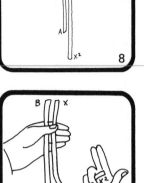

(1) Display the length of rope, holding it by the ends as shown. We will call the ends of the ropes A and B in the illustrations. End A is held in your left hand, and End B in your right.
(2) With your right hand, place End B into your left hand between your first and second fingers. End B is positioned as shown, overlapping End A. Hold End B in place with your left thumb as shown.

(3) Grasp End A with your right hand. (4) With End B held tightly by your left thumb, your right hand pulls End A down (toward yourself) as shown. As you pull the rope down, ask the spectator to tell you when to "stop" pulling.

(8) Adjust End X up next to End B and hold them with your left thumb and fingers. *To the audience, it will appear that you hold two separate long lengths of rope.*

(9) At this point, comment to the audience that the two ropes have not come out equal and you are a bit embarrassed by your "mistake." With that, grasp End X_2 in your right hand as shown, keeping the end well within the hand.

(10) Bring End X_2 up to meet End X_1 and grasp *both ends together* in your right hand, as shown in the illustration.

(5) As you pull End A, the loop in the rope will get smaller and smaller. The illusion created by this move is that the spectator is given a "free choice" as to where the rope will be cut. As you will see, *it makes no difference where he stops you.*

(11) As soon as you have both ends held firmly together within your right fingers, release your left hand and shake the rope open, holding it with your right hand so that it *appears* to be one long rope restored into a single length. *The effect is* <u>instant restoration</u>.

(6) When the spectator calls "Stop," release End A and *grasp the side of the loop closest to End B* (Point X in the illustration) as shown. Ask the spectator to cut the rope you hold between your hands (at Point X). If you study the illustration, you will see that THE SPECTATOR IS ACTUALLY CUTTING OFF ONLY A <u>SMALL PIECE OF ROPE</u> CLOSE TO END B — *not near the center of the rope as he thinks.*

Cut here

(12) Comment that "It wasn't a very good trick anyway," as you tug on the now "restored" rope.

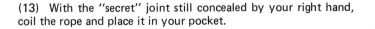

(7) As soon as the spectator makes the cut, release your right hand. This allows the "new" end, which we will call X_2, to fall next to End A. You now hold one *short* piece and one *long* piece of rope looped together in your left hand.

(13) With the "secret" joint still concealed by your right hand, coil the rope and place it in your pocket.

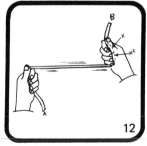

240

COMMENTS AND SUGGESTIONS

In both methods of the CUT AND RESTORED ROPE, after you apparently cut the rope into two pieces (Step 13 in the First Method, Step 8 in the Second Method), you are actually holding *a long piece of rope which is secretly looped with a short piece.* To the audience, it appears that you hold two separate long pieces of rope. At this point in the trick, because your left fingers conceal the interlocking loops, you may conclude the effect using either version of restoring the rope back to one long piece, as they are interchangeable.

If you restore the rope as described in the Second Method and you wish to continue with other rope tricks, you will need to dispose of the short end which extends from your right hand. A natural way to do this is to reach into your pocket to remove some object and simply carry the end of the "restored" rope and the short piece along. Then, when you remove your hand with the object, leave the short piece behind. The audience will not notice that the long rope has now become a bit "shorter" than before. If you use a pocket knife to cut the rope, this makes a logical item to remove from your pocket. You could also remove some small prop which you plan to use in your next trick, such as a ring, coin, or handkerchief. Another suggestion is to reach for some object on your table, carrying along the end of the rope and the short piece. When you pick up the object, you can leave the short piece on the table behind (or in) some prop that is already there.

Both methods of the CUT AND RESTORED ROPE are true classics of magic. Although quite simple, once learned they will become a permanent addition to your repertoire. Also, this is one of the few tricks that are just as effective when performed for a small intimate crowd as they are for large audiences. THIS IS A VALUABLE AND MUCH USED PRINCIPLE OF MAGIC. PRACTICE IT WELL BEFORE YOU PRESENT IT, AND — ABOVE ALL — DO NOT REVEAL ITS SECRET.

COMEDY CUT AND RESTORED ROPE

EFFECT

The performer gives a member of his audience a piece of rope approximately three feet in length and has the spectator cut the rope into two equal parts. After viewing the result, the magician decides to have the spectator cut the two pieces again, making four equal parts. Taking the four pieces of rope, the performer drops them one by one into an empty paper bag. Next, he closes the top of the bag and shakes it vigorously. The magician tells the spectator that, by waving the scissors over the bag, the rope will "mysteriously" restore itself to one piece. Upon opening the bag, the audience sees that the rope has restored itself, *but not in the way the magician intended.* Instead of *one* piece, the rope has "magically" *tied itself together* with *three* equally spaced knots. The bag is shown to be empty and is tossed aside. In order to solve this new problem, the magician simply gives the end of the "tied" rope a sharp pull. THE THREE KNOTS FLY OFF THE ROPE LEAVING IT COMPLETELY RESTORED!

SECRET AND PREPARATION

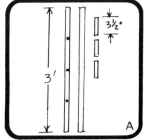

(A) Cut *two* 3-foot lengths of soft rope and *three* short pieces of rope about 3½ inches long. These short lengths will be used to form fake knots, which later "pop" off the rope. Stretch out one of the 3-foot lengths of rope and mark it lightly with a pencil in quarters as shown. These marks show you where to attach the fake knots which *apparently* divide the rope into four equal parts.

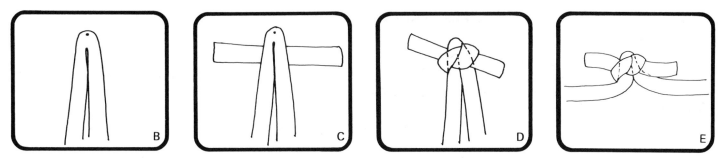

(B) First, to tie the fake knots, fold the long rope at one of the three pencil marks. (C) Then, tie one of the short pieces of rope . . .
(D) . . . *around* the folded rope as shown. (E) When you straighten the long rope, the knot will appear like this. If you pull on the rope, the knot will "pop" off.

(F) Tie the other two short pieces around the other two marked spots on the long rope. You now appear to have one long piece of rope made up of three short pieces knotted together.

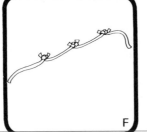

(G) You will also need a DOUBLE-WALLED BAG (see Page 357). Open the bag and place the prepared rope into the *main compartment* as shown. DO NOT PLACE IT INTO THE "SECRET" POCKET, *as this area will be used to conceal the cut pieces later in the routine.* Fold the bag flat and put it on your table.

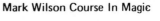

METHOD

(1) Invite a spectator to join you on stage so that you may teach him how to present a trick. Hand him the scissors and display the 3-foot length of rope to the audience. Turn to your volunteer and instruct him to cut the rope — first in half . . . (2) . . . and then into four equal parts.

(3) Pick up the paper bag and open it. *Be careful not to show the inside of the bag or you will expose the presence of the prepared rope.* Drop the four pieces of rope, one at a time, INTO THE SECRET COMPARTMENT OF THE BAG.

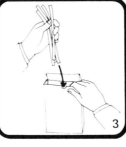

(4) Close the top of the bag and shake it so that the spectator can hear the rope inside. Tell him to wave the scissors over the bag, and the rope will restore itself — "as if by magic."

(5) Then, reach into the *main compartment* of the bag and remove *the prepared rope* (the one with the fake knots). Be sure to keep the secret pocket closed while you do this.

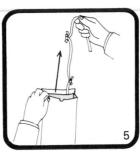

(6) Place the knotted rope aside and tear open the front of the bag to show it empty. (The cut pieces remain concealed in the "secret" pocket.) Set the bag aside and explain to the spectator that he almost made it — but it looks as if you will have to finish the trick for him.

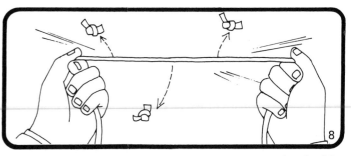

(7) Hold both ends of the prepared rope between your hands as shown.

(8) Now, pull sharply on the ends of the rope, *causing the fake knots to fly off the rope into the air.* The rope has become instantly restored! Give the rope to the spectator so he can "practice" at home and thank him for his assistance.

THE TRIPLE ROPE TRICK

This differs from a CUT AND RESTORED ROPE because no actual *cutting* is done. Instead, you start with *three* short lengths of rope and magically form them into one *single* long rope. One particular advantage to this mystery is that no scissors are needed; so you can carry the ropes in your pocket and work it anytime, anywhere.

EFFECT

The magician shows three pieces of rope that are about equal in length, pointing out that all three are knotted together at both ends. He unties one group of three knotted ends and then reties two of the ropes together again. Next, he unties the other group of three knotted ends, and reties two of these ropes together. This leaves the three ropes tied end to end, forming one long rope — *except for the knots!* The performer then coils the rope around one hand and removes a half-dollar from his coat pocket, which he waves over the rope. When the rope is uncoiled, *the knots have vanished* and the three short ropes have amazingly turned into one single length — which can be tossed to the spectators for examination.

SECRET AND PREPARATION

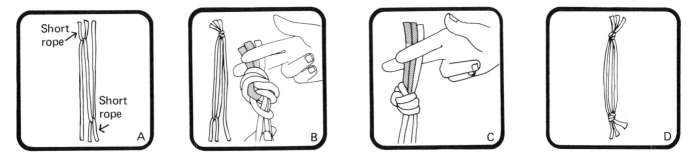

Actually, *one long rope* is used and *two short pieces.* The long rope is about three feet in length; the short pieces are each about four inches long. *(NOTE: The short pieces can be the leftover "ends" from the CUT AND RESTORED ROPE.)* The preparation for this trick is as follows:

(A)   Lay out the long rope in three sections. Then loop a short piece of rope in the two "bends" of the long piece as shown.   (B)   Tie the three upper ends (one end of the long rope and two ends of the short rope) into ONE SINGLE KNOT as shown. To the audience, these appear to be the ends of *three single ropes.* Only *you* know that *two* of the ends are from the *short rope* and the third is *one* end of the *long rope.*   (C)   This is how the knot looks when pulled tight.   (D)   Now, tie the other three "ends" together IN EXACTLY THE SAME WAY. This is all prepared before the performance. To your audience it appears that you have "three lengths of rope" — with their ends tied together. You are now ready for a real "fooler."

METHOD

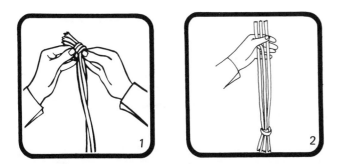

(1)   Display the "three ropes" to the audience. Then, with both hands, UNTIE THE LARGE KNOT AT ONE END. *Make sure not to reveal that two of the ends are from the short piece of rope.*   (2)   This done, hold the ropes in your left hand between your thumb and fingers as shown. Your left thumb clips the short loop above where the long rope loops over the short rope, concealing it from view with your left fingers.

(5)   Tie the short rope in a single knot around the long rope. Say, "I will tie two of the ropes together." Be sure to keep the small loop hidden by your fingers until the knot is tied. After that, it can be freely shown.

(6)   Grasp the remaining large knot and repeat Steps 1 through 5. Say, "Now I will tie these two pieces of rope together as well."

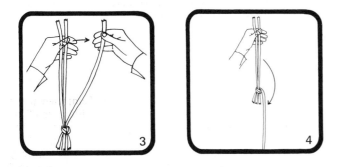

(3)   Let the end of the long rope drop, so that you are holding only the two ends of the short piece and the "looped over" part of the long rope.   (4)   After you drop the "long end," the rope should look like this.

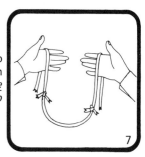

(7)   You now show what appears to be three short ropes knotted to form a single long one. *Actually, it is <u>one long rope</u> with two short ropes tied to look like "connecting" knots.*

(8) Hold one end of the rope in your left hand and begin coiling the rope around your left hand with your right hand. As you "wrap" it around, the rope naturally SLIDES THROUGH YOUR RIGHT HAND. When you come to the first knot, *keep it in your right hand,* secretly "slipping" it along the rope.

(9) When you come to the second knot, your right hand *slides it along in the same way.* THE AUDIENCE WILL THINK THAT THE KNOTS ARE STILL ON THE ROPE COILED AROUND YOUR LEFT HAND.

(10) As you complete the coiling, secretly slide <u>both knots</u> off the end of the rope.

(11) Remark that you will now use your "Magic Coin." Your right hand then goes into your right pocket — *where you <u>leave</u> the knots and <u>bring out</u> the half-dollar.*

(12) Make a "magical" wave of the coin over the rope. Then replace the coin in your pocket and unwind the rope from your hand, *showing the knots completely gone!*

(13) The three short ropes have been "magically" transformed into one single, long rope — much to the amazement of your audience!

COMMENTS AND SUGGESTIONS

The strong point of this clever mystery is that the "trick" is actually done *before you begin.* Therefore, you should stress that you have three single ropes at the start. If the audience wants you to repeat the TRIPLE ROPE, you can follow with the DOUBLE RESTORATION in which you actually cut a long rope into three short ones and then restore it.

TRIPLE ROPE — MULTIPLE "DO AS I DO" KNOT

With a receptive audience, you can amplify this effect by giving out three sets of knotted ropes letting *two* spectators follow along with you. Again, *your* ropes come out as one long piece and *theirs* do not. That is why you call it "Do As I Do" Knot.

METHOD

(1) In using three sets — one special and two regular — the selection procedure is simple and neat. If each spectator takes an ordinary set, you keep the special and proceed with your routine, having them both copy your moves.

(2) However, if Joe happens to take the special set, say, "You can see that your three ropes are knotted together at both ends." Then, take your set and give it to Joe, saying, "Now take my ropes and give yours to Tom . . ." As Joe gives the special set to Tom, take the ordinary set that Tom is holding, as you continue, ". . . so Tom can give his ropes to me."

(3) Briefly look at the set you just took from Tom; then give it to Joe, saying, "Now take Tom's ropes and give him mine." As Joe does that, take the special set that Tom has saying, "And Tom, give me yours." Then, speaking to both, you say, "Now that we have each checked *all three sets of ropes* to see that they are exactly alike, I want each of you to do <u>exactly</u> as I do."

COMMENTS AND SUGGESTIONS

In winding the coils around your left hand, be sure to tell your helpers to coil each knot inside the left hand, just as you do. Then go through the motion of bringing "Invisible Magic Dust" from your pocket and tell them to do the same. The only difference is that your powder works, while theirs doesn't. This is proven when you each uncoil your rope and you have one long, single length, free of knots, while theirs haven't changed at all. An optional ending is when you explain that your Magic Powder is "truly invisible," whereas theirs is "purely imaginary."

TRIPLE ROPE — "TIMES TWO"

This is a special form of presentation for the TRIPLE ROPE trick, especially suited for small or intimate audiences. It falls into the category of a Do As I Do effect, making it an ideal addition to the "audience participation" portion of your program.

SECRET AND PREPARATION

This time start with two sets of knotted ropes. One is the "special" type already described: _One long rope,_ with _two_ short loops, each looped to a portion of the long rope and knotted there to show three "ends." The second set consists of _three separate ropes,_ about the same length. These are actually knotted at both ends, so they look exactly the same as your faked set. You can identify the special set by making a small ink or pencil mark on one of the knots. The mark should be just large enough for you to notice. You then proceed as follows:

METHOD

(1) Bring out both sets of knotted ropes, remarking that each consists of _three short ropes_ knotted at both ends. Explain that _you_ intend to use one set in this mystery and the _spectator_ is to use the other. Tell the spectator that since both are exactly alike, he may choose either set.

(2) If he takes the _ordinary set,_ you keep the special set and tell him, "I want you to do exactly as I do. Untie your ropes like this." With that, you proceed step by step as already described with the "Three in One" effect.

(3) If he takes the _special set,_ the one that you should have, you can handle the situation quite easily. Say, "Good, now I want you to do just as I do. Give me your three ropes, so I can untie their ends, while I give you my three ropes, so you can untie them." Thus the exchange of ropes becomes the first step in the "Do As I Do" procedure and you simply carry on from there.

(4) Now proceed with the step-by-step process moving slowly and deliberately, so the spectator can copy your moves exactly. Since everyone sees that he has three separate ropes, they will assume that yours are the same.

(5) On the last step, you wrap the rope around your hand and then reach into your pocket to remove some "Invisible Magic Dust." The spectator, who has been duplicating your every move, will have to admit that he has no "Magic Dust" with him at the moment. Tell him to "pretend" that he has a pocketful and have him remove and "sprinkle" it on his rope as you do the same. (It is at this point that you leave the two knots in your pocket.) Your rope now comes out all in one piece while his is still in three pieces — proving that there is no substitute for "real" Invisible Magic Dust. Give the spectator a handful from your pocket along with the unrestored rope and tell him to take it all home and practice!

DOUBLE RESTORATION

As stated before, cutting and restoring a length of ordinary rope has become a classic feat of modern magic. Here is a method as simple as it is deceptive. What's more, this version enables you to "go one better" than the standard CUT AND RESTORED ROPE, because here you cut the rope twice — making three lengths instead of two — and then restore both cuts simultaneously.

EFFECT

The magician shows an ordinary rope about six feet in length, which he measures into three equal sections. He then ties both ends firmly around the center of the rope. When the rope is stretched between his hands, it is in three equal sections with the knots as dividing markers. The performer then cuts the rope near each knot so that the knots now connect the three pieces of rope. The magician then coils the rope loosely around one hand. With a little "Magic," the rope is uncoiled to reveal the knots have vanished — the three pieces of rope are completely restored to one long rope!

SECRET AND PREPARATION

(A) The secret of this effect is quite subtle, and — after you practice and learn it — the working is almost automatic. Beforehand, use a pen or pencil to make a small mark about 6 inches from each end of the rope. Make the marks just large enough so you can see them when you look for them. This done, you are ready to begin.

METHOD

(1) Display the rope to your audience by grasping one of the ends in your hand, allowing the rope to hang full length in front of your body as shown. Now, step on the loose end with your foot and give the rope a sharp upward pull to prove to the audience that the rope is genuine. From this point on, we will refer to the ends of the rope as A and B.

(2) Hold End A firmly in your left hand. Then loop End B over the top of your left fingers and pull End B down to the center of the lower loop as shown. This "measures" the rope into *three equal sections* as illustrated. The centers of the upper and lower loops are indicated as X and Y in the illustrations.

(3) Now, tie End A *around the bend in the loop* at Point X, using a single overhand knot as shown. Notice that the knot is in the center of the short section marked at the end of the rope.

(4) Here is a close-up view of the knot.

(5) Holding the knot in one hand, display the rope with the free end dangling next to the loop, showing the loop and the "free" end to be about equal in length.

(6) Now, *turn the rope over* so that End B and the center of the lower loop (Point Y) are on top as shown and then tie End B around Point Y in another single overhand knot. *At this point, both of your "secret" marks should be visible to you as indicated by the arrows in this illustration.*

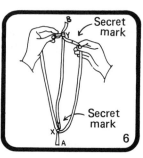

(7) When the rope is stretched between the thumbs and fingers of each hand, it can be shown in three distinct sections with the knots as dividing markers.

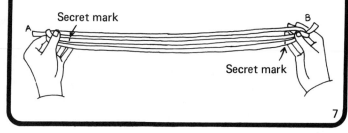

(8) With a pair of scissors, cut the rope at one of your secret marks near the knot. The spectators think you are cutting the main section of the rope. Actually, you have only cut off a short piece at one end. This creates the perfect illusion that you have a separate piece of rope hanging from the loop as illustrated.

(9) Now, turn the loop over so that the other knot is on top.

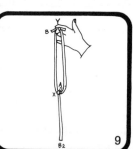

(10) Cut the rope at the other mark, stating that you have now cut the rope into *three* equal pieces.

(13) Now, begin to coil the rope around your left hand. When you come to the knots, pretend to wind them into the left hand. Actually, your right hand secretly retains the knots in the bend of the fingers and draws them along the rope completely off the end.

(11) The rope will now appear as shown here. It appears to the audience as if you actually cut the rope into three equal parts and tied them together. Unknown to your audience, the "twice cut" rope *is really already restored* — since the "knots" are just short ends tied around a single length of rope!

(14) With the knots concealed in your right hand, reach into your coat pocket for your "magic" coin. As soon as your hand is out of sight, exchange the knots for the coin. Immediately bring the coin into view, *leaving the knots behind in your pocket.* Wave the coin over the coiled rope as shown.

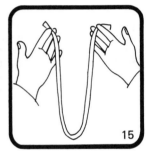

(12) Once again, allow the rope to fall full length in front of you and step on the lower end with your foot. Pull sharply on the rope as if to tighten the knots even more.

(15) Drop the coin back into your pocket and allow the rope to unwind from around your left fingers. Demonstrate the complete restoration of the rope by again testing it for strength.

COMMENTS AND SUGGESTIONS

At the finish of the trick, the rope will be a bit shorter than it was to start. No one will realize this as it is nearly impossible to estimate the length of a piece of rope without a frame of reference. Once the rope has been cut and knotted, you can purposely call attention to the length of the rope *as it will remain the same length from that point on,* thus adding to the deception. Each time you do the trick, the rope becomes about eight inches shorter (allowing four inches to be cut from each end) so, if you present the trick with a six-foot rope, it should be good for about four performances.

CUT AND RESTORED STRING

The following is one of those clever effects that can be presented anywhere and always leaves the spectators completely baffled. It might well be classified as a *close-up* version of the more familiar CUT AND RESTORED ROPE. However, the *method* for this effect is quite different, which makes the mystery all the more puzzling.

EFFECT

The magician calls attention to a single length of string which he proceeds to cut into two equal parts. He then gives one end of each of the "cut" strings to a spectator to hold. With everything in full view, the <u>spectator</u> instantly restores the twine to its original condition right before his own eyes. The stunned volunteer is then given the piece of string as a souvenir.

SECRET AND PREPARATION

(A) The secret of this trick depends on a *very clever principle* based on the properties of a certain type of common string which is *so obvious,* that it goes totally unsuspected by anyone. The string is the type which is composed of *many individual strands of twine* twisted together to form a multi-stranded string. This is sometimes referred to as "butcher's twine." It is usually thicker than ordinary string (like "kite" string) and is soft and white in color.

To perform this mystery, all you need is a length of this type of string approximately 18 inches long. For the purpose of explanation, we will refer to the ends of the string as X and Y.

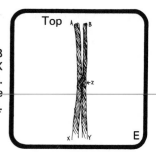

(E) NOTE: At this point, A and B form two "fake" ends of string, and X and Y (the real ones) the other ends. It appears that you have two separate strings. But, you're not through yet.

(B) Locate the *center* of the piece of string and *spread the individual strands open,* dividing the string into two equal sections of twine. We will refer to *these sections* as A and B.

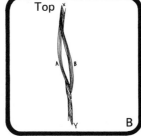

(F) Apply a very small dab of rubber cement to Ends X and Y and allow them to become nearly dry. Then, *attach the two ends* (X and Y) *together* — roll them between your fingers until they are joined.

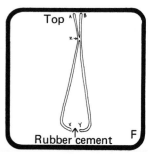

(C) Pull Sections A and B about five inches apart as shown. Then, slowly roll each section between your fingers so that they twist together to form *two new false ends*.

(G) The resulting product should look like *one continuous length of string as shown.* If done correctly, the "string" can be handled quite casually as you display it during the presentation.

(D) This done, adjust the entire affair so that the "two" newly formed string "ends" (AX and BY) run so close together at the place where they connect (letter "Z") that the secret connection between them is nearly impossible to detect.

METHOD

(1) To begin, display the prepared string casually calling attention to the fact that you hold only *one piece of string.* Then, as you prepare to cut the string, adjust your grip so that you hold it between the tips of your left fingers as shown here. Your thumb and first finger should cover the secret connection (Z).

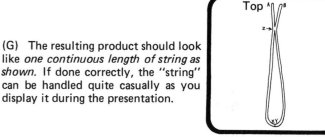

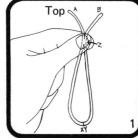

(2) With scissors cut the string (both pieces) near the bottom of the hanging loop *just above* Point XY. Let the glued joint (XY) drop to the floor leaving you two *new* "unglued" X and Y ends. *NOTE: This automatically removes the only gimmicked, non-examinable part of the string for the astonishing conclusion of the trick.*

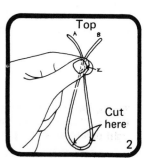

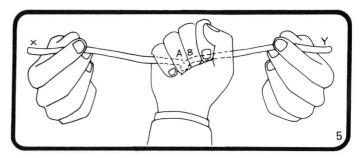

(3) Call attention to the *absolute fairness* of every move you make. The audience will be convinced that you have merely cut a single length of twine into two equal parts.

(5) Now, ask a spectator to grasp Ends X and Y. When he does you hold Ends A and B (and the secret connection Z) in your closed fist as shown.

(4) Place the scissors aside and display the two "separate" pieces of string. Be sure to handle the string(s) in a casual manner so as not to give the impression that you are concealing something from the audience — *but keep the strings together at the secret connection (Z).*

(6) Then tell him to *pull sharply* on the ends in opposite directions. When he does, release your grip on the string. Allow the secret connection to "untwist" and thus restore itself to its *original form* — the center of the string! The spectator will be astonished to see the strings "weld" themselves together as he pulls on their ends.

COMMENTS AND SUGGESTIONS

Stress the fact that the string actually "restores" itself while the *spectator holds both ends.* The beautiful thing here is that there are no secret "gimmicks" or extra pieces of string to get rid of. As you can see, this is another outstanding close-up mystery. Build it up properly, and you will be credited with performing a small miracle.

THREADING THE NEEDLE

EFFECT

The magician calls the audiences' attention to an ordinary piece of soft rope approximately three feet in length. He explains that even under the most adverse circumstances it is easy to *magically* "thread" a needle, IF you know the secret. To demonstrate, the magician forms a small loop from one end of the rope to represent the eye of a needle — the other end will substitute for the thread. The performer, with the loop in the left hand and the "thread" end of the rope in his right, makes a quick thrust at the loop. In spite of his speed and even though he may not even come near the loop, the needle has been magically threaded!

METHOD

(1) After displaying the rope to your audience, lay the rope over your left thumb so that Length A will measure approximately 12 inches and Length B will measure about 24 inches.

(2) Grasp Length B with your right hand and wrap the rope around your left thumb twice. BE SURE YOU WRAP THE ROPE AROUND YOUR THUMB IN THE DIRECTION SHOWN IN THE PICTURE.

(3) With your right hand, grasp Length B and twist the rope to form a loop about two inches high, as shown. This loop is lifted and placed between your left thumb and forefinger.

(7) As Length A passes between the left thumb and the left fingers, loosen your grip slightly by relaxing the left thumb as you pull Length A up sharply with the right hand.

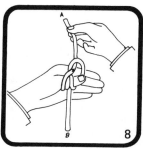

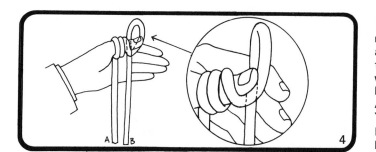

(4) Grip the loop between your left thumb and forefinger so that it protrudes over the top of the thumb. This loop now represents the "eye" of the needle. *NOTE: End B of the rope must be the side of the loop CLOSEST TO THE PALM OF YOUR LEFT HAND as shown by the dotted lines in 4.*

(8) The "X" part of Length A will now be through the loop and it will appear as if you have "threaded" the eye without even coming close with the thread. NOTE: THERE IS NOW ONE LESS TURN OF ROPE AROUND YOUR LEFT THUMB. YOU LOSE ONE OF THESE TURNS EACH TIME YOU "THREAD" THE NEEDLE.

(5) End A will now become the thread. Grasp A with your right thumb and fingers about one inch from the end. Then lift A *in front of* B and hold as shown.

(9) If you "unthread" the needle by really pulling End A back through the loop, you can immediately "magically" thread it again. When you do, the rope around your thumb will look like this. (Notice again that there is one less "turn" around your left thumb.)

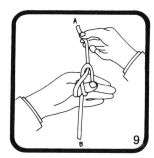

(6) *Steps 6 and 7 are the actual "threading."* With End A in your right hand, move that hand forward MISSING THE LOOP WITH THE END but allow the lower part of A (marked with an "X" in the illustration) to pass BETWEEN the left thumb and left fingers.

COMMENTS AND SUGGESTIONS

This effect is excellent when used in combination with other rope tricks to create an entertaining rope routine. On its own, it also makes a good "challenge" at a party, for no matter how hard anyone tries to duplicate your movements, he will find it impossible to "thread the eye of the needle."

When using the effect as a spectator challenge, be sure that he attempts the threading using Length B as the "thread." By substituting B for A, the trick becomes impossible to duplicate. You will also find, during practice, that you will be able to move your right hand as fast as you wish and still thread the needle — *as the end of the thread never actually passes through the needle anyway.* I have had a great deal of fun with this little trick over the years, and I am sure that you will too.

—MW

ONE HAND KNOT

EFFECT

The magician displays a 3-foot length of soft rope. Casually tossing the rope into the air, a genuine knot appears magically in its center.

METHOD

(1) Display a length of rope (a piece about 3 feet is best). Then drape it over your right hand with End A hanging between the third and fourth fingers and End B between your thumb and first finger. Although End A may be any length, End B *must not fall more than about one foot below your hand.*

(2) Now turn your right hand over and grasp Length B between the first and second fingers at "X" as shown.

(3) Now rotate your hand back up as shown holding B firmly between the first and second fingers.

(4) Simply allow the loop that has been formed around your right hand to fall off your hand.

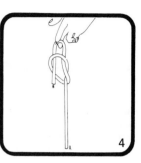

(5) The end of B will be drawn through this loop forming a knot in the rope. You may also "snap" the rope off your hand rather than letting it fall.

COMMENTS AND SUGGESTIONS

In order to disguise what is actually happening, practice the following movement: After grasping Length B firmly with the first and second fingers of the right hand (Fig. 2) throw the rope straight up into the air letting go of Length B *after* it has passed through the loop. The effect will be that the knot was tied *in the air.*

NOTE: The softer the rope, the easier this trick is to do. It will also work equally well with a soft handkerchief (silk is best) of the proper size.

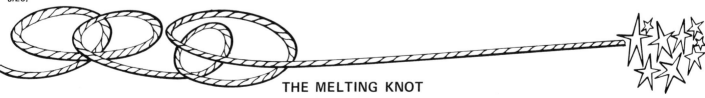

THE MELTING KNOT

EFFECT

The performer slowly and deliberately ties a knot in the center of a three-foot piece of rope. The audience watches as the magician gradually tightens the knot by pulling on both ends of the rope. The knot becomes smaller until, just before "cinching up" tight, it *melts away* into nothingness!

SECRET AND PREPARATION

Once again you will have use for that 3-foot length of soft rope. This mystery, combined with "Threading the Needle" and other such effects, makes an entertaining routine with just this short length of rope.

METHOD

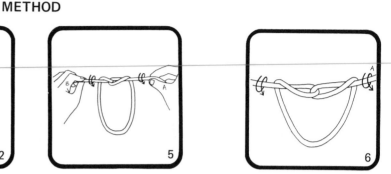

(1) Display the rope to the audience. (In the illustrations we will call the end in your left hand End A and the one in your right End B.) (2) With your right hand, bring End B around *behind* your left hand and *over the top* of End A. Place End B *between* your left first and second fingers and release your right hand. You should now be holding the rope as shown.

(5) You have now formed a "false" knot. In order to keep the knot from dissolving prematurely, you must "roll" the rope *with the thumb and first finger of each hand.* Roll or twist the rope *in the direction shown by the arrows* (toward yourself). (6) You can see the reasons for twisting the rope clearly here. The "rolling" action of the ends forces the false knot to ride *up* and *over* itself, thus maintaining its "knot" shape.

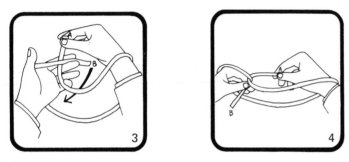

(7) When the knot is just about to tighten up, blow on it as you pull the ends. The knot seems to "dissolve" into thin air. Properly performed, the illusion is so perfect that you may immediately repeat the trick without fear of discovery.

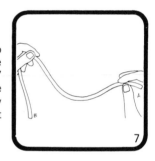

(3) Pass your right hand *through the loop of rope* and grasp End A between your right thumb and first finger. (4) Now pull Ends A and B apart. Hold End B with your left thumb and fingers. As you do this, pull End A *through the loop* and slowly separate your hands.

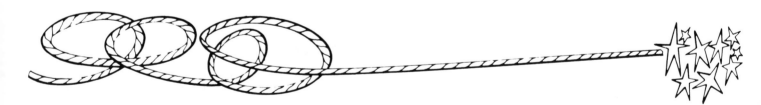

SHOELACE ROPE TIE

EFFECT

The magician displays a three-foot length of soft rope to his audience. Holding it between both hands, he skillfully ties a "bow knot" in the rope. The performer then threads the ends of the rope *through* the loops of the bows — and then pulls the ends so that a hopeless knot is formed in the center of the rope. The audience understands the magician's problem, for they have probably had this happen with their shoelaces many times. However, as if to defy the laws of nature, the magician causes the cumbersome knot to "dissolve" before the eyes of the audience!

METHOD

All you need for this clever effect is a length of soft rope approximately three feet in length.

 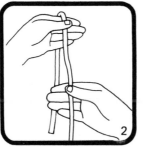  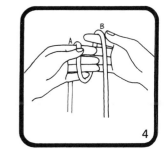

(1)   Display the rope to your audience and then lay it across the fingers of your right and left hands as shown. Your left hand is above your right hand, your palms face you and the backs of your hands are toward the audience.   (2)   Hold the rope in position by pressing your thumbs against the rope.   (3)   Now, move your right hand next to your left hand, allowing the rope to hook *underneath* the left fingers and *over the top* of the right fingers.   (4)   Then, move your right hand *behind your left hand* as shown in this illustration.

(5)   Now, clip the rope at Point A between the tips of your *right* first and second fingers. At the same time, grasp the rope at Point B with your *left* first and second fingers. (Study the drawing carefully.)

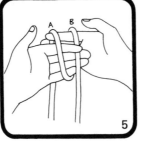

(9)   Then, with your *left* thumb and first finger, reach *through* the left bow (B), grasp the left end of the rope (C) . . .

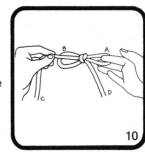

(6)   Hold the two points (A and B) tightly between the fingers of each hand and *begin to draw your hands apart.*

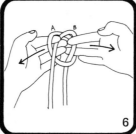

(10)   . . . and pull the left end of the rope (C) *back through the loop.*

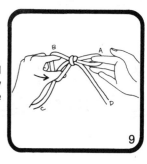

(7)   Continue to pull your hands apart, and a bow knot will begin to form in the middle of the rope.

(11)   With your *right* thumb and first finger, reach *through* the right-hand bow (A), grasp the right-hand end of the rope (D) . . .

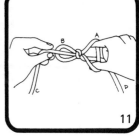

(8)   Now, gently pull the completed "bow knot" taut as shown.

(12)   . . . and pull that end of the rope (D) *back through the loop* (A).

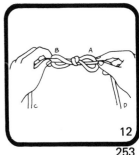

(13) Release the bow and gently pull on the ends of the rope causing the bow to "cinch up" and form a large knot in the center of the rope. *If you have followed the steps correctly, this knot will actually be a slip-knot or "dissolving" knot as magicians often call it.* Do not pull too hard on the ends or you will dissolve the knot too soon!

(14) Instead, display the "knot" to the audience as you comment about how bothersome a situation like this can be when it happens in everyday life. You might remark, "Being a magician comes in handy when this happens because all you have to do is to use the old 'knot-vanishing move' to get out of trouble." (As you say this, pull on the ends of the rope, and the knot will magically vanish.)

COMMENTS AND SUGGESTIONS

At first, when you start learning this clever effect, it may seem complicated and difficult to follow. Follow the pictures carefully. The tying of the bow and the pulling of the ends through the loops will be perfectly natural and easy and can be accompanied by a clever patter story — perhaps about how you became interested in magic as a child when you found that, in tying your shoes, the ends of the laces would slip through the bows, and you always ended up with a knot. But then *you began to study magic.* You discovered that by merely pulling on the ends of the laces and blowing on the knot at the same time (or saying the "magic words"), the knot would dissolve itself *as if by magic!*

THE RIGID ROPE

The legendary Hindu Rope Trick, wherein the fakir would throw a coil of rope into the air and cause it to remain suspended, has long been a mystery to which the exact method still remains questionable to this day. The following trick might well be considered a smaller version of this great mystery. It has the advantage that it can be performed anywhere — before small groups or larger audiences as well.

EFFECT

The magician displays a length of rope about 3 to 4 feet long. It appears to be normal in every respect and yet, upon his command, it becomes rigid and stands straight up from his fingertips. The performer passes his other hand around the rope on all sides, proving to the audience that the rope is unmistakably free from any threads or other hidden attachments. Then, with a mere wave of his hand, the magician causes the rope to gradually fall and return to its natural "flexible" state, right before the eyes of the spectators!

SECRET AND PREPARATION

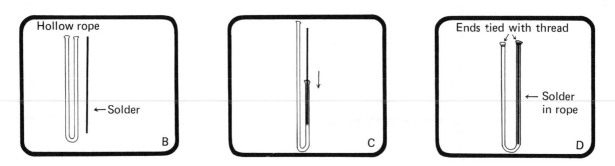

(A) To present this trick, it is necessary to construct a "special" rope. First, remove the inner core from a piece of rope approximately 4 feet long. (See "Coring" at the beginning of this section.) This leaves just the woven outer shell, which now forms a small hollow "tube" 4 feet long. (B) Next, cut a piece of solder wire (the kind of wire that is melted with a soldering iron to make electrical connections) so that it is <u>slightly shorter</u> than *half* the length of the rope. The solder should be about 1/16" to 1/8" in diameter and should be as straight as possible. (C) Now insert the piece of solder carefully *into* the hollow length of rope. (D) Tie off both ends of the rope with white thread. This will prevent the solder from falling out of the rope during the presentation.

METHOD

(1) Hold the prepared rope with one end in each hand as you display it to your audience. The end containing the solder is held in your left hand; the hollow end in your right. *Be sure to allow enough slack at the bottom of the rope so that it will curve naturally.*

(5) Release the upper end of the rope from your left fingers — it falls limp over your right hand. *At this point, the audience has seen that the entire length of rope is flexible.*

(2) Release the *hollow end* of the rope from your right fingers and let it hang freely as shown in the illustration. This subtly conveys to the audience that the rope is flexible.

(6) Reach down and grasp the *hollow end* with your left hand and raise it upward.

(3) Now grasp the rope with your right fingers slightly above the center of the rope. You will be able to feel the solder through the woven shell of the rope. At this point, your left hand *still retains its grip* on the "top" end of the rope.

(7) Release the *center* of the rope from your right fingers and allow the rope to hang *full length* from your left hand.

(4) Now, *relax the pressure on the solder* with your right fingers and allow the wire to secretly *slide down* into the bottom half of the rope.

(8) Now, grip the center of the rope once again between your right thumb and forefinger, but this time turn your right hand palm up so that your right thumb grips the rope from the audience side.

(9)   With your right hand still holding the center of the rope, release the hollow top end of the rope from your left hand and let it fall.

(12)   Now, slowly and dramatically, remove your left hand from the top of the rope. Hold the bottom of the solder in the top half firmly with your right hand. To the amazement of the viewers, the rope stays straight up — rigid! As the rope stands "unsupported" from your right hand, pass your left hand over the top and around all sides of the rope to prove that there are no outside connections responsible for this mystery.

(10)   Then grasp the bottom end *with the solder in it* with your left hand *palm up.*

(13)   To restore the rope back to its flexible state, *gradually* relax your grip on the solder with your right fingers. Allow the solder to *slowly* slide into the bottom half of the rope. *The effect will be that the rope gradually "wilts."* Gesture with your left hand as if the rope is always under your control as it loses its power to remain rigid.

(11)   HERE IS THE KEY MOVE IN THE TRICK. As you keep the *solder end* of the rope pulled taut between your hands, with your left hand swing *the solder end up* to the top and, at the same time, rotate the right wrist as shown. By the pressure of the fingers of both hands, <u>keep the solder in the "top" half.</u>

(14)   When the rope falls completely limp, grasp the hollow end of the rope with your left hand. With your right hand still retaining its hold on the rope, begin to coil the hollow half of the rope around your left fist. When you reach the solder half of the rope, *continue to wind the rope and the solder around your left fist.* Due to the softness of the solder, the rope, with the solder inside, will coil around your hand. Place the coiled rope in your pocket or on your table and take your bows.

EQUAL-UNEQUAL ROPES
"GEN" GRANT
EFFECT

The performer displays four lengths of rope by holding two ropes in each hand. Each pair is tied together in the center so that they form two sets of two ropes each. One of these sets consists of one long piece of rope and one short piece, while the other set contains two ropes exactly the same length. The magician asks for two volunteers to come up on the stage. Each is then given one set of ropes. The spectator on the right, who holds the long and the short pair of ropes, is asked to turn his back to the audience. The magician then pins one short and one long piece of ribbon to the back of his jacket to identify which set he holds. The volunteer on the left, who holds the two "equal" ropes, is marked by attaching two equal pieces of ribbon to the back of his coat. The magician points out that the volunteers are marked so that the audience can easily identify the location of each set of ropes, even when the backs of the spectators are facing them. The performer then has both spectators face the audience as he explains that he will cause something "magical" to happen. With that, the performer asks the volunteers to again turn their backs to the audience and to then untie their pairs of ropes. This done, the volunteers are asked to turn around and face the audience to show the ropes which they now hold. To the surprise of the audience, as well as the two volunteers, the two equal lengths of rope have "magically" exchanged positions with the two unequal pieces of rope!

SECRET AND PREPARATION

This clever mystery can most certainly be classified as a "self-working" trick, as the entire trick takes place in the hands of the spectators. The secret lies in the clever manner in which you have knotted the ropes before the show. For the trick, all you need are three pieces of soft rope about five feet in length and *one* piece of rope exactly half that long.

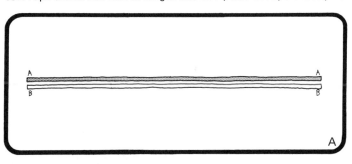

(A) To prepare, place two of the five-foot lengths side by side as shown. For the purpose of explanation, the ropes have been labeled A and B and, *for clarity only,* are shown in different colors. When performing the trick, all of the ropes must be the *same color.*

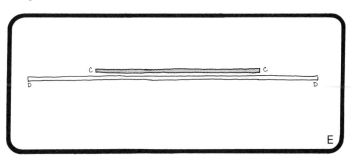

(E) The next step is to tie the two *unequal lengths* of rope together so that they look as if they are *equal* in length. To do this, place the short piece (C) next to the long piece (D). The short rope (C) must be *centered* between the ends of the long rope (D).

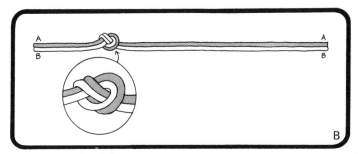

(B) Tie the two ropes together with a *single overhand knot* at a point approximately one third from the end as illustrated.

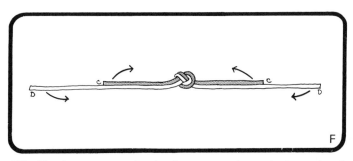

(F) Tie the ropes together in the center using a single overhand knot as shown.

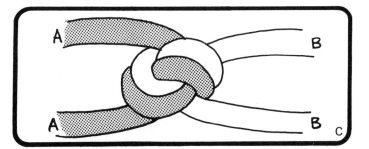

(C) Now, fold both ends of Rope B together, so that they run *side by side in the same direction.* Do the same with the ends of Rope A as shown in this illustration.

(G) Now, bring both ends of the short rope (C) together so they run *side by side,* and do the same with the ends of the long rope (D). Secure the ends in place with another overhand knot — the result will appear to be two *equal* pieces of rope tied together at their centers.

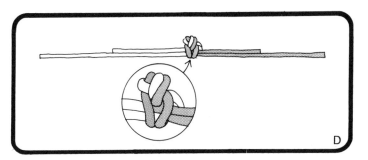

(D) Now, tie another overhand knot *on top of the first knot* to further confuse the spectators. *The result will appear to be one long and one short piece of rope tied together at the center.*

(H) Finally, you will need three pieces of colorful ribbon about two feet long, and a fourth piece about one foot long. Attach a small pin to the end of each ribbon and you are ready to present the EQUAL-UNEQUAL ROPES.

METHOD

(1) To begin, display the two sets of ropes as you ask for the assistance of two volunteers from the audience.

(2) Give the spectator to your *right* the set of ropes that <u>appears</u> to be the *unequal* lengths (actually the <u>equal</u> ropes), and to the volunteer on your *left,* give the set which appears to be two *equal lengths.*

(3) Have both assistants turn their backs to the audience and attach the corresponding lengths of ribbon to their coats. Have them turn back to face the audience as you explain that the ribbons will serve to identify which spectator holds which set of ropes.

(4) Instruct the spectators to again turn their backs to the audience and then to untie their ropes. If you wish, you can now state that something "magical" is going to happen. With that, instruct your volunteers to turn and face the audience — holding *one rope in each hand.* Sure enough, when they turn, the spectator on the left, instead of having two ropes of the same length, now has *one short* and *one long* rope — and the spectator on the right now has two ropes of the *same length.* The two sets of ropes have magically exchanged positions *while in the hands of the volunteers!*

COMMENTS AND SUGGESTIONS

This is a very clever "novelty" trick which always brings a laugh. Performed correctly, your two assistants themselves will not even get wise to the trick. With this type of knot, strange as it seems, when the spectators untie the knots, the ropes seem to change length <u>right in their hands</u> — and they will not be able to understand how it happened! Of course, *if you were to immediately repeat the trick,* they would watch the ends and no doubt figure it out. But the <u>first</u> time you work this, if you follow the instructions carefully, it will leave the volunteers as mystified as your audience — which, of course, enhances the total effect.

THE GREAT COAT ESCAPE

Audience participation is the theme of this mystery, since you work directly with one spectator and call upon another for further assistance. The GREAT COAT ESCAPE is an excellent trick for a small group and also can be presented just as effectively before a large audience, as part of your stage show.

EFFECT

The magician asks for the assistance of two gentlemen from the audience and requests that one of them remove his coat. The performer then displays two 8-foot lengths of rope which he proceeds to thread through the sleeves of the borrowed coat. The spectator is asked to put his jacket back on while holding the ends of the ropes in his hands. This leaves the spectator with the two ropes running through his sleeves and the ends of the ropes protruding from both cuffs. Two of the ropes, one from each sleeve, are then tied together in a single overhand knot in front of the volunteer. The knot is tightened. This draws the spectator's wrists together, thus imprisoning him — and the ropes — securely within his own jacket. However, when the ends of the ropes are pulled sharply by the magician and the other volunteer, the ropes seem to *penetrate* the spectator's body *visibly,* leaving him and his coat *entirely free of the ropes!*

SECRET AND PREPARATION

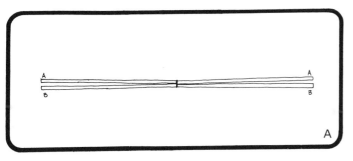

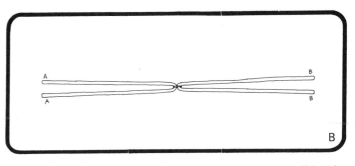

(A) The only items required to present this seemingly impossible mystery are two 8-foot lengths of soft rope and a small amount of ordinary white sewing thread. To prepare, lay the two lengths of rope *side by side* with their *ends even.* For the purpose of explanation, the two ropes have been labeled "A" and "B" in the illustrations. At the center of the ropes, tie a short piece of white thread *around both ropes,* forming a tight link that secretly holds them together.

(B) *NOTE: This "secret link" later will enable you to "double back" the ends of the ropes as shown here giving the appearance that the ropes are still running full length, side by side, as you will see.* You are now ready to proceed with THE GREAT COAT ESCAPE.

METHOD

(1) Pick up the two ropes and casually display them together with the secretly "linked" centers resting across the open fingers as shown.

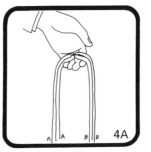

(4) *NOTE: In Illustration 4A, the fingers are purposely lowered to show the "secret link." Actually, the fingers should be closed around the centers of the ropes as shown in 4B so that the link is never seen.*

(2) Ask the spectator to remove his coat, and while he is doing so, transfer the ropes to your left hand, swinging them carelessly back and forth, while you reach for the coat with your right hand.

(5) With your right hand, take the spectator's coat and lift it so that your left hand can grip the coat by the collar, along with the "doubled back" centers of the ropes as shown. *The back of your left hand is toward the audience during this action and in Step 6 which follows.*

(3) During that action, slide your left fingers between the ropes of both sides of the "secret link," *doubling back the centers of the ropes* as shown. This brings *both ends* of Rope A to-gether at one side of the center link, and *both ends* of Rope B together at the other side. The "doubled" centers remain concealed in the bend of your left fingers. To the spectators, everything seems normal, as you still hold the ropes at the center with the four ends dangling from your left hand.

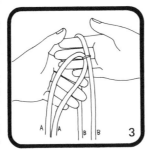

(6) Ask the spectator who lent you the coat to grasp the ends of one set of ropes (A) in his right hand and insert his right arm into the coat sleeve, *carrying the ends of the rope (A) along.* Note that your left hand still firmly holds and conceals the "doubled" centers of the ropes.

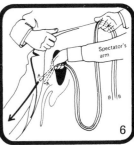

(7) As the spectator's right hand emerges from the sleeve, tell him to let go of the ends of the ropes so that they dangle from the sleeve. Then, bring your right hand up to your left and _transfer the centers of the ropes, along with the coat collar, into your right hand._ This frees your left hand, so it can open the left side of the coat as you ask the spectator to grasp the other ends (B) and carry them down his left sleeve. Then have him release those ends (B) as well.

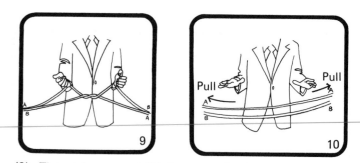

(8) As you adjust the spectator's jacket, _push the doubled centers (and the "secret link") inside his coat down below his coat collar_ between his coat and his shirt, where they are hidden beneath his coat behind his back.

(9) Then, take _one end (A)_ that protrudes from the spectator's _right_ sleeve and _one end (B)_ from his _left_ sleeve. Tie them together in a _single overhand knot_ in front of the spectator's body. _You must now have one End A and one End B paired up on each side of the volunteer._ By doing this, you have "cancelled out" the secret link in the center of the ropes. As soon as you have tied the single ropes together (one from each sleeve), give the left-hand pair of ropes (one End A and one End B) to the assisting spectator, and grasp the right-hand pair (the other End A and End B) in your own hands. This will position the bound volunteer between you and the other spectator. (10) Upon your command, you and the spectator holding the other ends both pull your ropes sharply in opposite directions. _This breaks the hidden thread,_ disposing of the secret link in the process. The two ropes will slide from the "bound" spectator's coat sleeves _completely releasing him from the rope!_ Your volunteers will be as mystified as your audience as to how you just accomplished an "impossible penetration."

COMMENTS AND SUGGESTIONS

Be sure that the two pieces of rope you use are soft. If the rope is too stiff, the centers will not "double" properly. For that reason, it is a good idea to "core" the ropes as described elsewhere in the Rope Section. Each rope should be approximately six to eight feet in length to allow for the crossing of the two ends that are tied. Extra length does not matter, as you and the other spectator can stand farther apart before you both pull the ropes.

Use a _fairly strong_ thread (or wrap a lightweight thread around several times) to tie the centers. This will assure that it will not break _before_ the ropes are pulled.

Keep a firm grip on the centers when you are holding them along with the coat collar, _particularly while the spectator is pulling the ropes down his sleeves._ Be sure to tell him not to release the ends until the ropes are completely through, so there will be no extra strain on them.

This is an excellent effect that uses a proven, practical, basic and very baffling magic principle. You can have great fun with THE GREAT COAT ESCAPE.

ROPE AND COAT RELEASE

EFFECT

The magician displays a wooden coat hanger, pointing out to his audience that the hanger supports two lengths of rope and thus is a convenient way for a magician to store his props. However, this so-called "convenience" has its problems, one of which the performer demonstrates.

Two spectators are invited to join the magician on stage. Borrowing one of the volunteers' jackets, the magician hangs it neatly on the coat hanger along with the two lengths of rope. The ends of both ropes are threaded through the sleeves of the borrowed coat. The magician takes _one_ rope from _each sleeve_ and ties them together, imprisoning the jacket on the hanger. The magician then hands a pair of rope ends to each volunteer as he supports the coat and hanger with his other hand. Then, upon the magician's command, the spectators pull the ropes in opposite directions. Magically, the ropes penetrate the hanger and the coat! The jacket is returned to the spectator unharmed and all of the equipment may be examined by the audience.

SECRET AND PREPARATION

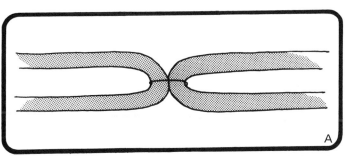

(A) Cut two pieces of soft rope approximately six feet in length. Now, fold each piece in the middle and tie them together with a *lightweight* piece of white thread as shown.

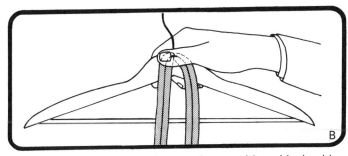

(B) It is best to use a wooden coat hanger with a wide shoulder support. You may already have one — if not, most clothing stores use this type for displaying men's suits. There are two important reasons for choosing this type of hanger: First, maximum protection for the spectator's jacket; and second, better concealment of the prepared ropes. Place the ropes around the coat hanger. Cover the "join" in the ropes (where the ropes are held together by the thread) with the thumb and fingers of your right hand as shown.

METHOD

(1) Ask for the assistance of two spectators, one of whom must be wearing a suitable coat. Borrow his jacket and place it on the coat hanger. *Keep the thread-connected loops to the rear of the hanger.*

(2) Have one of the volunteers hold the hanger, and drop the pairs of rope ends down the corresponding sleeves of the jacket as shown.

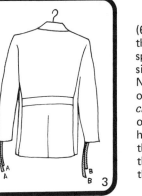

(3) Now turn the coat around and hand it back to the spectator to hold by the hook on the hanger. The secret thread "join" will now be concealed by the back of the jacket.

(4) With the back of the jacket facing the audience, pick up any *one* of the two ends from *each* sleeve and tie them in a *single overhand knot* as shown.

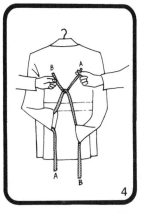

(5) THIS IS AN IMPORTANT POINT IN THE TRICK. When you tie the ends, you automatically *reverse their sides.* This means that the single end that is tied from the *left* sleeve is handed to the spectator on the *right,* and the single end from the *right* sleeve is given to the spectator on the *left.* Be sure "not" to recross the tied pair and defeat your purpose.

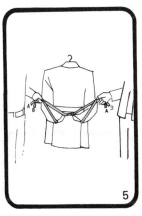

(6) Stand behind the coat and hold the hanger — making sure that the spectators are standing one on each side holding their ends of the ropes. Now, instruct the spectators to pull on their ropes. *This will cause the secret thread to break.* The two lengths of rope will appear to penetrate the hanger *and* the jacket! You now return the jacket to your volunteer and allow the audience to examine the ropes and the hanger.

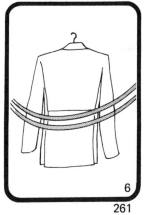

RING OFF ROPE

There are various tricks involving "rings" and "ropes," and this is one of the best. RING OFF ROPE has the impact of an impromptu effect when done at close range — yet it can also be performed before a fairly large group, with the assistance of two spectators from the audience, making it an equally good item for your stage show.

EFFECT

The magician borrows a finger ring from a member of the audience. He asks the spectator to thread it on a rope about three feet in length. Two spectators now hold the rope — one at each end — yet the performer causes the ring to magically "penetrate" right through the center of the rope! The ring is immediately returned to its owner. The ring can be thoroughly examined, along with the length of rope.

METHOD

(1) Hand one of the spectators a piece of rope about three feet long for examination as you ask to borrow a finger ring from any gentleman in the audience. Retrieve the now examined rope from the audience and invite a spectator to thread the borrowed ring on the rope.

(2) Lay the "threaded" ring and rope across your upturned right hand. The ring should rest near the base of your first finger, and the ends of the rope should hang down from both sides of your hand as shown.

(6) With the ring and rope held in this position, reach your left hand *across your right forearm* and grasp the dangling rope where it emerges from your right hand. Slide your left hand along the rope and give the right end of the rope to the spectator on that side. Ask him to hold that end. *NOTE: The illustration is from the spectator's viewpoint.*

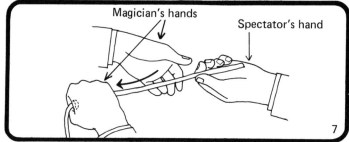

(7) After the spectator grasps the right end of the rope, slide your half-cupped left hand along the rope *bringing it beneath your right fist.*

(3) As you display the rope in this manner, remark that it would be impossible to remove the ring from the rope without sliding it off one of the ends. With that, close your fingers over the ring and turn your hand completely over so that the back of your hand is up. The ring should be held loosely by your first finger *near the very edge of your hand as shown.* (4) This illustration is a close-up view of how the ring should be held in your hand.

(5) *NOTE: To conceal the ring from the view of the spectators on your left, you can move your right thumb upward to fill in the open space where the ring might be seen in your hand.*

(8) <u>At the very moment your left hand arrives below your fist,</u> tilt your right hand slightly to the left and relax your right first finger. *Allow the ring to secretly drop from your right fist <u>into your left fingers.</u>* NOTE: This "drop" should be done smoothly and without hesitation. If your left hand pauses for even the slightest moment, you will "tip" the audience that something suspicious is happening. *THIS IS THE KEY "MOVE" FOR THIS TRICK.*

(9) *After* your left hand catches the ring, *raise your right hand upward.* Look directly into the eyes of the spectator *on your right* and say, "Hold your end a little higher."

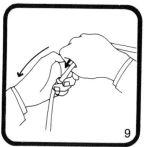

(10) NOTE: This is a good example of the use of "Misdirection" while the vital move of the trick takes place. By *looking* at the spectator and *directing a comment toward him,* you take his attention *off the rope* just long enough to make the secret "steal." Also, by raising your right hand upward, the attention of the audience *will follow that hand,* instead of your left hand, which secretly contains the ring.

(12) Bring your left hand up beneath your right fist. Quickly open both hands, placing your palms together so that the rope and the now "free" ring are trapped between them. Start to roll your hands back and forth as if to cause the ring to "dissolve" through the center of the rope.

(11) As you raise your right hand upward, your left hand (and the ring) slides down along the rope and secretly carries the ring *completely off the end of the rope.* Without hesitation, as you secretly hold the ring in the Finger Palm position, lift this end and give it to the spectator on your left. Tell him to hold the end firmly in his hand.

Spectator's hand

Magician's hand

(13) Lift your right hand to reveal the ring resting on your left hand next to the rope. Return the ring to its owner and pass the rope for examination.

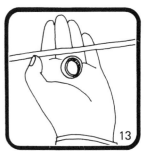

COMMENTS AND SUGGESTIONS

Although using a borrowed ring is best, the routine is just as effective with your own finger ring, or even a small curtain ring or a metal washer. At the finish, everything can be examined, just as with the borrowed ring, so the effect on the audience is the same. The vital point is to *make your presentation natural,* so that no one will suspect the "secret move." As you practice, and by working slowly and deliberately, you will find that the "steal" becomes easier and all the more deceptive. To "condition" the audience to the "naturalness" of your actions, you can introduce the following before actually performing the trick. Hold the threaded ring in your open right palm as in Step 2. Say to the spectator on your right, "I am going to give you *this end* of the rope." With that, reach over with your left hand and *start* to give him the right end but let it drop. Then say to the spectator on the left, "And I will give you *this* end," as you bring your left hand over and lift the left end of the rope and then let it drop. Then say, "And all the while, I will keep the ring tightly in my right hand." With that, you now, *for the first time,* turn your right fist downward. You are now all set to proceed, using *almost the same moves* with the ends of the rope, making the routine *entirely natural throughout.*

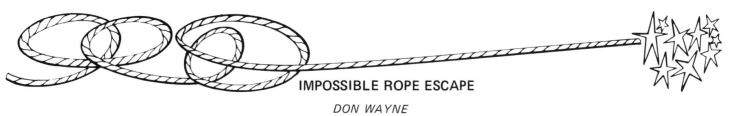

IMPOSSIBLE ROPE ESCAPE

DON WAYNE

EFFECT

The magician calls the audience's attention to two 5-foot lengths of unprepared rope. The performer then asks for the assistance of two spectators. Each spectator is handed one of the ropes for examination. While the spectators are busy with the ropes, the magician places a chair in the center of the stage. After the spectators have confirmed the unprepared nature of the ropes, the magician sits in the chair and allows the two volunteers to tie his knees and wrists together. When the spectators are satisfied that the performer is securely bound, they cover his wrists with a large cloth. *INSTANTLY,* one of the magician's hands is free—but before the spectators are able to remove the cloth, the performer plunges his hand back beneath the cloth. When the cloth is removed, the audience can see that the magician is *STILL BOUND AS TIGHTLY AS BEFORE.* The surprised spectators are asked to tie still another knot in the ropes above the magician's wrist. They then replace the cloth over his arms. Once more the performer escapes. But this time, upon lifting the cloth, *HE IS COMPLETELY FREE*—the ropes have apparently penetrated the magician's arms and legs as well!

SECRET AND PREPARATION

All you need for this excellent effect are two lengths of rope approximately 5 feet long, an opaque piece of cloth approximately 4 feet square and a chair.

METHOD

(1) Invite two members of your audience to join you on stage. Hand each of them one of the lengths of rope for their examination. While the two volunteers examine the ropes, place the folding chair at stage center.

(2) Take the rope back from the spectator on your right and drape it over the right hand as shown. We will call this Rope A. The middle of Rope A should rest on top of the first finger of the right hand near the thumb. Now, with the left hand, take the other rope from the spectator on your left. We will call this Rope B. Place the center of B between the first and second fingers of the right hand near the finger tips. Ropes A and B should now appear as shown.

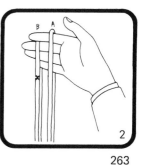

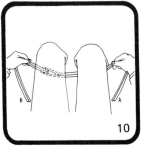

(3) The following series of moves will be made as you transfer the ropes from your right hand to your left. During this transfer you will be inviting the spectator on your left to cross in front of you so that he, and the other spectator, can "examine" the chair.

(9) Now reach behind your legs with your right hand and grasp both ends of Rope B. *Be sure to hold the "hooked" loops securely in your left hand.* Bring the ends of both A and B around your legs with the "hooked" loops behind your left knee as in the illustration. Now sit down and, at the same time, place the loops in the bend behind your left knee.

(4) With your left hand, grasp Rope B at a point about 6 inches down from the loop of the rope, which is shown as Point X, and allow Rope A to slide off your right first finger onto the loop formed by B, as shown.

(10) THE HOOKED LOOPS MUST BE POSITIONED DIRECTLY BEHIND YOUR LEFT KNEE SO THAT, AS YOU SIT DOWN, <u>THE LOOPS WILL BE HELD FIRMLY IN PLACE BY THE BEND IN YOUR LEG.</u> Slide your *left hand out* along the ropes to your left.

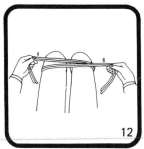

(5) With your right hand, pull Rope B up and over Rope A and down into the left hand to Point X.

(11) *ALSO NOTE: By holding the ropes as shown in Step 10 it appears to the audience that the two separate ropes pass <u>directly under your legs.</u>*

(6) Close the left fingers around the two "hooked" loops.

(12) Now cross the two pairs of ends up and over your knees. *Be sure that the left-hand Pair B crosses to the REAR of the right-hand Pair A as shown. Pull the ropes tightly in opposite directions. This action apparently binds the knees together.*

(7) To the audience the ropes will appear as if they *both pass straight through your left hand.*

(13) Then position your wrists on top of the ropes. STILL HOLD THE LOOPS FIRMLY WITH THE BEND IN YOUR LEFT KNEE.

(8) The two spectators will have examined the chair by now, so position yourself in front of the chair. Have the spectators stand, one on each side, beside you.

(14) Ask the spectator on your left to tie your wrists tightly using as many knots as he wishes.

(15) Ask the spectator on your right to cover your hands and knees with the cloth.

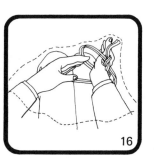

(16) Under cover of the cloth, *twist your wrists to the RIGHT.* You will find that your left hand will easily come free of the rope. Bring your left hand into view and adjust the cloth. This action will bring a laugh from the audience. Quickly place your hand back under the cloth *and into the ropes.* Twist your hands to the left to retighten the ropes.

(17) The spectator to your right is asked to remove the cloth. THE AUDIENCE WILL SEE THAT YOU ARE STILL SECURELY TIED. To make sure that you cannot escape, the spectator on your left is asked to tie another knot *on top of those already there.*

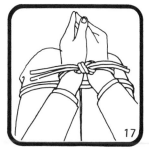

(18) After the new knot is tied, have the spectator on your right re-cover your hands with the cloth. As soon as you are covered, twist both hands to the right as in Step 16. This time release *both* your hands from the loop and bring them both into view on top of this cloth. During the laughter, grasp the ropes through the cloth and lift sharply, *as you relax your hold on the loops with your left knee.* The ropes will come completely loose — apparently having penetrated both legs.

(19) Stand up and drop the cloth containing the ropes on the chair seat. Thank your volunteers and congratulate them on tying you so well as they leave the stage.

SILK AND HANDKERCHIEF MAGIC

★ ★ ★

Tricks with handkerchiefs form quite a large category of magic and perhaps the most unusual. While it is possible to put card tricks, coin tricks, and even stage illusions in categories of their own, it is often difficult to classify a handkerchief trick exactly. Besides, there are distinctly different types of handkerchief magic, as will be seen.

Besides openly playing a major role in certain tricks, a handkerchief often serves as an important adjunct in other effects where its purpose is totally unsuspected. The broken and restored match is a typical example of this, wherein the secret depends on the handkerchief that is unobtrusively introduced into the routine.

The type of handkerchief to be used in certain tricks is also of importance. With effects involving knots, larger handkerchiefs are better. Houdini used huge handkerchiefs throughout his knot-tying routines that were a feature of his big show.

In other effects, cotton handkerchiefs are excellent—bandana type, polka dots or other designs aid concealment of small objects in their folds. For effects where the handkerchief seems totally unimportant, a plain white hankie is often best. At times you may borrow such handkerchiefs, so if you happen to bring but one of your own, nobody will suspect trickery.

In stage work before large audiences, some magicians go in for elaborate effects with colored silk handkerchiefs requiring special apparatus. Such handkerchiefs are popularly termed "silks" and should be made from thin silk with a very narrow hem. Being compressible, they are excellent for production effects in which very large silks with colorful ornamental designs may be used. For less elaborate effects, such as bare hand productions, vanishes, color changes, and the like, small silks are preferable. Silk effects really form a separate category of their own, and there's no question on that score. Hermann and Kellar both featured silk routines in their performances, and in later years, other magicians developed elaborate silk acts that helped them pave their roads to fame.

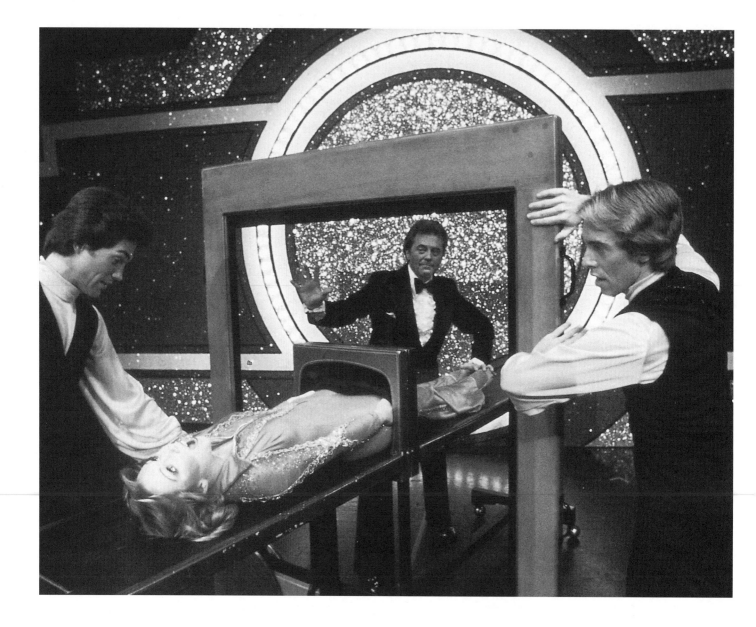

HYPNOTIZED HANDKERCHIEF

EFFECT

The magician displays a pocket handkerchief and twirls it between his hands in a "rope-like" fashion. Always under the performer's control, the handkerchief stands erect, bows to the audience, and moves back and forth in a very puzzling manner. He then attaches an "invisible" thread to the upper corner of the handkerchief and causes the handkerchief to follow his lead by pulling on the "magical" leash. Even after crushing the handkerchief down with his other hand, the magician cannot seem to discourage the persistant performance of the HYPNOTIZED HANDKERCHIEF.

METHOD

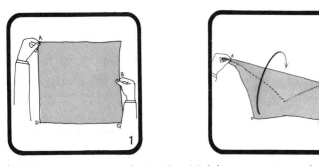

(1) Borrow a spectator's handkerchief (or use your own), and spread it open on the table. Now hold the left-hand corner (A) securely between your left thumb and fingers and grasp the *hem* at the *center of the right side* (B) with your right hand as shown.
(2) Pick up the handkerchief and hold it in front of you.

(3) Twirl the handkerchief between your hands ... (4) ... until the entire handkerchief is rolled in a tightly twisted rope-like configuration.

(5) As you continue to hold the "twisted" handkerchief, move your right hand *above* your left hand so that the right end (B) is directly above the left end (A) as shown.

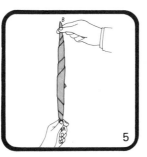

(6) Now, move your left hand up so that it can grasp the rolled handkerchief near the center. *Do not allow the twists in the handkerchief to "unroll" as you change the position of your left hand.* Your right hand maintains its grip on the *top* end (B).

(7) Pull the handkerchief "tight" between your hand ... then, slowly release the handkerchief from your right fingers. *It will stand erect as if "hypnotized."* (In reality, the natural rigidity given to the material by the many twists is what causes the handkerchief to maintain its upright position.)

(8) Pretend to pluck an imaginary strand of hair from your head and go through the motions of tying it to the upper end of the handkerchief (B). Holding the "free" end of this fictitious hair in your hand, slowly pull it towards your body. At the same time, draw your left thumb gently downward against your left fingers. The downward motion of your thumb will cause the handkerchief to obediently lean in your direction. NOTE: Practice will teach you how to synchronize the handkerchief's "leaning" movement with the pulling motion of the "invisible" hair in your right hand.

(9) Now move your right hand *and* the invisible hair forward, toward the spectators. To make the handkerchief lean away from you and follow the invisible tug, simply slide your left thumb up and forward on the center of the handkerchief.

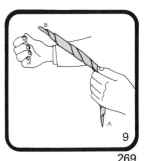

(10) Here is a more detailed illustration of the move required for Step 8. This shows how the left thumb pulls *down* on the center of the handkerchief to lean toward you.

(13) Now, in one swift downward motion, bring your right hand down on top of the handkerchief . . . crushing it between your right palm and the top of your left fist.

(11) And here is the action as your left thumb pushes *up and forward* on the center of the handkerchief, causing the handkerchief to lean away from you for Step 9.

(14) Quickly raise your right hand back up. As you do, secretly use your right fingers and thumb to straighten the handkerchief and . . .

(12) After repeating this back and forth pulling movement with the "invisible" hair several times, bring the handkerchief back to its original upright position. Then hold your right hand above the hypnotized handkerchief as shown.

(15) . . . bring the handkerchief back to its original "hypnotized" upright position. With practice you will learn to execute this upward movement so swiftly and smoothly that the handkerchief will appear to "bounce back" into shape on its own accord.

(16) To conclude the effect, snap the handkerchief open and offer it to the spectators for examination.

FATIMA, THE DANCER

EFFECT

As an interlude between effects, the magician tells the story of an exotic dancer named Fatima. Although she lived and danced many years ago, her exotic movements and high kicks have never been forgotten. To illustrate, the performer ties a knot in his pocket handkerchief — and then, with a twist and a twirl, he turns it into a doll-like replica of the famous dancer. To the accompaniment of a short poem, the magician seems to make the cloth figure come alive, dancing about between his hands, finishing in grand style with a *high, spinning kick!*

SECRET AND PREPARATION

This clever bit of business never fails to create interest and laughter. Since the handkerchief is completely unprepared, you are able to present this effect any time, with any handkerchief!

METHOD

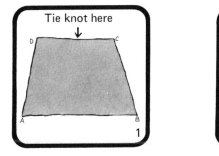

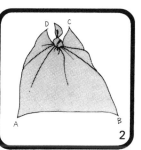

(1) Spread the handkerchief open and (2) tie a knot in the *center of one side* of the hem as shown. This knot represents the head of Fatima. Be sure that a small portion of the hem protrudes from the completed knot, forming a sort of "tail," which you can use to hold the handkerchief later.

(3) *NOTE: Be sure you do not tie the knot in one of the corners of the handkerchief, or the effect will not work. Tie the knot in the center of one of the side edges of the handkerchief as shown.*

(6) Now, bring Corners A and B together and grasp them *both* in your right hand as shown. With your left hand, grasp the "tail" of the knot (Fatima's head) between your left thumb and first finger.

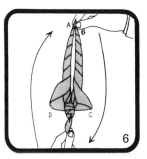

(7) Now, turn the entire affair *completely over.* This brings Corners A and B to the bottom and the knot to the top. If you use your imagination, you can see the form of a dancer created by the handkerchief.

(4) Grasp the two corners (A and B) on the *side opposite the knot* between the thumb and forefingers of both hands as shown.

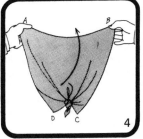

(8) By moving your hands back and forth, Fatima will dance about and swing her hips as if to keep time with the music. You can recite the following poem suiting the action to the words:

> *FATIMA was a dancer gay.*
> *For fifty cents she'd dance this way,*
> (Shake the figure)
> *But if a dollar you would pay,*
> (Release one leg)
> *She'd do "Ta Ra Ra Boom De Aye."*

NOTE: The high kick could also be done at the word "aye."

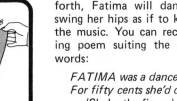

(5) Now, "twirl" the handkerchief away from you, causing the knotted portion of the handkerchief to spin around Ends A and B that you are holding. *Be sure to twirl the handkerchief as tightly as possible until it will no longer accept any additional twists in the material.*

(9) On the last line of the poem, to bring the dance to its grand finale, pull your left hand up and your right hand down. *At the same time,* release one of the bottom corners of the handkerchief (either A or B) from your right hand. The result will be a *high kick* and a *dramatic spin* — performed by Fatima at the peak of her career!

COMMENTS AND SUGGESTIONS

The clever poem was written by that excellent magician, showman, writer, and lawyer, William Larsen, Sr. and is still a favorite of his son, Bill Larsen, President of the Academy of Magical Arts in Hollywood.

THE DISSOLVING KNOT

EFFECT

During a routine with a silk handkerchief, the magician casually ties a knot in the center of the scarf. Then the knot simply "melts" away.

SECRET AND PREPARATION

You will require a handkerchief (silk is best) at least 18" square in order to present this trick effectively.

METHOD

(1) Grasp the diagonal corners of the handkerchief between the first and second fingers of each hand. (2) Now twirl the handkerchief into a loose "rope-like" configuration. We will call the end pinched between the first and second fingers of your left hand *End A,* and the end in your right hand *End B.*

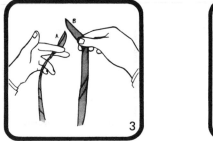

(3) Bring End B over toward your left and open the second and third fingers of your left hand as shown. (4) Lay End B *over* End A . . . passing End B *between* the second and third fingers of your left hand.

(5) Your right hand now reaches *through* the loop and grasps End A as shown. The third and fourth fingers of your left hand curl around the twisted silk below End A.

(6) After the third and fourth fingers of the left hand are closed around the handkerchief, *the second finger of your left hand "hooks" the silk just below where the two ends cross . . . below End B as shown.*

(7) THIS IS THE KEY MOVE. Now pull End A through the loop with your right hand. End B is held firmly by the thumb and first finger of your left hand. The third and fourth fingers of your left hand release their grip around the silk *as your left second finger hooks and pulls the lower portion of End B through the loop.* STUDY THE ILLUSTRATION CAREFULLY.

(8) As you continue pulling on End A, a knot will form *around the loop* held by the second finger of your left hand as shown. *When this knot is tight enough to hold its shape, remove your left second finger from inside the loop.*

(9) NOTE: You now have apparently tied a "real" knot in the handkerchief. Really you have cleverly (and secretly) tied a "slip" knot. If you were to pull on the ends of the handkerchief now the knot would "dissolve."

(10) Allow the handkerchief to hang freely from the thumb and first finger of your left hand.

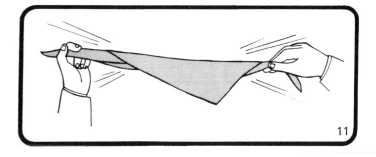

(11) Now grasp End A lightly with the thumb and first finger of your right hand. Hold the handkerchief horizontally in front of you and gently blow on the knot. At the same time, pull on the ends of the handkerchief and the knot will "dissolve" away!

COMMENTS AND SUGGESTIONS

The Dissolving Knot is one of the basic, classic effects in magic. It is important that you practice until you can tie the "Dissolving Knot" just as easily and quickly as you would a "real" knot. The ability to tie this trick knot will then become the basis for many other baffling effects. Two of these stunners are the tricks that follow.

THE KNOT THROUGH THE ARM

EFFECT

The magician displays an ordinary handkerchief. A spectator stands to the performer's left and is asked to extend his left arm about waist high. Grasping the diagonal corners of the handkerchief, the magician spins the scarf into a loose rope-like configuration. The handkerchief is now tied around the volunteer's wrist. With a sudden jerk, the handkerchief seems to visibly penetrate the spectator's arm leaving the magician with the undamaged handkerchief and the knot still intact!

SECRET AND PREPARATION

This effect is one of those beautiful little gems that can be done anywhere at any time. All that is needed is a large pocket handkerchief, a silk scarf, or an 18- or 24-inch square "magician's" silk handkerchief.

This trick is based on THE DISSOLVING KNOT, which you must learn first.

METHOD

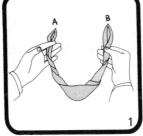

(1) Grasp the diagonal corners of the handkerchief and spin it into a loose "rope-like" configuration. In the illustration we have marked the two ends "A" and "B." Hold the handkerchief as shown.

(3) With the spectator's wrist still in position, insert your right hand through the loop and grasp End A. Pull this end back through the loop and tie the Dissolving Knot.

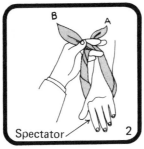

(2) Now, place the handkerchief around the spectator's left wrist and grasp both ends of the handkerchief in your left hand in preparation for the Dissolving Knot.

(4) *NOTE: As you pull the ends in opposite directions (End B to your right), be sure to retain the small loop in End A with the second finger of the left hand as described in the Dissolving Knot. This small loop will fall under End A between the handkerchief and the spectator's wrist. You can now pull on the ends to tie the handkerchief* <u>firmly</u> *around the spectator's wrist AS LONG AS YOU KEEP YOUR LEFT SECOND FINGER IN PLACE HOLDING THE SMALL LOOP. When the handkerchief is tightly around the spectator's wrist, remove your left second finger.*

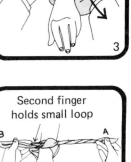

Second finger holds small loop

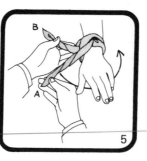

(5) Now with your right hand, swing End A to the left *around the spectator's wrist.* Continue to hold End A with your left hand. BE SURE THAT END B GOES <u>IN FRONT</u> OF END A as shown.

(8) Holding one end in each hand, pull up and out on *both ends* of the handkerchief. This "dissolves" the false knot around the wrist, creating a perfect illusion of the handkerchief penetrating the spectator's arm. The last (legitimate) knot is left in the handkerchief as a final convincer.

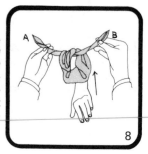

(6) After you have wrapped End B around the spectator's wrist, the entire affair should look like this.

(9) *NOTE: After you have tied BOTH knots, have the spectator grasp his hands together. In this way, you strengthen the mystery by making it impossible for the handkerchief to have been slipped over the end of the spectator's left hand when you perform the "penetration." Also, when tying the Dissolving Knot in Step 3, try to make it a bit off center so that End A is longer than End B as shown in Step 4. This is so you will have plenty of handkerchief left to wrap End A around the spectator's wrist the second time in Step 5.*

(7) Now tie a *single legitimate knot* on top of the Dissolving Knot. This will put End A in your <u>left</u> hand and End B in your <u>right</u>.

COMMENTS AND SUGGESTIONS

This is an excellent impromptu trick which can be performed for one person or, on stage, for a large audience. I have used it for many years, and it is well worth the small amount of practice necessary to learn it.

—MW

HANDKERCHIEF THROUGH HANDKERCHIEF

EFFECT

The magician displays two silk handkerchiefs. He twists one into a rope-like configuration and gives it to a spectator to hold outstretched between his hands. He then twists the second handkerchief in the same manner and ties it *around* the first handkerchief held by the spectator. The spectator is then asked to tie a knot in his handkerchief so that both handkerchiefs are securely bonded together. Under these impossible conditions, the magicians causes the handkerchiefs to seemingly "melt" apart — leaving their knots intact.

SECRET AND PREPARATION

In order to perform this trick, you must first have mastered THE DISSOLVING KNOT.

This illusion is an effective variation of the KNOT THROUGH ARM. You will require two large silk handkerchiefs. They should be at least 18" square and preferably of contrasting colors. In the illustrations, one of the handkerchiefs is light-colored and the other is dark-colored to make the description easier to follow.

METHOD

(1) Grasp the light-colored handkerchief by two diagonal corners and "twirl" it between your hands into a "loose rope." Hand it to a spectator and request that he hold it outstretched by those same corners as shown.

(2) Now twirl the dark-colored handkerchief in the same manner. Holding it by the ends, position it under the handkerchief being held by the spectator as shown.

(3) NOTE: In the illustration for Step 2, the spectator's hands that are holding the light-colored handkerchief have been omitted for clarity. You can also see from this illustration the similarity between this effect and the "Handkerchief through the Wrist." In this version, you are substituting the light-colored handkerchief for the volunteer's wrist.

(4) Utilizing the "Dissolving Knot" as described in Steps 3 and 4 in the "Handkerchief through the Wrist," tie the dark handkerchief around the light handkerchief.

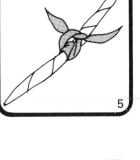

(5) With the fake knot cinched up tightly against the light-colored handkerchief, loop the dark handkerchief around the light handkerchief a second time and tie one legitimate knot just as you did in Steps 5, 6, and 7 in the "Handkerchief through the Wrist."

(6) Now ask the spectator to tie a knot in his handkerchief. As he does, you may find it necessary to hold the dark-colored handkerchief by its knot. There are two reasons why this may be necessary: First, to protect the fake knot from being pulled loose, and second, to prevent the spectator from tying his knot too tightly around your handkerchief. You can avoid this possibility by tying both knots yourself, but the effectiveness of the illusion is enhanced if the spectator ties the real knot in the light-colored handkerchief.

(7) Have the spectator hold the corners of the light handkerchief as you hold the corners of the dark handkerchief. With a gentle shaking motion, pull on the ends of your handkerchief and instruct the spectator to do the same. Your knot will "dissolve" and the two handkerchiefs will "magically" separate from each other. Because of the second "real" knot that you tied and the "real" knot that the spectator tied, you are both left with knots in your handkerchiefs! Done correctly, this is a beautiful and baffling mystery.

THE PENETRATING HANDKERCHIEF

Here is a simple but effective mystery involving objects easily found around the house. All you need is an ordinary drinking glass, two handkerchiefs, and a rubber band. This is another of those little "gems" from the inventive mind of "Gen" Grant.

EFFECT

The magician displays a drinking glass, holding it mouth up with the tips of his fingers. He then places a handkerchief into the glass and covers both this handkerchief and the glass with a *second* handkerchief. Next, he places a rubber band over the second handkerchief *and* the glass, thus sealing the first handkerchief inside the glass. Now, holding the glass from the outside, he reaches under the handkerchief for a brief moment and instantly withdraws the first handkerchief — the one that was sealed inside the glass! The outside handkerchief is removed and all may now be examined. AN IMPOSSIBLE PENETRATION!

SECRET AND PREPARATION

This trick depends entirely upon a simple "move" which involves secretly turning the glass upside down while it is being covered by the second handkerchief. *All of the illustrations are from the magician's point of view.*

METHOD

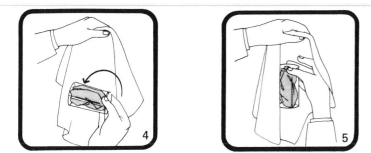

(1) Begin by holding the drinking glass, mouth up, at the tips of the fingers and thumb of your right hand as shown. (2) Display a handkerchief — this is the one that will later "penetrate" the glass. With your left hand, push it into the glass.

(7) As the glass turns over, your left hand finishes covering *both* the right hand and the glass. (8) After the glass is covered, grip the glass *through* the cloth with your left hand as shown.

(3) Pick up the second handkerchief with your left hand. Bring it up in front of the glass, *momentarily hiding the glass from the spectators' view.*

(9) Remove your right hand, casually showing it empty, and pick up the rubber band from the table. Spread the rubber band with your right fingers and place it around the handkerchief and the "top" of the glass (really the *bottom,* unknown to the spectators).

(4) NOW HERE COMES THE SECRET "MOVE." As you begin to cover the glass with the handkerchief, *your right hand slightly relaxes its grip on the bottom of the glass, allowing the glass to pivot between your thumb and fingers* (5) *until the glass has TURNED COMPLETELY UPSIDE DOWN.*

(6) *NOTE: The handkerchief inside the glass should be large enough so that it will not fall out when you turn the glass upside down.*

(10) With the empty right hand, reach underneath the covering handkerchief and grasp the first handkerchief — the one that is inside the glass. Pull it straight down into view. *To the audience it appears that the handkerchief has "magically" penetrated through the bottom of the glass!*

(11) Now with your right hand, reach under the covering handkerchief and grip the glass *in position to make the secret turn-over once again* — this time with the mouth of the glass (which is at the *bottom* because the glass is upside down) between the tips of your right thumb and fingers.

(12) With your left hand, grip the outer (second) handkerchief between the tips of the fingers at the very "top" of the covered glass (actually the "real" bottom) and pull the cloth *just enough to release the rubber band from around the glass* — and then *STOP*. Now, pause for a moment, *just long enough to allow the glass to PIVOT in the fingers BACK TO ITS ORIGINAL MOUTH-UP POSITION.*

(13) As soon as the glass is mouth up, draw the handkerchief away from the glass and all can be examined.

THE MAGICAL PRODUCTION OF A HANDKERCHIEF

EFFECT

The following effects comprise an entire routine for the "production" and "vanish" of a silk handkerchief. You will first learn how to fold the handkerchief so that you can produce it from the air. Then you will learn how to construct a "vanisher" to cause the handkerchief to disappear from your hands leaving them completely empty.

SECRET AND PREPARATION

To perform the production, it is best to use a handkerchief made of pure silk (the type sold by magic supply houses is best — these are called "silks"). A silk handkerchief can be easily folded in the special manner described here and it will spring open when it is produced. Also, a "magician's silk" can be more easily compressed so that it makes a smaller "package" . . . thus it can be more easily concealed for any production or vanish.

(A) Begin by placing the handkerchief flat on the table in front of you.

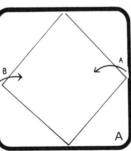

(B) Fold corners A and B into the center of the handkerchief. The corners A and B should just touch in the center of the handkerchief as shown.

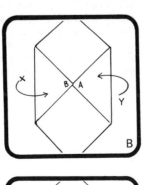

(C) Now grasp the handkerchief at points X and Y. Fold these two edges of the handkerchief into the center so that points X and Y touch. You'll notice that the handkerchief is getting thinner in width with each fold.

(D) Repeat the folding actions as you did in Steps B and C. Then, continue folding the edges of the handkerchief into the center until the folded handkerchief is about 3" wide.

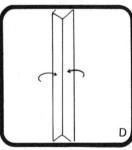

(E) Now fold the right-hand half of the handkerchief over *on top of the left-hand half*. The handkerchief should now be about 1½" wide.

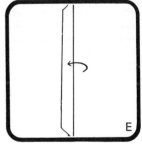

(F) Fold the bottom end of the handkerchief about an inch towards your right as shown. This forms a "tab" like protrusion which is labeled "T" in the illustration.

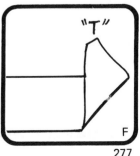

(G) Beginning at the bottom of the handkerchief, roll it up tightly so that the tab (T) protrudes from the bundle. Roll up the entire length of the handkerchief until it forms a tight little package.

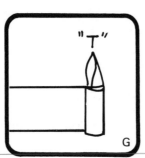

(I) With the handkerchief now properly rolled, it forms a tight little bundle which will not unroll until time for the production.

(H) The handkerchief should now look like this. Tuck the top "free" end of the handkerchief into the left-hand side of the rolled hank. (This is the side opposite the "tab.") You may use a blunt stick or other object to tuck this end down between the folds if you wish.

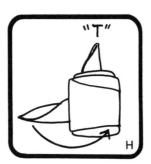

METHOD

(1) With the handkerchief folded and rolled into this compact bundle you are now ready for the production. Secretly obtain the bundle in your hand. (A good idea is to have the bundle hidden behind some prop on your table and then pick it up as you set down some other prop used in the preceeding trick in your show.) When you pick up the bundle, grasp the protruding tab (T) and hold it firmly in the crook of your thumb. Relax your hand so that it appears normal to the audience. Keep the back of your hand to the spectators so that no one can see the hidden bundle.

(3) Quickly bend your right fingers inward and grasp the end of the handkerchief between your first and second fingers as shown.

(2) To produce the handkerchief, if it is held in your right hand, turn your *right side* toward the audience. Make a "grabbing" motion in the air to your left with your right hand. As you do this, straighten out your fingers and snap your wrist sharply. This action will cause the bundle to unroll and open out quickly. You now have the handkerchief held at one corner by the crook of your right thumb.

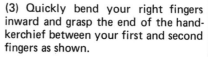

(4) Straighten out the fingers of your hand as you turn the hand palm up. The handkerchief is seen by the audience held at one end between the first and second fingers of your right hand. This completes the production sequence.

COMMENTS AND SUGGESTIONS

The "folding" and rolling of the silk handkerchief described here is a basic method used by magicians for making a handkerchief into a compact "self-contained" bundle. It has many other applications that you will use as you progress to more advanced effects in the Art of Magic.

THE VANISH OF THE HANDKERCHIEF

In order to vanish the handkerchief, you must first construct a *pull*. A "pull" is a clever device used by magicians that will enable you to cause the handkerchief to completely "disappear" in a startling manner.

SECRET AND PREPARATION

For the body of the "pull," you can use either a hollow rubber ball or a small plastic bottle.

(A) For the "ball pull," you must obtain a hollow ball that is small enough to be concealed in your hand, yet large enough to contain the handkerchief. Cut a small hole about 1" wide in the ball. This hole must be large enough for you to easily stuff the handkerchief into the ball. Then attach a length of strong, black round elastic on the other side of the ball — directly opposite the hole. Fasten a safety pin securely to the free end of the elastic.

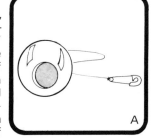

(C) *NOTE: You may construct either pull you wish, or you may find some other suitable container, such as the small metal cans which come with certain types of film, etc. In any event, the pull must be small enough so that it can be comfortably held in your fist. Just remember that if the pull is too large for your hand, your audience will see it, and the trick will be spoiled.*

(B) For the "bottle pull," obtain a small plastic bottle which will easily hold the handkerchief. (The best bottle is the kind with a snap-on or twist-on cap in which the bottom is as large as the top. These are often used as containers for pills. If you don't have one around the house, you can buy it from the pharmacist at your local drug store.) Make a small hole in the bottom of the bottle. Tie a large knot in one end of the elastic. Then, thread the other end through the mouth of the bottle and out the hole on the bottom. The knot will keep the end of the elastic from going through the hole, thus attaching it to the bottle. Tie a safety pin to the free end of the elastic.

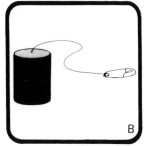

(D) After you have completed making the pull, fasten the safety pin to one of the rear belt loops of your trousers. Allow the elastic to run *beneath* the next two or three belt loops so that the pull will hang on your *left side near the seam of your trousers*. When performing the vanish, you must wear a coat or jacket so that the pull will be hidden from view.

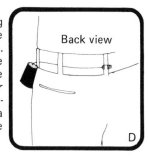

METHOD

(1) Assume that you are wearing the pull on your left side and have just produced the handkerchief from the air as described in the preceding trick. You are now prepared to vanish the handkerchief. Notice in the illustration that, as you produce the handkerchief, your left hand is momentarily hidden from the audience's view by your body.

(2) As you produce the handkerchief with your right hand, *secretly grasp the pull with your left hand.*

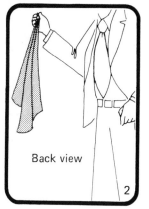

(3) *NOTE: At this point you should be giving your full attention to the handkerchief that is held in your right hand. At no time do you ever call attention to the hand containing the pull.*

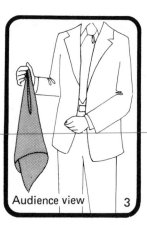

Audience view 3

(7) When the entire handkerchief has been pushed into the pull, relax the left-hand grip slightly. *The pull will fly secretly out of your hand and be carried inside your coat.*

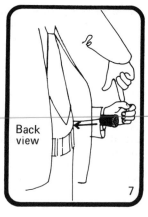

Back view 7

(4) Now turn your left side toward the audience as your left hand stretches the elastic attached to the pull. Your left hand should now be about six to ten inches away from your body.

Audience view 4

(8) *NOTE: You will have to experiment a little in order to get the elastic to the proper length to insure the maximum effect. The stretched elastic, when released, should cause the pull to go instantly inside the coat, while your left hand is held as if it still contained the handkerchief. During this action, your right index finger continues to pantomime the action of pushing the handkerchief into your closed left fist.*

(5) Place the handkerchief, which you are holding in your right hand, on top of your closed left fist. Use your right fingers to push the handkerchief into your closed left fist. Unknown to the audience, *you are pushing the handkerchief into the pull as well.*

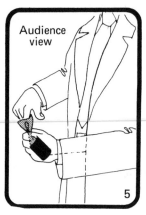

Audience view 5

(9) Continue the action, pretending to pack the handkerchief into your left fist with your right index finger. As you do this, *turn full front and extend both arms slightly away from your body* without any jerking or unnatural motions. The audience is led to believe that *the handkerchief is still held inside your left fist.*

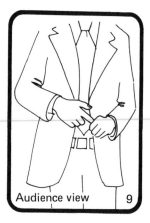

Audience view 9

(6) Here is a view of the action from the rear. The right fingers are pushing the handkerchief into the pull. Notice how the elastic runs from within your closed left fist, behind your left arm, and back inside your coat.

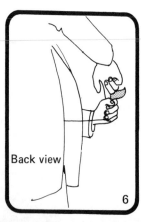

Back view 6

(10) You may now open your left hand to show that the handkerchief has vanished without a trace. This should catch your audience totally by surprise. You may wish to pull up both your coat sleeves to prove that the handkerchief has not gone "up your sleeve."

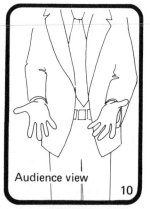

Audience view 10

COMMENTS AND SUGGESTIONS

It is important to remember when you release the pull, to do it in a natural manner so as not to arouse any suspicion. If the release is accompanied by any jerking of the hands, the audience may suspect "when" the dirty work was done. Remember to keep your left hand motionless when you let go of the pull. Don't worry about it; the elastic will do the work. Now that you know the moves, you can begin to practice the whole routine until the actions blend together to form a smooth, relaxed sequence.

The "pull" and the variations of the principle on which it is based are all derived from a basic magic concept with many important applications. Now that you know the important secret, you can devise many other ways to use this method of "vanishing" an object.

THE UNIVERSAL VANISHER

If you wish, you can construct a special UNIVERSAL PULL. This pull can be used to vanish a coin, button, ring, or practically any other small object as well as a handkerchief.

SECRET AND PREPARATION

(A) Make a small bag about 1½" by 2" out of black cloth as shown.

(B) Sew two stiff plastic shirt collar stays (or cut two strips from a sheet of stiff plastic) inside the hem around the mouth of the bag. This is done so that you can open and close the bag by squeezing it between your left thumb and fingers. Attach a length of black elastic to the bottom of the bag. Fasten a safety pin to the free end of the elastic.

(C) Arrange this special pull on your body exactly as you did for the handkerchief vanish pull just described.

METHOD

(1) For the most part, the vanish using the Universal Pull is handled just like the previous model. Stand with your right side toward the audience. Secretly obtain the cloth bag from your left side as your right hand picks up the item to be vanished from your table. Once you have a firm grip on the bag, turn your left side toward the audience. As you do this action, stretch out the length of elastic attached to the pull.

(2) Squeeze the bag with your left hand until the mouth opens wide enough to allow the object to be inserted inside. With your right hand, put the object into your closed left fist. *Unknown to the audience, you place the object into the cloth bag.*

(3) Once the object is "in the bag," relax your left fingers slightly so that the mouth of the bag will close up.

(4) You may then vanish the object just as you did the handkerchief, or you may use this other optional method. Extend your left arm in a throwing motion as you release the bag. The bag will fly, unnoticed, inside your coat. You can now turn full front and show both your hands to be completely empty.

THE SERPENTINE SILK

EFFECT

The magician displays a colorful silk handkerchief which he twirls into a loose rope-like configuration and then he ties a knot in its center. Holding the handkerchief at one end, the performer causes the handkerchief to *visibly* untie itself right before the unbelieving eyes of the spectators

SECRET AND PREPARATION

(A) You will need a silk scarf or magicians' silk handkerchief approximately 18'' to 36'' square and a spool of fine black nylon or silk thread. To prepare, attach one end of a six-foot length of thread to one corner of the silk handkerchief. In the illustrations that follow, this corner has been labeled A and the free end of the handkerchief is marked B. The other end of the thread must be securely fastened to the top of your table (a small thumb tack works well). Now, fold the handkerchief and place it on your table making sure that the thread is coiled next to the handkerchief as shown in the illustration. You are now ready to present this classic mystery.

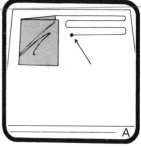

METHOD

(1) Pick up the folded handkerchief and stand approximately three feet in front of the table edge. Then, grasp Corner A in your right fingers and allow the silk to unfold in front of you. The thread should now be hanging at your right side *below your right arm.* Reach down and grasp the bottom of the handkerchief, Corner B, in your left hand and twirl the handkerchief into a loose rope-like configuration as shown. *The thread now runs across the top of your right thumb and under your right arm to the table top.*

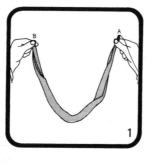

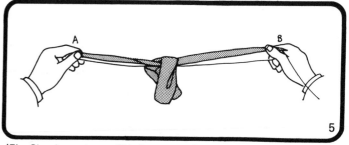

(5) Slowly and steadily draw your hands apart, forming a loose knot in the middle of the handkerchief. The thread sewn to Corner A will be drawn *through the knot* and should now run *over* your right thumb as shown.

(2) Now bring End A *across and over* End B as shown. As you do this, move your right hand so that the thread is being held in position *under* your right thumb.

(6) Release Corner A and allow the handkerchief to hang from your right hand. If you have performed all the steps correctly, the situation will be as follows: The thread, which is attached to Corner A, runs up and through the knot in the handkerchief.

(3) With your left hand reach through the loop formed by the handkerchief and . . .

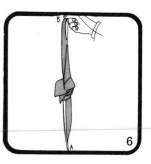

(7) From there, it travels *up* and *over* your right thumb and then *under* your right arm to the table.

(4) . . . grasp End A (and the thread) with the tips of your left fingers. Then pull End A back through the loop.

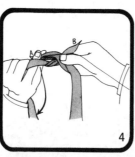

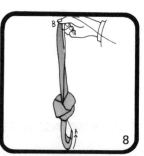

(8) Hold the handkerchief close to your body and move forward just enough to remove any remaining slack in the thread. Now, *by extending your right arm,* the thread will begin to pull End A upward as shown.

(9) As you move your arm farther from the table, End A will be drawn *into and completely through the knot* as shown.

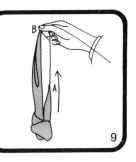

(11) ...*immediately release Corner B, let it fall from your hand, and grasp Corner A.*

(10) Now, by moving your body slightly forward, the thread will pull the rest of the End A portion of the handkerchief through the knot, causing it to *visibly dissolve.* As soon as Corner A reaches your right fingers . . .

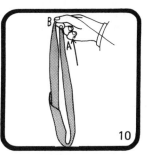

(12) You now hold the "untied" handkerchief by Corner A with Corner B hanging below as shown.

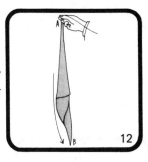

COMMENTS AND SUGGESTIONS

It will appear to the audience that the handkerchief has a life of its own and has wiggled out of its own knot. The position of the handkerchief at the end of the sequence leaves you all set to repeat the effect. This happens to be one of the rare cases in magic where repetition will help to build the mystery — but it is best to repeat the effect only once. At the conclusion, simply crumple the handkerchief and drop it on your table.

THE SERPENTINE SILK — SECOND VERSION

You may wish to try the SERPENTINE SILK by this alternate method. Use a shorter length of thread with a small plastic bead tied to the free end. The end with the thread does not run to the table as in the previous method. In this method, after the knot is tied, the bead is secretly held under your right foot. The tying of the knot is the same as before, as is the action of the untying of the knot except that this time you *lift your arm* instead of moving it forward. The benefit of this method is that you do not have to rely on a hookup to your table. With the bead-under-the-foot method, you can work the trick anywhere without fear of spoiling your set-up. You will, however, need a bit more distance from your audience as the thread is more visible since it is not hidden by your body.

THE PHANTOM

EFFECT

The magician removes his pocket handkerchief and spreads it open on the table in front of him. He then carefully folds over the four corners of the handkerchief creating a small, temporary pocket or "ghost trap" as the performer calls it. Grasping an obviously empty handful of air, the magician tells the audience that he has actually captured a *small phantom ghost*. Pretending to place his mysterious little friend inside the miniature trap, the "ghost" takes on a solid lifelike form which is clearly seen and heard through the fabric of the handkerchief. Yet, when the magician opens the handkerchief, the invisible phantom has escaped — leaving the handkerchief quite empty!

SECRET AND PREPARATION

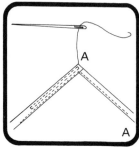

In this effect, as in THE BROKEN AND RESTORED MATCH, you need a gentleman's pocket handkerchief with a wide hem. To prepare, cut a length of coat hanger wire (or any similar thin, stiff wire) approximately 2½" long. Carefully insert the wire into the hem of the handkerchief at one corner (Corner A in the illustrations). Now sew the wire into place with a needle and thread. Fold the handkerchief and put it in your pocket. You will also need a common metal spoon. You are now ready to perform this excellent close-up mystery.

METHOD

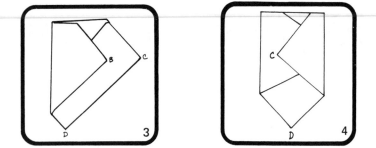

(1) To begin the presentation, remove the prepared handkerchief from your pocket and spread it open on the table in front of you. Corner D should be nearest you, pointing in your direction. Corner A, which contains the short length of wire, should be closest to the spectators. (2) With your right hand, grasp Corner A and fold it up and over to the center of the handkerchief as shown.

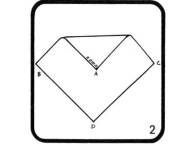

(3) Grasp Corner B in your left hand and fold it *over* Corner A as shown. (4) Now, grasp Corner C in your right hand and fold it over *both* Corners A and B so that it is even with the left edge of the handkerchief as shown. You will notice that the three folded Corners A, B, and C form a sort of "pocket" with the opening of the pocket facing you at Corner D.

(5) With your right hand, reach out and *pretend* to grasp something from the air. State that you have just caught a small "invisible ghost." Be sure your audience realizes that your hand is *quite empty* and that you are merely *pretending* to hold something in your hand.

(6) With your left hand, slightly raise the three folded corners (A, B and C), opening the "pocket" just enough to insert your right hand as if to give the illusive spirit a place to hide. Now, while your hand is inside the pocket, *grasp the secret wire that is sewn in Corner A and stand the wire upright, on its end.*

(7) As soon as the wire is secure in this position, remove your right hand from inside the pocket and release your hold on the handkerchief with your left hand. The wire will stand on its own accord due to the weight of the fabric. This creates the illusion of "something" within the folds of the handkerchief. With your left hand, lift Corner D and fold it up and over the opening of the pocket, thus imprisoning the "ghost" inside.

(8) The spectators will see a definite form inside the handkerchief, which you claim to be your little friend, the ghost. To further convince them of his presence, place the palm of your hand directly on top of the handkerchief, allowing the secret wire to press against the middle of your palm. Then, with a slight downward pressure, move your hand in a circular motion, thus creating the very eerie illusion of a *solid, round object* inside the handkerchief.

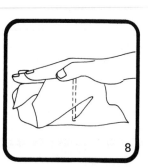

(9) The real convincer comes with this next move: Hold a spoon in your right hand — *then hit the end of the secret wire several times with the back of the spoon.* The noise created by the spoon against the hidden wire will convince the spectators — not only *visually,* but *audibly* as well — that you have really "captured" the small phantom.

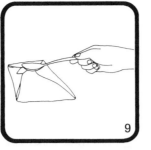

9

(10) To bring the mystery to its conclusion, set the spoon aside and quickly snap the handkerchief open, allowing the ghost to make his escape. Immediately show your hands and the handkerchief completely empty. Casually put the handkerchief in your pocket, leaving your audience totally baffled!

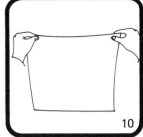

10

THE BROKEN AND RESTORED MATCH

EFFECT

The magician displays a wooden kitchen match and gives it to a spectator for examination. The performer then spreads out his pocket handkerchief on the table and places the match on the handkerchief near the center. He now folds the four corners of the handkerchief over the match so it is hidden from view. The magician asks the spectator to grip the match in both hands, through the folds of cloth, and break it into a number of pieces. Without any suspicious moves, the performer unfolds the handkerchief revealing the match *completely unharmed* — fully restored to its original condition!

SECRET AND PREPARATION

The secret to this mystery depends on the use of a certain type of handkerchief. It must be the kind which has a *wide hem* around the sides. This enables you to secretly conceal a duplicate match inside the hem. The audience is never aware of the duplicate match. NOTE: *Toothpicks* may also be used quite effectively in this trick instead of matches.

(A) To prepare, carefully insert the match into the open end of the hem of the handkerchief. Push it just far enough inside so that it is completely hidden from view. In the illustrations, the corners of the handkerchief have been labeled A, B, C, and D with the match inside the hem at Corner A. Fold the handkerchief and place it in your pocket and have a box of duplicate matches handy for the presentation.

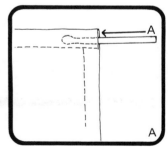

METHOD

(1) Display the box of matches and open it, requesting that a spectator select one match to use in the trick. This done, remove your handkerchief (with the secret match hidden in the hem) and spread it on the table in front of you. Place the handkerchief so that the hidden match is in the *lower right-hand corner* (A) nearest you. Now, take the match from the spectator and place it in the center of the handkerchief as shown. Note that both matches are running parallel to one another at the start.

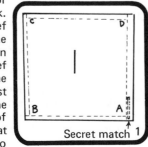

Secret match   1

(2) Now, fold Corner A up and over the center of the handkerchief placing the secret match by the selected match. Notice that the *selected* match and the *secret* match are now perpendicular to each other. This way, it will be easy for you to distinguish which match is which *without having to see them.* Now you can rely upon your sense of touch to tell them apart.

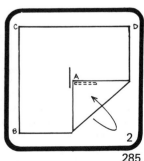

2

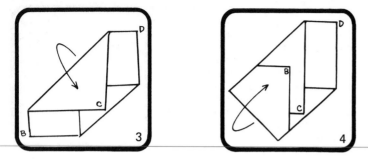

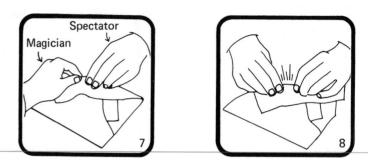

(3)   Next, fold the top left Corner C over the selected match and over Corner A as shown.   (4)   Then fold Corner B over Corners A and C as in the illustration.

(7)   Now, hand the match to the spectator and (8) instruct him to break it several times through the fabric of the handkerchief. *He believes he is breaking the same match which he just selected and watched you fold inside the handkerchief.*

(9)   When the spectator is quite satisfied that the match has been completely destroyed, slowly and deliberately unfold each corner of the handkerchief one at a time.

(5)   Finally, bring Corner D over Corners A, B, and C as shown.
(6)   Now, openly and deliberately grasp the *secret match* through the folds of the handkerchief and hold it between the thumb and fingers of both hands. You can be sure to grasp the secret match easily by simply "feeling" for the match that runs parallel to the edge of the table nearest you. *NOTE: The selected match remains within the handkerchief.*

(10)   As you unfold Corner C with your left hand, keep your right hand over Corner A to conceal any possible bulge or disconfiguration of the hem, due to the broken shape of the secret match. When you have completely opened the handkerchief, the audience will be amazed to see that the broken match is now completely restored.

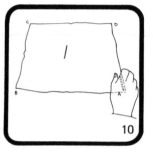

(11)   Immediately give the match to the spectator for examination. Hold up the handkerchief, shake it, and show it on both sides so that all can see that it is completely empty before you casually replace it in your pocket.

EGGS FROM NOWHERE

EFFECT

The magician calls attention to a woven basket and a folded handkerchief resting on his table. Picking up the handkerchief, he unfolds it and shows it to be quite ordinary by displaying both sides. Folding the handkerchief in half to form a sort of "pocket," the magician causes an egg to make its magical appearance inside and "allows" it to fall from within the folds of the handkerchief into the basket. Repeating the same procedure, *another* egg appears and is dropped into the basket. This production continues, egg after egg, until the audience is sure that the basket is *nearly full*. Setting the handkerchief aside, the magician removes one of the eggs from the basket and breaks it into a glass to prove that it is genuine. Then, picking up the basket, the magician throws the contents into the air *directly over the audience*. To their surprise — and relief — the eggs have magically transformed into a SHOWER OF CONFETTI!

SECRET AND PREPARATION

(A) The items necessary for this effect are an opaque handkerchief (a bandana is ideal), a medium-sized basket, a gentleman's hat or a similar sized box, and a plastic egg. This type of egg can be purchased from a novelty or "dime" store and is especially easy to find during the Easter season. The basket, hat, or box should be opaque, so that the spectators cannot see through, and deep enough to conceal a quantity of confetti and one *real* egg. You will also need some confetti (or just tear some paper into small pieces), a glass, and some fine sewing thread *which closely matches the color of the handkerchief.*

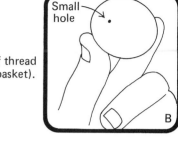

(B) To prepare, drill a small hole in one end of the hollow plastic egg as shown. Also cut a piece of thread about 12" long (the length of the thread will depend upon the size of the handkerchief and the basket).

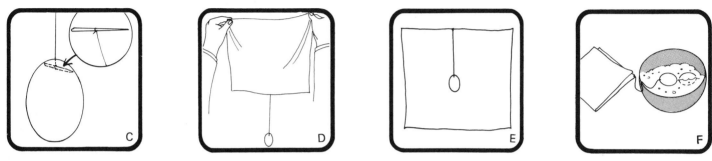

(C) Tie a short piece of toothpick to one end fo the thread. Push the toothpick through the hole in the egg, and the thread will be secured to the egg as shown. (You can also use transparent tape to secure the thread to the egg.) (D) Now, sew the other end of the thread to the *middle* of the hem of the handkerchief as shown. (E) As shown here, the length of the thread should be long enough to allow the egg to hang just below the center of the handkerchief. (F) Fold the handkerchief and place it on the table next to the basket. The thread should run *from* the handkerchief *into* the basket with the egg lying in the basket as shown. The basket should also contain a quantity of confetti and one real egg. *(NOTE: The real egg should be down in the confetti to protect it from the plastic egg when it falls into the basket.)*

METHOD

(1) To begin the presentation, pick up the handkerchief by the lower two corners (C and D) and display it on both sides as shown. The egg remains concealed in the basket.

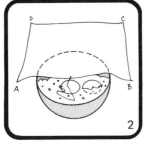

(2) Now lay the handkerchief partially over the basket with the top hem (the hem with the attached thread) draped across the opening of the basket. The center of this hem, where the thread is attached, should be *directly above* the plastic egg in the basket.

(3) Show your hands empty and grasp the handkerchief at Corners A and B as shown.

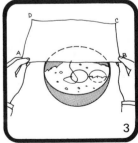

(4) Keep the top hem *stretched tightly between both hands* as you lift the handkerchief upward, away from the table and the basket. The thread will secretly draw the plastic egg *out* of the basket *behind* the handkerchief as shown. Keep the handkerchief stretched tightly so that you do not allow the weight of the egg to pull down the top hem of the handkerchief.

(5) Now, place the top corners (A and B) together in your left hand, hiding the plastic egg completely within the folds of the handkerchief. Hold both corners (A and B) with your left hand as you . . .

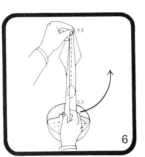

(6) . . . reach down with your right hand and grasp the two lower corners (C and D). (Be sure you have folded the handkerchief *around* the hanging egg.)

(7) Then swing those corners (C and D) upward — to your right — as shown.

(8) The folded handkerchief should now be broadside to the audience. Raise the right hand corners (C and D) slightly upward and gently shake the egg out of the handkerchief. The egg should fall into the basket and land safely on the confetti. YOU HAVE JUST "MAGICALLY" PRODUCED AN EGG FROM AN EMPTY HANDKERCHIEF!

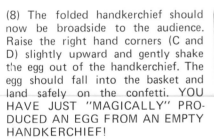

(9) After the egg lands in the basket, toss the right hand corners (C and D) of the folded handkerchief on the table in front of the bowl leaving the two top corners (A and B) in your left hand.

(10) Now, grasp the right Corner B in your right hand while continuing to hold the other Corner A in your left and draw your two hands apart as shown. *Be sure the entire bottom edge of the handkerchief (C and D) is resting in front of the bowl as you stretch the handkerchief open.*

(11) As you draw your hands apart, raise the top corners (A and B), *again secretly drawing the plastic egg out of the basket behind the handkerchief,* ready to make its magical reappearance.

(12) Repeat Steps 5 through 7 to fold the egg inside the handkerchief as you did the first time. Tilt the handkerchief, and a "second" egg (really the same egg) falls out.

(13) Follow the sequences as described from Step 9 through Step 12 for each egg you want to "produce." When you wish to conclude the production portion of the trick, repeat the procedure only through Step 11. At this point simply gather the handkerchief and place it aside, *with the plastic egg concealed inside its folds.*

(14) Now, remove the *real egg* from the basket and display it as you pick up the glass in your other hand. Then, deliberately break the egg in the glass, proving it to be genuine.

(15) For a conclusion, pick up the basket from your table and carry it toward the audience. They believe it is full of *real eggs.* Suddenly, toss the contents of the basket into the air above the audience *showering them with confetti!* If you have followed all of the steps correctly and practiced the trick well before you present it, you will now have a very surprised and very bewildered audience.

THE VANISHING GLASS

EFFECT

The magician openly exhibits an ordinary drinking glass. Covering the glass with a handkerchief, the performer lifts the glass into the air. The audience can plainly see that the glass is under the handkerchief. Suddenly, the magician throws the bundle high above his head. Instantly, the glass *vanishes* . . . allowing the empty handkerchief to flutter into the magician's hands.

SECRET AND PREPARATION

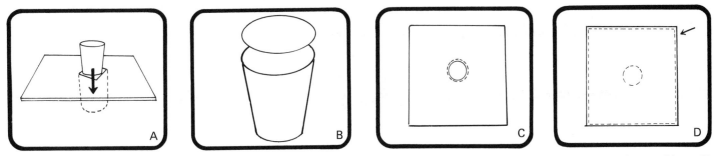

(A)   To present this effect, you must have a magician's table with a "well," like the one described elsewhere in the Course. You will also need an ordinary drinking glass. The glass must fit comfortably into the "well" in your table.

(B)   Cut a disc of plastic or cardboard just slightly larger than the mouth of the glass.

(C)   You will also need two matching handkerchiefs. (If possible, the handkerchiefs should have some kind of pattern or design on them.) Sew the disc to the center of one of the handkerchiefs.

(D)   Now cover the handkerchief and its attached disc with the duplicate handkerchief. Carefully sew the two handkerchiefs together around the edges with the disc sandwiched in between. Put the glass on your table with the folded handkerchief next to it and you are ready to perform.

METHOD

(1)   Pick up the glass and display it. Put the glass back on your table just in front of the "well." Now pick up the handkerchief. Snap it open so that the audience can see that it is apparently unprepared. Hold the handkerchief with the thumb and first fingers of each hand and position it behind the glass as shown.

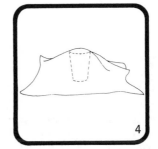

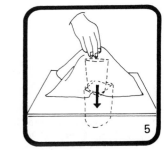

(4)   With the glass completely covered and the disc over the mouth of the glass, grasp the disc *and* the glass through the fabric of the handkerchief. *Without lifting the glass, slide it backward until it is directly over the "well" in your table.*   (5)   Now, while still holding onto the disc, LET THE GLASS SLIDE INTO THE WELL. *The disc will maintain the shape of the glass under the handkerchief.*

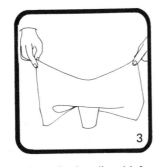

(2)   The next move is critical. As you place the handkerchief over the glass,   (3)   . . .be sure that the hidden disc *goes over the mouth of the glass.*

(6) Lift the handkerchief clear of the table and walk forward. The disc should be held lightly with your thumb and fingers *so that it appears that the glass is still under the handkerchief.*

(7) Throw the handkerchief high into the air. The effect upon an audience is that the glass *vanishes* into thin air. Crumple the handkerchief and drop it on your table.

COMMENTS AND SUGGESTIONS

Apparently having an object under a handkerchief or cloth after it has actually "gone" is an important basic principle of magic. This effect is a classic example of the use of this principle. The "secret disc" concealed in the handkerchief leads the audience to believe that the glass is still there long after it has gone. This subtle method will be of great value to you in the performance of many effects. There is even an "impromptu" version of the Vanishing Glass, which is described in the following.

THE VANISHING GLASS — IMPROMPTU VERSION

EFFECT

While seated at a table, the magician covers an empty glass with his pocket handkerchief. He raises the covered glass from the table and then throws the handkerchief in the air . . . *the glass has vanished.* The magician reaches under the table, directly below the spot where the handkerchief landed, and reproduces the glass. The glass has apparently penetrated the table!

SECRET AND PREPARATION

You will need the same special handkerchief with the disc sewn in it as described in The Vanishing Glass. You will also need a glass with the mouth approximately the same size as the disc. The effect is even better when this trick is performed in an impromptu manner . . . using an empty glass that is already on the table . . . for instance, after dinner or when you are seated with friends at a party.

METHOD

(1) The presentation of this effect is exactly the same as in Steps 1 to 4 of the VANISHING GLASS except, instead of dropping the glass into the well on your table, you merely move the handkerchief back past the edge of the table and drop the glass into your lap!

(2) This can be done quite effectively in the following manner. Cover the glass with the handkerchief, being sure that the disc is properly positioned over the mouth of the glass. Pick the glass and the handkerchief up in your right hand as shown.

(3) Now, as you hold the glass and handkerchief with your right hand, hold your left hand up, palm towards the spectators. Say, "As you can see, there is nothing in my left hand."

(4) *As you show your left hand, move the handkerchief and the glass back over the edge of the table so that the edge of the handkerchief is still touching the top of the table. As you display your empty left hand, DROP THE GLASS INTO YOUR LAP.*

(5) Holding the "secret" disc by the edges in your right hand, move the now "empty" handkerchief (as if it still covered the glass) back over the table.

(6) Say, "And, there is nothing under the handkerchief!" As you say this, at the same time, throw the handkerchief up into the air. Catch it as it comes down and show the handkerchief on both sides. Then drop it onto the table in front of you.

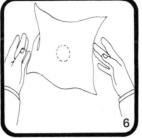

(7) Show both hands empty and reach under the table. As you do, say, "The reason that you don't see the glass any more is because it has gone right through the table . . . like this." As your hands go under the table, with your right hand pick up the glass from your lap and carry it under the table to a spot directly beneath the crumpled handkerchief. With a "pulling motion" apparently "extract" the glass from the table. Bring the glass out and set it on the table and put the handkerchief back in your pocket.

IMPROMPTU MAGIC

★ ★ ★

Here are some "quick tricks" that you can do anywhere at any time. Some are puzzles rather than tricks, others are more in the nature of stunts, but the majority are quite deceptive and all will arouse interest among people who see them. In fact, that is the great purpose of this branch of magic, for once you have gained people's interest with something trivial and find that they want to see more, you can go into your regular routine with confidence, since you know you already have a receptive audience.

Certain of these impromptu tricks are sometimes termed "ice-breakers" because when people seem cold or aloof, particularly at a party where very few know one another, they will often "thaw" quite rapidly when you show them a few bafflers. Also, some of these tricks, particularly the puzzle type, are expendable, in the sense that as a part of the presentation, you can explain them to your audience and they can use them to "puzzle" their friends as well.

This is quite important when you are doing magic for your friends, as they are very apt to ask you how some tricks are done and at times, you may find it difficult to refuse them. So, to keep from reaching the point where you have to choose between losing a good trick or a good friend, you can come up with one of these "quickies" to divert attention from something more important.

At the same time, as always, never explain any of the real "magic" bafflers. Keep these impromptu effects for yourself—because, as you advance in magic, you will find that some of the keenest spectators, when describing later what you did are apt to magnify trifling perplexities into near-miracles. When that happens, it is up to you, as a magician, to turn it to your own advantage.

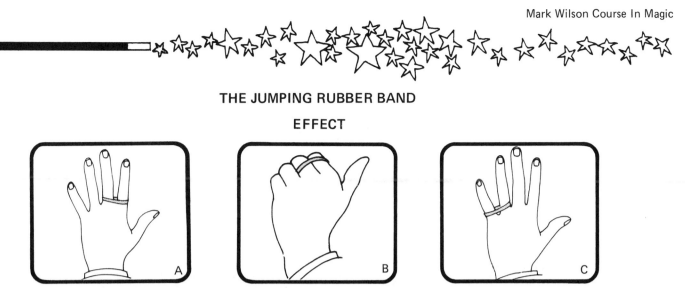

THE JUMPING RUBBER BAND

EFFECT

(A) The magician places a rubber band around his first and second fingers. (B) He closes his hand into a fist. (C) When he opens his hand, the band "magically" jumps to his third and fourth fingers. (A, B, and C show the spectator's viewpoint. In all the illustrations the magician's fingers are pointing "up.")

METHOD

(All illustrations are as the magician sees the trick.)

(1) Place the rubber band around the base of your first and second fingers on your left hand. If the band is too loose, you may put it around twice. Experiment with whatever rubber band you're using, so that you get the proper tension on the band. Your hand is toward the audience — and your palm faces you.

(2) Close your left hand into a fist by bending your fingers into your palm. At the same time, secretly use the first finger of your right hand to stretch the rubber band so that the tips of all four left fingers can be inserted into the rubber band.

(3) This is how your hand now looks to you. (To the audience, your hand will appear as in (B).)

(4) Now straighten out your fingers and the band will automatically jump to a new position around your left third and fourth fingers.

REVERSE JUMPING RUBBER BAND

EFFECT

The magician makes the rubber band jump *back* from his third and fourth fingers to his first and second fingers.

METHOD

(1) Simply reverse the procedure used for the first jump.

(4) Then, when you close your left hand, secretly insert the tips of all four left fingers as you did before.

(2) After the band has "jumped" to your third and fourth fingers, fold your hand into a fist again. As you do, use the first finger of your right hand to stretch the rubber band.

(5) When you straighten out your fingers, the band will jump *back* to your first and second fingers.

(3) Another way is to use your left thumb to stretch the band.

THE DOUBLE JUMPING RUBBER BAND
VERSION I

EFFECT

You can double the mystery of this trick by magically making two rubber bands change places.

METHOD

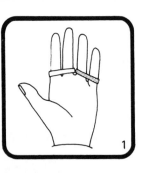

(1) Place *one* rubber band (a white one, for instance) around your left first and second fingers. Place a *second,* different colored rubber band (say a blue one) around your left third and fourth fingers.

(2) Before you close your hand into a fist, reach over with your left thumb and stretch the rubber band that is around the third and fourth fingers as shown.

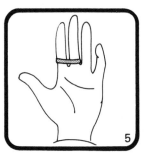

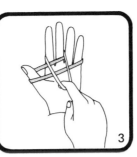

(3) Then, use your right first finger to pull the band that is around the first and second fingers of your left hand as shown.

(6) Call to the spectator's attention that the *white* band is around your first and second fingers, and the *blue* band is around your third and fourth fingers. To the audience, it looks like this.

(4) Now, secretly place the tips of all four fingers into BOTH rubber bands as you close your hand. The fingers of the left hand go into the opening indicated by the arrow.

(7) Now, just straighten out your fingers. THE BANDS WILL JUMP TO THE OPPOSITE FINGERS.

(5) At the same time that you insert the fingers of the left hand into the bands, release both the bands from your left thumb and from the first finger of the right hand. Your hand will look like this to you.

THE DOUBLE JUMPING RUBBER BAND
SECOND VERSION

EFFECT

The effect is the same as in the DOUBLE JUMPING RUBBER BAND described above; however, the "secret" method is slightly different.

METHOD

(1) Place the two rubber bands on your fingers as before.

(2) With the *first finger* of the right hand, secretly nip each of the bands.

(3) Then insert the *second finger* of the right hand into the loops formed by the right first finger and spread the loops open, using both right fingers.

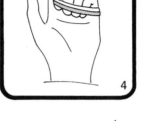

(5) Just straighten out your fingers in the usual way and the bands will change places.

(4) Fold your left hand into a fist and insert the tips of the left fingers into the opening formed by the right fingers. To you, your hand looks like this.

THE CHALLENGE JUMPING RUBBER BAND

EFFECT

This can be used as a follow-up for either the Regular or Double Jumping Rubber Bands. You explain that to make it *impossible* for the band to jump, you will encircle the tips of all of the fingers of your left hand individually with another rubber band.

METHOD

(1) Place an additional rubber band around the tips of the fingers of your left hand, as shown in the picture.

(2) Then proceed in exactly the same way as you did before: fold your hand into a fist, inserting the tips of the fingers into the band which is to jump. Straighten out your fingers, and behold — another minor miracle — the band jumped just as before!

The adding of the extra band to "lock in" the jumper is a clever touch which makes a simple trick into a very strong effect.

LINKING PAPER CLIPS

This is a most entertaining combination magic trick and puzzle. After you perform it, everyone will want to try it . . . and if someone should figure it out, don't worry — they'll have as much fun with it as you.

EFFECT

You show two paper clips and a dollar bill. Then you give the bill a three-way fold and use the clips to fasten the folds in place. As you pull the ends of the pleated bill, slowly but steadily the clips come closer together. You finish the pull with a sharp snap as the clips fly from the bill and land on the table . . . *linked together!*

METHOD

The trick is almost automatic. It depends entirely upon proper placement of the clips. Practice the setup until you can place the clips in position quickly and neatly, so observers will be unable to follow, and therefore find it difficult to duplicate the trick.

(1) Start by holding the bill open between both hands.

(6) Fold the left end of the bill over to the right as shown in the illustration.

(2) Fold one-third of the length of the bill over to the right as shown.

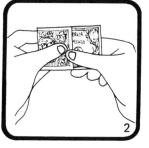

(7) Put the other paper clip on the bill from the top, thus holding this end in place, too. Clip together *just the two front folds*—those that are *toward you.*

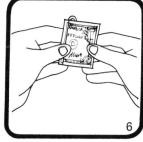

(3) Place one of the paper clips over this fold to hold it in place, and push it down so it is snug against the top edge of the bill.

(8) Again, the clip should be positioned near the end of the bill over its number value, as shown here.

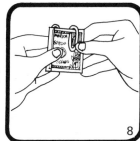

(4) The clip should be positioned near the end of the folded portion of the bill directly over the number that shows its value.

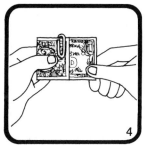

(9) *NOTE: If both clips have been properly placed the bill should look as shown in this view.*

(5) Now turn the bill completely *around* so you are looking at the other side. *Do not* turn the bill "upside down" in the process . . . the clip should still be at the top as shown.

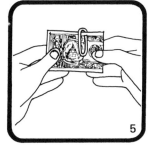

(10) Now firmly grip both ends of the bill near the top and start to pull them apart. As the bill unfolds, the clips will start moving together still pinned to the bill.

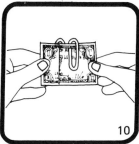

(11) When you reach the point where the clips are practically on top of each other, give the ends of the bill a sharp tug.

(12) The bill will open out and send the paper clips sailing across the table, linking them as they go!

COMMENTS AND SUGGESTIONS

The trick is particularly effective with "jumbo" clips, which are longer and wider so the linking can be followed easily. With ordinary paper clips, only a slight tug is needed; otherwise they may fly clear across the table as they link — and if they go off the edge, the effect will be weakened.

With practice, placing the clips in position becomes a simple and rapid process. If using small clips, you can put two on the top edge and another pair on the bottom edge. The tug will shoot them in opposite directions and each pair will be found linked.

LINKING PAPER CLIPS WITH RUBBER BAND

EFFECT

Here is a clever addition to the LINKING PAPER CLIP where the two clips mysteriously link themselves — but also link to a rubber band which was previously looped around the bill. This little twist not only takes the effect one step further, but also creates a very puzzling finish for the Linking Paper Clips.

METHOD

(1) Follow Steps 1 through 4 as already described in the Linking Paper Clips placing the first clip over the folded portion of the bill as shown.

(3) Fold back the right end of the bill and attach the second paper clip as you did in the original routine. If both clips and the rubber band have been properly placed, the bill should look like this.

(2) Now, loop a rubber band of the size shown around the *right end of the bill*. The rubber band should be slightly longer than the width of the bill so that a portion of the band hangs below the bottom edge of the bill.

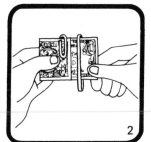

(4) Now, firmly grip both ends of the bill and pull them apart. The rubber band will remain looped around the bill with the paper clips linked to it in a chain as shown.

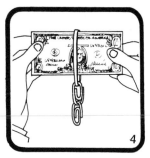

COMMENTS AND SUGGESTIONS

It is a good idea to practice this a few times until you understand "why" it works as it does. Once you understand the working, concentrate on placing the paper clips and the rubber band in *exactly the same position* every time you perform the trick. You can then succeed in baffling your audience without fear of any "mistake" in the handling of the props.

BAG TAG ESCAPE

EFFECT

The performer displays a typical paper tag and gives it to the nearest spectator to examine. A second spectator is given a length of string to examine. The tag and the string prove to be normal in every respect. The magician then proceeds to thread the string through the small hole in the tag. He then gives one end of the string to each spectator to hold. With the tag hanging in the center of the string, the magician covers the string and the tag with his pocket handkerchief. Reaching beneath the handkerchief, the performer "magically" removes the tag from the center of the string *without damage to either!* The spectators are left holding the now empty string suspended between them with no explanation for the mystery they have just witnessed.

SECRET AND PREPARATION

(A)   For this trick you will need to construct some small tags from cardboard. (Filing card stock is best.) The tags should be cut so that they measure approximately 3" x 1½" in size. Shape the tags by cutting off the two top corners at a 45-degree angle and then punch a hole in the center of the top edge of each of the tags as shown. The result will be a tag which closely resembles a standard baggage tag in every respect *except one.* Most standard tags are <u>heavily reinforced</u> around the small hole so that they will not tear when fastened to some object. This slight difference is what makes the entire effect possible. You will also need a piece of string about two feet long which you place on the table along with *one* of the tags. Place an ordinary handkerchief in your left pocket and a *duplicate tag* in your <u>right coat sleeve</u> so that it is out of view of the audience.

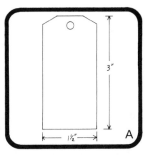

METHOD

(1)   To begin the presentation, ask for the assistance of two spectators. Hand one of the spectators the tag for examination and the other spectator the length of string. When they are satisfied that everything is unprepared, thread the string through the small hole at the top of the tag as shown in the illustration.

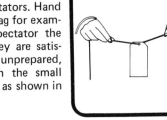

(4)   Carefully TEAR THROUGH THE TAG to the hole. Then remove the torn tag from the string.

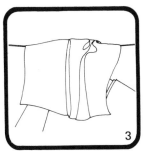

(2)   Now, give one end of the string to each spectator, leaving the suspended tag imprisoned on the string.

(5)   *NOTE: You may find it helpful to raise both hands slightly upward, thus lifting the handkerchief away from the tag. This will prevent the spectators from "seeing" the motion of what is actually taking place.*

(3)   Remove your handkerchief from your pocket, show it to be completely empty, and cover the tag *and* the center of the string as shown. Be sure the handkerchief is spread open enough to provide the "cover" necessary to conceal your hands beneath it. This done, reach under the handkerchief with both hands and grasp the tag near the hole at the top.

(6)   With the fingers of your right hand, secretly insert the <u>torn</u> tag *into your left coat sleeve.*

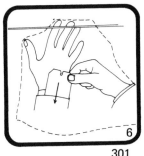

(7) Now exchange hand positions so that your left hand can withdraw the <u>duplicate</u> tag from your right sleeve as shown.

(8) NOW FOR THE STARTLING CLIMAX. Bring both hands into view along with the <u>duplicate</u> tag. Ask the spectators to look beneath the handkerchief to see if you actually removed the tag from the string as it appears. You may then offer the tag, the string, and the handkerchief for examination.

LIFESAVERS* ON THE LOOSE!

EFFECT

The magician displays an ordinary shoelace and hands it to a spectator for examination. Reaching into his pocket, the performer removes a new package of Lifesavers candy mints and gives it to another spectator to open. A number of the Lifesavers are then threaded onto the shoelace, and the ends of the lace are handed to two spectators to hold. Removing the handkerchief from his pocket, the magician covers the Lifesavers dangling in the middle of the lace, concealing them from view. Reaching under the handkerchief, the performer magically removes the imprisoned Lifesavers, leaving the now empty shoelace suspended between the two volunteers.

METHOD

(1) The only items required for this effect are an ordinary shoelace or a length of string and a package of Lifesavers or some similar candy with a hole in the center. To begin the presentation, hand the shoelace for examination as you introduce the package of Lifesavers and give them to another spectator to open.

(4) Now give both ends of the shoelace to a spectator to hold between his hands; *or,* give *one* end of the lace to one spectator and the *other* end to another spectator to hold. Either way, have the spectator(s) hold the ends far apart to allow enough space to drape your handkerchief over the suspended Lifesavers.

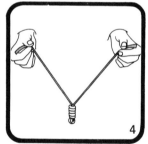

(2) Now pick up *one* of the Lifesavers and thread it on the shoelace as shown.

(5) Remove your handkerchief and cover the Lifesavers as shown. Be sure to spread open the handkerchief along the shoelace to provide enough "cover" for your hands when you place them underneath.

(3) With the candy suspended from the center of the lace, thread the remaining Lifesavers on the shoelace by running *both ends* of the lace through the holes in the candy as shown.

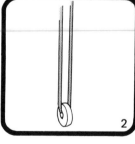

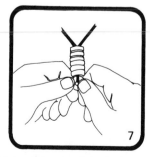

(6) Reach under the handkerchief with both hands and, (7) as soon as they are out of view, grasp the bottom Lifesaver between both hands and <u>break it</u> in half as shown.

(8) *NOTE: Try not to break it into little pieces as these can be difficult to conceal in your hand and may also fall to the floor during the presentation and spoil the trick.*

(10) Now, with your right hand (still concealing the broken pieces), lift the handkerchief away from the shoelace revealing the loose Lifesavers* in your left hand.

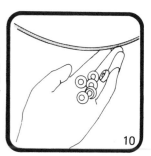

(9) Hold the broken pieces so that they are concealed in your curled right fingers. Allow the loose candy to slide from the shoelace into your left hand.

(11) Now, place the handkerchief back into your pocket *along with the broken pieces* and the mystery is complete.

COMMENTS AND SUGGESTIONS

This is truly an ideal "impromptu" mystery. All of the items are ordinary and easily obtainable. Just be sure to thread enough Lifesavers on the string, and no one will miss the broken one — which is the real secret of this clever mystery.

CORDS OF FANTASIA

EFFECT

The magician borrows two finger rings from members of the audience. Handing one of the spectators a pencil, the performer then displays two shoelaces. These laces are securely tied around the pencil. Both rings are threaded onto the shoelaces and held in place with an overhand knot. Under these conditions, even with the spectator holding onto the ends of the laces, the magician causes the rings to magically "melt" through the cords, leaving the rings, pencil and laces intact!

SECRET AND PREPARATION

All you require are a pencil, a pair of shoelaces and the two finger rings. All of the "props" are quite unprepared, and this clever effect can be presented "impromptu" at any time and any place that these common items can be obtained.

METHOD

(1) First, borrow two finger rings from members of the audience. Then have a spectator hold the pencil by the ends, between his hands. Now drape the two shoelaces over the pencil as illustrated. From this point on, we will refer to these as Lace A and Lace B.

(2) While the spectator holds the pencil, grasp both strands of Lace A in your left hand and both strands of Lace B in your right. Now tie a *single overhand knot* as shown.

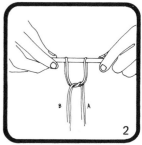

*® Lifesavers is a registered trademark of Lifesavers, Inc.

(3) Pull the knot up tight and ask the spectator to release his grip on the pencil. Turn the laces so that they are now parallel to the floor and the pencil is held by the laces in an upright position. Pull the laces tight on the pencil so that the pencil does not slide out. Now, hand the ends of the laces to the spectator.

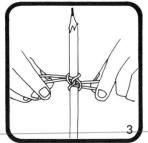

(8) With your right hand <u>firmly holding onto the knot</u>, with your left hand, pull the pencil out of the laces.

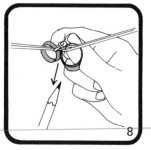

(4) Call attention to the two borrowed finger rings and thread them onto the laces. Thread one ring on each side of the pencil as shown. To do this, be sure to put *both* strands of Lace A through one ring and *both* strands of Lace B through the other.

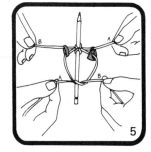

(9) Now thread the pencil *through* the rings. *NOTE: The right hand, which still holds the knot firmly, has been eliminated from this illustration for clarity.*

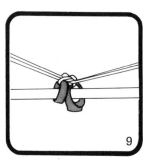

(5) You are now about to tie the rings in place. To do this, take *one* of the B ends and *one* of the A ends. *Then tie those ends in a <u>single overhand knot</u>* as shown. You will notice that when you tie this knot, you are *crossing* an A end with a B end. It makes no difference which of the two A ends or which of the two B ends you have chosen to tie. *Just be sure that you end up with one A end and one B end <u>paired on each side of the pencil</u>* as shown.

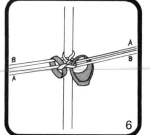

(10) Ask the spectator to pull on the ends of the laces. *At the same time,* <u>release</u> your grip on the knot held by your right hand. The illusion is perfect The rings seem to "melt" *right through the laces!*

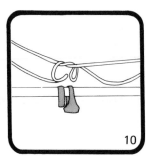

(6) Pull this new knot up tight. The rings will be jammed against the pencil. Now hand the ends back to the spectator so that he is now holding the entire affair as shown.

(11) The spectator is left holding only the two laces — the rings are on the pencil. Immediately allow the spectators to examine everything and return the rings to their owners with your thanks.

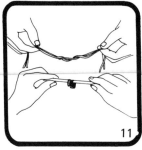

(7) Now with your right hand, *grasp the knot on the pencil as shown.* With your left hand, hold the pencil near the bottom and prepare to slip it free of the knot.

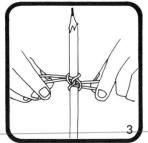

THE SUCKER TORN AND RESTORED NAPKIN

EFFECT

The magician announces that he is going to "teach" the audience how to perform a trick as he displays two paper napkins. One napkin he crumples into a ball and shows how he secretly "palms" it in his left hand. He explains that this is a "secret" napkin which no one in the audience is supposed to know about. The performer then tears the other napkin into a number of pieces. NOW FOR THE SECRET. The magician demonstrates exactly how he cleverly *switches* the torn napkin for the secret napkin. He even opens up the "secret" napkin to show how the torn pieces have supposedly been restored. The spectators, believing that they know how the trick is done, are warned by the magician that, if they should ever perform the trick, never to let anyone see the torn pieces in their hand. The performer explains that *if that should ever happen,* they would need to restore those pieces by "magic." With that, the magician opens the torn pieces revealing that *they too have been restored into a whole napkin!* It is then that the audience realizes *they have been taken in by the magician all along.*

SECRET AND PREPARATION

(A) To perform this highly entertaining effect, you will need three identical paper napkins. In this illusion, the napkins are numbered 1, 2, and 3. To prepare, spread open two of the napkins (1 and 2) and place one napkin (2) on top of the other napkin (1). Now, crumple the third napkin (3) into a ball and place it at the bottom center edge of the open napkins as shown.

(B) Starting at the top edge, roll the two open napkins down into a "tube" around the third napkin. This done, you are now ready to present the TORN AND RESTORED NAPKIN.

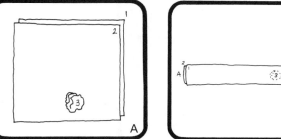

METHOD

(1) To begin, pick up the "tube" in your right hand near the center. Hold the tube so that End B is on top, and hold *the third napkin (3) through the other two napkins (1 and 2).* With your left hand, grasp the edges of the tube and start to unroll the open napkins (1 and 2) with your right hand. You should be able to feel the third napkin (3) inside as you unroll the tube. When the napkins are completely opened, secretly roll the inner crumpled napkin (3) into your right fingers so that it is hidden from the spectators.

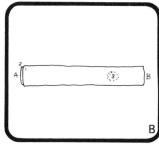

(4) Now, explain that the trick begins when the magician tears the whole napkin (2) into a number of pieces — which you proceed to do. Then, roll these torn pieces into a *small* ball.

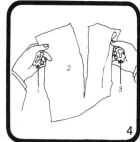

(2) Separate the two open napkins, taking one napkin (1) in your left hand and the other napkin (2) in your right. Announce to the audience that you are going to "teach them how to perform a trick."

(5) Here's how your hands should look from your point of view. The napkin (2) between the tips of your thumbs and fingers is the torn one, the napkin (1) in your left hand is the "secret" napkin *which the audience knows about,* and the napkin (3) in your right hand is the one *only you know about.*

(3) Explain that one of the two napkins (1) is a "secret" napkin and must be concealed in the magician's left hand until the proper moment. As you say this, with your left hand, crumple the left-hand napkin (1) into a ball. Then hold it in the curled fingers of your left hand (the same as the third napkin (3) in your right hand *of which the audience is totally unaware*). Explain to the audience that this "secret" napkin must be secretly "palmed" in the magician's left hand at all times as he performs the trick.

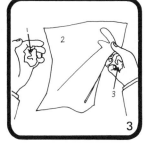

(6) As you are finishing, roll the torn pieces (2) into a ball and secretly add to them the whole napkin (3) in your right hand.

(7) You can now show *both napkins (2 and 3) together* as if they were *just the torn pieces.* As you display the supposedly torn pieces — really the torn pieces (2) and the third whole napkin (3) — turn your <u>right</u> hand so the audience can see that it is *quite empty.* THIS IS A VERY IMPORTANT PART OF THE TRICK. It convinces the audience that everything is "on the level" so that they will not suspect there is a *third* napkin.

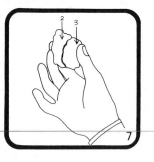

(8) Now, pretend to roll these "pieces" (Napkins 2 and 3) into a smaller ball. As you do, *secretly draw the torn pieces (2) downward behind your right fingers with your right thumb.* This leaves only the "whole" napkin (3) at the tips of your right fingers.

(9) Now, transfer *only* the "whole" ball (3) to the tips of your left fingers *as if it were the torn pieces.*

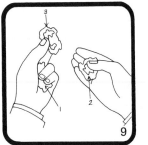

(10) *NOTE: The spectators think that you have merely placed the torn pieces — which they just saw you crumple into a ball — into your left fingers. Here is the <u>audience view</u> of this action.*

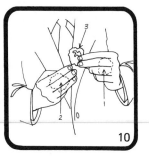

(11) Explain that when they (the spectators) perform the trick for their friends, they should have a coin in their right pocket to use as a sort of "magic wand." With your right hand reach into your right pocket and bring out the coin. When you do, LEAVE THE TORN PIECES (2) IN YOUR POCKET.

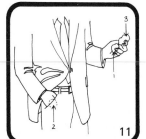

(12) *NOTE: The audience will not suspect anything because you have offered a <u>logical reason</u> for placing your hand in your pocket. This is a very important lesson to be learned by all magicians. <u>There must be a reason for every move you make.</u> Otherwise, you will arouse suspicion and, more than likely, spoil the entire effect.*

(13) At this point, the audience still believes that the torn pieces are held at the tips of your left fingers and the "secret" whole napkin is hidden in the curled fingers of the same hand. *Actually,* both of these napkins (1 and 3) are <u>whole.</u>

(14) Tell the spectators that the <u>real</u> reason for getting the coin is to direct the audience's attention <u>away</u> from the magician's left hand *so he can execute the "switch."* Explain that when your right hand reaches into your pocket, the spectators' eyes follow it, leaving your *left hand free to do the "dirty work."*

(15) Openly demonstrate this "dirty work" (the "switch") in the following manner: Slowly draw your left thumb and fingers down into your left hand (16) bringing the supposedly "torn pieces" (3) along.

(17) Now, move your thumb over to the "secret" napkin (1).
(18) Then, with the aid of your third and little fingers, raise this napkin (1) up to the tips of the fingers. Execute this series of moves slowly and deliberately *with the palm of your left hand toward the audience* to show them exactly how the "switch" is made.

(19) Explain to the audience that *at exactly the same time* the "switch" is being made in the left hand, the magician removes the coin from his pocket with his right hand. Then wave the coin over the napkin(s) and replace it in your pocket.

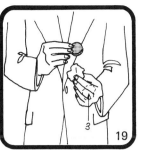

(21) Caution the spectators that they must always be very careful not to accidentally show the torn pieces concealed in their hand as they unfold the napkin — as that would be "very embarrassing." There is *one thing,* however, they can do to save themselves IF THAT SHOULD EVER HAPPEN.

(20) State that all that remains is to open the "secret" napkin and show it restored — as you do just that.

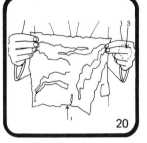

(22) The only thing a magician can do in that case is to *restore the torn pieces.* As you say this, open up the napkin (3) which the audience believes to be the torn pieces and *show it to be completely restored!* It is then that the spectators will realize *you have baffled them once again!*

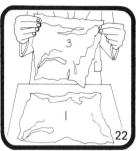

(23) Pick up both napkins (1 and 3) and hold one in each hand. Show both of your hands to be unmistakably empty as you toss the completely restored napkins to the audience.

RING ON WAND

EFFECT

The magician asks to borrow an ordinary finger ring from a member of the audience. For safe keeping, the ring is wrapped in a pocket handkerchief and given to another spectator to hold. The performer then displays an empty paper bag which he pierces on both sides with a pencil. The exposed ends of the pencil are then given to another volunteer to hold. This done, the performer asks the first spectator if he still feels the borrowed ring within the folds of the handkerchief. When the spectator replies, "Yes," the magician jerks the handkerchief from his hands only to find that the ring has vanished! The second spectator is instructed to hold the ends of the pencil tightly. The magician tears away the paper bag, *revealing the borrowed ring threaded on the pencil!* All of the props are handed for immediate examination as the ring is returned to its owner.

SECRET AND PREPARATION

The secret is in the use of a *second* finger ring and a previously prepared handkerchief. Purchase an average-sized, inexpensive ring. Avoid large costume jewelry. Also, you will need two identical pocket handkerchiefs. Prepare the handkerchiefs as described in THE SUPER DOOPER VERSATILE VANISHER. This "special" handkerchief can be shown as apparently unprepared, yet it actually contains the second finger ring in the secret pocket. Place the handkerchief in your top pocket or on your table along with a small ("lunch" size) paper bag and a pencil.

METHOD

(1) From a member of the audience, borrow a finger ring that most resembles the duplicate ring concealed in the secret pocket of the prepared handkerchief. Display the borrowed ring so that the audience can identify it later. Pick up the prepared handkerchief and spread it over the palm of your left hand. The concealed ring should be located in the right-hand corner, nearest you.

(2) Now, apparently wrap the borrowed ring within the handkerchief, as described in THE SUPER DOOPER VERSATILE VANISHER. Actually retain the *borrowed* ring in the Finger Palm position as you wrap the *duplicate* ring in the center of the handkerchief.

(3) Now, ask a spectator to grasp the (duplicate) ring through the folds of the handkerchief and hold it securely. The spectator believes he is holding the borrowed ring, so *do not* give the handkerchief to the owner of the ring as he might "feel" the ring and be able to tell that the ring inside is not his own.

(4) With the borrowed ring held secretly in your curled right fingers, place your right fingers (and the ring) inside the bag. Hold the open mouth of the bag toward the audience and show it to be empty and unprepared. *Be careful not to "flash" the borrowed ring as you handle the paper bag.*

(5) Now, pick up the pencil from the table as you continue to hold the bag at the top edge — fingers inside and thumb outside — *with the borrowed ring pressed against the inner wall of the bag by your right fingers.*

(6) Now pierce the point of the pencil through the side of the bag and *also through the ring inside.* The ring is now threaded on the pencil as shown. Without pausing, push the pencil on through the other side of the bag. *The ring is now secretly on the pencil — inside the bag.*

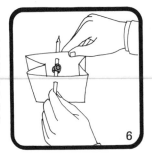

(7) *NOTE: The action of pushing the pencil through the bag (Step 6) should be executed quickly and smoothly so as not to alert the audience to any suspicious handling of the items.*

(8) Immediately remove your right hand and close the top of the bag. Then hand the whole affair to another spectator (the person you borrowed the ring from is best). Have him hold the pencil by the ends as shown.

(9) From this point on it is just a matter of presentation. Check with the spectator who is holding the handkerchief and ask him if he is still holding the ring. When he assures you that he is, take one corner of the handkerchief and snap it downward out of his grasp. To the audience the effect will be that the ring has apparently vanished from between the spectator's fingertips!

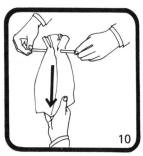

(10) Quickly turn to the other spectator. Grasp the bottom of the paper bag firmly in your right hand and give it a sharp downward pull, tearing the bag away from the pencil.

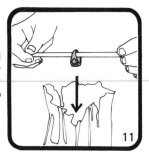

(11) The missing ring will be spinning on the pencil which the second spectator has been holding at both ends *even before the ring ever vanished* (or so they think)!

(12) Replace the handkerchief in your pocket as you ask the second spectator to return the borrowed ring to its lender. (Or have him verify that the ring on the pencil is his if he has been the "second" spectator.) The pencil, bag, and ring can then be examined by all.

THE JUMPING MATCH

EFFECT

The magician, during a casual encounter with a group of friends, announces that he has discovered a surefire method for checking his own pulse. After removing two ordinary wooden kitchen matches from his pocket, the performer places one across the palm of his left hand. He explains that his match will serve as the "counter." The second match is slipped under the first—for this demonstration it will serve as the "transmitter." As the spectators watch the counter, it is seen to bounce rhythmically as if counting out the heartbeats of the magician. Suddenly it stops, then beats erratically, creating a humorous finish to this puzzling feat. The spectators are handed the matches for examination and are challenged to try and duplicate the test. Of course, they can't, and the two matches will keep them busy for days in vain attempts to make the experiment work.

SECRET AND PREPARATION

Use large wooden kitchen matches for this effect. They are not prepared in any way and therefore can be borrowed. The secret to this experiment lies in your unseen manipulation of the "transmitter match."

METHOD

(1) Place the first or "counter" match across your left palm, as shown. Position the *end* of this match so that it is resting against the side of your first finger with the *head* of the match pointed toward you.

(2) The second or "transmitter" match is held between the thumb and first finger of your right hand. Your second finger *presses its nail against the back side of the match* as shown.

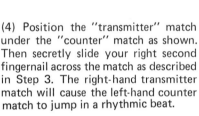

(3) If you now exert pressure against the match with the nail of the second finger, and slowly and imperceptively slide the match across the nail, the match will create the necessary unseen "pulses."

(4) Position the "transmitter" match under the "counter" match as shown. Then secretly slide your right second fingernail across the match as described in Step 3. The right-hand transmitter match will cause the left-hand counter match to jump in a rhythmic beat.

COMMENTS AND SUGGESTIONS

This fine pocket trick is completely impromptu, and can be very mystifying if done well. Large wooden kitchen matches are best since they show up better and make the "secret move" easier to perform. Remember that the counter match won't jump unless your right second fingernail is pressing firmly against its match when you slide it across.

Another patter theme for this effect is to explain that you have learned how to magically magnetize matches. Then rub the first (transmitter) match several times on your sleeve or the tablecloth. Sure enough, when you hold the "magnetized" first match up against the second (counter) match, it vibrates and shakes as if it really were impelled by some strange new power!

THE FLYING MATCH

EFFECT

The magician shows an ordinary book of paper matches. The book is opened and the matches, *all still attached to the book,* are counted for all to see. One match is removed from the book and the matchbook cover closed. The performer lights the match by striking it on the book and then blows the match out. He then makes the burnt match "vanish" as he throws it toward the matchbook. When the matchbook is opened by a spectator, *the burnt match is found inside, <u>attached</u> to the matchbook like the rest of the matches!* As an added convincer, the matches are counted and the number is found to be <u>the same as at the start of the effect.</u>

SECRET AND PREPARATION

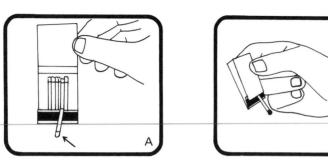

(A)   Before you perform this clever trick, you open the matchbook and bend one match in the first row "down" at the base as shown.
(B)   Now close the matchbook cover. The cover can't be tucked in because of the bent match, but don't worry about that yet. Take a *second* "lose" match, strike it, and set the head of the "bent" match on fire. Then quickly blow out both matches.   (C)   Now you must "hide" the burnt match that is still attached to the book. Place your left thumb on top of the matchbook so that it completely covers the bent match. The illustration shows how to conceal the match with your left thumb and hold the matchbook closed at the same time. With this "secret" preparation completed, you are now ready to perform.

METHOD

(1)   With the "bent" match concealed by your left thumb, open the cover of the matchbook with your right hand and ask a spectator to watch closely as you count the matches in the book. Be sure to keep the bent match hidden, and don't let the spectator take the matchbook from you as you count. Just hold the matchbook so that it's easy for the spectator to see the matches — then bend each match slightly forward with your right fingers as you count them.

(2)   *NOTE: It is best to have only 10 to 12 matches remaining in the book when you perform the trick. This gives fewer matches for you to count, and there is less chance for the spectator to see the "bent" match during the counting. Also, the smaller number of matches makes the reappearance of the burnt match even more startling.*

(3)   Now, with your right fingers, remove one match from the first row. This must be a match that is located *next to the hidden bent match*. Put this match on the table and close the matchbook cover.

(4)   As you close the cover, hold the book up in front of you so that the *back* of the book is toward the audience.

(5)   As your right fingers close the cover, your left thumb slips *under* the bent match and levers it upward *into the matchbook.*

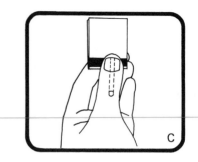

(6)   Immediately close the matchbook and tuck in the cover. The entire sequence takes but a few seconds and is hidden from the spectators, who see only the back of the matchbook.

(7)   Pick up the match you placed on the table (the one you just removed) and strike it on the matchbook. Let only the <u>head</u> of the match burn and then blow it out. Put the matchbook near the center of the table. *NOW FOR THE MAGIC!*

(8)   Pretend to pick up the match on the table with your right hand. Your right fingers really only *cover* the match and, as you slide your right hand back toward yourself . . .

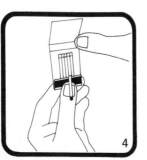

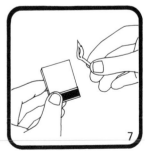

(9) ... the match is secretly swept *off the table* and falls into your lap.

(12) ... have *the spectator pick up the matchbook and open it.* Inside he will find what he thinks is the "original" match, now burnt and <u>firmly attached</u> with the rest of the matches to the matchbook.

(10) Hold up your right fingers *as if they contain the match.* Done correctly, the illusion of picking up the match is perfect.

(13) As a final convincer, *have the spectator count the matches.* He will find the number of matches to be the same as at the start of the trick!

(11) Apparently "throw" the burnt match (from your really empty hand) toward the closed matchbook. Show your right hand empty and ...

COMMENTS AND SUGGESTIONS

The vanish of the match, its reappearance in the matchbook, <u>and</u> the fact that the match is <u>burnt and attached to the matchbook</u> all add up to an outstanding close-up mystery.

DOTS MAGIC
(The Paddle Move)

After you become known as a magician, many times you will be asked to perform while you are seated at a table. The following effect teaches you a sleight (the Paddle Move) which is a magical "classic" that is ideal to be used under these very conditions.

EFFECT

The magician displays a clean table knife. After polishing both sides of the blade with his napkin, he attaches three red dots, one at a time, to the top surface of the blade. As he attaches each dot, three identical dots appear on the opposite side of the knife, one at a time, as if in sympathy with the first three dots. The magician hands the knife to a spectator seated near him and asks that he verify the existence of the duplicate set of dots. Upon retrieving the knife, the performer removes the top three dots from the blade and, magically, the bottom three dots vanish in sympathy. Suddenly all six dots reappear, three on each side of the knife blade. The magician now removes the dots one at a time from the top of the blade. As he removes each dot, the corresponding dot on the bottom vanishes in perfect synchronization. With the table knife now as clean as it was in the beginning, it is again handed to a spectator for examination.

SECRET AND PREPARATION

(A) The small circular "dots" needed for this effect are available at your local stationery store. They are "self-adhering" and come in several colors. Red has a high visibility and is therefore recommended for the trick, but any color will do. (If you wish, you can even cut dots out of gummed paper, but the "pressure sensitive" commercial dots can be much more easily attached and removed for this particular routine.) The dots selected should measure about ¼" in diameter.

(B) For practice purposes, prepare the table knife by placing three of the dots on one side of the blade as in Figure B. Then, turn the blade over so that the "blank" side is face up.

(C) NOTE: This next step is the classic *turn* entitled the "Paddle Move." After you have learned it, you will be able to show the <u>blank</u> side of the blade *twice* as you turn the knife over in your hand, *apparently showing <u>both</u> sides.* This will leave the spectators with the impression that they actually saw <u>both sides of the blade</u>. *This is the one <u>sleight</u> used in this entire routine. It is one of the most valuable principles in close-up magic.*

THE PADDLE MOVE

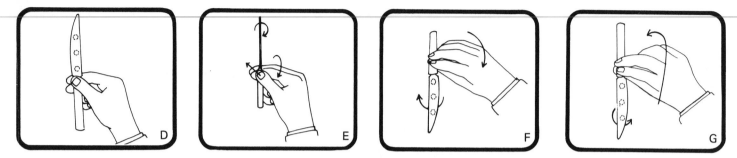

(D) To perform the Paddle Move, pick up the knife between the thumb and first two fingers of your right hand by the handle as shown. The blank side of the blade should be facing up. You will notice that the blade is facing away from you (pointing toward the spectators) and should be held at about waist level. You are about to turn the knife over so that the blade points toward you. In order to prevent the dots fastened on the bottom of the blade from being exposed, *you must simultaneously <u>revolve</u> the knife between your thumb and first two fingers as you turn the knife over.* (E) What happens is that your right thumb "rolls" the knife handle with your thumb and fingers *one-half turn to your left* (Illustrations E and F) . . . (F) . . . as you rotate the blade over so that it points <u>toward you</u> (Illustration F). (G) Then rotate the blade back toward the spectators. At the same time, execute Steps E and F *in reverse* and "roll" the knife back (to your right) with your thumb and fingers so that <u>the blank side is still up</u>. This is the Paddle Move. Practice in front of a mirror until you can execute the move smoothly. When properly done, the blade will appear to be blank on both sides. When you have mastered the Paddle Move, you will be ready to present this most clever and entertaining effect.

(H) Before the performance, place six of the dots in your wallet (or an envelope). After you are seated at the dinner table and have the opportunity, secretly attach three of the dots to the underside of the blade of your knife. You are now ready to perform a Minor Miracle.

The pictures describing the Paddle Move above as well as those in the Method which follows are from a point of view looking down on the magician's hand with the knife held horizontally over the surface of the table.

METHOD

(1) Stand up and display the knife to the spectators. By executing the "Paddle Move," show both sides of the blade to be empty. (Really, there are three dots on one side.) Now, wipe both sides of the blade, one at a time (really the same side twice, thanks to the Paddle Move), with your napkin to further create the illusion of a "clean" knife.

(3) Display the dot and execute the Paddle Move to apparently show the opposite side of the blade. To the audience it will appear that a duplicate dot has "magically appeared" on the other side of the blade.

(2) Remove the three remaining dots from your wallet and set them on the table. Now place one of these on the blank side of the blade directly in the center as shown.

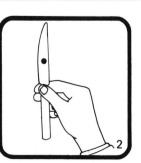

(4) Now return the knife to its original position and attach the second dot near the end of the blade as shown.

(5) Once again, execute the Paddle Move and apparently show the arrival of the second dot on the back of the blade.

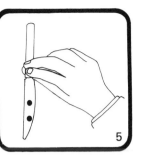

(10) Now, by executing the Paddle Move, you can show that the dots have not only magically returned, not only to the top of the blade, *but to the back as well.*

(6) Repeat Step 3 with the third and last dot again showing the knife on both sides. The spectators will now be convinced that the blade of your knife has three dots on both sides. At this point, *it actually does have three dots on both sides* because of the three "secret" dots you previously attached. You can now hand the knife to a spectator for examination.

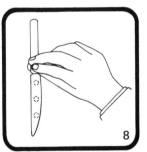

(11) *NOTE: At this point, you are set up for the sympathetic VANISH of the dots <u>one at a time</u> since the blade now has three red dots on the top surface only. Just repeat Steps 2 through 6 IN REVERSE.*

(7) As soon as the knife is returned to you, openly remove the three dots from the top of the blade and put them into your pocket.

(12) Begin by removing the center dot and executing the Paddle Move. It will appear as if the center dot vanished from the back of the knife as well.

(8) Execute the Paddle Move and show that the three dots on the back of the blade have sympathetically "vanished" as well.

(13) Now remove the dot closest to the handle and apparently show both sides as before. This will leave you with apparently one dot on the tip of both sides of the blade.

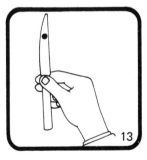

(9) Pick up your napkin and apparently wipe the blade clean. Under cover of this wiping action, turn the blade over. *The audience will be surprised to see that the three dots have reappeared on the knife!*

(14) Remove the last dot and slowly show both sides of the knife. The blade will be clean of spots and may now be handed to the spectator for examination.

COMMENTS AND SUGGESTION

As mentioned earlier, the Paddle Move is a classic sleight with many important uses in magic. Study the illustrations and practice the move until you can do it smoothly and almost without thinking. You will have learned an extremely valuable sleight that you will perform in many different effects as you progress through the wonderful world of Magic.

DOTS MAGIC — IMPROMPTU VERSION

DOTS MAGIC, as just described, can also be performed in a completely impromptu situation when you do not have the "commercial" dots with you.

EFFECT

The effect is the same as in DOTS MAGIC except that instead of dots, you cut or tear small squares of paper (a paper napkin works well) for use in the trick. The squares are attached to the knife by moistening them slightly using the tip of your finger to obtain a drop of water from your water glass and applying it to each square. The slightly dampened squares will now adhere to the blade of the knife.

SECRET AND PREPARATION

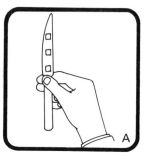

(A) If you have an opportunity to apply the three "secret" squares before the performance, you may utilize the same routine as described in DOTS MAGIC. If you do not have the time or opportunity to tear, moisten and apply the three extra squares, just start the routine from Step 10, using a total of three squares for the trick.

METHOD

(1) Openly attach the three squares to one side of the examined blade.

(2) Using the Paddle Move, you then show that three more identical squares have "magically" appeared on the opposite side of the blade.

(3) Now turn the blade over to show the spots to have vanished. Then use the Paddle Move to show the other side blank.

(4) After showing both sides of the blade blank (through the courtesy of the Paddle Move), the three squares reappear.

(5) Now proceed with Steps 12, 13, and 14, as the squares are openly removed from the top side of the blade and "sympathetically vanish" from the bottom side.

GLASS THROUGH THE TABLE

EFFECT

The magician states that he will cause a solid object to penetrate through the top of the table. With that, he places a coin on the table and covers it with a glass, mouth down. He then *covers the glass* with two paper napkins, which conceal both the glass and coin from view. The magician explains that, by mere concentration, he will cause the coin to "melt" through the top of the table. After several unsuccessful attempts, he explains that the reason for failure is that he forgot one of the most important parts of the experiment. He must first strike the top of the glass, giving the coin the momentum to penetrate the table. Suddenly, with a sharp downward motion of his hand, the performer smashes the glass and the napkins *flat on the table.* When the napkins are lifted, the coin is still there but THE GLASS IS GONE! Immediately, the magician reaches beneath the table and reproduces the same glass.

SECRET AND PREPARATION

The secret of this trick is based on a very clever principle. Due to the natural stiffness of the paper napkins, they will retain the form or shape of the glass *even if the glass is not within them.* This creates a very convincing illusion which makes this mystery possible. The glass should be smooth-sided so it slides easily from within the napkins. It should also be slightly smaller at the *base* than at the *mouth.* A glass which is approximately four or five inches tall works well. Also you need a coin (a half-dollar is a good size) and two ordinary paper napkins.

METHOD

(1) *You must be SEATED AT A CARD TABLE OR DINING TABLE to perform this close-up mystery.* Also, it is better if the spectators are also seated at the same table. With the glass, napkins, and coin lying on the table, tell the spectators that you will attempt to cause a solid object to pass through the top of the table.

(2) With that, place the coin directly in front of you, about 12 inches from the edge of the table. Then, cover the coin with the glass, *mouth downward.* Point out that the glass completely encloses the coin so that it is impossible for you to touch it.

(3) Next, open out both napkins, lay them on top of each other, and then over the glass as shown. Explain that the coin must be kept "in the dark" — so, you will cover the glass with the napkins.

(4) With both hands, pull the napkins downward around the glass. This makes the form of the glass clearly outlined through the napkins.

(5) With one hand, grip the top of the glass through the napkins and place your other hand around the mouth of the glass. Then, twist the glass as shown, *drawing the napkins tightly against the sides of the glass.* This helps to form the shape of the glass even more distinctly inside the paper napkins.

(6) This done, lift both the glass and the napkin together — to reassure the audience that the coin is still on the table.

(7) Once again, cover the coin with the glass and explain that through "deep concentration" you can cause the coin to penetrate through the table. All eyes will be fixed on the napkin-covered glass, waiting to see if the coin actually does as you say.

(8) Pretend to concentrate for a few seconds. Then announce that you think the coin has done its work. With your *right hand,* lift the napkins and glass revealing that the coin is still on the table. Act surprised, as if you actually expected the coin to be gone.

(9) Pick up the coin in your *left hand* as you remark that something seems to be wrong. *At the same time,* your right hand — holding the napkins and the glass — MOVES TO THE EDGE OF THE TABLE as shown. This motion of your right hand is completely natural, as it must move away to make room for your left hand, which picks up the coin. Your eyes, your gestures, *your total attention* should ALL BE DIRECTED AT THE COIN. This is MISDIRECTION!

(10) Here is a *side view* of the right hand holding the napkin-covered glass at the edge of the table. *Notice that the hand is actually resting on the table.*

(11) IT IS AT THIS TIME THAT THE "SECRET MOVE" TAKES PLACE. While the attention of the spectators is on the coin, the fingers of your right hand relax their grip on the glass through the napkin. *The weight of the glass will cause it to slide from within the napkins* INTO YOUR LAP.

(12) *The napkins retain the shape of the glass,* creating the illusion that the glass is still there.

(13) As the glass falls into your lap, raise your heels enough to bring your knees a bit higher than your lap. *This keeps the glass in your lap so it does not roll onto the floor.*

(17) SMASH THE NAPKINS FLAT ON THE TABLE WITH YOUR LEFT HAND. When this is done *fast* and *hard,* the reaction from the spectators will be one of complete astonishment.

(14) Here is the *audience view* of the performer as the "secret drop" takes place. *Notice how the left hand is forward,* FOCUSING ATTENTION ON THE COIN.

(18) Act puzzled for a moment. Then lift the napkins with your *left hand,* revealing the coin on the table. At the same time, your *right hand* grasps the glass in your lap and *carries it beneath the table,* as if reaching below the spot where you "smashed" the glass. Then bring your hand into view from beneath the table *with the glass.*

(15) *NOTE: The action of dropping the glass in your lap should take only a moment. As soon as the glass falls from the napkins, that is your cue to place the coin back on the table and cover it with the napkins (which apparently still contain the glass).*

(19) Place the glass on the table as you say, *"Now I remember* how the trick is done! It's the glass that is supposed to penetrate the table, *not* the coin."

(16) Explain that the trick failed because you forgot to strike the top of the glass. As you say this, raise your left hand above the glass and . . .

MENTAL MAGIC

★ ★ ★

This type of magic is unique because it depends on the effect created on the audience rather than the objects used. Instead of making things vanish and reappear or cutting them up and restoring them, you use them in special tests whereby you presumably "read people's minds." Since this goes along with modern talk of ESP, or Extra Sensory Perception, this type of magic has become so popular that some performers prefer to call themselves "mentalists" rather than magicians, as if they really were endowed with some supernormal power.

For practical purposes, however, it is better to inject a few mental effects at different parts of your performance and watch for audience reactions. If those prove favorable, add others to your program or play them up more strongly, until you strike the right balance. That, however, often depends upon the mood of your audience. Some people take mental magic so seriously that they don't care for anything else. If you run into people like that, you may just as well do a complete mental routine and forget your other tricks for the time being.

Most mental effects depend upon some secret that spectators are apt to overlook, so it is your job to see that they do exactly that. Never refer to a mental effect as a "trick." Call it a "test" or an "experiment" and in most cases, treat it rather seriously. If you run into complications or find that somebody is watching you too closely, don't try to work your way out of it as you would with other types of magic. Just put the blame on other people. Say that they are not "projecting" the right thoughts, or that you find it impossible to pick up the "impressions" that you need. That makes it look all the more genuine and gives you a chance to switch to another test.

THREE-WAY TEST

Reading a person's mind is surely a most effective way of demonstrating your magical powers. In this ESP experiment, using a small pad and pencil, you show your ability to predict and control the minds of three spectators. This effect requires a little closer study than most "magic" tricks, but it is well worth the sensational impact of your "magical mindreading."

THE EFFECT

(A)   In this mental effect, you demonstrate three different experiments in extrasensory perception. In the first experiment, you correctly determine the exact amount of change that a spectator has in his pockets.   (B)   In the second test, you receive a mental impression of an object that a spectator is thinking of before he picks it up in his hand.   (C)   And in the last experiment, you correctly predict which of three figure drawings a spectator will select from the table. With a small pad and pencil on your table, you are ready to begin.

THE METHOD

First explain that you are going to demonstrate three different forms of ESP, and to do this, you need three spectators to assist you — one person for each test. Then ask the members of the audience to assemble four or more small objects from around the room and place them on the table in front of one of the volunteers.

(1)   These can be any objects, as long as they are all different. Let's assume that the four items gathered are: ashtray, pen, matchbook and paper clip.

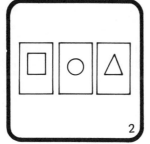

(2)   Next pick up the pad of paper and tear off three of the blank sheets. On one sheet of paper draw a circle; on the second, draw a square; and on the third, draw a triangle. Place these slips face up in a row in front of one of the other volunteers.

(3)   Ask the third spectator to reach in his pocket or purse and bring out all of the small change he has there. Tell him *not to count it* but to keep it held tightly in his closed fist.

(4)   You are now ready to begin the actual experiments. Explain that the first experiment is a test in *clairvoyance*, which is the ability to see hidden objects.

(5)   Pick up the pad and pencil and hold it so no one can see what you write. To the "money" spectator, say: "I am now going to write down my impression of the amount of change in your hand. "Obviously, you can't write this amount, because you don't know it yet! *Instead, draw a circle on the slip of paper.*

(6)   Now tear off the slip and fold it without letting anyone see what you have written. Say that you will call this first test "Test A" and that you will write the letter A on the outside of the slip. *Instead, you really mark it with the letter C.*

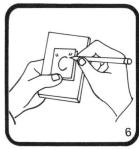

(7) After you have marked the slip, place it where it will be out of view of the spectators. (Be careful not to let anyone see the letter C on the slip of paper.) A drinking glass or coffee cup works well if it is the type you *can't see through*.

(8) Another suggestion would be to turn an ashtray or saucer upside down on the table and place the slips under it. It's not important where you place the slips *as long as the letters written on the outside cannot be seen by the spectators*. Let's assume you place the slips in a coffee mug.

(9) After the folded slip is in the mug, tell Person A to count his money out onto the table and leave it there for everyone to see. Let's say it comes to exactly $1.36.

(10) Now you turn to the second person and say, "I'm going to try a test in *telepathy* with you. This means that I can mentally pick up an impression that you *already* have in your mind. To do this, I want you to concentrate on one of the four objects on the table — the object *you are going to pick up in your hand*. Tell me when you have decided on the one you want, but *don't tell me* which object, and don't pick it up until *after* I have written down my impression."

(11) Then, instead of writing on the pad the name of one of the objects (because you don't know which one he's thinking of), *you write the amount of change that has been counted on the table from Test A — $1.36.*

(12) *NOTE: Learning information from one test and secretly using it in the next test is called the ONE-AHEAD PRINCIPLE.*

(13) Now tear off this sheet and fold it. Tell him that this is Test B and you will mark his slip with the letter B. But *instead of writing B, you mark it with the letter A.*

(14) Put this slip into the mug along with the other one.

(15) Now tell the spectator to pick up the object he was thinking of. Let's say he picks up the match book.

(16) Tell the third volunteer that you will do an experiment in *precognition*. This means you will *predict* a certain result before he knows what he is going to do.

(17) Pretend to write a prediction on the pad, but *really* write down the object that Person B is holding in his hand — the match book. *NOTE: Again you are using the ONE-AHEAD PRINCIPLE.*

(18) Now tear off the slip, fold it and say you'll call this Test C. Instead of marking the slip with the letter C, you mark it with the letter B as shown.

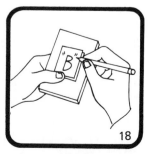

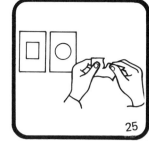

(19) Place this slip into the mug along with the other two.

(25) "Fine, I'll tear this one up and that leaves only two."

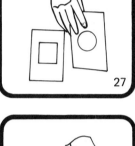

(20) Now you must maneuver the spectator into selecting the slip of paper with the circle on it. This is called "Forcing," although the spectator believes he is getting a free choice. The "Force" you will learn here is called the MAGICIAN'S CHOICE.

(26) Then ask him to *pick up* either one of the remaining slips of paper. Either one of two things will now happen.

(27) If he picks up the paper with the *circle* on it . . .

(21) Point out to the volunteer that you have drawn a different figure on each of the three papers on the table. Ask him to *point* to any one of the three slips. Now, one of several situations will arise:

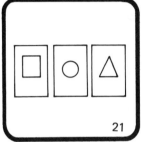

(28) . . . then you pick up the one remaining on the table and tear it up saying, "OK, the circle is the one you selected, so we won't need this one either."

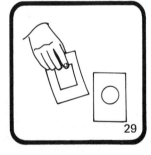

(22) *First Situation:*
If he points to the *circle,* say: "Would you pick up the slip that you have selected and hold it in your hand."

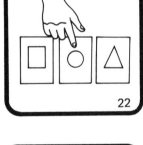

(29) If he picks up the paper *without the circle* on it, say:

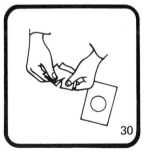

(23) When he does this, you pick up the other two slips and tear them up, saying: "We will not need these, so I'll tear them up."

(30) "OK, *you* tear up that slip, which leaves just the one on the table" (the circle).

(24) *Second Situation:*
If the spectator points to the *square* or the *triangle,* you pick up the one he points to and say:

(31) Now that you have successfully "Forced" the circle, you are ready for the "payoff." Pick up the mug and dump the slips onto the table. Ask each spectator to take the slip that has his letter on it and open it. When each slip is opened, all three of your tests prove to be correct!

COMMENTS AND SUGGESTIONS

This is a very strong trick. It can be performed anywhere; all you need are a pencil and some pieces of paper. There is no "sleight of hand" or special skill needed. But it is a trick that must be studied thoroughly and practiced until you can remember easily which part comes next — which letter to write on each slip, etc. After you have mastered it, you will be able to baffle your friends with one of the finest "mindreading" mysteries in the entire Art of Magic.

THE MAGAZINE TEST

Among mental mysteries, those in which a spectator does all the work can be rated among the best, for this apparently makes it impossible for the performer to inject any element of trickery. In fact, there are cases in which the magician does not even figure as a performer except to guide the spectator's actions. THE MAGAZINE TEST falls into that special category. You will find, however, that the effect does involve a small bit of work on your part, but this is mostly done beforehand. Hence, no one even knows about it, which makes it all the better for you.

EFFECT

The magician displays a sealed envelope and a current issue of a well known magazine. The performer explains to the audience that, prior to his appearance, he wrote one word on a white card and sealed it in an envelope. It is this envelope that he now hands to one of the spectators in the audience. A second spectator is asked to join the magician on stage and assist in a demonstration of the wizard's ability to "see into the future." The magician hands the magazine to the spectator along with a pencil or felt-tipped pen. In order not to influence the spectator's choice of a word from the magazine, the volunteer is asked to hold the magazine behind his back and mark a page at random with a bold X. Retrieving the now-closed magazine, the magician asks the first spectator to tear open the envelope he has held from the very start and read to the audience the predicted word. The magazine is then opened to the marked page. The spectators are surprised to see that the intersecting lines of the X *are directly through the identical word.*

SECRET AND PREPARATION

(A) Select a current issue of a magazine. Turn to any right-hand page located near the center of the magazine and draw a large X on the page. Make the mark so that the two lines of the X "cross" over a single word as shown. From this point on, we will refer to this word, "news," as the "Force Word."

(C) Now print the Force Word across the face of a white card and seal the "prediction" in an opaque envelope.

(B) NOTE: You should try marking the magazine page behind your own back before doing "The Magazine Test." In fact, several such trials are advisable in order to see just what a pair of crossed lines will look like when a spectator goes through the same procedure. Then, when you are ready to prepare the magazine that you intend to use in the test, you can copy one of your previous attempts, giving the lines slight curves or an irregular appearance to make them look authentic. Never have them cross exactly in the center of the "Forced" word. Hit near one end, or just above or below, yet close enough so everyone will agree upon that word.

(D) The final step is to prepare a pen or pencil in the same manner (so that it will not write) as for the "Double X Mystery" found elsewhere in the Course. *This prevents the spectator from actually making a mark on the magazine.* Be sure that this pen or pencil matches the one you used to mark the page.

METHOD

(1) Display the sealed envelope with the Force Word written on the card inside. Have a member of the audience hold the envelope. Pick up the magazine and demonstrate for the audience how you would like a spectator to mark the magazine page. Tell the spectator that you would like him to thumb through the magazine while holding it behind his back. Once he has selected a page, show him how he is to fold the *left-hand* pages of the magazine to the rear. This insures that the spectator will mark on a *right-hand* page of the magazine. (NOTE: Do not call them "left-hand" or "right-hand" pages. Just demonstrate what the spectator is to do so that, when he does "make his mark," it will be on the right-hand pages.)

(2) When you are sure that the spectator understands the proper procedure for marking the magazine, give him the *prepared* pen or pencil. (This is a good place for the "pencil switch" described in the "Super Double X Mystery.") Have him hold the magazine behind his back, select any (right-hand) page, fold the other (left-hand) pages out of the way, and mark the page with a large X. *The prepared pen or pencil will insure that no mark is made by the spectator.*

(3) Have him close the magazine before bringing it out from behind his back. Take the pen or pencil and the magazine from the spectator. *Put the pen or pencil away in your pocket as soon as you have finished this phase of the trick.* (You are now ready to later remove the ungimmicked pencil if you wish.)

(4) Call attention to the sealed envelope which is being held by a member of the audience. Emphasize that the envelope was given to the spectator before the magazine was marked! Have the person holding the envelope tear it open and call out the word written on the card inside.

(5) Give the magazine back to the spectator who marked the page and have him look through the pages until he locates the page he marked (or so he thinks!) with an X. When he has found it, have him call out the word which is indicated by that mark. *It will match the Force Word which was written on the prediction card!*

THE CURIOUS COINCIDENCE

When performing mental marvels, always remember that your main purpose is to create an effect in the minds of your audience, not to display skill or spring some quick surprise. In short, *method* is a secondary factor in any mental test and should be played down to such degree that no one will suspect that trickery is under way. That is the case with the effect that follows. Though the procedure is extremely bold, it will be free from suspicion if you adopt a matter-of-fact delivery.

EFFECT

Four identical pairs of papers bearing the names of past famous magicians are shown, along with two ordinary paper bags. One complete set of papers is put in a bag and given to a spectator. The other identical set of papers is placed in the remaining bag and held by the performer. The spectator and the performer each remove one of the folded papers from the bags and exchange their choices with one another. When the papers are opened and read aloud, they are found to match. This is repeated three more times with amazing results. The papers match perfectly each time.

SECRET AND PREPARATION

(A) For this amazing trick you will need two ordinary paper bags and two matching sets of papers bearing the names of famous magicians. (Any names or words may be used, such as famous singers or actors, presidents, cities — just use whatever best suits your act.) Make up two identical sets of papers. Write the names of the four magicians on the papers before folding each of them into quarters. Secretly prepare one set of papers as shown: The Dunninger paper is left unprepared. The Thurston paper has one corner folded up. The Houdini paper has two corners folded, and the Kellar paper has three folded corners. With the papers secretly prepared in this manner, you can tell at a glance which paper bears what name. This is your "key" to the trick; these prepared papers are the ones you will handle during the trick.

METHOD

(1) To perform the effect, place the unprepared set of papers into one bag and give it to the spectator to hold. Place the prepared set of papers in the other bag and hold it in your left hand.

(2) Instruct the spectator to remove one of the folded papers from his bag. You do likewise. As soon as you remove your paper, you will be able to tell at a glance which name is written inside because of the folded "key" corner(s). In the illustration, the paper with two folded corners — the "Houdini" paper — has been removed.

(3) Once you have removed a folded paper from your bag, place the paper in full view on the table.

(4) By now, the spectator has had time to remove a paper from his bag. Caution the spectator that he is not to open his paper yet.

(5) Take the spectator's folded paper from him. Instruct him to pick up your paper from the table and open it.

(6) While the spectator is unfolding the paper, you open the paper which you took from him. Because of your "key" corner-fold system, you already know what name appears on the paper held by the spectator. If you are not holding the matching paper, then you miscall the paper you hold. This means that if the paper you hold says "Kellar," as in the illustration, you say, "Houdini." The spectator will be amazed because he will believe that he holds the matching paper. After you have "miscalled" the paper you hold, fold it back up and place it aside on the table.

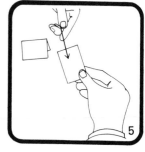

(7) Repeat the entire process with the three remaining pairs of papers. If by chance, the two of you remove identical papers, then you have an actual miracle. If not, simply miscall each paper as described in Step 6. The effect will work perfectly due to your corner-fold "key" papers. A little practice will show you how clever an effect you can make of this simple secret principle.

COMMENTS AND SUGGESTIONS

It is important that the slips not be examined or compared until *after* the effect is over. Keep the used slips in a confused pile on the table so that the spectators can't mentally pair up the slips at the trick's conclusion and discover one of your miscalls. Try this one a few times and you will be amazed at the startling effect it has on the spectators.

MILLION TO ONE

EFFECT

The magician shows the audience ten small cards with a large spot printed on the face of each card. These cards are placed on the table in a long straight row so that they alternate face up and face down. In this arrangement, the spectator can see five of the red spots and five of the red backs. The performer now asks one of the spectators to think of the color <u>blue</u>. As soon as the volunteer acknowledges, the magician asks him to call out a number between one and ten. With the number selected, the performer quickly points to the card that corresponds to the spectator's choice. To the complete surprise of the audience, this card proves to be the only blue card in the row.

SECRET AND PREPARATION

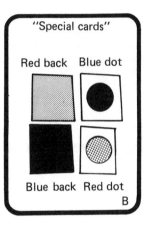

"Special cards"

Red back   Blue dot

Blue back   Red dot

B

(A)   The cards may be made from "index cards" or any type of stiff white cardboard. Use crayons or marking pens to color each card. Eight of the ten cards are alike. They all have a red spot on the face, and the backs are also colored red.

(B)   <u>The two remaining cards are prepared differently.</u> One card has a *red* spot on the <u>face</u> but the <u>back</u> is colored *blue*. The other special card has a *red* <u>back</u> and a *blue* spot on the <u>face</u>.

(C)   Arrange the ten cards in a stack in this manner: The top (uppermost) card is a regular card, <u>face up</u>. The second card from the top is also regular, <u>face down</u>. The third card is the *special* <u>blue-backed</u> card, face up. The fourth card is the other *special* card with the <u>blue dot</u>, face down. The fifth card is regular, face up. The sixth card is regular, face down. The seventh card is regular, face up. The eighth card is regular, face down. The ninth card is regular, face up. The last and tenth card is regular, face down.

METHOD

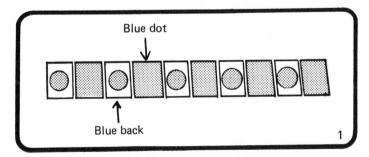

Blue dot

Blue back

1

(1)   Hold the cards in the prearranged order in your left hand. Now, with your right hand, deal the ten cards, starting at the top of the packet, onto the table from left to right. This means that the cards *alternate* face up and face down and that the two *special* cards will be in the <u>third and fourth positions from your left</u>.

(2)   After you have placed the cards on the table, ask a spectator to concentrate on the color "blue." Then have him call out any number between one and ten. You now proceed to *Force* one of the two specially prepared (blue) cards on the spectator.

(3)   After hearing the spectator's number, count the cards as follows. Here is a procedure for <u>whatever number the spectator calls</u>:

   NUMBER ONE — Begin with the card at the <u>left</u> end and *spell* "O-N-E," arriving at the third (blue-backed) card.

   NUMBER TWO — Begin at the <u>left</u> end and *spell* "T-W-O," arriving at the third (blue-backed) card.

   NUMBER THREE — *Count* "One, Two, Three" from the <u>left</u> arriving at the third (blue-backed) card.

   NUMBER FOUR — *Count* "One, Two, Three, Four" from the left, arriving at the fourth (blue-spotted) card.

   NUMBER FIVE — Begin at the left and *spell* out "F-I-V-E," arriving at the fourth (blue-spotted) card.

   NUMBER SIX — Begin at the left and *spell* "S-I-X," arriving at the third (blue-backed) card.

   NUMBER SEVEN — Have the <u>spectator</u> *count* from the <u>right</u> end of the row, and he will arrive at the fourth (blue-spotted) card.

   NUMBER EIGHT — Have the <u>spectator</u> *count* from the <u>right</u> end until he arrives at the eighth special (blue-backed) card.

   NUMBER NINE — Begin at your <u>left</u> end and *spell* "N-I-N-E," arriving at the fourth (blue-spotted) card.

   NUMBER TEN — Begin at your <u>left</u> end and *spell* "T-E-N," arriving at the third (blue-backed) card.

(4) After you have finished the spelling or counting, emphasize the fact that the spectator was given a <u>free</u> choice of any card. (Or so he thinks!) Now turn the chosen (Force) card over to show that the opposite side is <u>blue</u>.

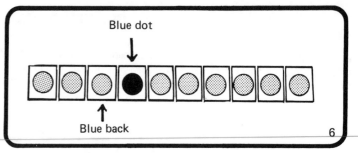

Blue dot

Blue back

6

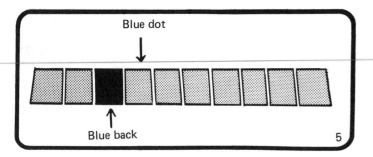

Blue dot

Blue back

5

(5) If the selected card is the *blue-backed* (third) card, turn all the cards which are face-up cards <u>face down</u> to show that all have <u>red backs</u> <u>except his chosen card</u>.

(6) If the selected card is the *blue-spotted* (fourth) card, turn all the cards that are face down <u>face up</u> *to show that all have red spots <u>except his chosen card</u>.*

(7) This final turning of the cards serves to convince the spectators that the cards are all identical *except* for the one card which he selected and conceals the fact that you are using one more specially prepared card. After this turn-over, gather up all the cards, being careful not to expose the remaining special (blue) card among the rest.

COMMENTS AND SUGGESTIONS

Carry the ten cards in their prearranged stack in a separate pocket so that you can remove the cards and place them on the table in a smooth, unhurried fashion. Practice placing the cards on the table until you can do it in a natural, relaxed manner. This effect can be presented either as a demonstration of ESP or as a magic trick. Never repeat this trick, or you will give away the principle used to force the special card.

THE GYPSY MINDREADER
(PSYCHOMETRY)

The subject of "psychometry" is based on the theory that objects belonging to a person, particularly those that he carries with him, can be identified as belonging to the person even when they are removed from the owner. For years, this was an old gypsy custom, depending on guesswork or trickery. Today, many people — including some professors — regard psychometry as a form of Extra-Sensory Perception (ESP). As such, it belongs in a program of mental magic, and the test about to be described is one of the best of that type.

EFFECT

Five plain white envelopes are distributed among the audience. Each recipient is asked to place a small article into his envelope and seal it. A volunteer gathers up the envelopes and thoroughly mixes them before handing them back to the performer. The magician openly places the envelopes into a clear glass bowl and explains to his audience that the little-explored subject of "psychometry" is based on the theory that, by handling articles belonging to a person, it is possible to gain a mental impression of the actual person, even though the articles are sealed in an envelope. In order to demonstrate the validity of this theory, the magician picks up one of the envelopes and holds it to his forehead. Without hesitation, he announces that the article inside the sealed envelope belongs to a young lady. The performer opens the envelope and allows the article to fall into his open palm. He closes his hand around the item and, apparently from the vibrations received from the article, proceeds to describe the owner in minute detail. Finally, the magician walks among the spectators and is mysteriously led to the surprised girl.

This demonstration is repeated using the four remaining envelopes and the objects they contain with the same unfailing accuracy.

NOTE: Properly performed, the above effect is one of the strongest mental feats available. Some professional magicians have built their entire reputation based on the above presentation. Again, it is important that you present this effect as entertainment, assuring your audience that it is merely a magician's demonstration of the phenomenon of psychometry.

SECRET AND PREPARATION

(A) You will need a number of plain white envelopes — "Letter" size, measuring approximately 3½" x 6½", are perfect for this effect. Four of the five envelopes are prepared by placing a small pencil dot in a *different corner* of each of the envelopes. The dots are put on the flap side of the envelope — one in each of the four corners. *They are made in pencil, lightly, so as not to be noticed by the spectators.*

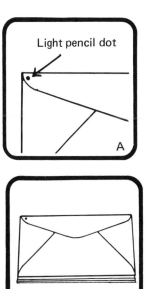

(B) Each of the four corner dots represents a different spectator. The fifth envelope is left unmarked. Stack the five envelopes so that the spectator number dots are arranged, clockwise from top to bottom, running one through five as shown.

METHOD

(1) Holding the envelopes in this prearranged stack, pass them out to the spectators, moving from left to right through the audience. *All you have to do is remember who gets each envelope.*

(2) After returning to the stage, instruct the five spectators to place a small object into their envelopes, seal them, and pass them to another spectator. This volunteer is asked to mix up the envelopes to his satisfaction and hand them back to you.

(3) Drop the envelopes into a clear glass container. As you remove the first envelope, turn it flap side up and locate the coded dot. You now know to whom this envelope belongs.

(4) Hold the envelope to your forehead and slowly reveal whether the object belongs to a man or a woman. An example might be as follows: "I'm getting a very strong vibration from this envelope. Yes, the article inside must belong to a gentleman in his late twenties or early thirties."

(5) At this point, tear open the envelope and allow the article to fall into your hand. After discarding the envelope, close your fingers around the item and begin to reveal details regarding this person's appearance (which you can see from the stage or, better yet, which you remember from when you handed out the envelopes).

(6) During this reading, start moving down into the audience and, as if being led by the vibrating force of the object in your hand, dramatically locate the owner.

(7) Repeat the demonstration with the four remaining objects. When you have finished, the audience will be left with a profound mystery that is quite different from any other effect on your program.

THE CENTER TEAR

This is without a doubt one of the simplest yet cleverest of all methods for learning the contents of a short message, a word or a number written by a spectator. Properly performed, it is so deceptive that your audience will have no idea that trickery is involved — with the result that many may be ready to accept it as a display of actual mindreading. Naturally, you should disclaim such power, yet at the same time keep the secret to yourself, thus adding to a very perplexing mystery.

EFFECT

The magician gives a spectator a square slip of paper and a pencil, telling him to write a name, a number, or even a brief message in the center. This is done while the magician's back is turned. Then the spectator folds the paper in half and then in quarters, so that the performer cannot possibly see the writing. The magician tears up the folded slip, and its pieces are openly dropped into an ashtray and burned. Yet the magician learns the spectator's message and reveals it!

SECRET AND PREPARATION

(A) To prepare for this trick, you will need to place a book of matches in your left trouser or coat pocket and you will need to have an ashtray handy.

(B) Cut out a small slip of paper approximately three inches square. *Draw a circle about 1¼ inches wide in the center of one side of the paper as shown.*

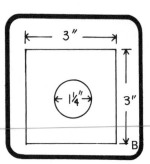

METHOD

(1) Give the paper to a spectator and instruct him to write a word or a short message within the "magic circle." Make sure that the spectator understands that you are not to see what he writes on the paper.

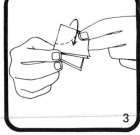

(2) When the message is complete, instruct the spectator to fold the paper in half so that his writing is within the fold.

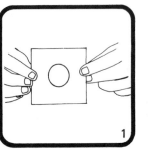

(3) Then have him fold the paper once again, so that it is in quarters.

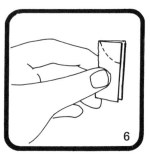

(4) Take the folded slip from the spectator. You can look at the packet and easily see which corner is actually the center "magic circle" of the piece of paper. *NOTE: Practice folding the paper yourself, and it will help you to instantly spot the desired corner.*

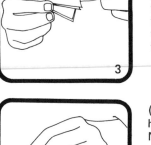

(5) When you have located the center corner of the paper, hold the folded packet so that the "magic circle" is in the upper right-hand corner facing you. With the packet held in this manner, tear it in half. This tear should leave the "magic circle" undamaged.

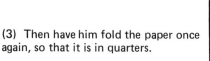

(6) Once you have torn the packet in half, place the left-hand pieces of paper behind the right-hand pieces. Hold all the pieces in your left hand. The "magic circle" should be at the top of the packet, and it should be nearest your body.

(7) Now rotate the packet a quarter-turn to the right and grasp it between both hands. The "magic circle" is still facing you, held by your right thumb and first finger. Holding the packet in this position, tear it in half once more.

(8) Again, place the left-hand pieces behind the right-hand pieces. Then take all the pieces in your right finger-tips. The "magic circle" is still facing you and is directly under your right thumb.

(9) Hold all the pieces in your right hand, between your thumb and fingers. Now position your right hand over the ashtray. Drop all of the pieces of paper except the "magic circle" which is held directly under your thumb, into the ashtray. As you release the pieces, use your thumb to slide the piece of paper containing the "magic circle" back toward the middle joints of your fingers.

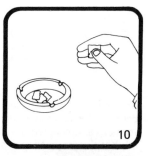

(10) You now secretly hold the "magic circle" concealed in your right fingers. The rest of the pieces of paper have fallen into the ashtray. The audience is unaware that you hold this paper (which contains the message) in your hand.

(11) With the "magic circle" safely hidden in your right hand, use your left hand to reach into your trouser pocket and take out the book of matches. Then use both hands to remove a match, strike it, and set fire to the piece of paper in the ashtray. Place the matchbook on the table with your right hand and use your left hand to hold the lighted match.

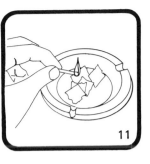

(12) While the spectators are concentrating on the burning pieces of paper, drop your right hand below the table and use your right thumb to secretly open up the "magic circle" hidden in your right fingers. As soon as you have read the message, quietly crumple up or refold the paper. As the paper continues to burn, pick up the packet of matches and place them *and the "magic circle"* in your right pocket. Concentrate deeply on the rising smoke before you reveal the words of the message!

COMMENTS AND SUGGESTIONS

The most important thing to remember is that your right hand, while it secretly holds the center portion of the paper, must be held completely relaxed and natural. Then, when you drop your right hand below the table to open up the paper and read the message, ask the spectators to focus their attention on the burning pieces of paper and the smoke as you casually glance at the message.

This is another "classic" method that is used not only by magicians, but also by fraudulent spirit mediums and psychics. Its great strength lies in that it uses only ordinary objects. With the proper "build-up," this simple effect can be made into a real miracle!

THE CENTER TEAR

"Standing" Variation

When working away from a table, as you occasionally may have to do, you can use the following subterfuge.

METHOD

(1) Light the match with your left hand, placing the match pack in your right hand, hiding the torn center.

(2) As you start to set fire to the pieces in the ashtray, place the matchbook on the table.

(3) Then purposely let the match go out, *while your right thumb is secretly opening the torn center.*

(4) Your right hand now picks up the match pack in order to strike another match. Both hands are needed for that action, particularly if the left hand dawdles while lighting the pieces in the ashtray, giving you an opportunity to read the message.

(5) Finally, the right hand can slide the match pack over the torn center, hiding it. You dispose of the torn center *by simply dropping it in your right pocket along with the match pack.*

SPECTRUM PREDICTION

PREDICTION effects form an important phase of Mentalism and therefore should be included on nearly every program. Moreover, where predictions are concerned, one good test definitely calls for another, because the more predictions you fulfill, the less chance there is that luck has anything to do with it. Any good prediction may puzzle your audience, but if you follow one with another, or even hit three in a row, people will really be bewildered. However, simply repeating the same prediction time after time is not the right policy. Some spectators lose interest when the same trick is repeated; others are apt to watch for a weak point and may be just sharp enough to spot it. So the answer is to have some special type of divination in reserve, differing from the rest in regard to objects used, as well as method. The SPECTRUM PREDICTION meets both those qualifications.

EFFECT

The magician displays eight brightly colored squares of cardboard and spreads them out on the table so that everyone can see that each square is a different color. The performer then writes a "prediction" on a piece of paper which he folds and gives to a member of the audience to hold. The colored chips are gathered together by a spectator and wrapped in the magician's opaque handkerchief. This same spectator is then asked to reach into the folds of the handkerchief and withdraw a single chip. This done, the prediction is unfolded and read aloud. The performer proves to be correct!

SECRET AND PREPARATION

(A) From a stationery or art supply store, obtain eight different colors of cardboard, or you may use colored "construction" paper, or even white cardboard which you color with paint, crayons, or ink. The colors you use are unimportant, but use easily recognizable colors such as: yellow, blue, green, red, orange, purple, black and white. In any event, make eight one-inch squares, all of a different color. You also need to cut eight more squares which *are all the same color.* For the purpose of explanation. let's assume that these additional squares are all red. *You, therefore, have eight different colored squares and eight squares which are all red.*

(B) You will also need two identical pocket handkerchiefs. Handkerchiefs made with a colored pattern work best. (Bandanas are good.) Now place one upon the other and sew them together exactly as shown by the dotted lines.

(C) You will notice that point "X" is the center of the handkerchief. The stitching along lines "XY" and "XZ" form a "hidden pocket" which can be opened at "AB." Now sew two small beads at the "A" and "B" corners. These beads will enable you to find the pocket opening quickly. (The beads are optional, but they do help greatly in locating the secret pocket at the proper time.)

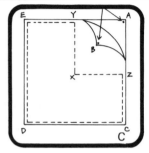

(D) *Place the eight red squares into the hidden pocket.* Grasp corners A and B and shake out the handkerchief. Place the prepared handkerchief into your inside coat pocket with corners A and B on top where you can grasp them easily so that the extra "secret" squares will not fall out when you remove the handkerchief.

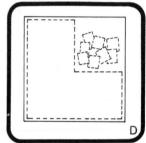

(E) Along with the eight squares of different colors, place a small pad of paper and a pencil on the table.

METHOD

(1) Call the spectator's attention to the colored squares. Pick up the pad and, without letting the spectators see what you are writing, write, "You will select the color red." Tear the "prediction" from the pad and fold it so that it cannot be read by the spectators. Hand the folded slip to one of the spectators to hold.

(2) With your right hand, reach into your inside coat pocket and grasp the prepared handkerchief by the small beads which are sewn into the Corners A and B. Withdraw the handkerchief, show it on both sides, and then gather all of the corners together forming a "bag" as shown.

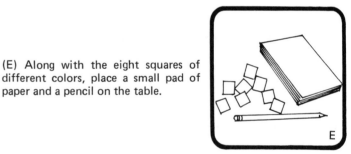

(3) Have the spectator pick up the colored squares from the table. You are holding the handkerchief by the corners in your right hand. With your left thumb and first finger, hinge down Corner D and allow the spectator to drop the squares into the handkerchief. *These squares do not go into the secret pocket.*

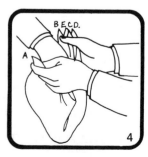

(4) Shake the impromptu bag, mixing the colored squares inside. *Now hinge Corner A down and allow the spectator to reach inside and remove a single square.* He will be reaching inside the hidden pocket which contains only red squares. *Be sure he removes only one of the squares.*

(5) Once the spectator has the red square in his hand, simply bunch up the handkerchief and put it back into your pocket, squares and all.

(6) Ask the spectator to unfold the slip of paper . . . again you have proven your "Magical Powers" . . . your prediction proves to be exactly correct!

COMMENTS AND SUGGESTIONS

The success of this trick depends upon handling the handkerchief in a natural, casual manner, so as to avoid suspicion. Since the handkerchief is a common article, it seems nothing more than a mere adjunct to the prediction, hence it is comparatively easy to focus attention on the colored squares at the outset and the prediction slip at the finish, leaving the spectator with one red square and the prediction.

If you have an *ordinary handkerchief* resembling the special double handkerchief, you can use it in some previous effect in which it plays an innocent part; then place it in your pocket afterward. When you bring out the *double handkerchief* for the SPECTRUM PREDICTION, everyone will suppose it to be the same one that you used before, so any suspicion will be lulled from the start. It is also a good plan to have eight extra squares of some color other than red, so that if you perform the prediction for the same group of people on another occasion, you can "Force" a different color.

SPECTRUM PREDICTION
"Number" Variation

A clever and simple variation of the SPECTRUM PREDICTION is the use of the numbers One through Eight written on separate slips of paper rather than the colored squares of cardboard used in the first version.

EFFECT

The magician displays a pad of paper and openly writes the numbers One through Eight on individual sheets of paper from the pad. After all of the papers have been numbered, each is folded, first in half and then into quarters, and the entire lot is placed into a makeshift bag constructed from the magician's handkerchief. The magician then writes an additional "prediction" number, which he does not let the audience see, on one more slip of paper. This is folded and handed to one of the spectators to hold. A second spectator is asked to select one of the eight slips from the handkerchief. After the slip is selected, the magician opens the handkerchief to show that only seven slips remain. The two spectators then open their papers. The slip containing the prediction is found to match exactly the "freely selected" number on the paper held by the second spectator.

SECRET AND PREPARATION

The secret of this trick is exactly the same as the SPECTRUM PREDICTION; however, it does have certain advantages and one disadvantage as well. The disadvantage is that the colored slips are perhaps more spectacular and can certainly be seen from a greater distance if you are performing for a large group. The number variation, however, has the advantage of the "look" of a totally impromptu mystery in that all of the props are ordinary objects as opposed to the specially colored squares. Also, in the following method, the handkerchief may be opened so that the remaining slips fall out after the second spectator has made his selection.

Before the show, on eight slips of paper write the same number — let's assume the number is *Five.* Fold all of the slips and place them in the secret pocket of the Double Handkerchief just as you did in Step D of the SPECTRUM PREDICTION. Then place the handkerchief in your pocket.

METHOD

(1) Display a pad of paper (this must be the same paper as the previously written and folded slips) and openly write the numbers One through Eight individually on different sheets from the pad. Write the number "1," tear that sheet off, fold it in half and then into quarters, and place it on the table. Then write the number "2," tear it off and fold it, and place it on the table with the first. Continue until you have eight separate slips with different numbers.

(2) Now, just as you did in Step 2 of the Spectrum Prediction, remove the handkerchief from your pocket and, as in Step 3, form the handkerchief into a bag by holding it by the four corners. Then place all eight slips into the main body of the handkerchief. *Do not put the slips in the secret pocket.*

(3) Now explain to the spectator what he is to do. Tell him that he is to reach into the handkerchief and remove *one* of the slips. He is to hold the slip tightly in his hand so that no one can see what number is written on it until the conclusion of the effect. As you explain to him what he is to do, *you demonstrate his actions at the same time.* Reach into the "bag" (be sure you reach into the main body of the handkerchief, not the secret compartment) and remove one of the regular slips. After explaining that he is to hold the slip tightly, put your hand back into the handkerchief apparently replacing the slip. *Really, you secretly hold the slip in the Finger Palm position and remove your hand as if it were empty.*

Finger Palmed slip

(4) *NOTE: You will find this quite easy to do as the spectators are not expecting trickery of any kind at this point.*

(5) Reach into your pocket and remove the pencil. *At the same time, leave the extra slip, which you have just palmed, in your pocket.* Gaze intently at the spectator who will select the slip as if to gain a "mental impression" of his future actions. Then pick up the pad with your other hand and write the prediction (the number "Five") on the pad. Tear off the slip, fold it, and hand it to some other spectator to hold.

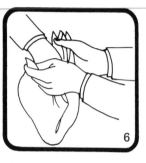

(6) Now ask the first spectator to reach into the handkerchief and remove one of the slips. Be sure that you open the handkerchief as you did in Step 4 of the Spectrum Prediction so that he will remove one of the Force papers.

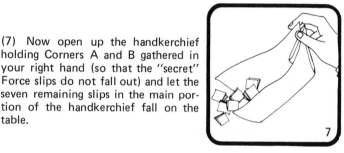

(7) Now open up the handkerchief holding Corners A and B gathered in your right hand (so that the "secret" Force slips do not fall out) and let the seven remaining slips in the main portion of the handkerchief fall on the table.

(8) Place the handkerchief in your pocket (along with the Force slips). Then, with your right hand, pick the slips up one at a time and count them, without unfolding them, from the table into your left hand. Indicate to the spectator that he could have had a free selection of any of the eight slips as you openly place the seven pieces of paper in your pocket.

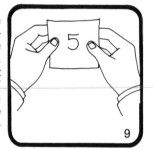

(9) Have the second spectator open the prediction slip and read the number aloud. Emphasize again the free selection that the first spectator had. Have him open his slip for the first time and read his "freely selected" number. The two numbers match! You have just presented what appears to be another completely impromptu Mental Miracle.

PING PONG PRESTIDIGITATION

Here is a comedy trick in which you let everyone in the audience in on the secret of the effect except for one person — a volunteer from the audience who assists you on stage. He is the only person who is deceived by your magical methods, creating a situation that develops into good fun for everyone.

EFFECT

The magician displays three pairs of different colored ping pong balls. One pair is white, one pair red, and one pair blue. The performer drops all six balls into a paper bag and invites two spectators on stage to assist in the effect. The spectator on the magician's left is asked to reach into the bag — without looking — and to remove any ball. No matter which ball he withdraws, the other spectator is always able to reach into the bag and remove the matching ball without looking inside the bag. The selected balls are replaced, and the trick is repeated over and over again with the same impossible results.

SECRET AND PREPARATION

What the first spectator doesn't know is that the entire audience and the other spectator on stage can see the colored balls all along through a secret "window" in the side of the bag! Because of the secret window, everyone sees how the trick works *except* for the spectator on the left who is unaware throughout the presentation that the bag is cleverly "gimmicked."

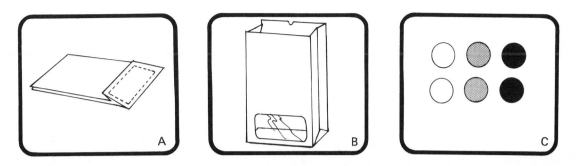

(A)   To prepare, obtain an ordinary brown paper bag, about the size of a standard "lunch bag," and cut a hole in the side of the bag as shown. The position of the hole should be such that it is completely hidden from view by the bottom portion of the bag when the bag is folded flat. This way the bag can be freely shown on both sides and handled quite casually before it is opened to begin the effect. (B)   This done, glue or tape a piece of transparent kitchen wrap (clear plastic) over the hole so that the balls will not fall out of the bag during the presentation. The construction of the bag is complete. As you can see, you formed a sort of "window" in the bag which allows you to see into the bag quite easily.   (C)   The next step is to purchase six ordinary ping pong balls. Prepare the three pairs of balls by painting or dyeing them in three brightly contrasting colors. Permanent ink marking pens also work well for coloring the balls and can be purchased at most stationery stores.

Instead of ping pong balls, you can use lightweight plastic or rubber balls which can be obtained at department or toy stores. Be sure they are all the same size and are made of the same material so that it is impossible to distinguish one color from another without looking at them. The construction of the props is now complete and you are ready to perform this clever comedy mystery.

METHOD

(1)   Invite two spectators on stage and position yourself between them, facing the audience. Display the balls and call attention to the fact that there are three pairs of different colored balls. Then pick up the bag and display it — folded flat — so that everyone (especially the spectator on the left) can see that it is quite "ordinary." Now, open the bag *so that the window faces the audience* (and not the spectator on your left) and openly drop the six balls into the bag. The audience will immediately see that the bag is gimmicked and will begin to see "why" as you continue.

(2)   Speaking to the spectator on your left, instruct him to reach into the bag — without looking — and remove *one* ball. *Tell him to keep it concealed in his closed hand so that only he knows its color.* Be sure to hold the bag so that the window is facing away from him so he cannot see that the bag is prepared.

(3)   After he removes the ball, swing your body to the right and explain to the other spectator that he is to concentrate very hard and then reach into the bag and try to remove the matching colored ball. *Be sure to hold the bag so that the window faces him.* He will "catch on" immediately once he sees the window in the bag. It is a simple matter for the volunteer to remove the correct ball, *as it will be the only ball inside the bag without a matching color.*

(4)   Once the second spectator has removed the ball, have both spectators openly display the two selected balls to the audience. Since the volunteer on your right has removed the correct ball, the two balls will match in color.

(5)   Now have, both spectators replace the balls in the bag and perform the effect a few more times. Each time the trick is successful, the reaction of the spectator on your left will become more and more humorous. Because he is unaware of the secret window, he will not be able to explain this seemingly impossible series of "coincidences."

COMMENTS AND SUGGESTIONS

At the end of the trick, you should humorously reveal the secret of the trick to the puzzled spectator by "accidentally" turning the window side of the bag toward him as you reach out to shake his hand. Then thank both of your volunteers for being such good sports as they return to the audience.

This is a good trick to work at a party when you are waiting for more people to arrive before you begin your regular show. After Mr. Left has been utterly baffled, you tell him that next time, he can play the part of Mr. Right. After some newcomers arrive, you repeat the trick, inviting one of them to serve as Mr. Left. Your former victim, now Mr. Right, then has the pleasure of seeing how nicely he was fooled the time before. This procedure can be repeated with other new arrivals, making an excellent prelude for your show.

NOTE: You must be careful in presenting tricks of this nature that you don't offend or insult the intelligence of the volunteer who is unaware of the working of the effect. Present the trick in a warm, humorous style so that the spectator does not get annoyed at the fact that he "can't see how it's done."

THE ENVELOPE STAND

With mental tests, it is always a good plan to use some simple props only if they make the presentation more direct and therefore more effective. When such devices actually aid in the deception without the audience realizing it, the effect is all the better. This applies strongly with THE ENVELOPE STAND, which is so named because it has much to do with the effect that follows.

EFFECT

The magician displays an attractive pasteboard stand with five numbered envelopes arranged on it. The performer announces that one of the sealed envelopes contains a *dollar bill* and the rest are *empty*. A spectator is given a free choice of any envelope. When the chosen envelope is opened, it is found to contain the dollar bill. It appears as if the magician has been able to influence the decision of the spectator.

SECRET AND PREPARATION

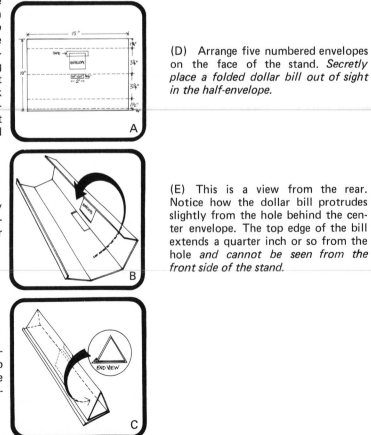

(A) Actually, all five envelopes are empty. The stand is constructed in such a way as to deliver the bill into any selected envelope. Construct the stand as shown. Use a piece of cardboard about 10" x 15" (depending upon the size of the envelopes). Cut out a hole in the center of the back of the stand. Then tape the lower portion of an envelope that you have cut in half to the back of the cardboard just below the opening.

(B) Fold the cardboard as shown by the dotted lines so that the half-envelope is hidden inside the triangular body of the stand.

(C) This illustration shows the completed stand. Notice the turned up "lip" located on the front edge of the stand. This ledge prevents the envelopes from slipping off the stand.

(D) Arrange five numbered envelopes on the face of the stand. *Secretly place a folded dollar bill out of sight in the half-envelope.*

(E) This is a view from the rear. Notice how the dollar bill protrudes slightly from the hole behind the center envelope. The top edge of the bill extends a quarter inch or so from the hole *and cannot be seen from the front side of the stand.*

METHOD

(1) To perform the trick, display the stand and call attention to the five numbered envelopes displayed on the stand. (Small "coin" or "pay" envelopes work best.) Announce that you have placed a dollar bill in only *one* of the envelopes prior to the trick. Predict that the dollar envelope will be chosen at random by a spectator. Select a spectator and allow him to choose any envelope. Give him the opportunity to change his mind if he wishes.

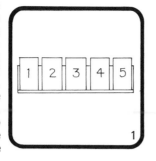

(5) Remove the selected envelope from the stand with the thumb and fingers of your right hand and, as you do, secretly grasp the upper end of the hidden bill with your right fingers. Hold it firmly behind the selected envelope as you remove the envelope from the stand, being sure not to expose the bill hidden behind it.

(2) Then remove all envelopes not chosen from the stand.

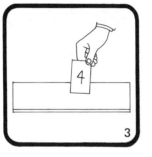

(6) Now casually transfer the envelope (and the hidden bill) to your left hand. The left thumb now holds the bill against the back of the envelope. This move gives the spectators a chance to see that both of your hands are empty. With your free right hand, tear off one end of the sealed envelope. Be sure not to prematurely expose the bill.

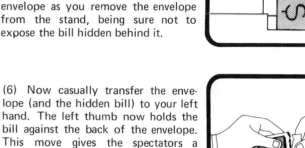

(3) *Place the selected envelope, in this case Number FOUR, <u>directly in front</u> of the secret hole in the stand.*

(7) Insert your right first and second fingers into the envelope and appear to remove the bill from inside. *Actually, you pull the bill out from <u>behind</u> the envelope using your right thumb.* Display the folded bill, held between the thumb and fingers of your right hand.

(4) Here is the rear view of the stand at this point in the routine. Notice how the bill in the half-envelope protrudes slightly from the hole in the stand.

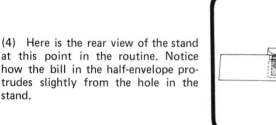

(8) Unfold the bill and show it to be authentic before you pick up the other four envelopes. Tear these envelopes in half to show that they are all empty — or better yet, have the spectators open and examine them. You may reward your spectator with the dollar as a souvenir if you wish. In any event, hand the remains of all of the envelopes out to your audience for inspection.

THE ENVELOPE STAND
"Bank Night" Variation

EFFECT

An effective comedy variation of this mystery can be worked with *four* spectators. The audience is informed that only one of the envelopes contains a real bill — the rest have only blank slips of paper. Each spectator will be allowed to choose any envelope, and they may change their minds as often as they wish. The performer states that *whoever picks the envelope with the dollar bill <u>can keep it</u>* and that he will keep only the final envelope for himself. Thus, the spectators do all of the "choosing." When each spectator opens his envelope, he finds a blank piece of paper the size of a dollar bill. The magician then opens his envelope and removes the "real" dollar bill!

SECRET AND PREPARATION

The trick works exactly the same as THE ENVELOPE STAND except that you must be sure that all the envelopes are opaque since the spectators will have an opportunity to handle them and change their minds, and thus perhaps "see through" an envelope made of light-weight paper. Cut <u>five</u> blank pieces of paper the same size as a dollar bill and place one in each of the five numbered envelopes. Conceal the dollar bill in the envelope stand as before.

METHOD

(1)   Explain that only <u>one</u> envelope contains a dollar bill and that the lucky spectator who selects it <u>will get to keep it.</u>

(2)   Have each spectator *call out the number of the envelope he wants.* When each makes his choice, <u>you hand the envelope to the spectator.</u> *(In this way, the spectators never have a chance to come near the Stand and discover its secret.)*

(3)   After each has decided which envelope he wants, position the remaining envelope in the center of the stand — <u>directly in front of the hidden bill.</u>

(4)   Emphasize the fairness of the selection and then have each spectator open his envelope — *one at a time.* <u>Now the suspense builds as the odds grow shorter</u> as the contents of each envelope are revealed.

(5)   *Just as the last spectator removes the blank paper, pick up your envelope and <u>steal the bill from the stand</u>.* All eyes will be on the spectator at this time, which will aid in the <u>misdirection</u> as you remove the remaining envelope *and* the bill.

(6)   Now open your envelope and remove (from behind) the "real" dollar.

(7)   Thank the spectators as you crumple up your envelope (with the last blank paper inside). Casually place the envelope on your table (or toss it off stage) as you display the dollar to the audience!

"BETCHAS"

★ ★ ★

In magical parlance, the term "Betcha" is short for "I'll bet you!"—which means that you, as the magician, would be willing to bet a spectator that you can do something that he can't. Of course, you don't have to make a bet to prove your point. You can go right ahead and do it, just for the fun of it. People appreciate that because, if they get fun out of watching magic, they want to see more. That works to your advantage as much as theirs.

Actually, a "Betcha" is more of a puzzle than a trick. If you lay a row of coins on a table and state that in three moves you can bring all the heads together and all the tails together, people may not believe you until you have done it. But once you have done it, you have shown them how to do it for themselves. With a full-fledged trick, it is different. You accomplish a seeming impossibility without disclosing the secret.

"Betchas," however, can prove both useful and effective, so it is wise to have them available. Practically every "Betcha" has some neat twist which gives it audience appeal, and some, if done smoothly and fairly rapidly, may even become tricks in their own right. Although you show people exactly what they are supposed to do, the moves may be too complex for them to follow. So instead of learning "how it's done," they only become all the more puzzled.

There are some other good reasons why "Betcha" should be cultivated. When performing before small groups, some people may want you to start before the rest are ready to watch. This can upset your routine, and it is also likely to interrupt a good trick at a crucial moment, spoiling the effect entirely. Even worse, you may have to do some of your tricks over to please people who weren't there to see them the first time, which can really detract from your performance and also give those who see them twice an opportunity to discover the secret.

So the best plan is to "warm up" with a few "Betcha"—getting people to try some trifling tricks for themselves, which will put them in a mood to appreciate the real magic that you show them later, when the group is fully assembled.

There are also times when you are starting an impromptu performance that somebody may come up with some trick of the "Betcha" type and try to steal some of your thunder. Even if you are familiar with this trick, it won't do any good to say so once your would-be rival has put it across. So the answer here is to come back with a few "Betchas" of your own, picking those that are so intriguing that you friends will forget the one they saw at the start.

Finally, "Betchas" are the real answer to the question that some friend is sure to ask—"Say! How about showing me how some of your tricks are done? Maybe just one trick that I could do myself . . ." Naturally, you won't want to lose a good trick by telling how it's done, but you won't want to lose a good friend either. So show him a few "Betchas." They're expendable!

THE IMPOSSIBLE PENETRATION

EFFECT

The magician displays two rolled up Dollar Bills. He places a bill in the crook of each of his thumbs, one bill in each hand. By grasping the ends of the bills with the *thumbs* and *second fingers* of the opposite hands, he is able to separate his hands — causing the bills to apparently pass "magically" through one another. The real mystery is that the spectators are unable to duplicate the feat.

METHOD

(1) Roll two Dollar Bills into tight cylinders and hold the bills in the crooks of the thumbs as shown.

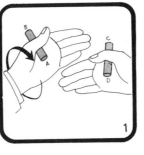

(2) Rotate your hands in opposite directions so that you can take the *left-hand* bill with the *right thumb* at A and the *right second finger* at B. At the same time, your left hand grasps the *right-hand* bill with the *left thumb* at D and the *left second finger* at C.

(3) Held correctly, your hands should look like this. To the audience, the illusion of the "linking" of your fingers and the bills is perfect.

(4) Rotate your hands in opposite directions as you pull your hands apart.

(5) The bills will free themselves and appear to "magically" pass through each other.

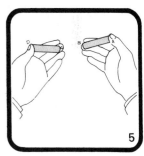

COMMENTS AND SUGGESTIONS

This effect can also be done with two corks, short pencils, or any small objects of the correct shape and size. Whatever you use, it's a very deceptive "quickie." Or it may be done as a "puzzle." In this case, you repeat the trick over and over as the spectators try to duplicate it. Each time do the "penetration" a little slower. Finally, someone will "get it" and start to fool the other participants. Present it this way at the next party you attend and see how much fun you will have!

THE IMPOSSIBLE KNOT

Tricks of the "Do As I Do" type are always effective, and this is one of the best. All you need are two ropes, each about three feet in length; one for yourself, the other for a spectator. With a little practice and one simple, secret move, you can baffle your audience time after time — to the point where they will actually fool themselves!

EFFECT

The magician holds a length of rope with one end in each hand. He invites a spectator to do the same with another piece of rope. Stating that it would be impossible to tie a knot in a rope without letting go of at least one end, the wizard proceeds to drape the rope over his arms, forming a series of simple loops and twists. This is done slowly, without letting go of the ends, so the spectator can copy *every move the magician makes* with his rope. Still holding both ends, the magician shakes the rope from his arms and — a knot appears "magically" in the center. No knot is formed in the spectator's rope, even though he is sure he has copied the magician's every move exactly.

METHOD

(1) Hold the rope near the ends between the thumb and first finger of each hand with the rope hanging below as shown.

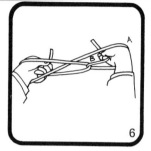

(2) Bring your right hand inwards (toward you) and drape the rope over your left wrist as shown.

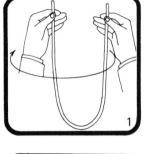

(3) Draw the right end of the rope downward and beneath the hanging loop. This divides the hanging loop into two sections, left and right.

(4) Insert your right hand (still holding the right end) through the *left* section of the loop; and, in the same continuous action, bring your hand back through the *right* section of the loop *nipping the rope at Point A* as shown.

(5) Without releasing either hand, move your right hand back to the right, bringing the "nipped" rope with it. Point A is now resting on the back of your right wrist. (NOTE: This is the only part of this excellent magical puzzle that is difficult to illustrate. Just try it with the rope in your hands until you hold the rope as shown in Step 5. Another way to describe Step 4 is that your right hand, still holding its end, goes into the loop and "picks up" Point A on the back of your right wrist. Point A is then pulled *out through the loop* to form the set-up shown in Step 5.)

(6) Move your right hand level with your left and pull the rope taut so it forms the "criss-cross" pattern between your wrists as shown. *Note that in the illustration a new spot is indicated on the rope, Point B. Point B is just below the end held by your right hand.* Now, relax the tension on the rope and tilt both hands forward and downward, so the *outside loops*, which are pressed against your wrists, begin to slide over the tops of your hands.

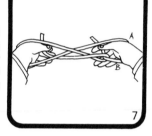

(7) YOU ARE NOW READY FOR THE SECRET MOVE. As the rope begins to fall off your wrists, your right hand prepares to *secretly release its end and grasp the rope at Point B* as described in Step 8.

(8) As the loops slide completely over and off of your hands, draw your hands apart. At the same time, *release the right end of the rope with your thumb and first finger, and secretly grasp Point B with your other three fingers.* Because of the "tossing" movement of the loops as they fall off your wrists, the audience is completely unaware of this small "move" which is the *whole secret of the trick.*

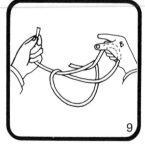

(9) As you draw your hands apart, the right end of the rope will automatically pull through the little loop forming a knot in the center of the rope.

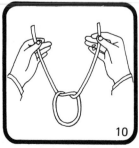

(10) Your right thumb and first finger immediately regain their original grip on the end of the rope so all looks the same — as the knot is formed.

COMMENTS AND SUGGESTIONS

All through the routine, you should emphasize that you *never release the ends of the rope.* Yet a knot still appears in the rope. That makes this an "Impossible Knot." Practice the moves until they become smooth and natural. When you present the effect, do each move *very slowly, step by step,* so the spectators can follow them easily. Your purpose is to show the audience exactly how to do it — *except for the final "toss"* where you "secretly" release the right end of the rope — enabling *you* to produce a knot where *everyone else* fails. Although they copy your moves with ropes of their own, they will always miss at the vital point — making the trick more baffling each time it is repeated. And then, to top off the IMPOSSIBLE KNOT, you can follow with ....

THE "DO IT YOURSELF" KNOT

To show the baffled spectators how "easy" the IMPOSSIBLE KNOT really is, the magician forms the preliminary loops with his own rope. He then hands the ends to the spectator *before* he "tosses" the rope from around his hands. When the spectator takes the rope from the performer's hands, he still finds that a knot has mysteriously appeared!

METHOD

(1) Simply go through all of the preliminary Steps 1 through 5 to the point where you have the two ends projecting from each hand, with the "loops" still around your wrists.

(2) Now, extend your hands and invite the spectator to take the ends of the rope, one end in each of his hands, and draw them apart himself. When he does, the knot will make its puzzling appearance!

COMMENTS AND SUGGESTIONS

The neat feature here is that the "Secret Move" is not necessary. The mere transfer of the ends to the spectator *before* you toss the rope off, sets up the formation of the knot. You can further emphasize that the ends of the rope *are never released,* just as with the IMPOSSIBLE KNOT.

Having shown the spectator "how easy it is," you can revert back to the original "Impossible Knot" routine. He will again find he cannot form a knot on his own.

Here, you can offer further help by having *him* go through the preliminary moves with his own rope. You then say to him, "I think you've got it!" Now *you* take the ends and take the rope from his hands to show the knot. Give him back the rope, and tell him to start again *now that he has found he can do it.* But when he tries, he fails as usual! This is a great "party" trick. Just have a number of ropes handy as everyone will want to try it!

TURNED-UP GLASSES

EFFECT

The magician places three glasses in a row on the table and announces that he will turn over two glasses at a time — and in three "moves" he will have them all facing *mouth upward.* Without hesitation he proceeds to do just as he said. At the end of the third move all three glasses are mouth up. This seems easy enough to accomplish, yet every time the spectators try to duplicate the performer's actions, something goes wrong. They always finish with the three glasses mouth down! No matter how often you repeat the effect, the spectators are unable to arrive at the same result as the magician and are left totally puzzled as to the reason why!

METHOD

(1) Arrange the three glasses *in the position shown here.* Cups A and C are mouth down at both ends of the row, and Cup B is mouth up between them. With the cups in this position, the stunt is really quite easy to accomplish. What the spectators do not realize is that *when you let them try it, the three glasses are not in this same starting position,* although it seems that they are.

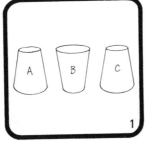

(2) To perform the feat, turn your hands thumbs down and grasp the two glasses at your right (B and C) and turn them over as shown.

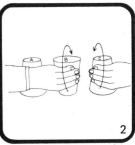

(3) The arrangement of the glasses should now appear as shown in the illustration. This completes move Number One.

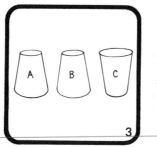

(7) This completes move Number Three. *All three glasses are now mouth upward.* You have performed the stunt, as you said you would, in only three moves.

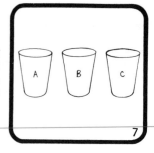

(4) Again, start thumbs down and grasp the two glasses at both ends of the row (Cups A and C) and turn them over as well.

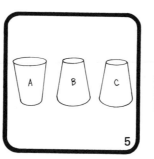

(8) Now for the "dirty work." To position the cups for the *spectator* to try, simply turn over the *center* glass as shown. Remember, when *you* performed the stunt you started with *one up* and *two down* — AND THAT WILL WORK. But *one down* and *two up* WILL NOT! Therefore, with the cups arranged as shown here, the spectator never will be able to perform the feat with the same results as you.

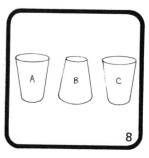

(5) Now the cups should be positioned as shown here. This completes move Number Two.

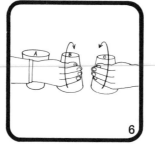

(9) If the spectator follows the series of moves *exactly as you did,* he will be left with the three glasses facing bottoms-up as shown here.

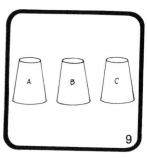

(6) Lastly, grasp the two glasses at the right (B and C) and turn them over, just as you did in move Number One.

(10) By turning over the center glass when all three are in this position, you regain your original position and your moves are ready-made.

(11) Then turn down the center glass, leaving the end ones up, and he is doomed to failure once again.

COMMENTS AND SUGGESTIONS

If you perform the stunt too many times, it is possible that your spectators will begin to "catch on" to the fact that you are changing the arrangement of the cups. It is usually best to do it just once; then let others try and fail. Give another quick demonstration later, but let others worry meantime. So use discretion in determining how many times to perform it for the same audience. You can vary your moves, starting with the two at the left instead of the right, if you wish, but speed is the factor that counts. People are then less likely to note the "difference" at the start, thanks to your casual turnover of the middle glass.

RUBBER BAND RELEASE

Here is another stunt which the magician is able to perform quite easily yet no one else is able to duplicate.

EFFECT

The magician displays an ordinary rubber band, twirling it between the first fingers of each hand. He then proceeds to touch the tips of his right thumb and first finger to the tips of his left thumb and first finger. Even though the tips of the performer's fingers remain touching, the rubber band instantly drops to the table. Yet, when the spectator tries to duplicate the stunt, the rubber band remains trapped between his thumbs and forefingers. No matter how many times the magician repeats the feat, no one else is able to perform it.

METHOD

(1) Begin by displaying the rubber band looped over the tips of your two first fingers as shown.

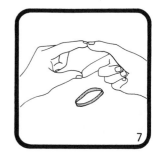

(5) *NOTE: This quarter turn move, as you <u>continue</u> to hold the band between your fingers, is the whole secret of the mystery. Later, when the spectator tries to duplicate your moves, he will neglect <u>to hold the finger and thumb of each hand together</u> and to execute the <u>quarter turn</u>. He will probably just touch both thumbs together and both first fingers together instead. Or, even if he touches the first fingers of each hand with the thumbs of the other hand, the trick is still impossible unless he <u>holds the band in place</u> as shown in Step 4.*

(2) Then rotate your fingers *around each other* as shown by the arrows — always keeping the rubber band lightly stretched between your fingers.

(6) To release the band, spread your thumbs and first fingers apart as shown. (7) The band will drop free to the table.

(3) Stop twirling the band and move both <u>thumbs</u> so that they touch the tips of the <u>first fingers</u> of the *same hand*. The band is now held between both hands as shown.

Fingers and thumbs touch

(8) This very puzzling stunt is quite difficult to figure out without being shown the proper procedure. Give the band to a spectator and encourage him to attempt to duplicate your moves. He will most surely be unable to do so as he will fail to touch the proper fingers together and make the correct moves in order to release the band from his fingers.

(4) HERE IS THE KEY MOVE. Rotate both hands a quarter turn in opposite directions so that you are able to touch the tip of your *left first finger* to your *right thumb* and the tip of your *right first finger* to your *left thumb* as shown. As you do this, <u>continue to hold the tips of the fingers of each hand together</u> as shown in Step 3.

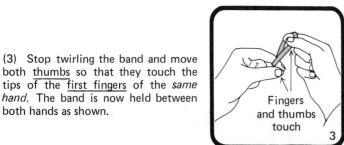

COMMENTS AND SUGGESTIONS

Experiment with the rubber band until you fully understand the *release positions* of the fingers. When you can perform the routine smoothly and without hesitation, you will be ready to present the stunt. This deceptive little maneuver will cause a stir among your friends and keep them busy for some time.

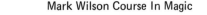

KNOT IN HANDKERCHIEF

EFFECT

Here is a quick and easy challenge which can be performed anywhere with any handkerchief. The magician wagers that he can tie a knot in a handkerchief *without letting go of either end* in the process. With that, he offers the handkerchief to anyone who wishes to try their luck before he attempts the seemingly impossible task himself. It soon becomes quite apparent that no one is able to perform the feat under those conditions. When all have tried and failed, the magician cleverly performs the stunt with ease and grace.

METHOD

(1) Hold the handkerchief at opposite corners and twirl it in a rope-like fashion between your hands. Then, place it on the table directly in front of you.

(2) In order to meet the terms of the challenge, before you pick up the handkerchief, *cross your arms as shown.*

(3) Now, lean forward until you can grasp *one end* of the handkerchief in *each hand.*

(4) With one end of the handkerchief held tightly in each hand, simply *uncross your arms.* As you do, the ends of the handkerchief will be drawn through your arms, creating a single knot in the center of the handkerchief — *without releasing the ends!*

(5) Immediately toss the handkerchief to your spectators as they will, no doubt, want to try the stunt themselves and later perform this "Betcha" for *their* friends.

Make At-Home Magic

★ ★ ★

When a magician speaks of "building an act," he may mean two different things. Usually, he means that he intends to choose certain effects or routines that can be "built" (combined) into a complete program. For instance, he might "build" a routine composed entirely of card tricks, or impromptu magic involving common objects such as coins, rings, string and handkerchiefs; or it could refer to a combination of larger and more elaborate effects. So, in this instance, "building an act" means that the magician is selecting which tricks to use for a particular performance.

The other definition of "building an act" means the actual construction of the magic apparatus to be used in a show. Here, instead of selecting the tricks he intends to do, the magician goes to his workshop and builds them. Every magician needs a "workshop," even if it is only a desk drawer containing old playing cards, envelopes, and sheets of construction paper along with scissors to cut them and colored pencils to mark them. But for more ambitious projects, you will require a well-equipped home workshop—either your own or one belonging to a friend who is mechanically minded.

Such "build-it-yourself" projects are covered in this section, which includes simple working plans and the magical effects that can be presented with the apparatus after it has been constructed. They have all been chosen because they are easy to build and effective when performed. If you feel that you require very special work, you can have the props built to order or buy them ready-made.

So, if you intend to "build an act," in both senses of the phrase, delve deeply into this section, and you will find it made to your order!

VASE OF ALLAH

EFFECT

The performer displays an attractive vase and a length of rope. The diameter of the rope is only about half the width of the mouth of the vase. The magician calls this to the audience's attention by inserting the end of the rope into the vase and then easily removing it. He then reinserts one end of the rope into the vase and *turns the whole affair upside down.* Yet, when the performer releases the rope, it remains suspended, hanging from the vase as if held there by some mysterious force. The performer then grasps the lower end of the rope and turns the vase right side up. Then, by holding *only* the end of the rope, he is able to swing the vase back and forth as if it were some sort of magical pendulum. The full weight of the vase will not break this strange power which now holds the vase to rope. Finally, the magician causes the rope to "lose its power" and *withdraws it effortlessly* from the neck of the vase. *Both the rope and the vase are immediately handed to the spectators for examination.*

SECRET AND PREPARATION

You will find that the items necessary to present this classic effect are very easy to acquire. First, you will need a long-necked flower vase (a "bud" vase is ideal) or a correctly shaped bottle. It must be opaque so that anything inside the vase will not be seen by the audience. The neck of the vase (or bottle) should be about twice the diameter of the rope which is used.

NOTE: Some salad dressing bottles work well for this effect. When you find one the proper size, you can paint it to make it opaque and also decorate it with "magical symbols" to suit your "patter" presentation.

You must also have a piece of rope about 2 feet long. (This is one of the few tricks in the Course in which hard or stiff rope works *better* than the soft magician's rope.) Lastly, you need a special item which is the secret of the trick. This is simply a *small cork or rubber ball* which is a little larger than half the diameter of the neck of the vase and will roll easily into the vase, where it remains throughout the presentation. Small rubber or cork balls can be purchased at many variety, drug or department stores, or you may carve a ball of the proper size from an ordinary bottle cork.

METHOD

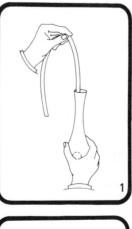

(1) Start with the "secret" ball inside the bottle as you casually display the vase and the rope to your audience. You will find that you can turn the vase in many directions without revealing the secret ball. Just be sure not to tip the bottle too far so that the ball does not roll out of the vase.

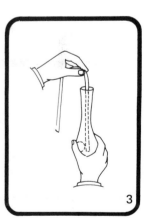

(3) As you demonstrate how the rope slides easily in and out of the vase, when you insert the rope for the last time, slide it into the vase until its end rests near the bottom of the vase as shown.

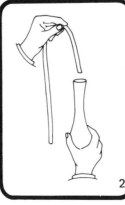

(2) Now, demonstrate how the rope fits loosely into the neck of the bottle. (This subtly shows the audience that it would be difficult to "jam" the rope into the vase without it being obvious to everyone watching.)

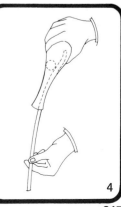

(4) Now, with the rope in this position, slowly invert the rope *and* the vase so that the vase is upside down. Hold the vase in one hand and the free end of the rope in the other hand. When you do this, the "secret" ball will roll *between* the rope and inner wall of the neck of the vase as shown.

(5) Slowly release your grip on the rope and it will seem to be held in place by a magical force (really by the secret ball). To assure that the rope remains in place, give it a slight pull on the end of the rope before you release it. This causes the ball to "wedge" securely in place.

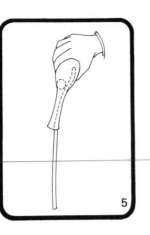

(7) To release the "mysterious force," grasp the vase in your hand and push the rope slightly into the vase — *just enough to cause the secret ball to fall down to the bottom of the vase and free the rope.*

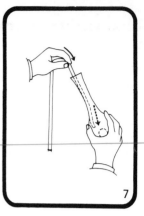

(6) Again, grasp the free end of the rope and turn the whole affair back over so that the vase is right side up. Then, hold the end of the rope in one hand and *release your grip on the vase.* You can now swing the vase back and forth while it remains suspended from the end of the rope!

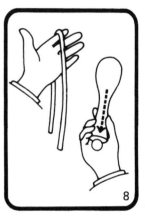

(8) Now, if you are performing close to the audience, *allow a spectator to pull the rope from the bottle.* (If not, just pull it out yourself.) As soon as he has the rope in his possession, *turn the bottle over* as if to show the bottom and *allow the secret ball to roll unseen into your curled fingers.* Then, hand the vase for examination as well.

COMMENTS AND SUGGESTIONS

Experiment with different sized balls until the trick works most effectively. Once you have determined the size that works best with your bottle and rope, make up several in case you lose one.

THE AFGHAN BANDS

EFFECT

The magician shows the audience a wide strip of cloth material that has been glued end to end to form a continuous loop of fabric. By tearing the loop lengthwise twice, the performer divides the circle into three separate rings of cloth. One of these rings is handed to a spectator, another is set aside, and the third ring the performer proceeds to again tear lengthwise down the middle. As he does this, the magician instructs the spectator to tear his ring of cloth in the same manner. As one would expect, the *magician* ends up with two *separate* rings of cloth. The *spectator,* however, manages somehow to create a *linked* chain of two rings.

The magician offers to give the spectator another chance and hands him the remaining single loop of cloth. As the spectator tears it down the middle, the audience anticipates that the circle will again become two linked rings. The final surprise, however, comes when the loop suddenly transforms into *one large, continuous circle of cloth — twice the size that it was at the start!*

SECRET AND PREPARATION

The cloth chosen for this effect must be a type that will tear easily. All *woven* fabrics tear in a straight line, but *knits* must be cut; so if you must purchase fabric, be sure it is a woven one. A lightweight cotton such as percale will tear the easiest, will be the least expensive to buy, and is available in many attractive colors and patterns. An excellent choice that will cost you nothing is to use strips cut from the remnants of worn bedsheets, which are usually made from percale.

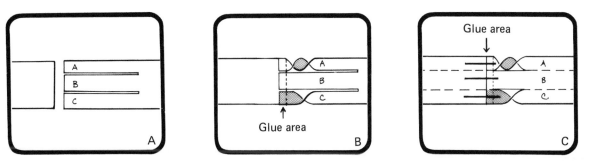

(A)　After you have found a material that works well, cut a strip of the cloth 36″ long by 6″ wide. At one end, cut two slits about 2½″ long, dividing the end of the strip into three 2″ wide bands. We will refer to these new bands as A, B, and C.　(B)　Give Band A a <u>full twist</u> (360 degrees) and glue it to the opposite end of the cloth strip as shown. Be sure to allow about ½″ overlap of gluing surface. Next, glue Band B <u>directly</u> to the other end of the strip <u>without twisting it</u>, as shown. Finally, give Band C just <u>one-half twist</u> (180 degrees) before gluing it to the opposite end of the loop.　(C)　The next step is to cut several slits about two inches long in the <u>exact center</u> of each band. <u>This slit must pass through the glue joint.</u> Study the illustrations for the correct location of these three slits. You are now ready to present THE AFGHAN BANDS. Special glues for fabrics are available where you buy the fabric. Or the ends of the strips may be sewn together.

METHOD

(1)　Holding the glued joints and the twists concealed in your right hand, display the loop of cloth to your audience. Call attention to the fact that the fabric is formed into one *continuous loop.*

(4)　Band B, being an unprepared section, will result in two *equal* and *separate* rings after the tear is completed as shown.

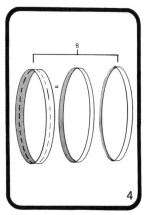

(2)　Now, tear Band C away from the main loop (the dotted lines in the illustration show the path of the tear) and drape it over your right arm, *concealing the twist in the crook of your elbow.*

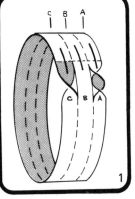

(5)　As the spectator completes the tearing of his Band A, the audience will expect the same result which you achieved. It comes as quite a surprise when the spectator ends up with two *linked* loops as shown.

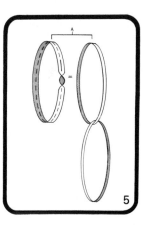

(3)　Now, tear the main loop again, separating Bands A and B as shown. Give Band A to the spectator and keep Band B for yourself. Call attention to the narrow slit in the middle of both bands and instruct the spectator to tear his Band A lengthwise into two parts while you do the same with your Band B.

(6)　Explain to the volunteer that, since there is still one loop remaining, you will give him another chance. Remove Loop C from your right arm and instruct him to tear it down the middle as before. The climax comes when Loop C transforms into *one large loop* right in the spectator's own hands!

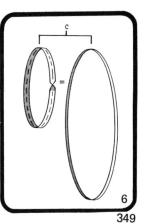

COMMENTS AND SUGGESTIONS

The AFGHAN BANDS can also be performed using strips of paper instead of cloth. The preparation is identical except that, instead of *tearing* the loops, you must *cut* them with a pair of scissors.

THE UTILITY CONE

Here is a clever utility prop which you can construct out of paper. (Construction paper and newspaper both work well, depending upon what "props" you will be using in the cone. If you use construction paper, you may wish to decorate it with a suitable design to help conceal the glued edges of the secret pocket.) When you have completed the construction of THE UTILITY CONE, you will have a very useful device which you can use to vanish things like a handkerchief, a card, stamps, and many other flat or comparable items.

EFFECT

The magician displays a sheet of newspaper. He folds the paper into the shape of a cone and then places a silk handkerchief (or other item) in the cone. Immediately the cone is opened up and shown on both sides. The handkerchief has completely vanished.

Here is the method for constructing a UTILITY CONE out of newspaper.

SECRET AND PREPARATION

(A) Obtain two *identical* pages of newspaper. Square the two pages together and place them so the identical sides are showing and the <u>long edges</u> of one side of the sheets is nearest you.

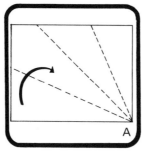

(D) Then make the third fold in the papers following the dotted line as shown. The cone, folded with both papers, should look something like this.

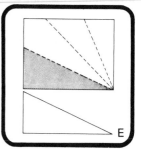

(B) Make the *first* fold in *both* of the papers as shown.

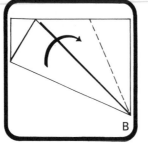

(E) Now, carefully unfold the two pieces of paper. Spread the papers out on the table in exactly the same position as in Step A. Pick up the top sheet of paper and carefully cut out Section X (indicated by the dark shading in the illustration) from this sheet. Once this is done, *discard the rest of this page.*

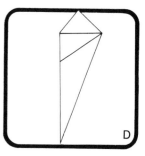

(C) Now make the second fold in the papers following the dotted line as shown.

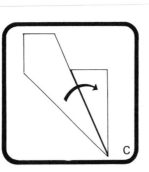

(F) You now have one complete sheet of paper and one extra piece, Section X, which matches a portion of the complete sheet. Glue this matching extra, triangular Section X on top of its identical portion of the side of the full-size page. Glue it along the *two long edges only* as shown. You now have created a "secret hidden pocket" in the newspaper page. If you place an object into the open top of the pocket, it will be hidden inside.

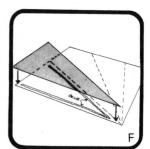

METHOD

(1) To perform the vanish, pick up the specially prepared newspaper page from your table. Hold the page with both hands so that the secret pocket faces the audience. Your right hand is positioned over the mouth of the secret pocket holding it closed, as shown. Use both hands to refold the paper *along the original fold lines*. When you have completed the folding, the opening to the secret pocket should be located at the mouth of the cone on the very inside fold of the paper. Position the cone so that the secret pocket is on the side of the cone *nearest you*.

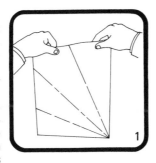

(2) Hold the body of the cone in your left hand. Insert your right fingers into the mouth of the cone and *open the secret pocket*. Do this in a casual manner, as if you are merely straightening up the cone a bit.

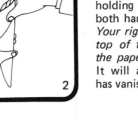

(3) After you have opened the secret pocket, remove your right hand from within the cone. Then, with your right hand, pick up the handkerchief from your table. Use your right fingers to push the handkerchief all the way down *into the secret pocket*.

(4) Once the handkerchief is securely inside the secret pocket, close the top opening of the pocket and hold it shut, pinching the top edges together between your right thumb and fingers. NOTE: Position your right hand with the fingers <u>inside</u> the cone and your thumb on the <u>outside</u>.

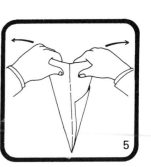

(5) <u>Without removing your right hand from this fixed position</u>, use your left hand to open out the piece of paper.

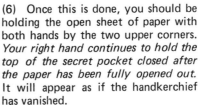

(6) Once this is done, you should be holding the open sheet of paper with both hands by the two upper corners. *Your right hand continues to hold the top of the secret pocket closed after the paper has been fully opened out.* It will appear as if the handkerchief has vanished.

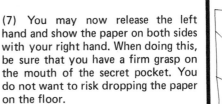

(7) You may now release the left hand and show the paper on both sides with your right hand. When doing this, be sure that you have a firm grasp on the mouth of the secret pocket. You do not want to risk dropping the paper on the floor.

COMMENTS AND SUGGESTIONS

If you wish, you may crush the paper into a ball before you casually toss it aside. This action serves to convince your audience that the paper is unprepared. *Pay very little attention to the paper once the "vanish" has been done.* Always handle the page of newspaper as if it were *totally* unprepared. There are many uses for THE UTILITY CONE. It makes an ideal magic "prop" because it appears to be so "ordinary" — just a sheet of paper!

THE SORCERER'S STAMP ALBUM
(SVENGALI BOOK)

EFFECT

The magician riffles through the blank pages of a stamp album showing it to be quite empty. He then places the album on his table where it remains *in full view of the spectators* throughout the presentation. The performer then displays a collection of loose stamps, which he pours into an empty paper cone. Immediately, the cone is snapped open. Instead of the stamps scattering all over the stage, they *vanish* in mid air! Without hesitation, the magician picks up the empty stamp album and slowly flips through the pages. Attached to the previously blank pages are the missing stamps — pasted in neat rows *completely filling the book.*

SECRET AND PREPARATION

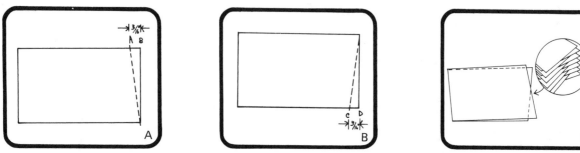

(A)   You will need to purchase enough black construction paper to make 20 sheets of paper approximately 8½ x 11 inches in size. Divide the pages into two equal piles of 10 pages each. Now, cut *all the pages* in one of these piles on a diagonal as shown in Fig. A. The angle of the cut is exaggerated in the illustration for clarity. The actual distance between A and B should be approximately 3/16". (B)   Next, cut the remaining 10 pages in the other pile as shown in Fig. B. Again, the distance between Points C and D should be about 3/16". (C)   Restack the prepared sheets *alternating* them so that every other sheet in the resulting stack is cut on the opposing diagonal as shown.

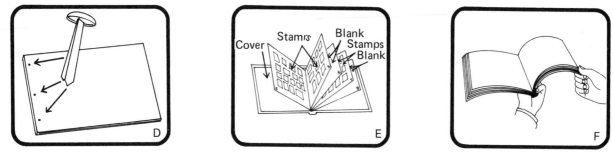

(D)   Without disturbing the arrangement of the sheets, punch three holes through the pages as illustrated and then bind the end of the "album" together with brass brads. A nice touch would be to cut two additional pages of contrasting color and use them as the front and back covers for your album. (E)   Your next step is to purchase several inexpensive packages of loose stamps. These can be found in hobby and department stores and, of course, stamp shops. Starting with the *back* side of the *first* sheet in the book (Page 2), paste the stamps in neat rows on this page and on the page directly across from it (Page 3). Leave the next pair of adjacent pages *blank* (4 and 5). Then, paste stamps on the *two adjacent pages* after those (6 and 7). Continue pasting stamps on *alternate pairs of adjacent pages* until you reach the end of the book. If you have done this correctly, the pages numbered 2 and 3, 6 and 7, 10 and 11, 14 and 15, and 18 and 19 *should contain stamps.* Pages 1, 4 and 5, 8 and 9, 12 and 13, 16 and 17, and 20 *should be blank.* (F)   You can now test your work by grasping the spine of the prepared volume in your left hand. Then, riffle through the pages with your right thumb — *at the lower corner* of the book. If all is well, the book will appear *empty*. Due to the diagonal cuts in the sheets, your thumb will only touch the blank pages as you riffle through the volume. The stamp-filled pages will automatically follow the blank pages as they flip unnoticed, two pages at a time, from one side of the book to the other.

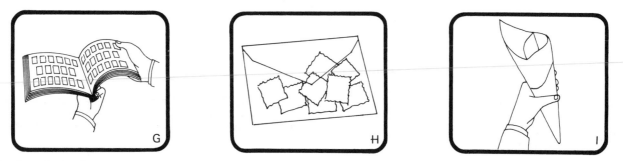

(G)   Now close the book and repeat the procedure, this time with your thumb riffling the book *at the upper corner*. The result should be that the entire book appears *completely filled with stamps.* (H)   You will also need a number of other duplicate loose stamps which you do not glue into the album. Place these into a transparent cellophane envelope or clear plastic bag. (A glass will also work well.) (I)   Finally, you will need to construct a "Utility Cone" which is explained in detail elsewhere in the Course. (J)   At the start, the prepared album and the Utility Cone should be on your table and the package of loose postage stamps in your coat pocket (or on your table). You are now ready to perform THE SORCERER'S STAMP ALBUM.

METHOD

(1) Pick up the album from your table and display it to the audience. Then, riffle through the pages by their <u>lower</u> corners allowing the spectators to clearly see that the album is "empty."

(2) Place the album in <u>full view</u> on the table. A good idea is to lean the album against something that is already on the table. The important part is that your audience *never loses sight of the book at any time during the presentation.*

(3) Display the package of loose stamps to the audience. Then pick up the Utility Cone from the table and openly pour all of the loose stamps from the package into the *secret pocket* of the cone.

(4) Now, make a magical gesture at the cone and then at the album. Immediately snap the cone open to show that the stamps have completely vanished! *Be sure to hold the secret pocket closed during this action.*

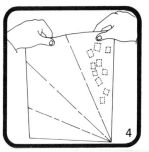

(5) Pick up the album and flip through the pages by their <u>upper</u> corners. The effect will be that the stamps have "magically" appeared" pasted to the previously empty pages of the stamp album!

COMMENTS AND SUGGESTIONS

Instead of constructing the stamp album yourself, you can purchase an inexpensive *photo album* from a stationery or department store. The kind with <u>black</u> pages is ideal. Also, be sure the album contains at least 20 sheets. The pages of most photo albums can be easily removed from the cover and then can be prepared in the same manner as described.

THE COMEDY CUT AND RESTORED PAPER
(CLIPPO)

EFFECT

The magician displays a single column cut from the classified section of a newspaper. Folding the paper strip in half, the performer cuts away the folded center leaving him with two separate strips of paper. When he "unfolds" the two individual strips, the performer finds that the news column has mysteriously restored itself back to one piece! It seems as though the ends of the strips have magically "healed" together. Somewhat puzzled at this strange occurrence, the magician repeats the cutting process, this time cutting the center fold at an angle. To everyone's surprise, when the paper is unfolded it is again found restored — *with a sharp bend in the center of the column!* Finally, the paper strip is cut for the last time, and is once again restored to its original form.

SECRET AND PREPARATION

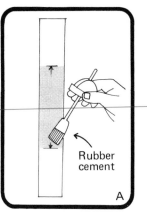

(A) This clever "cut and restored" effect works on the same principle as Inflation as described on Page 227. To prepare, with a pair of sharp scissors cut a single ad column from the classified section of a newspaper. The column should be about 24 inches in length or longer if possible.

Rubber cement

A

(B) Now, place the strip of paper on the table and apply a thin coat of *rubber cement* all along the center section of one side as shown and allow it to dry. Next, sprinkle a little talcum powder on the treated (rubber cement) area. Spread the powder over the entire surface with a tissue or soft brush. (The powder will prevent the treated surfaces from sticking together when the strip is folded in half.) This done, you are now ready to present this clever mystery.

METHOD

(1) Begin by displaying the paper strip as you make some comment about the large variety of items that you can find advertised in the newspaper. This is a good opportunity to inject comedy into the routine by pretending to read some humorous ads. These are really ads which you have memorized and should be as crazy and absurd as you can make them. As an example: "For Sale: Used tombstone — great buy for someone named Murphy!"

(4) Now, carefully open out the paper strip revealing it restored to one piece! Because of the rubber cement, the paper strips will stick together at the cut edges giving the illusion that the news column has restored itself. Even at a slight distance, no one will notice that the strip is secretly "joined" at the center.

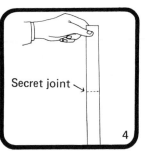

Secret joint

4

(2) After apparently reading the first ad from the center of the column, fold the news strip in half so the treated surfaces of the paper are together.

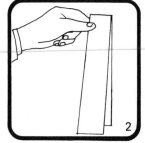

2

(5) Pretend to read another crazy ad and then fold the strip again and snip off another section from the center. This time, instead of cutting straight across, cut the paper at an *angle* to the right as shown.

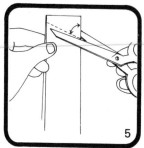

5

(3) Then, using the scissors, snip off the fold in the *center of the strip* making sure to cut *straight across* the paper. Make this cut in the pretense of cutting away the advertisement which you just read. The section which you cut away should be no more than a half-inch wide. *Make sure that the cemented areas are touching each other before making the cut.* Done openly and deliberately, there will be no question in the audience's mind that the strip has actually been cut into two pieces . . . which it has.

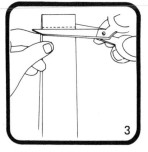

3

(6) When you open out the paper strip, the rubber cement will again restore the two pieces, *but the upper half of the paper will veer off to the right at a sharp angle!*

6

(7) Repeat the cutting process again. This time cut the strip at an angle to the left.

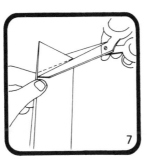

(9) Finally, fold the paper in half again and cut it for the last time — *straight across* — as in Step 3.

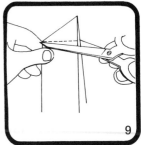

(8) When the paper is opened out, the upper half will veer off to the left as shown.

(10) When you open the paper strip, it will appear to be restored to its original condition in a straight column.

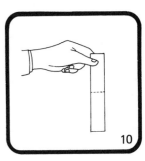

(11) To conclude, fold or crumple the piece of newspaper and place it aside, out of reach of the spectators.

COMMENTS AND SUGGESTIONS

You can also play the cutting of the paper for laughs by appearing to be confused every time you cut away a section of the paper. Each time you make a "mistake" you try to solve the problem by cutting a little more of the paper away. An audience is always amused when they think that the magician has made a mistake, so ham it up a bit, and your audience will enjoy the trick even more.

THE MAGIC CARD FRAME

EFFECT

The magician displays an empty picture frame. Covering the frame with a cloth, the performer picks up a deck of playing cards. The magician asks a spectator to select a card from the deck. The spectator is then requested to reveal the name of the chosen card. Turning to the covered frame, the magician lifts away the cloth. The audience sees that an oversized card has magically appeared imprisoned behind the glass in the previously empty frame. The Giant Card exactly matches the card selected by the spectator!

SECRET AND PREPARATION

(A) You will need an ordinary picture frame which you will change into a "Magic Card Frame." The frame should be of the size that holds an 8" by 10" picture. The type of frame you use should have a cardboard back, indicated by the letter "B" in the illustrations, and a glass front, indicated by the letter "D." You will need to turn the frame so that the "open" end will be at the *top*. This will require that you remove the "stand" that is attached to the back (B) that is used to hold the frame up and turn the stand around so that it matches the now "reversed" frame back (B). The stand now holds up the whole affair as it was originally intended to do. (For ideas for obtaining a frame, see Comments and Suggestions.)

(B) Now cut a square of black opaque cloth (felt is good) the width of the cardboard back of the frame (B). The cloth should be approximately one or two inches *longer* than the back (B). This piece of cloth is called the "flap" and is indicated by the letter "C" in the illustrations.

(C) Either glue a piece of cloth that *matches the flap* (C) onto the cardboard (B) which forms the back of the frame or paint it black.

(D) Next, attach a Giant playing card to the center of the cardboard back (B) so that it will face the audience.

(E) Assemble the frame as shown. The black cardboard back (B) with the Giant Card on it is slid into the frame (A). Carefully place the black flap (C) over the black cardboard back. Then slide the glass (D) into the frame *in front* of the flap. Leave enough of the flap cloth protruding from the top of the frame so that you can grasp it and pull it out of the frame later, as you will see.

(F) Viewing the frame from the front, it appears that the frame is empty, thanks to the black cloth flap that is in front of the Giant Card.

(G) Set this frame on your table, making sure that the part of the flap that extends from the top is folded out of sight behind the frame.

(H) You will also need an attractive cloth, a large handkerchief, or a square scarf. This must be large enough to completely cover the frame. Set the folded cloth and a regular deck of cards next to the frame on your table.

(I) You should have the duplicate card in the correct location in the deck for the "Force" which you will perform in Step 1 of the Method which follows. You are now ready to present this spectacular effect.

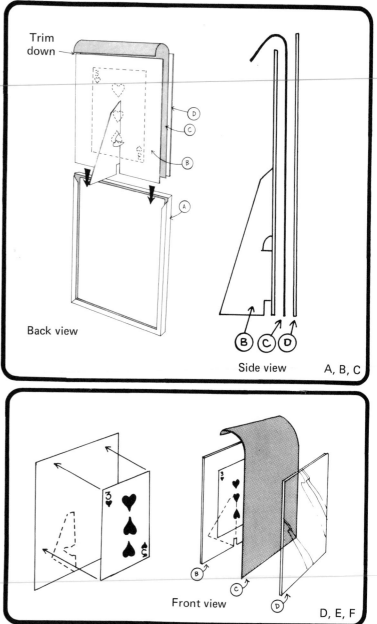

Trim down

Back view

Side view

A, B, C

Front view

D, E, F

METHOD

(1) Pick up the deck and ask a spectator to select a card. *You must now "Force" the duplicate of the Giant Card hidden in the frame.* Use any of the methods of forcing a card that are explained in the Course.

(2) After the duplicate card has been "selected" (really Forced), replace the remaining cards in their case. Ask the spectator to put his card in his pocket (or somewhere out of sight) so that there will be no possibility of your catching a glimpse of his selection.

(3) Now direct the audience's attention to the apparently empty frame on the table and cover it with the cloth.

3

(4) Ask the spectator to remove the card from his pocket and reveal its value to you and to the audience *for the first time.*

(5) Now, lift the cloth from the frame. As you do, *grasp the top edge of the black cloth "flap" through the fabric of the covering cloth and simultaneously* pull the flap from the frame *as you remove the covering cloth.* The flap will be concealed inside the cloth. The audience will be surprised to see the "magical" appearance of the Giant Card inside the frame. Casually discard the covering cloth with the secret flap inside. Have the spectator remove the selected card from his pocket to further confirm that the Giant Card matches the one he "freely selected" from the deck!

COMMENTS AND SUGGESTIONS

If you do not already have a suitable frame with which to make the trick, you can almost always find them for sale in local variety or department stores. They are called "Picture" or "Diploma" frames. The frame itself is made of metal and is complete with a glass front and a cardboard back. The bottom of the frame is open so that the glass and back can be removed. Just invert the frame and follow Steps A through G to make your MAGIC CARD FRAME.

THE DOUBLE-WALLED BAG

As the title of this next item might suggest, this is not a trick in itself, but rather a "magical" prop which will be very useful to you as a utility piece of equipment for switching one item for another or when used as a complete "vanish" for small objects. The strong point of this special bag is that it can be torn open after completing an effect to show it empty.

SECRET AND PREPARATION

(A) Acquire two identical paper bags. The brown "lunch bag" size available at any grocery is perfect. Cut one of the bags along the dotted line as illustrated. Save Part B and discard Part A.

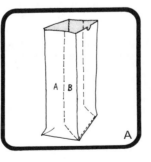

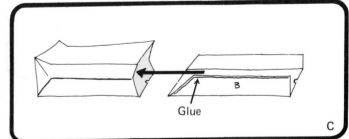

Glue

(C) Carefully slide Part B *into* the unprepared bag and align the top edges of both bags. Now press the glued edges of Part B to the bottom and sides of the unprepared bag. The edges of Part B are glued to the same "matching" parts of the inside of the unprepared bag.

(B) Spread Part B flat on the table and apply glue along the three edges as shown.

(D) You now have an ordinary looking paper bag as far as the audience is concerned — but you have added an undetectable "secret pocket."

Secret pocket

(E) Before its use in a trick, the bag should be folded flat. When you are ready to use it, just pick up the flat bag and open it. This helps give the audience the impression that it is just an ordinary paper bag. At the conclusion of the effect, you can tear away the *unprepared side* so that the spectators can see clearly into the bag. Make sure to keep the prepared side closed by holding it at the top edge with your hand. Some of the many uses of the bag will be explained in the following effects.

THE DOUBLE-WALLED BAG — VANISH

EFFECT

If you have constructed the Double-Walled Bag properly, you should have no trouble in causing an item to vanish from within the bag.

METHOD

(1) Let's suppose you are going to vanish a dollar bill. To do this, pick up the bag from your table and open it, *with the secret pocket side toward you.* Hold the bag with your left hand. Your left thumb should be located on the outside of the bag, while your left first finger is inside the "secret pocket" and your other three fingers are in the main compartment of the bag. This means that the mouth of the secret pocket is open. Keep the open bag tilted slightly away from the audience so that they do not see the double wall.

Secret pocket

(2) Pick up the dollar bill with your right hand. Place the bill *in the secret pocket* of the bag.

(3) With your left hand, place the bag on your table in full view and position the bag *so that the secret pocket is toward the rear.*

(4) When you are ready to make the bill vanish, pick up the bag, grasping the rear (secret pocket) side with your left hand so that the secret pocket is held <u>closed</u>.

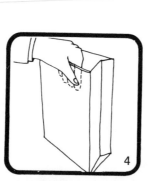

(5) *NOTE: When you pick up the bag, your left fingers grasp <u>both</u> the rear side of the bag <u>and</u> the extra flap of the secret pocket. You now hold the secret pocket closed between your left thumb and fingers.*

(6) Make a magical gesture to "make the bill vanish" and then grasp the front, <u>unprepared</u> edge of the bag with your right hand. Pull down with your right hand, tearing the unprepared side of the bag open down the center, exposing the empty interior. The dollar bill you placed inside the bag has "vanished."

(7) After showing the empty bag, crumple it up and place it aside on the shelf behind your magic table or just toss it off stage. Handle the bag naturally, but be careful not to expose the bill which is hidden inside the secret pocket.

THE DOUBLE-WALLED BAG — TRANSFORMATION

EFFECT

In addition to being able to *vanish* an object from within the special bag, you can also *transform* one object into a completely different one. The handling of the bag in both routines is practically identical.

SECRET AND PREPARATION

(A) For explanation purposes, assume that you wish to transform a silk handkerchief into a playing card. Place the playing card into the *main body* of the bag. Fold the bag flat and lay it on your table.

METHOD

(1) Pick up the bag, open it, and hold it with your left hand at the top just as you did in Step 1 of the "Vanish" so that the secret pocket is to the back. *NOTE: The secret pocket is open and is toward your body.*

(2) With your right hand, pick up the silk from your table and place it *into the secret pocket* of the bag.

(3) Place the bag on your table so that the secret pocket is still to the back, exactly as you did for the "Vanish" sequence.

(4) When you are ready for the transformation, pick up the bag with your left hand, *closing the secret pocket as you do* with your left thumb and fingers. This is exactly as in Step 4 of the "Vanish" routine.

(5) Reach into the bag with your right hand and remove the card secretly placed inside earlier. Show the card to the audience and place it on your table.

(6) Now grasp the front edge of the bag with your right hand and tear the bag open just as you did for Step 6 in the "Vanish." The bag appears to be empty — the silk handkerchief has "magically" turned into a playing card!

COMMENTS AND SUGGESTIONS

If the item which is preset in the main body of the bag is flat, such as a playing card, fold the bag flat prior to the performance. If the object is a *bulky item,* such as an orange, you will have to leave the bag standing open on your table. If you use a *heavy object* inside the bag, it is best that you perform the routine with the bag sitting on your table until <u>after</u> this object has been removed from the bag in Step 5. You can then pick up the bag and proceed to tear it open to show the interior.

THE SUN AND MOON

Here is a mystery which is sure to please any audience. It is a "comedy" effect, and centers around the apparent destruction of two sheets of tissue paper. One sheet is white, the other is any other contrasting color. Let's suppose that the other color is *red*.

EFFECT

Two sheets of tissue are shown front and back. The magician folds them into quarters and tears out the "centers". The torn sheets, along with their centers, are placed in a paper bag for their "magical" restoration. The wizard makes a "magical" gesture at the bag and, when the papers are removed, they are restored *except that the center portions are transposed!* Undaunted, the magician places the "mismade" tissues back into the bag. This time he holds the bag very still as he "MAKES THE MAGIC." The sheets of tissue are removed *again* from within the bag and opened out. This time they are completely restored to their original state. The bag is torn open to show it to be empty and the papers may be passed for examination.

SECRET AND PREPARATION

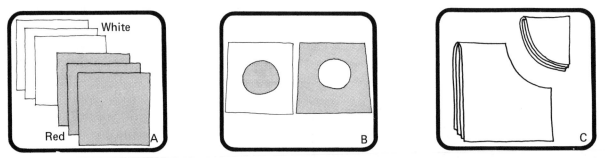

(A) You will need six sheets of tissue, three white and three red—about one foot square is a good size. The first pair of papers, consisting of *one white sheet* and *one red sheet* are unprepared. (B) The second "mismade" pair of tissues (one white, one red) have circles of the *opposite* color tissue pasted on them in the center on *both* sides. (C) To prepare the "mismade" tissues, carefully tear or cut *four* circles of the same size (two red and two white) out of other "matching" pieces of tissue. (D) Glue these circles, one on each side, in the center of the sheet of the *opposite* color. (E) The third pair of tissues, like the first pair, are unprepared.

(F) The paper bag is really the special DOUBLE-WALLED BAG which you have already learned to construct. Make the bag of a size which will easily accomodate *two sets* of the folded tissue papers in the "secret" compartment. (G) Fold the first pair of unprepared tissues into quarters. Do the same also with the second, "mismade" pair of tissues. (H) Put both these folded separate packets together and place them into the Double-Walled Bag. *Do not put these papers into the secret pocket.* PLACE THEM INTO THE LARGER SECTION OF THE BAG. (I) Fold the bag flat. This will conceal the presence of the papers which are secretly hidden inside. Fold the bag and place it on your table. Put the remaining (ungimmicked) pair of tissues on the table beside the paper bag.

METHOD

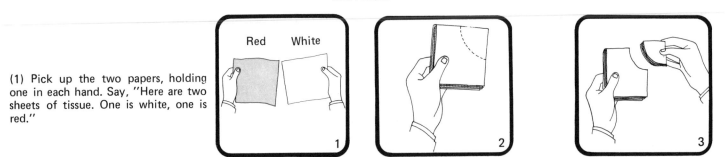

(1) Pick up the two papers, holding one in each hand. Say, "Here are two sheets of tissue. One is white, one is red."

(2) "I shall place the tissues together, fold them into quarters, and tear out the center portions." (3) As you say this, tear the "center corner" out of the tissues in a quarter circle as shown.

(4) *NOTE: When tearing the circles, try to make the torn "centers" approximately the same size as the center portions you pasted on the second "mismade" pair of tissues. You may have to practice tearing the tissues a few times before you can do this action automatically.*

(9) Act surprised as you look at the papers, wondering what went wrong. Place the tissues together and refold them into quarters. Hold the folded papers as shown in the illustration.

(5) Once you have removed the centers, open out the tissues and the centers. Display them to the audience.

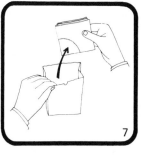

(10) "It seems I have made a terrible mistake. Wait a moment! Perhaps I can correct the situation." As you say this, *tear the centers out of the mismade tissues as shown.*

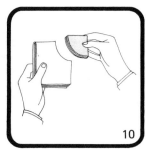

(6) Refold the tissues into quarters and put them, along with the center portions, into the bag. As you do this, PLACE THEM ALL INTO THE SECRET POCKET. Close the bag and shake it. Announce that, by making a *"MAGIC GESTURE"* and by "shaking" the bag, you will cause the tissues to restore themselves.

(11) Pick up the bag and place the torn tissues, *and their centers,* INTO THE SECRET POCKET. Say, "I know what happened, I *shook* the bag when the MAGIC was happening and the papers got a little mixed up."

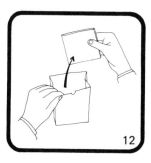

(7) Reach inside and REMOVE THE "MISMADE" PAIR OF TISSUES FROM THE BAG. Place the bag on the table *with the interior facing away from your audience.*

(12) Holding the bag very still, make a magical gesture at the bag. Then, TEAR OPEN THE BAG TO REVEAL THE REMAINING PAIR OF UNTORN TISSUES. *Be careful not to expose the extra tissues hidden in the secret pocket.*

(8) Open the "mismade" tissues to show your *mistake.* The papers are restored – BUT THE CENTERS ARE SWITCHED AROUND!

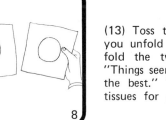

(13) Toss the torn bag aside before you unfold the two tissues. Now unfold the two papers, as you say, "Things seem to have worked out for the best." You can now hand both tissues for examination if you wish.

COMMENTS AND SUGGESTIONS

This trick will be very well received if you play it in a "tongue-in-cheek" fashion. The only thing you have to worry about is when you tear open the bag — be careful not to expose the "secret" pocket or its contents. This classic "comedy" effect gives you an opportunity to add as much "acting" as you wish to emphasize your "mistake" when you display the *mismade* tissues.

THE CUT AND RESTORED NECKTIE

EFFECT

The magician requests the assistance of a volunteer from the audience. Once on stage, the spectator is given a piece of rope to examine. After confirming that the rope is unprepared, the performer temporarily drapes the rope around the gentleman's neck so that the spectator may examine a very sharp pair of scissors. In order to demonstrate the efficiency of the scissors, the performer grasps both ends of the rope and, in one quick cut, he severs the rope in two places. Unfortunately, in his haste, *he also cuts through the spectator's tie —* which flutters to the floor. With a chagrinned look on his face, the magician sheepishly picks up the cut ends of the tie and hurriedly stuffs them into a paper bag along with the remaining portion of the tie which he has had the spectator remove. The embarrassed magician suggests that the volunteer take it to a seamstress for repair as the magician attempts to get *another* volunteer for the trick! Needless to say, his search for a new "volunteer" is remarkably unsuccessful. This leaves the magician only one recourse — that is to promptly restore the spectator's tie to its original condition. When the performer withdraws the once severed tie from the paper bag, it is found completely restored — leaving the bag absolutely empty — much to the relief of the spectator, the audience, *and* the magician!

SECRET AND PREPARATION

(A) You will need to purchase two *duplicate* neckties. It is not necessary to purchase expensive ties; in fact, this would hinder the effect. Expensive ties are generally <u>lined</u> and are more difficult to cut. A pair of sharp scissors is also essential to the working of this presentation, as any problems in cutting the tie *quickly* and *smoothly* spoils the comedy effect. In addition, you will also need to make one of the special Double-Walled Paper Bags as explained in the Course. The last item is a piece of soft rope approximately five feet long. If possible, the rope should have its "inner core" removed ("Coring") to make the cutting process easier. Now place *one* of the duplicate ties in the *main compartment* of the Double-Walled Bag along with the rope and scissors. The *secret pocket* in the bag is left *empty*.

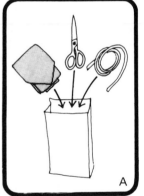

<u>Before the performance</u>, discreetly choose a member of the audience who appears to have an out-going personality to be your "partner" in this effect. Take him aside where the other spectators cannot see and have him put on the other duplicate tie. Explain to him exactly what will happen on stage and instruct him to volunteer to assist you when the time comes to present this effect. (Or arrange to "select" him yourself from the audience.) Tell him to act somewhat annoyed when he discovers that you have ruined his tie. He is to "play along" with the situation as it progresses to produce as much laughter and audience response as possible. Have your volunteer take a seat that is easily accessible to the stage and you are ready.

METHOD

(1) To begin the presentation, ask for the assistance of a member of the audience. As your pre-arranged "volunteer" arrives on stage, remove the length of rope and the scissors from the bag and place the bag aside. Ask the spectator to stand to your right and hand him the length of rope to examine.

(2) After he has confirmed that the rope is unprepared, drape it around his neck. The ends of the rope should extend below the edge of the tie as shown.

(3)   Now give the scissors to the spectator and ask him to verify their "sharp" condition. While he is looking at the shears, gather both ends of the rope in your left hand. As he hands the scissors back to you, explain to the audience how it will only take *one* cut to divide the rope into *three* parts. As you say this, open the scissors and pass the back blade behind the ends of the rope — *and the volunteer's tie* as shown.

(6)   After the comedy byplay with your volunteer, discard the rope and pick up the end of the severed tie from the floor. Ask the volunteer to remove what is left of his tie. Then place all the pieces of the tie into the *secret pocket* of the paper bag as shown.

(4)   With one quick cut, sever the rope *and* the tie, leaving you with two pieces of rope in your left hand *as the end of the spectator's tie flutters to the floor.*

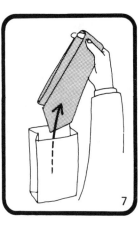

(7)   Offer the bag to the spectator suggesting that he have the tie mended by his wife or a local seamstress — as you quickly attempt to get another volunteer so you can repeat the trick! When the "tieless" spectator protests, explain that the only apparent solution to the dilemma is for you to use "a little more magic." Make a magical gesture at the bag, then reach into the bag and remove the whole duplicate tie from the *main compartment* of the bag.

(5)   NOTE: Now is the time when the acting ability of you and the spectator comes into play. You will, no doubt, get an immediate response when the audience realizes the terrible mistake you have made. You can then carry the humor of this misfortune as far as you wish. This is a wonderful opportunity to build the presentation into a complete "comedy of errors." One suggestion would be to *continue* cutting the tie into more pieces in an attempt to "make the trick work." You might even cut the remaining portion of the tie so it falls off the spectator, eliminating the need to have him remove it himself. (Be careful not to cut the spectator.)

(8)   Return the necktie to your assistant and tear the bag open to prove it is empty. *Be careful not to expose the pieces of the cut tie in the secret compartment.* Thanks to the Double-Walled Paper Bag and a more than helpful "volunteer," the audience will be again convinced of your remarkable abilities as a magical mystery worker!

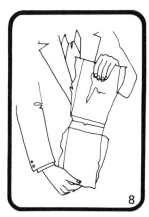

WINE GLASS PRODUCTION

EFFECT

This is excellent as an OPENING EFFECT. The performer freely displays both sides of an attractive handkerchief, showing it to be quite empty. He drapes the handkerchief over his open palm, and suddenly, a form is seen to appear under the fabric. When he lifts the handkerchief away, the spectators are astonished to see that a wine glass — *full of liquid* — has magically appeared and is resting upright on the magician's outstretched hand!

SECRET AND PREPARATION

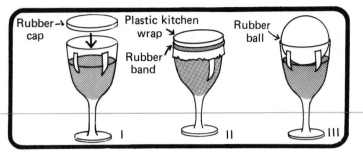

In order to present this startling effect, you will need the following items: A long-stemmed wine glass, an opaque handkerchief, about 24" square, a piece of material that *closely matches* the coat you will wear during your performance, and a soft plastic or rubber cover that fits snugly over the mouth of the wine glass. This cover serves to hold the liquid inside the glass before its "magical" appearance. Most camera stores carry various sizes of rubber *lens caps* which will fit tightly over the mouth of many standard size wine glasses. In place of the lens cap, you can use a sheet of *plastic kitchen wrap* held in place with a rubber band. Another excellent suggestion is to wedge a *rubber ball* into the mouth of the glass. In this case, in order to make an effective seal, you will have to experiment with different sized rubber balls until you find one that works well for retaining the liquid in the glass, yet can be quickly and easily removed without giving you any trouble.

(A)   The first step in the preparation of the wine glass is to cut a circular patch of cloth the same size as the bottom of the wine glass from the material that matches your coat. Glue the cloth circle to the bottom of the glass as shown.

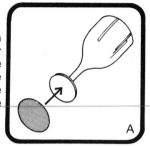

(B)   Next, fill the glass approximately three-quarters full of colored liquid and fasten the rubber cap (or whatever method you are using) in place, sealing the liquid inside.

(C)   Now, position the prepared glass under your left arm just below the shoulder with the <u>bottom</u> of the glass *facing the audience* as shown. (You can see why the fabric on the bottom of the glass must closely resemble your coat. Also, because you hold the glass under your arm, this must be the *opening effect* in your performance.) Place the handkerchief in your breast pocket and prepare to make your entrance.

METHOD

(1)   As soon as you arrive center stage, remove the handkerchief from your breast pocket and display it, holding it between both hands as shown in this <u>audience view</u>.

(3)   Keeping the handkerchief tightly stretched between your hands, cross your arms as shown. Your <u>right</u> hand moves <u>inward</u> *behind* your left arm, as your <u>left</u> hand swings <u>out toward the audience</u> to its new position in *front* of your right elbow. As you display the handkerchief in this position, your <u>right fingers</u> curl under the stem of the wine glass *secretly securing it between your right first and second fingers.* As soon as your fingers are around the stem of the glass, relax the pressure of your left arm. This allows the mouth of the glass to pivot downward *behind the right corner of the handkerchief* where it remains held by your right fingers concealed from the audience. Your left elbow also aids in concealing this action as you display the handkerchief.

(2)   Your thumbs should grip the handkerchief *over the top hem* with the rest of your fingers positioned <u>behind</u> the scarf as illustrated here from <u>your viewpoint</u>.

(4)   Now, uncross your arms and bring the handkerchief back to its original position. This action secretly carries the glass, in its inverted position in your right hand, behind the right-hand corner of the handkerchief.

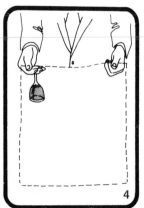

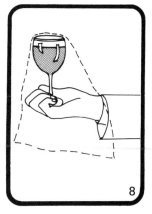

(5) The entire procedure of showing both sides of the handkerchief (Steps 1 through 4) must be performed in *one continuous flowing movement,* without directing any undue attention toward your right hand. Practice the "steal" before a mirror until you are exactly sure what "angles" are working against you. If the glass is "flashing" at any point during the steal, adjust your actions to correct the problem. Then, practice the steal over and over until you are able to execute the entire procedure smoothly and naturally.

(8) Repeat this move, but this time, as you lift the handkerchief, *bring the glass to an upright position* by curling the right fingers into your palm as shown. Now release the handkerchief as you did before; only this time, it falls over the upright glass *revealing the shape of the glass under the handkerchief.* This instant appearance is quite astonishing when performed correctly.

(6) Once you have executed the "steal," the glass should be hanging in its inverted position behind the right-hand corner of the handkerchief. Now, release your grip on the handkerchief with your right thumb (continue to hold the other corner with your left hand) and quickly slide your right hand forward to the center of the handkerchief, allowing the fabric to drape over your open hand and the glass as shown. Because the glass extends *downward* from your right hand, the effect to the audience is that the handkerchief is now covering your *empty* palm.

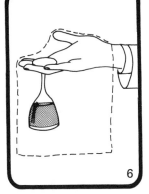

(9) With your left hand, grasp the rubber cap (or whatever you are using) *through the fabric of the handkerchief* and pull it from the mouth of the glass as you begin to lift away the handkerchief. Keep the rubber cap concealed within the folds of the material. Just as the handkerchief clears the glass, uncurl the fingers of your right hand allowing the glass to rest on your left palm as though it has just "magically" appeared in that position. Place the handkerchief aside (along with the rubber cap) and toast your audience as you drink the liquid to prove that it is genuine.

(7) Now, grasp the handkerchief at its center with your left fingers and lift it straight upward forming a sort of "tent" in the material of the handkerchief. Pause for just a moment and then <u>drop</u> the handkerchief, allowing it to <u>fall flat</u> against your palm once again. *Keep the glass hanging upside down from your right hand during this move.*

THE TAKE-APART VANISH

EFFECT

The performer displays a dove or small rabbit and openly places the animal into an attractive wooden box. Instantly, the box is taken apart — piece by piece — allowing the spectators to view all sides of the now dismantled container. Impossible as it seems, the animal has mysteriously vanished from within the box without a trace.

SECRET AND PREPARATION

To perform this astonishing vanish, you will need to construct a specially gimmicked wooden box. This box works on the same principle as a number of large stage illusions. The quality of the finished product will depend upon your ability as a craftsman. If you take your time in the construction of the prop, however, you will probably be using this vanish in your act for many years.

CONSTRUCTION

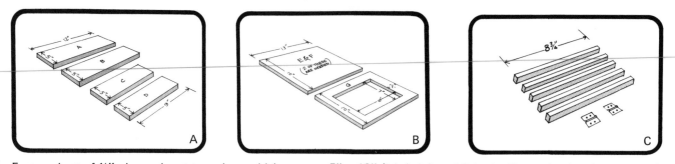

(A) From a sheet of ½" plywood, cut two pieces which measure 5" x 12" (labeled A and B in the illustrations) and two more pieces 5" x 9" (labeled C and D). (B) You will also need three 10" x 13" pieces of ½" plywood labeled E, F, and G. One of these pieces (G) has a 7" x 10" opening cut in the center leaving a 1½" border around the opening. (C) Next cut 5 strips of ¼" square soft pine 8¾" long. This type of wood can be purchased at most arts and crafts shops or obtained at any lumber yard. You will also need two 1½" butt hinges which can be purchased inexpensively at any hardware store. (The illustration shows this type of hinge.)

ASSEMBLY

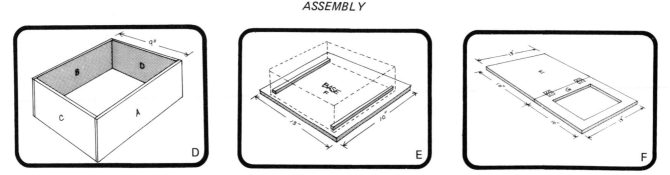

The assembly of the apparatus is quite simple. Take care, however, in fitting the parts together to guarantee the proper working of the equipment and to insure the overall attractiveness of the prop.

(D) Begin by constructing the rectangular frame of the box as illustrated, using Parts A, B, C, and D. Be sure that A and B overlap the ends of C and D so that the inside width of the frame is 9". (E) Next, attach two of the ¼" strips to the top surface of Part F, which serves as the removable bottom for the rectangular frame constructed in Step D. To insure exact alignment, center the frame on top of the board (F) and position the two strips along the inner walls of the frame as illustrated. Then, fasten these strips to the baseboard with wood glue and finishing nails. If done correctly, the frame should fit easily over the baseboard with the two strips serving to hold the frame in position during the presentation. (F) To construct the lid of the box, butt the long ends of E and G together and attach the two hinges as illustrated here. When E is hinged over — on top of G — the two boards should align evenly on all sides.

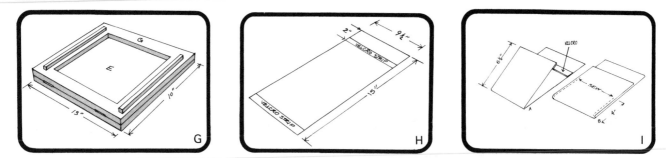

(G) Now, turn the unit over and attach two ¼" strips to the underside of Part G as shown here. To insure their exact alignment, follow the same procedure outlined in Step E. (H) The basic construction is now complete except for the addition of a secret cloth bag which is attached to the lid of the box. The bag should be constructed from a strip of strong, black material approximately 15" long by 9½" wide. Cut a strip of Velcro to fit across the full width of the cloth. (Or you may use snaps or a zipper.) Velcro can be obtained in the sewing notions section of department or yard goods stores. You will notice that the Velcro strip consists of two pieces of ribbon with fuzzy nylon loops which stick together. Each half of the Velcro strip has a different texture. Sew one side of the strip of Velcro across the width of the cloth approximately 2" from one end. Then sew the corresponding side of the Velcro strip (the one with the different texture) even with the edge of the opposite end of the cloth as shown. (I) Now fold the cloth over as shown and press the Velcro strips together. This fold will form a bag approximately 6½" deep and 9½" wide. Now, sew the two layers of material together along the sides of the bag — but only sew about 4" up from the fold which forms the bottom of the bag.

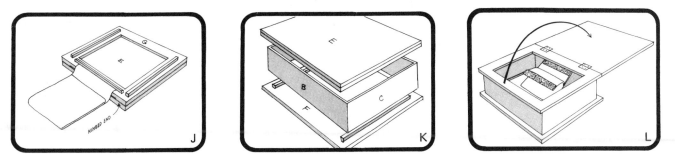

(J) Next, place the lid of the box on the table — bottom side up — *so that Part G of the lid is facing up.* Position the bag so that its upper edge lies over the *hinged side* of G as shown. Place the remaining ¼" strip of wood on top of the edge of the bag and secure the wood strip <u>and the bag</u> to Part G with glue and finishing nails as shown here. This strip must be properly positioned to insure the centering of the lid on the rectangular frame. The *construction* of the box is now complete, and you are ready to assemble the components into the finished product. (K) Place the baseboard F on your table with the ¼" strips facing up. Next, set the open frame on top of the baseboard; then, place the lid E on top of the frame. (L) Be sure that the bag hangs inside the frame and the hinges are nearest to the audience as shown. (M) If everything fits together well, paint the equipment in a decorative manner, and you are ready to present this most baffling vanish.

METHOD

(1) As you display the rabbit (or other small animal or object) to the audience, step to your table and open the lid of the box. The lid should open *away* from you *in the direction of the audience* as shown in Step L. Carefully place the rabbit into the black bag and press the Velcro strips together. This done, close the lid as if to prevent the rabbit from escaping.

(2) You are now ready to "vanish" the rabbit by showing all the sides of the box as you take it apart. Although this procedure can be executed by the magician alone, *the handling of the apparatus is easier and much less risky if you utilize the aid of an assistant.* With your assistant standing at your left, open the lid, Part E, completely so that the audience can see its top surface. Then grasp Part G by the *back edge* with your left hand and lift the entire lid assembly off the frame as shown. This will pull the bag — and the animal — out of the frame, *concealing it behind Part E.* The spectators have now seen <u>both sides</u> of the lid — which you give to your assistant to hold. Be sure not to let the audience catch a glimpse of the hidden bag as you hand the lid to your assistant.

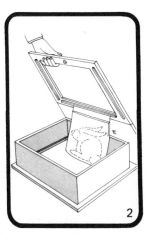

(3) Now direct your attention to the rectangular frame. *Lift it slowly from the baseboard <u>as though it contained the rabbit</u>.* Slowly move forward and then suddenly spin the frame between your hands showing it empty. Hang the empty frame over your assistant's free arm and once again direct your attention back to the table. Pick up the baseboard by tilting it toward the audience and hold it as though you were concealing something behind it. Take a few steps forward and then slowly turn the board over with a smile. The *total vanish* of the rabbit will leave the audience contemplating this mystery for a long time to come.

CONFETTI TO CANDY — FIRST VERSION

EFFECT

The magician displays a large bowl full of confetti and sets it on his table. (It can also be held by his assistant.) He calls his audience's attention to an empty paper cup. Plunging the cup into the bowl of loose confetti, the performer lifts the now full cup into the air and allows the confetti to shower back into the bowl. Once again the magician fills the empty cup with confetti, but this time, instead of pouring it back into the bowl, he covers the brimming cup with a handkerchief. Upon removing the handkerchief from the cup, the audience is surprised to see that the confetti has magically changed into candy! The candy is then passed out to the children in the audience.

SECRET AND PREPARATION

(A) In order to perform the effect, you will need the following:
1. Two medium-sized paper cups.
2. One cardboard lid that will fit into the mouth of one of the cups.
3. Several bags of confetti.
4. One large opaque bowl. This bowl must be large enough so that it will conceal one of the paper cups with enough room to spare for the confetti and the second cup.
5. An unprepared pocket handkerchief.
6. A bag of individually wrapped candies.

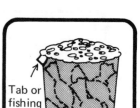

(C) Be sure that the tab or fishing line loop is protruding from the cup as shown.

(B) Your first project is to construct a "special" cup. Take the cardboard lid and glue a quantity of confetti to its upper surface. Most lids of this type have a small tab located on their outer rims. If yours does not have this tab, simply make a tab with cellophane tape or substitute with a loop of strong black fishing line. Now fill the cup with candy and press the confetti-covered lid into place as in the illustration. *NOTE: From this point on, we will refer to this prepared cup as Cup B and the unprepared cup as Cup A.*

(D) Fill the large bowl about half full of confetti. Then nestle Cup B deep enough into the bowl so that the audience cannot see the cup over the bowl's edge. (E) Place the bowl on your table with the empty cup (A) sitting beside it. Put the handkerchief into your left inside coat pocket (or on the table) and you will be ready to magically turn CONFETTI into CANDY!

METHOD

(1) Display the bowl and replace it on your table. Pick up Cup A, show it to be empty, and then, with a "scooping" motion, place it into the bowl and fill it with confetti. *Make sure that you don't accidentally expose Cup B during this maneuver.*

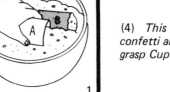

(4) *This time, leave Cup A under the confetti and, as you make the "scoop," grasp Cup B.*

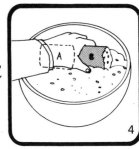

(2) Now pour the confetti back into the bowl from a sufficient height to dramatize the unprepared nature of the equipment.

(5) Bring the prepared Cup B into view with the excess confetti spilling from its lid. *NOTE: This action must be made in one flowing motion. If done properly, the audience will not be aware of the "switch" of the cups.*

STEPS 3, 4, and 5 ARE THE IMPORTANT MOVES IN THIS TRICK.

(3) Dip Cup A once again into the bowl as if to fill it with confetti.

(6) Brush off the excess leaving only the confetti that you previously glued to the lid. Hold the apparently confetti-filled cup up for all to see.

(7) Reach into your coat pocket and remove the handkerchief. Then, drape the handkerchief over the cup. Make a "magical gesture" toward the cup with your free hand or say a "magical word" to accomplish the small miracle.

(9) Lift the handkerchief *and the confetti-covered lid* off and away from the cup. Keep the lid concealed in the handkerchief as you drop them both into the bowl. All that is left is to reveal the "magical" change of the confetti to candy and pass it out among the children in the audience.

(8) Now grip the handkerchief *and* the tab underneath with the thumb and fingers of your right hand.

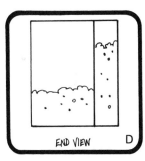

CONFETTI TO CANDY — SECOND VERSION

EFFECT

The effect in this version is identical to the First Version except that a box with a *transparent front* is used instead of an opaque bowl.

SECRET AND PREPARATION

(A) The cups are prepared in the same manner as described in the first version. In this variation, however, instead of the bowl, you must build a rectangular box approximately 12" long by 6" wide and 8" deep. The front of the box is open, and a piece of glass or clear plastic forms this side.

(D) Now place enough confetti in the rear compartment to fill it about half way.

(B) A second piece of glass or plastic is set into grooves 2" back from the front.

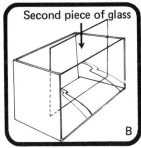

(E) Place the prepared Cup B in this back compartment. *Position it near the left side with its mouth facing left as shown.* The confetti in the front compartment conceals this cup (B) from view.

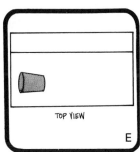

(C) Pour loose confetti into this front compartment until it is 3/4 full.

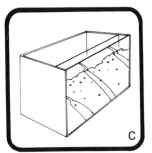

METHOD

The presentation is the same as in the First Version with the added advantage that the audience can actually see you dip up the confetti through the clear front in the box. At the same time, it gives you the ability to boldly make the "switch" of the cups right in front of them without being detected.

CONFETTI TO CANDY — THIRD VERSION

EFFECT

The effect to the audience is the same as in the previous two versions. You may use either the *bowl* or the *box with the clear front* for this method.

SECRET AND PREPARATION

(A) You will need to construct a special set of *nesting* paper cups for this variation. You will need two identical paper cups and one cardboard lid. Glue the confetti to the lid as before, but this time, cut the top rim off Cup B as shown.

Cut here

(C) When the lid is in position on Cup B and B is nested into Cup A, it will look as if you have only *one single cup full of confetti.*

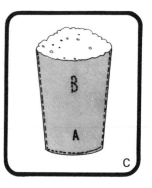

(B) This will enable Cup B to be nested into Cup A.

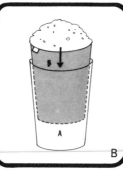

(D) Place the prepared Cup B into the container of your choice — hidden from view. Be sure it is positioned to your left so that there will be enough room for your hand and Cup A when they scoop up the loose confetti on the first pass.

METHOD

(1) Hold Cup A in your right hand. Show it empty and then scoop it up full of loose confetti as before. Pour the confetti back into the bowl.

(2) On the second "scoop," instead of exchanging the cups, simply scoop the loaded cup (B) into the empty cup (A) and lift the nested cups into view.

COMMENTS AND SUGGESTIONS

The advantage of this method is the elimination of any possible hesitation in the second scooping action. The combination of the glass-front box (Second Version) and the nested cups (Third Version) makes this clever effect even more baffling and foolproof. Performed correctly, it is well worth the small amount of time necessary to construct the various parts.

THANK YOU BANNER — FIRST METHOD

EFFECT

The magician displays a large square of velvet cloth and shows the audience that both sides are blank. He then gives the banner a sudden shake. As if by magic, the words "THANK YOU" magically appear on the previously blank surface of the material.

SECRET AND PREPARATION

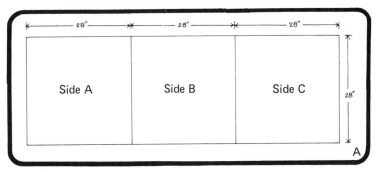

(A) You will need to purchase 2½ yards of black velvet or velveteen and cut a piece to measure 28" wide by 84" long. These dimensions give you a strip of cloth whose *length* is three times longer than its *width.* In the illustrations, the letters A, B, and C represent the three "sides" of the banner, each of which are 28" square.

(B) To make the banner, first spread the material out on the table or floor with the nap (the velvet surface) facing down. Then fold it across the width with the nap outside forming three equal square areas of cloth (Sides A, B, and C) that all hinge at a common point (X). If you have folded the fabric correctly, it should appear as illustrated in Step B. Study the picture and then pin the "sides" in place to see if you have folded the cloth as shown.

You will notice that the bottom half of Side A forms a sort of "flap" which, when folded up reveals Side B. When this "flap" is folded down, it *covers* Side B and *reveals* Side A again. (Side C is the blank "back" of the banner and does not change.) Insert a weight (Comments and Suggestions) between the layers of fabric in each bottom corner of the "flap" as shown and sew them in place with strong thread. These "weights" will cause the flap to drop smoothly and quickly when you make the "magical appearance" of the THANK YOU. They also help to pull the cloth downward so that Side A of the "flap" hangs straight as you display the banner to the audience after the "appearance." Now sew the banner together around the outside edges. *NOTE: Leave the hem open at the top edge of the banner where Side A and Side C come back to back. This leaves a sort of "secret pocket" between the two layers of material which you will use in the THANK YOU BANNER — SECOND METHOD described immediately after this effect.*

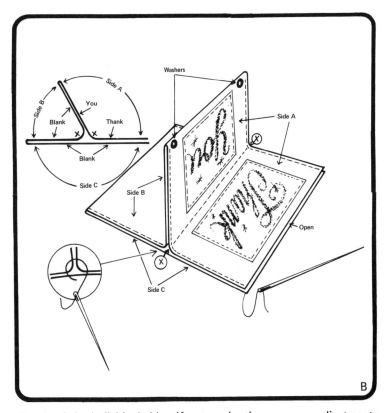

Then sew completely through the entire width of the banner at Point X where the three sides meet in the center. The line formed by sewing through the banner from X to X should be *exactly in the center of all three sides,* A, B, and C. Thus there should be precisely 14" between Line X-X and the ends of each of the individual sides. If not, make the necessary adjustments before sewing the banner together.

You will also need two pieces of black felt material that measure approximately two feet long and one foot wide. It is on these pieces of felt that the greeting or message (the "THANK YOU") that you wish to convey is written. One spectacular and attractive way of writing the words of the message across the felt is with an artists brush dipped in white glue. This done, sprinkle the glued surface with glitter and allow it to dry. Another method is to cut the individual letters of the message from a piece of brightly colored material and glue them to the black felt. With a little experimenting, you will discover other easy and practical ways of achieving the decorative results that will make an attractive-looking message on your banner.

Now, sew the felt to the top and bottom halves of Side A. As you see, the word "THANK" is positioned in the center of the top half of Side A and the word "YOU" on the bottom half. Be sure not to stitch through both layers of the banner when you sew on the felt pieces; *sew only through the material that makes up Side A.* Also, use only as many stitches as necessary to secure the felt pieces to the banner. This way they can be easily removed and replaced with other pieces that convey a different message. The construction of the banner is complete. You are now ready to present the THANK YOU BANNER.

METHOD

(1) Place the banner on a flat surface and fold the "flap" so that it covers Side A. Where the two weighted corners of the "flap" meet the upper half of Side A is now the "top" of the banner. When you are ready to present the trick, pick up one pair of these corners in your right hand and the other pair in your left hand and display Side B of the banner to your audience. *Be sure that Side B of the "flap" is closest to the audience.* Otherwise, your magical message will result in the appearance of the THANK YOU written upside-down across the banner — which is most embarrassing!

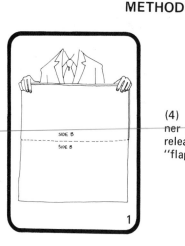

(2) Now cross your arms showing the audience the other side of the "blank" banner (Side C). *Be sure to keep the upper edges of both layers stretched tightly between your hands so the audience is not aware that you hold two separate layers of material together "as one."*

(3) Now, uncross your arms and bring the banner back to its former position as shown in Figure 1.

(4) All that remains is to give the banner a sharp SHAKE. At the same time, release your hold on the corners of the "flap."

(5) Retain a firm grip on the *upper corners* of Side A. The weights in the corners of the "flap" will cause it to drop with a snap, revealing the magical "THANK YOU" spelled out across the face of the now-exposed Side A.

COMMENTS AND SUGGESTIONS

When you are in the store to purchase the velvet or velveteen, ask for drapery weights. These are flat lead weights, usually square, with a cut-out in the center providing a bar by which they may be sewn to the fabric. If the fabric store does not have them, the curtain and drapery department of a large department store will. You could also use flat metal washers about 1" in diameter from any good hardware store, but they will be harder to sew on.

THANK YOU BANNER — SECOND METHOD

EFFECT

The magician displays a large, square cloth banner, showing the audience that both sides are blank. He then folds the banner in half and his assistant lowers two coils of rope into the folds of the material. With a snap, the performer flips the banner open. As if by magic, the rope mysteriously clings to the previously blank surface of the cloth, spelling out the words "THANK YOU" as a fitting close to the magician's performance.

SECRET AND PREPARATION

This is a clever variation of the THANK YOU BANNER. Instead of using glitter or cloth letters, however, sew or glue a length of soft rope to the black felt, spelling out whatever message or greeting you wish to convey. (Or you may sew the ropes directly to Side A of the banner.) Now, attach the felt pieces to the banner in their proper positions and you are ready to perform.

METHOD

(1) Hold the banner in the same starting position described in Step 1 of the THANK YOU BANNER, with Side A folded up concealing the message. Again, be sure that Side B of the "flap" is closest to the audience as you display the blank banner stretched between your hands. Now, display both sides of the apparently blank material to the audience to prove that it is "unprepared" as in Step 2.

(4) Now your assistant displays the two pieces of rope and apparently drops them into the folded banner. Actually, she places them into the "secret pocket" between the layers of material in the open hem where Sides A and C come together back to back.

(2) Have your assistant reach down and grasp the bottom corners of the banner (Side B) in both hands and fold the lower portion upward so that you can grasp these corners from your assistant — one in each hand.

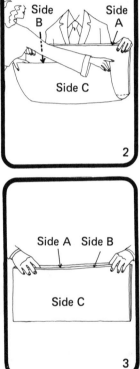

(5) All that remains is to give the banner a fast shake at the same time releasing your grip on the lower half of Sides B and C. Make sure, however, to retain a firm grip on the upper corners of Side A. The weights in the corners of the "flap" will cause the banner to open out with a snap, revealing the magical message spelled out across the face of the exposed surface.

(3) You now hold all three corners of Sides A, B, and C together in both hands. As you hold the folded banner, insert your first fingers between the faces of Side A (the side containing the message) in preparation for the flip when the message will be revealed.

(6) To the audience, the loose rope will appear to have magically arranged itself to form the words "THANK YOU." Actually, the loose rope is safely hidden within the secret pocket.

THANK YOU BANNER — THIRD METHOD

Instead of using a length of rope to form the magical greeting, you can purchase a quantity of glittering rhinestones at an Arts and Crafts shop or costume jewelry store and attach them to the black felt to spell out your message. The glittering stones create a brilliant display under the lights and can be seen clearly by everyone in the audience. To perform, simply fill a small brandy glass with the rhinestones. Then, after folding the banner in half as described above, your assistant pours the stones into the "secret pocket" at the open hem. When the banner flies open, the audience will see that the loose stones have magically attached themselves to the surface of the banner spelling out the words "THANK YOU."

VANISHING BOWL OF WATER

One of the most spectacular liquid tricks involves the vanish of a large bowl filled with water. The following is a simple, direct and very mystifying method for accomplishing this feat. It appears as if the bowl of water disappears right *under the noses of the spectators!*

EFFECT

The magician's assistant enters carrying a large bowl resting on a thin tray. The magician picks up a pitcher filled with water and pours the liquid into the bowl. The performer covers the bowl with an attractive cloth. He then picks up the covered bowl and walks forward into the audience. The cloth is snapped out into the air and the bowl of water has *vanished without a trace!*

SECRET AND PREPARATION

TO ACCOMPLISH THIS FEAT, YOU WILL NEED TO PREPARE THE BOWL, THE TRAY, AND THE CLOTH AS FOLLOWS: (A) THE BOWL: It is a good idea to use a lightweight metal, wooden or plastic bowl. The bowl must have a thin sheet of plastic glued over *half of the mouth of the bowl* as shown. The plastic will prevent the liquid from escaping when the bowl is tipped on its side. Position the plastic piece inside the rim of the bowl and use epoxy or waterproof cement to glue it in place. Also, obtain a strong metal "hook and bracket" combination from a hardware store. Mount the <u>hook</u> on the outside of the bottom of the bowl near the edge using epoxy or other strong cement as shown. (You may also use small nuts and bolts to secure the hook to the bowl. Just be sure to "waterproof" the holes with glue.) The bowl is now prepared for performance. (B) THE TRAY: The tray may be cut from 3/8-inch plywood and decorated to match the rest of your props (or buy an attractive metal, wooden or plastic tray). Mount the <u>bracket</u> on one side of the tray using short wood screws, epoxy or nuts and bolts. Paint the bracket the same color as the tray. The bracket and hook must be positioned so that you can hook the bowl secretly to the tray. Once this is done, you will be able to tip the tray "up," perpendicular to the floor, so that the bowl will be hidden from the audience. NOTE: When the tray is tipped in this fashion, the plastic piece in the top half of the bowl should be <u>lowermost</u>. *This will cause the liquid to remain trapped inside the bowl.* (C) THE CLOTH: The cloth is really two cloths, sewn together at the edges and has a cardboard or plastic disc *the same size as the mouth of the bowl* sewn into the center of the fabric, hidden between the two thicknesses of cloth.

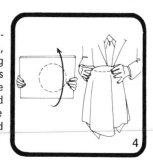

A B C

METHOD

(1) Have the bowl, the folded special cloth and a pitcher of liquid on your table. Your assistant enters at the proper time, carrying the tray. Place the bowl on the tray *secretly hooking it to the tray.* Pick up the pitcher and pour the liquid into the bowl. *NOTE: At this point, the <u>open half</u> of the mouth of the bowl is <u>toward</u> the audience.*

1

(2) Pick up the cloth from your table and unfold it. Handle the cloth so that you do not expose the "secret" disc sewn inside it.

2

(3) Use both hands to spread the cloth over the bowl and tray. Place the cloth over the bowl so that the disc is located *directly over the mouth of the bowl.*

3

(4) For this phase of the trick, TIMING IS CRITICAL. With both hands, grasp the *disc* as if you were picking up the *bowl.* Lift the disc upward as you turn to face the audience. At the same time that you lift the cloth (and the secret disc), your assistant tips the <u>front</u> edge of the tray upwards and takes one step back.

4

(5) This shows how the bowl, attached to the tray, swings to a position hidden by the bottom of the tray. *The piece of plastic glued in the mouth of the bowl prevents the liquid from escaping.*

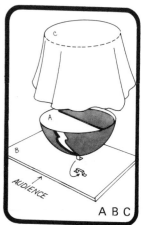
5

(6) Step forward as you hold what *appears* to be the bowl of liquid under the cloth (really just the disc). <u>The audience's attention will be entirely on you.</u> *This gives your assistant the opportunity to exit, secretly carrying the bowl of liquid hidden on the rear side of the tray.*

6

(7) Continue to walk forward until you are well into the audience (or near the front edge of the stage). You may wish to "stumble" slightly for effect as you near some members of the audience. This bit of comic action serves to reinforce to the rest of the audience that you are performing the delicate task of holding the bowl of liquid through the cloth. Suddenly, release your grasp on the disc and toss the cloth upward. As it descends toward the floor, catch one corner (or two corners if you wish) and snap the cloth back up into the air. *Show both sides of the cloth and toss it to your assistant.* Your audience will gasp in amazement at the apparant vanish of the bowl and the liquid in mid air!

COMMENTS AND SUGGESTIONS

If you have a FOO CAN (described elsewhere in the Course), you may wish to present it just prior to the BOWL VANISH. After openly filling the can with liquid, you proceed to show it to be empty — the water has vanished. At this point, your assistant enters with the bowl and tray. You then make the water "reappear" as you pour it from the FOO CAN into the bowl. Then proceed with the BOWL VANISH. Performed in this fashion, the two effects blend together in a smooth sequence which builds to a logical "magical" climax.

THE BUNNY BOX

EFFECT

This is a clever variation of the VANISHING BOWL OF WATER. In this adaptation, however, you vanish an attractive *box* which contains a rabbit (or other livestock) instead of the *bowl* of liquid. The method used for the vanish of the box is the same as for the bowl. You will find THE BUNNY BOX an excellent effect to perform for children as they are always delighted to see tricks with livestock.

SECRET AND PREPARATION

(A) Construct the box out of 1/4" pine or plywood to a size which suits the rabbit you wish to vanish. You will need to add some hardware to the box so that the lid can be locked shut. Then mount two metal hooks on the underneath side of the box. Position the two corresponding brackets on the plywood tray so that the hooks on the bottom of the box fit into them exactly. The box may now be hooked to the tray just like the bowl was in the previous "vanish." Drill a few air holes in the ends of the box so that your livestock can get plenty of air. Paint the box one color and the tray another, but select colors that match the rest of your props, so that the entire affair will blend in nicely with your other props.

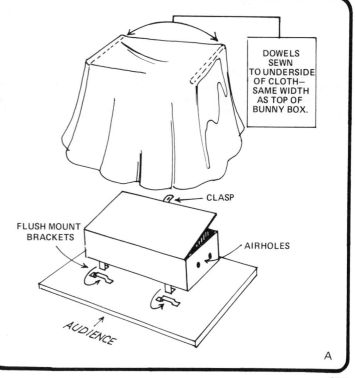

DOWELS SEWN TO UNDERSIDE OF CLOTH— SAME WIDTH AS TOP OF BUNNY BOX.

CLASP

FLUSH MOUNT BRACKETS

AIRHOLES

AUDIENCE

A

(B) Prepare the double cloth by sewing two dowels between the double cloth. (In the vanish, the *dowels* are used just as the *disc* was in the bowl vanish.) The dowels must correspond with the top outside edges of the box. By grasping the dowels, and stretching them tightly between your hands, you retain the *form* of the livestock box beneath the cloth.

METHOD

(1) Show the box and place it on the tray held by your assistant so that the hooks attach firmly to the brackets. Now gently place the bunny into the box. *Close the lid and fasten it securely before covering the box with the prepared cloth.*

(4) The timing of the tipping of the tray is the same as with the Vanishing Bowl of Water. At the proper moment, your assistant tips the tray before leaving with it. The box is secretly hidden on the rear side of the tray.

(2) Execute Steps 3 through 6 as explained in The Vanishing Bowl of Water.

(3) Grasp the two dowels through the cloth. Hold one dowel in each hand and stretch the cloth between the dowels as shown to retain the form of the box.

(5) Step toward the audience holding the cloth with the box apparently underneath. Toss the cloth into the air to cause the box *and* the bunny to vanish!

COMMENTS AND SUGGESTIONS

When you "vanish" the box and the bunny, grasp the cloth by one corner as it falls and snap it out sharply. You may now drape the cloth over one arm as you take your bow. This small addition of business is not always possible with the bowl vanish due to the large size of the disc sewn into the cloth. It can be done, however, with the livestock vanish because of the flexibility of the cloth containing the dowels. To see the magician drape the cloth over one arm before taking his bow not only creates an attractive picture, but also serves to convince the audience that the cloth is unprepared.

PRODUCTION BOX

EFFECT

On the magician's table rests what appears to be an ordinary shoe box. The performer picks up the box and shows it inside and out, proving it to be quite empty. Replacing the box on his table, the magician picks up the lid and allows the spectators to clearly see it on both sides as well. It is just what it appears to be — an ordinary cardboard lid to a shoe box. Placing the lid on the box, the magician picks up the container and displays it to his audience. Upon lifting the lid, the performer reaches into the previously empty box and removes a small live animal or any other similar sized item, much to the delight of the astonished spectators.

SECRET AND PREPARATION

The following is a simple but effective method to produce a live dove or other small animal. The items you will need for this effect are: a shoe box complete with lid, some black felt, a table, and, of course, the animal (let's assume it's a dove) to be produced.

(A) The first step in construction of the "production box" is to sew together a cloth bag made of strong black felt. Let's assume you will be using a standard shoe box with a lid that measures 12" x 6" x ¾". (The size of the lid determines the size of the bag you will make.) In this case, the bag should measure approximately 8" x 4". Cut an 8" square piece of felt and fold it in half. Now, sew up the *ends* of the folded square to form an 8" x 4" bag or pouch that is open at the top and large enough to contain the live dove. Sew a small dress snap in the center of the opening at the top of the bag, as shown in the illustration.

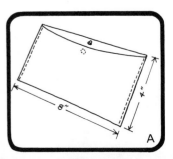

(B)   Next, cut a length of strong clear mono-filament fishing line or heavy thread. This line should be threaded through the lip of the lid and then sewn to the top corners of the bag as in the illustration.

(D)   This done, carefully load the dove into the bag and close the snap to prevent it from escaping. Then rest the lid of the box near the back edge of your table with the <u>inside</u> of the lid *facing up.* The bag containing the dove should be suspended *below the table top* as shown. Position the empty shoe box in front of the lid, and you are ready.

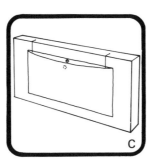

(C)   The exact length of the line must be determined through experimentation. The end result, however, should center the load bag on the back of the lid as shown.

METHOD

(1)   Begin by picking up the empty shoe box and displaying it on all sides. Make sure to give the audience a clear view of the inside of the box.

(4)   Release your grip on the lid and show your hands empty. Then lift the lid <u>just enough</u> so you can *rotate the lid completely over* and place it on the box. *Be careful not to raise the lid too high when you rotate it as that would lift the load bag out of the box where it would be seen by the audience.*

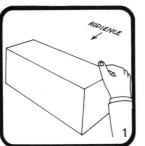

(2)   Replace the box on your table and pick up the lid. This is done by *tilting the lid forward before lifting it clear of the table.* The load bag will be lifted *unseen* into position <u>behind</u> the lid as shown.

(5)   Now pick up the covered box and display it freely on all sides. Then, place the box back on your table and raise the back of the lid with your left hand as shown. With your right hand reach into the box, open the snap, and remove the dove from the bag.

(3)   Keeping the inside of the lid facing the audience, lower the lid directly in front of the shoe box *allowing the load bag to secretly slip inside the box.* Now, stand the lid on its edge using the shoe box as a support.

(6)   To conclude the production, bring the dove into view and then close the lid of the box and take your bow.

COMMENTS AND SUGGESTIONS

The above principle may be applied to any size box. Simply adjust the dimensions of the load bag to fit the concealment area behind the lid.

It is a good idea to practice this production before a mirror and watch your angles. You will find that by *reversing* the procedure, a very effective <u>vanish</u> can also be presented with the same equipment.

THE SQUARE CIRCLE

EFFECT

The magician introduces his audience to an empty rectangular tube, one side of which is cut into an open grillwork or filigree pattern. A cylinder is next displayed and is also proven to be empty. The rectangular tube (the Square) and the cylinder (the Circle) are nested and placed on a small elevated stand. The spectators never lose sight of the cylinder, as its contrasting color can be clearly seen through the openings in the side of the rectangular cover. In spite of these impossible conditions, the performer succeeds in magically producing yards and yards of silk streamers and brightly colored scarves. The magician again proves both the Square and the Circle to be empty. After replacing the tubes, the magician produces a small bowl — complete with water and goldfish — which provides an effective climax to the SQUARE CIRCLE.

SECRET AND PREPARATION

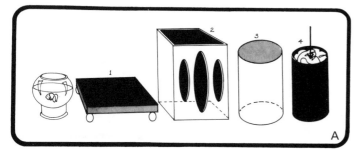

(A)   The equipment necessary to present this effect is illustrated in Figure A. The apparatus is divided into four parts. Item 1 is a small elevated stand, 2 is a rectangular tube with one side cut out in an attractive pattern, 3 is a cylinder of the appropriate size to fit inside the rectangle, and 4 is a smaller tube that will comfortably rest within the larger cylinder. From this point on, we will refer to the rectangular tube (Item 2) as the "Square" and the larger of the two cylinders (Item 3) as the "Circle." The small cylinder (Item 4) is never seen by the audience. Its function is to conceal the production articles, and we will refer to this piece as the "Load Chamber." The <u>top</u> surface of the small stand (Item 1), all of the <u>inside walls</u> of the Square except for the front "cut out" pattern, and the <u>outside</u> surface of the Load Chamber are covered with black velvet. The outside of the Square should be painted some bright color such as blue, green, or red. The Circle should be decorated in a contrasting color such as yellow, orange, or silver in order to be in direct contrast with the Square.

(B)   Let us assume that you will be finishing the trick with the production of the small fish bowl as described. Obtain a bowl that will just fit into the Load Chamber. Place it on the platform as shown. Fill the bowl approximately half full of water and then add several goldfish to complete the picture.

(C)   Place the black velvet-covered Load Chamber over the bowl. The silk handkerchiefs, streamers, or other production articles are packed inside the Load Chamber around (and carefully <u>over</u>) the fish bowl as illustrated.

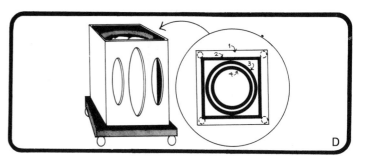

(D)   Now set the Square over the Load Chamber. You will see an amazing illusion. By viewing the set-up through the openings in the Square, the Square looks *quite empty.* Herein lies the secret to this effect. Now drop the Circle over the Load Chamber. Be sure the cut out front of the Square is facing your audience, and the entire arrangement will look as illustrated in Figure D. You are now ready to present THE SQUARE CIRCLE.

METHOD

(1)   Call the audience's attention to the equipment on your table. Lift the Square and show it freely to the spectators.

(2)   Drop the Square back on the Stand around the Circle. *Be sure the cut-outs are to the front.*

(3) Now lift the Circle from inside Square, *leaving the Load Chamber in place.* Thanks to the black velvet, *the Square appears to be empty.* Then make sure that the audience has a clear view through the empty Circle. AT THIS POINT, BOTH THE CIRCLE AND THE SQUARE APPEAR TO BE EMPTY.

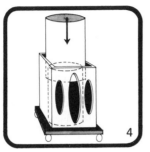

(4) Replace the Circle in the Square. The contrasting color of the Circle can be clearly seen by the audience as it is lowered into the Square. *Unknown to the spectators, you are covering the Load Chamber at the same time.*

(6) After all of these smaller items have been produced, show the Square and the Circle empty again by repeating Steps 1, 2, 3, and 4. After the audience is convinced that there is nothing left to produce, lift the Square and set it on its side as shown. This will leave only the Circle resting on the small base.

(7) Grasp the top edges of the Circle *and* the Load Chamber. *Now, lift them both together, as one unit, off the base.* The goldfish bowl will be revealed for the first time to a greatly surprised audience.

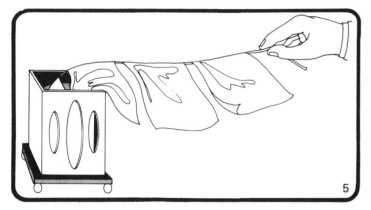

(5) Reach into the top of the Circle and "magically" produce the streamers, silk handkerchiefs. etc.

COMMENTS AND SUGGESTIONS

THE SQUARE CIRCLE is a tried and true classic magic prop. It can be made or purchased in many forms, designs, and sizes. In fact, you can easily even build one out of heavy cardboard that is big enough to produce a person! Be sure, as with all the other tricks you learn from the Course, to protect and never reveal the secret of THE SQUARE CIRCLE.

THE ALLAKAZAM HAT

INTRODUCTION

When I first succeeded in selling the *Magic Land of Allakazam* television series, the original contract was for a thirty-minute show to be aired every Saturday morning over the full CBS Television Network for 26 weeks. Although Nani and I had sold, produced, and performed in many of our own local television series and one syndicated series that was seen in a number of major cities throughout the United States, this was not only my first network series, but also the first time I had ever appeared on any network at all, even as a guest. At that time, unless you were a well established star with a proven show, the longest initial contract any show was likely to receive was 13 weeks. Therefore, we were quite lucky in being given 26 weeks to prove the entertainment value of the first network television magic series.

Nani and I assembled our first creative staff which consisted of a number of very talented people. Although our creative group enlarged and changed throughout the succeeding five-year run of the series (two years on the CBS network and three years on the ABC network), these magical talents remained with us throughout the entire period.

In order to present thirty minutes of magic every week, we not only had to devise many variations on standard tricks, but also create numerous original effects as well. One of the most practical and certainly the most used prop of the entire series was the ALLAKAZAM HAT.

The Allakazam Hat was created to fill a specific need. The show required a connective device which could produce, vanish or change objects; have a "magical" appearance; and be attractive, yet unique enough in design to fit into the overall concept and decor of the show. The Square Circle had the necessary "magical" properties, but the standard Square Circle design looked like nothing other than a magic prop — there was nothing that corresponded to it in "real life."

It was during one of our many extensive creative sessions that we decided that a unique "magician's hat" would be the ideal device — now how to do it? The Square Circle *principle* was an obvious "magical" answer, but it had one major drawback, *the rim of the hat!*

The problem caused by the rim was this: If the rim of the Hat (the Circle) were very large and the Hat were placed mouth upward inside the Square, then the Square could not be lifted off of the Hat because the rim would block it. We discussed the possibility of not showing the Square empty at all, merely lifting out the Hat and letting the viewers look into the Square through the grillwork in front to justify the "emptiness" of that portion of the apparatus. This was rejected for two reasons. First, merely *seeing* into the blackness of the Square without actually *showing* the Square empty would not be deceptive enough, particularly for a prop which we intended to use in many shows. Second, since television is two-dimensional and has no "depth" for the home viewer, this weakness would be doubly amplified.

As with most problems that you will come up against in magic, the answer was quite simple — *once you discover it!* We merely hinged the Square at the back, as you see illustrated in the explanation that follows. In this way, the Square could be removed from the back of the Hat rather than lifted over the top, *thereby eliminating the problem of the brim!*

As it turned out, this made the trick even stronger, and the Allakazam Hat became a regular effect on many of the Allakazam episodes that were seen by many millions of viewers every week. As a matter of fact, the Allakazam Hat became the "on camera" home of *Basil the Baffling Bunny,* the live rabbit who appeared in so many of our episodes, and was also on occasion the domicile of some of Basil's friends, such as *Doris the Daring Dove, Gertrude the Glamorous Guinea Pig, Harriet the Harmonious Hamster* and *Charles the Charming Chicken.* It was not, however, quite large enough to contain one of our most popular characters, our giant rabbit, *Bernard the Biggest Bunny in the Business!*

I feel sure that, at the end of the five-year run of the Allakazam series, because of the vast audiences available through the medium of television, the Allakazam Hat was the one magic prop that had been seen by more people throughout the world than any other magic prop in history.

If you should decide to make an ALLAKAZAM HAT for yourself, I hope that you will have great pleasure in presenting it and perhaps recall a bit of its history as you do. Of even more importance, I hope that this example of a "magical problem" and the technique we used to resolve it will help you to find solutions for some of the obstacles that you may encounter as you develop your own style and effects in the Art of Magic.

So here for the very first time is a complete description of how you can make and use an ALLAKAZAM HAT. Good Luck!

—MW

THE ALLAKAZAM HAT

EFFECT

The ALLAKAZAM HAT is a stylized, improved version of the SQUARE CIRCLE, which has been previously described. Since the secret is a refinement of principles you have already learned and you are also now familiar with the workings of the original trick, we will only discuss the *variations* involved in this particular form of equipment. NOTE: With the ALLAKAZAM HAT all of the parts should be made *larger* than a standard Square Circle, so that a sizable production of items is possible.

SECRET AND PREPARATION

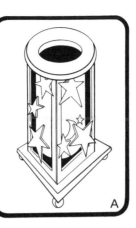

(A) In the ALLAKAZAM HAT, the "Circle" has been designed to look like a *magical hat* with its brim extending beyond the top edges of the "Square." The Square has been modified by cutting the open filigree into *two* adjacent sides. The corner between the cut out areas becomes the front of the Square, which gives a wide open view of the Hat inside.

(B) The load chamber is resting inside the Hat (Circle), as before; but the Square is made to *hinge* from the back corner as shown. In this way, the Square can be opened and removed from around the Hat, since the brim of the Hat prevents you from *lifting* the Square as in the original Square Circle routine.

METHOD

(1) To show the Square to your audience, simply hinge it open and lift it *back and away* from the Hat. You can then openly display it as shown.

(2) Replace the Square around the Hat. Then grasp the brim of the Hat with both hands. Lift the Hat up and out of the Square and show it empty. (The load chamber stays inside the Square as usual.)

(3) After replacing the Hat inside the Square, make your production as previously described. NOTE: The small amount of extra work involved in the construction of this "special version" of the Square Circle will not only result in a professional looking piece of equipment with maximum production space and deceptive values — but also allows you to present what is probably the most famous magic trick of all . . . *PRODUCING A RABBIT FROM A TOP HAT!*

THE ALLAKAZAM HAT — A VARIATION

Because of the unique construction of the ALLAKAZAM HAT there is a special "move" that can be easily added to the routine that will fool even those who know the secret of the regular Square Circle.

METHOD

(1) After you have removed the Square and shown it empty as in Step 1 of the previous routine, do not replace the Square around the Hat. *Instead, set the Square, still folded open, in front of the Hat as shown.*

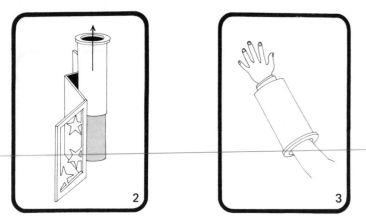

(5) Now pick up the Square, show it briefly again and then replace it around the Hat.

(2) Now pick up the Hat, *leaving the load chamber behind the solid sides of the open Square.* (3) These sides form a natural hiding place for the load chamber. Also, because of the "V" shaped area created by the solid sides, the "line of sight" for concealment of the load is also quite good.

(6) You have now shown *both* the Square *and* the Hat empty at *the same time . . .* thanks to the special Allakazam Hat move!

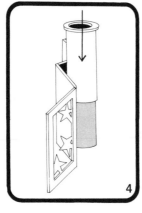

(4) Show that the Hat is completely empty . . . and then replace it behind the open Square . . . over the load chamber.

(7) Begin to make the production from the Hat. Then, after about half of the articles have been produced, pick up the Hat from inside the Square and show it empty again. Replace the Hat and continue with the rest of the "production." In this way you have now used the original Square Circle principle to add further to the deception.

MAGIC TABLE

If you intend to perform on a stage or for larger groups, you should have a "Magic Table." The following plans explain how you can easily and inexpensively build your own table in a style that is ideal for this purpose. It is attractive, simple to build and folds flat for travelling or storage between shows.

CONSTRUCTION

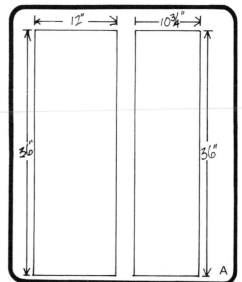

(A) The entire table is constructed from thick plywood and 1" x 2" clear pine stiffeners. Begin by cutting one piece of plywood 36" x 12" and another 36" x 10¾".

(B) Now take the 12″ width and add the 1″ x 2″ pine stiffeners as shown here. Attach the long stiffener "A," flush with the right side of the panel. Be sure to set the wooden stiffener marked "B," ½″ *below* the top edge of the panel as illustrated. Position the stiffener marked "C" 12″ below stiffener B. Stiffener D should be flush with the bottom edge of the panel. The next step is to install the stiffeners on the 10¾″ width. Stiffener A is attached to the left side of the panel. Stiffeners B, C, and D are attached as they were on the first panel. When finished, sand the panels smooth in preparation for painting.

(C) Butt the end of the 10¾″ panel next to the outer back edge of the 12″ panel . . .

(D) . . . and attach two hinges to the stiffeners as indicated. You will notice that both sides of the screen-like table base will now measure 12″. This hinging arrangement provides an automatic stop when opening the panels but allows them to be folded flat for storage.

(F) The second triangular section must be glued to the underside of the table top as illustrated in Figure F. This will insure the proper positioning of the top into the screen-like uprights. Now sand these parts thoroughly, and you will be ready for the final assembly.

(G) You will need 4 small "screen door" fasteners to hook the entire arrangement together. Two of these are mounted to the table top with the eyes positioned in the uppermost stiffener, A, as illustrated. As you can see from this diagram, these fasteners hold the top to the panels. The triangular piece fastened to the underside of the top prevents the panels from closing unexpectedly.

(H) This hook and eye arrangement is also used to secure the triangular shelf into position on top of the B stiffeners as shown in Step G.

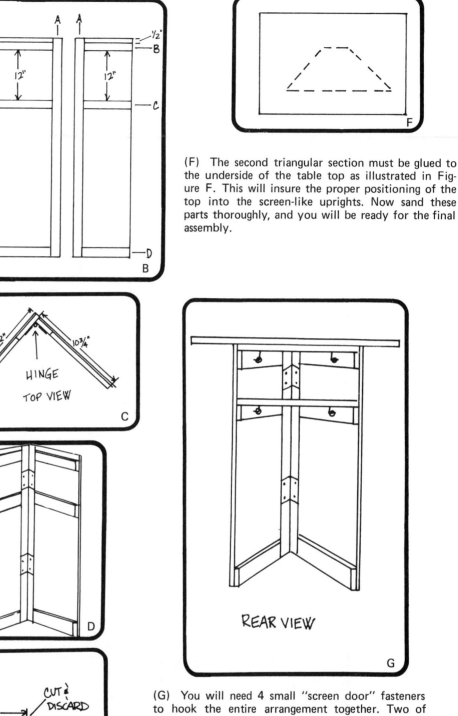

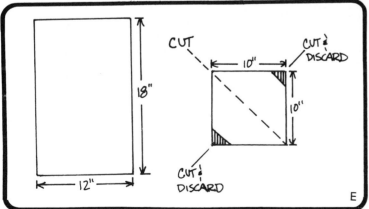

(E) In order to build the top and storage shelf, you will need to cut a piece of ½″ thick plywood 18″ long by 12″ wide and an additional piece 10″ square as in Figure E. The larger of the two pieces is utilized as the top of your table. The 10″ square must now be cut diagonally in order to form two triangular sections. One of these will serve as the *rear shelf* and rests on top of the C stiffeners.

(I) After you have positioned the fasteners and are satisfied with the rigidity of the equipment, you can begin to decorate the table. The first step is to paint the back side of the screen, the underside of the top, and the small triangular shelf "flat black." When these parts are dry, cover the *top* surface of your table with black felt and trim the *edges* with silver (or some other bright color) braid. The front surfaces of the screen can be decorated in any motif that you feel is attractive and suitable to your style of performance.

FRONT VIEW

I

THE BLACK ART WELL

The above title graphically describes a very useful addition to your magic table. Simply stated, a BLACK ART WELL is an "invisible hole" in the top of your table which enables you to vanish an object. The VANISHING GLASS described elsewhere in this Course can utilize a "well" of this nature.

CONSTRUCTION

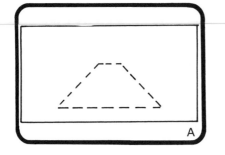

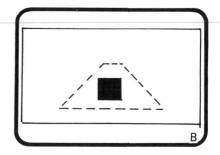

(A) Cut a piece of ½" thick plywood into a rectangular shape measuring 12" x 18". Now add a triangular section measuring 10" on each of the right-angled sides to the bottom of this new top in the same manner as you did with the regular top in Step F of the MAGIC TABLE.

(B) Now, cut a 3" square hole through *both layers* of your new top as illustrated.

(C) Sand the top smooth on all sides and then paint the entire unit flat black.

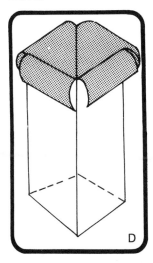

(D) You will need to sew up a square black velvet bag. This bag should measure 3" square and at least 7" deep as shown. Also, be sure that the soft (napped) side of the velvet is on the *inside surface* of the bag.

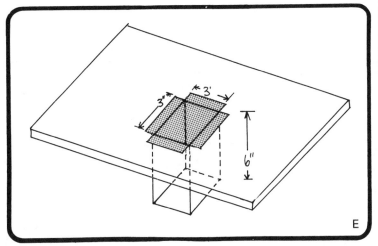

(E) Pull the bag up through the hole in your table top and staple it into position as illustrated. At this point, the well should measure 6" deep.

(F) It is now necessary to cover the entire table top with a piece of matching velvet measuring 12" x 18". This is best accomplished by gluing the fabric directly to the plywood top.

(G) Allow the adhesive to dry thoroughly and then *carefully cut out the excess material above the well with a sharp razor blade.*

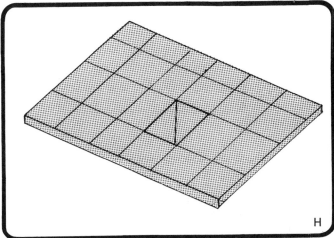

(H) In order to conceal the edges around the well, stretch bright colored braid across the top as shown here. You can attach this braid to the edges of the table by using small carpet tacks or staples. When you have completed the above, trim the edge of the top with a strip of matching braid.

(I) All that is left is to mount the two hooks to the underside of the completed top as described in the MAGIC TABLE.

MECHANICAL MAGIC

Although the following three tricks would be difficult to "Make At Home" — unless you are a skilled craftsman with a variety of tools — they have been included in this section for two reasons. First, they depend upon the *clever construction* of the prop, rather than on sleight-of-hand or misdirection, for their magical effect; and second, they incorporate *basic magic principles* which you should know and understand to aid your progress and help you to build a firm foundation in the Art of Magic.

THE DOVE PAN

If you are building your first magic act, here is an excellent, all-purpose utility prop which is very easy to use and which can be of great value to you. This trick, because of the huge magical "production" which is possible, makes a good closing (or opening) effect for any magical performance.

EFFECT

The magician displays an empty metal pan. A bit of tissue is placed in the pan and set on fire. The pan's cover is quickly clamped on the pan to smother the flames. When the cover is removed, the pan is seen to have become "magically" filled to the brim with candy, handkerchiefs, a dove, or a young rabbit — in fact, any item that would fit within the pan!

SECRET AND PREPARATION

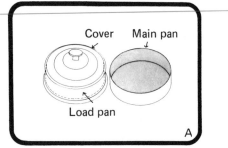

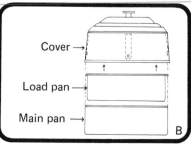

(A)   This is an extremely practical piece of magic equipment as it may be employed to make a variety of items "magically" appear. The "load" (the item(s) to be produced) is hidden *inside the cover of the pan.* When the cover is set over the pan, the "load" secretly goes into the pan. You can fill the "load pan" with anything from a duckling to a string of flags. Thus, this piece of magical apparatus is very useful because of the large "load" you are able to produce.

(B)   Here is an "exploded" view of the parts of the pan. As you see, there are three parts: (1) the "pan" which you display to the audience, (2) the cover, and (3) the secret "load pan" of which the audience is never aware. The load pan fits exactly into the "main" pan or can be secretly hidden inside the cover. The load pan is held inside the cover by metal stops located on the inner sides of the cover. The items to be produced are placed inside the "load pan" before the trick begins and then the "load pan" is inserted inside the cover. The cover and the main pan are both placed on your table.

METHOD

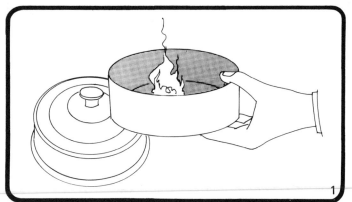

(1)   Pick up the main pan from your table. Show it to be empty and then place a small piece of crumpled tissue paper inside. Use a match to set the tissue afire. As the flames begin to rise, pick up the cover and quickly clamp it *over the main pan.*

(2)   When you put the cover on the main pan, the top edge releases the "load pan" from its secret position inside the cover. The "load pan" drops down *inside* the main pan — so that, when you remove the cover, the pan appears to have filled itself with the "load" items.

COMMENTS AND SUGGESTIONS

This clever piece of apparatus lends itself to almost any magical performance. You can use your imagination in determining what type of "load" is best suited for you. One inexpensive production can be to fill the pan with popcorn. This piece of equipment has long been a favorite with children and is very practical for the working magician.

THE FOO CAN

The vanish of a quantity of liquid has always been a favorite with audiences. Here is one of the simplest yet one of the most effective methods of accomplishing the feat.

EFFECT

The magician displays a tall metal canister. The canister is filled with water and immediately turned upside-down. The water appears to *vanish instantly* from within the can. The magician rights the container and then utters the proper magic words. As if by magic, the water *reappears* and is poured freely from the can.

METHOD

(1) This effect works with the aid of a specially constructed container called the Foo Can. The can is made with a double wall on one side so that the water can be trapped within a secret compartment. The dotted line in the illustration represents the "double wall" within the body of the can. Thus, if the can is rotated in the proper direction when it is turned upside-down, the water will be trapped inside.

(2) The can may be shown empty before the liquid is poured into the mouth of the can. You will have to experiment with the amount of liquid which can be held within the secret compartment. Be careful not to pour *too much* water into the can as the secret double-walled compartment is designed to hold only a certain amount of liquid.

(3) After the water is poured in, make a few "magical" passes over the can and perhaps tap it with your wand. Then pick up the can, holding it by the neck.

(4) Using both hands, tip the can *toward* the side with the double wall. This causes the liquid to begin to run *into the secret compartment.*

(5) As you turn the can over, all of the liquid is trapped within the secret compartment. The can may then be turned all the way upside-down, giving the appearance that the liquid has completely vanished.

(6) Now tip the can back until it assumes its original upright position. This allows the liquid to flow *out* of the secret compartment and *back* into the main body of the can.

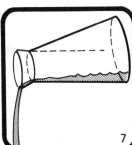

(7) If the can is now tipped to the side *away* from the double wall, the liquid will flow freely out of the mouth of the can — having "magically" reappeared!

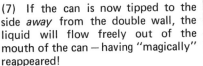

COMMENTS AND SUGGESTIONS

This is one of the oldest and most effective methods for vanishing a quantity of liquid. When the can is upside-down, demonstrating that it is empty (Step 5), you may wish to insert a wand (a pencil or any other suitable object will do) into the can. With the wand in this position, you may casually, *but carefully,* spin the "empty" can on the wand. This effective bit of business will convince your audience even more that the liquid has "vanished."

You may use this useful prop in conjunction with many other effects. For instance, you could perform the Foo Can effect first, followed by the VANISHING BOWL OF WATER. Follow the Foo Can routine until the water reappears in the container — then pour it directly into the "vanishing" bowl. After putting the Foo Can aside, you can proceed to vanish the bowl filled with water.

THE LOTA BOWL

EFFECT

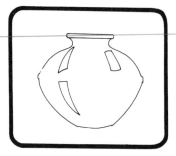

A large attractive bowl already filled to the top with water is displayed by the magician. He then proceeds to empty *all* the water out of the bowl. Yet, a number of times during the performance, the magician picks up the bowl and empties <u>more</u> water out of the "empty" bowl. The effect created is that the bowl "magically" <u>fills itself</u> — *over and over again*. In the end, the magician has apparently poured more water from the bowl than it could possibly hold!

SECRET AND PREPARATION

(A) This is an excellent "running gag" which can be easily added to any of your magical performances — particularly when you are appearing for large groups on a stage. (There are also "miniature" versions of the Lota Bowl for "close-up" shows.) The secret lies in the special construction of the bowl. It has a "double wall" built inside it which, because of the deceptive shape of the bowl, allows a great quantity of water to be hidden in a large secret compartment. A small hole (a) on the *outside* neck of the bowl controls the filling action of the water. Another small hole (b) *inside* at the bottom of the bowl allows the flow of the liquid *from* the secret compartment *into* the main body of the bowl.

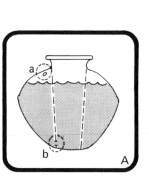

(B) To fill the bowl with water, you can hold it totally immersed in a bucket or sink *with both holes open.* Once this is done, wipe off the excess water from the outside of the bowl. Another more convenient but slower method of filling the bowl is to merely pour water *into the top* of the bowl from another container. When the bowl is "brim full," you must wait until a portion of water runs down into the secret compartment through the inside hole. Then you repeatedly fill the bowl back to the top as the water runs down seeking its own level. After repeated fillings, both the main body *and* the secret compartment will be full.

(C) Place the bowl on your table in preparation for performance. You must also have another container handy in which to pour the liquid from the bowl.

METHOD

(1) When you are ready to perform Lota Bowl, pick up the bowl from the table. *Place your thumb <u>over the outside hole in the neck</u> and pour "all" of the liquid from the bowl. This allows only the liquid <u>from the main body</u> to flow out of the bowl.*

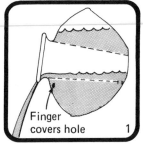

(3) The water will rise in the main body until it reaches the level of the liquid remaining in the secret compartment.

(2) Turn the "empty" bowl upright and place it back on your table. Because of the double-walled construction, the water from the secret compartment will run through the small hole *inside* the bowl into the main body.

(4) As soon as the main body of the bowl has "refilled" itself with liquid, you may pour out water again — *but be sure to cover the <u>outside hole</u> as you do.*

(5) The bowl will refill itself over and over again until almost all the water is exhausted from the secret compartment.

(6) *NOTE: Always place your thumb over the outside hole located in the neck <u>before</u> you pour out any liquid. This assures that <u>only</u> the water from the <u>main body</u> of the bowl is poured.*

COMMENTS AND SUGGESTIONS

As a container for holding the water that you pour out, a large FOO CAN is ideal. Now you can perform a double mystery. When all the liquid has been poured from the bowl into the FOO CAN, you then cause the liquid to *vanish completely* from the can!

SPONGE BALL MAGIC

★ ★ ★

Tricks with sponge balls represent a type of magic distinctively its own. With other articles such as cards, coins, thimbles, cigarettes, matches, and matchboxes, ways were designed to "palm" or manipulate such items purely because they were used in everyday life and were therefore natural objects to carry or borrow for magical purposes. Even the so-called magicians' "billiard balls" used in manipulative magic can be classed as something ordinary—for although they are smaller than the standard size, such balls are actually used on miniature pool tables. Sometimes they are even disguised as golf balls, being just about the right size.

But nobody ever heard of "sponge balls." That is, until magicians began carving them out of rubber sponges—simply because they were compressible and therefore could be handled in a special way. As the variety of different weights, textures, and compressibility of synthetic sponges increased, magicians found an ever-widening selection, and the "sponge balls" of today are much finer and easier to manipulate than their predecessors. "Magical" sponges today have a fairly solid look. This causes the average person to overlook the fact that they are remarkably compressible—which, of course, is the magician's reason for using them.

"Square" sponges are popular with many performers. These are actually cubical in shape and are handled the same as sponge balls. Since sponge ball routines are usually performed at a table, the square type has the advantage of never rolling off. Thus they are easier to use and to learn with. Square sponges are called sponge cubes, and are easily made by cutting soft foam rubber into one-inch cubes. Later you may wish to change to some other shape such as sponge balls which you can make yourself from soft sponge or buy from a magic supply house.

Whatever type you choose, you'll find the following routine well worth the effort required to learn it. Once you have seen the delighted response of your audience, chances are the sponges will become a permanent part of your act.

SPONGE SORCERY

EFFECT

The performer magically causes three sponges to appear, multiply, and vanish in an entertaining and amusing manner — they even seem to multiply in the hands of the spectator.

SECRET AND PREPARATION

Before the performance, place <u>three</u> of the sponge cubes in your right pants pocket and <u>one</u> sponge in your left pants pocket.

METHOD

Sponge balls are used in the following illustrations. To practice and present your routine, just use your sponge cubes in place of the balls as shown.

"A SPONGE APPEARS"

(1) With the four sponges located in your pants pockets as described, casually place your hand in your right pants pocket. Grasp one of the sponges in the Finger Palm Position and remove your hand, holding the sponge secretly. Then, reach into the air and "produce" it at the tips of your right fingers. You can also produce the sponge from the spectator's coat lapel, from behind his ear, or any other appropriate place.

(2) As you display the first sponge in your right hand, position it in readiness for the Finger Palm by placing it on your open hand at the base of the second and third fingers as shown. The left hand lies casually, palm down, on the table.

(3) Now, in one smooth, flowing movement, bring both hands together turning them over as you do. This is done in the <u>pretense</u> of gently tossing the sponge from your right hand into your left hand. But, instead of actually *tossing* the sponge in the left hand, it is *secretly retained* in the second and third fingers of the right hand — in the Finger Palm Position.

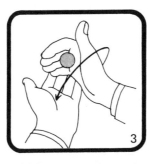

(4) Move your right hand away (with the sponge) as you close your left hand into a loose fist. The first finger of your right hand should casually point toward your left fist as shown in the illustration.

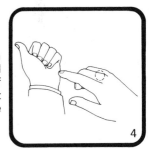

(5) Pause for a moment and then make a crumbling motion with your left fingers as if to cause the sponge to "dissolve" in your hand. Then, open your left hand to show that the sponge has vanished.

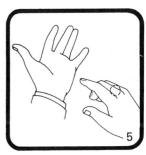

(6) *NOTE: What you have just done is the Basic Finger Palm Vanish with a sponge. Practice it with the sponge until it becomes smooth and convincing. When done correctly, the spectators should not suspect that you really retain the sponge in your right hand. The Finger Palm Vanish is described in detail in the Coin Section of the Course. The proper performance of this move is essential as it is used several times throughout the Sponge Sorcery routine. See Page 187 for the Finger Palm Vanish.*

"THE FLIGHT TO THE POCKET"

(7) Explain to the audience that often, when a sponge vanishes, it manages to reappear in your *right pocket.* Reach into your right pants pocket (being careful not to flash the "vanished" sponge that is now concealed in your right fingers) and grasp one of the two sponges that are left in that pocket.

(8) Openly remove this sponge — still keeping the <u>first</u> sponge Finger Palmed — from your pocket and display it in your right fingertips. *Again, be careful not to let the audience see the sponge Finger Palmed in your right hand as you display the other sponge.* The effect is that you vanished a sponge from your left hand and caused it to reappear in your pants pocket.

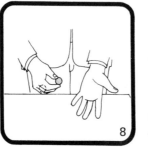

"GUESS WHICH HAND"

(9) Upon completing "The Flight to the Pocket," you now hold one sponge at your right fingertips and one sponge secretly in the Finger Palm position of the same hand. Openly place the sponge from your right fingertips into the palm of your left hand as shown.

(10) Close your left hand into a fist and hold it *palm up* in front of you as shown. Then, close your right hand and hold it *palm down* next to your left fist. *The audience still believes that only <u>one</u> sponge is being used and that it is in your <u>left</u> hand.*

(11) Now, strike both fists together several times and hold your hands "crossed" at the wrist as shown. Explain how this seems to have a "strange effect" upon the location of the mischievous sponge. With that, ask the spectator which hand he thinks the sponge is in.

(12) The answer will probably be, "In your left hand." *No matter which hand the spectator says,* uncross your hands and open your <u>left hand</u> — revealing the sponge still there.

(13) Tell the spectator that it really didn't matter which hand he chose; he would have been correct in either case. With that, turn your right hand palm up and open the fingers revealing the other sponge. *It appears that this "strange effect" you spoke about has caused <u>one</u> sponge to multiply into <u>two!</u>*

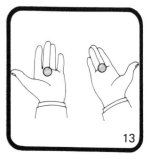

"SPECTATOR'S DOUBLES"

(14) Place the *left*-hand sponge on the table and hold the *right*-hand sponge in position for the Finger Palm Vanish.

(15) Now, you pretend to place the sponge in your left hand. Actually you execute the Finger Palm Vanish, secretly retaining the sponge in your right hand. *Remember that each time you perform this vanish, your left hand should be closed in a loose fist <u>as if it actually contained the sponge.</u>*

(16) Without hesitation, move your right hand toward the sponge lying on the table. *Be careful not to expose the sponge Finger Palmed in your right hand.*

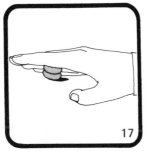

(17) As your right hand arrives above the sponge on the table, secretly place the Finger Palmed sponge directly *on top* of the sponge on the table.

(22) Tell the spectator that you intend to cause the sponge which you are holding to travel *invisibly* from your hand into his closed fist.

(18) Now, by drawing your right hand along the table, the sponges will roll toward the tips of your right fingers, where they can be picked up together as one sponge. Because of the soft texture of the sponges, when they are pinched together slightly, this will appear to be just *one* sponge.

(23) Again, make a crumbling motion with your left fingers and open your hand to show it empty. Ask the spectator if he felt anything happen in his hand. Whatever his answer, tell him to open his hand revealing the two sponges.

(19) As you display the two sponges (as one) at the tips of your right fingers, ask the spectator to open his right hand and hold it palm up above the table.

"TRANSPOSITION IN YOUR HANDS"

(24) Take both sponges from the spectator and place them on the table in front of you about 12 inches apart. Then, turn your hands palm up and openly place the back of your hands on top of the sponges as shown. This is the *starting position* for the next series of moves.

THE FOLLOWING STEPS (25 through 36) ARE A CLEVER SEQUENCE OF MOVES DESIGNED TO CONFUSE AND AMAZE THE SPECTATORS.

(20) Now, place the sponge(s) in the spectator's hand as you state, "Here, *you* hold this sponge in your hand while I hold the other." At this point, the spectator *thinks that you still hold one sponge in your left hand* and that you are merely giving him the other sponge to hold, *when actually you are giving him both sponges.*

(25) First, raise your right hand, turn it over, and pick up the sponge that was beneath it with the tips of your right thumb and finger.

(21) Now, instruct him to close his fingers around the sponge and squeeze it tightly so it would be impossible for you to remove it without his knowledge. *Be sure you maintain a firm grip on the two sponges until the spectator's fingers are completely closed around them.* Then, and only then, should you remove your fingers from his fist.

(26) Second, *without lifting your left hand from the table,* rest the sponge in the palm of your left hand. Then, close your hand into a fist over your right fingers *and* the sponge. As you do this say, "The *right* sponge goes in the *left* hand . . ." Then, withdraw your right fingers actually *leaving the sponge in your closed left hand.*

(27) Third, raise your <u>left</u> fist off the table and pick up the sponge that was beneath it with the tips of the <u>right</u> fingers. Then, close your <u>right</u> fingers into a fist around the sponge. Hold your right fist next to your left fist as you say, ". . . and the *left* sponge goes in the *right* hand."

(32) Rest the sponge in the palm of the <u>left</u> hand and close your left fingers over your right fingers and the sponge. Again you say, "The *right* sponge goes in the *left* fist . . ." This time, however, *instead of leaving the sponge in your left fist, as you with-draw your right hand, <u>secretly retain the sponge between your right thumb and fingers</u>.* Be sure to keep your right fingers together so the audience cannot see the sponge between them.

(28) You now hold one sponge in each hand as shown in the illustration.

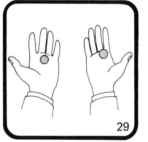

(33) Immediately move your right hand away from your closed left hand, <u>secretly carrying the sponge in your right hand as shown</u>. *Direct your complete attention toward your left hand as if it really contained the sponge.* As your right hand moves away, draw your right thumb inward moving the sponge slightly deeper into your hand where it will not be seen by the spectators.

(29) Now open both hands together revealing the two sponges, one in each hand. So far, NO "MAGIC" HAS HAPPENED! State that you will now do the *same thing again.* Unknown to the audience, this "trial run" is a very important part of the mystery that is about to take place. By first executing this series of moves *without any magic,* you *condition* the spectators to expect the same results next time.

(34) Now, raise your left hand and, with your right fingers, pick up the sponge which lay beneath it. When you pick up the "left-hand" sponge, secretly add the palmed "right-hand" sponge to it (just as you did in Step 18).

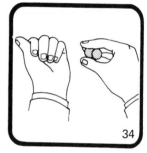

(30) Again, place both hands on top of the two sponges in starting position for the same series of moves.

(35) Now, close your <u>right</u> hand into a fist around the *two* sponges. Hold your right fist next to your left fist as shown. To the audience you have apparently just repeated Steps 24 through 28, and they think that you now hold one sponge in each hand.

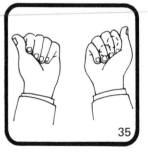

(31) Again, raise your <u>right</u> hand, turn it over and pick up the sponge beneath it in the tips of the <u>right</u> fingers (just as you did in Step 25).

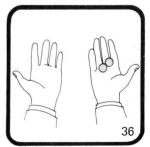

(36) Make a crumbling motion with your left fingers — open your left hand to show that the sponge has *vanished.* Then, slowly open your right hand — revealing *both* sponges! *It appears as though one sponge has jumped "invisibly" from your left hand into your right hand!*

"IMPOSSIBLE PENETRATION"

NOTE: IF YOU HAVE BEEN <u>SITTING</u> AT A TABLE AS YOU PERFORM THE TRICK, YOU MUST NOW <u>STAND UP</u> FOR THE NEXT PORTION OF THE ROUTINE. Steps 36 through 44 are all shown from the <u>SPECTATOR'S VIEWPOINT</u>.

(41) With that, move your right hand (which secretly holds the other sponge) in front of your left pants pocket. *Your left hand is still inside your pocket.* Now, with your right hand, press the sponge against your pants leg next to where your left hand is inside your pocket.

(37) After the "Transposition in Your Hands," place one sponge on the table and keep the other sponge in your right hand in position ready for the Finger Palm Vanish.

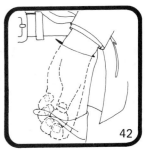

(42) Inside your pocket, your left thumb and fingers *grasp the sponge through the fabric* and hold it between the folds of the cloth so that it is *concealed from view by the material.* As soon as the sponge is in position, move your right hand away from in front of your pant leg. The "pinched" section of the fabric will look like a fold in the cloth.

(38) Execute the Finger Palm Vanish, pretending to place the sponge in your left hand but actually retaining it Finger Palmed in your right hand.

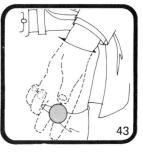

(43) Immediately begin a "back and forth" rubbing motion with your left fingers. At the same time, relax your grip on the sponge through the fabric. This will cause the sponge to slowly emerge into view <u>as though it were penetrating right through the cloth.</u> *NOTE: This illusion is very effective — don't worry if the sponge is not completely hidden in the folds of the fabric before you remove your right hand. It will just appear that the "penetration" of the cloth started when you first placed your right hand on your pants leg.*

(39) Hold your closed left hand in a loose fist as if it actually contained the sponge and casually move your right hand (with the Finger Palmed sponge) away. *Again, be sure to direct your <u>complete attention</u> toward your left fist.*

(44) When the sponge emerges almost totally into view, grasp it in your right hand and pull it away from the pocket. At the same time, *your left hand secretly secures the sponge already in that pocket in the Finger Palm position.* While all the attention is on the sponge in your right hand, remove your left hand from your pocket with the new "secret" sponge.

"THE SPECTATOR'S HAND REVISITED"

(40) Place your left hand (which supposedly contains the sponge) into your left pants pocket as you explain that your clothes are made of a "special material."

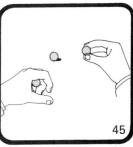

(45) There are now *three* sponges in play, although the audience is aware of only *two.* One sponge is on the table, another is held at the tips of your right fingers, and the "secret" sponge is Finger Palmed in your left hand.

(46) Call attention to the sponge in your right hand. While the audience is looking at it, with your left hand pick up the sponge on the table and add the "secret" sponge to it.

(51) Once the spectator has a firm grip on the sponges, reach into your right pants pocket and remove the *fourth sponge* from your pocket. Openly display the sponge as you say, "You may be wondering how all this is happening. Well the secret is that I have a *third* sponge which nobody knows about."

(47) With your left hand, you now display the sponge which was on the table *and* the secret sponge as *one*, holding them with your left thumb and fingers. At this point you actually hold three sponges (one in your right hand and two in your left). *To the audience it appears that you hold only one sponge in each hand.*

(52) With that, execute the Finger Palm Vanish, pretending to place the sponge into your left hand but actually retaining it in the Finger Palm position in your right hand.

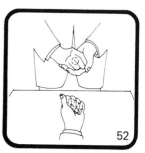

(48) Transfer the two sponges in your left hand to your right hand, *placing them directly on top of the sponge in your right fingers.* Say, "Now I would like you to hold these two sponges."

(53) Casually drop your right hand to the table and move your closed left fist next to the spectator's hand.

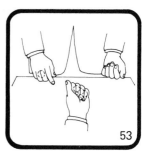

(49) Move your right hand (which now holds the three sponges) toward the spectator and ask him to open his hand so that he may take the sponges from you.

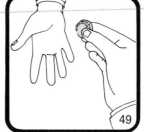

(54) Make the crumbling motion with your left fingers and open your hand to show it empty. Instruct the spectator to open his hand revealing *all three sponges*. It appears that the third sponge has flown invisibly from your fingers into the spectator's hand.

(50) Place *all three sponges* in the spectator's hand. Instruct him to close his fingers around them. Tell him to squeeze his fist tightly to make sure that you cannot remove them. *Again, remember to wait until the spectator's hand is <u>completely closed</u> before releasing your grip on the sponges.*

"TWO IN THE HAND, ONE IN THE POCKET — PHASE ONE"

(55) After "The Spectator's Hand Revisited," there are *four* sponges in use, although the audience is only aware of *three*. The next sequence begins with the three sponges in a horizontal row in front of you and the fourth sponge held secretly in your curled right fingers.

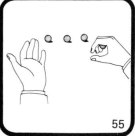

(56) With your right hand pick up the sponge at the right end of the row, and execute the "two-as-one" pick-up (Step 17). In your right hand you now hold two sponges together (as one).

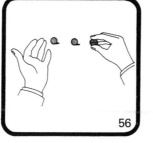

(57) Place the two sponges in the palm of your left hand and close your left fingers around them as you say, "One in the hand."

(58) Withdraw your right hand from your left fist. Then pick up another of the sponges on the table with your right hand as shown.

(59) Move your right hand toward your left fist. Open your left fingers *just enough* to place the sponge in your left hand. Say, "Two in the hand." Close your left fingers around the *three* sponges and withdraw your right hand from your left fist.

(60) Pick up the remaining sponge in your right hand.

(61) Openly place the last sponge into your right pants pocket. Say, "And one in the pocket." As your hand reaches in your right trouser pocket, *do not leave the sponge in your pocket.* Instead, hold it in the Finger Palm Position and *remove your hand from your pocket secretly carrying the sponge along.* The audience will believe that you merely placed the sponge in your pocket.

(62) Now, ask the spectator, "How many sponges are in my hand?" The answer will be, "Two." With that, open your left hand revealing *three* sponges — as you remark, "Maybe I went too fast. I'll do that again."

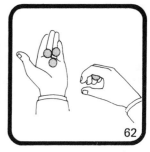

"TWO IN THE HAND, ONE IN THE POCKET — PHASE TWO"

(63) With your left hand, place the three sponges in a horizontal row on the table as in Step 55. The fourth sponge is secretly held in the curled fingers of your right hand.

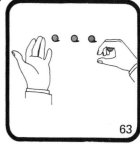

(64) As before, execute the "two-as-one" pick-up with the sponge on the right as in Step 56.

(65) Place the two sponges (as one) in your left hand and close your left fingers into a fist around them (as in Step 57). Say, "One in the hand."

(66) Withdraw your right fingers from your left fist and pick up another sponge with your right hand (as in Step 58).

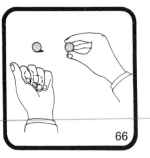

(67) Open your left fingers just enough to place the sponge into your left fist as you did in Step 59. Say, "<u>Two</u> in the hand."

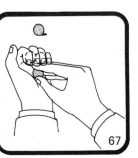

(68) Now pick up the remaining sponge in your right fingertips (as in Step 60).

(69) Say, "And <u>one</u> in the pocket." Openly place this sponge into your right pants pocket, the same as in Step 61 — BUT THIS TIME, LEAVE THE SPONGE IN YOUR POCKET.

(70) Withdraw your right hand from your pocket and gesture toward your fist. *Make the gesture in a way that the audience can see that your <u>right hand is quite empty</u>*. Do not call special attention to your right hand — merely show it in an open and casual manner so that there is <u>no question</u> that it is <u>empty</u>.

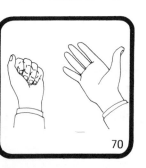

(71) As you gesture ask, "How many in the hand?" The answer will probably be "Two." The spectators are so baffled by this time, however, that there is no predicting what they will say! In any event, open your left hand revealing all three sponges. Now say, "Let's try just once more."

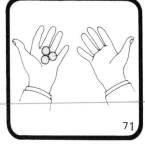

"THE TOTAL VANISH"
NOW FOR A "SMASHING" CLIMAX TO THE ROUTINE.

(72) At this time, there are only three sponges remaining. With your left hand place them on the table in a row as you did before.

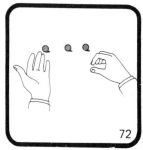

(73) Begin again, just as you did before, by picking up the sponge on the far right with your right thumb and fingers. Rest this sponge on the palm of your open left hand as shown.

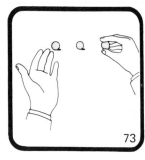

(74) Now close the fingers of the left hand around the sponge *and* the fingers of your right hand. *Your right fingers <u>retain</u> their grip on the sponge.* "One in the hand." <u>Your right fingers continue to hold the sponge inside your closed left hand.</u>

(75) Now, *instead of leaving the sponge in your left hand,* SECRETLY RETAIN THE SPONGE IN YOUR RIGHT FINGERS AS YOU WITHDRAW YOUR RIGHT HAND FROM YOUR LEFT FIST.

(76) To keep the sponge concealed from view during this procedure, as you withdraw your hand, move your right thumb slightly inward, rolling the sponge behind your right fingers out of sight.

(80) <u>Without pausing</u>, pick up the remaining sponge in your right hand. Do <u>not</u> execute the "two-as-one" pick-up — just keep the two "palmed" sponges behind your fingers and openly pick up the third sponge, holding it at the fingertips of your right hand.

(77) Without hesitation, move your right hand toward the next sponge and *execute the "two-as-one" pick-up.*

(81) <u>Immediately</u>, place your right hand into your right pants pocket. Say, "And the <u>last</u> sponge goes in the pocket." Now *leave <u>all three sponges</u>* in your pocket as you . . .

(78) With the two sponges held together (as one) in your right hand, open your left fist *just enough to place your right fingers into your hand.* Say, "<u>Two</u> in the hand." Once again, your thumb secretly draws *both sponges* behind your right fingers out of view . . .

(82) . . . remove your right hand from your pocket. With your right hand, gesture toward your left fist *so the audience can see that your right hand is <u>quite empty</u>.*

(79) . . . as you withdraw your right fingers from your left hand and close your left hand into a loose fist.

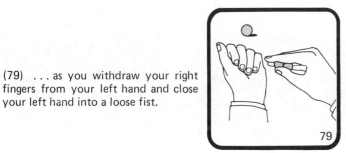

(83) Ask, "How many in my hand?" By now, the audience will probably answer "Three," thinking that they know what is going to happen. Whatever the number given say, "No, actually they are all gone — because <u>that was the end of the trick</u>." With that, open your left hand to show that all three sponges have *vanished,* bringing the routine to a startling climax!

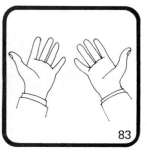

COMMENTS AND SUGGESTIONS

It is generally good policy to avoid handling sponges either too boldly or too cautiously. A quick thrust of the hand excites suspicion, and so does a tight squeeze of the sponge itself when the performer is actually giving the spectator two as one. A casual in-between course is best, particularly when done in an unhurried manner. In fact, the correct preliminary procedure will do much toward dispelling suspicion on the part of the spectators.

If a sponge is held lightly at the fingertips, with absolutely no pressure, no one is apt to regard it as compressible; and later, when two are shown as one, correct pressure of the thumb and fingers can give the "double" ball a distinctively "single" appearance. While a natural, unhurried motion of the hand is sufficient to cover the deception, larger loads depend upon fuller compression for complete concealment.

It is a good idea when practicing, to break the routine down into smaller units. Then, learn each phase before you go on to the next. The "Sponges" is undoubtedly one of the finest close-up tricks in magic. Each effect in this routine can be performed separately — and, as you will see when you perform it for your friends, the entire routine is constructed in a logical progression, building to a perfect climax — truly a masterpiece of magic!

BILLIARD
BALL MAGIC

★ ★ ★

Very few magicians have performed tricks with full-sized balls, as they are too large and too heavy to handle except with oversized hands and a powerful grip. However, modern pool tables that come in less than standard sizes are supplied with numbered balls that are proportionally smaller and therefore, can be manipulated effectively, but magicians prefer to work with lighter balls made of wood, plastic or rubber.

These run in sizes from larger golf balls down to marbles; but generally speaking, the medium sizes are easier to handle. This may sound odd, but if you try out the various sizes, you will soon realize why. The medium-size ball has a more gradual curvature than its smaller counterpart—making it easier to grip by the basic palming methods described in this section. That is from the magician's viewpoint; while from the spectators' viewpoint, a similar situation applies. The larger the ball, the greater the effect, as it is more surprising to see a magician "vanish" a golf ball than a marble.

The answer to this is twofold: If you are planning a billiard ball routine in which you have the choice of sizes, pick the largest you can handle comfortable and go right ahead. Making that decision is easy enough when you are familiar both with the necessary moves and the effect that the audience expects. Such factors are covered in individual descriptors that follow.

THE CLASSIC PALM
Using a Ball

If you wish to learn Billiard Ball manipulation, you must first learn to "palm" a ball properly. To *palm* is to hold a ball (or any object) secretly in your hand so that the audience does not know it is there. As you practice, you will probably find it is easier to palm a ball than to palm, for instance, a coin. The curved surface of the ball gives you an opportunity for a much better grip, and since the entire surface of a ball is the same, spherical, it is not necessary to hold it by any particular side. You should also develop the skill required to palm a ball with *either* hand.

Probably the oldest method of "palming," and certainly one of the most useful, is known as the CLASSIC PALM.

METHOD

(1) Hold the ball in the center of your palm by a slight contraction of your thumb and little finger. This causes the two masses of flesh on the opposite sides of the palm to exert a slight pressure on the ball — enough to hold it firmly in place while the hand is moved about.

(2) If this seems a bit difficult at first, you should experiment with different-sized balls until you find the one best suited to your hands. Here is how your hand should look from the audience's view. You must avoid holding your hand with the thumb and fingers *stiff* or *abnormally separated*. The most important point of all is that the hand palming the ball *must always look RELAXED and COMPLETELY NATURAL.*

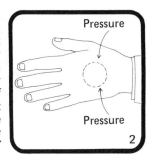

COMMENTS AND SUGGESTIONS

If the ball is properly palmed, you should be able to make a variety of gestures with your hand, move your fingers, and so on, without arousing suspicion. Most of the time when using the CLASSIC PALM, you will find it advisable to keep the hand that is holding the ball close to your body *and always keep the back of your hand* to the audience — for any "flash" of the ball will ruin the illusion. You should practice and learn the CLASSIC PALM as it is one of the most basic and versatile sleights in magic.

LET ME EMPHASIZE AGAIN, THE MOST IMPORTANT POINT OF ALL — THE HAND CONTAINING THE BALL (OR WHATEVER ELSE YOU ARE PALMING) MUST ALWAYS LOOK RELAXED AND COMPLETELY NATURAL. THAT IS THE TRUE SECRET, NOT ONLY OF THE CLASSIC PALM, BUT OF PALMING OF EVERY KIND.

THE CLASSIC PALM VANISH

EFFECT

This is a basic sleight for causing a ball (or any small object) to "disappear" from your hand. It utilizes the CLASSIC PALM and should be practiced until it can be performed smoothly with almost no conscious effort.

METHOD

(1) Stand facing the spectators with both hands at about waist level. Hold the ball in the palm of your right hand as shown. Your left hand is also held palm up, ready to receive the ball.

(2) Rotate your right hand over so that your right fingers point to the left and . . .

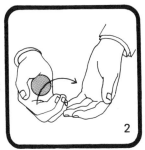

(3) . . . let the ball drop (or roll) into your left hand. Your left fingers should be pointing toward the audience when you drop the ball into your left hand as shown.

(7) Again, *with the very same movement as in Steps 2 and 3,* the right hand turns until the back of the hand is toward the audience. As the right hand turns, *the ball is secretly retained in the right hand in the Classic Palm.* Your left fingers bend slightly, as if receiving the ball.

(4) Now repeat the exact same procedure but from *left to right.* Hold both hands palm up, then rotate your *left* hand and drop the ball back into your *right* hand. Do this "back and forth" tossing motion several times.

(8) Move your right hand up and from your left hand, retaining the ball in the Classic Palm. Your left hand quickly closes into a loose fist, *as if the left hand is holding the ball.*

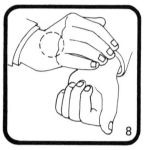

(5) NOW FOR THE VANISH. Hold the ball on the palm of your right hand just as before, but be sure it is in position so that you may retain it easily in the Classic Palm. As usual, the left hand is held open waiting to receive the ball.

(9) Your right hand assumes a relaxed position and casually points to the left fist. The fingers of the left hand make a "crumbling" motion, as if you were slowly crushing the ball.

(6) Turn your right hand at the wrist as if you were going to drop the ball into your left hand.

(10) Your right hand drops to the side of your body in a casual manner as you *concentrate all of your attention on your left hand.* Slowly open your left hand to reveal the ball has "vanished."

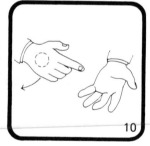

(11) Your right hand can now reproduce the ball from behind your right knee, from under your left elbow, or any appropriate place you may wish.

COMMENTS AND SUGGESTIONS

The CLASSIC PALM VANISH is a very versatile and deceptive sleight that can be performed with almost any small object. Practice the moves so that they can be done in an easy, natural manner — as if you are merely tossing the ball back and forth between your hands — finally ending with the ball in your closed left fist (really it is secretly held in the Classic Palm in your right). The tossing *conditions* the audience to believe that the ball is contained in the left hand. Your concentration on your closed left hand furnishes the *misdirection.* Combine these two deceptive elements with *practice* and you will have a truly "magical" vanish.

THE FRENCH DROP
Using a Ball

This is one of the most deceptive of all vanishes. Along with the Classic Palm, it surely ranks among the most practical and widely used sleight-of-hand moves.

EFFECT

The magician holds a ball in the left hand. He takes the ball in his right hand — makes a crumbling motion — and causes the ball to vanish!

METHOD

THE ILLUSTRATIONS ON THE *LEFT* SHOW THE <u>MAGICIAN'S</u> VIEW AND THOSE ON THE *RIGHT* SHOW THE <u>VERY SAME MOVE</u> FROM THE <u>SPECTATOR'S</u> VIEWPOINT.

MAGICIAN'S VIEW   *SPECTATORS' VIEW*

(1) Hold the ball between your left thumb and fingertips as shown. Your hand is held palm upward and your thumb and fingers point up. Display the ball to your audience.

(2) Bring your hands together. Your left hand continues holding the ball as in Step 1 as your right hand approaches and then covers the ball as shown. Tuck your right <u>thumb</u> *under* the ball as your <u>fingers</u> *encircle* the ball over the top.

(3) Apparently close your right fingers around the ball — this momentarily conceals the ball from the audience's view. At that very moment, release the ball from your left thumb and fingers and allow it to drop secretly into your left hand. If your left hand is held correctly, the ball will fall into the Finger Palm position. When it does, curl your left fingers loosely around the ball. *Close your right hand around the space between your left thumb and fingers where the ball was before you secretly dropped it AS IF TO TAKE THE BALL.*

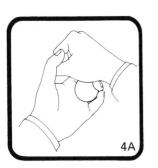

(4) Turn your *right* side toward the audience as you *appear to take the ball away in your right hand.* Keep your left hand with its palm toward you as you continue to hold the ball secretly in the Finger Palm position. Your right hand moves to the right, closed into a loose fist *as if it contained the ball.*

MAGICIAN'S VIEW

SPECTATORS' VIEW

5A

5B

(5) The first finger of your left hand points at your closed right hand *as you direct <u>all of your attention</u> to your right hand.* Make a "crumbling" motion with your right hand as if the ball were turning to dust.

6A

6B

(6) Continue pointing with your left hand as you open your right hand to show that the ball has completely "vanished." (The ball is still secretly Finger Palmed in your left hand.) You can now reproduce the palmed ball with your left hand in any way that you wish.

FIST VANISH

This is another basic sleight which will enable you to vanish a ball or other small object in a very deceptive manner.

EFFECT

The magician places a ball on top of his left fist, and then takes it away with his right hand. When the hand is opened, the ball has vanished.

METHOD

(1) Stand with your *left side* toward the spectators. Hold your left hand in a loose fist with the *back* of your hand toward the audience. Place the ball on top of the fist with your right hand. Display the ball atop your left fist, then start to move your right hand toward the ball. Rotate your right hand so that the back of your hand is toward the audience as shown.

1

(3) <u>Without moving your left fingers,</u> move your <u>left thumb</u> just enough to allow the ball to drop secretly into your left hand, which holds the ball in the curled fingers. *Close your right hand as if it were grasping the ball.*

3

(2) Bring your open right hand against the top of your left fist so that your right first finger is resting on your left first finger and your right thumb touches your left thumb. Begin to curl your right fingers around the ball. The ball should now be out of the sight of the audience, hidden by the right hand.

2

(4) Move your right hand, *which pretends to hold the ball,* up and away from your left fist. Your left hand secretly holds the ball in the Finger Palm position. Extend the first finger of your left hand and point to your right hand. *Follow your right hand with your eyes.*

4

(5) Turn your closed right hand, which apparently holds the ball, so that its palm and closed fingers are facing the audience.

(9) Your right fingers curl around the ball, pretending to take it, as in Step 3. At the same time, your left thumb relaxes a bit, *allowing the ball to drop secretly into your left fist.*

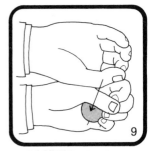

(6) Slowly open your right hand and reveal that the ball has vanished.

(10) As in Step 4, your right hand moves away as if it holds the ball. Be sure *your eyes follow your right hand* as your left first finger casually points to your right fist.

(7) To conclude the trick, you can move the left hand, which contains the Finger Palmed ball, down behind your leg and reproduce the ball from behind the left knee.

(11) Slowly open your right hand to reveal the disappearance of the ball as described in Steps 5 and 6.

(8) The following are illustrations of Steps 1, 3, and 4 *as seen from the magician's viewpoint.* The ball is on top of your left fist as your right hand approaches the ball as in Step 1.

(12) Now reproduce the ball from behind your left knee as explained in Step 7.

COMMENTS AND SUGGESTIONS

This is a very basic and useful sleight. Practice it and you will find that it can be done with almost any small object.

CHANGE-OVER PALM

This is a very useful sleight that can be used *before* the production or *after* the vanish of a ball.

EFFECT

The magician shows both hands to be empty — yet he has a ball palmed secretly in one hand.

MAGICIAN'S VIEW

METHOD

SPECTATORS' VIEW

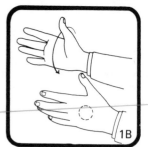

(1) Stand with your left side toward the audience. The ball is held secretly in the Classic Palm in your *left* hand. Show your *right* hand empty. Rotate your hand so that the audience may see both sides.

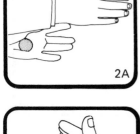

(2) After showing your right hand empty, place your left first finger on the base of your right palm at the wrist as shown.

(3) Now turn your body to the *left* so that your <u>right</u> side faces the audience. As you turn, your hands will naturally come together in front of your body.

(4) Your left palm, which contains the ball, will be facing your right palm when you are half way through the turn. At that moment the tips of the fingers of both hands are pointing toward the audience. Be sure to keep the tips of the fingers of both hands *together* (the right fingertips touch the left fingertips) to prevent anyone from seeing a "flash" of the palmed ball as you turn your body from right to left.

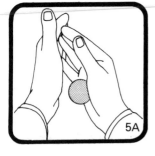

(5) As you turn, when the palms of your hands are together, <u>secretly</u> <u>transfer</u> the ball from the Classic Palm in your left hand to the Classic Palm in your right hand.

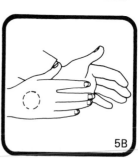

(6) Once the ball is held in the Classic Palm in your right hand *and* your right side is toward the audience, move your right hand back toward your body. Your hands are now *reversed* from the position they were in in Step 1. The ball is palmed in your *right* hand as the *left* hand is now shown empty on both sides.

(7) You have now shown *both hands empty* — yet you have a ball (or any other small object) secretly palmed in your right hand!

THE FINGER ROLL FLOURISH

EFFECT

This is a beautiful "flourish" to add to your Billiard Ball repertoire. The ball rolls rapidly from finger to finger convincing your audience that you possess great skill as a manipulator. This feat requires practice — so be prepared to devote considerable time to it so that your hands become accustomed to the ball and to the series of finger positions. After you once work out the basic moves, you will find that it becomes easier and easier to do. Practice it well and you will have a bit of manipulative magic of which you can be justly proud.

METHOD

(1) Begin the "roll" with the ball held between your right thumb and first finger with the back of your hand toward the audience. Swing your second finger under the ball (it does not touch the ball) toward the right until it reaches your thumb.

(2) Now hold the ball *between your first and second fingers,* and *release* your thumbs' grasp on the ball.

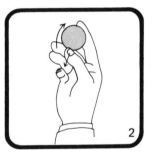

(3) The ball is now held between your first and second fingers. Move your second finger to the left "rolling" the ball on your first finger. At the same time, your third finger moves to the right to meet the first finger. *Your third finger has not yet touched the ball.*

(4) Swing your first finger to the left rolling the ball until it touches your third fingertip. You now hold the ball between your second and third fingers. Remove your first finger from the ball.

(5) As you hold the ball between your second and third fingers, swing your second finger to the left as you did with the first finger in Step 4. At the same time, bring your little finger to the right and under but not touching the ball yet.

(6) Continue to swing your second finger to the left until its tip touches your little finger. Clip the ball between your third and fourth fingers, and release your second finger's hold on the ball.

(7) You now hold the ball clipped between your third and little fingers. Now pivot your little finger *around behind* your third finger. This rolls the ball to the *back* of your third finger.

(8) Continue to move the little finger around *behind* the third finger. Move your second finger *behind* your third finger *and* the ball until you can clip the ball between the third and second finger — with the ball resting on the *back* of your third finger. As soon as the ball is held between the second and third fingers, release the little finger's grip on the ball.

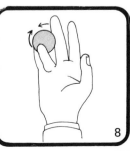

(9) The ball is now held between your second and third fingers *on the back of your hand.* Swing your third finger in an arc to the right rolling the ball around *behind* your second finger. Your first finger moves left *behind* the ball *and* your second finger, *but does not touch the ball.*

(11) You now hold the ball between the tips of your first and second fingers. You have executed the complete Finger Roll. The ball was rolled down the *front* of your hand, *around* your third finger, and then rolled on the *back* of your hand to the position it now occupies.

(10) Continue with the third finger rolling the ball around behind the second finger until the tips of the third and first finger touch. Then, clip the ball between the tips of your first and second fingers and remove your third finger from the ball.

(12) Now repeat Steps 3 through 10 in quick succession a few more times to further display this spectacular flourish.

(13) *NOTE: After Step 11, DO NOT USE YOUR THUMB. The ball is pivoted between your first and second fingers (around your second finger) for its repeat journey.*

COMMENTS AND SUGGESTIONS

This flourish may seem difficult, if not impossible, at first. Do not become discouraged. Experiment with balls of different sizes until you find the right size for your hands. (Rubber balls are easier and sponge balls are the easiest of all.) Carry a ball with you and practice whenever you can — I'll bet that sooner than you think, you will be able to perform the FINGER ROLL FLOURISH like a professional.

THE MARK WILSON BILLIARD BALL ROUTINE

This is an entire BILLIARD BALL ROUTINE made up of a number of vanishes, productions, and multiplications. The routine is described exactly as I have presented it for many years, and thus has been well tried and tested. I have performed it on all of the major television networks, on hundreds of local television shows, in thousands of "live" appearances, and in many countries throughout the world. It is extremely practical and, although it requires practice, it is not nearly as difficult as you may assume when you first read it, and it certainly is not as difficult as it appears to the audience.

For the routine, you will require a standard set of Magicians' Billiard Balls. This consists of three *solid* balls and one *"shell."* A *shell* is actually a hollow half-ball into which one of the solid balls may be secretly inserted. When the solid ball is inside the shell, the two appear to be only one ball. This is the basic secret of the BILLIARD BALLS and, as you will see, is used in a number of different ways throughout the routine.

Rather than teach you the sleights that go to make up the routine individually, I have described them all in sequence as they occur in the presentation (with the exception of the CHANGE-OVER and the FIST VANISH, which are standard ball sleights, and the CLASSIC PALM, all of which have been previously described). In this way, you can see how each sleight fits in context into the routine and how each move blends with the next to create a truly outstanding sleight-of-hand presentation. In learning the routine, you should practice one phase at a time — learn it — and then move on to the next sequence.

—MW

EFFECT

The magician shows both hands empty and states, "I would like to show you a trick in which I reach out into the air and produce a ball." He then does just that — he produces a solid ball from the air. The performer explains that he will now make the ball *vanish* on the count of "three." He tosses the ball into the air as he counts "one" — and then catches the ball between his hands as it descends. He tosses it again and counts "two." On the count of "three," the magician *apparently* tosses the ball into the air with his right hand, whereupon it "vanishes." His hand, however, suspiciously strikes his right back pocket as he makes this third upward throw. The audience assumes that instead of "vanishing" the ball, the magician has cleverly slipped the ball into his back pocket. Rather jokingly, the performer confirms the spectators' suspicions by removing the ball from that very pocket.

The magician, however, quickly re-establishes his ability by rapidly producing *two more* solid balls from the air, giving him a total of three.

Pretending to hear someone in the audience question whether the balls are solid, the magician, who now holds the three balls between the fingers of his right hand, takes one of the balls in his left hand and apparently "throws" it to a member of the audience. Actually, when he makes the throwing motion, the audience is surprised to find that his left hand is empty — the ball has vanished!

Continuing as if nothing out of the ordinary has happened, the magician requests that the spectator to whom he tossed the "invisible ball" examine it and then toss it back to him. When the spectator throws the imaginary ball back to the magician, he "catches" it out of the air — back in its solid, *visible* form.

Replacing the ball between the other two held in his right fingers, the wizard explains that he will demonstrate something that his viewers should never do. Taking one of the balls from his right hand with his left, he apparently places the ball in his mouth — whereupon he swallows it! Then, showing his left hand empty, the performer reaches down into the waistband of his trousers — where his shirt meets the top of his belt — and openly removes the apparently swallowed ball!

The magician goes on to explain that what he "really wanted to do" was to produce a ball from the air. The magician then reaches out into the air with his left hand and produces yet a *fourth* ball from the air. This is placed in the last remaining space between the fingers of his right hand. *STARTING WITH ONLY HIS EMPTY HANDS, THE MAGICIAN HAS NOW MAGICALLY PRODUCED FOUR BALLS FROM THE AIR!*

Now for the second half of the routine. First the magician removes one of the balls from between the fingers of his right hand with his left. Then, by merely squeezing it. "dissolves" it completely away.

Then with a slight wave of the right hand, one of the three remaining balls vanishes. Reaching behind his left knee with his left hand, he reproduces the vanished ball. This ball he openly places in his left coat pocket (or in a bowl, hat, or some other container on his table).

The magician is now left with two balls in the right hand. After rearranging them so that they are held side by side, one of them visibly vanishes and is reproduced, this time not from behind his knee, but from the magician's right elbow.

Now for a little "magical" byplay. The magician displays the two balls in his right hand as he swings both arms down so that his hands are beside his knees. With a wave of his right hand, one of the two balls disappears and is reproduced from behind his left knee. This is repeated several times. As soon as the ball is replaced by the left hand into the right, one of the balls in the right vanishes and is reproduced behind the magician's left knee.

After several unsuccessful attempts to keep the two spheres in his right hand, the magician places one of the balls into his pocket. He now explains that he will be unable to perform the trick that he had planned to do with this last ball because he does not have on his "special coat." Yet, despite the magician's explanation as to why he cannot present this last mystery, he proceeds to do exactly what he said ' couldn't — which brings the routine to a clever, happy, and inexplicable conclusion.

SECRET AND PREPARATION

As stated above, you will need one set of multiplying Billiard Balls. First, place one of the balls *and* the shell (with the ball *inside* the shell) in your right back trouser pocket. One of the two remaining solid balls is placed inside the waistband of your pants, between your pants and shirt. (This will be directly behind where your belt buckle is located if you are wearing a belt.) The remaining solid ball is either placed in your left coat pocket or in a location on your table so that it is hidden by some other prop and where it may be easily obtained when necessary.

METHOD

IN ALL OF THE ILLUSTRATIONS FOR THIS ROUTINE, THE SHELL IS A DARKER COLOR THAN THE BALLS SO THAT YOU CAN KEEP TRACK OF ITS POSITION DURING THE PRESENTATION.

PHASE ONE

(1) Secretly obtain the ball from your left coat pocket (or from behind the object on your table) and hold it in the Classic Palm in your left hand as your left arm hangs casually at your side.

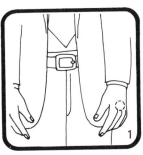

(2) NOTE: There are any number of clever ways of obtaining the ball without the audience's knowledge. For instance, you may replace some small object used in a previous trick in your left coat pocket and secretly palm the ball before you remove your hand. The same holds true if you are replacing an object on the table, which gives you a similar opportunity to secretly obtain the ball. If you are using the routine as an opening effect, for which it is quite well suited by the way, then enter from the left side of the stage with the ball *already palmed* in your left hand.

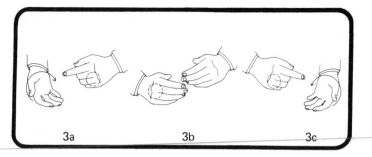

3a   3b   3c

(7) Immediately toss the ball in the air again as you count "two." Again catch the ball exactly as you did before with both hands.

(3a) In any event, with the ball secretly palmed in your left hand, show both hands "empty" using the Change-Over Palm already described in the Billiard Ball Section of the Course. In this case, start with your left side toward the audience. Point to your right hand with your left first finger as you turn your right hand over showing both sides. It is undoubtedly empty! Then rotate your whole body so that your right side is toward the audience. (b) During the "turning" movement, it is quite natural that your hands approach each other, palm to palm, as you secretly execute the Change-Over. (c) Now you can show your left hand on both sides — it too is "empty" (since the ball is now palmed in your right hand). Point at your left hand with your right first finger to further direct (and "misdirect") the audience's attention.

(8) Now you apparently toss the ball in the air for the third and last time. *What you actually do, however, is to retain the ball in your left hand in the Classic Palm.* Your right hand, apparently containing the ball, makes an exaggerated sweep, first downward behind your body, and then up into the air as if to toss the ball. However, your right hand strikes your pants in the area of your right back pocket as it passes behind you. The right hand then continues its motion of tossing the ball up in the air. You count "three."

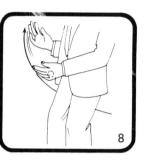

(4) Explain to the audience, "I would like to show you a trick in which I reach out into the air and get a ball — like this!" With your right side still to the audience, reach out with your right hand and produce the ball "from the air."

(9) Make this third toss an obviously suspicious move (and thus quite different from the first two "tosses") because you want the audience to believe that you cleverly placed the ball in your right back pocket.

(5) NOTE: It is important that this, and all of the following "productions" be presented so that you apparently do "pluck" the ball from the air (as opposed to merely "seeing" it in your hand). To do this, the fingers and thumb of your right hand reach down and obtain the ball from the Classic Palm as your hand begins its motion away from your body to your left. As your hand moves, *look at the exact spot in the air where the ball is going to come from, as if you already see it there.* It is important, as your hand reaches the top of its swing for the "grasp," that the ball "appear" at the tips of your fingers *just as your hand starts its downward motion.* In this way, you apparently "pluck" the ball from the air. (Just imagine that you were going to "pick" an apple from a tree. First your eyes would see the apple. Then, your hand would reach for it. *Your eyes would remain on the apple — not on your hand —* until your hand reached the apple and "picked" it from the tree. Then your eyes would follow the apple.)

(10) Smile and say, "I see — you think the ball went into my back pocket. Well you are right!" Reach into your back pocket and remove *the ball and the shell* and . . .

(11) . . . display them as *one ball* between your right first finger and thumb. (At this point, you have one ball palmed in your left hand and the ball and shell displayed as one ball in your right hand.)

Ball and shell held as one ball   11

PHASE TWO

(6) Now explain that you will make the ball *vanish* when you count to "three." Turn your left side to the audience and hold the ball in your right hand. The left hand is held waist high with its back to the spectators.

Toss the ball two or three feet in the air with your right hand. Then catch the ball with *both* hands, being sure to keep the back of your left hand to the audience.

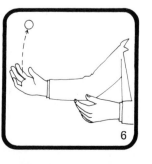

PHASE THREE

(12) Keep the left side of your body toward the audience. Say, "Actually that isn't the trick that I wanted to do. The trick I wanted to do is the one where I reach into the air and produce a ball!" As you say this, with your left hand (which has a ball secretly retained in the Classic Palm) reach out and produce the ball from the air on your right side.

PHASE FOUR

(13) Display this "new" ball (really the <u>first</u> ball) and . . .

(14) . . . then place it between your right <u>first</u> and <u>second</u> fingers.

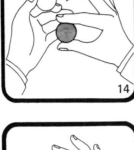

(15) As you <u>openly</u> place the ball between your right first and second fingers, <u>secretly</u> steal the ball out of the shell with the second, third, and fourth fingers of your left hand. Then, use the fingers of your left hand to press the ball into the Classic Palm position.

(16) NOTE: THE PRECEDING "STEAL" (STEP 15) IS ONE OF THE KEY MOVES IN THE BILLIARD BALL ROUTINE.

(17) Here is a side view of this important move. This is how <u>you</u> see the "steal" as you hold your hands about shoulder high on your right side.

(18) Separate your hands so that your left hand is positioned about waist high as your right hand holds what appears to be two solid balls (actually only one ball and the shell. The left hand secretly holds the other solid ball in the Classic Palm).

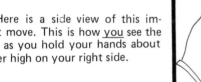

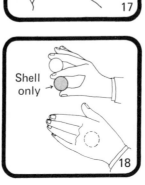

Shell only

(19) *NOTE: Be sure to keep the <u>back</u> of your left hand toward the audience. Also be sure that you keep the <u>full front</u> of the <u>shell</u> facing the audience at all times, <u>particularly when it does not contain a solid ball</u>, so that the audience cannot see that it is merely a half ball.*

(20) Here is a <u>rear</u> view of the situation at this point. The <u>shell</u> is held between your right thumb and first finger and the <u>solid ball</u> is gripped between your right first and second fingers. Another solid ball is secretly held in the Classic Palm in your left hand.

(21) Repeat the line you just said before with the following variation. "If you didn't see that — I will do it again. The trick I <u>really</u> wanted to do is the one where I reach out into the air and produce a ball like this!" As you say the above, reach out with your left hand and "produce" the palmed ball.

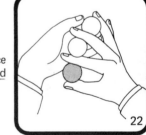

PHASE FIVE

(22) Display the ball and then place it between your right <u>second</u> and <u>third</u> fingers as shown.

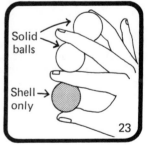

(23) You now appear to be holding three solid balls in your right hand. Actually, you hold two balls and one shell.

Solid balls

Shell only

(24) *You are now apparently going to "throw one of the balls to a member of the audience." <u>Actually</u> you will make the ball "vanish" and throw an "invisible" ball to the startled spectator. During this entire sequence it is important to remember that the left side of your body is toward the audience.*

(25) *Here is what you really do.* Move your left hand to a position so that it covers the two lowermost balls held in the right hand (actually the shell and one ball). You now *appear* to take the ball from between your right first and second fingers with your left hand.

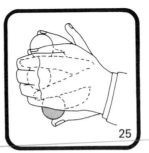

(31) Move your closed left hand down and away, *held as if it contained a ball.*

(26) *NOTE: In Steps 27, 28, and 29, the left hand has been removed from the illustration so that you can better understand the action of the right hand.*

(32) *NOTE: THE PRECEDING (STEPS 27, 28, 29, AND 30) IS A KEY MOVE IN THE BILLIARD BALL ROUTINE.*

(27) What you really do is the following important secret move. Your right second finger rotates downward (toward the floor) and lowers the solid ball held between your right first and second fingers *into the shell.*

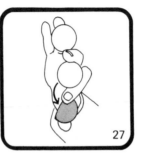

(33) Keep your right hand motionless, held about shoulder high directly to your right side. Continue to swing your left hand down so that it is held about waist high with the left fingers pointing up as if you are about to toss the ball to the audience. Say, "I can see that some of you think that the balls are not solid. Here — catch!"

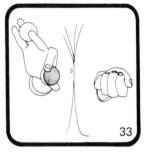

(28) Once the ball has been pivoted *all the way into the shell,* the ball is held inside the shell by your right thumb and first finger as shown.

(34) Pretend to toss the ball to one particular spectator. He, and the rest of the audience, will see as you make the throwing motion that there is *nothing in your left hand.* The ball has either "vanished" or become "invisible." Make no comment about this but, addressing yourself to the person in the audience to whom you apparently "threw" the ball, say, "Now when you are through examining it, please throw the ball back."

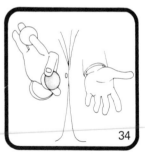

(29) As soon as the ball is inside the shell, *bring your right second finger back up to the position where it was before.* Remember, all of this action is covered by your left hand which . . .

PHASE SIX

(35) As if to occupy your time while the spectator "examines" the ball, bring your left hand back up to your right hand. Take the ball from between your right second and third fingers and transfer it down one notch so that it is held between your right first and second fingers.

(30) . . . has apparently removed the ball from between your right first and second fingers. *Actually, your left hand is empty.*

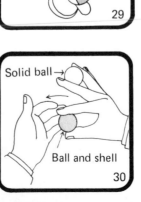

Solid ball →

Ball and shell

(36) As you do this, *steal the ball out of the shell with your left fingers as you did in Step 15.*

(37) Now, keeping the back of your left hand to the audience, bring your left hand (which secretly contains the just stolen ball in the Classic Palm) down to about the level of your waist.

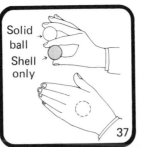

(38) Addressing the spectator to whom you threw the "invisible" ball say, "Are you through with the ball? Then would you please toss it back." The spectator may "play along" and pretend to throw the invisible ball to you (usually this is the case) or he may just sit there! In any event, reach out in the air with your left hand and *pretend to catch the ball,* really "producing" it as you did before at the tips of your left fingers. Say, "Thank you," to the spectator as you display the ball at your left fingertips.

PHASE SEVEN

(39) Now, reach up and place this ball between your right <u>second</u> and <u>third</u> fingers. You apparently have three solid balls held in your right hand. (Actually, you hold <u>two</u> balls and the <u>shell</u>.)

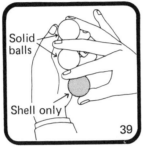

(40) Now move your left hand in front of your right hand just as you did before and perform Steps 27, 28, 29, and 30, *apparently* taking the ball from between your right first and second fingers into your left hand. *You actually pivot that ball down into the shell as you did before.*

(41) You now have two balls showing in your right hand. (Really one of the balls is the shell with a solid ball inside.) Your left hand appears to be holding one ball, but it is really empty.

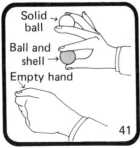

(42) Keeping the back of your left hand to the audience, bring your closed left fist up to your mouth. Now pantomime the action of placing the ball from your left hand into your mouth. As soon as you do this, turn the palm of your left hand toward the audience — showing it to be empty — as you apparently hold the ball in your closed mouth.

(43) *NOTE: As shown in the illustration for Step 42, you should bring your right hand down and hold it <u>in front of your body</u>. This "pivoting" move with your right hand is fully explained in Step 53.*

(44) Now with your tongue, push out your left cheek as if it contained the ball. Then repeat the same motion with your tongue on the inside of your right cheek. Now make a very obvious "swallowing" motion — just as if you have swallowed the ball!

(45) Look a bit dismayed. Then, with your empty left hand, reach down and remove the ball from the waistband of your trousers. (This is the ball which you preset and has been there from the start of the routine.) Your audience will think you were extracting the "swallowed" ball from your stomach.

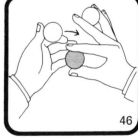

PHASE EIGHT

(46) Display the ball and place it between your right first and second fingers.

(47) As you do this, *steal the ball out of the shell with your left hand* as in Step 15.

(48) You now appear to be holding three solid balls in your right hand. (You really hold two balls and the shell. Your left hand secretly holds one ball in the Classic Palm.)

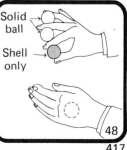

(49) Here is the view from the rear with the palmed ball hidden in your left hand.

(55) You are now in an ideal position to make a slight bow toward the audience as you hold the four balls in front of your body. If you have performed the routine correctly up to this point, you are sure to get applause (which, by the way, you certainly deserve!).

NOW FOR THE SECOND HALF OF THE ROUTINE.

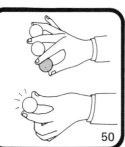

(50) Say, "However, the trick that I really wanted to show you is the one in which I reach out into the air and produce a ball." With your left hand, reach into the air and produce the fourth ball.

(56) Pivot your right hand back out so that the four balls are held as before on the right side of your body about shoulder high.

PHASE NINE

(51) Then place the ball between the third and little fingers of your right hand.

(57) Reach up with your left hand and cover the two lowermost balls. Execute Steps 27, 28, 29, and 30 as you *apparently* take the ball from between your right first and second fingers into your left hand. *(Actually, you pivot the ball down into the shell.)*

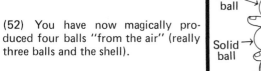

Solid ball
Solid ball
Solid ball
Shell only

(52) You have now magically produced four balls "from the air" (really three balls and the shell).

(58) Move your left hand down and away as if it contained the ball . . .

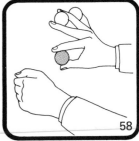

(53) You are now going to give the audience *a direct applause cue.* To do this, pivot your right hand down and around so that it is held in front of your body. *You must make this move without exposing the "half-ball" shell.* Just swing your right hand down and then back up in a half-circle as shown in the illustration. *Be sure to keep the front of the shell toward the audience at all times.*

(59) . . . until your left hand is in front of your body. Hold your left hand just as you did before you tossed the "invisible" ball into the audience. This time, however, make a "squeezing" motion with the left hand as if grinding the ball to dust.

(54) After you "pivot" your hand down, it will appear as shown here.

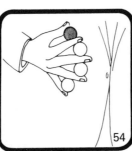

(60) Then slowly open your left hand to show that the ball has vanished.

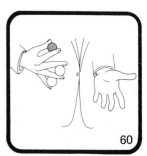

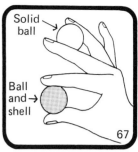

(61) *NOTE: In Steps 59 and 60, you may either leave your right hand held out to your right as shown in Step 59 or pivot it down in front of you as shown in Step 60.*

(67) . . . down into the shell. *It will appear as if the ball held between your right first and second fingers visibly vanishes.*

(62) After the audience sees that your left hand is completely empty, move your left hand back up to your right and grasp the ball that is located between your right <u>third</u> and <u>little</u> fingers.

(68) This "visible" variation on Steps 27, 28, and 29 is another key move in the Billiard Ball Routine.

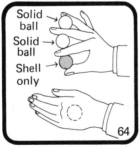

(63) Move this ball down to the position between your right first and second fingers. As you do this, *steal the ball from the shell as you did in Step 15 and hold it in the Classic Palm.*

(69) With your left hand, reach down behind your left knee and produce the palmed ball. Apparently this is the ball that has "vanished" from your right hand and has now "reappeared" from behind your left knee.

(64) Display what appears to be three balls in your right hand. (Actually, you hold two balls and the shell. Your left hand has one ball held secretly in the Classic Palm.)

PHASE TWELVE

(70) Display this ball in your left hand and then drop it into your left coat pocket (or place it in some receptacle such as a bowl or a hat on your table).

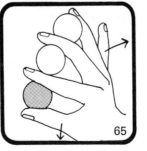

(65) Now wave your right hand up and down as you perform the *same move* that you did in Steps 27, 28, and 29 — *except this time you do it WITHOUT THE COVERING OF YOUR LEFT HAND.*

(71) Now move your left hand up to your right hand and take the ball that is located between your right second and third fingers and move it down one notch so that it is held between your right first and second fingers *in readiness for the same visible vanish that you just performed in Steps 65, 66, and 67.*

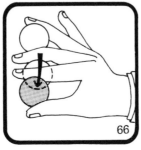

(66) Just as you did in Step 28, with your right second finger roll the ball that is held immediately above the shell . . .

(72) At the same time that you place the ball between your first and second fingers, *secretly steal the ball from the shell as you did in Step 15.*

(73) Exhibit the two visible balls in your right hand. (*Actually*, you hold one ball and the shell. Unknown to the audience, you have one ball secretly held in the Classic Palm in your left hand.)

(74) Wave your right hand up and down as you did in Step 65 and execute Steps 66 and 67.

(75) Here is a side view as you roll the ball held between the first and second fingers down into the shell.

(76) Here is a side view at the completion of the move. Again, you have apparently caused a ball to "visibly" vanish at the tips of your right fingers.

(77) With your left hand, reach behind your right elbow and "reproduce" the ball (really the ball you were holding in the Classic Palm in your left hand).

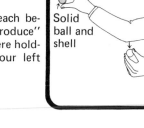

PHASE THIRTEEN

(78) Now for a bit of "magical fun" with the Billiard Balls. Display the solid ball you now hold in your left hand and then place it between the first and second fingers of your right hand. *At the same time, steal the ball from the shell as you did in Step 15.*

(79) You now apparently hold two balls in your right hand. (Actually you hold one ball and the shell. Another ball is held secretly in the Classic Palm in your left hand.)

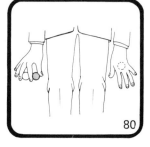

(80) Now pivot your right hand down so that it is beside your right knee. Your left hand also swings down so that it is on the other side of your body beside your left knee.

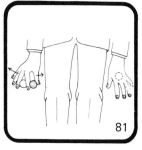

(81) Move the right hand away from your right knee and make a slight "tossing" motion toward your left.

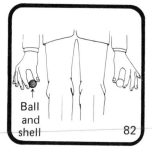

(82) As you do this "toss," pivot the ball that is held between the right first and second fingers into the shell. (This is the "visible" vanish again as in Steps 66 and 67.) Immediately, reach behind your left knee with your left hand and apparently reproduce the ball.

PHASE FOURTEEN

(83) You may now repeat this same effect by placing the ball held in your left hand back between your right first and second fingers. (The hands can remain down by your legs during this procedure. It is not necessary to return the right hand to its shoulder height position.) When you place the ball between the first and second fingers of your right hand, repeat Step 78 and steal the other ball from the shell. You are now set for the "Ball through the Knees" effect again.

(84) Make the "tossing" motion with your right hand beside your right knee. At the same time, pivot the ball between your right first and second fingers into the shell and reproduce the palmed ball from behind your left knee with your left hand.

(85) *NOTE: Here is an opportunity to add comedy to the act if you wish. This can be presented as a "perplexing situation" during which you apparently cannot control the balls — as one continues to vanish from your right hand and reappear behind your left knee. Or you may wish to make this appear to be a "magical transposition" which is under your control at all times. The choice is yours and should be made to fit the style of your presentation.*

(86) After several repetitions of the "Ball through the Knee," stop when you have one ball in each hand. (<u>Really</u> you have the ball and shell in your right and a solid ball in your left.) Place the *ball and shell,* as one, into your right coat pocket (or into the receptacle).

PHASE FIFTEEN

(87) You are now left with one ordinary ball which you display in your left hand. Say to the audience, "I am sorry that I will not be able to perform the last trick that I wanted to do for you with this ball — but you see, I don't have on my 'special coat.' If I had on my special coat, you wouldn't know it — but it would have a <u>tube</u> that runs *down* my right sleeve, *across* my back, and then *down* my left sleeve . . .

(88) . . . like this." As you make this statement, openly transfer the ball to your right hand and hold it at your right fingertips. Then use your left first finger to trace the path of the non-existent "tube" down your right sleeve and across your back. Then extend your left arm as if to display where the tube would be if you had on your "special coat."

(89) Continue by saying, "You see, if I had on my special coat, I could take the ball in my right hand like this. It would travel *down* the tube and come out here." As you say this, perform the following action. Close your left hand into a fist. Place the ball, which is being held at the right fingertips, on top of your left fist. Then with the right hand, apparently grasp the ball, really performing the Fist Vanish that is described earlier in this section of the Course.

(90) Extend your right arm so that it is held as shown, with your right hand apparently containing the ball. Your left fingers should be extended and the ball held secretly in the Classic Palm. Swing your left hand down as shown so that it is extended to your left completing the "tube." *Be sure to keep the back of your left hand to the audience so as not to expose the palmed ball.*

(91) Squeeze your right fingers together and then turn your right-hand palm toward the audience to show that it is empty. Then the left hand apparently "receives" the ball that has traveled down the nonexistent tube.

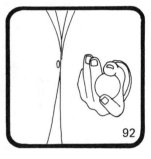

(92) Still holding your left hand extended, turn it around so that your left palm is to the audience and display the ball at the left fingertips.

(93) Bring both hands in front of your body and say, "I am sorry that I do not have on the special coat, so *I can't do that one for you today — <u>but maybe next time!</u>*"

(94) Then drop the ball in your pocket or the receptacle for the conclusion of an extremely clever sleight-of-hand routine with the classic Billiard Balls.

COMMENTS AND SUGGESTIONS

Along with the CUPS AND BALLS, the BILLIARD BALLS is another true Classic of Magic. Before you attempt to present the routine, be sure that you have practiced it well. As you can see, there are a number of sleights that are repeated several times. However, the entire routine has been designed so that each move is natural and there do not appear to be any unnecessary motions or suspicious moves.

In selecting your Billiard Balls, you should try to obtain a set which fits your hands well, as they are available in different sizes. The criterion here is that you must be able to comfortably hold the four balls (really the *three* balls and the *shell*) individually between your right fingers as shown in Step 52 of the routine.

Routines with Billiard Balls are literally endless. I am sure you will think of many variations and devise your own routine as you practice and progress with this classic effect.

CUPS
AND BALLS

★ ★ ★

We must delve far back into antiquity to learn the origins of magic. There, perhaps, to our surprise, we will learn that the mysteries known to the ancients were the largest and the smallest, with virtually none in between. The reason for this was that they did not class them all as "magic." The larger effects were regarded as miracles because they were seen only in the pagan temples where doors opened with a sound resembling a peal of thunder and life-sized statues poured water on a fire when it was kindled on an altar. These were the equivalent of our modern stage illusions, and their purpose was to excite the awe of the populace.

So much for the large effects. The small were feats performed by jugglers who claimed no supernatural powers but merely embellished their usual juggling routines with feats of sleight-of-hand, the commonest being to put a pebble under one cup and have it disappear from there only to be found beneath another. This was practiced by the ancient Egyptians, later by the Greeks, and by Roman times, such deceptions were known as *acetabularii.* The name is derived from the cups they used which were called *acetabula.* Times had changes by the Middle Ages, though not too greatly. Jesters and minstrels were performing their share of magic along with jugglers, and in many instances, cups and balls had become their mainstay. Numerous old prints dating from around the year 1500 and continuing onward show performers at tables manipulating conically shaped cups with small balls made of cork, which was the one great improvement over the pebbles used in ancient times. The cork balls were light, and therefore easy to manipulate, much to the amazement of the onlookers. And the trick itself was so good that it underwent practically no improvement during the next 400 years.

Professor Hoffman, in his famous book *Modern Magic* which appeared in 1878, devoted an entire chapter to the cups and balls, classing the trick as "the groundwork of legerdemain," and "the very earliest form in which sleight-of-hand was exhibited." He recommends the use of tin cups and cork balls of various sizes and describes a series of passes for the secret transfer of the balls from cup to cup that follow the pattern of the past four centuries.

Improvements have been made, however, since Hoffman's time. Nickel- and chromium-plated cups have replaced the old tin variety along with those of other materials that make handling easier. Balls of soft rubber have supplanted the old cork type, also with good results. Routines have been simplified and modernized to suit the needs of today's close-up workers so the descriptions that appear in the following section might prove amazing, even to Professor Hoffman as well as to his predecessors of the centuries before.

CUPS AND BALLS

This classic of magic deserves a top rating, for although it dates back to ancient times, it has still maintained its popularity throughout the centuries. Even though it is among the oldest of magical effects, it always seems new. The following routine gives the appearance of requiring great skill, yet actually the basic moves are comparatively simple. This is due largely to the fact that the CUPS AND BALLS combines *misdirection* with the element of *surprise* so that the spectators never know what to expect next.

EFFECT

On the table before the magician are three empty cups and three small colored balls. The performer positions the three balls in a horizontal row and places a cup, mouth down, behind each ball. He then places one of the balls on top of the center cup and stacks the remaining two cups on top of the first, imprisoning the ball between them. Upon lifting the stack of cups as a group, the ball is found to have mysteriously penetrated *through* the center cup and now rests on the table. This baffling process is repeated with the two remaining balls until all three balls have magically gathered beneath the stack of cups. The magician then varies his procedure by causing a single ball to vanish from his hand and appear beneath the center cup on the table.

Next he places a ball beneath each cup. He then mysteriously causes the ball under the center cup to vanish and join the ball under the right-hand cup. From there, it vanishes once again, and reappears with the ball under the left-hand cup. The performer then places the three balls in his pocket — one at a time — only to find that they have once again appeared beneath the cups on the table. This procedure is repeated once more, when suddenly the performer reveals the surprise appearance of three full-size lemons — one beneath each cup.

SECRET AND PREPARATION

(A) You will need to acquire the proper type of cups in order to perform this routine effectively. These cups should nest within each other easily and leave enough space between each cup to permit the concealment of a ball between them. (See Comments and Suggestions.) You will also need four small identical balls of the appropriate size to be used with the cups. The only other props you need are three ordinary lemons (or a lemon, a small potato and an onion, or three small rubber balls, etc.) The primary requirement for these props is that each can fit easily inside one of the cups.

(C) Now turn the entire stack mouth up and drop the three remaining balls into the top cup of the stack. Throughout the presentation, the audience should only be aware of three balls. A primary secret to the entire routine is the hidden "fourth" ball.

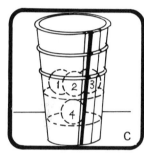

(B) To set up the apparatus for the start of the routine, place one of the cups mouth down on your table and put a ball on top of it. Now nest the other two cups on over the first, concealing the ball between the first and second cups.

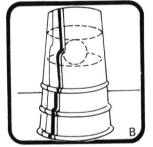

(D) At the start, have the three lemons in your right jacket pocket, and you are ready. The lemons are not used until the final phase of the routine, but it is a good idea to practice with them in position so that you become used to their presence as you practice.

NOTE: TO MAKE CUPS AND BALLS EASY TO LEARN, THE ROUTINE HAS BEEN BROKEN DOWN INTO SEPARATE PHASES. LEARN EACH PHASE BEFORE PROCEEDING TO THE NEXT, AND THEN PRACTICE THE ENTIRE ROUTINE FROM THE START TO FINISH UNTIL EACH PORTION BECOMES SMOOTH AND NATURAL.

METHOD

PHASE 1 — "PENETRATION"

All of the illustrations in this phase are from the audience's viewpoint.

(1) Stand at the table with the spectators across from you. Pick up the cups with your left hand and tip the three balls from the top cup of the stack onto the table. With your right hand arrange the balls in a horizontal row. The stack of nested cups is held in your left hand so that the bottom of the cups slants toward the table and the mouth of the cups tilts slightly up toward you as shown. *This angle is important in order to prevent the audience from seeing into the cups during the performance of the following steps.*

(2) With your right hand, draw the *bottom* cup from the stack downward as shown.

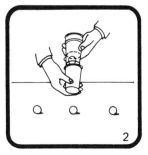

(3) *In one continuous flowing motion,* turn the cup *mouth down* and place it on the table behind the ball at the *right* end of the row.

(9) NOTE: It is important that the placement of the individual cups on the table be executed at the *same exact pace* so as not to attract undue attention to the center cup.

(4) Now remove the *second* cup from the stack in the same manner and . . .

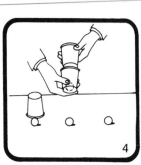

(10) The three cups are now mouth down on the table with the extra ball secretly under the center cup. The three visible balls are positioned in front of the cups as shown.

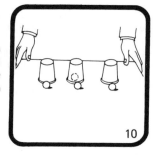

(5) . . . place it *mouth down* on the table behind the *center* ball.

(11) You are now ready to execute the first trick — the Penetration. Pick up the *right-hand ball* and place it on top of the *center* cup.

(6) *NOTE: You can now see why the cups must be tilted slightly toward you, since this cup is concealing the fourth "secret" ball. If this step is executed in a smooth, unbroken motion, the secret ball will be secretly carried along inside the cup to the table unnoticed by the spectators.*

(12) Then, lift the *right-hand cup* and nest it over the *center* cup imprisoning the ball between the two cups as shown.

(7) Next grasp the last cup in your right hand and . . .

(13) Now pick up the *left-hand cup* and add it to the stack.

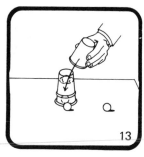

(8) . . . place it *mouth down* behind the ball at the *left* end of the row.

(14) With your right first finger, tap the top cup of the stack and say, "I'll make the first ball penetrate the cup."

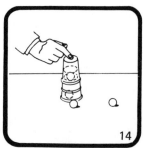

(15) Without hesitation, lift the *entire stack* of cups with your left hand, revealing the ball on the table beneath them. *To the spectators, it will look as if the ball you placed on the center cup "penetrated" the solid bottom of the cup and landed on the table!*

(16) Holding the three cups together in your left hand, turn your left hand palm up so that the cups are positioned just as they were in Step 1.

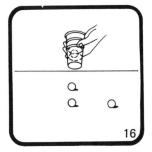

(17) *You are now going to repeat the same series of moves that you used in Steps 2 through 8.* Remove the bottom cup and place it mouth down on the table to your right. Then remove the second cup (which now contains the secret ball) and set it mouth down over the ball that just penetrated the cup in the previous sequence. *Unknown to the audience there are now two balls under this cup instead of one.* Then, place the last cup mouth down behind the left-hand ball. The situation should be as shown here.

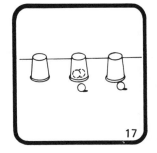

(18) You are now ready to execute the *second* penetration. Pick up the ball in front of the center cup and place it on top of the center cup.

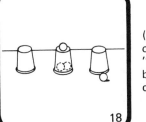

(19) Now, nest the other two cups, one at a time, over the center cup — and the ball — just as you did in Steps 12 and 13.

(20) Tap the top cup once with your right finger and say, "Now I'll make the *second* ball penetrate the cup."

(21) Immediately lift the stack of three cups revealing the two balls beneath them. To the audience, it appears as if the ball on the second cup penetrated through the cup to join the other ball beneath it.

(22) Once again turn your left hand palm up, holding the cups in the basic starting position as in Step 1.

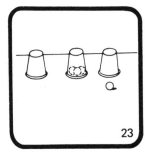

(23) Now repeat the same sequence again (Steps 2 through 8), placing the cups — one at a time — mouth down on the table. *Be sure to place the second cup containing the secret ball over the two balls which have already "penetrated" through the cup.*

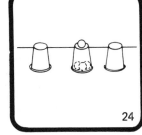

(24) You now repeat the same series of moves (Steps 9 through 15) to "penetrate" the last ball. Pick up the ball and place it on top of the center cup.

(25) Then, nest the other two cups over the ball and tap the top cup to make the ball "magically penetrate" the cup.

(26) Lift the stack to reveal all three balls on the table, beneath the center cup!

NOTE: BEFORE CONTINUING, BE SURE YOU HAVE MASTERED THE FIRST PHASE OF THE ROUTINE. WHEN YOU CAN PERFORM IT SMOOTHLY AND WITH CONFIDENCE FROM START TO FINISH, THEN YOU ARE READY TO MOVE ON TO THE SECOND PHASE.

PHASE 2 — "INVISIBLE FLIGHT"

All of the illustrations in Phase 2 are from the audience's viewpoint!

(27) With the left hand holding the stack of cups in the basic starting position, arrange the three balls on the table in a horizontal row before you. Now place the three cups, one at a time, mouth down behind the three balls as shown here. *The secret ball will once again be carried along, unnoticed, inside the center cup to the table.*

(28) With your right hand, pick up the ball in front of the center cup and display it briefly on your right fingers in readiness for the Finger Palm Vanish.

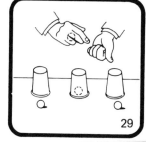

(29) Now apparently transfer the ball to your left hand. Really execute the Finger Palm Vanish as described in the Coin Section (See Page 187.) The audience will believe that you have merely placed the ball into your left hand. *Actually, the ball is secretly retained in the fingers of your right hand.*

(30) Casually lower your right hand and make a tossing motion with your left hand as if to throw the ball invisibly from your left fist into the center cup.

(31) With your left hand, lift the center cup and roll the ball slightly forward to reveal its "magical" arrival.

(32) Then, set the center cup on the table, mouth down, behind the center ball. *This is a very important phase of the routine as it allows you to get the secret ball out of the cups and into your hand where you can use it to execute the next series of "impossibilities" described in Phase Three.*

(33) Still holding the secret ball in the Finger Palm position in your right hand, pick up the ball in front of the cup on the right with the tips of your right thumb and fingers as shown.

PHASE 3 — "ANY CUP CALLED FOR"

In Phase 3, the illustrations are both from the audience's and the magician's viewpoint as indicated.

(34) Here is a view of this action from your point of view. Notice how the *visible* ball is held between the thumb and first finger while the *secret* ball is still concealed in the curled fingers. As you pick up the ball, your left hand grasps the right cup near the mouth as shown.

(35) Now, tilt the cup back toward you *leaving the rear edge of the cup resting on the table.* At the same time, allow the visible ball to roll alongside the secret ball in your curled fingers.

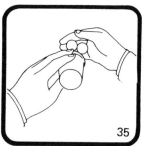

(36) Without hesitation, slip *both balls* well under the front edge of the cup as shown.

(42) As soon as your fingers are well beneath the cup, remove your thumb from the ball and hold the ball with your right fingers as shown. Withdraw your hand secretly carrying the ball along. *As you withdraw your hand from beneath the cup, be sure to tilt the back of your hand toward the audience so no one will see that you still hold the ball in your fingers instead of leaving it under the cup.*

(37) Here is a view of this action from the spectators' point of view. *The audience will believe that you are placing only one ball under the cup.*

(43) Immediately lower the front edge of the cup to the table as you remove your fingers — and the ball — from beneath the cup. *The audience believes that you merely placed the second ball under the center cup.*

(38) As you hold the balls under the cup, tilt the cup down and withdraw your fingers *leaving both balls beneath the cup.*

(44) Without hesitation, move your right hand (still concealing the ball) to the last visible ball which you pick up with your right thumb and fingers (just as you did in Step 33) as your left hand grasps the cup.

(39) Without pausing, pick up the ball in front of the center cup with the tips of your right thumb and fingers, just as you did the first ball in Step 33. At the same time, grasp the center cup in position to apparently repeat the previous series of moves as when you placed the ball(s) under the right cup.

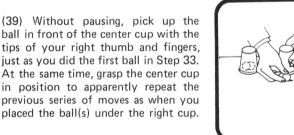

(45) You are now going to repeat Steps 34 through 38 with the third cup. With your left hand, tip the third cup back on its edge and place *both balls* under the cup, "as one," as shown in this illustration from your point of view.

(40) Here is the situation as seen from your point of view. Notice how the ball is held against the second and third fingers with your thumb.

(46) Here is the same action as seen from the audience point of view. *To the spectators, it should appear as if you are merely placing a single ball under the third cup, just as you did with the other cups.*

(41) Now, tip the center cup back on its edge and move your right fingers and the ball under the front edge of the cup as shown.

(47) Now, lower the front edge of the cup allowing it to drag *both balls* from your fingers as you withdraw your hand.

(48) As soon as your fingers clear the front edge of the cup, set the mouth of the cup down flush with the top of the table.

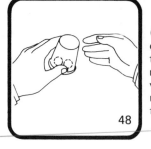

(49) *NOTE: At this point, the audience believes that you have simply placed one ball under each of the three cups. Actually, you have two balls under both end cups and nothing under the center cup.*

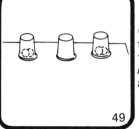

(50) State that you will cause the ball under the *center* cup to vanish and appear beneath *whichever end cup the spectator wishes.* Assuming the spectator chooses the right-hand cup, slowly tip over the center cup allowing your audience to see that the ball which you placed under that cup has vanished. *Leave the center cup on its side on the table as shown.*

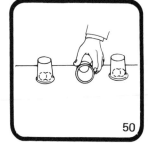

(51) Then, tip over the selected cup (in this case the right-hand cup) to reveal the mysterious arrival of the missing ball, *apparently joining the ball already under that cup.*

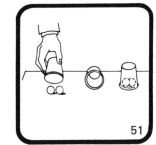

(52) With your right hand, pick up one of the two balls and display it at the base of your curled fingers in readiness for the Finger Palm Vanish. As you display the ball, make some comment about how difficult it is to keep track of that particular ball.

(53) With that, apparently transfer the ball into your left hand, executing the Finger Palm Vanish. *Actually, the ball is secretly retained in your right fingers as shown.*

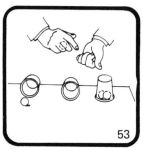

(54) Your left hand (which the spectators believe contains the ball) makes a tossing motion toward the left cup. As you "toss" the ball, open your left hand showing that the ball has vanished. At the same time, your right hand drops casually to your right side, carrying the secret ball with it.

(55) With your empty left hand, tip the left cup over revealing the missing ball to complete the sequence.

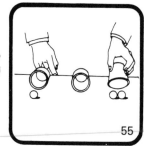

NOTE: AFTER MASTERING THIS PHASE, COMBINE THESE THREE PHASES INTO A SMOOTH ROUTINE. WHEN YOU HAVE ACCOMPLISHED THIS AND FEEL CONFIDENT OF ALL OF THE MOVES, YOU WILL BE READY TO LEARN PHASE FOUR.

PHASE 4 — "THE REPEAT PRODUCTION"

In Phase 4, all of the illustrations are from the audience's viewpoint.

(56) After the conclusion of Phase 3, rearrange the three visible balls in a horizontal row and place one cup mouth down over each ball as shown. *The secret ball is still concealed in the curled fingers of your right hand.*

(57) With your *left* hand, lift the cup on the *right*.

(58) Without pausing, turn the cup *mouth up* and transfer it to your *right* hand which contains the secret ball.

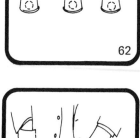

(59) Without hesitation, pick up the ball that was under the cup with your left fingers. *At the same time, release your grip on the palmed ball in your right hand and allow it to roll secretly into the cup as shown.*

(60) In a smooth, unbroken motion with your right hand, turn the cup mouth down and place it on the table in its former position. If the action of setting the cup down is done properly, *the ball will remain hidden in the cup as the mouth of the cup comes to rest on the table.*

(61) At this point, you have apparently lifted the right-hand cup, picked up the ball that was under it, and replaced the cup on the table. *Really you have secretly "loaded" the fourth ball into the cup.*

(62) Once the cup is on the table, openly transfer the ball from your left hand to your right hand.

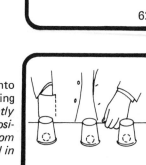

(63) Now place your right hand into your coat pocket, apparently leaving the ball there. *Actually, you secretly retain the ball in the Finger Palm position and remove your right hand from your pocket with the ball concealed in your right fingers.*

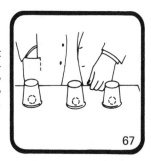

(64) NOTE: Steps 57 through 63 are the key moves in Phase 4. *The audience will be convinced that the first cup is empty and the ball is now in your pocket.*

(65) Now, repeat this same sequence of moves (Steps 57 through 63) with the *center* cup, secretly loading the extra ball into the cup as you apparently place the visible ball in your pocket.

(66) Once again repeat the same sequence (Steps 57 through 63) with the last (left) cup *up to the point where your hand is in your coat pocket apparently leaving the last ball there.*

(67) The situation at this point should look as shown in this illustration. *Unknown to the audience, there is one ball under each cup and the extra ball is in your coat pocket with the three lemons.*

The audience thinks you have placed all three balls, one at a time, in your right coat pocket. Really, you have secretly loaded the balls back under the three cups. If you wished, you could stop now by merely revealing the "return" of the three balls. However, you don't make that revelation quite yet, as you continue to Phase Five.

NOTE: THE NEXT SERIES OF MOVES IS BASED ON THE SAME SECRET "LOADING" PROCESS WHICH YOU HAVE JUST LEARNED. PRACTICE THEM THOROUGHLY UNTIL YOU CAN LOAD EACH CUP QUICKLY AND SMOOTHLY WITHOUT UNDUE ATTENTION TO YOUR RIGHT HAND.

PHASE 5 — "THE LEMON SURPRISE"

(68) When your right hand is in your pocket in Step 67, *release* the ball and *grasp* one of the three lemons, curling your fingers around it as far as possible. Now, remove your hand from your pocket, secretly holding the lemon, and let your hand fall casually to your side. *Be sure to use a lemon (or any other suitable small object) which can be totally concealed from view as you hold it in your hand as shown.*

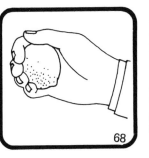

(69) As your right hand secretly holds the lemon, grasp the cup on the *right* with your *left* hand in readiness to lift it from the table. Then, as you lift the cup to reveal the ball beneath it, bring your right hand up from your side, making sure to keep the back of your hand to the audience. *The surprise appearance of the ball under this cup will draw the eyes of the audience to the table.*

(70) In the same motion, your left hand *turns the cup mouth upward* and places it into your right hand as shown here from your viewpoint. Be sure the fingers and the back of your right hand completely cover the top of the cup so that the audience cannot see *between* your hand and the mouth of the cup.

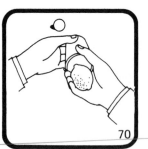

(71) This shows the action from the spectators' point of view. *IT IS VERY IMPORTANT THAT YOU PRACTICE THESE CRITICAL MOVES BEFORE A MIRROR IN ORDER TO OBSERVE THE AUDIENCE'S VIEW OF THE PRESENTATION AS WELL AS YOUR OWN.*

(72) *As soon as you transfer the cup to your right hand, move your left hand to the table and pick up the now visible ball. At the same time, allow the lemon to drop unseen into the cup.*

(73) From your point of view, this "loading" action looks like this. *Be sure to keep the mouth of the cup tilted toward you during this procedure.*

(74) As you lift the ball from the table with your left hand, "swing" the cup mouth down and place it on the table with your right hand as shown here. The important point here is to execute this movement *smoothly* and *quickly,* keeping the lemon well within the cup and out of sight of the audience.

(75) Now, openly transfer the ball from your left hand to your right hand and place it in your right coat pocket. While your hand is in the pocket, *grasp another lemon* in readiness to "load" the next cup.

(76) Now, repeat the exact same sequence (Steps 68 through 75) with the center cup. Just go back to Step 68 and repeat all of the steps through Step 75 with the second cup, *ending with a lemon secretly loaded under the cup* and your right hand in your pocket grasping the third lemon.

(77) Now repeat Steps 68 through 75 with the third (left) cup, *ending with a lemon secretly loaded under it as well.*

(78) When the last ball is placed in your pocket, leave it there and remove your empty right hand. The three mouth-down cups now each conceal a lemon beneath them. *The audience believes that you merely placed the three balls back into your pocket and that the cups are now empty.*

(79) To bring the routine to its startling and spectacular conclusion, ask a spectator if he thinks there is a ball under *any* of the cups. No matter what his answer, lift the cup he points to, *revealing the lemon beneath it!* The appearance of the first lemon will catch your spectators completely off guard.

(80) Then, without hesitation, quickly lift the other two cups, one at a time, *revealing the other two lemons.*

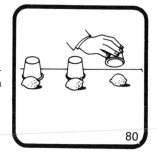

COMMENTS AND SUGGESTIONS

The CUPS AND BALLS is probably the oldest and certainly one of the most popular tricks in magic. The necessary props (three cups and four balls) may be purchased at any good magic supply company. For practice purposes, and even for your first performances, a very practical set of "cups" may be made from paper cups. The heavy paper kind are best — the type used for coffee or other hot beverages. They are strong, usually have a slightly recessed bottom, and often have "fold out" handles, which you leave "folded in." The cups can be decorated by painting them an attractive color if you wish.

The balls of a professional set may be made of cork, hard rubber, or often are a knitted or crocheted cover over a cork ball. You may also make your first set of these as well. Balls made from sponge rubber are excellent for practice. They are quite easy to make and equally easy to handle during the presentation.

Though the basic moves are relatively simple, they should be practiced until they become almost automatic in order to blend into a convincing routine. Any hesitation on your part may detract from the effect, as the whole purpose is to keep just enough ahead of the spectator so that he is constantly wondering what will happen next. In placing the balls beneath the cups, or pretending to do so, the moves must be *natural* and *identical* to one another. Once your actions become automatic, the vital moves will begin to feel more casual and less conspicuous and therefore less likely to arouse suspicion. Another reason for continued practice is that of gaining self-confidence. When first performing the CUPS AND BALLS, you yourself may wonder just why the routine deceives people. This is particularly true when you "load" the lemons at the finish. Having watched the small balls jump from cup to cup, spectators become so caught up with the action of the balls on the table they are never ready for the unexpected appearance of the lemons.

The CUPS AND BALLS is especially suited for performance when seated at a table but, it can be worked just as well when standing at a table. Any points of individuality that you may add to the routine will most likely prove helpful. Some performers like to vary it by using either hand to turn over a cup, even though the hand may have a ball palmed at the time. Just think of the CUPS AND BALLS as *your* trick, to be done the way you like it most. Once you have mastered the CUPS AND BALLS, you will be able to present one of the finest and most respected effects in the Art of Magic.

MAGICAL ILLUSIONS

★ ★ ★

In magical terms, an "illusion" is any trick or effect involving a human being, most notably an appearance, vanish or transformation. The term has been extended to include large animals and sizeable objects as well, while many unique effects, such as levitation, where a girl is floated in mid-air, or a "spook" cabinet, in which ghostly phenomena occur, also fall into this category. Formerly such effects were called "stage illusions," but today, some are presented in night clubs and outdoor shows or under almost any circumstances, hence "Magical Illusions" is a better way to define them.

From your standpoint, as a magician, the introduction of illusions can always be considered if they are in keeping with your act or suited to the circumstances under which you perform. If your specialty is impromptu magic, you naturally can't jump into illusions as part of your regular act. But an impromptu worker who is going to a large party, or putting on a children's show will often take alone some showy tricks, such as a box for the production of colorful silk handkerchiefs or the vanish of a rabbit.

Once such a step is taken, it can lead to more, and when audiences like tricks with small or middle-sized apparatus, it is a foregone conclusion that they will like illusions as well. If you can set up your act to produce an assistant as an opening number or early in the show, you may find it highly effective. If working on a platform or a stage where you have the benefit of a curtain, you can "close in" and work in front of the curtain with smaller magic. In the meantime, your assistant—or assistants—can be setting up your next illusion.

Two factors are important when considering the inclusion of illusions in a show: One is expense; the other, portability. It is unwise to spend times as well as money building illusions unless you feel sure you can use them often enough to make it worthwhile. Similarly, it is a mistake to make an act too big for the places you expect to play, or to run up extra costs for transporting you equipment. Such points have been considered in designing the illusions that appear in this section. All are inexpensive to construct and light to carry, so, if you plan to perform before large audiences, you can't go wrong on either count!

THE ARABIAN TENT ILLUSION
"GEN" GRANT

This is a very effective illusion which, once again, comes from the mind of that outstanding magical inventor, Gen. Grant.

EFFECT

The magician calls the audience's attention to a stack of heavy cardboard sheets. The performer displays each part and begins to fit them together one at a time. The spectators soon realize that the magician is building a small tent. With the four walls standing intact, the performer positions the roof, which completes the structure. Almost instantly, the magician lifts the roof *revealing the magical appearance of a lovely young lady from within the tent!*

SECRET AND PREPARATION

A very inexpensive and practical way to build this illusion is out of heavy cardboard. If you decide, after presenting the effect, to incorporate the illusion as a permanent part of your show, you can rebuild the equipment using wooden frames made of 1" x 2" pine covered with colorful lightweight canvas.

(A) If you plan to use cardboard as your building material, it must be strong and sturdy. You can buy *new* cardboard at wholesale paper supply houses or from companies that manufacture large cardboard cartons. A local printer is an excellent person to help you find a source of supply for for the cardboard sheets you will need. Also, moving and storage companies usually have large cardboard boxes for sale. On the other hand, you may wish to build your first illusion from materials that cost little or nothing. In this case, obtain a large cardboard box or shipping carton such as the kind in which stoves, refrigerators, furniture, and other large items are shipped.

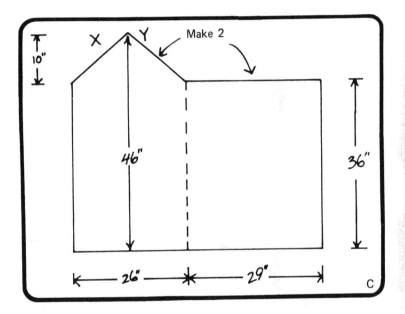

(B) The only other items you will need for this illusion are some strong paper or cloth tape with which to make the "hinges" that hold the various parts together and, if you wish, some paint and brushes to decorate the final prop.

(C) After you have obtained your materials, from the cardboard cut out *two* identical pieces as shown here. If your cardboard is not exactly the dimensions shown here, don't worry. The parts just need to be large enough to hide your assistant as you perform the routine as outlined under *METHOD.*

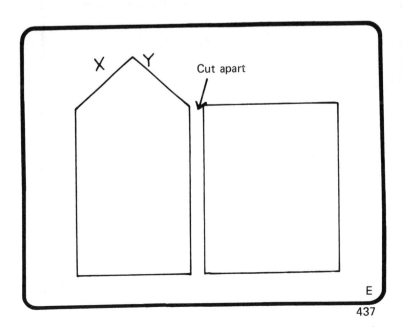

(D) Fold the two parts where indicated by the dotted line in Figure C.

(E) If you find that the board is too stiff to make a clean fold, it may be necessary to cut the piece in two as shown in Figure E . . .

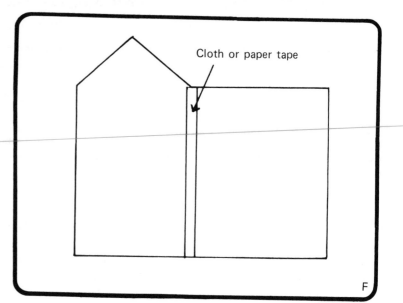

(F) ... and then "hinge" them back together with a wide band of paper or cloth tape. When you have them completed, these parts make up the four *walls* of your tent.

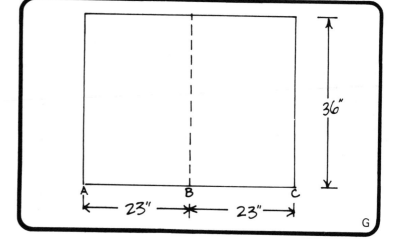

(G) Next cut out one piece of board as shown here. This is the *roof* of the tent. It must also be folded as indicated by the dotted line. If necessary, cut and hinge the two parts with tape as suggested in Steps E and F.

(H) *NOTE: Be sure that the two sides of the roof (A to B and B to C) are the same size and that they are each approximately 2" longer than the top of the tent's walls (X and Y) on which the roof will rest after you have assembled the tent.*

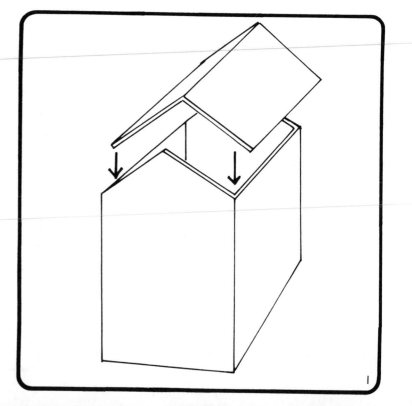

(I) Check to see that all parts fit well to make up the completed tent. Then decorate the tent to fit the patter theme that you will use for the trick (Circus Tent, Haunted House, Doll House etc.).

(J) *NOTE: This type of cardboard will take paint very well so don't hesitate to use it. Any slight warping that may occur can be cured by bending the part in the opposite direction to the warp. However, if you paint both sides of the board, the possibility of warping is minimized. You can also use "contact paper" or colored paper to decorate this illusion.*

(K) After your construction and decoration are completed, stand the roof on end like a two-fold screen. Fold the two side pieces flat and lean them against the left side of the roof as shown. The girl must be secretly positioned behind the roof section as illustrated by the circle in the "overhead" view shown in Figure K.

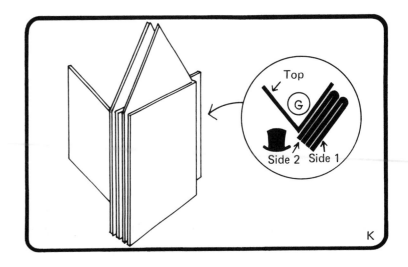

NOTE: IN THESE PICTURES, AND IN ALL THOSE THAT FOLLOW, THE LOCATION OF THE MAGICIAN IS INDICATED BY THE TOP HAT AND YOUR BEAUTIFUL GIRL ASSISTANT BY THE LETTER "G."

METHOD

(1) After the curtain opens, explain that you are going to do a little "Magical Construction." Take the first folded part (one of the sides of the tent), open it out and allow the spectators to see it on all sides. Position this piece as illustrated in the circular insert picture.

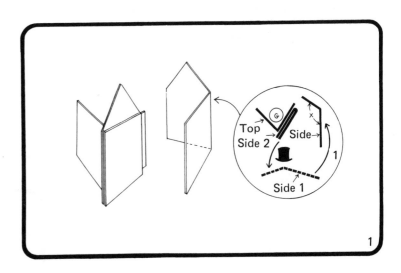

(2) *NOTE: The piece shown by the DASHES in the picture is the SIDE when you are showing it to the audience during the MIDDLE of Step 1. Also, when you study the insert drawing, you will see that the back of this side is left "open" when you place it in position on the floor. There is a very important reason for this, as you will see. Also note that the longer side of Side 2 is pointing directly at the audience.*

(3) *Immediately* pick up the second folded section (the other "side") and display it to the audience. Turn, and position it exactly as illustrated here.

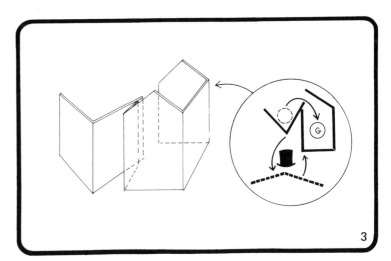

(4) It is at this precise moment that the girl moves secretly from *behind* the roof *into* the "tent" as shown in the insert drawing. This move is masked from the audience by the arrangement of the top and the two sides as you can see from the encircled diagram in Step 3.

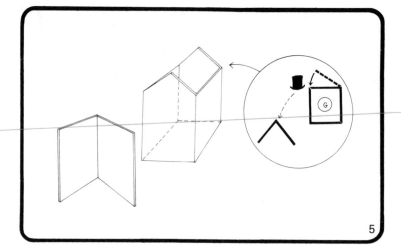

(5) Now quickly walk around the tent circling to your left. As you do, openly close the gap in the rear panel as you pass as if merely straightening the sides. Cross on the right of the tent and then pick up the roof section and display it.

(6) After showing the roof to the audience, set it in place on top of the tent. (Be careful not to move the sides and expose the presence of the girl inside.)

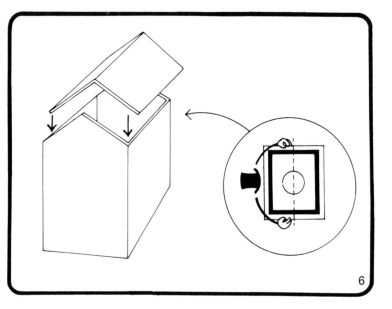

(7) Make a magical gesture toward the tent and then suddenly lift the roof section. At the same time, have the girl stand erect. *She has just magically appeared!*

(8) During the applause, hinge open the front panel and allow the girl to step forward for a bow.

THE HAUNTED HOUSE

MARK WILSON

EFFECT

The magician calls attention to the stacked sections of a miniature house with weird decorations and hooded figures peering from windows with broken shutters. He states that this is a replica of a haunted house that is waiting for a ghost to rent it, so that strange manifestations can take place within its musty walls and beneath its ramshackle roof. The magician decides to play the part of a ghost by putting on a sheet. Thus attired, he sets up the walls and finally picks up the roof and puts it in place. Continuing his ghostly act, he walks around the house, then makes weird gestures and suddenly raises the roof. To the audience's amazement, who pops up but the magician himself! Then, stepping from the house, he grabs the ghost before it can get away. When the sheet is whisked clear, the "ghost" proves to be a beautiful young lady, who takes a bow along with the magician.

SECRET AND PREPARATION

(A) The equipment for this startling effect is the same as used in the ARABIAN TENT ILLUSION which has been previously described. The only change required will be in the decoration of the parts.

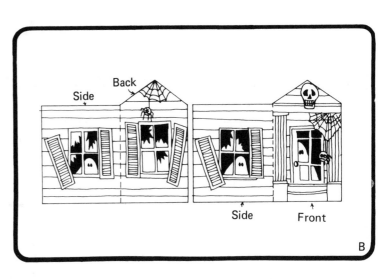

(B) This is an appropriate design for the "walls" of the House.

(C) The roof should be painted to look like worn shingles as shown here.

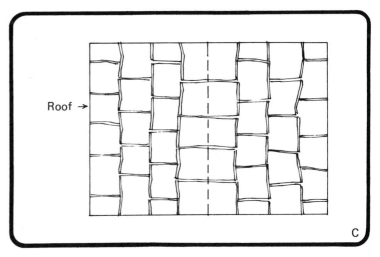

(D) You will need *two identical* white sheets. The size of the sheets is determined by your and the assistant's heights. *Be sure to make the ghost costumes long enough to touch the stage floor so that your feet do not show.* The eye holes should be cut as shown. You should also pin the sides of the sheets together and sew the material so that it forms make-shift "sleeves" as well.

(E) The parts of the Ghost House should be arranged exactly the same as in the ARABIAN TENT ILLUSION at the start. The girl should be wearing her "ghost" sheet and be positioned behind the roof as before. Now drape the duplicate sheet over your arm and make your entrance.

NOTE: WE WILL ASSUME THAT YOU ARE FAMILIAR WITH THE METHODS USED TO PRODUCE THE GIRL IN THE ARABIAN TENT ILLUSION SO THE FOLLOWING WILL EXPLAIN ONLY THIS STARTLING VARIATION.

METHOD

(1) Call attention to the vertical stack of parts on stage. Unfold the sheet and cover yourself completely. Make sure the eye holes line up properly. Then lift the first section (the back and left side of the House) from the stack as in Step 1 of the Tent.

(2) Now display and position the second side (the front and right side of the House) just as in Step 2.

(3) The illustration here gives you a back view of the situation at this point in the presentation.

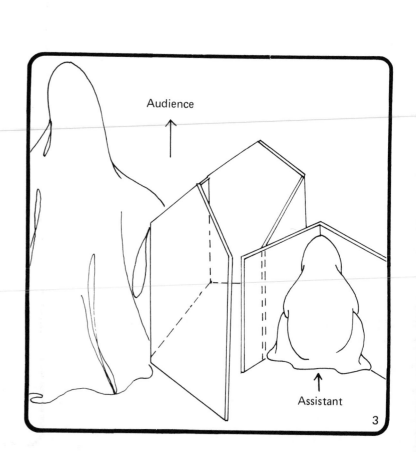

(4) After the second side is in place, circle the illusion to your left and end up standing *directly behind the concealed girl assistant.*

(5) *NOTE: It is very important at this point in the illusion that you don't look down and give away the presence of the girl to the audience. YOU ARE ABOUT TO MAKE THE MOST CRITICAL MOVE IN THIS PRESENTATION — and any hesitation will mean failure.*

(6) Stoop down behind your assistant *and* the folded roof as shown. Keep your arms to your sides, for as soon as you are out of sight, *the girl assistant grasps the outer edges of the roof as illustrated.* The audience will believe that these are *your hands,* since they are completely unaware of the concealed "duplicate" ghost.

(7) Quickly crawl into the "House" as shown here. (This is the same secret move the girl made in the "Tent.")

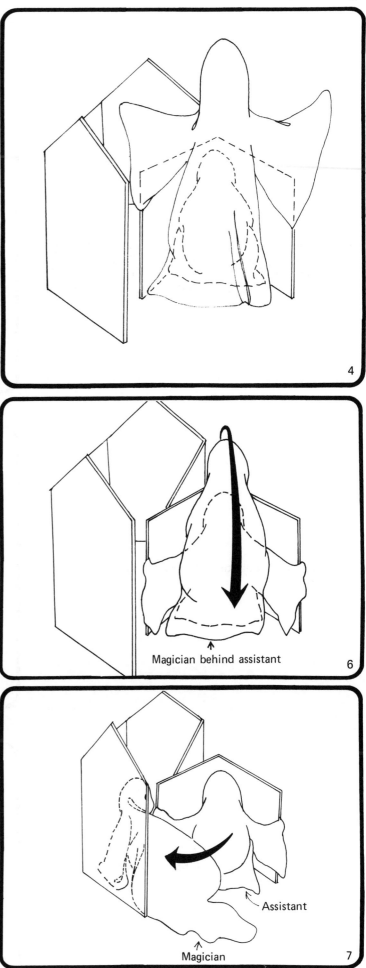

Magician behind assistant

Assistant

Magician

(8) *As soon as you are inside the House, your assistant immediately stands up, picking up the roof as shown here.*

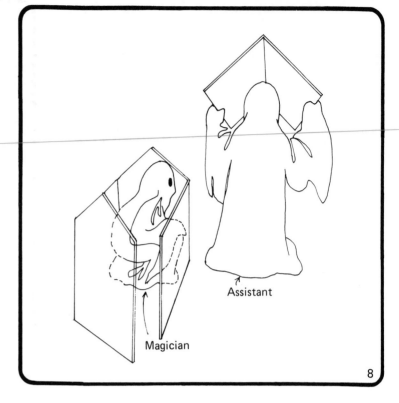

(9) *NOTE: YOU AND THE GIRL MUST PRACTICE THIS MANEUVER UNTIL IT BLENDS INTO <u>ONE FLOWING MOTION</u>. THIS MOVE IS SO DECEPTIVE THAT, IF DONE CORRECTLY, THE AUDIENCE WILL BELIEVE THAT <u>YOU NEVER LEFT THEIR SIGHT</u>.*

(10) The ghost (really the girl) now displays the roof *as if she were you.*

(11) She then sets the roof back down on the floor (slightly away from the House). Circling to her left, she closes the rear gap in the back wall of the House.

(12) Next she places the roof into position on the House.

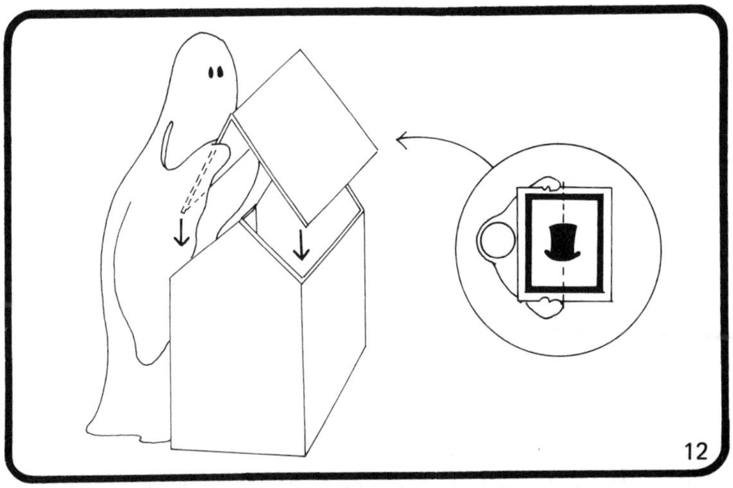

(13) NOTE: Steps 10, 11, and 12 of this routine are a slightly different sequence from their counterpart in the "Tent" routine.

(14) Making one more circle around the "Haunted Mansion," she prepares to lift the roof. During the time it takes her to complete this circle, *you carefully remove your ghost costume.* (<u>Don't hit the sides of the House.</u>)

12

(15) As soon as she lifts the top, you stand erect. If you have executed the illusion properly up to this point, the reaction of utter disbelief of the audience will be immediate. During the applause, quickly step out of the House *from the back* so as not to reveal your ghost costume in the House.

15

(16) <u>Now unveil the girl!</u> This *second* surprise will boost the reaction so that you may both take the bows.

16

COMMENTS AND SUGGESTIONS

Much depends on how the magician plays his part as the "ghost" when presenting this striking illusion. By having the sheet handy at the start, he can put it on immediately and begin a weird pantomime. But another way is to have the sheet hanging over the second wall, so the magician can put the first side of the House in position *before* he comes to the sheet and decides to play the "ghost."

Also, the girl must copy the magician's gestures *exactly,* once she appears in his place, so the audience will be held in suspense until the climax. By taking her time in parading around the assembled House, she can give the magician ample opportunity to dispose of his ghost costume. There is definitely no need to hurry, for, if spectators suspect that somebody is due to appear from the House, the one person they *won't* expect is the *magician* — so the longer the suspense, the stronger the climax.

THE VICTORY CARTONS ILLUSION

"GEN" GRANT

For a quick and surprising way to produce a girl from nowhere, this is ideal, both from the standpoint of its surprising magical effect, its portability, and its inexpensive cost. In addition, it can be set up in a matter of moments and worked on any stage or platform where your audience is located in front, making it a valuable feature for your magical program.

EFFECT

The magician displays two large cardboard boxes. Both boxes are folded flat and held upright by the magician's assistant. The tops and bottoms of the boxes have been removed so that actually the boxes are rectangular tubes which fold along their seams. The magician takes the first box from his assistant and opens it out into a square. Obviously, nothing of any size could be concealed inside since the box has been folded "flat" from the beginning. The second box is then also opened. To prove even more convincingly that it too is completely empty, the magician and his assistant show the audience a clear view through the ends of the box. The second box, being slightly larger than the other, is then placed over the first box. The two "nested" boxes are now revolved to show the audience all sides. It seems impossible that anything could be concealed within the cardboard containers. Yet, upon the magician's command, a beautiful young lady makes her appearance from within the boxes!

SECRET AND PREPARATION

(A) All you need are two large cardboard boxes of the size shown and the proper amount of rehearsal with your assistants. As you can see from the dimensions on the illustration, one of the boxes must be slightly larger so that one will fit over the other box. We will call the inner or smaller box No. 1 and the larger box No. 2.

From corrugated paperboard or any lightweight material, make two boxes as described. The sides are held together with heavy paper or cloth tape. The boxes are both 36 inches high. The smaller box is 28 inches square, and the larger 30 inches as shown. Neither box has a top or bottom — so actually they are large rectangular tubes. The smaller box has an opening cut in one side. The opening is 24 inches high by 20 inches wide with a 3-inch "lip" around the sides and bottom and a 9-inch lip at the top. The audience is *never aware* of this opening. The boxes must fold "flat" as shown.

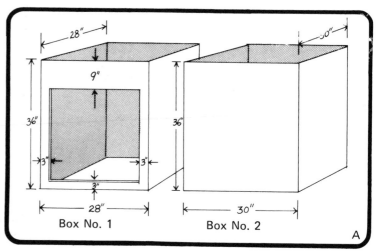

Box No. 1   Box No. 2

METHOD

(1) Fold both boxes flat and stand them on end with the prepared box (No. 1) nearest the audience. The "secret" opening in Box No. 1 must face to the rear. Box No. 2 is directly behind it. Your assistant should stand at the right side of the cartons supporting them in their vertical position. Step 1 shows the "backstage" view with the proper position of the two containers at the start. Unknown to the audience, the girl is crouched behind the two cartons as shown.

1

(2) To begin the presentation, call attention to the two flat-tened containers. Lift the front box (No. 1) and open it out into a square as shown. *Be sure to keep the "secret" opening to the back so that the audience cannot see it.*

(3) Place the box (No. 1) in the position illustrated, *so that it overlaps the left edge of the other box (No. 2)* which is still held by your assistant. As soon as Box No. 1 is open and on the floor, *the girl crawls from behind the other, still "flat" box (No. 2) through the "secret" opening into the "open" Box No. 1.* Because the boxes overlap, the movement of the girl from behind the closed box (No. 2) into the open box (No. 1) will not be seen by the audience. Your position at the left of the open box (No. 1) will also help to hide the girl's movement from any spectators watching from that side. Your assistant's body helps hide the girl's movement from the right side.

(4) After the girl enters the open box (No. 1), your assistant immediately lifts the other box (No. 2) and hands it to you. *This action must be done smoothly — with perfect coordina-tion between you and your assistant.* With the help of your assistant, open Box No. 2 and tilt it on its side — allowing the audience to see completely through the box. Now, slide Box No. 2 over the prepared box (No. 1) which now conceals the girl.

(5) With the aid of your assistant, revolve the nested cartons one complete turn to show the audience all sides of the cardboard containers. Since the outer container conceals the cut out portion of the inner box, everything appears quite normal. *Be sure to keep the bottoms of the boxes on the floor as you turn them so that you do not expose the girl's feet.*

(6) Upon your command, the young lady quickly stands up — apparently having "magically appeared" inside the two empty boxes! You and your assistant now help the young lady out of the box by holding her beneath the arms as she "jumps" out of the box. (See Comments and Suggestions.) Your male assistant can now carry the equipment safely off stage as the audience applauds this startling illusion.

COMMENTS AND SUGGESTIONS

Although the construction and the presentation are comparatively simple, this illusion must be carefully rehearsed until you can perform it in a brisk, straightforward manner. *Coordination* and *timing* on the part of the magician and both of his assistants is the vital factor. Any *hesitation* at the wrong moment may arouse audience suspicion that could otherwise be avoided, and the same applies to too much *haste.* As an example of proper timing, the girl should begin to enter the smaller box (No. 1) while you are adjusting it to its proper position overlapping the other, still flat box (No. 2). In this way, if the girl hits Box No. 1 as she enters through the opening, the motion will be attributed to your handling of the box. The quicker the girl enters the open smaller Box No. 1, the better. Your male assistant can then *immediately* pick up the larger box, with less chance that anyone will guess its real purpose — which was to conceal the girl behind it. You can then slow down the pace while showing the large box (No. 2) *as the real work is now done.* Revolving the boxes is very effective because, when the spectators think back later, they will be sure that each box was shown "clear through" and "all around" at the start.

THE MYSTERY OF THE MAGICAL MUMMY

EFFECT

The performer unfolds an attractive piece of cloth measuring approximately 6 x 8 feet in size. A male assistant, standing to the magician's left picks up the left top corner of the loose material and stretches it tightly between the performer and himself. Upon the magician's command, the assistant "rolls" himself into the cloth and then turns his body so that the material is wrapped tightly around him. The performer walks quickly around the "mummy-like" figure and then grasps the loose end of the cloth. With a broad flourish, the fabric is unrolled from the body within. When the cloth falls free, the audience is surprised to see a beautiful young lady standing in place of the male assistant!

SECRET AND PREPARATION

(A)   The only prop you will need is a 6- x 8-foot piece of cloth. If you are presenting this illusion in your home, you can use a blanket or a sheet. For stage use, however, an attractive, opaque piece of fabric is far better.

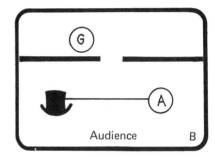

(B)   This *first version* of the MUMMY is the method for presenting the effect in your home. Select a room in the house where there is a door or archway located approximately in the center of a wall as shown here. The girl should be hidden behind this wall and to the right of the door as illustrated. Your male assistant, who, by the way, should be close to the same height as the girl, is standing to your left with the folded cloth over his arm. The spectators must be located in front of you, so that the door is obscured by the cloth when you and the assistant hold it up between you as shown in Step 1 that follows.

METHOD

IN THE CIRCULAR INSERTS, IN ADDITION TO THE LOCATIONS OF YOU (TOP HAT) AND YOUR BEAUTIFUL GIRL ASSISTANT (G), YOUR MALE ASSISTANT IS SHOWN AS "A."

(1)   Take the cloth and open to your left. Your male assistant (A) grasps the fabric by the top left corner and stretches it between you both as shown. This action must place the archway *directly behind the cloth* as illustrated in Step B above. *Also, be sure that the bottom edge of the fabric is touching the floor.*

(2)   As soon as the cloth is in position, the girl (G) leaves her hiding place and positions herself *directly behind the cloth.*

(3) STEPS 3 AND 4 ARE THE IMPORTANT SECRET MOVES IN THIS ILLUSION. On your command, the male assistant openly steps around the left edge of the cloth and stands behind the fabric as shown. *You and he must keep the cloth tightly stretched while he moves.*

(4) As your male assistant moves out of sight behind the cloth, the girl takes a new position *between* the male assistant and the cloth, as shown here. The male assistant has allowed her room in this area by extending his left arm and taking an unseen step backward. The girl, in the meantime, grasps the side of the cloth with her right hand at Point X as shown in the illustration. The assistant's left hand should curl the top corner of the cloth inward *just prior to the girl's move* in order to conceal his own hand from the audience's view.

(5) *NOTE: All of the above (Steps 3 and 4) take only a second or two and must be executed without hesitation. The flow of action should continue smoothly into the following steps.*

(6) As soon as the girl (G) takes hold of the cloth, the male assistant (A) quickly and secretly exits through the arch.

(7) Simultaneously, *the moment the assistant is out of sight through the door,* the girl begins to wrap herself into the cloth until she is standing next to you.

(8) *NOTE: The effect to the audience at this point is that the male assistant simply stepped behind his edge of the fabric and immediately wrapped himself in the cloth.*

(9) Now walk around the "mummy" and grasp the loose end of the cloth. *At this point in the presentation the audience does not anticipate the final result, so you should play it up to the fullest.*

(10) Start to unwrap the figure, slowly at first, then gradually increase your tempo until the concealed girl is about to be revealed. With a flourish, whip the remaining cloth away and dramatically point up the magical appearance of the young lady.

COMMENTS AND SUGGESTIONS

For an added climax, the male assistant can do a "run around" and make a surprise appearance in the audience. A "run around" means that as soon as the assistant is out of sight through the doorway, he literally runs through (or outside) the house by some route that the spectators cannot see and secretly enters at the back of the audience. If the physical set-up of the house is right, the assistant may have time to actually *sit down in the audience.* The viewers are concentrating on the action "on stage" and will not notice this new arrival. Then the assistant can loudly *lead the applause* until he is discovered by the now doubly amazed spectators!

THE MYSTERY OF THE MAGICAL MUMMY
Second Version

EFFECT

The effect in this variation is identical to that of the first version; however, this is the presentation as designed for use *on stage* in a theater. Therefore the placement of assistants and the "sightline" controls must be changed. We will assume that you are now completely familiar with the first version and move directly into the description of this new method.

SECRET AND PREPARATION

This on-stage version of the "Mummy" must be performed in a theater with vertical legs (side curtains) as shown in the illustrations. The right center "leg" will serve as a replacement for the doorway used in the first method. The girl is hidden behind this leg as shown.

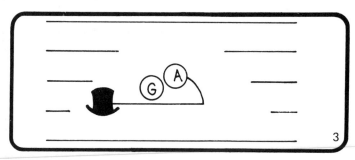

METHOD

NOTE: ALL ILLUSTRATIONS ARE FROM THE OVERHEAD POINT OF VIEW IN ORDER TO DIAGRAM THE MOVES MORE CLEARLY.

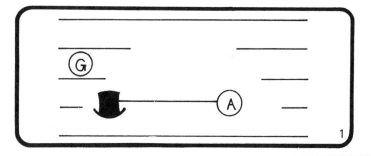

(1) Stretch the cloth between you and your male assistant (A). It is important that *you* are standing so that your body and the cloth *mask the on-stage edge of the right center leg as illustrated.* This will protect the girl's unseen entrance from the curtain to her new position behind the cloth in Step 2.

(3) At this point, upon your command, the assistant steps behind the cloth in the same manner as in the first version.

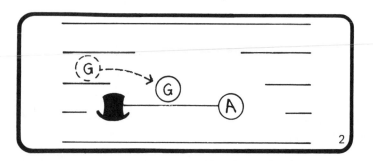

(2) As soon as the cloth is stretched, *with its bottom edge resting on the stage floor,* the girl secretly moves into position behind the cloth.

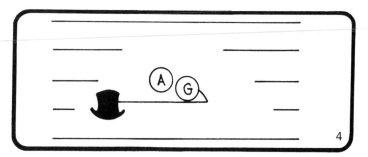

(4) The girl immediately takes her position *between* the assistant and the cloth as shown and substitutes her own grip on the top corner of the cloth for that of the assistant as before.

452

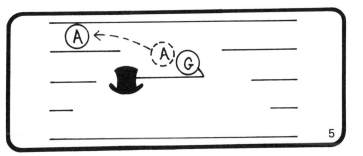

(5) The assistant makes his quick exit *into the wings* as illustrated.

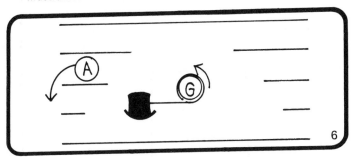

(6) *Simultaneously with the assistant's unseen exit,* the girl starts to wrap herself into the cloth. In the meantime, the male assistant is making a rapid (but hidden) journey around the outside of the theater (or through a hallway, etc.) so that he will be ready for his "magical reappearance" from behind the audience

(7) When the girl has utilized approximately one-half of the material, you carry the right end of the cloth in and around the girl as shown. *This serves the purpose of positioning you away from the wings.*

(8) Now unwrap the figure until the girl has been magically revealed.

(9) During the audience's surprise reaction, point dramatically to the rear of the theater as your vanished assistant makes his unexpected appearance by running down the aisle among the members of the unbelieving audience!

THE CURIOUS CABINET CAPER
EFFECT

A tall, slender, attractive cabinet is revealed in the center of the stage. The magician and his male assistant spin the equipment so that the audience can see it on all sides. The performer opens the front and then the back doors which allows the spectators a clear view through the cabinet. The magician even walks through the empty cabinet and then he and the assistant close the doors. Instantly the front door bursts open, revealing the magical appearance of a beautiful girl!

SECRET AND PREPARATION

(A) This effective production is quite easy to build. The illusion's dimensions and materials are as follows: The cabinet should measure approximately 2½ feet square by 6 feet tall and rest upon a castered platform about 5 feet square. The doors hinge open from *diagonal corners* as illustrated. In order to save weight, the cabinet may be made of ¼-inch thick plywood framed in 1" x 2" pine. The base should be made of ½-inch thick plywood with vertical framing underneath to prevent sagging with the girl's weight.

(B) After the construction is complete, decorate the cabinet in a style that blends with the theme of your presentation.

METHOD

For simplicity and clarity the male assistant is not shown in the illustrations. All of his actions can be clearly followed from the written description.

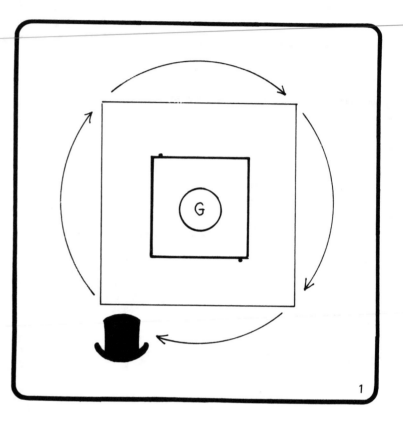

(1) The girl is loaded into the cabinet off stage. On your cue, the illusion is wheeled rapidly to the center of the stage. You and your assistant then spin the cabinet — showing all sides.

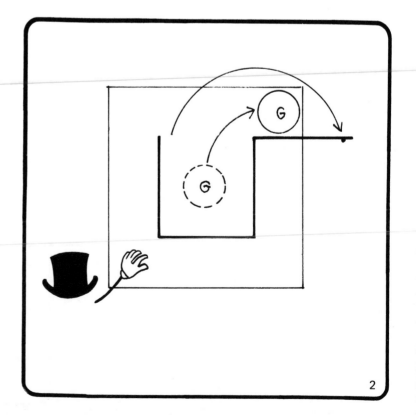

(2) The assistant opens the back door. Immediately the girl moves secretly from inside the cabinet to a new position *behind* this door as shown.

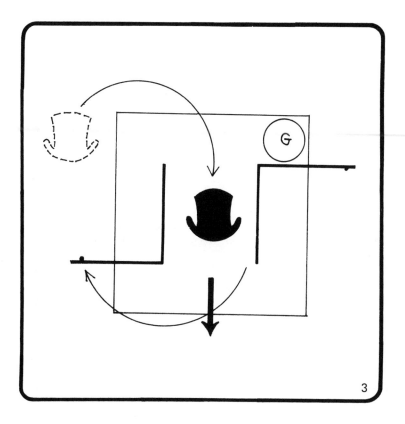

(3) Almost simultaneously, you walk around to the back of the illusion and quickly step through the cabinet *pushing the front door open toward the audience as you exit.*

(4) Your male assistant has moved forward and is now standing at attention to the left of the front door.

(5) You are standing to the right and pointing out the empty interior of the illusion. The girl is hidden behind the open back door.

(6) THIS NEXT STEP IS IMPORTANT. Since both you and your assistant are standing to the front of the illusion, the proper timing in closing the doors is essential. You close the front door first — as your assistant moves to close the back door. *The time it takes for your assistant to get into position will create the fraction of a second necessary for the girl to step back into the cabinet.* If these moves are properly timed, the effect will be that both doors are closed simultaneously.

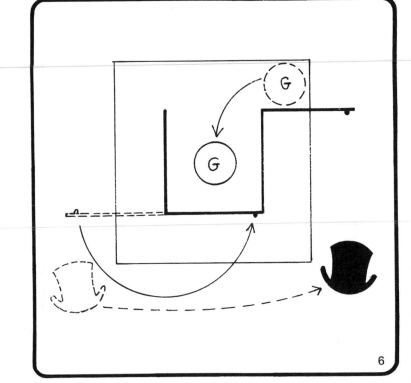

(7) You and your assistant step away from the cabinet. The girl flings open the front door, making her magical appearance!

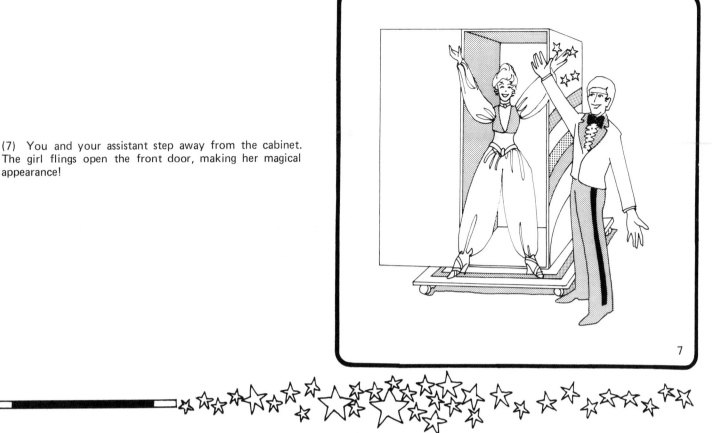

7

MUMMY'S CASKET

EFFECT

A tall, slender cabinet decorated to resemble an Egyptian Mummy Casket, is wheeled on stage by the magician's assistant. All sides of the equipment are shown to the audience prior to opening front and back doors. As you might expect, the casket contains a cloth-wrapped mummy covered with the dust of ages past. The assistant carefully removes this relic as the magician steps through the cabinet brushing away the imaginary cobwebs. The audience can see completely through the casket as the performer walks through it. Together, the magician and his aid reposition the mummy inside the casket and close the doors. Once again, they revolve the equipment to prove to the audience that the mummy is safely sealed inside its tomb. Suddenly the doors are opened revealing the startling transformation of the mummy into a beautiful young girl dressed in the ancient style of an Egyptian princess.

SECRET AND PREPARATION

(A) The equipment and the method are basically the same as in the CURIOUS CABINET CAPER. The only difference is in the decoration of the equipment and the additional task of constructing a replica of an Egyptian mummy. There are several ways in which to construct the "mummy." The best method, but unfortunately the most difficult, is to build a wire form in the shape of a person approximately 5' 3" tall and then completely wrap the finished form in wide surgical gauze. The second method is to sew up a cloth dummy of the same height as the girl and stuff this large doll with lightweight foam rubber. Wrap the dummy figure with gauze as before. The last, but least desirable method is to simply cut out an outline of the figure in ¼" thick plywood. Wrap this silhouette with gauze as in the first two descriptions. Remember, whichever method you choose, to keep the figure as light as possible. Also, lightly spray the completed figure with black or gray paint to "age" it. Now attach a thin piece of wire to the top of the mummy's head as shown.

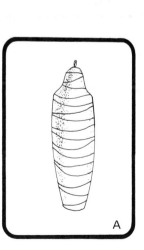

A

(B) This wire should be of the proper length to suspend the figure from a hook fastened to the inside top of the casket as shown in Step 3 of Method.

(C) A metal ring should now be sewn to the *back* of the mummy in the position diagrammed.

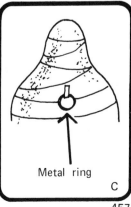

Metal ring

C

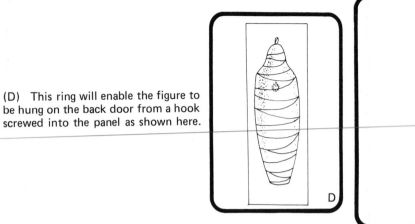

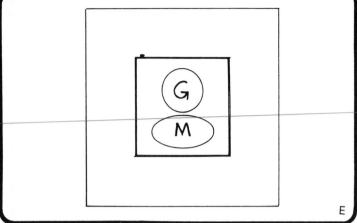

(D) This ring will enable the figure to be hung on the back door from a hook screwed into the panel as shown here.

(E) To present the illusion, first, hang the mummy from the top of his head inside the casket. Place the girl in the cabinet so that she stands behind the suspended figure as shown in this diagram. Then close both doors and have your assistant wait for your cue.

METHOD

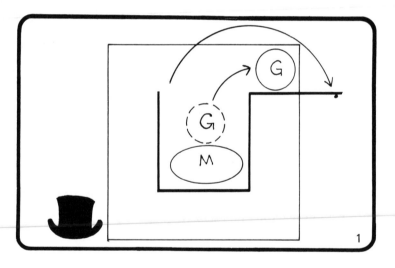

(1) After you have verbally introduced the illusion to your audience, the assistant wheels the equipment on stage so that it stands to your left. Together you revolve the cabinet. Your assistant steps back and opens the *rear* door. The girl shifts to her new position behind this door as shown.

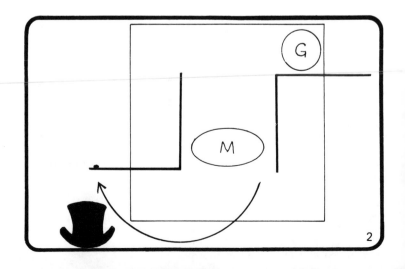

(2) *As soon as the back door is open,* your assistant moves back into position near the front of the equipment. Simultaneously with his forward movement, you open the front door.

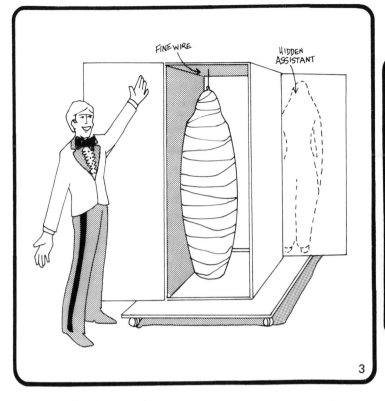

(3) Here is the audience's view at this point in the presentation.

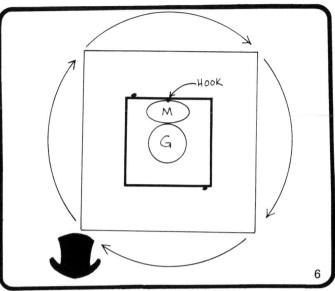

(6) Now revolve the cabinet in order to assure your audience that the mummy is still inside. During this rotation, *the girl unhooks the mummy from the top and fastens it by the ring on the back door* as illustrated.

(4) Your assistant reaches into the cabinet and removes the wrapped figure. This clears the way for you to walk into and through the empty cabinet as you did in Step 3 of the Curious Cabinet Caper.

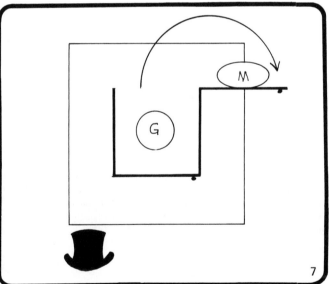

(7) Your assistant moves to the rear and opens the back door as before. This time, however, the *mummy* swings into concealment behind the back door.

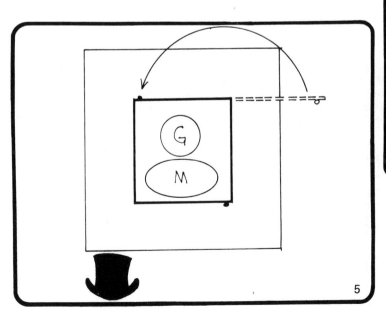

(5) As you exit from the front, turn and help your assistant in repositioning the mummy in the casket. As soon as the figure is secure, close the front door. Your assistant moves directly to the rear. The girl has already moved back into the casket by the time your assistant can close the back door.

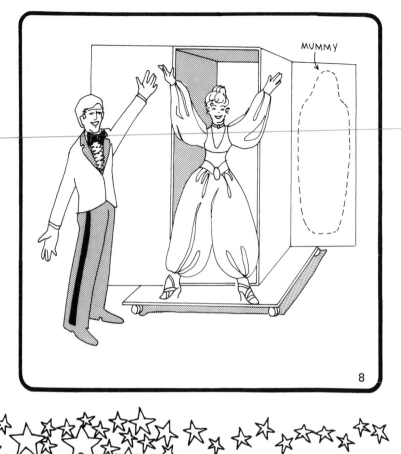

(8) As soon as your assistant has opened the back door completely, you immediately swing the front door wide open — the transformation of the mummy into the beautifully alive girl will shock the audience into real applause.

WHO'S THERE

This is the modern equivalent of one of the popular cabinet illusions featured in big-time magic shows that worked on full-size stages in large theaters. It usually required several assistants to move a cabinet around so that the magician could open the door and show it empty. Here, the illusion has been reduced to simply a *door,* a *frame,* and a *curtain* — making it easy to do and light to handle. The effect is nearly the same, but it is enhanced by the simplicity of the equipment itself.

EFFECT

Standing on stage is a full-sized door mounted in a thin door frame. The magician's attractive assistant opens the door revealing a curtain hanging across the threshold. Drawing the drape aside, the girl walks through the door and around its skeleton framework. The audience can see that the doorway is quite normal and totally unprepared. Without hesitation, the assistant redraws the curtain and closes the door so that everything is exactly as it was originally. Immediately a loud knocking sound is heard coming from the other side of the door. The assistant swings the door open and there stands the magician — making his first appearance onstage in a startling and amazing manner.

SECRET AND PREPARATION

(A) The equipment necessary to present this illusion is quite simple and easily constructed. As you can see from the illustrations, the door is mounted in a simple frame, which in turn is, anchored securely to a thin platform for sturdiness. An opaque curtain is hung from a rod at the top of the frame where it will not interfere with opening and closing the action of the door. *The curtain must be long enough so that it touches the surface of the platform.* This will prevent the spectators from seeing behind or under the curtain when the door is open.

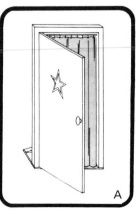

(B) Here is a "backstage" view of the doorway. The angle brackets serve to support the apparatus in its upright position and keep the framework from moving about when the door is open.

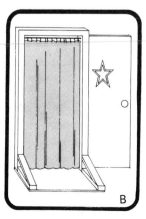

METHOD

(1)   At the start, the door should be in its closed position with the curtain drawn closed also. You (the magician) should be standing on the back edge of the platform behind the center fo the curtain as shown from this top view.

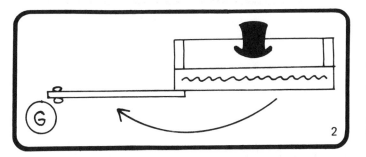

(2)   To present the illusion, the girl (G) steps to the front of the framework and opens the door to its maximum capacity as shown. You should still be concealed by the closed curtain at this point in the presentation.

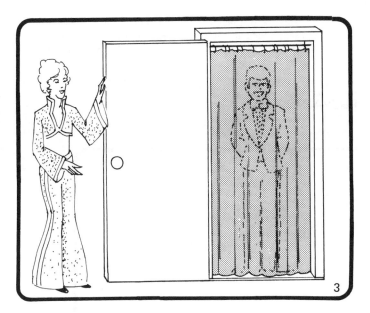

(3)   Here is the audience's view of the situation at this point. You can now see why it is important that the curtain is long enough to touch the platform.

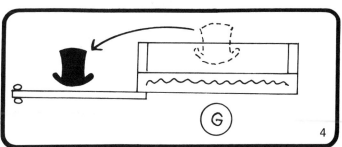

(4)   As soon as the door is completely open, quickly and quietly move to a new position behind the open door as shown. *At the same time,* your assistant crosses in front of the framework to a position in front of the closed curtain. Practice exact timing with your assistant so that *both* moves are perfectly synchronized, thus eliminating any hesitation in the presentation.

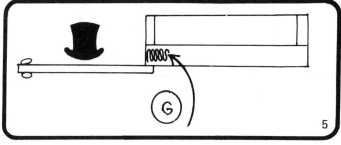

(5)   *Immediately* your assistant draws the curtain open as illustrated.

(6)   From the spectators' point of view, the doorway appears to be quite empty. Your assistant immediately walks through the open doorway and turns to face the audience proving that everything is just as it appears. Be sure that she does not glance in your direction. After a brief pause, she walks back through the threshold and closes the curtain.

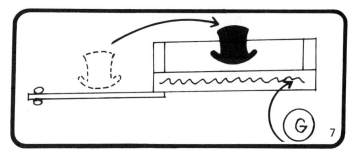

(7)   At this point, you return quickly to your former position behind the curtain.

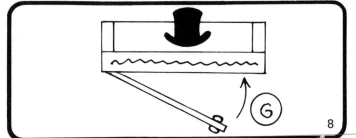

(8) During your move, your assistant walks from in front of the curtain to the edge of the open door and closes it. As soon as you hear the door click shut, pull the curtain open and begin to knock loudly on the back of the door.

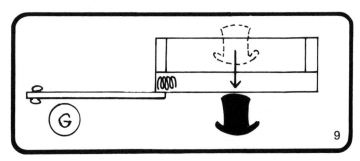

(9) With this as her cue, your assistant swings the door open.

(10) You immediately step through the doorway in a grand gesture making your magical appearance on the stage.

TIP-OVER TRUNK

EFFECT

An attractive trunk is shown and revolved by the magician and his assistant. All sides are displayed to the audience. The trunk is even tilted on its side, permitting a clear view of the top. In this position, the lid is raised, giving the spectators an opportunity to view the trunk's empty interior. Closing the lid, the magician and his assistant return the trunk to its original upright position. Immediately the top of the trunk bursts open, revealing the magical appearance of an attractive young lady!

SECRET AND PREPARATION

(A) The dimensions of the trunk shown here are for instructive purposes only. You will notice that two hinges, indicated by the letter "C," hold the trunk to the platform by its bottom front edge. This allows the performer and his assistant to "tip" the trunk over (hence the name) on the base and, at the same time, keep the trunk in place on the platform. The two handles mounted on the front edge of the lid make it convenient for the magician to open the lid while the trunk is "tipped" on its side. The casters fastened to the four corners of the base permit the easy rotation of the trunk during the performance.

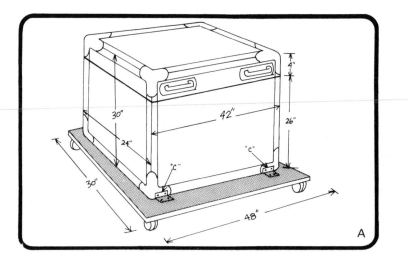

(B) In this illustration you can see that the trunk actually has no bottom. The shaded area represents the top surface of the platform. The upright panel marked "A" is mounted permanently to the top surface of the platform and held in this position by Sections B1 and B2 which are also permanently attached to the platform and to Panel A. These end pieces (B1 and B2) are cut into a pie wedge shape in order to allow the bottom back edge of the trunk to pass over them during the "tipping" action. A length of webbing (or lightweight chain) is attached to the lid as illustrated to prevent the lid from falling too far back and shearing the hinges when the lid is open.

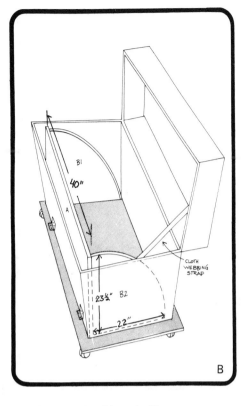

(C) When the trunk has been tipped over on its side as in Figure 3, *the upright Panel A becomes the bottom of the trunk.* The magician is then free to lift the lid as illustrated and allow the audience a clear view into the trunk's empty interior.

METHOD

(1) With the girl concealed in the trunk, the entire affair is rolled on stage so that it stands between you and your assistant. The two of you now revolve the trunk, showing all sides.

(2) With the front now facing the audience, with the aid of your assistant, grasp the handles at the back and tip the trunk forward on its base. *Be sure to keep the lid closed as you tip the trunk or the audience will see the false bottom swinging into position.* When the trunk is on its side, swing the lid open and allow the audience to see that the inside of the trunk is empty.

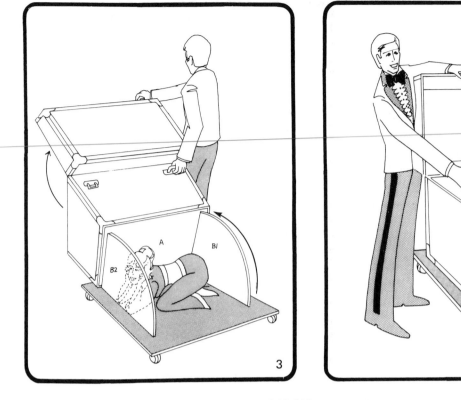

(3) This is a backstage view and shows how the girl is hidden behind the false bottom (A). Depending upon the "line of sight" of your audience, you and your assistant should stand next to the open trunk, one on each side, to hide the two end supports (B1 and B2) which also conceal the girl.

(4) Now close the lid and set the trunk upright on its base. Step in front of the trunk, turn and clap your hands. On this cue, the girl stands erect, pushing open the lid, which flies back into the hands of your waiting assistant.

(5) NOTE: In order to give the girl a graceful exit from the trunk, it will be necessary for you and your assistant to vault her out in a strong, sweeping motion so that she lands on both feet to conclude her dramatic "magical" appearance.

An interesting term used by professional illusionists that is appropriate here is *"Box Jumpers."* A Box Jumper is the assistant, who helps the magician by conveniently appearing, vanishing, being divided into two or more parts and then becoming "magically" restored, and so on during the illusion show. You can see from the "exit" the girl makes from the TIP-OVER TRUNK after she appears just how these talented ladies acquired that unusual nickname.

THE FARMER AND THE WITCH

"GEN" GRANT

EFFECT

From the large crowd of eager volunteers, the magician selects one boy and two girls to participate in the next mystery. On a small table to the performer's right, place two costumes. One represents a *witch*, the other an old *farmer*. The girl is selected by the magician to play the part of the witch. She is sent back stage with the appropriate cloak and mask, in the company of the other girl, whose job is to act as *wardrobe mistress*. While the girl is backstage slipping on her costume, the magician gives the farmer's costume to the boy who will be playing the part of the farmer in the story the magician is about to tell. The old witch enters and the boy exits to allow the wardrobe mistress to dress him as the farmer. After a bit of funny by-play, all three children are standing around the magician, the farmer smoking his pipe, the witch brandishing her broom and the wardrobe mistress observing all their antics. Suddenly, the witch waves her broom at the farmer. Upon removing the farmer's costume, the audience is surprised to see the *girl,* who moments before had been the witch. The second surprise comes when it is discovered that the witch's costume now covers the *boy,* who had been the farmer. Through all the applause and laughter, the children are thanked for their participation and excused from the stage.

SECRET AND PREPARATION

(A) This highly entertaining and portable illusion is made up of the following elements: one broom, *two identical* witches' costumes complete with hooded masks and one farmer's outfit with mask to match.

NOTE: All of the costumes should be made so that they can be quickly slipped on over the children's clothes.

(C) The farmer's mask may be purchased from a novelty store. Be sure that the mask is opaque except for the eye, nose, and mouth openings. Fashion a hood of the same blue material and stitch it around the edges of the mask. The addition of a bandana around the neck is a nice touch. Just be sure that the entire mask assembly can pass freely over a child's head.

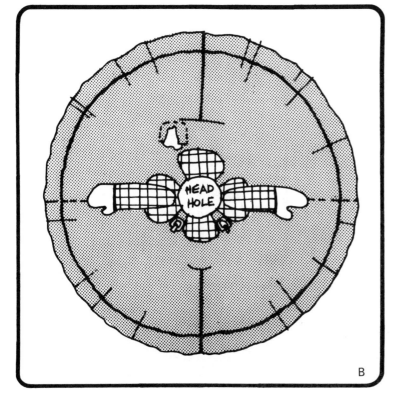

(B) To create the farmer's costume, you will need to purchase a quantity of blue cotton material and sew it into a large circle as shown. The hole in the center is passed over the child's head and allows the material to fall around his shoulders and hang to the floor. For a more charming look, you can add the shirt and hands as illustrated. The shirt can be made of a red and white checkered material and appliqued to the blue cape. NOTE: The arms and hands are not real, but merely designs made from the material.

(D) The completed costume, when worn, should look like this.

(E) The *two* identical witches' costumes are made in the same manner as just described, except that in this case, select a black material for the background color to accentuate the patches as illustrated.

(G) The completed costume will look like this. The broom is held *through the fabric of the cape* as shown.

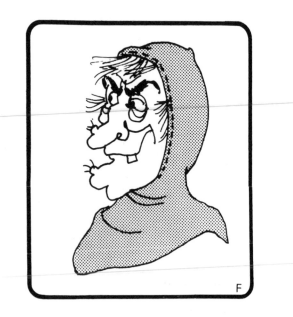

(F) The mask should look like a witch and be completed with a black hood. You will notice that all the hoods (the farmer and the two witches) extend well below the neck in order to cover any possibility of seeing the child through the hole in the center of the cape.

(H) Now place *one* of the witch's costumes and the farmer's costume on your table. The *second* witch costume and the broom are stationed back stage on your left with an assistant.

METHOD

All of the following illustrations are diagrammed from an overhead view. In this way, you can more clearly visualize the sequence of events as it takes place. The boy is represented by the "B," the girl who is to play the witch by the "G," the girl who is to play the wardrobe mistress by the "W," and your assistant by the "A."

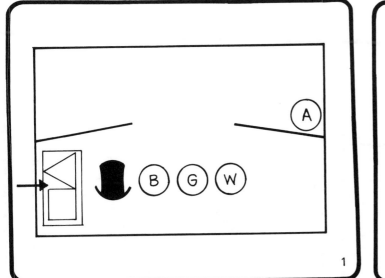

(1)   Request the assistance of two girls and a boy from your audience. At this point you will usually be mobbed with volunteers. Select three that are very close to the same height — thank and excuse the rest. The table containing the costumes is to your right. The three children should be standing on your left.

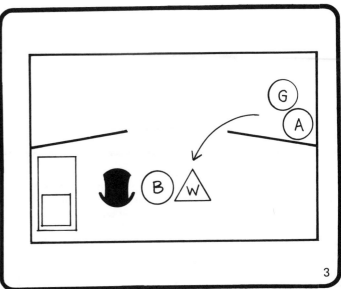

(3)   What *actually* takes place is that your assistant costumes the wardrobe mistress in the *witch's* outfit and sends her back on stage as diagrammed here. (The "triangle" represents one of the *witch's* costumes.)

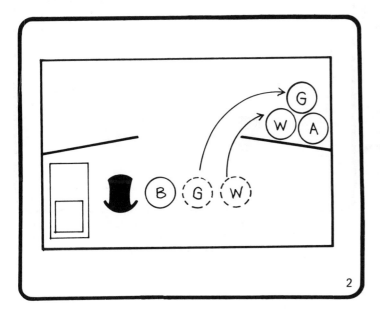

(2)   Hand the witch's costume and mask to the girl chosen to act as wardrobe mistress and send her *with the second girl, who is to play the witch,* back stage to change.

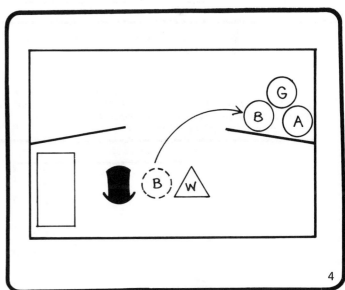

(4)   As soon as the "witch" (really the wardrobe mistress) appears on stage, the boy is sent back with the farmer's costume so that he can be quickly dressed.

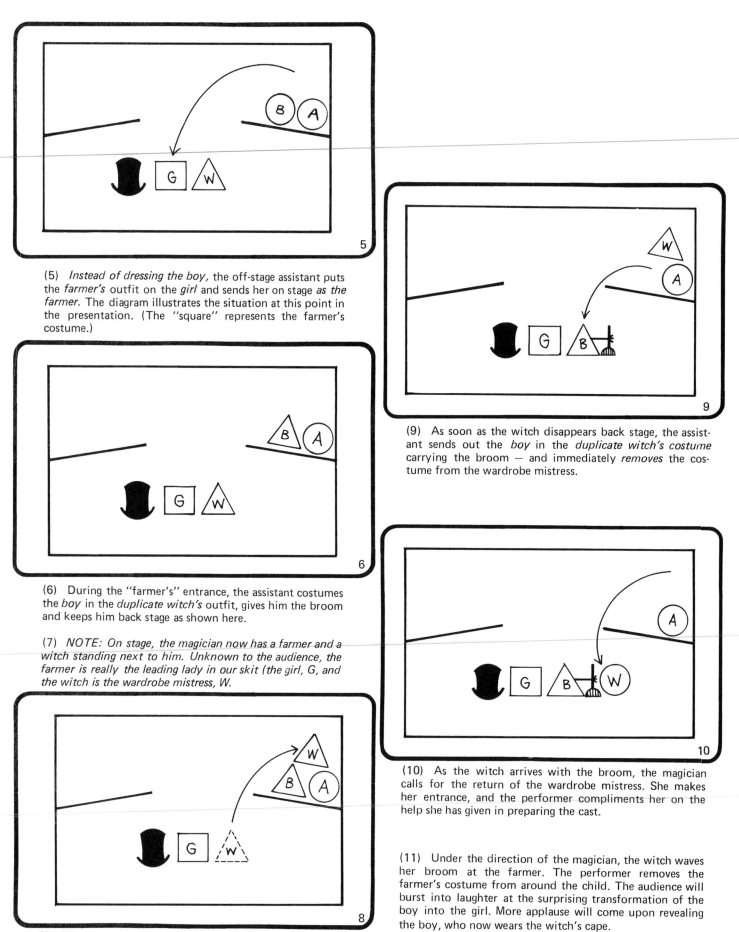

(5) *Instead of dressing the boy,* the off-stage assistant puts the *farmer's* outfit on the *girl* and sends her on stage *as the farmer.* The diagram illustrates the situation at this point in the presentation. (The "square" represents the farmer's costume.)

(6) During the "farmer's" entrance, the assistant costumes the *boy* in the *duplicate witch's* outfit, gives him the broom and keeps him back stage as shown here.

(7) *NOTE: On stage, the magician now has a farmer and a witch standing next to him. Unknown to the audience, the farmer is really the leading lady in our skit (the girl, G, and the witch is the wardrobe mistress, W.*

(8) The performer turns to the witch telling her that she has forgotten her broom and sends her back stage to get it, as shown here.

(9) As soon as the witch disappears back stage, the assistant sends out the *boy* in the *duplicate witch's costume* carrying the broom — and immediately *removes* the costume from the wardrobe mistress.

(10) As the witch arrives with the broom, the magician calls for the return of the wardrobe mistress. She makes her entrance, and the performer compliments her on the help she has given in preparing the cast.

(11) Under the direction of the magician, the witch waves her broom at the farmer. The performer removes the farmer's costume from around the child. The audience will burst into laughter at the surprising transformation of the boy into the girl. More applause will come upon revealing the boy, who now wears the witch's cape.

COMMENTS AND SUGGESTIONS

This exchange is a real puzzler. Its principle has been used by magicians for many years — and it has been presented in glamorous variations by some of the great showmen in our industry. Gen Grant's version is a classic, mystifying, and practical use of this clever concept in a very colorful and entertaining presentation.

THE SUSPENSION ILLUSION

For centuries, tales were told of Hindu fakirs who could levitate themselves and remain suspended in mid-air for hours or even days. Such exaggerated reports caused the magicians of Europe and America to devise their own methods of presenting this fanciful effect, but in its ultimate form, the illusion was costly, difficult to transport, and could only be presented on a fully equipped stage in a large theater. In contrast, the version about to be described is inexpensive, portable, easy to set up, and can be presented on practically any stage that has drapes and on which the "angles" (line of sight) are those normally found in a theater.

EFFECT

The magician calls the audience's attention to a thin board resting on two small, sawhorse-like supports. These supports are positioned at the ends of the board and elevate it to a height of approximately 3 feet. This equipment is standing in the middle of the stage, and the audience can see the basic simplicity of the arrangement. An attractive young lady makes her entrance and sits comfortably on the board. With the aid of the magician, the girl turns and positions herself horizontally on the board. Walking behind the girl and leaning over her body, the performer apparently hypnotizes the girl. Her arm falls limply over the side of the board as her eyes close. Carefully placing her arm next to her body, the magician moves to the girl's feet and slowly removes the sawhorse from beneath this end of the board. Magically, and with only the support of the single sawhorse, the girl remains suspended as if being held in balance by an unseen force. Passing his hands under the suspended girl, the magician carefully removes the last sawhorse. The audience is stunned to see that the sleeping girl is now "floating on air" with no other support than the magician's will!

Again, the performer passes his hands under and over the young lady's suspended figure, proving to the audience that she is truly "levitated." Quickly replacing the supports beneath the board, the magician snaps his fingers and awakens the young lady. She stands and bows to the applauding spectators.

SECRET AND PREPARATION

NOTE: Since this is one of the true classics of magic, it is important that you construct this illusion with care. Any skimping or make-do arrangements will only spoil a great effect.

(A) Figure A tells the whole story. Except for the 12" x 54" x ¾" plywood board, the entire structure is made up of hardened steel 2" wide by ¼" to ½" thick. The board is fastened to the top extension arm by two heavy angle brackets (A and B) as illustrated. After construction, paint the entire unit flat black, then cover the board with a good quality black felt. Trim the edge of the board with a 5-inch fringe as illustrated. This fringe conceals the steel support directly under the board. You will also require an attractive carpet that can be thrown over the floor supports of the apparatus and two lightweight sawhorses that are the correct height to *apparently* support the board. In fact, the board is *always* supported by the secret device located behind the curtain. Paint these supports white (or leave them their natural light color of unfinished wood) in order to create the contrast necessary to help divert the spectators' eyes from the board. If the black felt-covered board is also trimmed with black fringe, the audience, many times, will leave the theater with the impression that the girl was only supported by the two white sawhorses.

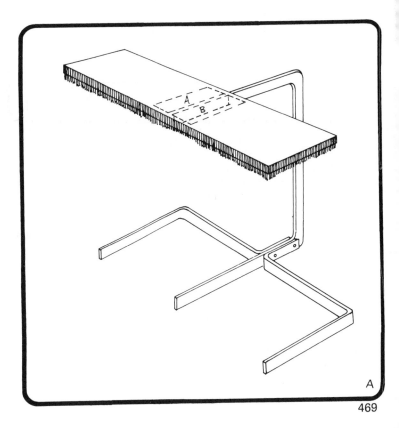

A

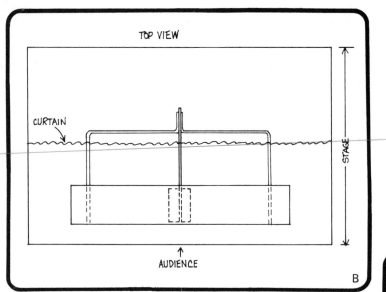

(B) You will also require a curtain directly behind the illusion as shown in the top view. The support arm for the board must extend through the curtain as shown. The brighter the color of this curtain, the better. The object here is to create a brilliant area behind the girl giving the audience the impression of a clean separation.

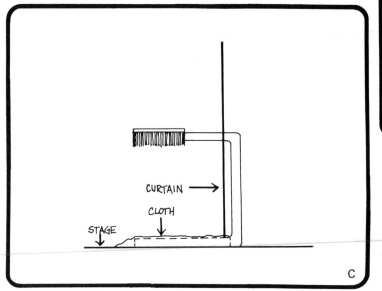

(C) The equipment is positioned on stage as shown in this side view. You will notice that the support arm extends through the center slit in the backdrop. The floor supports extend under the bottom edge of the curtain and are disguised with the small carpet.

(D) Now place the two sawhorses under the ends of the board as in Figure D. The effect will be as illustrated.

METHOD

(1) Introduce the girl to your audience and have her sit on the center of the board. Take hold of her ankles and help her in positioning her feet near the left end support.

(2) Walk around the front side of the equipment and assist the girl in leaning back until she is resting flat on the board with her neck just above the sawhorse support at that end.

(3) Now move around the head end of the board until you are standing behind the girl and the board. The hidden arm of the equipment will be next to your left wrist.

(4) The following move will help establish separation between the girl and the curtain. Lean over the young lady and apparently hypnotize her. As she closes her eyes, have her drop her right arm limply off the board. This diversion gives you an excuse for moving back to the front of the girl in order to replace her arm next to her side.

(5) After repositioning the girl's arm, move to the end of the board supporting her head. Reach under it, remove the sawhorse, and set it aside.

(8) Pass your hands over and under the suspended figure.

(6) Step around *behind* the girl at the head end of the board and pass your hands over and under the suspended figure.

(7) Now move back around to the *front* and cross over to the foot end of the equipment. Gently slide the last sawhorse from beneath the board, *leaving the girl apparently suspended in the air!*

(9) Quickly replace the foot support. Then cross over to the other side and slide the second sawhorse under her head. Snap your fingers as if to awaken the girl and then help her to her feet as you take your bows.

REPUTATION
MAKERS

★ ★ ★

REPUTATION MAKERS

You will find magic can help you in many ways. With what you learn in this course, you can entertain almost anybody, any time, in any country in the world. The following pages teach you a number of excellent tricks not previously covered in the course. I call them "Reputation Makers." But, even more importantly, you'll learn how magic can be useful in different situations, for different people, of different ages, to help you achieve your goals.

Let me give you an example. Performing a bit of magic has gotten me tables in restaurants that were "fully booked," rooms in hotels that had "no vacancies," and seats on trains and airplanes where there were "none available." Magic worked for me, not just in places where I may have been known before as a magician, but in foreign countries where they had no idea who I was. It wasn't me, it was the magic.

Now I would like to pass on to you how you can use your magic in different situations. This is knowledge gained from researching and studying literally thousands of tricks and illusions, and then presenting the best of these under many varying conditions. Here's how the need for so many different tricks came about.

In the past, great magicians traveled from city to city, showing the same magic to new audiences, year after year. That was wonderful for them. The more you perform any magic effect, the better you become at presenting it. Every time you do a trick for an audience of any size you learn something: what works … what doesn't work … what gets a laugh … what just lays there and dies. It is performing experience that teaches you how to better present that trick next time.

On the other hand, when you perform on a television series, you must present new material every week. We were constantly revising old or creating new magical effects week after week for the entertainment of repeat television audiences. I was always happy when we concluded a television show on which everything seemed to go well. But that nice feeling left quickly when I realized we had to do it all over again the following week, with all new material.

When we moved from our local television series to the CBS network for *The Magic Land of Allakazam,* we had a fine creative staff. It consisted of Bev Bergeron, known to millions as "Rebo the Clown," John Gaughan, Leo Behnke, Bob Towner, and Bob Fenton. Although the group enlarged and changed during the five-year run of the show, these fine magical talents remained for the entire series.

Our creative group, drawing from our background of magical knowledge, perusing books and working with new and existing props and illusions, was able to devise, develop, and construct a steady succession of baffling mysteries. Almost every one of the illusions featured Nani Darnell. (In magic terminology, an illusion is a large magic effect that utilizes someone in addition to the magician, like Floating a Lady in the Air.) Fortunately, Nani is a beautiful and versatile performer who was a professional entertainer and nationally recognized dancer before becoming my wife. With the constant creation and testing of new illusions and their performance, some only once for television, Nani Darnell Wilson set a new record for having been in and out of more different illusions than anyone in history.

Although I did not realize it at the time, we were ushering in a new era in the history of magic. Because *Allakazam* was the first network magic television series, we were bringing modernized versions of classic magic, and new effects as well, to people in their own homes every week. It was estimated that in one week, more viewers watched our show than the total number of people who saw Houdini during his entire lifetime.

It was after we completed the five-year run of *The Magic Land of Allakazam,* that our magic business really expanded. Our "Hall of Magic" at the New York World's Fair, was seen by more than two million people. The "Magic of the Telephone" for A.T.T. at the Hemisfair in San Antonio, Texas, debuted our patented Cinillusion process. We supplied major productions for corporate sales meetings and feature attractions for trade shows, fairs and exhibitions, along with continuing magical revues for some of America's leading amusement parks. We produced the first, full-color, magic television specials, *The Magic Circus,* and a series of five-minute/half-hour television shows, *The Magic of Mark Wilson*. I had offices in Los Angeles, New York and Chicago.

The point of all this is, I had learned that "magic" can be much more than just good entertainment. Although performance of magic was the end result of our efforts, it was *sales magic* that greatly helped in getting those contracts in the first place. Now I would like to show you how to put that kind of magic to work for you. Let me explain.

I think the best way to convey this knowledge is with some specific examples. **Magic for Children** covers the three ways you can present your magic for youngsters. **After Dinner Magic** is another special category and **Party Magic** explains what works for a number of different kinds of affairs. In **Sales Magic Secrets,** you'll see how magic can improve your sales meetings, group presentations, networking and trade shows. Magic can help you in all of these various situations. Here's a good example, **The Challenge Coin Vanish.**

THE CHALLENGE COIN VANISH

This is one of the easiest of tricks in this course. Yet, properly presented, it appears to be one of the most amazing and difficult feats of magic, comparable to those professional magicians practice for years to perfect. It illustrates three major principles in the performance of magic. One is *presentation.* "It's not what you do, but the way that you do it," as someone said long ago. The second is the clever *secret.* The third, an important component of many tricks, is *misdirection.*

EFFECT:

"I will now demonstrate one of the most baffling feats of prestidigitation ever attempted, I will perform it under the strictest test conditions. You all will be the judges. You will remember and tell your grandchildren about what you are about to witness. You will see it, but you won't believe it."

You continue, "This silver coin is a half a dollar." (This will work with any coin, a poker chip, a small ball, a crumpled up dollar bill … any small object.) You hand the coin to a spectator. "Would you please examine the coin."

"This is an ordinary pocket handkerchief." You display a handkerchief on both sides. "Please examine the handkerchief. You will find it is perfectly normal. There are no trapdoors, mirrors, ducks or elephants concealed inside."

"To eliminate any of the usual skullduggery, I am removing my coat and rolling up one sleeve of my shirt to isolate this hand from all outside contact." With your sleeve now rolled up, you hold out your left hand and show it on both sides. "You'll see why in just a moment."

"Have you thoroughly inspected the coin? Is it exactly what it appears to be, a regular coin, is that correct?" The man replies, "Yes, it is." "And you madam, do you find that to be a run of the mill pocket handkerchief?" The lady confirms that is exactly what it is.

"Now, I want you to watch this very closely. Would you please place the coin on my left hand." You extend your open hand, palm up. The spectator places the coin on your palm. (Image 1)

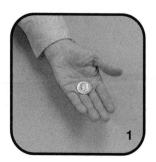

"You can all see the coin is truly there, on my hand. Now, would you, oh beautiful lady, drape the handkerchief over my hand and, thus, over the coin as well." The lady does this. (Image 2)

"It is important that you watch me closely. You all saw the coin on the palm of my hand, but I want your confirmation that it is still there."

"Would you, young lady, please feel and see that the coin is still in my hand. You could just feel the coin through the cloth of the handkerchief, but I want you to be absolutely sure it is still there by feeling under the handkerchief to confirm the coin's continued presence in my hand."

The lady reaches under the hank and states that the coin is still there. (Image 3)

You have two more spectators substantiate her statement by reaching under the cloth and feeling the coin.

You continue, "I have now proven, without a question of a doubt, the coin is resting on my hand. Watch even more closely than before, because ladies and gentlemen, I will now make that coin disappear!"

Your right hand has never been near your left hand since the coin was placed by a spectator on the palm of your left hand. You make a magical gesture or say some ancient "magic word." "And now, the coin is totally gone. It has disappeared into thin air. I can see, you may not believe me."

You go back to the lady who placed the handkerchief over your hand. "Would you please, slowly, remove the handkerchief!" She removes the handkerchief. Sure enough your hand is totally empty!

"As you see, the coin has completely vanished." You now show both your hands on both sides. "There is no possible explanation. The coin is gone. It must be magic."

"However, there are some rules those of us with great magical ability must obey. When we make something vanish, the cardinal discipline is we must bring that very same item back! You can see that if any object, no matter how small, were to be permanently eliminated from this dimension, it could cause the whole universe to go out of balance. We wizards know and live by this principle. Therefore, of necessity, I must make that very same coin reappear. Let's retrace our steps."

You extend your empty hand, palm up, toward the woman holding the handkerchief. "Would you check to see there is absolutely nothing hidden in the handkerchief, and nothing in my hand." She confirms your statement. "Now, please cover my hand, just as you did before," which she does.

"I know you may not believe what you have seen. You must confirm the emptiness of my hand, before I conclude this extraordinary demonstration." You approach those spectators who felt the coin in your hand before. "Please check under the handkerchief, as you did before. Is my hand completely empty?" All three confirm your hand is empty, there is nothing there.

"Now for the unbelievable ending. To you this has appeared to be a bizarre experiment. To me it is but a simple demonstration of the inherent magical powers within us all. Watch closely as I will now make that coin reappear."

You say the "magic word" again. (Perhaps this time you say it backwards. After all, this is to make the coin reappear.) Addressing any spectator you say, "Please remove the handkerchief." Sure enough, there, on the palm of your hand, is the coin!

"As you can see, the coin has now returned from the atmosphere to the hand of its master. As I told you when we started, you would see it but you would not believe it!"

You bow and say, "I thank you for all your attention." You can end by saying, "next show at five o'clock," or whatever, which will give a happy ending to your magical extravaganza.

SECRET:

As I told you, this is a very simple trick and quite easy to perform. What really happens is, unknown to the audience, one of the spectators acts as your secret accomplice. The last person who feels under the handkerchief and states that they feel the object in your hand is your collaborator. What they really do, when they reach under the handkerchief, is take the coin away in their hand. They keep the coin until it's time for you to make it "reappear." Your unknown protege is the last person to confirm your hand is "empty." What they actually do, when they reach under the handkerchief, is replace the coin on your palm.

Basically, that's it. That's the secret. As you see, it is quite simple and very easy to do. However, the success of the secret depends on your *presentation,* and a little *misdirection.*

THE PRESENTATION

It is the eloquence of your narration that first misleads the audience and elevates this effect to a small miracle. Your overly-elaborate phrasing intentionally leads viewers down the wrong track. Rolling back your sleeve adds to the mystery. Frankly, the true secret is so elemental, and the answer so compounded by your elaborate presentation, most people never arrive at the very simple solution.

Your presentation is in the same genre as those delivered by the wonderful wizard in *The Wizard of Oz.* As you may recall, Dorothy, the lion, tin man and scarecrow discovered that the wizard didn't have any real magical powers, but maintained his position as Exalted Ruler of Oz with his grandiose statements and (questionable) magical demonstrations. Actually, rulers, charlatans, mountebanks and magicians have been using these mythical presentations for centuries. And now it's your turn!

I have performed this effect many times. Let's suppose you are at a party. You can usually "set up" the person who will secretly help you, even when you don't know anyone at the party before you arrive. Of course, your accomplice can always be your host or the person who has invited you to the party. You can even explain everything on the phone beforehand, if you wish.

However, I have found it is usually better to recruit someone you haven't met before. If your "secret help" comes from someone you (apparently) don't even know, this becomes an even more sensational feat of magic. If you have the opportunity, explain your need to someone at the party discreetly. Everyone I have ever given this opportunity has accepted. Your new undercover associate doesn't even need any actual rehearsal. Just explain exactly what you want him or her to do.

THE MISDIRECTION

Here's where the misdirection comes in. As you perform this effect, be careful to always keep your right hand away from your left hand after it is covered by the handkerchief. This seemingly adds to the impossibility of the vanish and reappearance of the coin. Actually, it gives you the opportunity to perform the two important misdirections.

FIRST MISDIRECTION

When your unknown accomplice places her hand under the handkerchief to "feel" the coin in your left hand, you raise your right hand. You say, "As you have seen, my right hand has not even touched the hand covered by the handkerchief." As you say this, look at your right hand. As with all misdirection, *the audience will look where you look.*

That is when your confidential cohort secretly takes the coin out of your hand.

Your secret assistant does not need to "palm" the coin. Just hold the coin in their hand when they take their hand out from under the handkerchief. (Image 4)

This is a picture of your secret assistant's hand from underneath. (Image 5)

When your secret assistant says, "Yes, I feel the coin," it's the *third* confirmation that you are still holding the coin. Their action and their statement are almost redundant. Their removal of the coin will never be noticed.

SECOND MISDIRECTION

You use the same kind of misdirection for the reappearance of the coin. As your secret assistant is reaching under the handkerchief, secretly replacing the coin in your hand, raise your right hand in the air again. Flex your fingers several times and say, "Notice that my right hand is also empty. I do not wish for you to assume this is a mere sleight-of-hand trick." Be sure to look at your right hand when you say this. The misdirection is perfect. Now anyone can remove the handkerchief and all will see the coin has returned!

USING THE CHALLENGE COIN VANISH

There are many excellent opportunities to present this trick. Not only will you have a lot of fun doing it, even the selection of your secret collaborator can be beneficial.

For instance, let's say you are on a sales call. Your confederate can be the boss's secretary. You may have a unique opportunity to arrange everything with her as you wait in the outer office for your appointment. Depending upon the situation and the personalities of the people involved, this may work very well.

Or, better yet, your accomplice can be the boss himself. Assume you've made your business card appear by magic and perhaps done another magic effect or two during your meeting. The boss may ask if you would perform some of your magic for his office staff. Of course, you will be happy to fulfill his request. Ask him if he will be your clandestine confidant when you do the magic for his associates and quickly explain to him his part in **The Challenge Coin Vanish**. I have always found the executive is delighted to help. He will enjoy himself even more as he secretly participates in the mystery.

This can lead to another way this sneaky deception can improve your relationship with the company even more. After you (and the boss) perform the trick for his employees, you offer to teach the trick to everyone, so they can do that magic for their friends and family. You ask the boss if it is all right with him if you reveal the secret. He will always say "yes." When you think about it, what else is he going to say? He can't really say "no," his employees would not understand why he kept this unique opportunity from them.

When you explain that your "secret helper" was the boss, everyone will laugh. You will cement your relationship, not only with the executive who helped you, but with all of his employees as well. Many of them will do the trick for their family and friends. When they do, they will remember who taught it to them. You'll get a wonderful reception the next time you visit that company.

Please understand, one of the most important rules of magic is to never reveal any of the secrets. Maintaining the mystery of the magic is one of the most important principles of our art. You may well ask, why is it all right to teach **The Challenge Coin Vanish**? Good question.

It's because this effect is basically a "magic gag," It depends upon having an unknown accomplice who tells a fib about feeling the coin. When they say, "Yes, the coin is there," they are lying and secretly taking the coin out of your hand.

Throughout the ages, magicians have often used audience members as "stooges," "plants," "sticks," or whatever the current name is at that time, as confederates. Quite possibly, ancient priests used this type of bogus testimony to prove their god given powers to the masses. Charlatans and con men often employ unknown confederates.

Frankly, I don't like magic that depends upon someone telling a lie about some amazing effect I have just presented. If I show a playing card and say, "Is this the card you selected?" If that spectator lies and says "yes" to any card I display, that is not my kind of magic.

On the other hand, after performing **The Challenge Coin Vanish,** when you explain to the spectators exactly what happened, you can add, "The moral of what you have just seen is, *don't trust anybody.*" You will not only get a good laugh, but might actually be helping some in your audience analyze a future real life situation.

As an example, the principle of "not telling the truth," on which this trick is based, creates the kind of conflicting courtroom testimony judges must evaluate every day to reach just decisions. Law schools can use the trick to illustrate how witnesses can be misled in their "Eye Witness Testimony" classes. In mystery stories a key person not telling the truth is often used to explain what appeared to be an inexplicable event, such as the strange disappearance of the crown jewels from the sealed safe, or how the victim was murdered while alone in a "locked room."

If you are teaching magic to a class which consists of students of any age, be they in grade school, high school or college, or if they are Ph.D.'s, professors, or corporate executives, **The Challenge Coin Vanish** is an excellent way to start. You begin your teaching by explaining that presenting "magic" is quite different from that of any other form of entertainment. Then you vanish the coin and make it reappear under "challenge" conditions.

The class will be totally bamboozled (except for your secret assistant). Your explanation reveals that the students were baffled, not by your great magical skill, learned through years of practice, or by some complicated or expensive magic prop. The magic they witnessed was based entirely upon the "secret." If they had known that secret in advance, there would have been no magic. This is an excellent way to begin any magic instruction class, which visually illustrates the importance of the "secret" in magic.

MAGIC FOR CHILDREN

Let's say you want to perform your magic to make children happy. There are three ways you may channel your wonders. *Entertain* them with magic ... *Teach* them the magic ... *Learn* the magic together. The age of the children and your goals for them determines which of these avenues will work best for you.

1. *Entertain children with magic.* Magicians have always been primarily known as entertainers. With your wizardry you can fascinate one or two children or an assemblage of youngsters. The most basic trick for a single child or two is when an adult vanishes a coin and finds it behind a child's ear. Fathers, grandfathers and favorite uncles have been doing that for centuries. An easy method for accomplishing this is **The French Drop** (Page 186). There are other sleights which accomplish this same thing, such as **The Pinch and Drop Vanish** (Page 189) and **The Finger Palm Vanish** (Page 187). Some other tricks with coins for a single child or small group are **The Coin Through Leg** (Page 195), **Coin-A-Go-Go** (Page 197) and **Continuous Coins** (Page 200). Of course, almost any effect in this course can be performed to a single child. As with all of the other magic, it's up to you to decide what will work best for your small viewers.

If you are appearing for a larger group of children, say, at a birthday party, there are many tricks that will work beautifully. Every trick in this course can be entertaining, but some work particularly well for younger folks. There is: **Fatima the Dancer** (Page 270) in which you make a little dancing doll from an ordinary handkerchief. When you perform **The Sorcerer's Stamp Album** (page 352), you magically transfer postage stamps from a paper cone into a previously empty stamp album. Any of the versions of **Confetti to Candy** (Pages 367 through 371) are enjoyed by youngsters. All of these effects are, in a way, the fulfillment of children's dreams.

2. *Teach children magic.* Over the years, I have often been told something like this, "I know only one trick. My grandfather used to do it. I still remember how happy I was when he taught it to me. Now I do it for my kids."

When you have learned and practiced the magic this course, you might like to teach some magic to children. You can deliver your instruction to an individual child or to a classroom full of youngsters. What you teach is determined, primarily, by the age of the students.

The Cut and Restored String (Page 247) is an excellent effect, easily understood by students. Because the only prop is a piece of string (and some glue) it's easy for the children to take home and show their family what they learned today. Another good "teaching" trick is **Magically Multiply Your Money** (Page 181), a basic sleight-of-hand effect. The first magic trick I ever learned, which was taught to me by my great, great aunt when I was a small boy, was **The Broken and Restored Match** (Page 285). I'm still doing it and teaching it as well.

There is one effect I have found that can be easily taught to children of all ages of (and it works well for adults, too). It is **The Jumping Rubber Band** (Page 293). There are three follow up effects, **Reverse Jumping Rubber Bands** (Page 295), **Double Jumping Rubber Bands** (Page 297), and **The Challenge Jumping Rubber Band** (Page 298). These are all simple, easily-taught tricks, which only require a few rubber bands. Children are delighted to learn these effects and show them to their friends. Perhaps, a few generations from now, they will teach magic with rubber bands to their children.

Another method of "teaching" is for you to act as the child's co-star as you both perform the magic together for family and friends. Or the child can become the magician and you assume the roll of the magician's assistant. Your choice of either of these approaches depends upon the age, physical ability, and psychological orientation of the child. The major advantage here is when an adult and a child are presenting the magic together, whether the grown-up is the co-star or the magician's assistant, the adult can assure that everything is done correctly to make the magic work.

Let me give you an example. In the presentation of the hypnotized handkerchief (page 269), the handkerchief can be held by the child, who then does all of the "magic." If the child is not old enough, or for some other reason has a problem performing the trick, the handkerchief can be held by the adult as the co-star or as the assistant. The child, with appropriate gestures, hypnotizes the handkerchief. The handkerchief then magically "moves" (in the adult's hand) under the spell cast by the child, with the "handling" really done by the adult.

Another example, the props in **The Sorcerer's Stamp Album** (page 352) can be easily made and shared in the presentation between both the child and the adult as co-stars. Or, the child plays the part of the magician and the props are all handled entirely by the adult, acting as the assistant. Either way, you are assured everything will be presented correctly. When the spectators give their applause, it can give some sorely needed recognition to the young magician … something the child might need and will always remember.

3. *Learn magic together.* Often it is good to have a partner in any learning situation. If you are going on a diet, lifting weights or learning Latin, having a partner can help. When I first became interested in magic, after baffling my parents with a few simple tricks, I teamed up with my best friend, Malcolm Ogden to learn more magic. We studied together and practiced what we had learned on each other. We criticized the other guy's magic and had a lot of laughs while we were doing it. When we thought we were good enough to start doing shows, we appeared together as "Malcolm and Mark" (He got first billing because he was bigger than I!)

Learning magic together is an excellent way to create bonding between an adult and a child. This course works well for that. Both the child and the adult not only learn *how* to perform the tricks, they also learn the *secrets* together. They have pledged, to each other, not to reveal those secrets to anyone, which strengthens the bonding even more.

Let's say a child's home is divided by divorce. Father has custody one day a week, usually on weekends. He and the child have gone to all the amusement parks and seen most of the suitable movies. A better relationship might be developed if some of that valuable time was spent studying magic together. In addition to strengthening the bonding between them, what they learn together will be pleasantly remembered as the child matures.

Of course, any of the tricks in this course can be learned with another person. Some particularly good ones for that are **Threading the Needle** (Page 249), **One Hand Knot** (Page 251), **The Melting Knot** (Page 251) and **The Shoe Lace Rope Trick** (Page 252). For these effects you need only two pieces of rope, each about three feet long. The pictures in course show exactly how to do everything. The two pieces of rope allow both the parent and child to learn at the same time. Sometimes the adult will achieve success first. But, more often than not, it will be the child who figures everything out. When one "teaches" the other exactly how it works, it strengthens the bonding between them even more.

THE COWBOY ROPE TRICK

Of course, some tricks can be presented almost anywhere. **The Cowboy Rope Trick** can be performed for an individual child or a theater full of children. It can be adapted to fit any of the categories listed above. All you need is a piece of rope and a pair of scissors. It's incredibly easy to do. Its appeal is based on the story you deliver, which adds significantly to the magic.

EFFECT:

"Let me show you something very interesting with a piece of rope." You display a six-foot length of rope. "How many of you have seen a cowboy on television? Good." (In the following description, to each of the children's responses to your questions, you give an appropriate reply). "Now, cowboys always carry ropes, but the don't call them ropes. Do you remember what they do call them?" The children will respond. "That's right, (or whatever …) they call them lariats or lassos. Now a lariat or a lasso is a rope that has a loop in the end like this." You tie one end of the rope to the middle of the rope, forming a loop.

"The cowboys twirl the lasso or the lariat around like this and what do they catch with it?" Again the children respond with many different answers. Often they will say, "people" or "another cowboy." "Well, yes, sometimes, if they're not careful, they may catch another cowboy, but usually they catch cows. That's why we call them cowboys. If they caught rabbits, we would call them rabbitboys."

"The cow doesn't like getting caught by the cowboy and always tries to get away. That makes the rope tight around the cow's neck. The cow really doesn't like that. So, the cowboy takes a pair of scissors and cuts the cow loose, like this." You cut the rope in two where the loop is tied. You now have what appears to be two pieces of rope tied together in the middle. "That makes the cow happy because she's loose, but the cowboy is unhappy because his lasso is in two pieces."

"You know what the cowboys do? They bring the rope to me. I wrap the rope round my hand like this. Then I reach in my pocket and I get a pinch of magic dust. I always carry some magic dust for problems like this."

You reach into your pocket for the imaginary magic dust, which you show to the children between your pinched fingers. "Do you see the magic dust?" You will either hear "yes" or "no," or usually both. Either way you go on to explain, "That's right, because the magic dust is invisible. I just sprinkle it on the rope like this." You pretend to sprinkle the dust on the rope around your closed hand.

"Then I ask the cowboy to hold on to the end of the rope. Would you hold this for me please?" The youngster you have selected holds on to the end of the rope, which is still wrapped around your hand. This is a good opportunity to use the birthday child, or the person for whom the party is being held. As he or she hold on to the end of the rope, you let it unroll it from your hand. Everyone can see that the rope has been restored to one long piece!

"You see, it's the magic dust that makes the rope come out all in one piece. That means cowboys don't have to use as many ropes, which cuts down on the price of beef, and that's why you can have hamburgers for supper!"

SECRET:

The Cowboy Rope Trick is very easy to do. The rope should be about six feet long. (Image 1)

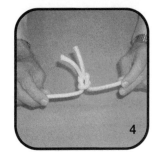

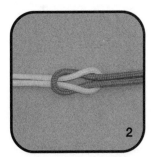

When you tell the story and make the loop, you tie one end of the rope to the middle of the rope. Just be sure to tie a square knot. In the picture, we have used two different colored ropes to make the square knot, so you can see exactly how it looks. (Image 2)

When you cut the rope, it appears you have cut the rope in the middle. You are really only cutting a short piece from the end of the rope. (Image 3) Be sure to cut in the correct place on the rope, beside the knot. If you cut the rope on the wrong side of the knot, you really will cut the rope in the middle. Tying a square knot makes it easier to cut the rope in the correct place.

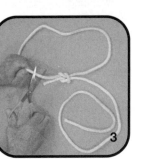

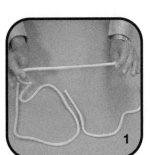

Display the "cut" rope to the audience (Image 4).

Then pull on the rope (Image 5) . . .

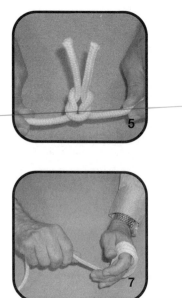

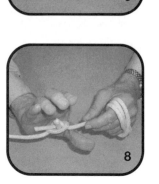

. . . which "upsets" the square knot and makes it into a slip knot (Image 6). Now you can easily slide the knot along the rope.

With your right hand, begin to wrap the rope around your left hand. (Image 7)

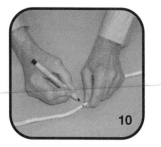

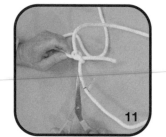

As you pull the rope through your right hand, secretly slide the knot along the rope. (Image 8) Keep the knot hidden in your right hand as you slide it along. (Image 8) (I have raised my fingers in the picture to show you the knot.)

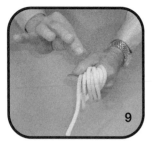

As you complete the winding, slide the knot off the end of the rope secretly in your right hand. Without pausing, reach your into your right pocket and say, "I need some magic dust." Leave the knot in your pocket and bring out the (imaginary) magic dust. Pretend to sprinkle it on the rope. (Image 9) Have someone hold the end of the rope as you uncoil it from your left hand. The children will see the knot has vanished and the rope is completely restored! The rope can then be tossed to the audience for examination.

Another way to be sure you cut the rope at the right place is also explained in **The Double Knot Restoration.** (page 245)

For this method, before the show, make a small mark about 5 inches from one end of the rope. (Image 10) That is the end that you tie to the middle of the rope to make the "loop."

After you tie the knot, cut the rope at the secret mark. (Image 11) This will assure you only cut off the short end piece.

In **The Double Rope Restoration** on page 247, pictures 13, 14, and 15 show wrapping the rope around your hand to secretly slide the knot off of the rope.

Here is an example of how magic can be added to a wide area of interest to children, teenagers and adults, utilizing all of the three methods outlined above. That is magic specifically selected for summer camps.

MAGIC FOR CAMPERS

Every year, there are thousands of summer camps attended by millions of children and teenagers. Investigating some of possibilities for the instruction of magic to campers, I conducted a number of teaching seminars for camp owners, executives and camp directors. I taught them magic tricks that I thought were suitable for campers and they gave me insight into how that magic could be of help to them for their particular needs and goals. Here are some of the conclusions the camping people reached and conveyed to me at the end of the seminars.

"Magic can be inexpensively incorporated into camping programs."

"It was easy to understand, so campers can learn easily and take magic skills home and show their friends."

"Learning magic can help increase a camper's social skills and self-confidence."

"Magic can help counselors 'bring out' a shy kid or a homesick scout."

"Magic can be used to gain the attention of staff members and/or campers to emphasis important points."

Most of the magic I taught in the seminars was easy-to-do and could be performed with inexpensive items such as rubber bands, paper clips, paper cups, rope, etc.—all items easily found by campers when they returned home. In this way, the campers can show their friends and family the magic they learned at camp, which helps create lasting memories of their camping experience. There are many such tricks in the course.

Some of the magic taught in the seminar required a bit more preparation or larger props. All of these tricks could be easily learned and then performed by the camp directors for their staff or by the staff members for campers. Each effect could be used to emphasize an important point such as fire safety, teamwork, rewards for effort, etc. Such effects as **The Comedy Cut and Restored Rope** (page 241), **The Comedy Cut and Restored Paper** (page 353) and **The Rope and Coat Release** (page 260) worked well for this. Another example is **The Magic Card Frame** (page 355) which does not have to be as small as shown in the picture, but can be made in any size from an appropriately-sized picture frame, which can then magically produce any graphic to highlight a specific goal. The opportunities to use magic to emphasize particular points are many.

Also included were some illusions which could be inexpensively made from cardboard boxes, corrugated board, bed sheets, etc. Then the camp could put on their own magic show. The show could be performed by the camp staff, or the councelors could teach the magic to campers so the youngsters would become the "magicians." The end result would be a magic show performed for other campers or for the camper's parents, who come on the last day to pick up their children.

Such illusions as **The Arabian Tent** (Page 437) and **The Haunted House** (Page 441) can be made inexpensively from corrugated board or foam core. A bit more elaborate is **The Mummy's Casket** (Page 449) which can be made quite inexpensively by the counselors or the campers. For **The Victory Cartons Illusion** (page 446) all that is needed are two large corrugated boxes which can be easily found. **The Mystery of the Magical Mummy** (page 449) requires only a large bedspread or sheet. The conclusion of that illusion is explained on page 451. The person the audience thought was wrapped inside the cloth turns out to be somebody else. Then, when that person comes running from behind the watching campers or makes some other miraculous appearance, it lends a terrific finale to the show.

Now here's a trick that will work well at any camp, and most any other place as well.

TIC TAC TOE PREDICTION

Here is an excellent effect that very few people have ever seen, and even fewer know how to perform. It can be presented in almost any conditions for any size audience.

EFFECT:

You offer to play a game of tic-tac-toe with a spectator. The spectator will have complete freedom of choice, making his or her mark in any of the squares. You state you have made a prediction of exactly how that game will be played, where each X and each O will be on the board. You hold up an envelope which contains your prediction and give it to someone in the audience to hold.

Then, you play a standard game of tic-tac-toe with any spectator. And yet, when your prediction is removed from the envelope, it proves to be entirely correct!

SECRET:

You can write up the prediction at home or somewhere out of sight of the spectators before you present the trick. Now, all you have to do is make sure the tic-tac-toe game you play with the spectator ends up looking just like your prediction … and it will! Here's what you do.

METHOD:

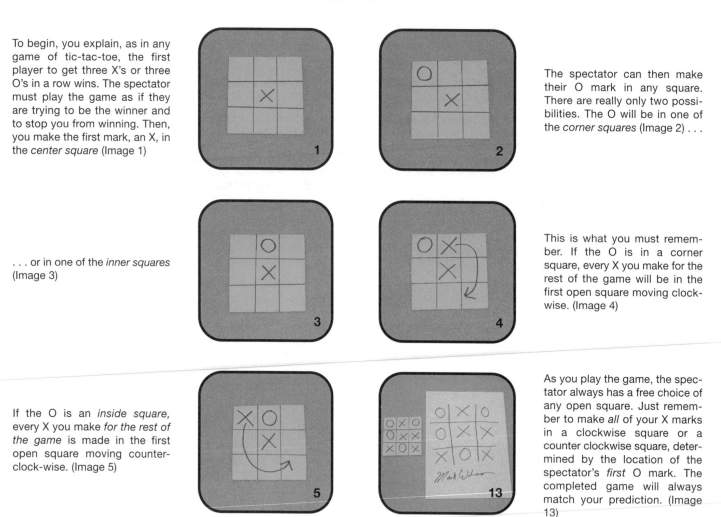

To begin, you explain, as in any game of tic-tac-toe, the first player to get three X's or three O's in a row wins. The spectator must play the game as if they are trying to be the winner and to stop you from winning. Then, you make the first mark, an X, in the center square (Image 1)

The spectator can then make their O mark in any square. There are really only two possibilities. The O will be in one of the corner squares (Image 2) . . .

. . . or in one of the inner squares (Image 3)

This is what you must remember. If the O is in a corner square, every X you make for the rest of the game will be in the first open square moving clockwise. (Image 4)

If the O is an inside square, every X you make for the rest of the game is made in the first open square moving counter-clock-wise. (Image 5)

As you play the game, the spectator always has a free choice of any open square. Just remember to make all of your X marks in a clockwise square or a counter clockwise square, determined by the location of the spectator's first O mark. The completed game will always match your prediction. (Image 13)

To practice, play both sides of the game and you will see it always comes out exactly the same. Here is the progression on a game in which the spectator's first mark is in the corner square. Then, all of the X's are made in a clockwise square. (Images 6 through 12)

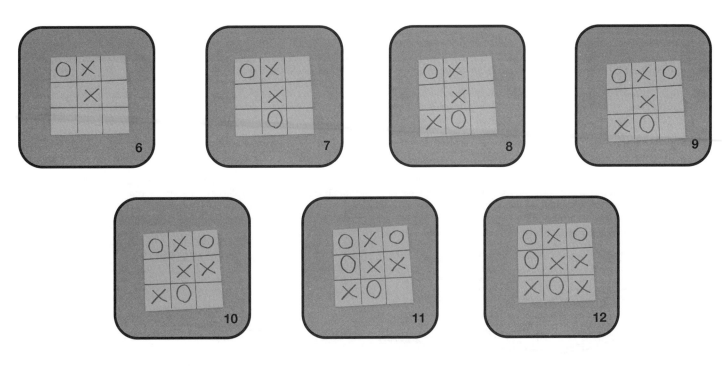

There is one more thing you can do to make your prediction even more impressive. You can sign your name on the bottom of the prediction. Still, the game you play with the spectator will match your prediction exactly, The reason is, there is no special "top" or "bottom" to a game of Tic Tac Toe. The game is "square", so any of the sides can be the top or the bottom. You must remember that, in your prediction, the three top squares are O/X/O. When you have finished playing with the spectator, before you reveal your prediction, turn the spectator's game so that O/X/O is the top. Then that game will match your prediction perfectly.

AFTER DINNER MAGIC

Performing a few baffling magic tricks as you sit at the dinner table is a natural. I've called this section **After Dinner Magic,** because that's the time your magic usually works best. When you are dining in a home, everyone, particularly mom if it's a family affair or your host if it's not, will be more interested in seeing that the food on the table is warm, rather than being distracted by your wizardry. After the meal, things are different. The dishes are cleared. You've had dessert (if you're lucky). Now is time for your magic.

In a restaurant, the timing can be different. There's a period between when the order is placed, until it is served. Sometimes this bit of time works well for magic. If the dining is preceded by a social get-together, that can be a good place to start. However, the safest time may be "after" dinner in a restaurant as well. Homes, restaurants, picnics, buffet-type affairs and banquets all have varying schedules, so it's up to you to select the most appropriate time, as well as the best possible magic for the occasion.

What you do is wide open, as well. There are several unique advantages in being seated at the dinner table when you fascinate the folks with your sorcery. For one thing, the table is right in front of you. You don't have to move the furniture or redo the landscape. That table is the perfect place for your "close-up" miracles. The viewers are seated there, so they can see everything very well. They are relaxing after a good meal. They are ready to be entertained.

Another advantage, there is a secret move many magicians use in their close-up performance called "lapping." Lapping is when you secretly drop some small object into you lap, or secretly pick-up something from your lap. You must be seated at a table to do any kind of lapping. Since that's exactly where you are, there is no suspicion, so performance of this particular ploy works wonderfully at the dinner table.

As an example, **The Glass Through Table** (page 314) is a true classic of magic. It's in the **Impromptu Magic** section of the course, because everything you need, the glass, a couple of paper napkins and any coin are all readily available. Images 11 and 12 in **The Glass Through Table** description show the lapping of the glass. In images 17 and 18, you see how you secretly pick up the glass from your lap to show everyone it has (apparently) penetrated the table.

There are many other tricks in the course that can be done with items usually found on or near the table. **The Turned Up Glasses** (page 341) uses only three regular drinking glasses and **The Knot in Handkerchief** (page 344) can be done with a cloth napkin. These are two of the many "Betcha" possibilities. **Roll the Bills** (page 222) is another excellent choice. Then there's **Dots Magic** (page 311) and **Dots Magic Impromptu Version** (page 314) where all of your magic is done with a dinner table knife and a few small pieces of paper.

If you just happen to have a deck of cards in your pocket or purse, some of your excellent card tricks can occupy the entire evening. Another good selection are tricks with **Sponge Balls**. In **Sponge Ball Magic** (page 391) you learn many powerful effects. Each of those tricks can stand alone or be presented as part of a routine. Then your magic can be made to fit the time available.

The Cords of Fantasia (page 303) works beautifully at the dinner table. You can usually borrow the necessary finger rings and have the guest on each side of you hold the cords, as you perform the magic. It's great entertainment based on a century-old principle of magic.

The Flying Match (page 309) should be performed only by adults because it involves the use of matches. It is one of the best after dinner magic effects. If you are in a restaurant, they will almost always have personalized match books. Do the "secret preparation" before dinner or excuse yourself from the table for a moment to set it up. The table is a perfect place for the effect, which uses lapping to make the match vanish. When that burnt match reappears, attached to the matchbook with all of the other unburnt matches, you will have made a powerful impression with your magical powers.

The following is ideal for performing after dinner.

THE RING ON THE ROPE

Now you will learn one of the most baffling close-up magic tricks I have ever had the privilege of performing. I learned it first when I was thirteen years old and worked as the "magic demonstrator" in Douglas Magicland, the magic shop in my home town, Dallas, Texas. I have been puzzling audiences with this trick ever since. I'm sure you'll find it a valuable magical asset.

One of the great advantages of the Ring on Rope is you do it with four ordinary articles that you can find anywhere. They are a piece of rope about 2 feet long (you can use a shoe lace or a ribbon), a large safety pin, a handkerchief or cloth napkin, and a ring about the size of a finger ring, to as large as a curtain ring or harness ring. Everything can be examined before and after the trick, because they are exactly what they appear to be, just four ordinary objects.

EFFECT:

You tell the viewers that they are going to see a visual impossibility, so they should watch very closely. You show the four items and suggest the spectators examine everything. Ask if you may borrow someone's finger ring (A man's wedding ring works very well for this, but it will work with any ring).

You place all of the items on the table in front of you. (Image 1)

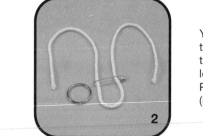

You put the safety pin (It's good to use a large safety pin for this) through the rope twice, making a loop as shown in the picture. Place the ring beside the loop. (Image 2)

Call to the spectator's attention, the ring is not on the rope. Also, emphasize that the ends of the rope will always be visible as you perform this seeming miracle.

Show the handkerchief on both sides and place it over the rope and the ring As you do this, it is most important that the spectator always sees both ends of the rope at all times.

The handkerchief now covers the rope and the ring. The ends of the rope are not covered by the handkerchief. You reach under the handkerchief with both hands. (Image 3) The viewers can see your hands are moving under the handkerchief. You explain you are now doing the "magic. "

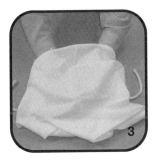

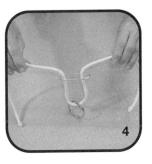

After thirty seconds or so, you say, "I have completed the magic." Ask the spectator, "Have the ends of the rope have been completely visible at all times?" The answer is, "Yes." "And yet, the ring is now on the rope." You pull the rope out from under the handkerchief. Sure enough, the impossible has happened, the ring is on the rope. (Image 4)

SECRET:

Before I explain the secret, let me assure you, at the conclusion of the trick, the ring is really on the rope. These are all ordinary objects, there are no "duplicates." All these items can be borrowed, if you wish. There are no suspicious moves. The secret is so subtle and so rational, "the Ring on the Rope" is really is one of the masterpieces of the art of magic.

METHOD:

Here is the closely guarded secret to this unbelievable trick. Everything the spectators see is exactly as described in the Effect. When you place both of your hands beneath the handkerchief, here's what you do.

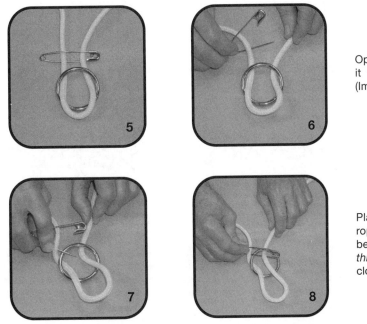

First, slip the ring over the top of the loop of rope. (Image 5)

Open the safety pin and remove it from one side of the rope. (Image 6)

Slide the ring a short distance down the rope, past the place on the rope where you removed the pin. (Image 7)

Place the pin back through the rope in the same place it was before. *Do not put the pin through the ring.* Fasten the pin closed. (Image 8)

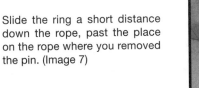

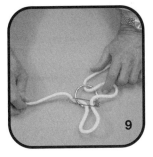

Both of your hands are still under the handkerchief. Pull a bit of the rope through the ring and insert the first finger of your left hand just above the place where you refastened the pin as shown in the picture. (Image 9) As you see, your finger is between the pin and the ring and the rope runs around it. *Study the picture so you will put your finger in the correct place.* Press the tip of that left finger down on the table. You should learn to do this by "feeling" what you are doing, so you do not need to look under the handkerchief.

You now state, "Although the ends of the rope have been visible at all times, impossible as it seems, the ring is now on the rope." (Actually, the ring is not on the rope, but *you want the spectators to believe you have already performed the "magic."*)

To show everyone that the ring is on the rope, you pull the rope out from under the handkerchief. To do this, remove your right hand from under the handkerchief, pick up the end of the rope on the right side and pull the rope out from under the handkerchief.

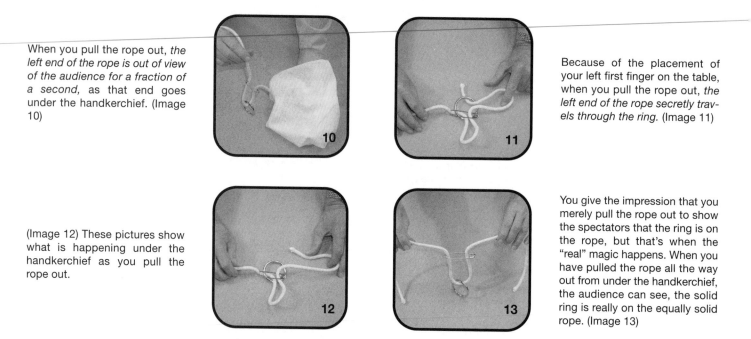

When you pull the rope out, *the left end of the rope is out of view of the audience for a fraction of a second,* as that end goes under the handkerchief. (Image 10)

Because of the placement of your left first finger on the table, when you pull the rope out, *the left end of the rope secretly travels through the ring.* (Image 11)

(Image 12) These pictures show what is happening under the handkerchief as you pull the rope out.

You give the impression that you merely pull the rope out to show the spectators that the ring is on the rope, but that's when the "real" magic happens. When you have pulled the rope all the way out from under the handkerchief, the audience can see, the solid ring is really on the equally solid rope. (Image 13)

Before you perform "the Ring on the Rope" for anyone, I would sincerely appreciate your learning and practicing this trick thoroughly. That way we will all protect the secret to this astonishing effect.

PARTY MAGIC

Parties can be ideal for your magic. There are many different types of parties and just as many different kinds of magic. The magic you do at any get-together is determined by three criteria. One is the age of your audience… young, old, all around the same age, or spanning many generations. The second is the type of occasion… birthday party, bar mitzvah, retirement celebration, church affair, or grand extravaganza. The third is the performing conditions… intimate gathering, walk around, stage setting, indoor or outdoor. Whatever these criteria are, they establish what magic will work best for you at that particular party.

Let's assume you are attending a gathering that would really appreciate a good card trick. You've got lots of them. There are many excellent effects in the chapter in this course.

The Fantastic Five (page 32) is a good start for your initial card routine. This can be followed by **Turn Over Card** (page 34) during which you have apparently made a mistake, but are saved by the magic. **You Do As I Do** (page 44) was one of the first card tricks I ever learned. It takes two decks of cards. If you wish, both decks can be borrowed from the host at the party. In any event, the effect is outstanding. There are many other terrific self-working card tricks.

Here is a self-working card trick with an exceptionally powerful effect and many endings, one after another. The final climax provides a super conclusion. Properly presented, this effect, alone, can make you the hit of the party.

FURTHER THAN THAT

This is an excellent trick you can do with any deck of cards. It has not just one, but a whole series of magical endings. You'll see why it really deserves the name "Further Than That."

EFFECT:

Holding a deck of cards, you say, "Perhaps the oldest card tricks is one in which the magician has you freely select any card from the deck, and then tells you what card you selected. But the trick I'll show you now *goes further than that*."

While saying this you spread the cards from hand to hand, as if you were going to have one selected by the spectator. (Image 1) But don't have one chosen, just keep the deck in your hands.

"Please name a small number." Pause for just a brief moment as if you are making up your mind. "Why don't you select a number between 10 and 20. What is the number? I'll count that number of cards from the deck." Let's assume the spectator says "Fifteen." You count off 15 cards, one at a time, from the top of the deck, placing them in a stack on the table. (Image 2)

Say each card's number as you count them, "1,2,3, etc." Set the deck down and point to the top card of the stack. "This could be the card you selected, but *this trick goes further than that*." "To make this a truly random selection, we'll add together the two digits that make up the number 15. That would be a one and a five. When you add those numbers together it totals 6."

Pick up the packet of 15 cards and count off six cards, one at a time, to the table. Say the number of each card as you deal them, "1, 2, 3, 4, 5, 6." (Image 3)

Keep the balance of the packet in your left hand. Show the top card of the six cards on the table and say, "This is the card you selected. I will not look at the card. Remember it … it is very important that you remember it." (Image 4)

Show the "selected" card, the Ace of Spades, to the spectator. You know it is the ace of spades, but hold the card so you cannot see its face. Replace the selected card on top of the stack on the table.

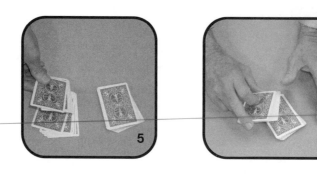

Place the cards in your hand on top of the stack of cards on the table. (Image 5)

Pick up the stack of cards from the table and place it on top of the deck. (Image 6)

"If I were to tell you now which card you freely selected, that would be a good trick. But *this trick goes further than that*." "Your card is somewhere in the deck. I don't know what card you selected. But let me show you something I have learned as I studied magic." Hold the deck beside your ear and riffle the corner of the deck with your thumb. "I'll let the deck tell me the name of your card."

Now hold the deck in front of you and speak to the deck, "Yes deck, I hear you." To the spectator, you say, "The deck tells me you selected the Ace of Spades, is that right?" When the spectator says, "Yes," you say, "Now that would be an excellent conclusion to this trick. But *this trick goes further than that*."

"I will now find your card by magic. I'll just spell the name of your card. It was an ace … A … C … E …"

From the top of the deck, count off one card for each letter. When you say, "A," you count one card to the table in a pile slightly to your right. Say "C" and place the second card on top of the "A" card. The "E" card goes on top of the other two. (Image 7)

"And the suit was spades. I'll spell spades." From the top of the deck, count one card for each letter, into a pile slightly to the left, "S … P … A … D … E … S …" (Image 8)

"Having spelled its name, we find your selected card is right here on top of the deck!" Turn over the top card, it is the Ace of Spades. (Image 9) Place the ace on the table between the two stacks of cards "And that would be a great ending. Except *this trick goes further than that*."

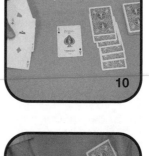

"Look, these cards are the other three aces." Turn the three ace cards in the right side stack face up. (Image 10) "Locating all four aces would be a wonderful ending! *But this trick goes further than that*."

"The suit of your card was spades. And look, these cards are, all spades!" Turn over the stack of cards on your left to show they are all spades. (Image 11) "That would be a really tremendous ending, *but this trick goes further than that*."

"If I deal the next four cards from the deck and combine them with the Ace of Spades, like this …" From the top of the deck, deal the next four cards face down in front of the Ace of Spades on the table. (Image 12)

"Then we would have," turn the cards face up, (Image 13) "a royal flush, which always wins, *and you can't go any further than that!*"

SECRET:

As you see, with **Further Than That,** you apparently reach the end of the trick several times. Each false conclusion builds to a really grand climax. You might think, because of its powerful effect on the audience, this trick may be very difficult to do, requiring a great deal of practice. Actually, this is one of the very best self-working card tricks. Just follow the directions and it performs itself! This effect was originally devised by the creator of many clever and ingenious tricks, Stewart James.

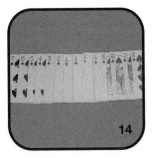

Unknown to the audience, before you perform the trick, you arrange (stack) the top cards of the deck like this:

Top card 7S, 6S, 5S, 4S, 3S, 2S, AH, AC, AD, AS, KS, QS, JS, 10S. Bottom card (Image 14)

Your audience must not be aware that the deck is "stacked." If you wish, you can just take the stacked deck out of the card case, as you begin the presentation.

The only magic in the routine is that the Ace of Spades is "forced" on the spectator, which is automatic in the routine. It uses The 10-20 Count Force, which is fully explained on page 78. The spectator is free to name any number between 10 and 20. You count that many cards from the deck, one at a time, to the table. Then you total the two digits of the selected number and count that number of cards from those you just counted to the table. This will automatically force the tenth card, the Ace of Spades.

To learn this trick, all you need to do is stack the deck as shown and follow the directions. Everything happens automatically. This trick has a terrific built-in presentation, which always gets laughs and has a powerful ending. It will be a real "reputation maker" for you.

After you learn a few card sleights, the number of possibilities is increased even more. An easily learned sleight is **The Hindu Shuffle.** (page 46). You can control a selected card with **The Hindu Key Card Location** (page 49) or a group of cards using **The Hindu Shuffle—Bottom Stock Control** (page 56). You can "force" a card with **The Hindu Flash Force** (page 52), and magically make a red-backed deck change into a blue backed deck employing **The Hindu Color Change** (page 53). You can even make two different colored decks change places by learning **The Color Changing Decks—Two Deck Version** (page 55). All of these, and a lot more, can be performed using only this one sleight.

Of course, it's not just card tricks, there are many other magic effects in the course that work beautifully at parties. An excellent choice is **The Sucker Torn and Restored Napkin** (page 305), which you can perform with whatever paper napkins are available at the affair. **The Three Way Test** (page 318) is a great baffler which can be done with just pieces of paper, predicting three items to be selected by the party goers. One of the strongest effects at any party can be **The Cut and Restored Neck Tie** (page 362). Although it does take a bit of preparation and some cooperation from your "victim," the effect is really hilarious and has a great pay off.

EFFECT:

This baffling prediction can be terrific at parties. You write a prediction on a piece of paper, fold the paper and hand it to a spectator to hold. Then five different numbers between 1 and 25 are selected, at random, by members of the audience. These numbers are added together to reach an even more random total. Your prediction, which has been in the spectator's position since long before any of the numbers were chosen, is revealed to the audience. They are amazed to see that your prediction is entirely correct!

PRESENTATION:

For selection of the numbers, you use the Random Number Selector chart, which is a display of the numbers 1 through 25 arranged in 5 horizontal rows with 5 numbers in each row. (Image 1) The chart can be printed on a postcard-sized card, on a large display board, or displayed in any size in between, just so it is large enough to be seen by the people in your audience.

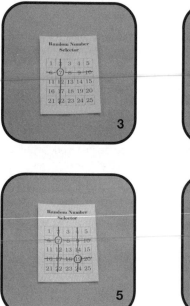

Ask a spectator to call out any number from 1 to 25. You circle that number on the Random Number Selector chart. (Image 2)

Then you cross out all of the numbers in the row, (going across the chart) and all of the numbers in the column (going up and down the chart) of the selected number. (Image 3)

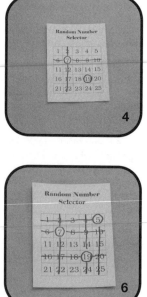

You ask another spectator to select any other number that has not been marked off of the chart. You circle the selected number (Image 4) . . .

. . . and mark off all the other numbers in the row and column of that number. (Image 5)

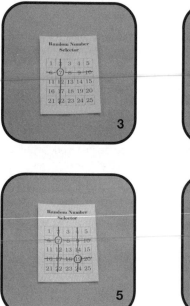

You ask a third audience member to select any number that has not been eliminated. You circle that number and mark off its appropriate row and column. (Image 6)

You do the same with a fourth spectator, marking off the selected numbers in the row and column. (Image 7)

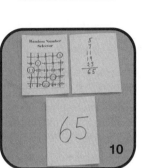

The last number, which would be the fifth choice, is actually the only remaining open number on the chart. You circle that number. (Image 8)

You now make a list of the five numbers that have been "selected." Then you add those numbers together for a total. (Image 9)

Sure enough, that total is exactly what you have written as your prediction! (Image 10)

SECRET:

This effect is based on a little known mathematical principle. The working of the trick is totally automatic. Each spectator has a free choice of any number from 1 to 25. Then any other number that has not been crossed out can be selected by a spectator. As the numbers are chosen, you eliminate all of the other numbers in the row and the column of each selected number. Interestingly, when those five "selected" numbers are added together, the total will always be 65.

If you are performing this for only one person, she or he can make all of the number selections. Or, this magical mystery can be performed in a giant auditorium, an arena or a coliseum. For a larger group, I recommend you have different audience members select each number, which strengthens the effect. Just be sure the display chart of the 25 numbers is visible to everyone.

If the numbers are on a small card or drawing pad, you can hand the Random Number Selector chart to the audience for marking. If the spectators follow your directions as they select the five numbers, and mark out the rows and columns correctly, you don't even need to know what numbers they have selected. The total will always total 65. This makes a very strong presentation.

The main problem I have found in handing the chart to the spectators for marking is that the audience members must be correct in crossing out both the rows and the columns of the numbers they select. If someone doesn't get that part right, it throws the whole effect out of whack, and your prediction will be wrong. So, I feel it is better if you do the marking. The choice of all the numbers is done by the audience. You do the marking, so the rows and columns are marked off correctly.

You can make Random Number Selector charts on a copy machine. Or, you can scan the chart into your computer and print out copies. For business or promotional purposes, let's say you are using a bingo-sized card for the chart. Then you can have your name printed on the top or bottom of the card. You can put more information, your address, or any other promotional material you wish on the back of the card. You can leave the card with your host, the birthday party celebrant, the person who booked the show, etc.

You can do the trick even if you don't have any cards printed. On a sheet of paper, draw the lines and put in the numbers. It will take you a few minutes, but this is an excellent trick.

Actually, every trick in this course can be adapted and performed at various get-togethers. It's up to you to choose what will work best for you. The magic you present at parties will not only add to your social life, as your ability to present the magic increases, these affairs can also be consistent income producers for you, if you wish.

SALES MAGIC SECRETS

Everybody sells something and everybody wants to sell more of it. You may sell a product or a service. If you are not directly involved in sales, you are selling your wonderful personality or the excellent work you do for the company. The response you get from the other kids, your team-mates, your family, your fellow workers in the production line, or your peers at the university … whoever it is that you work with and for … is important to your life. In other words, no matter what kind of work you do, whether it's white collar at the office, blue collar at the factory or no collar at all at the swimming pool, there are people you want to please. You want those people to appreciate what you do. They should recognize you as an individual, not just part of the operation.

Magic can help you do that. You see, now you are on your way to being a "special" person. Those "amazing" things you do will gain you that recognition, which can be a unique advantage over your competition, whatever that competition is.

Of course, you must decide what magic is best to help you achieve your goals in the conditions in which you find yourself. As an example, let's say you are a salesman and you need to get in to see the purchasing agent at a major corporation, someone you have never met before. You are in the waiting room with several other people who would like to do that very same thing.

Just suppose, between those incoming phone calls the receptionist is taking, you show her a simple trick, like **The Linking Paper Clips** (Page 298). The effect requires only one dollar bill and two paper clips. You can supply the dollar bill. She will have the paper clips. When you snap those paper clips off of the dollar bill and they are "magically" linked together, she is intrigued! You do it again, and this time you add a rubber band to the bill. When the clips are magically linked, they are also attached to the rubber band! See Page 300.

Now here's where your magic can really help: You volunteer to teach her exactly how to magically link those paper clips, so she can show it to her family when she gets home tonight. She's happy because you brought a little joy to her day. You've just gained a definite advantage over all those other people waiting to get in.

This is a large company you are calling on and making this sale is important. Many are still waiting, but you're on your way down the hall to meet that purchasing agent. While you're walking to his office, he gets a call from an even higher executive of the company. They'll talk while you wait with his secretary, outside his office. The secretary thought he was going to be meeting with you and has nothing particular to do at the moment. You have another opportunity.

You could tell her a joke, but you're not sure she would laugh at it. You could sing her a song. (With my voice, that would be a really dumb idea. She might call security and then I'd never get in to see anybody in that company again.) Or you could do a simple magic trick, something like **Sponge Ball Magic** (Page 391).

That trick is actually a series of effects made into a routine. You can stop the magic at any time, when her boss is ready to see you. If you do those tricks well, there's a very good chance, when she ushers you into see him, she will make a favorable comment about what she has just seen. You begin your relationship with this gentleman on a very pleasant note … and that's good.

So you've finally gotten in to see the purchasing agent. Now it's time to present your products, your competitive advantages, and the excellence of the company you represent. If appropriate, there are many points you can illustrate or emphasize "by magic." For a starter, you can magically imprint your business card for him.

At the end of this section I'll teach you how to "magically" print your business card. It's easy to do, you can present it in less than one minute, it immediately establishes your "magical powers" and adds to the possibility that the potential customer will keep your business card, not throw it away.

When the person with whom you are meeting sees your magic, quite often they will call some of their associates into their office, or take you where there are a number of company employees, and ask you to do your magic for them.

An excellent series of magic effects I have used in this kind of situation are **The Dissolving Knot** (page 272), next **The Knot Through Arm** (Page 273), followed by **The Coin Through Handkerchief** (page 178), concluding with **The Hypnotized Handkerchief** (Page 269). These can be combined into one fast moving routine. I do the magic with my pocket handkerchief and a half dollar, both of which I always have with me. I have performed these tricks in business meetings around the world.

YOUR MAGIC WILL OPEN MANY DOORS

Many times, when I'm seeing a doctor or a dentist, and I present a bit of magic, they will call in their nurses and technicians. An auto shop foreman will assemble his mechanics. In my initial meeting with Frito Lay, I had to come back very early the next morning to perform a few tricks at the Morning Meeting. At a giant silk mill in China, I was asked to perform on the dusty factory floor for the production workers. At the conclusion of the International Air Show in Paris, Martin-Marretta Company held a reception in the large mezzanine ballroom of the Eiffel Tower. I was asked to perform some of my magic for the many different small groups of guests, all speaking many different languages, gathered for the huge affair. Remember, the more people you entertain with your magic, the better impression you will make on the client and the more they will like you and the product or services you are selling.

SPEECHES AND PRESENTATIONS

Here's another effective way to apply magic. Let's say you are the new Chief Executive Officer of the company, making an important speech to the company employees concerning the exciting future their company now has with the new operational procedures you have installed. You've been preparing this presentation for weeks. It's important that it be a success, not just for the bright future you are predicting, but, perhaps even more importantly, so your associates will see you as a person, not just the new boss.

Near the beginning of your presentation you display three short pieces of rope. You explain that each rope represents one of the three major divisions of the company: Sales, Production, and Management. You show that the three ropes are exactly the same length. Each rope is two feet long.

You explain how each of the three divisions must work closely with the other two for any company to achieve maximum success. "In the best of all worlds, Sales must not outstrip Production. Production must keep up with Sales. The positive interaction between Sales and Production must be optimized by Management."

You expound on the important role of each division of their company. Nearing the conclusion of your presentation, you say, "Under our reorganization, these three divisions are combined, integrated, and coordinated as never before, into one dynamic, seamless organization."

To demonstrate how effective these changes will be, you, amazingly, turn those three short pieces of rope into one strong, six-foot long rope. This graphically illustrates the importance of what you have brought to the company. You've smoothed out the rough spots and added continuity and strength to the organization. You've also shown your own personality to the employees in a very positive way. (**Triple Rope Trick**, Page 242)

You can do the triple rope trick with two ropes or four ropes, if that better illustrates your theme. It is quite easy to do and the ending is powerful. You can perform it for one person or for a large audience. When the three short ropes become one long rope, if you're doing it for an individual, you can leave the rope as a souvenir. In a corporate meeting, you can hand the rope to the next speaker on the bill, or toss it out to the audience. It is a powerful effect.

IF YOUR CUSTOMERS COME TO YOUR BUSINESS

Let's say you are not the new CEO. Perhaps you are a barber, work in a restaurant or own a shoe store. Your customers come to you. That's where magic can give you a definite competitive advantage over that other company down the street, your competition.

Many previous customers that you've done a bit of magic for will come back to your business because they would like to see another trick. "Let's go get our ice cream sundae from that guy who has the shop on the corner. I'm gonna ask him if he can make those three short ropes into one long rope, like he did last time. Remember, he gave me the long rope. When I got home, I cut it up but it didn't go back together. Or maybe he'll show us a new trick. Come on, let's go." This is an example of how that same bit of magic that worked well to illustrate a speech can be adapted to other situations. Every trick in this course can do that. Just use your imagination.

Perhaps you'd like to be the most popular baby sitter in town. "We need a babysitter for Saturday night. Let's ask Julie. Last time she taught Sally and Johnny how to make rubber bands jump around on their fingers. They've done it now for all their friends and for Grandma and Grandpa when they came over to visit last week. Let's get her again. Maybe she will teach the kids another trick." **The Jumping Rubber Band**, page 295, can easily be taught to someone else and particularly fits the need in this instance.

The following could be a recorded message on a phone answering machine. "Hi Ed, it's Joe. I'm calling you from the car. I'm on my way from my office to meet you for dinner. Let's meet at the ABC Bar & Grill, you know where it is. I was there last week and that guy Frank, the bartender, did the darndest card trick. He and I each selected the very same card from two different deck of cards. I want you to see it. I'll meet you there at eight." When Ed meets Joe, Frank will perform **You Do As I Do** (Page 44). It's really a great trick and it's what is bringing Joe and Ed in tonight.

TRADE SHOWS AND NETWORKING

Magic can be used to great advantage in trade shows and networking events, helping you to attract more potential customers and to deliver your sales message more effectively.

Let's say you're standing in your company's booth at a trade show. Several conventioneers are looking at your product. You introduce yourself and shake hands. Then, unmistakably showing both of your hands empty, you reach into the air and produce a number of dollar bills. You explain that, "If you use our company's product, which is on display right here in our booth, you will get the same results."

You have just performed, **Bills From Nowhere** (Page 223). You loaded the rolled up bills in the fold of your left arm when you saw those customers coming. You're free to shake hands, show both of your hands empty and produce those bills from the air. You don't ordinarily see someone pulling money out of thin air at a trade show, or anywhere else for that matter. Those folks will remember you and your product … and that's why you are there.

There are many tricks in the course you can use for trade events and networking. Any of the cut and restored rope effects, beginning on page 237, can be used to illustrate many sales points, marketing plans or corporate promotions. If you have a little more time available, **Roll the Bills** (Page 222) is an excellent "betcha." You then explain it to the visitors, who will roll the bills for their friends. When they do this, they'll remember they learned that "betcha" from you.

MAGIC BUSINESS CARD PRINTING

EFFECT:

Whether you go to your customers, or they come to you, they will all remember you and your business. You know why they remember you? Because they've all kept your business card. You printed the card, by magic, right in their own hand. They're still talking about it. Your magic is working for you.

"Let me give you my business card." You remove three blank business cards from your pocket or business card case. "Oh, that's right, the printer forgot to print the cards. Let me just double check."

"Let's see. One, Two, Three cards." You count the cards, one at a time, and (apparently) show the three cards are all blank on both sides.

"They're blank all right. I have an idea. Would you hold out your hand for me please." You place one of the cards on the spectator's outstretched palm. "Please place your other hand on top, like this." "Now, turn both of your hands over." You indicate what you want. "I'll add a little magic." You make a magical gesture, or say a magic word. "Let's see what happened. Please take your top hand away." The spectator is greatly surprised to discover the formerly blank card is now your printed business card! As the spectator looks with amazement at your business card, you say, "It's a good thing I know some magic!"

SECRET:

To do this trick, all you need is one of your regular business cards and two blank business cards to match. There are several ways to obtain blank business cards.

You can ask the company that printed your business cards to send you some blank cards or include some blank cards with your next order of business cards.

You can create blank cards from your existing business cards. All you do is glue two of your business cards together, face to face. When you glue together the printed sides of two of your business cards, they appear to be one blank card. You can use any kind of glue, rubber cement, paste, etc. Make two of the "blank" cards, add one of your regular business cards and that's all you need.

An excellent way to make your own business cards is to use blank business card stock and print them on your computer printer. You can buy blank business card stock at any office supply store. Use an unprinted sheet for the blank cards. Usually, each sheet carries ten cards. From one printed sheet and two unprinted sheets, you can make ten sets of the three cards.

A few requirements for the cards ...

The paper stock on which the cards are printed must be thick enough so, when you look at the printed card from the back, you cannot see through the card and tell that it is printed on the other side.

The blank cards must look the same on both sides. Some business cards are glossy on one side and dull on the other. Or, the color or the finish of the stock may vary from one side to the other. Because of the way you show the three cards "blank" on both sides, the sides must all appear to be the same.

The design (printing) on your card should not extend to the edge of the card. That's because the requirement for your business cards for this trick is the same as for playing cards. As stated in Card Definitions under "White Bordered Back Cards" on page 19. "A white bordered back is essential in the performance of many of the tricks described in this course. This is because, when a card is reversed (turned face-up in a face-down pack), it will not be noticeable because the white edges of the face are the same as the white border of the pattern back." The same is true of the business cards used for Magic Business Cards printing.

METHOD:

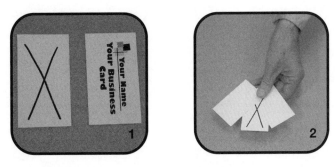

For these instructions, we have put an "X" on the blank side of the printed card. (Image 1)

Before you present the effect, place your printed business card face down, between the blank cards. (Image 2)

I often carry my business cards in a leather or plastic business card case. That is not needed for the trick, but it is a convenient way of carrying your cards. Or, the cards can just be in your pocket.

When you remove the three cards from your business card case or pocket, they are stacked one on top of the other. (Image 3)

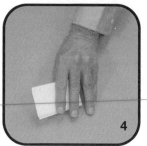

You can show the stack on both sides, because the printed card is concealed between the two blank cards. (Image 4)

You talk about the printer having delivered blank cards, as you show the stack on both sides.

Here's how you display, individually, that the three cards are all blank. "Let me double check." Hold the stack of three cards in your left hand, with the printed card face down between the other two. Say, "One" and push off the top card of the stack of three with your left thumb and take it with your right thumb on top and fingers underneath. (Image 5)

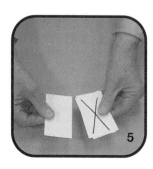

Show the card in your right hand on both sides by turning your hand over. (Image 6)

Turn your hand back as it was before. You have shown the card blank on both sides.

Now comes the only "move" in the routine. Count "Two," and place the top card of the two in your left hand, (that's the card with the printing on it), on top of the card in your right hand. (Image 7) The printing is now face down on the top card of the two in your right hand.

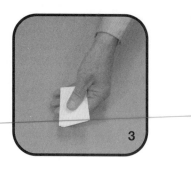

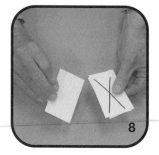

Then turn your right hand over, as you did before, showing the blank back of the business cards you hold in that hand. (Image 8) *To the spectators it appears you have shown both of the cards blank on both sides. What you're actually showing is the back of the first card you put in your right hand, again.* You have now, apparently, shown the two cards in your right hand are blank.

Say, "Three," but *do not* place the card in your left hand into your right hand. When you say, "Three," *turn your left hand over* to show the other side of that card, which is also blank. (Image 9) *To the spectators, you have shown all three cards blank on both sides!*

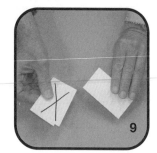

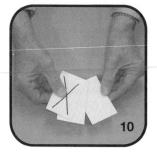

Place the card in your left hand, *under* the two held in your right hand. (Image 10) To the spectator say, "Would you please hold out your hand like this." Show what you want the spectator to do by holding out your left hand, palm up. The spectator holds out his or her hand.

With your left hand, remove the two bottom cards from the stack of three in your right hand and casually show those two cards blank on both sides. (Image 11) Put them away in your pocket, or just drop them on the table. *Everything* the spectator has seen so far are *blank cards*.

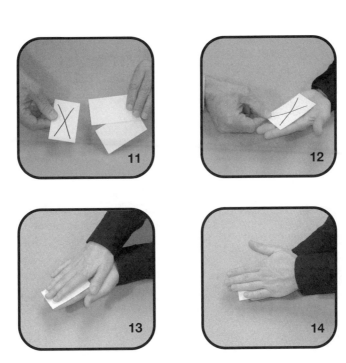

Place the printed card face down on the spectator's palm. (Image 12)

"Please place your other hand on top like this." (Image 13) You demonstrate what you want with your hands.

"Just turn both hands over like this," Again you demonstrate with your hands. The printed card is now face up in the spectator's hand. (Image 14)

"I'll use a little magic." Make a magic gesture, say a magic word, your company's name or whatever is appropriate for the occasion. "Please remove your top hand."

When the spectator removes their hand, they are always greatly surprised to see they are holding your imprinted business card. (Image 15) The effect is that the blank card was printed while in their own hands. With a little practice, this entire affect can be done in less than one minute. It's really a terrific trick.

I perform this effect often, because it is an excellent way to give out my business card. I have refined the method several times. Originally, I started with a more difficult sleight using several more blank cards. Then I incorporated the "Olram subtlety" move. ("Olram" is Marlo spelled backwards, named after its inventor, Edward Marlo, who is legendary in the creation of many excellent sleights and tricks primarily with playing cards.)

Showing the three cards totally blank is quite easy. Just follow the directions. This trick is so strong, often you will be asked, by the person in whose hands the card was "printed," "Would you do that for my boss?" Because you are always happy to oblige, it is good to have several sets of three cards with you, ready to go. I always carry 4 or 5 sets in my pocket or business card case.

Magically "printing" your blank business card, right on the customer's hand, serves a number of purposes.

Delivering your business card magically is much better than just handing your card to a client.

Printing your business card is entertaining, memorable and impressive, because the "magic" seems to happen as the spectator holds the blank card.

The magic happens quickly. You can do the effect in less than one minute.

It immediately proves your magical powers.

Because the magic is with your business card, which they receive and keep, the customer is less likely to throw it away. "How did you do that? It must be some kind of special invisible ink. I'll keep it and see if it fades out." And, that's good!

THE MAGICAL BOTTOM LINE

In addition to helping you achieve specific sales goals, your magic will help you in another, more subtle way. "People do business with people they like," is certainly true. If they like you, they are more likely to buy your product. If they don't like you, you'll have a hard time making any sale.

Here's an example. Many times I have gone to a restaurant where the food was excellent, but the waiter was so rude I never went back to that establishment again. And the reverse is true as well. In some restaurants, the food may not be wonderful, but, if your waiter is very personable and efficient, you feel as if you've really selected the right place for that dinner. You'll be back.

It's that same way with your customers. Your magic has made you a special person. You've entertained them. You've made their day a bit better. They like you. And remember, when they like you, they are more likely to buy your product. It has always been that way.

The bottom line is, because of the magic you do, your customers will remember you and your product. They will be delighted to see you the next time you call. They will probably say, "What are you going to do for me this time?" ... Study this course; practice the tricks; learn the magic; add your own presentation ... and you will be ready. And that's good!

THE LAST TRICK IN THE BOOK

I have saved this trick for last. It is ideal for just about any occasion. You can present it in Carlsbad Caverns, on a cruise ship in the middle of any ocean or on a jet plane thirty thousand feet high in the air. It works with foreign currency as well as U.S. dollars. You can do it anywhere, anytime, for just about anyone. It is truly a reputation maker.

THE CHAPSTICK CAPER

What you will learn now is one of the finest magic tricks I know. I have created this routine over the years, which I first did with a whole borrowed bill appearing in a lemon. This is a greatly improved version which uses only two ordinary objects, a dollar bill, and, of all things, a tube of Chapstick. The spectators see no "magic" props. (I have included an optional vanish for the dollar bill which uses a "trick" handkerchief.) You can easily carry the effect with you anywhere and perform it for only a few people or, with the proper staging, present it in a large theater. When you tear the borrowed bill in half, it is very funny for everyone except the lender. What happens after that is impossible. Frankly, I thought for a long time before I decided to include this in the course. It does require some practice, but it is truly sensational magic. Let me tell you the effect, and you'll see why.

EFFECT:

"Let me show you a magic trick that I'm just learning. To do it I need my magic wand." You feel in your pockets (a lady can look in her purse). "I don't seem to have my magic wand with me today, but I do want to show you this trick ..." As if the thought is just occurring to you, "Tell you what, let's use this Chapstick as the magic wand." You remove a Chapstick from your pocket and hand it to a spectator. A standard Chapstick is black with a white tip, the same color scheme as most magic wands. "Please hold this for me for a moment. It's smaller than my regular magic wand, but I think it will work. Now, I'll show you what I've learned."

"I'd like to borrow a dollar bill. I could do the magic with a larger denomination bill, but since I'm just learning, I guess I'd better stick to a dollar." Someone will volunteer a dollar, which can be pretty funny in itself.

"Thank you … oh, I'm sorry, I forgot your receipt." To the surprise of everyone, particularly the person who just lent you the bill, you visibly tear the bill in half. "Here's your receipt. I hope I'm remembering correctly what I'm supposed to do." You hand half of the now torn bill to the startled spectator. "I'll use these halves of the bill for the magic."

"Please crumple your half into a small ball. I'll do the same with mine." As you say this you have been crumpling the half bill into a very small ball. "Now hold your half tightly in your closed hands. I'll hold the other half." You hold the crumpled bill tightly in your closed left hand as the spectator does the same with their half.

"Now folks, here comes that wonderful magic I was telling you about. You have one half of the bill in your hand, and I have the other half in mine. Believe it or not, I'm going to make my half travel, invisibly, to your half and then reunite both halves into one bill. Everyone watch closely."

You point to the person holding the Chapstick and say, "Please wave the magic wand over both of our hands." That person waves the Chapstick as requested. This will always get a laugh.

"Here comes the first part of the magic." You open your left hand and they see that it is empty. To emphasize the effect, you show your right hand is empty, too. "As you see, my half has vanished."

Obviously elated by your success in making half of the dollar vanish, you continue, "Now, ladies and gentlemen, you may have seen a lot of magic in your lives. You've seen some good tricks and you've seen some bad tricks, but I'm going to show, the greatest miracle you have ever seen! If you open your hand, you will see the bill is completely restored! Unfold the bill and raise it high over your head so we can all see this wonder." During your soliloquy, the person holding the half bill has opened it. Sure enough, what he is holding is exactly the same as he had before, it's still only half a bill.

You say sheepishly, "Whoops, it didn't work." You pause for a moment and deliver a line that has been getting me laughs for many years, "I think it would work better with a larger bill. Does anyone have a twenty dollar bill I can borrow?"

Everyone will laugh. No one will volunteer another bill. You will, however, hear a lot of interesting comments from the spectators. Whatever they say, you respond, "Yes, I see what you mean. No one wants to lend me any more money. I better try to do that trick again. Crumple the half bill up in your hand as we try this one more time."

To the Chapstick-holding spectator you say, "Please wave that small magic wand over my friend's hand THREE times." In desperation you add, "And say any magic word you can think of." Whatever the person says gets a laugh, even if they say nothing. "Now, look and see what has happened. Three's the charm …" As the spectator unfolds the bill and finds he's still holding only half a bill, you add "… but not this time."

"This is pretty embarrassing. In his magic course, Mark Wilson told me this would work. I better try some of my own magic. Perhaps this will help. Would you please open the Chapstick." Your volunteer takes off the top of the Chapstick. Inside is not the usual contents of the tube, but something with a greenish color that may be paper. "Let's see what that is. Please remove the contents, I don't want to touch it." To strengthen the magic, it is important that you not touch the small rolled-up piece of paper the spectator is taking out of the Chapstick. "Now would you please open that little package." The person unrolls the paper. It is one half of a dollar bill.

"Now we must check to see if that just happens to match the other half of the bill." Speaking to the now much happier spectator from whom you borrowed the bill. "I don't see how they could match, because I handed this person the magic wand, I mean the Chapstick, before I borrowed the bill from you." This statement emphasizes the impossibility of the magic everyone is seeing.

"There are two ways to see if those halves match. One is by checking the serial numbers. There is a serial number on both halves. Do you see it on yours? It 's on the gray side of the bill, right above the green seal. The other serial number is just below the black seal on your half. Now, most serial numbers start with a letter. Is there a letter? And is there one on yours? Very good. Now, would you both say the letter and then read the numbers off, both of you at the same time. And the letter is …"

At this point both spectators will say the same letter and continue with the same numbers. As they read the numbers together, everyone now knows the numbers on both half bills are exactly the same.

"And the other way to check is to put the two halves together and see if they match." The half found in the Chapstick is returned to the person who lent you the bill. Everyone can see that the halves match perfectly. Then you say to the person who lent you the bill, "Thank you. I couldn't have done this without your help. You are going to get all of my borrowing business from now on."

Remember, the Chapstick is handed to the spectator before the dollar bill is borrowed and never leaves the spectator's hand until he removes the half bill. At the conclusion, the two halves of the bill match perfectly. Correctly performed, this is one of the strongest effects in the world of magic, a real "Reputation Maker."

CHAPSTICK CAPER EXPLANATION

To perform this caper, you must do only two sleights. (If you use the trick handkerchief to make the bill vanish, only one sleight.) They are both easy to do, and do not requiring any great finger dexterity. Both sleights are primarily based on timing. With a little practice, you will get them exactly right.

SECRET:

Before the show, you must really tear a dollar bill in half. Use a bill that is slightly aged so it will match the bill you borrow, even if it is a new or an old bill. Put the right torn half of that bill in your right coat or pants pocket. The left torn half of the bill you place inside an empty tube of Chapstick. (You do not have to use Chapstick. You can use any container for the "magical" reappearance of the "vanished" half of the torn bill. It could be an aspirin box, a sealed envelope, or any suitable object. I think the Chapstick is particularly good because of its small, round design, which is like a little magic wand. Also, they are found in the pants pockets or purses of many people.)

PREPARATION:

If you use a Chapstick, you must first remove the lip balm from the tube. You can use a small knife, a stick, a pair of tweezers or even a strong tooth pick, anything small enough to reach inside the Chapstick. The bottom of the lip balm is in a small round base that rests within the tube. After you remove all of the lip balm use a paper towel or tissue to clean the inside and outside of the tube.

You are going to put the left half of the bill into the Chapstick. But, before you insert it, crumple the half bill into a small ball. The reason you crumple the half bill before you put it in the Chapstick, is it then appears to be the same crumpled half bill that vanishes from your hand and "reappears" in the Chapstick. Unroll the crumpled half bill, fold and roll it into the round shape required to insert it into the empty Chapstick. The half bill must fit far enough down in the Chapstick so you can replace the top of the tube. Put the "loaded" Chapstick in your left side pants pocket. Do not crumple the right half bill that you put in your right pocket. The spectator will crumple that half into a small ball during the routine.

An advantage of crumpling both halves of the bill during the routine is, at the conclusion of the trick, it greatly disguises the age of the bill, so they appear to be the two halves of the bill you borrowed from the spectator.

ROUTINE:

You borrow a dollar bill from someone in the audience. Display the bill between your right and left hand with the picture of George Washington facing the audience. (Image 2) You apparently tear the bill in half. You have really not torn the bill at all.

THE MAGIC TEAR

Here's what you really do. Let's assume you are right handed. Face the audience and hold the bill a little below your eye level (Image 2). You appear to tear the bill apart in the middle with a downward motion of your right hand.

Your left hand remains in place. Move your right hand down and slightly toward you as you (apparently) tear the bill into two parts. (Image 3)

As you make the "tearing" motion, what you actually do is slide your right hand down the bill, and fold the bill in half. The half in your right hand folds towards you and behind the other half held in your left hand. (Image 4) Your left thumb holds the now folded bill in place in your left hand.

When you make the phony tear, hold the bill tightly enough so your right thumb makes a scraping noise rubbing on the bill as your right hand slides down. It sounds exactly as if the bill is being torn into two parts.

Let me emphasize, all of this is much more difficult to explain than it is to do. Practice with a real bill. Learn the movements of your hands from the pictures. Practice the move slowly at first, then learn to do it quickly. The entire tearing action takes about one second. Because of the visual effect of the "tearing" movement you make with your hands and the sound your thumb makes moving down the bill, the spectators see and hear everything, just as if you were actually tearing the bill in half.

You should learn the "tearing" move before you learn the rest of the trick. As you practice, you may, accidentally, really tear a bill in half. I certainly did that several times as I was learning. Put that bill back together with clear Scotch tape and practice with another bill!

There is one additional thing you must do. That is to hold the half of the bill you tore before the show in your right hand when you do the fake tearing move. Here's how you do it.

When you receive the borrowed bill from the spectator, take it from them with your left hand. As you do this, place your right hand into your right side pocket and grasp the half bill you put there before the show. (Image 5)

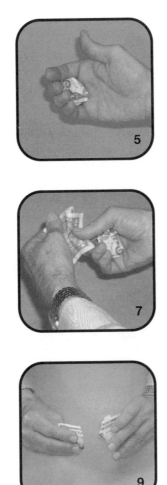

Your right hand holds the half bill in your fingers as you do the tearing with the borrowed bill. (Image 6) After the fake tear, you will have the folded whole bill in your left hand and that half bill in your right hand.

Don't let holding the half bill in your right hand when you make the tear scare you. Just hold the bill with your fingers as you make the "tear." (Image 7)

After the tear is completed, you can now show there is a "half bill" in each of your hands. (Image 8)

Your right hand shows the torn half bill. Your left hand reveals a part of the folded whole bill. (Image 9)

Hand the half bill in your right hand, as the "receipt," to the lender. (Image 10)

Now you must vanish the borrowed bill held in your left hand. Explain that you will now crumple up your half of the borrowed bill, and ask the spectator to do the same with theirs. As you crumple it, do not let the spectators see you have a whole bill. As you will see when you try it, you can crumple the bill into such a small ball, the spectators will think it is only half a bill. Place the crumpled bill on your open right hand. Have the spectator place their crumpled bill on their open hand. (Image 11)

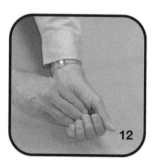

Say to the lender, "Please hold your half tightly in your closed hand, and I'll hold the other half." As you say this, you (apparently) place the bill held in your right hand into your left hand, which you close into a fist. Actually, you perform **The Finger Palm Vanish,** page 187 and secretly retain the bill in your right hand. This should be done casually, not as if you are performing any "sleight of hand." The move looks like this, (Image 12) as you (apparently) put the small rolled up ball of a bill into your left hand, but really keep the bill in your right hand in the finger palm position. (Image 13)

Immediately reach your right hand into your right coat or pants pocket, as if you are looking for the magic wand. Leave the bill in your pocket as you say, "Oh, that's right, you have my magic wand," as you remove your now-empty hand from your pocket. This is a very clever excuse for reaching into your pocket, which works beautifully in this routine.

If you would prefer not to do the finger palm vanish to make the bill disappear, you can use **The Coin Vanishing Handkerchief** (page 191). Instead of a coin, you sew a folded piece of paper the size of a dollar bill into the corner of the handkerchief. At this point, the spectators think you have one half of the bill in your closed left hand (which is really empty), and the other half is held by the lender. Actually, you have already done all the magic. What's left is the spectacular reveal.

You announce the great magical miracle they are all about to see. You ask the person with the Chapstick to wave it over the lender's hand and then over yours. Slowly open your left hand. It is empty! To emphasize the vanish, you show your right hand is also empty. To the viewers, the half bill has vanished!

Ask the spectator to show everyone the bill is now restored. The lender unfolds the bill and finds it is still only half a bill! (Image 13)

You appear to have made a terrible mistake. Say you will try it one more time. Have the lender hold the half bill tightly again. Ask the wand holder to wave the Chapstick three times over the lender's hand. Again, the trick doesn't work. It is still only half a bill. Apparently, you are in big trouble.

You ask the person holding the Chapstick to look inside the tube. They find the half bill. (Image 14)

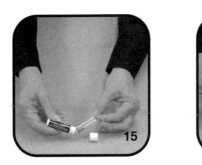

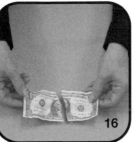

When everyone sees that the halves match perfectly, they will know you have just performed a real miracle! (Image 15)

Please study and practice this amazing trick before you present it. When you do, it will be one of your best "Reputation Makers."

YOUR FUTURE IN MAGIC

In looking toward your future in magic, you may find that magic itself can shape it for you. That rule has held true for many years, and numerous instances could be cited to prove it: How men who intended to be doctors, lawyers, or scientists turned to magic as a profession. In contrast, there have been magicians who abandoned the stage to become doctors, lawyers, ministers, or professors. The reasons for this are that the study and practice of magic can develop versatility, the ability to handle emergencies while under pressure and to recognize coming trends, and perhaps most importantly, how to appear before and speak to groups of people, both large and small, which can be a definite asset in almost any career you may choose.

Interest in magic has expanded so rapidly that it has become an adjunct not only to professions, but, most certainly, to social life as well. Salesmen, executives, and educators can use it to advantage. Anyone versed in magic will find it helpful in making contacts in almost any line. Moreover, the demand for magic has increased so greatly that it can be turned to profit as a sideline.

First, you must learn to do magic. The fact that you are studying this course shows that you have already made progress in that direction. You should learn it in a comprehensive way, for two reasons: One, many phases of magic, particularly misdirection and showmanship, apply to small tricks as well as large, so anything you learn from one will be helpful toward the other. Two, only by trying your hand at different types or styles of magic can you find the one to which you are best suited, for audience reaction to your work is what counts. Get people talking about you and the way you do your magic rather than about the tricks you perform. That will enable you to find your place in magic according to your own individuality.

Harry Houdini originally billed himself as the "King of Cards" but dropped it when he found that his Escape Act created a sensation. T. Nelson Downs was so successful as the "King of Coins" that he retired early with a fair-sized fortune. Then, in later years, he took up card work and became one of the best in the business.

Where you go from there will be largely up to you. Once you have a working pattern and style, you can decide whether to regard magic simply as a fascinating hobby, a form of social contact and enjoyment, a paying sideline, or an outright profession. New fields are constantly developing within the realm of magic. The demand for new tricks has attracted inventors, stimulated the manufacture of special apparatus, and magic dealers are increasing steadily. So if you have talents in any of those fields, they may be worthy of consideration.

The choice is yours, so make the most of it!